# Vintage Aircraft
# Recognition Guide

**Jane's Recognition Guides**

**Jane's**

# Vintage Aircraft
**Recognition Guide**

Tony Holmes

**Collins**

First published in 2005 by **Collins**

HarperCollins Publishers
77-85 Fulham Palace Road
Hammersmith
London w6 8jb
UK
www.collins.co.uk

HarperCollins Publishers Inc
10 East 53rd Street
New York
NY 10022
USA
www.harpercollins.com

www.janes.com

ISBN: 0-00-719292-4
ISBN-10: 0-06-081896-4 (in the us)
ISBN-13: 978-0-06-081896-8 (in the us)

HarperCollins books may be purchased for
educational, business or sales promotional
use. For information in the United States,
please write to: Special Markets
Department, HarperCollins Publishers,
Inc., 10 East 53rd Street, New York, NTY
10022.

Printed and bound in Scotland by Scotprint

05 06 07 08      10 9 8 7 6 5 4 3 2 1

# Contents

# A-Z of Aircraft

8

# Introduction

You hold in your hands an all-new addition to the familiar, and highly successful, range of *Jane's Recognition Guides*. Unlike its well-established 'older brother', the *Jane's Aircraft Recognition Guide*, which details all the world's flying types both large and small, this particular volume focuses on almost 500 aeroplanes that are either airworthy or on display in museums.

When compiling this first edition of *Jane's Vintage Aircraft Recognition Guide*, I have set out to produce a book which will hopefully be of use to those who regularly visit airshows or aviation museums, as well as perhaps cultivating further awareness of the subject with individuals who have only a passing interest in aircraft. Therefore, you will find entries for one-off gems such as the Sukhoi su-2 sitting alongside firmly established favourites like the Supermarine Spitfire.

The gulf in terms of performance between the aircraft featured is just as wide, as chapter one is full of World War 1 types that struggled to reach 120 mph with a tailwind, yet Chapter 4 includes details of the world's fastest interceptor (miG-25) and reconnaissance aircraft (sr-71). Such differences are also apparent in terms of size too, with the entry for the diminutive Aerospace ct-4 'plastic parrot' basic trainer being separated from Antonov's an-22 Antei behemoth only by the latter's anachronistic an-2.

All of these aeroplanes have one thing in common, however. They can be found in a museum or being flown by private individuals/organisations or still in military service somewhere in the world today.

I have been rather liberal in my interpretation of the word 'vintage' when it has come to choosing the 460+ aircraft that grace the pages of this book. One of the definitions within the *Modern Oxford Dictionary* for the word vintage is, 'characterised by maturity, enduring quality, excellence'. Certainly all of the aeroplanes within the volume are mature by any yardstick. Indeed, even the youngest of them – Mikoyan's MiG-29 – made its first flight in October 1977, and numerous examples now reside in museums in Russia and other former eastern bloc countries. Each and every aircraft possesses the enduring qualities embodied in them by the individuals that built them and the men and women that flew them both in war and peace. Finally, the term 'excellence' can be applied both to the aircraft themselves in respect to their design, and the service they gave to their countries. Some, like the Supermarine Swift, did not serve for long, and were perhaps less than successful in their designed roles. Nevertheless, they deserve their place in the aviation museums of the world.

A significant number of the fighters, bombers, transports and helicopters featured in the final two chapters of *Jane's Vintage Aircraft Recognition Guide* are still very much in military service today. Indeed, aeroplanes such as the C-130 Hercules, F-15 Eagle, F-16 Fighting Falcon and Tornado will remain in the vanguard of such air arms as the US Air Force and Royal Air Force well into the 21st century. Yet, despite their unmatched performance as fighter-bombers or tactical transports, each of these types is at least several decades old in terms of design concept. Early examples of these aircraft can also be found on display in museums in Europe and North America. Therefore, they deserve their place in this book, even if the term 'vintage' jars somewhat when applied to an F/A-18 Hornet or MiG-31!

As with my previous *Jane's Recognition Guides*, this book would have been much poorer in terms of its photographic content had it not been for the massive contribution made by the following individuals:

Shlomo Aloni, Daniel Brackx, Rob Fox, Cory Graff, Mike Hooks, Phil Jarrett, Otger van der Kooij, Cliff Knox, Phil Makanna, Peter March, Wojtek Matusiak George Mellinger, Paul Nann, Michael O'Leary, Juoko Ravantti, Ian Sayer, Paul Thompson, Mike Vines and Simon Watson. These individuals have travelled the world photographing aircraft both on the ground and in the air, and this book reveals the diversity and breadth of their work.

Finally, I would like to thank my editor, David Palmer, at Collins. He has endured the late delivery of this book with the good humour of a true editorial professional!


Tony Holmes
December 2004

For my young sons Thomas and William, who already
know their Spitfires from their Hurricanes.

# World
# War 1
# Aircraft

# Airco (de Havilland) DH 4 UK

two-seat, single-engined biplane bomber

The first British aircraft to be expressly designed as a day bomber, Airco's DH 4 was the company's response to an Air Ministry request issued in early 1916. Unusual for its clean tractor layout, as opposed to the rotary-dominated aircraft of the period, the DH 4 was also unique in having a wide separation between the pilot and observer. The latter was adopted to give the pilot the best possible field of view and the observer the best field of fire. Such an arrangement made it difficult for the crew to communicate, and the petrol tank fitted in the space was judged to be a safety hazard by the Americans, who had chosen the DH 4 to be their principal warplane. British-built examples started reaching the Western Front in March 1917, and improved US-built DH 4s, fitted with the vastly superior 400 HP Liberty engine (and dubbed the 'Liberty Plane' as a result), went into mass production later that year. No fewer than 4846 American DH 4s were eventually built, and they saw widespread service, both in military and civilian hands, post-war.

SPECIFICATION:

**ACCOMMODATION:**
pilot and gunner/observer in tandem

**DIMENSIONS:**
LENGTH: 30 ft 8 in (9.35 m)
WINGSPAN: 42 ft 5 in (12.95 m)
HEIGHT: 11 ft 0 in (3.35 m)

**WEIGHTS:**
EMPTY: 2387 lb (1082 kg)
MAX T/O: 3472 lb (1575 kg)

**PERFORMANCE:**
MAX SPEED: 136 mph (219 kmh)
RANGE: endurance of 3.75 hours
POWERPLANT: Liberty 12A
output: 400 hp (298 kW)

**FIRST FLIGHT DATE:**
August 1916

**ARMAMENT:**
two fixed Marlin 0.30-in machine guns forward of cockpit and twin manually-aimed Lewis 0.303-in machine guns for gunner/observer on Scarff ring; bomb load of 460 lb (209 kg) on fuselage and wing racks

**FEATURES:**
Biplane wing layout; pilot and gunner/observer sat some distance apart; inline engine; rectangular radiator; exposed exhaust stubs

# Airco (de Havilland) DH 9  UK

two-seat, single-engined biplane bomber

When the British government ordered the Royal
Flying Corps to be doubled in size in the wake of
audacious German bombing raids on Britain in
1917, one of the types developed specifically for
mass production was the Airco DH 9. Effectively an
improved DH 4, which had originally been
produced in late 1916 to answer an Air Ministry
request for a new day bomber, the DH 9 was
powered by the unreliable Siddeley Puma engine.
The latter was installed in a Germanic style, with
exposed cylinder heads. Efforts to cure the engine
maladies saw the overall horsepower of the Puma
reduced to such a degree that early examples of the
DH 9 were dangerously underpowered. The aircraft
suffered from having a lower ceiling and reduced
manoeuvrability in comparison with the DH 4, but
factories had already been geared up to build vast
quantities of DH 9s, so production went ahead
nonetheless. Equipping units of the Independent
Air Force and regular squadrons, the DH 9's
unreliability got so bad that DH 4 production
commenced once again in early 1918.

SPECIFICATION:

**ACCOMMODATION:**
pilot and gunner/observer in
tandem

**DIMENSIONS:**
LENGTH: 30 ft 5 in (9.29 m)
WINGSPAN: 42 ft 11 in (12.80 m)
HEIGHT: 11 ft 3.5 in (3.45 m)

**WEIGHTS:**
EMPTY: 2230 lb (1011 kg)
MAX T/O: 3790 lb (1719 kg)

**PERFORMANCE:**
MAX SPEED: 113 mph (181 kmh)
RANGE: endurance of 4.5 hours
POWERPLANT: Siddeley Puma
OUTPUT: 230 hp (171.50 kW)

**FIRST FLIGHT DATE:**
July 1917

**ARMAMENT:**
one fixed Vickers 0.303-in
machine gun forward of cockpit,
one or two manually-aimed Lewis
0.303-in machine guns for
gunner/observer on Scarff ring;
bomb load of 460 lb (208 kg) on
fuselage and wing racks

**FEATURES:**
Biplane wing layout; pilot and
gunner/observer sat close
together; inline engine; exposed
exhaust manifold and cylinder
heads forward of cockpit

# Airco (de Havilland) DH 9A  UK

two-seat, single-engined biplane bomber

As described in the previous entry, the original DH 9 was plagued by serious defects with its Siddeley Puma inline engine. Despite these problems, 3200 examples had been built by the time the DH 9 was replaced by the redesigned 9A, developed by Westland Aircraft. Pairing a completely reworked airframe with the more powerful, and reliable, Rolls-Royce Eagle or American-built Liberty 12 inline engines, the DH 9A (nicknamed the 'Ninak') proved to be the best strategic bomber in service in 1918. Operating in close formation at 17,000 ft, DH 9A squadrons (previously equipped with DH 9s) were extremely effective at performing the daylight bombing mission with the RAF's Independent Air Force in France in the final months of the war. By November 1918, some 885 DH 9As had been built by Westland, and a further 1600 were produced by a dozen manufacturers for post-war use with the RAF as the standard overseas utility machine. In this role, it saw further combat in 'hotspots' throughout the British Empire into the late 1920s.

## SPECIFICATION:

**ACCOMMODATION:**
pilot and gunner/observer in tandem

**DIMENSIONS:**
LENGTH: 30 ft 3 in (9.22 m)
WINGSPAN: 45 ft 11.5 in (14 m)
HEIGHT: 10 ft 9 in (3.32 m)

**WEIGHTS:**
EMPTY: 2695 lb (1223 kg)
MAX T/O: 4645 lb (2107 kg)

**PERFORMANCE:**
MAX SPEED: 123 mph (197 kmh)
RANGE: endurance of 5.75 hours
POWERPLANT: Rolls-Royce Eagle or Liberty 12
OUTPUT: 400 hp (298 kW)

**FIRST FLIGHT DATE:**
March 1918

**ARMAMENT:**
one fixed Vickers 0.303-in machine gun on fuselage side, one manually-aimed Lewis 0.303-in machine gun for gunner/observer on Scarff ring; bomb load of 450 lb (204 kg) on fuselage and wing racks

**FEATURES:**
Biplane wing layout; pilot and gunner/observer sat close together; inline engine; rectangular radiator

# Albatros D Va  GERMANY

single-seat, single-engined biplane fighter

The Albatros D V was derived from the highly successful D III, which had helped the German *Jastas* wrest control of the skies over the Western Front from the Allies following the scout's combat debut in the summer of 1916. Having to rely on a higher compression ratio version of the D III's Mercedes D IIIA powerplant due to the unreliability of a replacement geared engine, the D V introduced still more trademark Albatros streamlining to further improve the scout's performance. Reaching the frontline in May 1917, the D V remained in full production until the Armistice some 18 months later. Although hugely successful in combat, the Albatros scout had an unfortunate habit of literally falling apart when subjected to sustained manoeuvring, and the strengthened D Va was hastily rushed into service in the late summer of 1917. Nevertheless, the scout's lower wing still remained weak, and in 1918 pilots were prohibited from performing prolonged dives. Despite these shortcomings, over 1500 D V/Vas saw service on the Western Front.

SPECIFICATION:

**ACCOMMODATION:**
pilot

**DIMENSIONS:**
LENGTH: 24 ft 0 in (7.33 m)
WINGSPAN: 29 ft 8 in (9.04 m)
HEIGHT: 9 ft 4.25 in (2.85 m)

**WEIGHTS:**
EMPTY: 1511 lb (687 kg)
MAX T/O: 2066 lb (937 kg)

**PERFORMANCE:**
MAX SPEED: 116 mph (187 kmh)
RANGE: endurance of 2 hours
POWERPLANT: Mercedes D IIIa
OUTPUT: 185 hp (140 kW)

**FIRST FLIGHT DATE:**
Spring 1917

**ARMAMENT:**
two fixed Spandau 7.92 mm machine guns forward of cockpit

**FEATURES:**
Biplane wing layout; exposed engine cylinder heads and exhaust forward of cockpit; tail skid; streamlined, plywood-skinned and oval-sectioned fuselage

# Aviatik D I  AUSTRIA-HUNGARY

single-seat, single-engined biplane fighter

German Dipl Ing Julius von Berg created the D I for Aviatik in early 1917, the aircraft subsequently becoming the first indigenously designed machine to be put into mass production by the Viennese company. The D I evolved from several previous one-off prototypes produced in 1916, and featured a deep fuselage and thin wings in order to take advantage of the thermal currents encountered over the Austrian Alps – the fighting ground of the Austro-Hungarian *Luftfahrttruppe* in their struggle with the Allies. Entering frontline service in the autumn of 1917, the D I was manufactured by no fewer than five companies, aside from Aviatik. Some 700 examples were eventually built, these featuring various engine configurations and armament. Although initially plagued by structural weaknesses, the D I matured into a sound fighter, featuring excellent manoeuvrability and a high rate of climb. Nevertheless, concerns over the aircraft's fragility, and continual overheating problems with the D I's Austro Daimler engine plagued the machine throughout its service life.

SPECIFICATION:

**ACCOMMODATION:**
pilot

**DIMENSIONS:**
LENGTH: 22 ft 6 in (6.86 m)
WINGSPAN: 26 ft 3 in (8.00 m)
HEIGHT: 8 ft 2 in (2.48 m)

**WEIGHTS:**
EMPTY: 1345 lb (610 kg)
MAX T/O: 1878 lb (852 kg)

**PERFORMANCE:**
MAX SPEED: 115 mph (185 kmh)
RANGE: endurance of 2.5 hours
POWERPLANT: Austro-Daimler
OUTPUT: 200 hp (149 kW)

**FIRST FLIGHT DATE:**
24 January 1917

**ARMAMENT:**
two fixed Schwarzlose 8 mm machine guns forward of cockpit

**FEATURES:**
Biplane wing layout; plywood fuselage skinning; flat-sided fuselage; prominent fairing over engine cylinder heads; tail skid

# Avro 504 UK

two-seat, single-engined biplane trainer; single-seat fighter; two-seat bomber

The RFC/RAF basic trainer throughout World War 1 and up to 1924, the Avro 504 was built to the tune of 8970 airframes between 1913 and 1933! The aircraft was designed by the pioneering A V Roe, who originally thought that he would be lucky to sell six examples of his new machine. Versions A to H were constructed between 1913 and 1917, and although best remembered for its work in the instructional role, the early marks were actually employed during the first months of World War 1 as reconnaissance-bombers. Indeed, an Avro 504A was the first Allied aircraft to be shot down (on 22 August 1914) during the conflict, and a 504B dropped the first bombs on Germany a short while later. The definitive 504K was ushered into service in 1918, this version boasting a universal engine mounting which allowed the basic airframe to be powered by any one of several differing types of rotary engine. The final variant was the Armstrong Siddeley Lynx-powered 504N, which entered production in 1927 and served with the RAF's Central Flying School well into the 1930s.

SPECIFICATION:

**ACCOMMODATION:**
two pilots in tandem

**DIMENSIONS:**
LENGTH: 29 ft 5 in (8.97 m)
WINGSPAN: 36 ft 0 in (10.97 m)
HEIGHT: 10 ft 5 in (3.17 m)

**WEIGHTS:**
EMPTY: 1231 lb (558.38 kg)
MAX T/O: 1829 lb (829.63 kg)

**PERFORMANCE:**
MAX SPEED: 95 mph (152.9 kmh)
RANGE: 250 miles (400 km)
POWERPLANT: Clerget, Le Rhône, Warner Scarab, Gnome Monosoupape, Armstrong Siddeley Lynx
OUTPUT: (Le Rhône engine) 110 hp (82.7 kW)

**FIRST FLIGHT DATE:**
18 September 1913

**ARMAMENT:**
Manually aimed Lewis 0.303-in machine gun on upper wing. Manually aimed Lewis 0.303-in machine gun in front cockpit. Four 20-lb bombs under wings.

**FEATURES:**
Biplane wing (of equal span) layout; skid between undercarriage (not on 504N); radial engine; tail skid

# Breguet 14 FRANCE

two-seat, single-engined biplane bomber

The best French day-bomber and reconnaissance aircraft to see combat in World War 1, the Breguet 14 saw considerable action with French, Belgian and American units on the Western Front in the final two years of the conflict. The aircraft was designed with its powerful and efficient Renault 12 water-cooled engine positioned ahead of the wing, rather than behind in typical pusher configuration – official regulations dictated that all French bombers had to be pushers, as anti-aircraft gunners were permitted to fire on aircraft of non-pusher layout, as these we typically German! Constructed largely of the new light allow Duralumin, the 14.A2 reconnaissance, B.2 bomber, B.1 single–seat bomber and BN.2 two-seat nightfighter were built in quantity by no fewer than eight manufacturers in France between late 1916 and mid-1926. Examples served with 93 French *escadrilles* on most fronts, and by war's end 5500 had been built. The 14 remained in production until 1926, by which time a further 2700 had been delivered for both military and civilian use.

SPECIFICATION:

**ACCOMMODATION:**
two pilots in tandem

**DIMENSIONS:**
LENGTH: 29 ft 1.25 in (8.87 m)
WINGSPAN: 48 ft 11.5 in (14.91 m)
HEIGHT: 10 ft 9.75 in (3.3 m)

**WEIGHTS:**
EMPTY: 2513 lb (1140 kg)
MAX T/O: 4144 lb (1880 kg)

**PERFORMANCE:**
MAX SPEED: 112 mph (180 kmh)
RANGE: 435 miles (700 km)
POWERPLANT: Renault 12 Fe
or 12 FCX
OUTPUT: 300 hp (224 kW)

**FIRST FLIGHT DATE:**
21 November 1916

**ARMAMENT:**
one fixed Vickers 0.303-in machine gun on fuselage side and two Vickers or Lewis 0.303-in machine guns on pivoted mount for observer; racks under lower wings for 32 17.6 or 22 lb bombs

**FEATURES:**
Biplane wing (with slight back staggering) layout; louvred engine cowlings; prominent horn-like exhaust stack; tail skid

# Bristol F2B Fighter UK

two-seat, single-engined biplane fighter

Built to replace the obsolete two-seat BE and RE types which had become 'Fokker fodder' over the Western Front, Bristol's F2B Fighter first entered service in June 1917. It too initially suffered at the hands of the Albatros scouts, although crews quickly turned the tables when they realised that the F2B had the speed and manoeuvrability only previously found in single-seat fighters. Pilots flew aggressively as if in a Camel or SE 5A, aiming their fixed weapons, while their observers took shots at fighters that latched onto the tail of the F2B. Using these new tactics, the aircraft proved so effective that it began to produce aces with scores that rivalled those of single-seat fighter pilots – the greatest exponent of the F2B, Canadian Lt Andrew McKeever, scored 30 victories with No 11 Sqn. The aircraft remained in production until December 1926, by which time some 5100+ had been delivered. Post-war, the F2B was used in the Army Co-operation and training roles, where its durability ensured its survival in Iraq and the North-West Frontier of India until 1931.

SPECIFICATION:

ACCOMMODATION:
pilot and gunner in tandem

DIMENSIONS:
LENGTH: 25 ft 10 in (7.87 m)
WINGSPAN: 39 ft 3 in (11.96 m)
HEIGHT: 9 ft 9 in (2.97 m)

WEIGHTS:
EMPTY: 1930 lb (875 kg)
MAX T/O: 2800 lb (1280 kg)

PERFORMANCE:
MAX SPEED: 125 mph (201 kmh)
RANGE: endurance of 3 hours
POWERPLANT: Rolls-Royce
Falcon III
OUTPUT: 275 hp (205 kW)

FIRST FLIGHT DATE:
25 October 1916 (modified F2A)

ARMAMENT:
one fixed Vickers 0.303-in
machine gun forward of cockpit
and single or twin Lewis 0.303-in
machine guns on Scarff ring for
observer; racks under lower
wings for 12 20 lb bombs

FEATURES:
Biplane wing layout; louvred
engine cowlings; lower wings not
faired into fuselage; oval-shaped
radiator; flat-sided fuselage;
tail skid

# Caudron G 3 FRANCE

two-seat, single-engined biplane reconnaissance aircraft

Caudron brothers Gaston and René were among the most successful of Allied aircraft designers in the early years of World War 1. Demand for their aircraft proved to be so great that they allowed them to be built by rival companies without licence. This resulted in vast quantities of their G 3 design being produced. The latter was the ultimate development of the preceding Caudron C, D and E types, which had been built pre-war. Combining the unique pusher configuration with a tractor powerplant, the G 3 made its service debut with the French air force in 1914, and was duly purchased in modest numbers by the RFC, as well as the Belgians, Italians and Russians. Used as a reconnaissance platform and basic trainer, the G 3 was produced in significant numbers – Caudron alone built 1420, and several small production batches were competed in the UK. Some 38 French *escadrilles* operated G 3s at some stage during World War 1.

SPECIFICATION:

ACCOMMODATION:
pilot and gunner in tandem

DIMENSIONS:
LENGTH: 21 ft 3 in (6.40 m)
WINGSPAN: 44 ft 6 in (13.40 m)
HEIGHT: 8 ft 3 in (2.50 m)

WEIGHTS:
EMPTY: 933 lb (420 kg)
MAX T/O: 1577 lb (710 kg)

PERFORMANCE:
MAX SPEED: 70 mph (112 kmh)
RANGE: endurance of 4 hours
POWERPLANT: Gnome
OUTPUT: 80 hp (59.6 kW)

FIRST FLIGHT DATE:
Late 1913

FEATURES:
Biplane wing layout; pusher configuration, but with tractor engine; half-cowled radial engine

# Curtiss JN-4 Jenny USA

two-seat, single-engined biplane trainer

America's most successful training aircraft of
World War 1, the Curtiss JN-4 was an improved
version of the JN-3, which had itself been
developed through the combination of the best
features of the preceding J and N models. The
Jenny relied heavily on the incredibly robust
Curtiss OX-5 engine for its success in the
instructional role. The entry of America into World
War 1 in April 1917 resulted in orders for the Jenny
that totalled over 6000 examples by the time
production ended soon after the November 1918
Armistice. Having been the most widely used
trainer in both the US Army and Royal Canadian
Air Force in World War 1, the Jenny became the
most influential type in the post-war development
of aviation in North America, when hundreds of
surplus machines were sold cheaply to private
buyers. Helping to establish civil aviation across
this vast continent, the Jenny also became the
favourite mount of the 1920s Barnstormers, who
enjoyed great popularity during the decade.

SPECIFICATION:

ACCOMMODATION:
two pilots in tandem

DIMENSIONS:
LENGTH: 27 ft 4 in (8.34 m)
WINGSPAN: 43 ft 7 in (13.31 m)
HEIGHT: 9 ft 11 in (2.77 m)

WEIGHTS:
EMPTY: 1580 lb (716.88 kg)
MAX T/O: 2130 lb (966.16 kg)

PERFORMANCE:
MAX SPEED: 75 mph (120 kmh)
RANGE: 250 miles (400 km)
POWERPLANT: Curtiss OX-5
OUTPUT: 90 hp (67 kW)

FIRST FLIGHT DATE:
Early 1916

FEATURES:
Biplane wing layout, with upper
wing of greater span; exposed
engine cylinder heads and
exhaust forward of cockpit; tail
skid

# Fokker D VII GERMANY

single-seat, single-engined biplane fighter

Created by Fokker's highly talented design team, the prototype D VII was completed in great haste in late 1917 so that it could enter the German D-Type standard fighter competition held at Adlershof in January/February 1918. Emerging the clear winner, the design boasted a simple, yet strong, welded-steel tube fuselage and cantilever wing cellule. It was put into widespread production by Fokker, as well as by licensees Albatros and O.A.W. Once committed to frontline service with *Jagdgeschwader* I in May 1918, the D VII proved to be one of the best fighting scouts in service with either side. Indeed, it was claimed that the Fokker could make a good pilot into an ace, and it set the standard against which all new fighters were measured for over a decade. Precise production figures have been lost, but it is thought that somewhere in the region of 3200 D VIIs were ordered and 1720+ delivered before the Armistice. Proof of the fighter's formidable reputation came when the Allies stated in the surrender terms dictated to Germany that all surviving D VIIs had to be handed over.

SPECIFICATION:

ACCOMMODATION:
pilot

DIMENSIONS:
LENGTH: 22 ft 9.66 in (6.95 m)
WINGSPAN: 29 ft 2.333 in (8.90 m)
HEIGHT: 9 ft 0 in (2.75 m)

WEIGHTS:
EMPTY: 1508 lb (684 kg)
MAX T/O: 2006 lb (910 kg)

PERFORMANCE:
MAX SPEED: 117.5 mph (189 kmh)
RANGE: endurance of 1.5 hours
POWERPLANT: Mercedes D IIIaü
OUTPUT: 180 hp (134 kW)

FIRST FLIGHT DATE:
December 1917

ARMAMENT:
two fixed Maxim LMG 08/15 7.92 mm machine guns forward of cockpit

FEATURES:
Biplane wing layout; axle fairing structure; exposed exhaust manifold and cylinder heads forward of cockpit; tail skid

# Halberstadt CL IV GERMANY

two-seat, single-engined biplane fighter

Built by Halberstädter Flugzeugwerke as a higher-performance derivative of the successful CL II close air support fighter, the CL IV commenced flight-testing in February 1918. Both types had been developed from the unsuccessful D IV single seat fighter, the CL concept seeing a raised ring mounting being built into the fuselage behind the cockpit. The CL II earned a reputation for excellent manoeuvrability, an exceptional rate of climb and a wide field of view for the gunner which allowed him to engage attacking fighters with confidence.

Despite relying on the same Mercedes D III engine that powered the CL II, the CL IV had better performance thanks to its lighter airframe. Proof of these improve-ments came when frontline *Schlachtstaffeln* commented on the aircraft's fantastic handling qualities and rate of climb following its combat debut in May 1918. No fewer than 700 were ordered, and deliveries were still in progress when the Armistice came into effect in November 1918.

SPECIFICATION:

ACCOMMODATION:
pilot and gunner in tandem

DIMENSIONS:
LENGTH: 21 ft 5.5 in (6.54 m)
WINGSPAN: 35 ft 2.75 in (10.74 m)
HEIGHT: 8 ft 9 in (2.67 m)

WEIGHTS:
EMPTY: 1605 lb (728 kg)
MAX T/O: 2354 lb (1068 kg)

PERFORMANCE:
MAX SPEED: 104 mph (168 kmh)
RANGE: endurance of 3.25 hours
POWERPLANT: Mercedes D IIIa
OUTPUT: 160 hp (119 kW)

FIRST FLIGHT DATE:
February 1918

ARMAMENT:
two fixed Maxim LMG
08/15 7.92 mm machine guns
forward of cockpit and single
Maxim LMG 14 machine guns on
flexible ring for observer; fuselage
racks for anti-personnel grenades

FEATURES:
Biplane wing layout; rear-mounted gun ring; exposed exhaust manifold and cylinder heads forward of cockpit; flat-sided fuselage; tail skid

# Halberstadt C V  GERMANY

two-seat, single-engined biplane reconnaissance aircraft

Designed by the Halberstädter Flugzeugwerke primarily for long-range, high-altitude reconnaissance and photographic operations, the C V prototype began testing in early 1918 and made its debut on the Western Front in the mid summer of that year. The aircraft boasted considerable span, high-aspect-ratio wings, and these proved to be hugely efficient at the altitudes – 20,000 ft+ – at which the C V found itself regularly operating. The aircraft's high-compression Benz Bz IV also played a significant part in the Halberstadt's ability to attain these rarified heights. The final months of the war saw the C V operating alongside the Rumpler C VII, both types providing vital photographic intelligence for the beleaguered German troops along the Western Front. Despite increasing Allied opposition in the air, and near constant retreating on the ground, the C V-equipped units stuck grimly to their task until the end of the war.

SPECIFICATION:

ACCOMMODATION:
pilot and observer in tandem

DIMENSIONS:
LENGTH: 22 ft 6.3 in (6.90 m)
WINGSPAN: 45 ft 6 in (13.90 m)
HEIGHT: 10 ft 9.9 in (3.35 m)

WEIGHTS:
EMPTY: 2068 lb (938 kg)
MAX T/O: 3016 lb (1368 kg)

PERFORMANCE:
MAX SPEED: 106 mph (169 kmh)
RANGE: 312 miles (500 km)
POWERPLANT: Benz Bz IV
OUTPUT: 220 hp (164 kW)

FIRST FLIGHT DATE:
Early 1918

FEATURES:
Wide-span biplane wing layout;
exposed horn-type exhaust
manifold and cylinder heads
forward of cockpit; tail skid

# Hanriot HD 1 FRANCE

single-seat, single-engined biplane fighter

A contemporary of the Sopwith Pup and Nieuport 17, the Hanriot HD 1 was the first fighter to be produced by the Société Anonyme des Appareils d'Aviation Hanriot. Designed by Emile Dupont in early 1916, the HD 1 was passed over by France's *Aviation Militaire* in favour of the Nieuport 17 and SPAD VII, both of which entered production ahead of the Hanriot. It was, however, welcomed by the Belgian and Italian air forces, and almost 900 examples were built under licence by the Societá Nieuport Macchi in Italy between 1917 and 1919. Used in greater numbers than any other fighter type on the Italian front, the HD 1 was the mount of choice for most leading aces of the *Aeronautica del Reggio Escercito*. Around 125 examples were also supplied to Belgium's *Aviation Militaire Belge* from August 1917, where the fighter enjoyed great success when flown by balloon-busting ace Willy Coppens. Remaining in use in Belgium and Italy into the early 1920s, the final HD 1s to see frontline service were the 16 supplied to the Swiss *Jagdflieger-Kompagnien* from Italian stocks in 1921.

SPECIFICATION:

ACCOMMODATION:
pilot

DIMENSIONS:
LENGTH: 19 ft 2.25 in (5.85 m)
WINGSPAN: 28 ft 6.50 in (8.70 m)
HEIGHT: 9 ft 7.50 in (2.94 m)

WEIGHTS:
EMPTY: 983 lb (446 kg)
MAX T/O: 1437 lb (652 kg)

PERFORMANCE:
MAX SPEED: 115 mph (184 kmh)
RANGE: 224 miles (360 km)
POWERPLANT: Le Rhine 9Jb
OUTPUT: 120 hp (89.50 kW)

FIRST FLIGHT DATE:
Summer 1916

ARMAMENT:
one fixed Vickers 0.303-in machine gun forward of cockpit

FEATURES:
Biplane wing layout; close-cowled rotary engine; flat-sided fuselage; tail skid, head fairing aft of cockpit

# Junkers J 9 (D 1) GERMANY
single-seat, single-engined monoplane fighter

Unique in being the only all-metal cantilever monoplane fighter to make it into frontline service on either side in World War 1, the Junkers J 9 (designated D 1 in military service) reached the German *Idflieg* in small numbers just prior to the Armistice. Evolved from the J-series monoplanes which had preceded it in 1915-17, the J 9 featured the distinctive corrugated skinning which characterised virtually all of Hugo Junkers' early machines. The prototype J 9 participated in the 2nd D-Type contest held at Adlershof in May-June 1918, and combat pilots that flew it rated it totally unsuitable for frontline service as a fighter. However, because its metal construction made it relatively invulnerable to machine gun fire, the *Idflieg* chose the J 9 as a specialised 'balloon attack' machine. Sixty were ordered between May and November 1918, and by February 1919 40 had been delivered. There is no record of the J 9 being used in combat in World War 1, but a handful saw action with the *Flugpark* Sachsenberg in Kurland against Bolshevik insurgents in 1919.

SPECIFICATION:

**ACCOMMODATION:**
pilot

**DIMENSIONS:**
LENGTH: 23 ft 9.333 in (7.25 m)
WINGSPAN: 29 ft 6.333 in (9.00 m)
HEIGHT: 8 ft 6.333 in (2.60 m)

**WEIGHTS:**
EMPTY: 1442 lb (654 kg)
MAX T/O: 1839 lb (834 kg)

**PERFORMANCE:**
MAX SPEED: 140 mph (225 kmh)
RANGE: endurance of 1.5 hours
POWERPLANT: BMW III
OUTPUT: 185 hp (134 kW)

**FIRST FLIGHT DATE:**
Early 1918

**ARMAMENT:**
one or two fixed, forward-firing, Maxim LMG 08/15 7.92 mm machine guns forward of cockpit

**FEATURES:**
Monoplane wing layout; corrugated metal skinning overall; exposed horn-type exhaust manifold and cylinder heads forward of cockpit; tail skid

# Luft-Verkehrs Gesellschaft C VI GERMANY

two-seat, single-engined biplane reconnaissance bomber

A versatile reconnaissance bomber from Germany's most successful World War 1 bomber constructor, the C VI was the most advanced of the C-type aircraft to see wartime service. With its lineage stretching back to the C I of 1915, the final variant benefitted from the introduction of the new Benz Bz IV engine in early 1918.

Very similar in layout to the preceding C V, the C VI was lighter and more compact overall, thus improving its serviceability. Capable of carrying 250 lb of bombs, the aircraft saw widespread service on the Western Front in the final months of the war, although it never totally replaced the ubiquitous C V – despite Johannisthal-based LVG managing to build 1100 C VIS by the Armistice.

SPECIFCATION:

**ACCOMMODATION:**
pilot and observer/gunner in tandem

**DIMENSIONS:**
LENGTH: 24 ft 5.25 in (7.47 m)
WINGSPAN: 42 ft 7.75 in (13.03 m)
HEIGHT: 9 ft 2.25 in (2.80 m)

**WEIGHTS:**
EMPTY: 2090 lb (948 kg)
MAX T/O: 3036 lb (1377 kg)

**PERFORMANCE:**
MAX SPEED: 106 mph (169.6 kmh)
RANGE: endurance of 3.5 hours
POWERPLANT: Benz Bz IV
OUTPUT: 200 hp (149 kW)

**FIRST FLIGHT DATE:**
Late January 1918

**ARMAMENT:**
one fixed, forward-firing, Maxim LMG 08/15 7.92 mm machine gun and single Parabellum machine gun on flexible ring for observer; fuselage racks for 250 lb bombload

**FEATURES:**
Biplane wing layout, with both wings of equal span; exposed horn-type exhaust manifold and cylinder heads forward of cockpit; tail skid

33

# Martinsyde F 4 Buzzard  UK

single-seat, single-engined biplane fighter

Fast, manoeuvrable and boasting a fantastic rate of climb, the Martinsyde Buzzard was considered by many to be the best British single-seat fighter in production at the end of World War 1. The ultimate development of the wartime Martinsyde F series of fighter that traced their lineage back to the Elephant of 1915, the Buzzard was powered by a 300 hp Hispano-Suiza 8Fb eight-cylinder inline engine. The latter had been chosen as a replacement for the Rolls-Royce Falcon, which had originally powered the near-identical F 3. However, the Bristol Fighter had priority when it came to the supply of Falcon engines, so the F 3 airframe was reworked to take the 8Fb, and redesignated the F 4. The Air Ministry ordered 150, and the first F 4 unit was scheduled to form in April 1918. Production delays and the late delivery of engines put paid to this, and a mere seven had been handed over to the RAF by November 1918 against orders placed for 1450! Some 370+ Buzzards were eventually built, but few saw service with the RAF, which had in the meantime opted for the inferior Sopwith Snipe.

SPECIFCATION:

ACCOMMODATION:
pilot

DIMENSIONS:
LENGTH: 25 ft 5.5 in (7.76 m)
WINGSPAN: 32 ft 9.5 in (9.99 m)
HEIGHT: 8 ft 10 in (2.69 m)

WEIGHTS:
EMPTY: 1811 lb (821 kg)
MAX T/O: 2398 lb (1088 kg)

PERFORMANCE:
MAX SPEED: 132 mph (212 kmh)
RANGE: endurance of 2.5 hours
POWERPLANT: Hispano-Suiza 8Fb
OUTPUT: 300 hp (224 kW)

ARMAMENT:
two fixed Vickers 0.303-in
machine guns forward of cockpit

FIRST FLIGHT DATE:
October 1917

FEATURES:
Single bay biplane wing layout;
closely-cowled inline engine; tail
skid; head fairing aft of cockpit

# Maurice Farman HF 20  FRANCE

two-seat, single-engined biplane reconnaissance/light bomber aircraft

A whole series of quintessentially French pre-war and early war pusher biplanes were produced by Henri and Maurice Farman, these machines performing all manner of reconnaissance, light bombing and training roles well into 1916. Capable of producing ten machines per day in their separate factories in Billancourt, the Farman brothers stuck to a tried and tested layout for their various aircraft types. Most had a canard elevator in front of the crew nacelle, with the engine mounted in pusher fashion immediately behind the two-man crew. Single and twin fin designs were used in equal measure, as were a variety of water-cooled vee-8 engines. Sluggish and unstable, yet thoroughly reliable, examples of the Farman MF 7/11 and HF 20 were licence-built in Britain, Italy and Russia, as well as in several other countries. Seen as the main Allied combat aircraft in World War 1 until at least mid-1915, carrying out reconnaissance and day/night bombing, examples of the MF 7/11 and HF 20 soldiered on as trainers into 1918.

SPECIFICATION:

ACCOMMODATION:
pilot and gunner/observer in tandem

DIMENSIONS:
LENGTH: 32 ft 3 in (9.84 m)
WINGSPAN: 53 ft 5 in (16.30 m)
HEIGHT: 10 ft 5 in (3.20 m)

WEIGHTS:
EMPTY: 1378 lb (625 kg)
MAX T/O: 2050 lb (930 kg)

PERFORMANCE:
MAX SPEED: 69 mph (110 kmh)
RANGE: endurance of 5 hours
POWERPLANT: Renault R 80
OUTPUT: 79 hp (59 kW)

FIRST FLIGHT DATE:
1913

FEATURES:
Biplane wing layout; pusher configuration; exposed engine; central nacelle

# Morane-Saulnier Type AI FRANCE

single-seat, single-engined parasol monoplane fighter

Deemed superior to both the SPAD XIII and the Nieuport 28 following its first flights in August-September 1917, the radically configured Morane-Saulnier Type AI parasol fighter appeared to have a bright future ahead of it. However, the aircraft proved to be a disappointment once examples entered frontline service early the following year. Some 1000+ examples were constructed by Morane-Saulnier, and a number of new *escadrilles* were formed specifically to operate the AI. Yet it had been relegated to the advanced training role by mid-May 1918, replaced by the more conventional SPAD XIII. The official reasons for the AI's rapid demise remain obscure to this day, although sources at the time stated that the aircraft had suffered structural failures in flight, and the type's 150 hp Gnome Monosoupape rotary engine had proven temperamental in frontline service. Re-engined with the less powerful, but more reliable, Le Rhône 9Jb or 9Jby, the AI (redesignated the MoS 30 E I) served as an advanced trainer with the *Aviation Militaire* well into the 1920s.

SPECIFICATION:

ACCOMMODATION:
one pilot

DIMENSIONS:
LENGTH: 18 ft 6.2 in (5.65 m)
WINGSPAN: 27 ft 11 in (8.51 m)
HEIGHT: 7 ft 10.5 in (2.40 m)

WEIGHTS:
EMPTY: 912 lb (414 kg)
MAX T/O: 1486 lb (674 kg)

PERFORMANCE:
MAX SPEED: 137 mph (221 kmh)
RANGE: endurance of 1.75 hours
POWERPLANT: Gnome
Monosoupape 9Nb
OUTPUT: 150 hp (112 kW)

FIRST FLIGHT DATE:
August 1917

ARMAMENT:
one fixed Vickers 0.303-in
machine gun forward of cockpit

FEATURES:
Single parasol wing layout; close-cowled rotary engine; tail skid; circular fuselage

# Nieuport 10.C1 FRANCE

two-seat, single-engined biplane fighter/reconnaissance/bomber

The first in a long line of successful military aircraft built by Nieuport, the 10 was reputedly derived from a one-off racing special designed by Gustave Delage for the cancelled 1914 Gordon-Bennett contest. The first examples to enter service in May 1915 were two-seaters built for the observation role, but these aircraft were quickly modified into single-place configuration through the simple expedient of fairing over the front seat. With the addition of an overwing Lewis machine gun, the Nieuport 10 became a fighter. This armament was also employed by those machines that remained true to the original design, the observer being forced to stand erect through a hole in the upper wing in order to fire the gun! Aside from its use by the French, the Nieuport 10 also saw combat on the Western Front with the Royal Naval Air Service. Licence production was undertaken in Italy and in Russia, with the 10s being built in the latter country. Indeed, Russian production continued until 1920 – long after Nieuport had replaced the aircraft with much newer designs.

SPECIFICATION:

**ACCOMMODATION:**
pilot and observer/gunner in tandem

**DIMENSIONS:**
LENGTH: 22 ft 2.5 in (7.00 m)
WINGSPAN: 25 ft 11 in (7.90 m)
HEIGHT: 8 ft 10.25 in (2.70 m)

**WEIGHTS:**
EMPTY: 904 lb (410 kg)
MAX T/O: 1455 lb (660 kg)

**PERFORMANCE:**
MAX SPEED: 91 mph (146 kmh)
RANGE: endurance of 3 hours
POWERPLANT: Gnome or Le Rhône
OUTPUT: 80 hp (59.5 kW)

**FIRST FLIGHT DATE:**
Late 1914

**ARMAMENT:**
one fixed Lewis 0.303-in machine gun on upper wing

**FEATURES:**
Sesquiplane wing layout, with narrow-chord lower wing; close-cowled rotary engine; tail skid

# Nieuport 11 FRANCE

single-seat, single-engined biplane fighter

One of the most important fighting scouts of World War 1, the Nieuport 11 was a scaled-down version of the 10. Dubbed the *Bébé* by those who flew it, early examples of France's first purpose-built fighter reached the *Aviation Militaire* in January 1916. Highly manoeuvrable and fast for its time, the 11 blunted the Fokker Eindecker menace which had terrorised Allied aircraft in the skies over the Western Front since mid 1915. Like the 10 before it, and the numerous Nieuport fighter types which followed, the 11 derived its remarkable manoeuvrability from the trademark sesquiplane wing layout adopted by chief designer Gustave Delage. This proved to be both its strength and its weakness, however, as the lower wing (which had exactly half the surface area of the upper wing) had a nasty habit of twisting and breaking off under stress. Aside from its use by the French, examples were also supplied to the Royal Naval Air Service. Licence production also took place in Russian and Italy, 543 examples being constructed in the latter country.

SPECIFICATION:

**ACCOMMODATION:**
one pilot

**DIMENSIONS:**
LENGTH: 18 ft 6 in (5.64 m)
WINGSPAN: 24 ft 8 in (7.52 m)
HEIGHT: 7 ft 10.5 in (2.40 m)

**WEIGHTS:**
EMPTY: 705 lb (320 kg)
MAX T/O: 1058 lb (480 kg)

**PERFORMANCE:**
MAX SPEED: 104 mph (167 kmh)
RANGE: endurance of 2 hours
POWERPLANT: Le Rhône
OUTPUT: 80 hp (59.5 kW)

**FIRST FLIGHT DATE:**
Late 1915

**ARMAMENT:**
one fixed Lewis 0.303-in machine gun on upper wing

**FEATURES:**
Sesquiplanel wing layout, with narrow-chord lower wing; close-cowled rotary engine; tail skid; single gun in overwing position

# Nieuport 28.C1 FRANCE

single-seat, single-engined biplane fighter

The last Nieuport fighter to reach the frontline during World War 1, the 28.C1 was also the first aircraft from this manufacturer to feature a two-spar lower wing with a chord almost equal to the upper flying surface, rather than the company's trademark sesquiplane configuration. Built to replace earlier Nieuport and SPAD designs, the 28.C1 was deemed to be unsuitable by the French and issued instead to the American Expeditionary Force (AEF). The latter received 297 examples from March 1918, equipping four pursuit squadrons. However, the fighter suffered from traditional Nieuport frailty, and a number were lost when upper wing fabric was shed in extended dives or during vigorous high-g manoeuvring. These limitations greatly reduced the 28.C.1's effectiveness in combat over the Western Front, and early encounters with the superb Fokker D VII saw the French fighter coming off decidedly second best. A spate of engine fuel line fires added to the scout's growing list of woes, and by August 1918 surviving 28.C1s had been withdrawn.

SPECIFICATION:

ACCOMMODATION:
one pilot

DIMENSIONS:
LENGTH: 21 ft 0 in (6.40 m)
WINGSPAN: 26 ft 9.25 in (8.16 m)
HEIGHT: 8 ft 2.5 in (2.50 m)

WEIGHTS:
EMPTY: 961 lb (436 kg)
MAX T/O: 1539 lb (698 kg)

PERFORMANCE:
MAX SPEED: 123 mph (198 kmh)
RANGE: endurance of 1.5 hours
POWERPLANT: Gnome
Monosoupape 9N
OUTPUT: 150 hp (112 kW)

FIRST FLIGHT DATE:
June 1917

ARMAMENT:
two fixed Vickers 0.303-in
machine guns, one forward of
the cockpit and one on upper
left fuselage side

FEATURES:
Biplane wing layout; close-cowled
rotary engine; tail skid; circular
fuselage; machine guns forward
of the cockpit and on upper left
fuselage side

# Pfalz D XII GERMANY

single-seat, single-engined biplane fighter

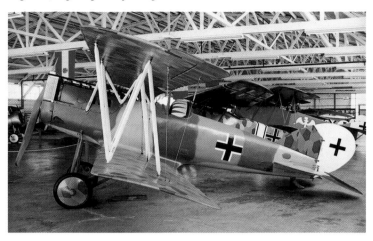

German manufacturer Pfalz Flugzeugwerke of
Speyer had been established in 1913 specifically to
build aircraft for the Bavarian Flying Service.
Administered by the Bavarian government, the
company supplied its aircraft exclusively to
Bavarian units in the early war years. Pfalz built a
series of fighter prototypes during the war, only
two of which made it into frontline service. The
D XII was the final Pfalz design to see combat, the
aircraft being strongly influenced by the company's
most successful model, the D III of 1917. A
participant in the 2nd D-Type contest of May 1918,
the Daimler D IIIa-powered D XII was one of the
winning designs. Pfalz received a contract for 500
examples, and production aircraft reached the
Western Front in quantity in August 1918. *Jasta*
pilots were never keen on the D XII due to its poor
control response, most preferring the Fokker D VII.
Nevertheless, by October 1918 180 D XIIs had been
issued to 11 units, although the Armistice abruptly
ended the Pfalz's combat career.

SPECIFICATION:

**ACCOMMODATION:**
pilot

**DIMENSIONS:**
LENGTH: 20 ft 10 in (6.35 m)
WINGSPAN: 29 ft 6.333 in (9.00 m)
HEIGHT: 8 ft 10.25 in (2.70 m)

**WEIGHTS:**
EMPTY: 1578 lb (716 kg)
MAX T/O: 1977 lb (897 kg)

**PERFORMANCE:**
MAX SPEED: 106 mph (170 kmh)
RANGE: endurance of 1.5 hours
POWERPLANT: Daimler D IIIa
OUTPUT: 170 hp (126.7 kW)

**FIRST FLIGHT DATE:**
Spring 1918

**ARMAMENT:**
two fixed Maxim LMG
08/15 7.92 mm machine guns
forward of cockpit

**FEATURES:**
Double-bay, biplane wing layout;
exposed exhaust manifold and
cylinder heads forward of cockpit;
tail skid

# Royal Aircraft Factory BE 2 UK

single/two-seat, single-engined biplane fighter/reconnaissance/bomber

Britain's first purpose-built military aircraft, the BE (Bleriot Experimental) was actually designed by Geoffrey de Havilland and F M Green at the Royal Aircraft Factory (RAF) in August 1911. The improved BE 2 evolved from the original prototype one year later, and three RFC squadrons had been equipped with production examples by 1913. The BE 2a and 2b then followed, the latter being built as a bomber capable of carrying up to 100 lbs of ordnance. Renowned for its stability in flight, the BE 2 was the perfect reconnaissance platform for artillery spotting. However, this very trait made the aircraft easy pickings for the Fokker Eindecker fighter when it appeared over the Western Front in 1915. In a forlorn attempt to make the type more manoeuvrable, and therefore capable of defending itself against aerial attack, RAF designers introduced ailerons and more powerful engines with the production of the BE 2c, 2d and 2e. The BE 2 was kept in production much longer than it should have been, with 3500 eventually being built up to 1917.

SPECIFICATION:

ACCOMMODATION:
single pilot, or pilot and gunner/observer in tandem

DIMENSIONS:
LENGTH: 29 ft 6.5 in (9 m)
WINGSPAN: 35 ft 0.5 in (10.68 m)
HEIGHT: 10 ft 2 in (2.10 m)

WEIGHTS:
EMPTY: 1274 lb (578 kg)
MAX T/O: 1600 lb (726 kg)

PERFORMANCE:
MAX SPEED: 70 mph (113 kmh)
RANGE: endurance of 3 hours
POWERPLANT: RAF 1a
OUTPUT: 90 hp (67 kW)

FIRST FLIGHT DATE:
February 1912

ARMAMENT:
crew's small arms, and mounting in front cockpit for Lewis 0.303-in machine gun; bomb load of 100 lb (45 kg) on fuselage racks

FEATURES:
Biplane wing layout; inline engine; exposed exhaust manifold and cylinder heads forward of cockpit; skid between undercarriage

# Royal Aircraft Factory RE 8 UK

two-seat, single-engined biplane reconnaissance/bomber

Designed as a long overdue replacement for the
thoroughly obsolete BE 2, the RE 8 (Reconnaissance
Experimental) was built in considerable numbers
over a short period of time. Developed in the
winter of 1915-16 in response to a RFC requirement
for a reconnaissance aircraft that could defend
itself, the RE 8's layout was strongly influenced by
the now discredited BE 2. However, as with the
latter type, the RE 8's lack of speed and
manoeuvrability rendered it vulnerable to attack.
Production examples reached the frontline in early
1917, and a series of crashes marred the type's
service introduction as inexperienced pilots
struggled to cope with the aircraft's poor handling
characteristics. Despite these failings, the RE 8 was
still deemed to be a vast improvement over the
hated BE 2C, and 4100 were produced between 1916
and 1919. Of this total, 67 per cent saw action over
the Western Front, as the RE 8 became the most
widely used British reconnaissance/bomber. In
November 1918, it was in service with 21 units,
although all had been retired by November 1920.

SPECIFICATION:

ACCOMMODATION:
pilot and gunner/observer in
tandem

DIMENSIONS:
LENGTH: 32 ft 7.5 in (9.98 m)
WINGSPAN: 42 ft 7 in (13.01 m)
HEIGHT: 11 ft 4.5 in (3.48 m)

WEIGHTS:
EMPTY: 1803 lb (817 kg)
MAX T/O: 2869 lb (1301 kg)

PERFORMANCE:
MAX SPEED: 109 mph (174 kmh)
RANGE: endurance of 2.75 hours
POWERPLANT: RAF 4a
OUTPUT: 150 hp (112 kW)

FIRST FLIGHT DATE:
17 June 1916

ARMAMENT:
one fixed Vickers 0.303-in
machine gun on port fuselage
side and one manually-aimed
Lewis 0.303-in machine gun on
Scarff ring for gunner/observer;
bomb load of 260 lb (118 kg) on
fuselage and wing racks

FEATURES:
Heavily staggered biplane wings
of unequal span; inline engine;
exposed exhaust manifold and
cylinder heads forward of cockpit;
large air scoop above engine

# Royal Aircraft Factory SE 5a UK

single-seat, single-engined biplane fighter

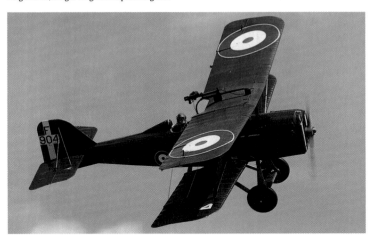

The SE 5a was easily the most successful warplane designed by the Royal Aircraft Factory at Farnborough. Although less nimble than its frontline contemporary, the Sopwith Camel, the SE 5a enjoyed the inherent stability of all previous RAF designs, thus making it easier to fly. It could out-dive and out-climb the Camel and sustain more combat damage, yet remain intact despite performing high-g manoeuvres. The aircraft's only failing was its geared Hispano-Suiza 8A engine. This suffered from chronic unreliability, and these problems were only solved when Wolseley re-engineered the engine as the direct-drive W 4a Viper. This too endured its fair share of teething troubles, but these were eventually overcome. The SE 5a was developed from the original SE 5, which entered frontline service in March 1917. The improved SE 5a reached the RFC in June 1917, and it soon became a favourite with Allied aces. Some 5125 SE 5as were built in less than 18 months and these were issued to 22 British and American squadrons on the Western Front.

SPECIFCATION:

**ACCOMMODATION:**
one pilot

**DIMENSIONS:**
LENGTH: 20 ft 11 in (6.38 m)
WINGSPAN: 26 ft 11 in (8.11 m)
HEIGHT: 9 ft 6 in (2.89 m)

**WEIGHTS:**
EMPTY: 1531 lb (694 kg)
MAX T/O: 2048 lb (929 kg)

**PERFORMANCE:**
MAX SPEED: 120 mph (193 kmh)
RANGE: endurance of 2.25 hours
POWERPLANT: Hispano-Suiza 8B or Wolseley w.4a Viper
OUTPUT: 200 hp (149.3 kW)

**FIRST FLIGHT DATE:**
12 January 1917

**ARMAMENT:**
one fixed Vickers 0.303-in machine gun on port fuselage side and one Lewis 0.303-in machine gun on Foster mount on upper wing; bomb load of 100 lb (44 kg) on fuselage racks

**FEATURES:**
Equal span biplane wing layout; inline engine; exposed exhaust manifold; fabric-covered head fairing behind cockpit

# Sopwith Baby UK

single-seat, single-engined biplane fighter

The Sopwith Baby was a more powerful version of
the company's Schneider seaplane fighter, which
was in itself a derivative of Sopwith's Schneider
Trophy-winning Tabloid of April 1914. The Baby
was powered by a 110 hp Clerget nine-cylinder
rotary engine in place of the Schneider's 100 hp
Gnome Monosoupape, and 110 examples were
ordered for the RNAS. These were delivered by
Sopwith between September 1915 and July 1916,
after which a further 71 were built by Blackburn.
Aside from the engine change, Sopwith also
introduced ailerons instead of wing warping for
lateral control. Fitted with floats, the Baby was
widely used by the RNAS in conjunction with
patrolling ships enforcing a blockade of North Sea
ports. The aircraft was also used to escort
vulnerable two-seaters attacking coastal targets
and was embarked in early seaplane carriers. The
latter sailed in the North Sea and the Mediterranean on anti-Zeppelin patrols, while land-based
Sopwith Babys conducted patrols from Dunkirk
until replaced by the Sopwith Pup in July 1917.

SPECIFICATION:

ACCOMMODATION:
one pilot

DIMENSIONS:
LENGTH: 23 ft 0 in (7.01 m)
WINGSPAN: 25 ft 8 in (6.90 m)
HEIGHT: 10 ft 0 in (3.05 m)

WEIGHTS:
EMPTY: 1226 lb (556 kg)
MAX T/O: 1715 lb (778 kg)

PERFORMANCE:
MAX SPEED: 100 mph (161 kmh)
RANGE: endurance of 2.25 hours
POWERPLANT: Clerget
OUTPUT: 110 hp (82.7 kW)

FIRST FLIGHT DATE:
September 1915

ARMAMENT:
one fixed Lewis 0.303-in machine
gun mounted on upper wing

FEATURES:
Equal span biplane wing layout;
three floats; closely cowled radial
engine, with lower cylinders
exposed

# Sopwith 1 ¹/₂ Strutter  UK

two-seat, single-engined biplane fighter/bomber

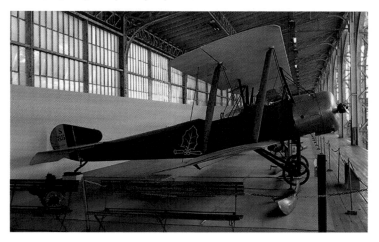

Its unusual named derived from the unique arrangement of its cabane wing bracing struts, the 1 ¹/₂ Strutter was the first British aircraft to be built with a synchronised gun as standard equipment. It was also the RFC's first true two-seat fighter to attain series production. Designed and built for the Admiralty by Sopwith as the LCT (Land Clerget Tractor), delivery of the aircraft began in February 1916. The 1 ¹/₂ Strutter was used by the RNAS both as a fighter escort and a bomber. Of the first 150 built for the RNAS, 77 were transferred to the RFC to boost squadron strength on the Western Front. Despite soon being outclassed by German fighting scouts, production of the 1 ¹/₂ Strutter continued well into 1917. More than 1500 were built in the UK, but this number was far surpassed by licence production in France, where around 4500 were made by no fewer than seven companies. The US government procured 514 from French stocks in late 1917 for its fledgling Air Service, and further 1 ¹/₂ Strutters were supplied to the Belgians and Russians.

SPECIFICATION:

**ACCOMMODATION:**
pilot and gunner/observer in tandem

**DIMENSIONS:**
LENGTH: 25 ft 3 in (7.69 m)
WINGSPAN: 33 ft 6 in (10.21 m)
HEIGHT: 10 ft 3 in (3.12 m)

**WEIGHTS:**
EMPTY: 1305 lb (592 kg)
MAX T/O: 2150 lb (975 kg)

**PERFORMANCE:**
MAX SPEED: 100 mph (161 kmh)
RANGE: endurance of 3.75 hours
POWERPLANT: Clerget 9B
OUTPUT: 130 hp (96.6 kW)

**FIRST FLIGHT DATE:**
December 1915

**ARMAMENT:**
one fixed Vickers 0.303-in machine gun forward of cockpit and one manually-aimed Lewis 0.303-in machine gun on Scarff ring for gunner/observer; bomb load of 260 lb (118 kg) in internal fuselage bay

**FEATURES:**
Equal span biplane wing layout; unique cabane struts between wings; closely cowled radial engine; tail skid

45

# Sopwith Pup UK

single-seat, single-engined biplane fighter

Essentially a scaled-down, single-seat, derivative of Sopwith's 1 1/2 Strutter, the much-loved Pup was initially known as the Scout. However, due to its small size and strong family resemblance to the Strutter, it was quickly dubbed the 'Pup' – an appellation which eventually became official. Ordered by both the RFC and RNAS, the first Pups reached the Western Front in September 1916, and remained in frontline service until rendered obsolete by SE 5as and Camels in the late summer of the following year. Blessed with excellent flying control response, and genuinely loved both those that flew it, some 1770 Pups were eventually built. Although replaced on the Western Front in the autumn of 1917, Pup production continued into 1918 in order to satisfy the demand for UK Home Defence fighters to engage marauding German bombers and Zeppelin dirigibles. The type was also a favourite with instructors at training squadrons. Aside from operating with RNAS units on land, a number of Pups were also embarked on the Royal Navy's trio of aircraft carriers from early 1917.

SPECIFICATION:

ACCOMMODATION:
one pilot

DIMENSIONS:
LENGTH: 19 ft 3.75 in (5.89 m)
WINGSPAN: 26 ft 6 in (8.08 m)
HEIGHT: 9 ft 5 in (2.87 m)

WEIGHTS:
EMPTY: 787 lb (357 kg)
MAX T/O: 1225 lb (556 kg)

PERFORMANCE:
MAX SPEED: 111 mph (179 kmh)
RANGE: endurance of 3 hours
POWERPLANT: Le Rhône 9C
OUTPUT: 80 hp (59.6 kW)

FIRST FLIGHT DATE:
February 1916

ARMAMENT:
one fixed Vickers 0.303-in machine gun forward of cockpit; anti-airship armament of four Le Prieur rockets, two per interplane struts

FEATURES:
Equal span biplane wing layout; closely cowled radial engine; tail skid

# Sopwith Triplane UK

single-seat, single-engined triplane fighter

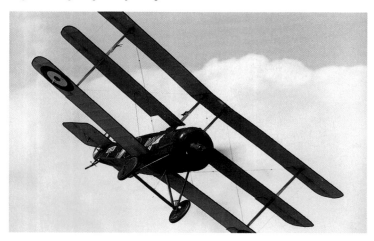

Built as a replacement for the Pup, the Triplane boasted a superior rate of climb and greatly improved manoeuvrability thanks to its extra wing. Indeed, when the type made its combat debut with the RNAS in late 1916, the Triplane could easily out-climb any other aircraft operated by either side over the Western Front. Aside from its use by the RNAS, the Triplane was also due to serve with the RFC, but a deal struck in February 1917 saw the Navy exchange all its SPAD VIIs for the Triplanes then on order for the RFC. This agreement resulted in the planned production run for the Triplane being reduced to just 150. Nevertheless, the design had a great impact when it finally met the enemy – so much so that the German High Command immediately ordered their manufacturers to produce triplane designs to counter the Sopwith fighter, the most famous of which was the Fokker Dr I. Naval squadrons on the Western Front began replacing their Triplanes with Camels from July 1917 onwards, and the last examples in frontline service were flown by UK Home Defence units.

SPECIFICATION:

**ACCOMMODATION:**
one pilot

**DIMENSIONS:**
LENGTH: 18 ft 10 in (5.74 m)
WINGSPAN: 26 ft 6 in (8.08 m)
HEIGHT: 10 ft 6 in (3.20 m)

**WEIGHTS:**
EMPTY: 993 lb (450 kg)
MAX T/O: 1415 lb (642 kg)

**PERFORMANCE:**
MAX SPEED: 116 mph (187 kmh)
RANGE: endurance of 2.75 hours
POWERPLANT: Clerget 9B
OUTPUT: 130 hp (96.6 kW)

**FIRST FLIGHT DATE:**
28 May 1916

**ARMAMENT:**
one (sometimes two) fixed Vickers 0.303-in machine gun forward of cockpit

**FEATURES:**
Equal span, staggered triplane wing layout; closely cowled radial engine; tail skid

# Sopwith Camel UK

single-seat, single-engined biplane fighter

The most famous British fighter of World War 1, the Camel was also the most successful design to see service with either side in respect to the number of victories – 1294 aeroplanes and three airships. The Camel was the first fighter to boast two Vickers machine guns synchronised to fire through the propeller arc. The humped fairing covering the breeches of these weapons actually provided the inspiration for the fighter's unique sobriquet, which, like the Pup, went from being an unofficial appellation to its official name. Although the Camel boasted a fearsome reputation in combat, its exacting handling characteristics took a heavy toll on poorly trained novice pilots. Nevertheless, almost 5500 Camels were eventually built, with the Sopwith design seeing service on the Western Front from May 1917. It was also flown by UK Home Defence units and saw action on the Italian front with RFC/RAF squadrons. Land-based RNAS Camel squadrons patrolled the North Sea coast prior to being amalgamated into the newly-formed RAF on 1 April 1918.

SPECIFICATION:

**ACCOMMODATION:**
one pilot

**DIMENSIONS:**
LENGTH: 18 ft 9 in (5.72 m)
WINGSPAN: 28 ft 0 in (8.53 m)
HEIGHT: 8 ft 6 in (2.59 m)

**WEIGHTS:**
EMPTY: 929 lb (421 kg)
MAX T/O: 1453 lb (659 kg)

**PERFORMANCE:**
MAX SPEED: 113 mph (182 kmh)
RANGE: endurance of 2.5 hours
POWERPLANT: Clerget 9B,
Bentley B.R.1 or Le Rhône
OUTPUT: 130 hp (96.6 kW)

**FIRST FLIGHT DATE:**
22 December 1916

**ARMAMENT:**
two fixed Vickers 0.303-in machine guns forward of cockpit; optional underwing racks for four 25 lb (11.3 kg) bombs

**FEATURES:**
Equal span, staggered biplane wing layout; closely cowled radial engine; fairing 'hump' over gun breeches; tail skid

# Sopwith Snipe UK

single-seat, single-engined biplane fighter

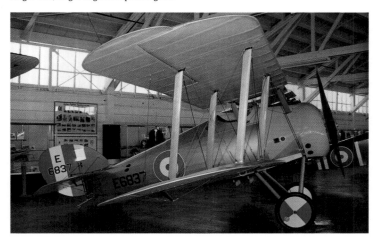

Conceived as a replacement for the Camel, and designed from specifications given to Sopwith by the Air Board in early 1917, the Snipe looked every bit the big brother of the company's famed fighting scout. The specification called for a fighter that could attain 135 mph at 15,000 ft, sustain an average rate of climb of 1000 ft per minute above 10,000 ft and cruise at 25,000 ft. The aircraft also had to have an endurance of three hours. Once in service, the Snipe proved unable to reproduce any of these figures, despite being powered by the 230 hp Bentley BR2 engine.

Despite these shortcomings, the RAF voiced its approval of the machine, and the Snipe was put into large-scale production. Of the 4500 ordered, 487 had been built by the end of December 1918, and production continued into the early 1920s. The first examples started to arrive in France in August 1918, and No 43 Sqn was the first to swap its Camels for Snipes. A total of 1100 Snipes were eventually built for the RAF, and the fighter remained in service until 1926.

SPECIFICATION:

ACCOMMODATION:
one pilot

DIMENSIONS:
LENGTH: 19 ft 10 in (6.04 m)
WINGSPAN: 31 ft 1 in (9.47 m)
HEIGHT: 8 ft 3 in (2.51 m)

WEIGHTS:
EMPTY: 1312 lb (595 kg)
MAX T/O: 2020 lb (916 kg)

PERFORMANCE:
MAX SPEED: 121 mph (195 kmh)
RANGE: endurance of 3 hours
POWERPLANT: Bentley BR2
OUTPUT: 234 hp (172 kW)

FIRST FLIGHT:
September 1917

ARMAMENT:
two fixed Vickers 0.303-in machine guns forward of cockpit

FEATURES:
Equal span, staggered biplane wing layout; closely cowled radial engine; fairing 'hump' over much of the guns; rounded fuselage; tail skid

# SPAD VII

single-seat, single-engined biplane fighter

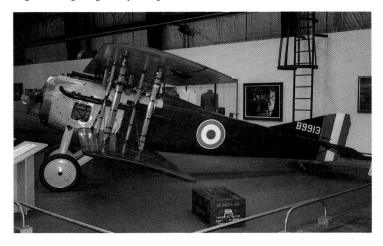

The end result of the design trend of 1915-16 which saw heavier, more powerful and less agile fighting scouts appearing from the warring nations of Europe, the SPAD VII was easily France's most successful aircraft of this period. Powered by the superb, but often temperamental, Hispano-Suiza V8 engine, the 150 hp SPAD VII prototype had flown for the first time in April 1917. The aircraft had an impressive top speed in both level flight and in the dive, but lacked the manoeuvrability of contemporary Nieuports. However, combat reports received from the front had suggested that pilots valued high speed over agility, hence the heavy fighter route chosen by SPAD. Production examples first saw combat in the summer of 1916, but the delivery tempo was slow due to production difficulties with the scout's V8 engine. The SPAD VII entered combat with both the French *Aviation Militaire* and the RFC at much the same time, and once its engine maladies had been corrected, the fighter enjoyed great success over the Western Front.

SPECIFICATION:

ACCOMMODATION:
one pilot

DIMENSIONS:
LENGTH: 19 ft 11.3 in (6.08 m)
WINGSPAN: 25 ft 8 in (7.82 m)
HEIGHT: 7 ft 2.75 in (2.20 m)

WEIGHTS:
EMPTY: 1102 lb (500 kg)
MAX T/O: 1552 lb (704 kg)

PERFORMANCE:
MAX SPEED: 132 mph (212 kmh)
RANGE: endurance of 1.85 hours
POWERPLANT: Hispano-Suiza HS 8Aa
OUTPUT: 150 hp (134 kW)

FIRST FLIGHT DATE:
April 1916

ARMAMENT:
One fixed Vickers 0.303-in machine gun forward of cockpit

FEATURES:
Equal span biplane wing layout; closely cowled engine; circular frontal radiator; exposed exhaust manifolds; reduced upper wing/cockpit clearance; tail skid

## SPAD XIII FRANCE

single-seat, single-engined biplane fighter

Derived from the SPAD VII and limited-edition XII, the XIII was developed to make use of the powerful 200 hp Hispano-Suiza 8B engine. Dubbed the 'geared SPAD' due to the arrangement of its powerplant, the XIII bore a striking resemblance to the earlier VII, but was larger overall. The extra performance offered by the 8B engine allowed company designers to fit two Vickers 0.303-in machine guns into the XIII, and the *Aviation Militaire* ordered 8470 examples to be built. However, a combination of manufacturing problems and chronic engine reliability severely hampered the delivery process, and of the 2200 XIIIs that SPAD had promised to supply by March 1918, just 764 had been built and only 300 were in operational service. With the engine woes eventually rectified, production finally began to meet demand in the spring of 1918, SPAD churning out 11 XIIIs a day until manufacturing ceased in 1919. Aside from its use by French *Escadrilles*, British, Italian, Belgian and American units also saw action with the SPAD.

SPECIFICATION:

**ACCOMMODATION:**
one pilot

**DIMENSIONS:**
LENGTH: 20 ft 6 in (6.25 m)
WINGSPAN: 27 ft 1 in (8.25 m)
HEIGHT: 8 ft 6.5 in (2.60 m)

**WEIGHTS:**
EMPTY: 1326 lb (601 kg)
MAX T/O: 1888 lb (856 kg)

**PERFORMANCE:**
MAX SPEED: 135 mph (218 kmh)
RANGE: endurance of 1.67 hours
POWERPLANT: Hispano-Suiza 8B
OUTPUT: 200 hp (149 kW)

**FIRST FLIGHT DATE:**
4 April 1917

**ARMAMENT:**
two fixed Vickers 0.303-in
machine guns forward of cockpit

**FEATURES:**
Equal span biplane wing layout; closely cowled engine; circular frontal radiator; exposed exhaust manifolds; reduced upper wing/ cockpit clearance; tail skid

# Thomas-Morse S-4 USA

single-seat, single-engined biplane fighter trainer

The Thomas-Morse Aircraft Corporation formed in January 1917 when the English-born Thomas brothers went into partnership with the American-based Morse Chain Company. Their chief designer was B D Thomas (no relation), who had previously worked for Curtiss on the JN-4 Jenny. His first offering for his new employer was also a trainer in the form of the single-seat S-4 scout, this diminutive machine being ordered by the US Signal Corps to the tune of 100 examples for use as an advanced trainer. Designated S-4BS, these aircraft were powered by the Gnome Monosoupape rotary, although the engine proved to be a less than successful choice thanks to its propensity for oil leaks. So bad was the problem that the follow-on batch of 400 S-4CS, ordered in January 1918, utilised the less powerful, but infinitely more reliable, Le Rhône 4C. Used exclusively in America, the 'Tommy', as it was dubbed in service, was soon retired after the Armistice, and many surplus machines found gainful civilian employment as air racers or in film work well into the 1920s.

SPECIFICATION:

**ACCOMMODATION:**
one pilot

**DIMENSIONS:**
LENGTH: 19 ft 10 in (5.82 m)
WINGSPAN: 26 ft 6 in (8.01 m)
HEIGHT: 8 ft 1 in (2.73 m)

**WEIGHTS:**
EMPTY: 940 lb (426.38kg)
MAX T/O: 1330 lb (603.28 kg)

**PERFORMANCE:**
MAX SPEED: 97 mph (155.2 kmh)
RANGE: endurance of 2 hours
POWERPLANT: Gnome Monosoupape and Le Rhône 4C
OUTPUT: 100 hp (74.5 kW) and 80 hp (59.5 kW) respectively

**FIRST FLIGHT DATE:**
June 1917

**FEATURES:**
Equal span biplane wing layout; closely cowled radial engine; tail skid

# Inter-War Aircraft

# Avro 621 Tutor UK

two-seat, single-engined biplane trainer

The Tutor was built as a replacement for the company's veteran 504K/N, many of which were still in use with RAF flying training schools in the late 1920s. Following an evaluation of the new machine by the Aircraft and Armament Experimental Establishment in December 1929, the RAF chose the Tutor as its new basic trainer. A trial batch of 21 was initially ordered, and following their successful introduction into service at the Central Flying School (CFS), a further 373 Tutors were taken on strength between 1934 and 1936. Possessing excellent handling characteristics, CFS Tutors were regularly put through their aerobatic paces at numerous air pageants and RAF displays throughout the 1930s. The aircraft also proved popular with overseas air arms too, the South African Air Force actually operating locally-built Tutors. The advent of monoplane fighters like the Hurricane and Spitfire sounded the death knell for the Avro biplane trainer as the decade drew to a close, and by 1939 most had been replaced by Miles Magisters.

SPECIFICATION:

ACCOMMODATION:
two pilots in tandem

DIMENSIONS:
LENGTH: 26 ft 6 in (8.08 m)
WINGSPAN: 34 ft 0 in (10.36 m)
HEIGHT: 9 ft 7 in (2.92 m)

WEIGHTS:
EMPTY: 1844 lb (836 kg)
MAX T/O: 2458 lb (1115 kg)

PERFORMANCE:
MAX SPEED: 122 mph (196.7 kmh)
RANGE: 250 miles (402 km)
POWERPLANT: (Mk 19/T 21)
Armstrong Siddeley Lynx IVC
OUTPUT: 240 hp (179 kW)

FIRST FLIGHT DATE:
December 1929

FEATURES:
Biplane wing layout; tandem
cockpits; radial engine; N-shaped
bracing struts

# Avro Anson UK

six-seat, twin-engined monoplane trainer/communications aircraft

Derived from Avro's 652 airliner, the Anson claimed two firsts when it entered military service in March 1936. It was not only the RAF's first monoplane design, the Anson was also the air force's first aircraft to boast a retractable undercarriage. Its principal user pre-war was Coastal Command, whose squadrons employed the aircraft in the general reconnaissance and search and rescue roles until 1942. Soon after the outbreak of World War 2, the Anson was chosen as a standard training aircraft for the British Commonwealth Air Training Plan, and it was in this instructional role that the aircraft really excelled. Indeed, it was so successful that a second production line was set up in Canada in order to satisfy the demand for new aircraft. The Anson's fuselage shape was revised with the advent of the Mk XI/XII, and its reliability and docile handling ensured that the design remained in production until May 1952 – a total of 11,020 Ansons were built. The T 21 was finally retired from RAF service in June 1968.

SPECIFICATION:

**ACCOMMODATION:**
crew of up to six in training role, seats for up to eleven in communications configuration

**DIMENSIONS:**
LENGTH: 42 ft 3 in (12.88 m)
WINGSPAN: 56 ft 5 in (17.20m)
HEIGHT: 13 ft 1 in (3.99 m)

**WEIGHTS:**
EMPTY: 5375 lb (2438 kg)
MAX T/O: 8000 lb (3629 kg)

**PERFORMANCE:**
MAX SPEED: 188 mph (303 kmh)
RANGE: 790 miles (1271 km)
POWERPLANT: (Mk 19/T 21) two Armstrong Siddeley Cheetah 15s
OUTPUT: 840 hp (626.4 kW)

**FIRST FLIGHT DATE:**
24 March 1935

**ARMAMENT:**
one fixed Vickers 0.303-in machine gun in fuselage to left of cockpit and one turret-mounted Vickers 0.303-in machine for gunner/observer; bomb load of 360 lb (163 kg) on wing racks

**FEATURES:**
Monoplane wing layout; retractable undercarriage; twin radial engines; fabric covered wings and fuselage

# Boeing Model 100 (F4B-1/P-12B) USA

single-seat, single-engined biplane fighter

Built as the private venture Model 100 by Boeing in 1929, this machine was a natural successor to the company's F2B/F3B naval fighters of several years earlier. The new design's big advantage over its predecessors was its smaller and lighter airframe, which combined with Pratt & Whitney's latest specification Wasp radial to produce an aircraft that was 32 mph faster than the Boeing fighters then in service. After testing two prototypes, the US Navy ordered 27 F4B-1s, followed in 1931 by 46 F4B-2s (fitted with engine cowls, Frise ailerons, a tailwheel and a supercharged engine), 21 F4B-3s with a new light-alloy monocoque fuselage and 92 F4B-4s with a wider fin.

In a rare display of service unity, the US Army Air Corps also ordered the Model 100, which it duly designated the P-12 – Army Air Corps purchases consisted of 90 P-12BS, 96 P-12CS, 35 P-12DS, 110 P-12ES and 25 P-12FS. These machines differed only in minor detail from their Navy brethren. Used throughout the 1930s, the last F4BS/P-12s were phased out of service in 1941.

SPECIFICATION:

**ACCOMMODATION:**
pilot

**DIMENSIONS:**
LENGTH: 20 ft 1 in (6.12 m)
WINGSPAN: 30 ft 0 in (9.14 m)
HEIGHT: 9 ft 7 in (2.92 m)

**WEIGHTS:**
EMPTY: 1758 lb (797 kg)
MAX T/O: 2536 lb (1150 kg)

**PERFORMANCE:**
MAX SPEED: 171 mph (275 kmh)
RANGE: 371 miles (597 km)
POWERPLANT: Pratt & Whitney
R-1340-8 Wasp
OUTPUT: 500 hp (373 kW)

**FIRST FLIGHT DATE:**
6 May 1929 (F4B-1)

**ARMAMENT:**
two fixed 0.30-in machine guns
forward of cockpit; bomb load of
500 lb (226 kg) on wing racks or
underfuselage

**FEATURES:**
Biplane wing layout; uncowled
radial engine; arrestor hook
(naval variant)

# Boeing/Stearman Model 75 USA

two-seat, single-engined biplane trainer

Created by the Stearman Aircraft Company (which was bought by Boeing in 1934) utilising the firm's Model C as a base, the x70, as it was designated by the manufacturer, was submitted as a contender for the USAAC's primary trainer requirement of 1934. It was therefore rather ironic that the first service to show interest in the design was the US Navy, which ordered 61 (designated NS-1s) in early 1935. Following a prolonged evaluation of the x70, the USAAC bought an initial batch of 26 (which it designated the PT-13) in 1936. This small quantity reflected the paucity of the funding then available to the Army Air Corps, but all this changed with the outbreak of World War 2 – 3519 PT-17s were built in 1940 alone. Numerous military designations were given to the Model 75 (as it was officially known after 1939), these usually denoting the aircraft's engine fitment. Canadian machines were given the appellation Kaydet, a name which is now universally applied to all Model 75s. By the time production ceased in early 1945, over 10,000 had been built.

SPECIFICATION:

ACCOMMODATION:
two pilots in tandem

DIMENSIONS:
LENGTH: 25 ft 0.25 in (7.63 m)
WINGSPAN: 32 ft 2 in (9.80 m)
HEIGHT: 9 ft 2 in (2.79 m)

WEIGHTS:
EMPTY: 1936 lb (878 kg)
MAX T/O: 2717 lb (1232 kg)

PERFORMANCE:
MAX SPEED: 124 mph (200 kmh)
RANGE: 505 miles (813 km)
POWERPLANT: Continental R-670 or Lycoming R-680
OUTPUT: 220 hp (164 kW)

FIRST FLIGHT DATE:
December 1933 (Stearman x70)

FEATURES:
Biplane wing layout; uncowled radial engine; N-shaped bracing struts

# Boeing P-26 USA

single-seat, single-engined monoplane fighter

The iconic P-26 started life as the Model 248 in September 1931. Featuring an advanced monoplane layout and all-metal construction, the prototype was flown on 20 March 1932 with the designation XP-936. This was changed to XP-26 when the aircraft was purchased by the USAAC, the latter placing an order for 111 examples of the improved Model 266 (P-26A in Army Air Corps service). By 30 June 1934 all production aircraft had been delivered. A further 25 were built as P-26B/CS, these featuring modified powerplants and armament. Twelve export P-26s were also constructed as the Model 281, eleven of these going to China and the twelfth machine being sent to Spain for evaluation. Dubbed the 'Peashooter', P-26s were supplied to 17 USAAC squadrons. By 1940 the aircraft had been relegated to service with units in the Philippines and Central America, and a small number attempted to defend Manila and Bataan from Japanese aerial attacks in 1941-42. A handful of airworthy P-26s soldiered on with the air forces of Panama and Guatemala into the 1950s.

SPECIFICATION:

ACCOMMODATION:
pilot

DIMENSIONS:
LENGTH: 23 ft 10 in (7.26 m)
WINGSPAN: 27 ft 11.5 in (8.52 m)
HEIGHT: 10 ft 5 in (3.17 m)

WEIGHTS:
EMPTY: 2196 lb (996.1 kg)
MAX T/O: 3015 lb (1367.6 kg)

PERFORMANCE:
MAX SPEED: 234 mph (376.6 kmh)
RANGE: 560 miles (901 km)
POWERPLANT: Pratt & Whitney R-1340-27 Wasp
OUTPUT: 600 hp (447.4 kW)

FIRST FLIGHT DATE:
20 March 1932

ARMAMENT:
two fixed Browning
0.30-in machine guns
in forward fuselage

FEATURES:
Monoplane wing layout;
Townend ring-cowled radial
engine; spatted fixed
undercarriage; prominent
headrest

# Breguet XIX  FRANCE

two-seat, single-engined biplane reconnaissance bomber

Designed as a replacement for the successful Breguet 14, the XIX was produced in even larger numbers, and in more variants, than its Great War predecessor. The XIX featured a strong Duralumin structure which gave the aircraft an empty weight almost identical to the 14. However, its improved strength and more powerful engine meant that the XIX could carry 60 to 80 per cent more fuel and bombs. Proving the type's outstanding performance, the prototype duly set a series of world records. The most famous of these was the flight made by long-range XIX *Question Mark*, which was the first aircraft to cross the North Atlantic westbound – it also made many flights in excess of 5000 miles. By the end of 1926 Breguet had built 1100 A-2 reconnaissance and B-2 bomber versions for the *Armée de l'Air* and nine other air forces. Further examples were built under licence in Yugoslavia, Turkey, Spain, Belgium, Greece and Japan. The XIX remained in frontline service with the *Armée de l'Air* until 1939, and Turkish examples survived well into the late 1940s.

SPECIFICATION:

**ACCOMMODATION:**
pilot and gunner/observer in tandem

**DIMENSIONS:**
LENGTH: 31 ft 2.5 in (9.52 m)
WINGSPAN: 48 ft 8 in (14.85 m)
HEIGHT: 10 ft 11.5 in (3.34 m)

**WEIGHTS:**
EMPTY: 2645 lb (1200 kg)
MAX T/O: 4850 lb (2200 kg)

**PERFORMANCE:**
MAX SPEED: 137 mph (220 kmh)
RANGE: 497 miles (800 km)
POWERPLANT: Renault, Lorraine or Hispano-Suiza vee-12
OUTPUT: 375 to 600 hp (279.6 to 447.4 kW)

**FIRST FLIGHT DATE:**
May 1922

**ARMAMENT:**
one fixed Vickers 0.303-in machine gun on fuselage side and on pivoted mount for observer; racks under lower wings for 1543 lb (700 kg) of bombs

**FEATURES:**
Biplane wing (with slight back staggering) layout; close-fitting engine cowlings; tail skid, Duralumin fuselage

# Bristol Bulldog IIA  UK

single-seat, single-engined biplane fighter

Designed to meet RAF Specification F 9/26, which called for a day and night fighter, Bristol's Type 105 Bulldog I was initially produced as a private venture. First flown on 17 May 1927, the prototype was not an official contender for F 9/26, but following its evaluation by the RAF, service test pilots reported that it was superior to seven of the designs put forward to meet the specification. Indeed, it was only matched by the Hawker Hawfinch, and the 105 was chosen for series production as the Bulldog II. Featuring a longer rear fuselage, the Mk II entered RAF service in May 1929, and by the time production ended two years later, 293 had been built. The bulk of these were Mk IIAs, featuring a larger fin and wider track undercarriage. Fifty-five two-seat trainers were also built. Nine fighter squadrons were equipped with Bulldogs, which remained in frontline service until 1936, providing 70 per cent of the UK's fighter defences. A further 131 Gnome-Rhône Jupiter-powered Bulldogs were exported to countries including Estonia, Denmark, Sweden, Latvia and Siam.

SPECIFICATION:

**ACCOMMODATION:**
pilot

**DIMENSIONS:**
LENGTH: 25 ft 2 in (7.7 m)
WINGSPAN: 33 ft 10 in (10.3 m)
HEIGHT: 8 ft 9 in (2.7 m)

**WEIGHTS:**
EMPTY: 2222 lb (1008 kg)
MAX T/O: 3530 lb (1601 kg)

**PERFORMANCE:**
MAX SPEED: 174 mph (280 kmh)
RANGE: 350 miles (563 km)
POWERPLANT: Bristol Jupiter VIIF
OUTPUT: 490 hp (365.3 kW)

**FIRST FLIGHT DATE:**
17 May 1927

**ARMAMENT:**
two fixed Vickers 0.303-in machine guns on fuselage sides; racks under lower wings for 80 lb (36.4 kg) of bombs

**FEATURES:**
Biplane wing layout; exposed radial engine; extended twin exhaust pipes below forward fuselage; fabric-covered fuselage and wings

# Bücker Bü 131 Jungmann/CASA 1.131E GERMANY & SPAIN

two-seat, single-engined biplane trainer

The Jungmann was employed as a basic trainer by both civil and military flying schools in Germany from late 1934 onwards. The initial production version (Bü 131A) relied on the 80 hp (60 kW) Hirth HM 60R inline engine, but a later variant (and all export models) made use of the more powerful HM 504A-2 powerplant. Aside from its success in its own native land, the Jungmann garnered impressive foreign sales, with eight European nations obtaining aircraft in substantial quantities prior to the outbreak of war. Bücker also concluded a licence deal with Japan, where 1037 were constructed for the Army (as Ki-86As) and 200+ for the Navy (designated K9W1S). The trainer remained in service with the Luftwaffe throughout World War 2, although it was eventually replaced by Bücker's Bü 181 Bestmann. The humble Jungmann also fulfilled an offensive role, dropping light bombs on Soviet troops during nocturnal nuisance raids. Post-war, the design was resurrected in Czechoslovakia, Hungary and Spain, and many remain airworthy today.

SPECIFICATION:

**ACCOMMODATION:**
two pilots in tandem

**DIMENSIONS:**
LENGTH: 21 ft 8 in (6.60 m)
WINGSPAN: 24 ft 3.25 in (7.40 m)
HEIGHT: 7 ft 4.5 in (2.25 m)

**WEIGHTS:**
EMPTY: 860 lb (390 kg)
MAX T/O: 1499 lb (680 kg)

**PERFORMANCE:**
MAX SPEED: 115 mph (185 kmh)
RANGE: 404 miles (650 km)
powerplant: Hirth HM 504A-2
OUTPUT: 105 hp (78 kW)

**FIRST FLIGHT DATE:**
27 April 1934

**FEATURES:**
Biplane wing layout; cowled inline engine; exhaust stubs below engine; canted-in mainwheels on fixed undercarriage; tailwheel

# Bücker BÜ 133 Jungmeister/CASA ES-1 GERMANY & SPAIN

single-seat, single-engined biplane trainer

Similar in overall configuration to the Jungmann, the Jungmeister was designed and built at Bücker's then-new Rangsdorf factory, which had been opened in order to allow the company to cope with the overwhelming demand for its BÜ 131 trainer. Whereas the latter had been designed for the basic training role, the smaller and more powerful BÜ 133 was aimed at the more advanced student, being fully aerobatic. The Luftwaffe soon ordered the Jungmeister into volume production following its evaluation in 1935-36, the type being used extensively by pilots destined to fly single-seat fighters. Although the prototype and early production BÜ 133As relied on the 135 hp (101 kW) Hirth HM 6 inline engine, the major production variant (C-model) was fitted with the more powerful Siemens sh 14A-4 radial – as were the 47 licence-built machines (designated BÜ 133Bs) produced for the Swiss Air Force by Dornier-Werke. CASA of Spain also built a similar number of BÜ 133Cs for the Spanish Air Force, who designated them ES-1s.

SPECIFICATION:

ACCOMMODATION:
pilot

DIMENSIONS:
LENGTH: 19 ft 8.25 in (6 m)
WINGSPAN: 21 ft 7.75 in (6.60 m)
HEIGHT: 7 ft 2.5 in (2.20 m)

WEIGHTS:
EMPTY: 937 lb (425 kg)
MAX T/O: 1290 lb (585 kg)

PERFORMANCE:
MAX SPEED: 137 mph (220 kmh)
RANGE: 311 miles (500 km)
POWERPLANT: Siemens SH 14a-4 and Franklin 6a-650-c1 (BÜ 133f of the 1960s)
OUTPUT: 160 hp (119 kW) and 220 hp (164 kW) respectively

FIRST FLIGHT DATE:
1935

FEATURES:
Biplane wing layout; close-cowled radial engine; raised fuselage rear decking; mudguards fitted to mainwheels; tailwheel

# Curtiss NC-4  USA

six-seat, four-engined biplane long-range patrol flying-boat

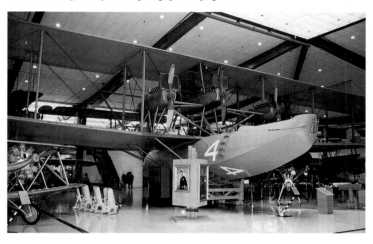

Famed for being the first aircraft to complete a crossing of the Atlantic (in stages), the Navy/Curtiss flying-boat was developed in response to Germany's successful U-boat campaign of 1917. The aircraft had to be able to fly across the Atlantic, as there was no space available for flying-boats to be shipped to the UK. Such a machine needed an endurance of 15-20 hours, which meant that it would have to be large, multi-engined and rugged enough to endure forced landings at sea.

Curtiss was alone amongst US manufacturers in having experience of building such aircraft, and it produced a 28,000-lb biplane based on the US Navy's hull design. Designated the NC for Navy and Curtiss, the first example completed its maiden flight on 4 October 1918. Too late to see action in World War 1, three NC flying-boats nevertheless set off across the Atlantic on a proving flight in May 1919. Only NC-4 made it to the UK, however. Six more NC flying-boats were built post-war, and these remained in service into the late 1920s.

SPECIFICATION:

**ACCOMMODATION:**
two pilots, navigator/nose gunner, radio operator and two flight engineers

**DIMENSIONS:**
LENGTH: 68 ft 3 in (20.8 m)
WINGSPAN: 126 ft 0 in (38.4 m)
HEIGHT: 24 ft 6 in (7.49 m)

**WEIGHTS:**
EMPTY: 15,874 lb (7200 kg)
MAX T/O: 26,386 lb (11,968 kg)

**PERFORMANCE:**
MAX SPEED: 85 mph (136 kmh)
RANGE: 1470 miles (2352 km)
POWERPLANT: three Liberty 12s
OUTPUT: 800 hp (596.5 kW)

**FIRST FLIGHT DATE:**
4 October 1918

**ARMAMENT:**
Single 0.30-in machine guns on pivoted mount for observer/gunner in bow and rear hull cockpits

**FEATURES:**
Biplane wing layout; laminated wood veneer flying-boat hull; three tractor engines between the wings; wingtip sponsons

# Curtiss F6C Hawk USA

single-seat, single-engined biplane fighter

Just as Boeing succeeded in selling versions of its biplane fighters to the Navy, so too did rival manufacturer Curtiss. The breakthrough came in March 1925 when the Navy ordered nine F6C-1 Hawks, which were effectively navalised versions of the USAAC's P-1 Hawk. The primary difference between the two aircraft was that the F6C-1 could be fitted with Macchi floats for water-borne operations. Two of these machines were delivered with arrestor hooks and strengthened landing gear for carrier deck trials. These proved successful, and 35 F6C-3s were ordered in early 1927. A further 31 Pratt & Whitney R-1340-powered F6C-4s were ordered following the Navy's decision to standardise on air-cooled radials for its aircraft. Although lighter and more manoeuvrable than the Curtiss-powered F6C-3s, the -4s were deemed obsolete by the time production examples reached the fleet. Following their replacement by the Boeing F4B, a number of F6Cs were used as advanced trainers, while others were passed on to the Marine Corps.

SPECIFICATION:

ACCOMMODATION:
pilot

DIMENSIONS:
LENGTH: 22 ft 6 in (6.86 m)
WINGSPAN: 31 ft 6 in (9.60 m)
HEIGHT: 10 ft 11 in (3.33 m)

WEIGHTS:
EMPTY: 1980 lb (898 kg)
MAX T/O: 2785 lb (1263 kg)

PERFORMANCE:
MAX SPEED: 155 mph (249 kmh)
RANGE: 361 miles (581 km)
POWERPLANT: Curtiss V-1150-1
(F6C-1/3) or Pratt & Whitney
R-1340 (F6C-4)
OUTPUT: 435 hp (324.37 kW) and
410 hp (305.73 kW) respectively

FIRST FLIGHT DATE:
Autumn 1925

ARMAMENT:
two fixed Browning 0.30-in
machine guns on upper fuselage

FEATURES:
Biplane wing layout; close-cowled
inline engine (F6C-1/3) and ringed
radial engine (F6C-4); arrestor
hook

# Curtiss P-6E Hawk  USA

single-seat, single-engined biplane fighter

The P-6E was the final production machine in this series, which could trace its history back to the P-1 of 1925. The Hawk was created when Curtiss married the engine, cowling, three-bladed propeller and main undercarriage of its XP-22 fighter prototype with the airframe of the YP-20 in the autumn of 1931. The end result was designated the XP-6E, and the USAAC ordered it into limited production. Like previous Curtiss fighter designs, only a small number of P-6Es were built – 46 were delivered from 2 December 1931. The aircraft differed from previous Hawk fighters by having an underbelly radiator and single-strut undercarriage. Most P-6Es were issued to the 1st Pursuit Group at Selfridge Field, Michigan, or the 8th Pursuit Group at Langley Field, Virginia. The P-6E was a contemporary of the Boeing P-12 in USAAC service, and the two types were the principal biplane fighters in the US in the inter-war years. A handful of surviving P-6Es remained in service as communication 'hacks' in 1938, after which they were quietly retired.

SPECIFICATION:

ACCOMMODATION:
pilot

DIMENSIONS:
LENGTH: 23 ft 2 in (7.06 m)
WINGSPAN: 31 ft 6 in (9.60 m)
HEIGHT: 8 ft 10 in (2.69 m)

WEIGHTS:
EMPTY: 2699 lb (1224.3 kg)
MAX T/O: 3392 lb (1538.6 kg)

PERFORMANCE:
MAX SPEED: 197 mph (317 kmh)
RANGE: 570 miles (917 km)
POWERPLANT: Curtiss V-1570-23
OUTPUT: 600 hp (447.4 kW)

FIRST FLIGHT DATE:
Autumn 1931

ARMAMENT:
two fixed Browning 0.30-in
machine guns on upper
fuselage sides

FEATURES:
Tapered biplane wing layout;
single-strut, spatted
undercarriage; underbelly
radiator; close-cowled inline
engine

# Curtiss F9C Sparrowhawk USA

single-seat, single-engined biplane fighter

Only eight F9C Sparrowhawks were built for the US Navy, the aircraft being designed to meet a lightweight shipboard fighter requirement. The latter called for the production of a very small aircraft, yet despite being just 20 ft long and with a wingspan of only 25 ft, the XF9C-1 proved too large for the Navy! However, these modest dimensions meant that the Sparrowhawk was small enough to pass through the hangar door built into the Navy dirigibles USS *Akron* and *Macon*.

These airships were constructed with hangar space for four aeroplanes each, which were launched and retrieved by means of a trapeze. The aircraft would hang from the trapeze by a skyhook fitted to the upper wing. Curtiss also raised the aircraft's top wing by four inches and fitted a more powerful Wright radial. Six production F9C-2s were ordered in October 1931, and the first hook-on to *Akron* was made on 29 June 1932. No Sparrowhawks were lost when *Akron* crashed in 1933, but four were destroyed with the loss of *Macon* two years later.

SPECIFICATION:

**ACCOMMODATION:**
pilot

**DIMENSIONS:**
LENGTH: 20 ft 7 in (6.27 m)
WINGSPAN: 25 ft 5 in (7.75 m)
HEIGHT: 10 ft 11.5 in (3.34 m)

**WEIGHTS:**
EMPTY: 2089 lb (947 kg)
MAX T/O: 2770 lb (1256 kg)

**PERFORMANCE:**
MAX SPEED: 176 mph (284 kmh)
RANGE: 350 miles (563 km)
POWERPLANT: Wright R-975-E3
OUTPUT: 438 hp (326.6 kW)

**FIRST FLIGHT DATE:**
12 February 1931

**ARMAMENT:**
two fixed Browning 0.30-in machine guns on upper fuselage

**FEATURES:**
Biplane wing layout, with upper wing gull-shaped; N-shaped bracing struts; spatted undercarriage; close-cowled radial engine; skyhook assembly above upper wing

# Curtiss Hawk III  USA

single-seat, single-engined biplane fighter

The Hawk III was the export version of the US Navy's unsuccessful F11C-3/BF2C-1, 27 examples of which saw brief service in 1934-35 until grounded by an incurable sympathetic wing vibration. This was caused by the engine at cruising rpm, and Curtiss found that it could only be eradicated by replacing the metal wing structure with wood. The first export of a Hawk III was a single example sold to Turkey in April 1935, followed by 24 to Thailand and 102 to China – 90 of the latter machines were assembled by the Central Aircraft Manufacturing Company in Hangchow. Finally, Argentina purchased ten Hawk IIIs in May 1936. Used as a fighter-bomber, the aircraft's most distinguishing feature was its manually-operated retractable main undercarriage members, which were accommodated in a deepened forward fuselage. Most Chinese Hawks were destroyed fighting superior Japanese aircraft in 1937-38, and the handful of survivors were replaced by superior Soviet fighters. A number of Thai Hawks survived in service post-World War 2, however.

SPECIFICATION:

ACCOMMODATION:
pilot

DIMENSIONS:
LENGTH: 23 ft 5 in (7.14 m)
WINGSPAN: 31 ft 6 in (9.60 m)
HEIGHT: 9 ft 9.5 in (2.98 m)

WEIGHTS:
EMPTY: 3213 lb (1457 kg)
MAX T/O: 4317 lb (1958 kg)

PERFORMANCE:
MAX SPEED: 240 mph (386 kmh)
RANGE: 575 miles (925 km)
POWERPLANT: Wright SR-1820F-53
OUTPUT: 785 hp (585.3 kW)

FIRST FLIGHT DATE:
Early 1933

ARMAMENT:
two fixed Browning 0.30-in machine guns on upper fuselage; racks under lower wings for 400 lb (181.4 kg) of bombs

FEATURES:
Biplane, staggered wing layout; N-shaped bracing struts; retractable undercarriage; close-cowled radial engine

# Curtiss o-52 Owl USA

two-seat, single-engined parasol heavy observation aircraft

Built by Curtiss Wright in response to a US Army requirement for a two-seat observation aircraft, the Owl was a very capable machine with good low-speed manoeuvrability and landing characteristics. Designated the Model 85 by the company, the all-metal design relied on full-span automatic leading edge slots working in conjunction with wide-span trailing edge flaps to achieve low-speed agility. Ordered into production in 1939, a total of 203 o-52 Owls were built for the US Army from 1940 onwards, although none actually saw frontline service – 19 of these machines were eventually passed on the Soviet Union. Following the US entry into World War 2, the Army Air Force determined that the o-52 did not possess sufficient performance for combat operations overseas, resulting in the Owls being relegated to flying courier duties within America. A small number also flew short-range submarine patrols over the Gulf of Mexico and Atlantic and Pacific Oceans soon after war was declared. By late 1942 virtually all o-52s had been retired.

## SPECIFICATION:

**ACCOMMODATION:**
pilot and observer in tandem

**DIMENSIONS:**
LENGTH: 26 ft 4 in (8.03 m)
WINGSPAN: 40 ft 9.50 in (12.43 m)
HEIGHT: 9 ft 3.25 in (2.83 m)

**WEIGHTS:**
EMPTY: 4231 lb (1919 kg)
MAX T/O: 5364 lb (2433 kg)

**PERFORMANCE:**
MAX SPEED: 220 mph (354 kmh)
RANGE: 700 miles (1127 km)
POWERPLANT: Pratt & Whitney R-1340-51 Wasp
OUTPUT: 600 hp (447 kW)

**FIRST FLIGHT DATE:**
1938

**ARMAMENT:**
one fixed Browning 0.30-in machine gun on upper fuselage and one Browning 0.30-in machine gun

**FEATURES:**
Parasol wing; retractable undercarriage; close-cowled radial engine; tailwheel

# Curtiss SNC USA

two-seat, single-engined monoplane advanced trainer

This rather obscure aircraft was ordered by the US Navy in 1940 to fulfil the scout trainer role, its layout being based on the Curtiss CW-21 fighter of 1938. Unlike the latter machine, the SNC had tandem cockpit arrangement and an engine of far less power – a 420 hp (313 kW) Wright Whirlwind in place of the 1000 hp (744 kW) Cyclone from the same manufacturer – as befitted its training role.

Unofficially named the 'Falcon', the SNC was fully equipped to undertake instrument flying, high altitude training, air gunnery and bomb delivery. An initial contract for 150 aircraft was placed with Curtiss in November 1940, followed by subsequent orders for 150 and 5 the following year. With the delivery of the 305th SNC in late 1941, the production line was terminated. The SNC was soon replaced by navalised versions of the ubiquitous T-6 Texan, known as the NJ/SNJ in Navy service.

SPECIFICATION:

**ACCOMMODATION:**
two pilots in tandem

**DIMENSIONS:**
LENGTH: 26 ft 6 in (8.08 m)
WINGSPAN: 35 ft 0 in (10.67 m)
HEIGHT: 7 ft 6 in (2.29 m)

**WEIGHTS:**
EMPTY: 2610 lb (1184 kg)
MAX T/O: 3626 lb (1645 kg)

**PERFORMANCE:**
MAX SPEED: 201 mph (323 kmh)
RANGE: 515 miles (829 km)
POWERPLANT: Wright R-975-E3 Whirlwind 9
OUTPUT: 420 hp (313 kW)

**FIRST FLIGHT DATE:**
1939

**FEATURES:**
Monoplane wing; retractable undercarriage; close-cowled radial engine; tailwheel, tapered rear fuselage

# de Havilland DH 82 Tiger Moth UK

two-seat, single-engined biplane trainer

Derived from the highly successful civilian DH 60G Gipsy Moth, the Tiger Moth differed from its predecessor in having staggered and swept-back wings (which allowed the parachute-equipped occupant to exit the machine in a hurry), an inverted engine to aid visibility over the nose and strengthening to the wings and fuselage in order to allow the aircraft to operate at a higher all up weight. Designated the DH 82, the prototype completed its maiden flight on 26 October 1931 and entered service with the RAF the following month.

De Havilland further improved the trainer three years later when it mated the more powerful Gipsy Major engine with a slightly modified Tiger Moth fuselage (wooden rear fuselage decking in place of fabric), the new version being designated the DH 82A. The final variant to reach series production was the winterised DH 82C, built by de Havilland Aircraft of Canada. A staple trainer for virtually all Allied air arms during World War 2, over 8500 Tiger Moths were eventually built.

SPECIFICATION:

ACCOMMODATION:
two pilots in tandem

DIMENSIONS:
LENGTH: 23 ft 11 in (7.29 m)
WINGSPAN: 29 ft 4 in (8.94 m)
HEIGHT: 8 ft 9.50 in (2.68 m)

WEIGHTS:
EMPTY: 1115 lb (506 kg)
MAX T/O: 1770 lb (803 kg)

PERFORMANCE:
MAX SPEED: 109 mph (175 kmh)
RANGE: 302 miles (486 km)
POWERPLANT: de Havilland Gipsy
III (DH 82) or Gipsy Major
(DH 82B/C)
OUTPUT: DH 82 120 hp (89 kW),
DH 82B 130 hp (97 kW),
DH 82C 145 hp (108 kW)

FIRST FLIGHT DATE:
26 October 1931

FEATURES:
Swept-back biplane wing layout;
cowled inline engine; single
exhaust stub below starboard side
of engine; tail skid

# de Havilland DH 89 Dominie UK

five/six-seat, twin-engined biplane trainer/communications aircraft

The military version of the pre-war Dragon Rapide airliner, the Dominie was initially produced to meet the same Air Ministry Specification as the Anson. As previously mentioned, the monoplane design was chosen for the general reconnaissance task, and de Havilland had to be satisfied with selling a handful of DH 89Ms (as the military Rapide was designated) to the Spanish government for use in Morocco. However, all was not lost for the Rapide as it was selected by the RAF to fill the role of communications aircraft – several DH 89s were purchased in 1937-38, whilst in 1939, a further 17 were acquired for wireless training.

At this time the trainer variant was designated the Dominie Mk I, whilst the communications version was christened the Dominie Mk II. The type remained in production until July 1946, some 475 Dominies being built for the RAF and Fleet Air Arm. A number of pre-war civil Rapides were also impressed into RAF service alongside the purpose-built Dominies during the early years of World War 2.

## SPECIFICATION:

**ACCOMMODATION:**
crew of up to six in training role, seats for up to ten in communications configuration

**DIMENSIONS:**
LENGTH: 34 ft 6 in (10.52 m)
WINGSPAN: 48 ft 0 in (14.63 m)
HEIGHT: 10 ft 3 in (3.12 m)

**WEIGHTS:**
EMPTY: 3230 lb (1465 kg)
MAX T/O: 5500 lb (2945 kg)

**PERFORMANCE:**
MAX SPEED: 157 mph (253 kmh)
RANGE: 570 miles (917 km)
POWERPLANT: two de Havilland Gipsy Queens
OUTPUT: 400 hp (298.2 kW)

**FIRST FLIGHT DATE:**
17 April 1934 (civilian Dragon Rapide)

**FEATURES:**
Biplane wing layout; two close-cowled inline engines; spatted undercarriage; tail wheel

# Dewoitine D 26 FRANCE & SWITZERLAND

single-seat, single-engined parasol fighter trainer

Based on the Dewoitine D 27 III parasol fighter, which entered service with the Swiss Air Force in 1931, the D 26 was a dedicated training variant built in limited numbers (11) under licence by EKW of Switzerland. Whilst the frontline fighter was fitted with a 500 hp (372.6 kW) Hispano-Suiza 12Mb V12, the D 26 was equipped with a radial engine from the same manufacturer that produced exactly half the horsepower. The Dewoitine machine proved to be the perfect training tool for future *Fliegertruppe* fighter pilots, and despite the D 27 IIIs being replaced in 1940 (and finally scrapped in 1944) by Bf 109ES bought from Germany, the D 26s remained in service until late in the decade. Of the eleven originally built, no fewer than six survived military service to be sold into private hands in Switzerland between 1949 and 1951.

SPECIFICATION:

ACCOMMODATION:
pilot

DIMENSIONS:
LENGTH: 21 ft 6 in (6.40 m)
WINGSPAN: 33 ft 9.5 in (10.30 m)
HEIGHT: 9 ft 1.5 in (2.78 m)

WEIGHTS:
EMPTY: 2046 lb (930 kg)
MAX T/O: 2350 lb (1065.96 kg)

PERFORMANCE:
MAX SPEED: 120 mph (192 kmh)
RANGE: 230 miles (368 km)
POWERPLANT: Hispano 9QA
OUTPUT: 250 hp (186.3 kW)

FIRST FLIGHT DATE:
1928

FEATURES:
Parasol wing layout; uncowled
radial engine; tail wheel

# Douglas B-18 Bolo   USA

six-seat, twin-engined bomber/transport/anti-submarine aircraft

A military adaption of Douglas's successful DC-2 commercial transport, the B-18 (designated the DB-1 by its manufacturer) was the winner of the 1934 multi-engined bomber competition staged by the US Army Air Corps to find a replacement for its Martin B-10. The new machine had to be able to carry one tonne of bombs over 2000 miles at a speed in excess of 200 mph. Drawing heavily on its experience with the DC-2, Douglas's DB-1 boasted the wings of the civilian airliner combined with a deeper and fatter fuselage that contained a bomb-bay. Although the DB-1 was outclassed by the Boeing Model 299 (later to be redesignated the B-17) in the competition fly-off, it was substantially cheaper. The crash of the prototype Model 299 in October 1935 sealed the order in favour of the Douglas, and 132 B-18s were built in 1937-38. A further 217 improved B-18As were also delivered between April 1938 and January 1940. Obsolete as a bomber by 1940, a number of B-18s were destroyed in the attacks on Pearl Harbor and the Philippines in December 1941.

SPECIFCATION:

**ACCOMMODATION:**
two pilots, navigator/bombardier and three gunners

**DIMENSIONS:**
LENGTH: 56 ft 8 in (17.31 m)
WINGSPAN: 89 ft 6 in (27.3 m)
HEIGHT: 15 ft 2 in (4.63 m)

**WEIGHTS:**
EMPTY: 15,719 lb (7130 kg)
MAX T/O: 27,087 lb (12,286 kg)

**PERFORMANCE:**
MAX SPEED: 217 mph (347 kmh)
RANGE: 1150 miles (1840 km)
POWERPLANT: two Wright R-1820-45s
OUTPUT: 1860 hp (1387 kW)

**FIRST FLIGHT DATE:**
April 1935

**ARMAMENT:**
three Browning 0.30-in machine guns in the nose, dorsal and ventral positions; maximum bomb load of 4400 lb (1995 kg) carried in bomb-bay

**FEATURES:**
Monoplane wing layout; retractable undercarriage; twin radial engines; nose turret

# Douglas B-23 Dragon USA

six-seat, twin-engined bomber/transport/anti-submarine aircraft

The B-23 Dragon was essentially a reworked and improved B-18. Produced as a result of the success of the multi-engined B-17, which had been built at the same time as the B-18, the Dragon boasted a new, more aerodynamic fuselage, greater wingspan and taller vertical tail unit – it was also the first US bomber built with a tail gunner's position. All of these modifications were meant to make the bomber a better performer, and when married to the greater power of the twin Wright R-2600s, Douglas felt sure that they had an aircraft to rival the Flying Fortress. However, flight trials soon revealed less than inspiring performance figures, particularly in light of combat information reaching America from Europe in relation to bomb load and range. The B-23 was quickly passed over in favour of newer medium bombers under development, and only 38 were eventually delivered. These machines saw limited service as coastal patrol aircraft along the Pacific seaboard, whilst 12 were later converted into utility transports (designated UC-67s).

SPECIFICATION:

ACCOMMODATION:
pilot, navigator, bombardier, radio operator, camera operator, tail gunner

DIMENSIONS:
LENGTH: 58 ft 4 in (17.78 m)
WINGSPAN: 92 ft 0 in (28.04 m)
HEIGHT: 18 ft 6 in (5.64 m)

WEIGHTS:
EMPTY: 19 059 lb (8645 kg)
MAX T/O: 30 475 lb (13 823 kg)

PERFORMANCE:
MAX SPEED: 282 mph (454 kmh)
RANGE: 1455 miles (2342 km)
POWERPLANT: two Wright R-2600-3 Cyclones
OUTPUT: 3200 hp (2366 kW)

FIRST FLIGHT DATE:
27 July 1939

ARMAMENT:
three Browning 0.30-in machine guns on flexible mounts in the nose, dorsal and aft fuselage positions, and one Browning 0.50-in machine gun in tail; maximum bomb load of 4000 lb (1814 kg) in bomb-bay

FEATURES:
Monoplane wing layout; retractable undercarriage; twin radial engines; nose and tail guns

# Fairchild PT-19, PT-23 and PT-26 Cornell USA

two-seat, single-engined monoplane trainer

Procured by the USAAC in order to better prepare trainee pilots destined to fly monoplane aircraft in the frontline, the PT-19 started life as the private-venture M-62. Evaluated in 1939, the trainer was ordered into series production in 1940 and entered service as the PT-19 Cornell later that same year – some 270 were built before the re-engined PT-19A came on line in 1941. Over 3700 PT-19AS were built, but by 1942 production was being seriously affected by a shortage of Ranger inline engines. With engineless airframes backing up at three assembly lines, a solution to the problem was needed quickly, so Fairchild simply fitted an uncowled Continental R-670 radial to a standard PT-19A and produced the PT-23. The 'new' aircraft proved to be so successful that a further 6000 were delivered before production finally ceased in 1944. The Canadians also found the Fairchild design ideal for the Commonwealth Air Training Scheme, Fleet building substantial quantities of the PT-23 (Cornell I – 93 examples) and PT-26A/B (Cornell II – 1057 examples) under licence.

SPECIFICATION:

**ACCOMMODATION:**
two pilots in tandem

**DIMENSIONS:**
LENGTH: 27 ft 8.5 in (8.45 m)
WINGSPAN: 36 ft 0 in (10.97 m)
HEIGHT: 7 ft 7.5 in (2.32 m)

**WEIGHTS:**
EMPTY: 2022 lb (917 kg)
MAX T/O: 2736 lb (1241 kg)

**PERFORMANCE:**
MAX SPEED: 122 mph (196 kmh)
RANGE: 400 miles (644 km)
POWERPLANT: Ranger L-440 or Continental R-670
OUTPUT: 200 hp (149 kW) and 220 hp (164 kW) respectively

**FIRST FLIGHT DATE:**
March 1939

**FEATURES:**
Monoplane wing layout; fixed undercarriage; close-cowled inline (PT-19) or exposed radial (PT-23) engines; tandem open cockpits

# Fairey IIID UK

three-seat, single-engined biplane reconnaissance land/seaplane

One of the most important types in the Fleet Air Arm (FAA) inventory between 1924 and 1930, the IIID was the penultimate example of the famous III series of land/seaplanes built by Fairey over a 20-year period commencing in 1916. Strongly built and immensely reliable, the IIID was flown either with a wheeled undercarriage from shore stations or aircraft carriers, or with floats as a seaplane catapulted from warships. The aircraft's primary missions were reconnaissance and gunnery spotting, crews being trained to search out enemy fleets and relay the fall of shot to battleships and cruisers tasked with engaging the enemy.

The prototype IIID was built in seaplane configuration in early 1920, and early examples reached the FAA in 1924. A total of 207 IIIDs were delivered to the FAA, with the final examples being built in 1926. The aircraft saw service with the Royal Navy in the Far East, the Mediterranean and in home waters. The IIID was replaced in FAA service from 1928 by the IIIF, which was Fairey's final III series machine.

SPECIFICATION:

**ACCOMMODATION:**
pilot, observer and gunner

**DIMENSIONS:**
LENGTH: 37 ft 0 in (11.27 m)
WINGSPAN: 46 ft 1.25 in (14.05 m)
HEIGHT: 11 ft 4 in (3.47 m)

**WEIGHTS:**
EMPTY: 3248 lb (1473 kg)
MAX T/O: 4918 lb (2230 kg)

**PERFORMANCE:**
MAX SPEED: 106 mph (169.6 kmh)
RANGE: 550 miles (880 km)
POWERPLANT: Rolls-Royce Eagle VIII or Napier Lion
OUTPUT: 375 hp (279 kW) and 450 hp (335 kW) respectively

**FIRST FLIGHT DATE:**
August 1920

**ARMAMENT:**
One fixed Vickers 0.303-in machine gun forward and one Lewis 0.303-in machine gun on flexible mount for gunner

**FEATURES:**
Biplane wing layout; inline engine with exposed cylinder banks; floats on seaplane variant

# Fairey Battle UK

three-seat, single-engined monoplane light bomber

The Battle was one of the key types chosen by the Air Ministry for the re-equipment of the rapidly expanding RAF of the late 1930s. Designed to meet the requirements of Specification P 27/32. The aircraft carried twice as many bombs as the Harts and Hinds it was to replace and was 50 mph faster. An order was placed for 655 aircraft, and production Battle IS entered squadron service in March 1937. Fifteen units within Bomber Command had re-equipped by mid 1938, and upon the outbreak of World War 2, Battles of No 226 Sqn became the first RAF aircraft sent to France. This unit, along with nine other Battle squadrons, formed the van-guard of the Advanced Air Striking Force in France in 1939-40. Following early skirmishes during the 'Phoney War', the RAF realised that the Battle was underpowered, and lacked the speed and defensive armament necessary to perform unescorted daylight operations. Horrendous losses to German flak and fighters in May 1940 confirmed this, and surviving Battles were employed as gunnery trainers and target tugs in Canada and Australia.

SPECIFICATION:

ACCOMMODATION:
pilots, bomb aimer and gunner

DIMENSIONS:
LENGTH: 42 ft 2 in (12.85 m)
WINGSPAN: 54 ft 0 in (16.46 m)
HEIGHT: 15 ft 6 in (4.72 m)

WEIGHTS:
EMPTY: 6647 lb (3015 kg)
MAX T/O: 10,792 lb (4895 kg)

PERFORMANCE:
MAX SPEED: 241 mph (388 kmh)
RANGE: 900 miles (1450 km)
POWERPLANT: Rolls-Royce
Merlin I/II/III or IV
OUTPUT: 1030 hp (768 kW)

FIRST FLIGHT DATE:
10 March 1936

ARMAMENT:
One fixed Vickers 0.303-in machine gun in starboard wing and one Vickers K gun on flexible mount for gunner; maximum bomb load of 1000 lb (454 kg) in inner wing cells

FEATURES:
Monoplane wing; semi-retractable undercarriage; close-cowled inline engine; fixed tailwheel; long canopy

# Fleet Finch CANADA

two-seat, single-engined biplane trainer

The origins of the Finch can be traced back to Consolidated's then President, Major Reuben H Fleet, who believed that there was a gap in the civil market in North America for a basic trainer. However, with the first prototype built and tested, Consolidated's management decided not to enter the field of light aviation, so the Major established Fleet Aircraft and build the trainer independently. Six months later, Consolidated yet again changed its mind and bought Fleet out, duly setting up a factory for trainer construction in Canada. Sold in modest numbers throughout the 1930s on both sides of the border, the trainer was finally evaluated by the RCAF in Model 10 form in September 1938. Following the trials, the air force stipulated that certain strengthening modifications must be carried out to enable the aircraft to perform aerobatics when fully equipped with military equipment. Known as the Model 16, and christened the Finch I in RCAF service, 606 were eventually built between 1939 and 1941.

SPECIFICATION:

**ACCOMMODATION:**
two pilots in tandem

**DIMENSIONS:**
LENGTH: 21 ft 8 in (6.60 m)
WINGSPAN: 28 ft 0 in (8.53 m)
HEIGHT: 7 ft 9 in (2.36 m)

**WEIGHTS:**
EMPTY: 1122 lb (509 kg)
MAX T/O: 2000 lb (908 kg)

**PERFORMANCE:**
MAX SPEED: 104 mph (167.3 kmh)
RANGE: 320 miles (512 km)
POWERPLANT: Kinner B-5
OUTPUT: 125 hp (93.25 kW)

**FIRST FLIGHT DATE:**
September 1938

**FEATURES:**
Biplane wing layout; uncowled radial engine; N-shaped bracing struts; tailwheel

# Focke-Wulf FW 44 Stieglitz GERMANY

two-seat, single-engined biplane trainer

The humble FW 44 Stieglitz (Goldfinch) basic
trainer first took to the skies in the late summer of
1932. Despite its conventional appearance, the
prototype aircraft proved to be extremely difficult
to fly, and it was left to recently-arrived designer
Kurt Tank to sort the trainer out. This he duly did,
and the revised FW 44 was subsequently ordered
into series production not only for the newly-born
Luftwaffe, but also for the ostensibly civilian-run
*Deutsche Verkehrsfliegerschule* and the *Deutsche
Luftsportverband.*

Focke-Wulf followed up the radial-powered FW
44 with the Argus AS 8 inline-engined B- and E-
models, small numbers of which were also issued
to Luftwaffe training units. However, the company
returned to the Siemens sh 14a radial again for the
remaining variants, with the C-, D-, F-, and
J-models being built in substantial quantities until
the end of the war. Licence production was also
undertaken in a number of foreign countries,
whilst numerous other air arms bought FW 44s
directly from Focke-Wulf.

SPECIFICATION:

**ACCOMMODATION:**
two pilots in tandem

**DIMENSIONS:**
LENGTH: 23 ft 11.5 in (7.30 m)
WINGSPAN: 29 ft 6.5 in (9.00 m)
HEIGHT: 8 ft 10.25 in (2.70 m)

**WEIGHTS:**
EMPTY: 1157 lb (525 kg)
MAX T/O: 1985 lb (900 kg)

**PERFORMANCE:**
MAX SPEED: 115 mph (185 kmh)
RANGE: 419 miles (675 km)
POWERPLANT: Siemens sh 14a
OUTPUT: 150 hp (112 kW)

**FIRST FLIGHT DATE:**
Late Summer 1932

**FEATURES:**
Biplane wing layout; uncowled
radial engine; N-shaped bracing
struts; tailwheel

# Fokker D.XXI  THE NETHERLANDS

single-seat, single-engined monoplane fighter

The last single-engined fighter to carry the famous Fokker name, the D.XXI was a fixed undercarriage monoplane fighter that was effectively obsolete by the outbreak of World War 2. Built in small numbers, and only used by three air arms, the type nevertheless acquitted itself well in Dutch hands before being totally overwhelmed during the May 1940 *Blitzkrieg*. The first D.XXIs had been ordered to fill a requirement expressed by the Netherlands East Indies Air Service in the mid-1930s, and the first examples entered Dutch service in the Netherlands in early 1938. Licence-built examples were also produced concurrently by VL in Finland, and some 90 D.XXIs were delivered. The final foreign user of the Fokker fighter was Denmark, who bought two directly from the Dutch company and then built a further ten. Danish D.XXIs saw little action during the German invasion in the spring of 1940, but the Finnish examples inflicted heavy casualties on Soviet forces for much of World War 2. Indeed, the final Finnish D.XXI was not retired from service until 1951.

SPECIFICATION:

ACCOMMODATION:
pilot

DIMENSIONS:
LENGTH: 26 ft 11 in (8.20 m)
WINGSPAN: 36 ft 1 in (11.00 m)
HEIGHT: 9 ft 8 in (2.95 m)

WEIGHTS:
EMPTY: 3197 lb (1450 kg)
MAX T/O: 4519 lb (2050 kg)

PERFORMANCE:
MAX SPEED: 286 mph (460 kmh)
RANGE: 578 miles (930 km)
POWERPLANT: Bristol Mercury VII/VIII
OUTPUT: 830 hp (619 kW)

FIRST FLIGHT DATE:
27 March 1936

ARMAMENT:
four 7.7 mm or 7.9 mm machine guns in wings, or two 7.9 mm machine guns and two 20 mm cannon in wings

FEATURES:
Monoplane wing; spatted undercarriage; close-cowled radial engine; tailwheel; fixed tailwheel

# Gloster Gauntlet  UK

single-seat, single-engined biplane fighter

The last open-cockpit biplane fighter to serve with the RAF, Gloster's Gauntlet started life as the ss (single-seat) 18 of 1929. Built to Air Ministry Specification F 9/26, the aircraft was powered by a Bristol Mercury IIA engine and armed with two Vickers machine guns. The prototype was progressively modified over the next four years until it was chosen by the Air Ministry in ss 19B form to replace the Bulldog. The first 24 examples built (designated the Gauntlet I) boasted wheel spats, although two follow-on orders in 1935 for a total of 204 Gauntlet IIs deleted this fitment.

A number of late-build Mk IIs also featured a Fairey-Reed three-blade, fixed-pitch metal propeller in place of the original two-blade Watts wooden type. No 19 Sqn became the first unit to receive Gauntlet Is in May 1935, and, at peak strength, Gauntlets equipped 22 British squadrons at home and in the Middle East. They remained in the frontline inventory in the latter theatre until July 1940. Gauntlets also saw service in Australia, South Africa, Rhodesia, Denmark and Finland.

SPECIFICATION:

ACCOMMODATION:
pilot

DIMENSIONS:
LENGTH: 26 ft 2 in (7.97 m)
WINGSPAN: 32 ft 9.5 in (10 m)
HEIGHT: 10 ft 4 in (3.18 m)

WEIGHTS:
EMPTY: 2775 lb (1260 kg)
MAX T/O: 3970 lb (1801 kg)

PERFORMANCE:
MAX SPEED: 230 mph (370 kmh)
RANGE: 460 miles (740 km)
POWERPLANT: Bristol Mercury VIS-2
OUTPUT: 645 hp (481 kW)

FIRST FLIGHT DATE:
August 1933 (ss 19B)

ARMAMENT:
two Vickers 0.303 in machine guns in fuselage sides

FEATURES:
Biplane wing layout; cowled radial engine; tailwheel; open cockpit

# Gloster Gladiator UK

single-seat, single-engined biplane fighter

The Gladiator started life as a company private venture, Gloster basing its new ss 37 very much on its predecessor, the Gauntlet. Although equipped with four guns, the design still embraced the 'old' technology of doped fabric over its wood-and-metal ribbed and stringered fuselage and wings. Following its first flight in September 1934, the Gladiator I was put into production and 231 examples were built. The fighter made its service debut in January 1937, and went on to fly with 26 RAF fighter squadrons. The later Mk II was fitted with the Bristol Mercury VIIIA engine and a three-bladed metal Fairey-Reed propeller, and 252 new-build machines were delivered. Sixty arrestor-hooked Sea Gladiators were also delivered to the Royal Navy, plus a further 165 Mk Is and IIs were sold to foreign customers. A considerable number of Gladiators were still in service when war broke out in September 1939, and although virtually obsolete, they gave a good account of themselves in France, the Middle East, over Malta and in East Africa.

SPECIFICATION:

**ACCOMMODATION:**
pilot

**DIMENSIONS:**
LENGTH: 27 ft 5 in (8.36 m)
WINGSPAN: 32 ft 3 in (9.83 m)
HEIGHT: 10 ft 4 in (3.15 m)

**WEIGHTS:**
EMPTY: 3450 lb (1565 kg)
MAX T/O: 4750 lb (2155 kg)

**PERFORMANCE:**
MAX SPEED: 253 mph (407 kmh)
RANGE: 428 miles (689 km)
POWERPLANT: Bristol Mercury VIIIA/AS or IX
OUTPUT: 840 hp (626 kW)

**FIRST FLIGHT DATE:**
12 September 1934 (SS 37)

**ARMAMENT:**
four 0.303 in machine guns in nose and under wings

**FEATURES:**
Biplane wing layout; cowled radial engine; tailwheel; enclosed cockpit

# Grumman JF/J2F Duck USA

three-seat, single-engined biplane utility amphibian

Grumman's first amphibian, the Duck, was heavily influenced by the company's FF-1 and F2F carrier-based fighters of the early 1930s. Grumman also borrowed ideas from the US Navy's then current amphibian, the Loening OL-9, with the end result being the XJF-1. Flight testing revealed no serious problems with the new amphibian, and the Navy ordered 27 Ducks, the first of which was delivered in late 1934. The J2F was vastly superior to the OL-9, possessing a better rate of climb, greater maximum speed and increased service ceiling.

Fulfilling both the general utility role and observation mission, the Duck was procured in steady numbers for almost a decade, with the Coast Guard and Marine Corps also receiving examples. Grumman built its last Ducks (J2F-5s) in 1941, after which a further 330 (J2F-6s) were constructed by the Columbia Aircraft Corporation. The aircraft saw service both in Europe and the Pacific during World War 2, flying anti-submarine and coastal patrols, air-sea rescue missions, reconnaissance flights, target towing and casualty evacuation.

SPECIFICATION:

**ACCOMMODATION:**
pilot, observer/gunner and radio operator

**DIMENSIONS:**
LENGTH: 34 ft 0 in (10.36 m)
WINGSPAN: 39 ft 0 in (11.89 m)
HEIGHT: 13 ft 11 in (4.24 m)

**WEIGHTS:**
EMPTY: 4400 lb (1996 kg)
MAX T/O: 7700 lb (3493 kg)

**PERFORMANCE:**
MAX SPEED: 190 mph (306 kmh)
RANGE: 750 miles (1207 km)
POWERPLANT: Wright R-1820-54 Cyclone 9
OUTPUT: 900 hp (671 kW)

**FIRST FLIGHT DATE:**
24 April 1933

**ARMAMENT:**
one Browning 0.30 in machine gun on flexible mounting for observer; two 100-lb (45 kg) bombs on underwing racks

**FEATURES:**
Biplane wing layout; cowled radial engine; single main float, into which main wheels retract

# Grumman F3F USA

single-seat, single-engined biplane fighter

The portly F3F was the last biplane interceptor to operate from the deck of an American carrier. Built as an improved F2F, with a longer fuselage, greater wingspan and more powerful Pratt & Whitney (F3F-1) or Wright Cyclone (F3F-2/-3) engine, some 54 F3F-1s and 108 F3F-2/3s served with frontline Navy and Marine Corps units from 1936 through to 1941. The 27 F3F-3s ordered by the Navy on 21 June 1938 were the last biplane fighters to be built for any of the US armed services.

During the F3F's brief time in the frontline (both ashore and at sea aboard the Navy's carriers *Yorktown*, *Saratoga*, *Ranger* and *Enterprise*), the Grumman design proved both rugged and highly manoeuvrable, and many of the US Navy's most influential fighter leaders of World War 2 (Butch O'Hare and Jimmy Thach, to name but two) 'cut their teeth' operationally with the F3F in the years leading up to 1941. By the time of the Japanese attack on Pearl Harbor, none of the 117 F3Fs still in service with the Navy were assigned to frontline units.

SPECIFICATION:

**ACCOMMODATION:**
pilot

**DIMENSIONS:**
LENGTH: 23 ft 0 in (7.01 m)
WINGSPAN: 32 ft 0 in (9.75 m)
HEIGHT: 9 ft 4 in (2.84 m)

**WEIGHTS:**
EMPTY: 3254 lb (1476 kg)
MAX T/O: 4750 lb (2155 kg)

**PERFORMANCE:**
MAX SPEED: 234 mph (376 kmh)
RANGE: 1130 miles (1818 km)
POWERPLANT: Wright R-1820-22 Cyclone (F3F-2)
OUTPUT: 950 hp (708 kW)

**FIRST FLIGHT DATE:**
20 March 1935 (XF3F-1)

**ARMAMENT:**
two fixed Browning 0.30 in machine guns forward of cockpit

**FEATURES:**
Biplane wing layout; cowled radial engine; retractable undercarriage; enclosed cockpit; arrestor hook

# Grumman JRF Goose USA

seven-seat, twin-engined monoplane utility amphibian

Initially built as a private venture for the civil market of the late 1930s, the G-21 Goose evoked immediate interest within the US military, with the Navy ordering one for evaluation in 1938. Designated the XJ3F-1, the prototype was followed by 20 JRF-1AS in 1939 upon the completion of the former's successful flight test programme. The first examples were employed as general transports, target tugs and photographic platforms by both the Navy and Marine Corps. The next batch of ten, designated JRF-4S, could carry bombs or depth charges, and these were followed by variants for the Coast Guard and USAAC (where they were designated OA-9/-13S). The build up to war in 1941 resulted in Grumman introducing the improved JRF-5, of which 184 were eventually built. At least 56 of these were supplied to the RAF as Goose I/IAS in 1943, and they performed navigational training, air-sea rescue and general ferrying duties. After the war the surviving JRFS were sold into civilian hands, and many were re-engined with turbine powerplants to increase their longevity.

SPECIFICATION:

**ACCOMMODATION:**
crew of two and up to five passengers

**DIMENSIONS:**
LENGTH: 38 ft 6 in (11.73 m)
WINGSPAN: 49 ft 0 in (14.94 m)
HEIGHT: 16 ft 2 in (4.93 m)

**WEIGHTS:**
EMPTY: 5425 lb (2461 kg)
MAX T/O: 8000 lb (3629 kg)

**PERFORMANCE:**
MAX SPEED: 201 mph (323 kmh)
RANGE: 640 miles (1030 km)
POWERPLANT: two Pratt & Whitney R-985-AN-6 Wasp Juniors
OUTPUT: 900 hp (670 kW)

**FIRST FLIGHT DATE:**
June 1937

**ARMAMENT:**
two 250-lb (113 kg) bombs or depth-charges on underwing racks

**FEATURES:**
High monoplane wing layout; cowled radial engine; floatplane hull, into which main wheels retract

# Hawker Tomtit UK

two-seat, single-engined biplane trainer

Built as a replacement for the Avro 504 series of
elementary training aircraft, the Tomtit entered RAF
service in late 1928. It had been one of two designs
(the other was the Avro Trainer, which was the
forerunner of the Tutor) selected by the Air
Ministry for small-scale production and extended
trials with the air force. Once on strength with the
RAF, the Tomtit revealed excellent handling
qualities, thanks in no small part to the Handley
Page type automatic slots fitted to the upper wings.
Between November 1928 and 1931 just 25 Tomtits
were built to an Air Ministry order, split into three
batches.

The first of these were mostly delivered to No 3
Flying Training School at RAF Grantham in early
1929, whilst other examples were also flown by the
Central Flying School at RAF Wittering. With Avro's
Tutor being picked as the successor to the
company's 504N in 1929, the Tomtit was not put
into mass-production by Hawkers, who were
already fully pre-occupied building Hart light
bomber and fighter variants for the RAF.

SPECIFICATION:

**ACCOMMODATION:**
two pilots in tandem

**DIMENSIONS:**
LENGTH: 23 ft 8 in (7.25 m)
WINGSPAN: 38 ft 6 in (8.71 m)
HEIGHT: 8 ft 8 in (2.68 m)

**WEIGHTS:**
EMPTY: 1100 lb (499 kg)
MAX T/O: 1750 lb (794 kg)

**PERFORMANCE:**
MAX SPEED: 124 mph (198.4 kmh)
RANGE: 350 miles (560 km)
POWERPLANT: Armstrong Siddeley
Mongoose IIIC
OUTPUT: 150 hp (112 kW)

**FIRST FLIGHT DATE:**
Early 1928

**FEATURES:**
Biplane wing layout; tandem
cockpits; radial engine;N-shaped
bracing struts; tail skid

# Hawker Hart  UK

two-seat, single-engined biplane light bomber

Hawker's family of fighters and bombers of the
1930s were some of the most stylish aircraft ever to
wear the RAF roundel. The first to emerge in 1928
was the Hart day bomber. So advanced was this
machine that it actually outpaced the RAF's main
fighter of the day, the Bristol Bulldog. Designed in
response to Air Ministry Specification 12/26, the
Hart was chosen as the new standard light day
bomber after the RAF staged competitive trials
between the Hawker design and rival prototypes
from Avro (Antelope) and Fairey (Fox II). Fifteen
development aircraft were built by Hawkers, and
these were issued to No 33 Sqn in April 1930 as
replacements for the unit's Hawker Horsleys.
Following the successful completion of the service
trial, large-scale production commenced, and more
than 500 Harts were built. Seven home-based
frontline units were equipped with the aircraft
between 1930 and 1936, and eight Auxiliary Air
Force squadrons operated the Hart from 1933 to
1938. Harts. The aircraft also saw service overseas
in India and the Middle East.

SPECIFICATION:

ACCOMMODATION:
pilot and observer/gunner

DIMENSIONS:
LENGTH: 29 ft 4 in (8.93 m)
WINGSPAN: 37 ft 3 in (11.35 m)
HEIGHT: 10 ft 5 in (3.2 m)

WEIGHTS:
EMPTY: 2530 lb (1148 kg)
MAX T/O: 4554 lb (2066 kg)

PERFORMANCE:
MAX SPEED: 184 mph (298 kmh)
RANGE: 470 miles (756 km)
POWERPLANT: Rolls-Royce
Kestrel IB
OUTPUT: 525 hp (391 kW)

FIRST FLIGHT DATE:
June 1928

ARMAMENT:
one fixed Vickers 0.303-in
machine gun in left fuselage side
and one Lewis 0.303-in machine
gun on pivoted mount for
observer; racks under lower
wings for 500-lb (227 kg)
bombload

FEATURES:
Biplane wing layout; close-cowled
inline engine; N-shaped bracing
struts; tail skid

87

# Hawker Demon UK

two-seat, single-engined biplane fighter

Impressed with the speed of the Hart light bomber, the RAF chose to purchase a fighter variant. The aircraft revived a tradition in the Air Force for two-seat fighters which had been absent since the retirement of the Bristol Fighter in the mid 1920s. Christened the Demon, the aircraft featured two fixed forward-firing guns and a cutaway rear cockpit with a tilted gun-ring to improve the arc of fire. The first production machines entered service in May 1931 and a total of 190 Demons had been built by the time production ended in December 1937.

From October 1936, all Demons built by Boulton Paul were fitted with a Frazer-Nash hydraulic gun turret. Aircraft fitted with this equipment were know as Turret-Demons in RAF service. Seven frontline and five Auxiliary Air Force units operated Demons between 1931 and 1939, and like the Hart, the aircraft also saw service in the Middle East. The Demon had been replaced by the Blenheim IF fighter by the outbreak of World War 2.

SPECIFICATION:

ACCOMMODATION:
pilot and gunner

DIMENSIONS:
LENGTH: 29 ft 7 in (9.05 m)
WINGSPAN: 37 ft 3 in (11.35 m)
HEIGHT: 10 ft 5 in (3.20 m)

WEIGHTS:
EMPTY: 3319 lb (1505 kg)
MAX T/O: 4668 lb (2117 kg)

PERFORMANCE:
MAX SPEED: 182 mph (291 kmh)
RANGE: 470 miles (756 km)
POWERPLANT: Rolls-Royce Kestrel V
OUTPUT: 560 hp (417 kW)

FIRST FLIGHT DATE:
March 1931

ARMAMENT:
two fixed Vickers 0.303-in machine guns in fuselage sides and one Lewis 0.303-in machine gun on ring-mounting or hydraulic turret for gunner; racks under lower wings for 500-lb (227 kg) bombload

FEATURES:
Biplane wing layout; close-cowled inline engine; N-shaped bracing struts; tail skid; cutaway rear cockpit

# Hawker Nimrod UK

single-seat, single-engined biplane fighter

The Nimrod started life as the HN 1 Norn, the Air Ministry issuing fleet fighter Specification 16/30 in August 1930 based on the already extant Hawker design. Although effectively a naval counterpart of the RAF's Fury I, the Nimrod was not simply a clone of the quintessential interwar biplane fighter. It had wings of greater span to improve slow speed handling on the approach to the carrier deck, an arrestor hook, a radio and flotation boxes in the wings and fuselage.

In November 1931 the first six service examples replaced the Fairey Flycatchers within 402 Fleet Fighter Flight, and a second production batch of 26 aircraft was completed by the following year. Service experience resulted in a number of improvements being incorporated into the follow-on Nimrod II, including the fitment of a headrest and an arrestor hook, a modified tail section and wing sweep-back. The first Mk IIs were delivered in March 1934. The last Nimrods were replaced by Sea Gladiators in May 1939, leaving the survivors to see out their days as trainers with the Fleet Air Arm.

SPECIFICATION:

**ACCOMMODATION:**
pilot

**DIMENSIONS:**
LENGTH: 26 ft 6.5 in (8.09 m)
WINGSPAN: 33 ft 6.75 in (10.23 m)
HEIGHT: 9 ft 10 in (3 m)

**WEIGHTS:**
EMPTY: 3115 lb (1413 kg)
MAX T/O: 4059 lb (1841 kg)

**PERFORMANCE:**
MAX SPEED: 196 mph (315 kmh)
RANGE: 305 miles (488 km)
POWERPLANT: Rolls-Royce Kestrel IIMS
OUTPUT: 525 hp (391 kW)

**FIRST FLIGHT DATE:**
14 October 1931

**ARMAMENT:**
two fixed Vickers 0.303-in machine guns in fuselage side

**FEATURES:**
Biplane wing layout; close-cowled inline engine; N-shaped bracing struts; tail skid; arrestor hook; central underfuselage radiator housing

# Hawker Hind UK

two-seat, single-engined biplane light bomber

Developed by Hawkers in 1934 at the request of the RAF to serve as a replacement for the Hart, the Hind was powered by the fully supercharged Kestrel v and featured the cut-away gunner's cockpit utilised by the Demon. An interim machine that saw widespread use until the new generation of monoplane bombers entered service in the late 1930s, the Hind made its RAF service debut with Nos 18, 21 and 34 Sqns in late 1935. The aircraft had replaced the last frontline Harts in Bomber Command by the end of 1936, and new units were formed to operate the 338 Hinds that had been issued to Bomber Command by the time production ended in 1937 – the Auxiliary Air Force flew a further 114, split between 11 squadrons. However, within 12 short months the Hawker biplane had been all but replaced in the frontline by the Battle and the Blenheim. Although obsolete, surplus Hinds proved to be capable trainers, and they served in this role until 1939. A number of Hinds were also exported, including 20 to the Royal Afghan Air Force in 1939.

SPECIFICATION:

ACCOMMODATION:
pilot and gunner

DIMENSIONS:
LENGTH: 29 ft 7 in (9.05 m)
WINGSPAN: 37 ft 3 in (11.35 m)
HEIGHT: 10 ft 7 in (3.26 m)

WEIGHTS:
EMPTY: 3251 lb (1474 kg)
MAX T/O: 5298 lb (2403 kg)

PERFORMANCE:
MAX SPEED: 186 mph (297 kmh)
RANGE: 430 miles (688 km)
POWERPLANT: Rolls-Royce Kestrel v
OUTPUT: 640 hp (477 kW)

FIRST FLIGHT DATE:
12 September 1934

ARMAMENT:
one fixed Vickers 0.303-in machine gun in left fuselage side and one Lewis 0.303-in machine gun on ring-mounting for gunner; racks under lower wings for 500-lb (227 kg) bombload

FEATURES:
Biplane wing layout; close-cowled inline engine; N-shaped bracing struts; cutaway rear cockpit; tail wheel

# Junkers Ju 52/3m/CASA 352L  GERMANY & SPAIN

19-seat, three-engined monoplane transport/bomber aircraft

The German equivalent of the DC-3/C-47, the Ju 52/3m tri-motor boasted rugged construction thanks to Junkers' trademark corrugated skinning technique. The aircraft started life as a single-engined airliner in 1930, but after a production run of just six Ju 52s Junkers decided to evaluate a three-engined version, powered by 550 hp Pratt & Whitney Hornet radials. The results were so successful that the single-engined variant was immediately superseded by the Ju 52/3mCE. The Luftwaffe was an early recipient of the Ju 52/3mGE, initially operating it as a stop-gap bomber after Junkers had re-engined the aircraft with more powerful BMW 132A-3 radials. By 1939 there were close to 1000 Ju 52/3ms in military service or ready for the call up from Lufthansa. The type went on to become the 'workhorse' of the Luftwaffe during World War 2, performing all manner of missions from troop transport to mine-sweeping on all war fronts. An estimated 4845 were built between 1932 and 1944, and post-war construction continued in both France and Spain.

SPECIFICATION:

**ACCOMMODATION:**
crew of two and seating for up to 17 passengers

**DIMENSIONS:**
LENGTH: 62 ft 0 in (18.90 m)
WINGSPAN: 95 ft 11.5 in (29.25 m)
HEIGHT: 18 ft 2.5 in (5.55 m)

**WEIGHTS:**
EMPTY: 12,610 lb (5720 kg)
MAX T/O: 23,149 lb (10 500 kg)

**PERFORMANCE:**
MAX SPEED: 171 mph (275 kmh)
RANGE: 800 miles (1287 km)
POWERPLANT: three BMW 132TS (Ju 52/3M) or ENMA Betas (CASA 352L)
OUTPUT: 2490 hp (1856.7 kW) and 2250 hp (1677 kW) respectively

**FIRST FLIGHT DATE:**
April 1931

**ARMAMENT:**
single MG 15 7.92 mm machine guns on flexible mounts in dorsal cockpit and ventral 'dustbin' positions; maximum bomb load of 3307 lb (1500 kg) carried in bomb-bay

**FEATURES:**
Monoplane wing layout; fixed undercarriage; exposed tri-motor radial engine layout; unique Junkers corrugated skinning

# Junkers Ju 86 GERMANY

four-seat, twin-engined monoplane bomber

Designed as both a bomber and a civil airliner, the Ju 86 was one of the most advanced machines in Europe at the time of its first flight on 4 November 1934. Featuring double-wing flaps and outward retracting main gear legs, the diesel-engined Ju 86D-1 entered production in late 1936. Upon its arrival in the frontline, the Junkers bomber replaced the Dornier Do 23 and Junkers Ju 52/3M as the Luftwaffe's standard heavy bomber. The *Condor Legion's* combat experiences with the Ju 86D in Spain during the civil war showed that the aircraft was slow and vulnerable to aerial attack, so Junkers produced the Ju 86E with powerful BMW radial engines. Both D- and E-models saw action in Poland in September 1939, but the bomber was replaced by the He 111, Do 17 and Ju 88 over the following months. Junkers then worked on a high altitude, pressurised version for photo-reconnaissance and bombing missions. Also featuring a wider wingspan, the Ju 86P/R remained in German service into 1943, by which time close to 500 examples of all variants had been built.

## SPECIFICATION:

**ACCOMMODATION:**
pilot, bomb aimer/navigator and dorsal and ventral gunners

**DIMENSIONS:**
LENGTH: 58 ft 7.5 in (17.87 m)
WINGSPAN: 73 ft 10 in (22.50 m)
HEIGHT: 16 ft 7 in (5.05 m)

**WEIGHTS:**
EMPTY: 11,354 lb (5150 kg)
MAX T/O: 17,770 lb (8060 kg)

**PERFORMANCE:**
MAX SPEED: 202 mph (325 kmh)
RANGE: 932 miles (1500 km)
POWERPLANT: two Junkers Jumo 205CS
OUTPUT: 1200 hp (894 kW)

**FIRST FLIGHT DATE:**
4 November 1934

**ARMAMENT:**
single MG 15 7.92 mm machine guns on flexible mounts in nose, dorsal cockpit and ventral 'dustbin' positions; maximum bomb load of 2205 lb (1000 kg) carried in bomb-bay

**FEATURES:**
Monoplane wing layout; retractable undercarriage; closely faired inline (Ju 86D) or radial engines (Ju 86E/K); twin tail fins

# Klemm Kl 35 GERMANY

two-seat, single-engined monoplane trainer

Formed in 1926, Klemm Leichtflugzeugbau GmbH's first aircraft was the Kl 25 two-seat monoplane trainer/tourer, released soon after the company's establishment. This highly successful machine was built to the tune of 600 airframes over the next decade, inspiring the company to produce a successor in the mid-1930s. Christened the Kl 35, the first prototype completed its maiden flight in 1935. Again, the new Klemm design was a tandem two-seater of wooden construction, although this time the aircraft was fitted with an inverted gull wing and an inline engine. The first production version was the Kl 35B, which was built between 1935 and 1938. The principal model used by the Luftwaffe was the Kl 35D, which had the spatted undercarriage of the civil Klemm replaced with a strengthened unit that could be adapted for use with wheels, floats or skis. It remained in service as a primary trainer with numerous Luftwaffe pilot training schools right up the end of World War 2, and was also used by the air forces of Sweden, Hungary, Rumania and Czechoslovakia.

SPECIFICATION:

**ACCOMMODATION:**
two pilots in tandem

**DIMENSIONS:**
LENGTH: 24 ft 7.25 in (7.50 m)
WINGSPAN: 34 ft 1.5 in (10.40 m)
HEIGHT: 6 ft 8.75 in (2.05 m)

**WEIGHTS:**
EMPTY: 1014 lb (460 kg)
MAX T/O: 1654 lb (750 kg)

**PERFORMANCE:**
MAX SPEED: 132 mph (212 kmh)
RANGE: 413 miles (665 km)
POWERPLANT: Hirth HM 60R
OUTPUT: 80 hp (60 kW)

**FIRST FLIGHT DATE:**
March 1935

**FEATURES:**
Inverted gull wing layout; fixed undercarriage; close-cowled inline engine; tandem open cockpits

# Martin B-10B USA

four/five-seat, twin-engined bomber

The first all-metal monoplane bomber to enter full scale production for the US Army Air Corps, the Martin B-10 was the most successful variant of the hugely significant family of bombers built by the Baltimore-based Glenn L Martin company in the 1930s. Derived from the Model 123, which featured such advances as cantilever monoplane wings, flaps, stressed-skin construction, advanced engine cowls, retractable landing gear, an internal bomb-bay with power-driven doors and variable-pitch propellers, the B-10 was much faster than the USAAC's pursuit fighters of the day.

Some 103 B-10Bs were built, the first of which arrived at Wright Field in July 1935. Production deliveries to Langley Field began in December of that year and were completed by August 1936. The B-10 remained in frontline service until replaced by B-17s and B-18s in the late 1930s, after which it performed secondary roles such as target towing. A further 189 B-10s were sold (as Model 139s) to the Dutch East Indies, Argentina, China and Turkey.

SPECIFICATION:

**ACCOMMODATION:**
pilot, bombardier/gunner, navigator, radio operator and rear gunner

**DIMENSIONS:**
LENGTH: 44 ft 9 in (13.68 m)
WINGSPAN: 70 ft 6 in (21.51 m)
HEIGHT: 15 ft 5 in (4.72 m)

**WEIGHTS:**
EMPTY: 9681 lb (4391 kg)
MAX T/O: 16,400 lb (7439 kg)

**PERFORMANCE:**
MAX SPEED: 213 mph (341 kmh)
RANGE: 1240 miles (1984 km)
POWERPLANT: two Wright R-1820-33s
OUTPUT: 1550 hp (1156 kW)

**FIRST FLIGHT DATE:**
June 1934 (YB-10)

**ARMAMENT:**
three Browning 0.30-in machine guns on flexible mounts in the nose, rear cockpit and rear ventral hatch positions; maximum bomb load of 1000 lb (454 kg) carried in bomb-bay

**FEATURES:**
Monoplane wing layout; retractable undercarriage; twin radial engines; nose turret, bomb-bay

# Messerschmitt Bf 108 Taifun/Nord 1002 Pingouin

GERMANY & FRANCE

four-seat, single-engined monoplane utility aircraft

Built to compete in the *Fourth Challenge de Tourisme International* held in 1934, the Bf 108 was streets ahead of its contemporaries thanks to features like its retractable undercarriage and all-metal construction. Although the Messerschmitt was unsuccessful at the competition, over 30 aircraft were ordered in 1935 for private use, predominantly in Germany. Its high performance made the Bf 108 a natural choice for record flights, and one such machine christened *Taifun* (Typhoon) was flown by German aviatrix Elly Beinhorn from Berlin to Constantinople in a single day. In honour of this success, Messerschmitt named all of its Bf 108s Taifun. The Luftwaffe was quick to appreciate the performance of the Bf 108, and the aircraft was acquired in quantity for the communications role. By 1942 the Taifun assembly line had moved to the SNCAN factory near Paris, and it was this French connection which kept the aircraft in production after the German defeat. Re-engined with a Renault powerplant, 285 Nord 1001/1002s were built to add to the 885 completed between 1934 and 1945.

SPECIFICATION:

**ACCOMMODATION:**
one pilot and three passengers

**DIMENSIONS:**
LENGTH: 27 ft 2.5 in (8.29 m)
WINGSPAN: 34 ft 10 in (10.62 m)
HEIGHT: 7 ft 6.5 in (2.30 m)

**WEIGHTS:**
EMPTY: 1941 lb (880 kg)
MAX T/O: 2987 lb (1355 kg)

**PERFORMANCE:**
MAX SPEED: 186 mph (300 kmh)
RANGE: 621 miles (1000 km)
POWERPLANT: Argus AS 10C
(Bf 108B) or Renault 60-11
(Nord 1002)
OUTPUT: both 240 hp (179 kW)

**FIRST FLIGHT DATE:**
June 1934

**FEATURES:**
Monoplane wing; retractable main undercarriage; close-cowled inline engine; fixed tailwheel

# Miles Hawk Trainer III/M 14 Magister  UK

two-seat, single-engined monoplane trainer

Like most RAF trainers of the inter-war period, the Magister was a military development of a civilian design – in this case the Miles Hawk trainer. To meet Air Ministry Specification T 40/36, which covered the acquisition of a monoplane elementary trainer for the RAF, Miles had to increase the size of the Hawk's tandem cockpits and make provision for the fitment of blind flying equipment. The first examples of the all-wooden trainer were delivered in May 1937, but within months of their arrival a number had been lost as a result of their failure to recover from spinning. Following extensive trials, Miles redesigned the rear fuselage and decking of the aircraft and fitted a larger rudder, raised tailplane and anti-spin strakes. The new machine was redesignated the M 14A, and it remained in production until 1941. A total of 1229 Magisters were built, and they served with many Elementary Flying Training Schools and the Central Flying School. Finally retired from the RAF in 1948, a large number of Magisters continued to fly as civilian trainers well into the 1950s.

SPECIFICATION:

ACCOMMODATION:
two pilots in tandem

DIMENSIONS:
LENGTH: 24 ft 7.5 in (7.51 m)
WINGSPAN: 33 ft 10 in (10.31 m)
HEIGHT: 6 ft 8 in (2.03 m)

WEIGHTS:
EMPTY: 1286 lb (583 kg)
MAX T/O: 1900 lb (862 kg)

PERFORMANCE:
MAX SPEED: 132 mph (212 kmh)
RANGE: 380 miles (612 km)
POWERPLANT: de Havilland
Gipsy Major I
OUTPUT: 130 hp (96.9 kW)

FIRST FLIGHT DATE:
20 March 1937

FEATURES:
Monoplane wing; fixed spatted main undercarriage; close-cowled inline engine; tailwheel

# Morane-Saulnier MS 230 FRANCE

two-seat, single-engined parasol advanced trainer

This distinctively Gallic-looking aircraft was designed by Morane-Saulnier to meet a French Air Ministry requirement, issued in 1928, for a basic training aircraft that boasted a decent performance. The end result was the MS 230, which mated the manufacturer's trademark parasol configuration (as seen on its fighter designs of the period) with a 250 hp (186.4 kW) Salmson radial engine. Warmly received by the French, more than 1000 were built during the 1930s, with the *Armée de l'Air* using the MS 230 not only for advanced pilot training but also as a platform for general observation and gunnery work. The MS 230 was superseded by the generally similar (although both larger and lighter) MS 315 in 1932, and aside from those examples operated in France, a number were exported to Romania, Greece, Belgium and Brazil.

SPECIFICATION:

**ACCOMMODATION:**
two pilots in tandem

**DIMENSIONS:**
LENGTH: 22 ft 9 in (6.93 m)
WINGSPAN: 35 ft 2 in (10.72 m)
HEIGHT: 9 ft 9.33 in (2.98 m)

**WEIGHTS:**
EMPTY: 1835 lb (832.35 kg)
MAX T/O: 2558 lb (1160.30 kg)

**PERFORMANCE:**
MAX SPEED: 127 mph (204 kmh)
RANGE: 350 miles (560 km)
POWERPLANT: Salmson 9ab
OUTPUT: 250 hp (186.4 kW)

**FIRST FLIGHT DATE:**
February 1929

**FEATURES:**
Parasol wing layout; fixed undercarriage; uncowled radial engine; tail wheel

# Naval Aircraft Factory N3N USA

two-seat, single-engined biplane trainer

The Naval Aircraft Factory (NAF) was created in 1918 to enable the US Navy to design and manufacture aircraft uniquely tailored to its needs, and during the inter-war years it did just that, producing a series of flying-boats and a carrier-based fleet fighter. The final NAF design to be mass-produced was the N3N primary trainer, which was built to replace the Consolidated NY-2s and -3s of the 1920s. The prototype XN3N-1 flew for the first time in August 1935, and following successful trials in both land- and seaplane configurations, an order for 179 production N3N-1s was placed. The first examples were powered by the Wright J-5 radial, although this obsolescent powerplant was replaced towards the end of the initial production run by the R-760 Whirlwind from the same source. This engine swap resulted in a designation change to N3N-3, and a further 816 trainers were procured from 1938 onwards. The N3N remained in the primary training role with the Navy until 1945, when all but a handful of the survivors were promptly declared surplus and sold to civilian operators.

SPECIFICATION:

**ACCOMMODATION:**
two pilots in tandem

**DIMENSIONS:**
LENGTH: 25 ft 6 in (7.77 m)
WINGSPAN: 34 ft 0 in (10.36 m)
HEIGHT: 10 ft 10 in (3.30 m)

**WEIGHTS:**
EMPTY: 2090 lb (948 kg)
MAX T/O: 2792 lb (1266 kg)

**PERFORMANCE:**
MAX SPEED: 126 mph (203 kmh)
RANGE: 470 miles (756 km)
POWERPLANT: Wright J-5 and Wright R-760-96 Whirlwind
OUTPUT: 220 hp (164 kW) and 240 hp (179 kW) respectively

**FIRST FLIGHT DATE:**
August 1935

**FEATURES:**
Biplane wing layout; uncowled radial engine; N-shaped bracing struts; floats for seaplane variant

# North American BT-9/-14/Yale I USA

two-seat, single-engined monoplane trainer

The BT-9 was the USAAC version of North American Aviation's (NAA) private-venture NA-16 basic trainer. Flown in prototype form in April 1935, the NA-16 revealed performance figures near equal to the Army Air Corps' frontline combat aircraft of the time. Ordered into production as the BT-9, the USAAC took delivery of its first example in April 1936. A total of 226 BT-9s were built in three different variants (A-, B- and C-models), whilst the US Navy received 40 NJ-1s, fitted with a 600 hp Pratt & Whitney R-1340 Wasp radial in place of the 400 hp (298 kW) Wright unit. NAA then produced the BT-14, which had its fabric fuselage covering replaced with lightweight metal sheeting. The aircraft also featured a 450 hp Wright R-985 engine. Some 251 were produced for the USAAC, and export orders for the trainer were received from several nations, including France, which bought 230. When the latter country was invaded by Germany in June 1940, 119 undelivered aircraft were acquired by Britain and passed on to the Royal Canadian Air Force, which christened them Yale Is.

SPECIFICATION:

ACCOMMODATION:
two pilots in tandem

DIMENSIONS:
LENGTH: 27 ft 7 in (8.39 m)
WINGSPAN: 42 ft 0 in (12.80 m)
HEIGHT: 13 ft 7 in (4.13 m)

WEIGHTS:
EMPTY: 3314 lb (1500 kg)
MAX T/O: 4471 lb (2030 kg)

PERFORMANCE:
MAX SPEED: 170 mph (274 kmh)
RANGE: 882 miles (1420 km)
POWERPLANT: Wright R-975-7 (BT-9) and Wright R-985-11 (BT-14)
OUTPUT: 400 hp (298 kW) and 450 hp (336 kW) respectively

FIRST FLIGHT DATE:
April 1935

FEATURES:
Monoplane wing; fixed undercarriage; close-cowled radial engine; tailwheel

# North American NA-50/-68 and P-64 USA

single-seat, single-engined monoplane fighter

A low-cost fighter derived from the NA-16 trainer, the NA-50 was aimed at smaller air forces which had neither the cash nor the technical expertise to operate the latest monoplane fighters emerging from Europe and the USA. Using the trainer as a base, NAA designers reduced the seating to one, made the undercarriage retractable, fitted a more powerful Wright R-1820 engine and armed the fighter with two 0.30-in machine guns. Only seven NA-50s were built in response to an order placed by Peru in January 1938. Used in combat against Ecuador in 1941, the last examples were retired 20 years later. The NA-68 was very similar to the NA-50 (the former had a longer chord cowling, redesigned wingtips and tail surfaces and two underwing-mounted 20 mm cannon, as well as the 0.30-in guns), the Royal Siam (Thai) Air Force ordering six in 1939 for delivery in 1941. However, Siam was invaded by Japan before it could take delivery of the fighters, and they were used by the USAAC (with the designation P-64) in the advanced fighter trainer role instead.

SPECIFICATION:

**ACCOMMODATION:**
pilot

**DIMENSIONS:**
LENGTH: 27 ft 0 in (8.23 m)
WINGSPAN: 37 ft 3 in (11.35 m)
HEIGHT: 9 ft 0 in (2.74 m)

**WEIGHTS:**
EMPTY: 4660 lb (2114 kg)
MAX T/O: 5990 lb (2717 kg)

**PERFORMANCE:**
MAX SPEED: 270 mph (435 kmh)
RANGE: 630 miles (1014 km)
POWERPLANT: Wright R-1820-77 Cyclone 9
OUTPUT: 870 hp (649 kW)

**FIRST FLIGHT DATE:**
early 1939

**ARMAMENT:**
two 20 mm cannon in underwing pods and two fixed Browning 0.30-in machine guns in the wings

**FEATURES:**
Monoplane wing; retractable undercarriage; close-cowled radial engine; tailwheel

# North American O-47 USA

three-seat, single-engined monoplane observation aircraft

The O-47 was developed by General Aviation in response to a US Army specification for an observation aircraft. The aircraft broke the mould for this type of machine, for unlike its predecessors, it was a low-wing monoplane with an enclosed cockpit, rather than an open-cockpit parasol/biplane design. The USAAC was pleased with the field of view for the observer, who had a glazed underfuselage station immediately beneath the cockpit. NAA was contracted to build 109 O-47As in February 1937, and subsequently increased the order to 164 aircraft. These machines were powered by 975-hp Cyclones, while 74 additional O-47Bs featured a 1060-hp R-1820-57 engine. Large-scale training exercises in 1941 demonstrated the short-comings of the O-47, with commercially available light aeroplanes proving more capable of operating with ground troops and fighters and twin-engined bombers showing greater ability to perform reconnaissance and photographic duties. Thus, during World War 2, O-47s were restricted to coastal and anti-submarine patrols, and towing target tugs.

SPECIFICATION:

**ACCOMMODATION:**
pilot, observer and gunner

**DIMENSIONS:**
LENGTH: 33 ft 7 in (10.24 m)
WINGSPAN: 46 ft 4 in (14.12 m)
HEIGHT: 12 ft 2 in (3.71 m)

**WEIGHTS:**
EMPTY: 5980 lb (2712 kg)
MAX T/O: 7636 lb (3463 kg)

**PERFORMANCE:**
MAX SPEED: 221 mph (355 kmh)
RANGE: 750 miles (1207 km)
POWERPLANT: Wright R-1820-49 Cyclone
OUTPUT: 975 hp (727 kW)

**FIRST FLIGHT DATE:**
mid-1935

**ARMAMENT:**
one fixed Browning 0.30-in machine gun in starboard wing and one Browning 0.30-in machine gun on flexible mount in rear cockpit

**FEATURES:**
Monoplane wing; retractable undercarriage; close-cowled radial engine; deep centre fuselage, fixed tailwheel

# Northrop A-17A USA

two-seat, single-engined monoplane attack aircraft

Developed from the Gamma transport as a private-venture light attack aircraft, the Northrop Gamma 2C was acquired for evaluation by the USAAC in June 1934. Designated the YA-13, the aircraft was re-engined and redesignated the XA-16 soon afterwards. Northrop was issued with a contract to build 110 A-17s in 1935, and the first production A-17 was delivered to the USAAC in December of that year. That same month, Northrop was awarded a second contract for the improved A-17A.

The new version had a retractable undercarriage and was powered by the 825-hp Pratt & Whitney R-1535-13 engine. A total of 129 were built, although only 93 saw service with the USAAC. They were returned to Douglas (which had had acquired 49 per cent of the Northorp A-17 stock in 1937) for sale to the UK and France. The RAF designated the aircraft the Nomad I, and transferred all 60 it received to the South African Air Force. Further export examples were built by Douglas, with small numbers being sold to the Netherlands, Argentina, Iraq, Norway and Peru.

# Polikarpov I-16 USSR

single-seat, single-engined monoplane fighter

The world's first cantilever low wing monoplane and retractable undercarriage fighter to enter frontline service, the I-16 was an incredibly advanced design for its time, but by the outbreak of World War 2, it had been well and truly left behind by more modern fighter types. Despite this fact, the I-16 still equipped two-thirds of all Soviet air force fighter units at the time of the German invasion in June 1941. The first I-16s entered service in the USSR in 1935, the fighter being powered by a reverse-engineered Wright Cyclone (designated the Shvetsov M-25).

Throughout its long production life, the I-16 was upgraded through the fitment of uprated engines and improved armament. The I-16 first saw action with the Republican forces in the Spanish Civil War, 278 being supplied by the USSR. It was also primary Soviet fighter during the Nomonhan Incident with Japan in 1939. Later that same year the I-16 bore the brunt of the fighting with Finland in the Winter War of 1939-40, before being thrown into the fray against the Luftwaffe in June 1941.

SPECIFICATION:

**ACCOMMODATION:**
pilot

**DIMENSIONS:**
LENGTH: 19 ft 11.15 in (6.07 m)
WINGSPAN: 29 ft 6.33 in (9.00 m)
HEIGHT: 8 ft 4.75 in (2.56 m)

**WEIGHTS:**
EMPTY: 2976 lb (1350 kg)
NORMAL LOADED: 3781 lb (1715 kg)

**PERFORMANCE:**
MAX SPEED: 273 mph (440 kmh)
RANGE: 497 miles (800 km)
POWERPLANT: Shvetsov M-25A
OUTPUT: 750 hp (578 kW)

**FIRST FLIGHT DATE:**
31 December 1933

**ARMAMENT:**
two fixed ShKAS 7.62 mm machine guns in nose and two in wings; provision for two-six underwing 82 mm rockets or up to 441-lb (200 kg) of bombs under wings

**FEATURES:**
Monoplane wings; retractable undercarriage; close-cowled radial engine; tail skid; open cockpit

# Polikarpov I-152 (I-15bis) USSR

single-seat, single-engined biplane fighter

Although Polikarpov earned the distinction of building the world's first 'modern' monoplane interceptor in the I-16, it was also a major manufacturer of biplane fighters as well. Indeed, the revolutionary I-15 had flown just prior to the I-16, its distinctive 'gulled' upper wing and I-type interplane struts giving the barrel-shaped fighter a distinctive appearance. Blessed with incredible manoeuvrability, a respectable top speed and potent armament, the I-15 proved popular in the USSR and in Spain, where it saw much action in the Spanish Civil War. As a result of feedback from the latter conflict, Polikarpov redesigned the I-15 without the 'gulled' upper wing centre section, which pilots criticised for restricting their view on take-off and landing. The I-15 was replaced on the production line by the I-15bis (later redesignated the I-152) in late 1937. The fighter was used in the same conflicts as the I-16, often flying into action along-side the monoplane. Although production ended in 1939, substantial numbers of I-152s remained in service with the Soviet air force well into 1942.

SPECIFICATION:

ACCOMMODATION:
pilot

DIMENSIONS:
LENGTH: 20 ft 7 in (6.27 m)
WINGSPAN: 33 ft 5.5 in (10.20 m)
HEIGHT: 9 ft 2.25 in (2.80 m)

WEIGHTS:
EMPTY: 2888 lb (1310 kg)
MAX T/O: 4044 lb (1834 kg)

PERFORMANCE:
MAX SPEED: 230 mph (368 kmh)
RANGE: 280 miles (450 km)
POWERPLANT: Shvetsov M-25B
OUTPUT: 750 hp (559 kW)

FIRST FLIGHT DATE:
early 1937

ARMAMENT:
two fixed ShKAS 7.62 mm machine guns in nose and two in wings

FEATURES:
Biplane wings; fixed undercarriage; close-cowled radial engine; tail skid; single wing struts

# Polikarpov I-153 (I-15ter) USSR

single-seat, single-engined biplane fighter

The final word in the Polikarpov family of biplane fighters, the I-153 boasted a considerably more powerful Shvetsov radial and a retractable undercarriage, as a well as the 'gull' wing centre section. Despite other manufacturers the world over embracing the monoplane fighter that he had pioneered in the early 1930s, Nikolai Polikarpov refused to abandon the biplane layout, and the first I-153s entered frontline service as late as May 1939. Polikarpov delivered its last I-153 in late 1940, and although in production for barely 18 months, no fewer than 3437 had been built in that time. Examples were supplied to China in 1940, which used them against the Japanese in a repeat of the Nomonhan Incident of the year before. Finland also made use of 11 captured examples following the 1939-40 Winter War.

Heavily involved in the opening months of the war on the Eastern Front, I-153s remained an important part of the Soviet fighter force into 1942, when they were relegated to the no less hazardous ground attack role.

SPECIFICATION:

ACCOMMODATION:
pilot

DIMENSIONS:
LENGTH: 20 ft 3 in (6.17 m)
WINGSPAN: 32 ft 9.75 in (10.00 m)
HEIGHT: 9 ft 2.25 in (2.80 m)

WEIGHTS:
EMPTY: 3200 lb (1452 kg)
MAX T/O: 4652 lb (2110 kg)

PERFORMANCE:
MAX SPEED: 280 mph (450 kmh)
RANGE: 292 miles (470 km)
POWERPLANT: Shvetsov M-62R
OUTPUT: 1000 hp (746 kW)

FIRST FLIGHT DATE:
mid-1938

ARMAMENT:
four fixed ShKAS 7.62 mm or 12.7 mm machine guns in nose; max bombload of 441-lb (200 kg) or six 82 mm rocket projectiles under wings

FEATURES:
'Gulled' biplane wings; retractable undercarriage; close-cowled radial engine; tail wheel; single wing struts

## P.Z.L. P.11C POLAND

single-seat, single-engined gull-winged monoplane fighter

The final incarnation of the P.Z.L. family of high-wing fighters that could trace its lineage back to the two-seat P.W.S.1 of 1927, the P.11 was the staple fighter of the Polish Air Force when Germany invaded on 1 September 1939. Effectively an upgraded P.7 with a more powerful Bristol Mercury engine in place of the Jupiter VIIF from the same source, the P.11 entered service in 1933. Capable of reasonable speeds, highly manoeuvrable and well armed, the P.Z.L. fighter was also licence-built in Romania, where it was re-engined with the Gnome-Rhône Mistral/Jupiter. After several years out of production, P.Z.L. was ordered to re-open the line as it became obvious that war with Germany was inevitable. The new P.11g was to be powered by the 840 hp Mercury VIII engine, but it had only flown in prototype form by the time of the invasion. Despite being outclassed by their opponents in Bf 109s and Bf 110s, the 12 squadrons of P.11s that opposed the German assault on Poland claimed 125 Luftwaffe aircraft destroyed for the loss of 114 of their own number.

SPECIFICATION:

ACCOMMODATION:
pilot

DIMENSIONS:
LENGTH: 24 ft 9.25 in (7.55 m)
WINGSPAN: 35 ft 2 in (10.72 m)
HEIGHT: 9 ft 4.25 in (2.85 m)

WEIGHTS:
EMPTY: 2529 lb (1147 kg)
MAX T/O: 3968 lb (1800 kg)

PERFORMANCE:
MAX SPEED: 242 mph (389 kmh)
RANGE: 435 miles (700 km)
POWERPLANT: P.Z.L. Mercury
VS2/VIS2
OUTPUT: 600-645 hp (447-481 kW)

FIRST FLIGHT DATE:
August 1931

ARMAMENT:
two fixed Wzor 37 7.7 mm
machine guns in forward
fuselage and two in wings;
maximum load of 110-lb (50 kg)
bomb under each wing

FEATURES:
'Gulled' monoplane wing; fixed
undercarriage; close-cowled
radial engine; tail skid; raised
head rest

# Republic (Seversky) AT-12 Guardsman USA

two-seat, single-engined monoplane advanced trainer

Built as a two-seat development of the USAAC's P-35 fighter of 1937, the privately-funded 'Convoy Fighter' was designated the 2PA by its manufacturer. Like the single-seater, this aircraft had two 0.30-in or 0.50-in machine guns fitted in the wings, plus a flexibly-mounted 0.30-in weapon in the rear cockpit. Two 2PAs were sold to the Soviet Union in 1938, together with a manufacturing licence. Some 52 examples were ordered by Sweden the following year, while 20 were also clandestinely bought by the Imperial Japanese Navy for use over China. However, the 2PA's lack of manoeuvrability and poor rate of climb saw it swiftly relegated from the role of escort fighter to reconnaissance mount over central China. The 2PA eventually joined the ranks of the USAAC in late 1941, when all bar two of the 52 aircraft ordered by Sweden were hastily requisitioned by the Army Air Corps and pressed into service following events in the Pacific. Given the designation AT-12, these aircraft saw limited flying as advanced trainers and general communications hacks.

SPECIFICATION:

ACCOMMODATION:
pilot and instructor/gunner in tandem

DIMENSIONS:
LENGTH: 26 ft 11 in (8.20 m)
WINGSPAN: 36 ft 0 in (10.97 m)
HEIGHT: 9 ft 9.5 in (2.99 m)

WEIGHTS:
EMPTY: 4581 lb (2078 kg)
MAX T/O: 7658 lb (3474 kg)

PERFORMANCE:
MAX SPEED: 316 mph (508 kmh)
RANGE: 1150 miles (1850 km)
POWERPLANT: Pratt & Whitney R-1830-S3C Twin Wasp
OUTPUT: 1100 hp (820.6 kW)

FIRST FLIGHT DATE:
Late 1937

ARMAMENT:
two fixed Browning 0.30-in or 0.50-in machine guns in wings, plus a flexibly-mounted Browning 0.30-in machine gun in the rear cockpit; provision for up to 350-lb (158 kg) of bombs under wings/fuselage

FEATURES:
Monoplane wing; retractable undercarriage; close-cowled inline engine

# Ryan PT-16/-20/-21/-22 and NR-1 Recruit and S-T-3 USA

two-seat, single-engined monoplane trainer

The USAAC's first monoplane primary trainer, the PT, can trace its ancestry back to the Ryan's S-T two-seater design of 1933-34. Highly successful in its civil form, the Ryan garnered military interest in 1939 when the USAAC began looking around for a new primary trainer. A solitary example of the S-T-A was acquired (redesignated the XPT-16), and it was thoroughly tested. A further 15 were purchased to allow a wider evaluation to be completed, and in 1940 an order for 30 was received.

After taking delivery of these machines, the USAAC decided that the more powerful Kinner radial would endure the rigours of training better than the Menasco inline engine, and the 100 PT-21s ordered in 1941 were delivered with the radial powerplant. The PT-12 was so successful that Ryan received an order for 1023 , which were designated PT-22 Recruits. The US Navy also ordered 125 (designated NR-1s), which were near identical to the PT-22. Operated primarily by civilian-run flying training schools, the last PTs were retired towards the end of World War 2.

## SPECIFICATION:

**ACCOMMODATION:**
two pilots in tandem

**DIMENSIONS:**
LENGTH: 22 ft 5 in (6.83 m)
WINGSPAN: 30 ft 1 in (9.17 m)
HEIGHT: 6 ft 10 in (2.08 m)

**WEIGHTS:**
EMPTY: 1313 lb (596 kg)
MAX T/O: 1860 lb (844 kg)

**PERFORMANCE:**
MAX SPEED: 131 mph (211 kmh)
RANGE: 352 miles (566 km)
POWERPLANT: Menasco L-365-1 (PT-16 and -20), Kinner R-440-3 (PT-21 and NR-1) and R-540-1 (PT-22 and S-T-3)
OUTPUT: 125 hp (93 kW), 132 hp (98 kW) and 160 hp (119 kW) respectively

**FIRST FLIGHT DATE:**
3 February 1939

**FEATURES:**
Monoplane wing; fixed spatted main undercarriage; close-cowled inline (PT-16/20) or exposed radial (PT-21/22) engine; tailwheel

# Seversky P-35A USA

single-seat, single-engined monoplane fighter

The P-35 was the first fighter produced by Seversky (later Republic) of Farmingdale, Long Island. The work of chief designer Alexander Kartveli, the P-35 was the USAAC's first single-seat all-metal fighter with both a retractable undercarriage and an enclosed cockpit. The P-35 started life as the SEV-1XP, which was one of several machines built by Seversky and flown as prototypes and race aircraft. The P-35 beat the Curtiss Hawk Model 75 for the 16 June 1936 US Army contract for 77 fighters, the first of which was delivered to Wright Field for testing. Sweden also placed an order for 120 P-35s, designated EP-106s by Seversky (and J9s by the Swedes), although only 60 had been delivered when the US government enforced an embargo in October 1940. The remaining aircraft were impressed into USAAC service as P-35As. By late 1941 about 50 ex-Swedish Seversky fighters remained in service with the 24th PG in the Philippines, and these were destroyed attempting to stave off the Japanese invasion launched on 7 December that year.

SPECIFICATION:

ACCOMMODATION:
pilot

DIMENSIONS:
LENGTH: 26 ft 10 in (8.18 m)
WINGSPAN: 36 ft 0 in (10.97 m)
HEIGHT: 9 ft 9 in (2.97 m)

WEIGHTS:
EMPTY: 4575 lb (2075 kg)
MAX T/O: 6723 lb (3050 kg)

PERFORMANCE:
MAX SPEED: 310 mph (499 kmh)
RANGE: 950 miles (1529 km)
POWERPLANT: Pratt & Whitney
R-1830-45 Twin Wasp
OUTPUT: 1050 hp (783 kW)

FIRST FLIGHT DATE:
Late 1935

ARMAMENT:
two fixed Browning 0.30-in
forward fuselage and two fixed
0.50-in machine guns in wings;
provision for up to 350-lb (158 kg)
of bombs under wings/fuselage

FEATURES:
Monoplane wing; retractable
undercarriage; close-cowled
inline engine

# Stampe sv4 BELGIUM & FRANCE

two-seat, single-engined biplane trainer

Designed by Belgian de Havilland importer Jean Stampe, it is not surprising to find that the sv4 bears more than a passing resemblance to the DH 82 Tiger Moth. First flown in May 1933, the trainer also shares a similar powerplant with its British contemporary. The sv4 was ordered by both the Belgian and French air forces in the late 1930s, but before large-scale production commenced the Stampe factory was seized by the Germans in May 1940.

In 1944 French manufacturer Nord resurrected the design, and over the next two years 70 were built with the designation sv4c. These machines differed from the pre-war Stampe through the fitment of the Renault 4 Pei engine, the bulk of the Nord-built aircraft being shared between the *Armeé de l'Air* and French flying clubs. Jean Stampe returned to business soon after World War 2 when he formed Stampe et Renard in Belgium, his new company completing an order for 65 sv4Bs for the Belgian air force. Unlike the French aircraft, these machines had an enclosed cabin for both cockpits.

SPECIFICATION:

ACCOMMODATION:
two pilots in tandem

DIMENSIONS:
LENGTH: 22 ft 10 in (6.96 m)
WINGSPAN: 27 ft 6 in (8.38 m)
HEIGHT: 9 ft 1 in (2.77 m)

WEIGHTS:
EMPTY: 1056 lb (480 kg)
MAX T/O: 1716 lb (780 kg)

PERFORMANCE:
MAX SPEED: 112 mph (180 kmh)
RANGE: 300 miles (480 km)
POWERPLANT: de Havilland Gipsy Major 10 (sv4/sv4B) and Renault 4 Pei (sv4c)
OUTPUT: 130 hp (97 kW) and 140 hp (104.9 kW) respectively

FIRST FLIGHT DATE:
May 1933

FEATURES:
Swept-back biplane wing layout; cowled inline engine; fixed undercarriage; tail skid; enclosed cockpits (Belgian sv4)

# Supermarine Stranraer UK

six-seat, twin-engined biplane reconnaissance flying-boat

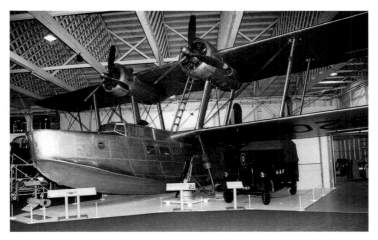

The Stranraer was the final biplane flying-boat to be designed by the legendary R J Mitchell of Supermarine Spitfire fame. Initially designated the Southampton V, and thus revealing its lineage to the RAF's most successful inter-war flying-boat design, the Stranraer had little in common with the Supermarine machine of ten years earlier. It was officially renamed the Stranraer in August 1935. Strongly influenced by the preceding Scapa flying-boat, the all-metal Stranraer was appreciably larger. The Air Ministry ordered 17 Stranraers in August 1935, and the first of these entered service with No 228 Sqn in 1936. Three more units would receive Stranraers, and Nos 201 and 209 Sqn retained the flying-boats until the summer of 1940, when they re-equipped with Sunderlands and Lerwicks, respectively. The Stranraer was also built under licence by Canadian Vickers, with some 40 examples being produced between 1938 and 1941. Flying anti-submarine patrols along Canada's east and west coasts, five units operated the obsolescent flying-boats until April 1944.

SPECIFICATION:

**ACCOMMODATION:**
two pilots, navigator/nose gunner, radio operator and two flight engineers

**DIMENSIONS:**
LENGTH: 68 ft 3 in (20.8 m)
WINGSPAN: 126 ft 0 in (38.4 m)
HEIGHT: 24 ft 6 in (7.49 m)

**WEIGHTS:**
EMPTY: 15,874 lb (7200 kg)
MAX T/O: 26,386 lb (11,968 kg)

**PERFORMANCE:**
MAX SPEED: 85 mph (136 kmh)
RANGE: 1470 miles (2352 km)
POWERPLANT: three Liberty 12S
OUTPUT: 800 hp (596.5 kW)

**FIRST FLIGHT DATE:**
1935

**ARMAMENT:**
Single 0.30-in machine guns on pivoted mount for observer/gunner in bow and rear hull cockpits; up to 1000 lb (454 kg) of bombs on wing racks

**FEATURES:**
Biplane wing layout; laminated wood veneer flying-boat hull; three tractor engines between the wings; wingtip sponsons

# Supermarine Walrus UK

four-seat, single-engined biplane air-sea rescue and reconnaissance amphibian

Designed as a private venture amphibian suitable for catapulting from warships, the Walrus was originally known as the Seagull v. Very different from the manufacturer's previous Seagull designs, which were made of wood, featured open cockpits and had tractor engines, the Mk v had a pusher engine, a metal hull and an enclosed cockpit. The prototype was flown on 21 June 1933 and the first 24 Seagull vs built were purchased by the Royal Australian Navy. The prototype was tested by the Air Ministry in 1933, and an order for 12 aircraft placed in May 1935. Christened the Walrus, the first two were completed in March 1936 and supplied to the Fleet Air Arm's catapult flights.

A further 739 Walruses would be built over the next eight years, the aircraft becoming the 'eyes of the fleet' as a spotter-reconnaissance platform. Seeing action in every theatre of war, the Walrus proved a dependable servant in all climates. The RAF also procured enough Walruses to equip 12 squadrons tasked with performing the air-sea rescue mission for downed aircrew.

SPECIFICATION:

**ACCOMMODATION:**
pilot, navigator/gunner and two passengers

**DIMENSIONS:**
LENGTH: 37 ft 3 in (11.35 m)
WINGSPAN: 45 ft 10 in (13.97 m)
HEIGHT: 15 ft 3 in (4.65 m)

**WEIGHTS:**
EMPTY: 4900 lb (2223 kg)
MAX T/O: 7200 lb (3266 kg)

**PERFORMANCE:**
MAX SPEED: 135 mph (217 kmh)
RANGE: 600 miles (966 km)
POWERPLANT: Bristol Pegasus VI
OUTPUT: 775 hp (578 kW)

**FIRST FLIGHT DATE:**
21 June 1933

**ARMAMENT:**
Single Vickers or Lewis K 0.303-in machine gun on flexible mount for observer/gunner in bow and one or two similar weapons in midships; underwing racks for up to 760-lb (345 kg) of bombs or depth charges

**FEATURES:**
Biplane wing layout; flying-boat hull; pusher engine between the wings; wingtip sponsons; retractable undercarriage

# Vickers Vimy  UK

three-seat, twin-engined biplane heavy bomber

Built to take the war to the heart of Germany, only three production Vimys had reached the RAF by the time the signing of the Armistice brought World War 1 to an end on 11 November 1918. The aircraft would enjoy a long association with the RAF post-war, however. The prototype made its first flight in November 1917, powered by two 207 hp Hispano-Suizas, and the following Mks II and III featured 290 hp Sunbeam Maori and 310 hp Fiat engines, respectively. It was not until the advent of the Mk IV, fitted with 360 hp Rolls-Royce Eagle VIIIs, that the potential of the Vimy was realised. Around 300 were built, although contracts for many more were cancelled after the end of the war.

No 58 Sqn was the first unit to attain operational status with the aircraft in July 1919, the Vimys replacing the squadron's O/400s. A further seven units would re-equip with the Vickers bomber, three of these in Eqypt, three in England and one in Northern Ireland. In 1924-25, the Vimy was replaced in frontline service by the Virginia.

SPECIFICATION:

ACCOMMODATION:
pilot, navigator/bomb aimer, gunner

DIMENSIONS:
LENGTH: 43 ft 6.5 in (13.27 m)
WINGSPAN: 68 ft 0 in (20.73 m)
HEIGHT: 15 ft 0 in (4.57 m)

WEIGHTS:
EMPTY: 7104 lb (3222 kg)
MAX T/O: 12,500 lb (5670 kg)

PERFORMANCE:
MAX SPEED: 103 mph (166 kmh)
RANGE: 900 miles (1448 km)
POWERPLANT: two Rolls-Royce Eagle VIIIs
OUTPUT: 720 hp (537 kW)

FIRST FLIGHT DATE:
30 November 1917

ARMAMENT:
Up to four manually aimed Lewis K 0.303-in machine guns on flexible mounts for navigator/gunner in nose, rear upper and ventral or beam positions; internal bomb cell and underwing racks for up to 4804-lb (2179 kg) of bombs

FEATURES:
Biplane wing layout; pusher engines between the wings; skid between undercarriage; tail skid

113

# Vought SB2U Vindicator  USA

two-seat, single-engined scout/dive-bomber

The US Navy's first monoplane scout-bomber, the
Vindicator was the end result of an order placed
with Vought in 1934 for two prototype carrier-based
aircraft. The order called for the construction of a
biplane (XSB3U-1) and a monoplane (XSB2U-1), which
would then conduct comparative flight trials before
a production order was placed. Both flew in early
1936, and the all-metal XSB2U-1 soon proved its
superiority – the Navy ordered 54 SB2U-1s in
October of that year. Deliveries began in December
1937, and a year later 58 SB2U-2s were purchased.
Finally, in late 1940, 57 SB2U-3s were ordered, these
featuring more armour, heavier gun armament
and increased fuel capacity. The SB2U-3 was the
first version to be named the Vindicator, and this
was retrospectively applied to all surviving SB2Us.
By 1940, the aircraft equipped seven fleet units,
with the Marine Corps receiving the SB2U-3s.
Marine Vindicators saw action from land bases
during the early months of the Pacific War but they
had been largely replaced on carrier decks by the
superior Douglas SBD Dauntless at the end of 1941.

SPECIFICATION:

ACCOMMODATION:
pilot and gunner

DIMENSIONS:
LENGTH: 34 ft 0 in (10.36 m)
WINGSPAN: 42 ft 0 in (12.80 m)
HEIGHT: 10 ft 3 in (3.12 m)

WEIGHTS:
EMPTY: 5634 lb (2555 kg)
MAX T/O: 9421 lb (4273 kg)

PERFORMANCE:
MAX SPEED: 243 mph (391 kmh)
RANGE: 1120 miles (1802 km)
POWERPLANT: Pratt & Whitney
R-1535-96 Twin Wasp Junior
OUTPUT: 825 hp (615 kW)

FIRST FLIGHT DATE:
4 January 1936

ARMAMENT:
one fixed Browning 0.30-in
machine guns in nose and one
Browning 0.30-in machine gun
on flexible mount in rear cockpit;
maximum load of 1000-lb
(454 kg) on racks under wings
and fuselage

FEATURES:
Monoplane wing; retractable
undercarriage; close-cowled
radial engine; fixed tailwheel;
aerial mast forward of cockpit

# Vultee BT-13/-15 and SNV-1/-2 Valiant USA

two-seat, single-engined monoplane trainer

The most produced basic trainer in the USA during World War 2, the Valiant can trace its lineage back to Vultee's BC-3 basic combat trainer. Tested by the USAAC in 1938, the BC-3 was fitted with retractable landing gear and a powerful 600 hp Pratt & Whitney Wasp engine. The evaluation showed that the aircraft had perfect handling characteristics but that the landing gear need not be retractable or the powerplant so big. Vultee duly fitted oleo-pneumatic shock-struts and bolted a Pratt & Whitney Wasp Junior 'up front'. The end result was the BT-13 Valiant, and the USAAC ordered 300 in September 1939. A follow-on variant fitted with a different version of the Wasp Junior engine was then procured to the tune of 6407 examples. The rapidity at which these airframes were built resulted in a shortage of Wasp engines, thus forcing Vultee to create the Wright R-975-11 Whirlwind 9-powered BT-15 instead. The US Navy procured well over 1500 Valiants, which it designated the SNV-1/2. By the time production ceased in 1944, 11,000+ Valiants had been built.

SPECIFICATION:

ACCOMMODATION:
two pilots in tandem

DIMENSIONS:
LENGTH: 28 ft 10 in (8.79 m)
WINGSPAN: 42 ft 0 in (12.80 m)
HEIGHT: 11 ft 6 in (3.51 m)

WEIGHTS:
EMPTY: 3375 lb (1531 kg)
MAX T/O: 4496 lb (2039 kg)

PERFORMANCE:
MAX SPEED: 180 mph (290 kmh)
RANGE: 725 miles (1167 km)
POWERPLANT: Pratt & Whitney
R-985-AN-1 Wasp Junior (BT-13
and SNV-1/-2) and Wright R-975-11
Whirlwind 9 (BT-15)
OUTPUT: both 450 hp (336 kW)

FIRST FLIGHT DATE:
24 March 1939 (BT-13)

FEATURES:
Monoplane wing; fixed
undercarriage; close-cowled
radial engine; fixed tailwheel;
aerial mast forward of cockpit

# Westland Wapiti UK

two-seat, single-engined biplane utility aircraft

Built to replace the venerable DH 9A, Westland's Wapiti incorporated as many parts from the de Havilland bomber as possible. The Yeovil-based manufacturer was thoroughly familiar with the "Nine-Ack", as it had built 390 for the RAF and subsequently spent a decade reconditioning them for service overseas. Thus, Westland was ideally placed to offer the Air Force a replacement machine when the Air Ministry issued a specification for a successor to the DH 9A in 1926. The new aircraft had to be able to carry a bigger load with better reliability. The prototype first flew in 1927, and it saw off rival designs to secure an order for 25 Wapiti Is for trials in Iraq. The Mk I featured wooden wings and rear fuselage, while the follow-on Mk II switched to all-metal construction – this version was used in the UK with the Auxiliary Air Force. The Mk IIA, with the 550 hp Jupiter VIII engine, was the principal overseas variant, serving in India and Iraq. By the time production ended in 1932, 517 had been built. Retired from the Auxiliaries in 1937, Wapitis lingered on in India until 1939.

## SPECIFICATION:

**ACCOMMODATION:**
pilot and observer/gunner

**DIMENSIONS:**
LENGTH: 32 ft 6 in (9.90 m)
WINGSPAN: 46 ft 5 in (14.14 m)
HEIGHT: 11 ft 10 in (3.60 m)

**WEIGHTS:**
EMPTY: 3280 lb (1487 kg)
MAX T/O: 5400 lb (2449 kg)

**PERFORMANCE:**
MAX SPEED: 140 mph (225 kmh)
RANGE: 360 miles (580 km)
POWERPLANT: Bristol Jupiter VIII
OUTPUT: 480 hp (358 kW)

**FIRST FLIGHT DATE:**
early 1927

**ARMAMENT:**
two fixed Vickers 0.303-in machine guns on left fuselage side and one Lewis 0.303-in machine gun on ring-mounting for gunner; racks under lower wings for 580-lb (263 kg) bombload

**FEATURES:**
Biplane wing layout; exposed radial engine; tail skid; fixed undercarriage

# World
# War 2
# Aircraft

# Aeronca O-58 and L-3/-16 Grasshopper USA

two-seat, single-engined high-wing liaison/observation aircraft

In an effort to hastily acquire a light aircraft for observation/liaison duties in the frontline in the final months of peace in 1941, the US Army evaluated four designs from established American manufacturers Piper, Taylorcraft and Aeronca. The latter's offering was the Model 65, which was a modified version of its commercially available two-seat trainer. The aircraft was designated the O-58 by the USAAC and 400+ were purchased in three versions – in 1942 their designation was changed from O (for Observation) to L (for Liaison). A further 1030 were built before production ceased in 1944, these aircraft seeing action with US forces across the globe. Post-war, further aircraft were built both for the civil and military markets, with the US Army designating its version the L-16. An engineless version of the Model 65 was also produced in 1942 when the US Army expanded its glider pilot training programme. Aeronca built 250 TG-5 gliders, and they played an integral part in the training of pilots who would later make assault landings in Occupied Europe.

SPECIFICATION:

**ACCOMMODATION:**
pilot and passenger in tandem

**DIMENSIONS:**
LENGTH: 21 ft 0 in (6.40 m)
WINGSPAN: 35 ft 0 in (10.67 m)
HEIGHT: 7 ft 8 in (2.34 m)

**WEIGHTS:**
EMPTY: 835 lb (379 kg)
MAX T/O: 1300 lb (590 kg)

**PERFORMANCE:**
MAX SPEED: 87 mph (140 kmh)
RANGE: 200 miles (322 km)
POWERPLANT: Continental O-170-3 (O-58/L-3) and Continental O-205-1 (L-16)
OUTPUT: 65 hp (48.9 kW) and 90 hp (67 kW) respectively

**FIRST FLIGHT DATE:**
1941

**FEATURES:**
High-wing layout; tandem cockpits; fixed landing gear; extensive cockpit glazing

# Airspeed Oxford UK

six-seat, twin-engined monoplane trainer and light transport

Produced as a military version of Airspeed's Envoy light transport, the Oxford was an important wartime trainer. The RAF's first twin-engined monoplane advanced trainer, it was used to instruct aircrew in twin-engined flying, radio and navigation, gunnery and bombing. The prototype Oxford was first flown on 19 June 1937, and entered service with the RAF's Central Flying School five months later. By World War 2 400+ were in service, and further contracts were placed with Percival, Standard Motors and de Havilland as the Oxford became an important tool in the Empire Air Training Scheme. Some 8568 Oxfords were built, with the final example being handed over in July 1945. Of this number, 391 were supplied to the Royal Australian Air Force and 700 to the South African Air Force. The main Oxford variants were the Mk I bombing and gunnery trainer (fitted with a dorsal turret), the Mk II pilot, navigation and radio trainer, the Cheetah-engined Mk III, and the Mk v pilot, navigation and radio trainer, with Pratt & Whitney Wasp engines.

SPECIFICATION:

ACCOMMODATION:
pilot and seats for up to five students/passengers

DIMENSIONS:
LENGTH: 34 ft 6 in (10.51 m)
WINGSPAN: 53 ft 4 in (16.25 m)
HEIGHT: 11 ft 1 in (3.38 m)

WEIGHTS:
EMPTY: 5670 lb (2572 kg)
MAX T/O: 7600 lb (3447 kg)

PERFORMANCE:
MAX SPEED: 188 mph (302 kmh)
RANGE: 550 miles (885 km)
POWERPLANT: two Armstrong Siddeley Cheetah xs
OUTPUT: 750 hp (560 kW)

FIRST FLIGHT DATE:
19 June 1937

ARMAMENT:
Mk I had a dorsal turret fitted with a single Browning 0.303-in machine gun

FEATURES:
Monoplane wing layout; rectractable landing gear; two close-cowled radial engines; fixed tailwheel

# Arado Ar 196 GERMANY

two-seat, single-engined maritime reconnaissance floatplane

Replacing the Heinkel He 60 biplane as the standard catapult-launched floatplane embarked on the Kriegsmarine's capital ships, the Ar 196 flew an assortment of combat missions during World War 2. Capable of flying coastal patrol, submarine hunting, light bombing, general reconnaissance and convoy escort sorties, the Arado floatplane entered service in August 1939. The first vessel to take its Ar 196A-1s to sea was the pocket battleship *Graf Spee*, which embarked two in the autumn of 1939. The battleships *Bismark* and *Tirpitz* could carry six Arados each, the battlecruisers *Gneisenau* and *Scharnhorst* four and smaller pocket battleships and cruisers two. Shore-based aircraft were also operated from coastal ports on the Channel, Baltic, North Sea and Bay of Biscay coasts, as well as in the Balkans and Mediterranean. Aside from its use with the Luftwaffe, the Ar 196 also served with the co-belligerent air forces of Romania and Bulgaria in the Adriatic and Black Sea. A total of 392 Ar 196s were constructed by Arado, 23 by SNCA in Vichy France and 69 by Fokker in Holland.

SPECIFICATION:

**ACCOMMODATION:**
pilot and gunner in tandem

**DIMENSIONS:**
LENGTH: 36 ft 1 in (11.00 m)
WINGSPAN: 40 ft 8.25 in (12.40 m)
HEIGHT: 14 ft 7.25 in (4.45 m)

**WEIGHTS:**
EMPTY: 6593 lb (2990 kg)
MAX T/O: 8225 lb (3730 kg)

**PERFORMANCE:**
MAX SPEED: 193 mph (310 kmh)
RANGE: 665 miles (1070 km)
POWERPLANT: BMW 132K
OUTPUT: 960 hp (716 kW)

**FIRST FLIGHT DATE:**
May 1938

**ARMAMENT:**
two fixed MG FF 20 mm cannon in wings, one fixed MG 17 7.92 mm machine gun in starboard forward fuselage and on flexible mounting in rear cockpit; maximum bomb load of 220-lb (100 kg) on underwing racks

**FEATURES:**
Monoplane wing layout; tandem cockpits; twin floats; close-cowled radial engine; extensive cockpit glazing

# Avro Lancaster UK

seven-seat, four-engined monoplane heavy bomber

The Lancaster was literally the 'phoenix that rose from the ashes' of the disastrous Manchester programme of 1940-41. The latter machine was powered by two Rolls-Royce Vultures, and boasted a layout near-identical to the Lancaster, but was plagued by grave engine reliability problems. Avro realised that its airframe design was essentially right, however, and turned to Rolls-Royce and demanded access to its Merlin powerplant. The Manchester had been chronically underpowered, so Avro ensured that its replacement suffered no such problems by installing four Merlin xs. The prototype flew on 9 January 1941, an order for 1070 bombers was placed just months later and the first production machines emerged that October. Some 59 Bomber Command units saw service with the Lancaster, flying 156,000 sorties and dropping 608,612 tons of bombs and 51 million incendiaries. A total of 7377 airframes were built, this number being split between five marks. Post-war, Lancasters survived in maritime patrol, transport and test trials roles until the late 1950s.

## SPECIFICATION:

**ACCOMMODATION:**
pilot, flight engineer, navigator, bomb aimer/nose gunner, wireless operator, dorsal and tail turret gunners

**DIMENSIONS:**
LENGTH: 69 ft 6 in (21.18 m)
WINGSPAN: 102 ft 0 in (31.09 m)
HEIGHT: 20 ft 0 in (6.10 m)

**WEIGHTS:**
EMPTY: 36,900 lb (16,738 kg)
MAX T/O: 70,000 lb (31,751 kg)

**PERFORMANCE:**
MAX SPEED: 287 mph (462 kmh)
RANGE: 2530 miles (4072 km)
POWERPLANT: four Rolls-Royce Merlin 24 engines
OUTPUT: 5120 hp (3849.6 kW)

**FIRST FLIGHT DATE:**
9 January 1941

**ARMAMENT:**
nose and dorsal turrets with two Browning 0.303-in machine guns and tail turret with four Browning 0.303-in machine guns; maximum bomb load of 14,000 lb (6350 kg) in bomb-bay

**FEATURES:**
Monoplane wing layout; four close-cowled inline engines; twin tail layout

# Beech UC-43/GB-2 Traveller USA

four-seat, single-engined liaison/communications biplane

The first design put into production by Beech, the Model 17 Staggerwing established itself in the US civil market of the 1930s. The aircraft offered both comfort and performance to its occupants, and these attributes also appealed to senior US military officers. The US Navy initially acquired a handful (which it designated GB-1s) for the VIP transportation role in 1939, and with the outbreak of war two years later, it purchased 300+ examples – designated GB-2s – 105 of which were in turn supplied to the Royal Navy. The USAAC also acquired three D17Ss in 1939, which were designated YC-43 Travellers. Three years later a production order for 27 UC-43s was placed with Beech, followed by two subsequent requests for 75 and 105 Travellers, which brought total USAAF procurement to 207 aircraft. A large number of civilian Staggerwings (434 had been built by Beech up to 7 December 1941) were also pressed into military service. Production of civil Staggerwings recommenced in August 1945, and the last example left the Beech assembly line in 1948.

SPECIFICATION:

ACCOMMODATION:
pilot and seats for up to three passengers

DIMENSIONS:
LENGTH: 26 ft 2 in (7.98 m)
WINGSPAN: 32 ft 0 in (9.75 m)
HEIGHT: 10 ft 3 in (3.12 m)

WEIGHTS:
EMPTY: 3085 lb (1399 kg)
MAX T/O: 4700 lb (2123 kg)

PERFORMANCE:
MAX SPEED: 198 mph (319 kmh)
RANGE: 500 miles (805 km)
POWERPLANT: Pratt & Whitney R-985-AN-1 Wasp Junior
OUTPUT: 450 hp (335.3 kW)

FIRST FLIGHT DATE:
4 November 1932 (civilian Beech 17 Staggerwing)

FEATURES:
Staggered biplane wing layout; rectractable landing gear; close-cowled radial engine; single wing struts

# Beech Model 18 USA

eight-seat, twin-engined monoplane light transport and trainer

Like the Model 17 Staggerwing, the Beech Model 18 started life as a transport aimed at the American civil market of the late 1930s. Similarities between the two Beech designs did not stop there, however, for like the Staggerwing, the first examples of the Model 18 ordered by the USAAC in 1940 operated in the staff transport role. Designated the C-45, over 250 were procured for VIP and utility transportation. Some of these aircraft were also passed on to the RAF/Fleet Air Arm/RCAF under Lend-Lease. The final transport version built for the USAAF was the C-45F, which was produced to the tune of 1137 examples – all C-45s were redesignated UC-45s in 1943. Two years earlier, Beech had produced the Model 18-based AT-7 navigation trainer, and the USAAC took delivery of 549. Following in the AT-7's footsteps was the AT-11 Kansan bombing/gunnery trainer, of which 1582 were built. Finally, the US Navy/Marine Corps also procured 1500+ Model 18s, which it designated JRBs (equivalent to the USAAF's C-45) and SNBs (AT-7/-11). US military use of the aircraft lasted into the late 1960s.

SPECIFICATION:

ACCOMMODATION:
pilot and seats for up to seven
students/passengers

DIMENSIONS:
LENGTH: 34 ft 3 in (10.4 m)
WINGSPAN: 47 ft 8 in (14.5 m)
HEIGHT: 9 ft 8 in (2.95 m)

WEIGHTS:
EMPTY: 6175 lb (2801 kg)
MAX T/O: 8727 lb (3959 kg)

PERFORMANCE:
MAX SPEED: 215 mph (346 kmh)
RANGE: 850 miles (1368 km)
POWERPLANT: two Pratt & Whitney
R-985-AN-1 Wasp Juniors
OUTPUT: 900 hp (670.6 kW)

FIRST FLIGHT DATE:
15 January 1937 (civilian Beech 18)

FEATURES:
Monoplane wing layout;
rectractable landing gear; two
close-cowled radial engines;
twin tail layout

# Bell P-39 Airacobra USA

single-seat, single-engined monoplane fighter

The P-39 introduced the concept of both the centrally-mounted powerplant and the tricycle undercarriage to fighters, the aircraft's configuration stemming from its propeller hub-mounted T9 37 mm cannon. In order to allow the weapon to be housed in the nose, the P-39's engine was moved aft to sit over the rear half of the wing centre-section. This shifted the aircraft's centre of gravity, hence the tricycle undercarriage. Unfortunately, the P-39's design was not matched by stunning performance, particularly above 14,000 ft, where its normally-aspirated Allison V-1710 struggled. Ironically, following a service evaluation of the YP-39, Bell was told by the USAAC that a turbocharged version of the V-1710 was not needed! Once the fighter entered service the wisdom of this decision was called into question. Indeed, so compromised was the P-39 that it was relegated to close air support duties. Operating at lower altitudes over the Eastern Front, the Soviet air force did, however, achieve great success with the fighter from 1942.

SPECIFICATION:

ACCOMMODATION:
pilot

DIMENSIONS:
LENGTH: 30 ft 2 in (9.19 m)
WINGSPAN: 34 ft 0 in (10.36 m)
HEIGHT: 11 ft 10 in (3.61 m)

WEIGHTS:
EMPTY: 5645 lb (2560 kg)
MAX T/O: 8300 lb (3765 kg)

PERFORMANCE:
MAX SPEED: 386 mph (621 kmh)
RANGE: 650 miles (1046 km)
POWERPLANT: Allison V-1710-85
OUTPUT: 1200 hp (895 kW)

FIRST FLIGHT DATE:
6 April 1938 (XP-39)

ARMAMENT:
one American Armaments
Company T9 37 mm cannon and
two Browning 0.50-in machine
guns in nose and two or four
Browning 0.30-in machine guns
in wings; one 500-lb (227 kg)
bomb on centreline rack

FEATURES:
Monoplane wing layout;
rectractable, tricycle landing gear;
inline engine; 'car door' entry to
cockpit; carburettor intake fairing
behind cockpit

# Bell P-63 Kingcobra USA

single-seat, single-engined monoplane fighter

Although the P-63 looked like an enlarged
Airacobra, it was in fact an all-new design that had
a superior turn of speed at all altitudes. Christened
the Kingcobra, the fighter drew on modifications
incorporated into the P-39's original replacement,
the cancelled XP-39E. However, unlike the latter
design, the P-63 was more than just an Airacobra
fuselage with new semi-laminar flow wings – the
fighter was appreciably larger, and boasted an
Allison V-1710-93 engine that could be boosted to
1325 hp in flight. Although 3300 P-63s were built in
several different versions, by the time the first
production examples began to reach the USAAF in
October 1943, the P-51B, P-38H and P-470 had
successfully filled the air force's requirement for a
frontline fighter. Most Kingcobras were therefore
made available for lend-lease purchase, and the
Soviet air force happily snapped up 2400 examples.
A further 300 went to Free French units in the
Mediterranean, but the primary customer – the
USAAF – restricted its use of the Kingcobra to
training squadrons in America.

SPECIFICATION:

ACCOMMODATION:
pilot

DIMENSIONS:
LENGTH: 32 ft 8 in (9.96 m)
WINGSPAN: 38 ft 4 in (11.68 m)
HEIGHT: 12 ft 7 in (3.84 m)

WEIGHTS:
EMPTY: 6375 lb (2892 kg)
MAX T/O: 10 500 lb (4763 kg)

PERFORMANCE:
MAX SPEED: 410 mph (660 kmh)
RANGE: 2200 miles (3540 km)
POWERPLANT: Allison V-1710-93
OUTPUT: 1325 hp (988 kW)

FIRST FLIGHT DATE:
7 December 1942

ARMAMENT:
one American Armaments
Company T9 37 mm cannon and
two Browning 0.50-in machine
guns in nose and two underwing
Browning 0.50-in machine guns;
bombload of up to 1500-lb (681
kg) on underwing/fuselage racks

FEATURES:
Monoplane wing layout;
rectractable, tricycle landing gear;
inline engine; 'car door' entry to
cockpit; carburettor intake fairing
behind cockpit

# Bell P-59 Airacomet USA

single-seat, twin-engined jet monoplane fighter

America's first jet fighter, the Bell P-59 was built around the revolutionary Whittle turbojet, unveiled to the US Government by Britain in September 1941. Of conventional design, the fighter was powered by two General Electric Type IAS (redesignated J31s). Flight development went smoothly, with three prototypes and 13 evaluation airframes being delivered by late 1944. It was realised at an early stage of the flight development programme that the Airacomet boasted a performance inferior to many frontline piston-engined fighters of the day, so the production aircraft subsequently acquired were relegated to the fighter trainer role. The first production P-59A was delivered to the USAAF in August 1944, and of the 20 that were built, three went to the US Navy as the XF2L-1. The P-59B replaced the A-model soon after, and a further 30 were delivered before the remaining 50 on order (plus an expected follow-on batch of 250) were cancelled in October 1944. Most production P-59Bs were assigned to the USAAF's 412th Fighter Group for use as drones or controllers.

SPECIFICATION:

ACCOMMODATION:
pilot

DIMENSIONS:
LENGTH: 38 ft 10 in (11.83 m)
WINGSPAN: 45 ft 6 in (13.97 m)
HEIGHT: 12 ft 4 in (3.76 m)

WEIGHTS:
EMPTY: 8165 lb (3704 kg)
MAX T/O: 13 700 lb (6214 kg)

PERFORMANCE:
MAX SPEED: 413 mph (665 kmh)
RANGE: 525 miles (845 km)
POWERPLANT: two General
Electric J31-GE-3/5s
OUTPUT: 4000 lb st (18.0 kN)

FIRST FLIGHT DATE:
1 October 1942

ARMAMENT:
one American Armaments
Company T9 37 mm cannon and
three Browning 0.50-in machine
guns in nose; two underwing
racks for up to 500-lb (227 kg)
of bombs

FEATURES:
Monoplane wing layout;
rectractable, tricycle landing gear;
twin jet engines; engine intakes
at wing roots

# Boeing B-17 Flying Fortress  USA

ten-seat, four-engined monoplane heavy bomber

Built as a private venture by Boeing in response to a USAAC requirement for a Martin B-10 replacement, the Model 299 was first flown on 28 July 1935. The USAAC was impressed by the new bomber, and although not chosen to replace the B-10, the aircraft had elicited enough interest for Boeing to receive an order for 13 YB-17s, followed by 39 near-identical B-17Bs. By mid-1940 the Flying Fortress had been improved with the addition of two extra guns and more powerful engines. Designated the B-17C, 20 were exported to Britain for service with the RAF. Lessons learned from the European conflict saw Boeing 'beef up' the armour fitted to future models, as well as add extra guns and self-sealing fuel tanks. The end result of these changes was the B-17E, 512 of which were built in 1941-42, followed by the B-17F, which had a redesigned nose to incorporate a 0.50-in machine gun, a strength-ened undercarriage to cope with increased bomb loads and Wright R-1820-97 engines. The final version to see mass-production was the chin-turreted B-17G, 8680 examples of which were built.

## SPECIFICATION:

**ACCOMMODATION:**
pilot and co-pilot, flight engineer, navigator, bombardier/nose gunner, radio operator/dorsal gunner, two waist gunners, ball turret gunner, tail gunner

**DIMENSIONS:**
LENGTH: 74 ft 4 in (22.66 m)
WINGSPAN: 103 ft 9 in (31.62 m)
HEIGHT: 19 ft 1 in (5.82 m)

**WEIGHTS:**
EMPTY: 36,135 lb (16,391 kg)
MAX T/O: 65,500 lb (29,710 kg)

**PERFORMANCE:**
MAX SPEED: 287 mph (462 kmh)
RANGE: 2000 miles (3219 km)
POWERPLANT: four Wright R-1820-97 Cyclones
OUTPUT: 4800 hp (3580 kW)

**FIRST FLIGHT DATE:**
28 July 1935

**ARMAMENT:**
twin Browning 0.50-in machine guns in chin, dorsal, ball and tail turrets, plus one in nose, radio compartment and waist positions; bomb load of 12,800 lb (5800 kg) in bomb-bay

**FEATURES:**
Monoplane wing; four radial engines; large vertical tail surface

# Boeing B-29 Superfortress  USA

eleven-seat, four-engined monoplane heavy bomber

Boeing's response to the USAAC's request for a long-range strategic bomber to replace the B-17, the B-29 concept was devised soon after the Flying Fortress entered service. Initially hindered by the lack of a suitable powerplant, the very long-range bomber project was resurrected in 1940 when manufacturers were invited to tender proposals. Only Consolidated and Boeing produced flyable prototypes, and although the former's XB-32 Dominator flew first, it was plagued by development problems. Boeing, however, was able to convince the USAAC that it could deliver production versions of its Model 345 (designated the XB-29 by the military) by 1943, and it won the contract for 1500+ bombers before the prototype had even flown. Production B-29s were delivered from late 1943 onwards, and by the spring of 1944 the Super fortress was bombing targets in the Pacific. The aircraft played as great a part as any weapon in ending the conflict with the Japanese. Although production ceased in May 1946 after 3970 B-29s had been built, the type enjoyed a long career in the USAF post-war.

## SPECIFICATION:

**ACCOMMODATION:**
pilot, co-pilot, flight engineer, navigator, bombardier, radar operator, radio operator, central fire controller, right and left gunners, tail gunner

**DIMENSIONS:**
LENGTH: 99 ft 0 in (30.18 m)
WINGSPAN: 141 ft 3 in (43.05 m)
HEIGHT: 29 ft 7 in (9.02 m)

**WEIGHTS:**
EMPTY: 70,140 lb (31,815 kg)
MAX T/O: 124,000 lb (56,245 kg)

**PERFORMANCE:**
MAX SPEED: 358 mph (576 kmh)
RANGE: 3250 miles (5230 km)
POWERPLANT: four Wright R-3350-23 Duplex Cyclones
OUTPUT: 8800 hp (6564 kW)

**FIRST FLIGHT DATE:**
21 September 1942

**ARMAMENT:**
turrets with Browning 0.50-in machine guns on top/bottom of fuselage, tail turret with 20 mm cannon/Browning 0.50-in machine guns; 20,000-lb (9072 kg) bombs in bomb-bay

**FEATURES:**
Monoplane wing layout; four radial engines; large vertical tail

# Boulton Paul Defiant UK

two-seat, single-engined monoplane fighter

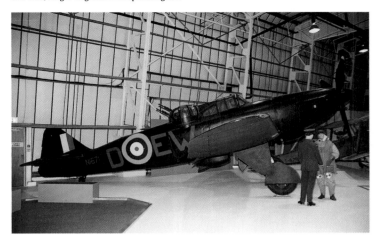

The Defiant enjoyed a less than successful career as a frontline fighter over southern England during the summer of 1940. Built to combine the strengths of new monoplane fighter design with turret weaponry, the Defiant struggled against single-seat opposition due to the weight of its two-man crew and primary armament. First flown in August 1937, and entering service in December 1939, the Defiant initially enjoyed success against German fighters surprised by its turret armament. However, once these same pilots learned that the aircraft had no forward-firing guns, they tailored their tactics accordingly, inflicting heavy losses on the Defiant. Removed from daylight operations, surviving Defiant Is (723 built) and new Mk IIs (210 built) equipped 13 newly-formed nightfighter squadrons, and between the autumn of 1940 and early 1942, the aircraft enjoyed some nocturnal success. An unarmed target-tug variant was also built in 1941, 140 TT Is being produced. Around 150 Defiant Is were also modified for this role, being redesignated TT IIIs.

SPECIFICATION:

ACCOMMODATION:
pilot and turret gunner

DIMENSIONS:
LENGTH: 35 ft 4 in (10.77 m)
WINGSPAN: 39 ft 4 in (12.00 m)
HEIGHT: 12 ft 2 in (3.70 m)

WEIGHTS:
EMPTY: 6078 lb (2757 kg)
MAX T/O: 8318 lb (3773 kg)

PERFORMANCE:
MAX SPEED: 304 mph (489 kmh)
RANGE: 465 miles (748 km)
POWERPLANT: Rolls-Royce Merlin III
OUTPUT: 1030 hp (768 kW)

FIRST FLIGHT DATE:
11 August 1937

ARMAMENT:
four Browning 0.303-in machine guns in dorsal turret

FEATURES:
Monoplane wing layout; rectractable landing gear; close-cowled inline engine; turret behind cockpit

# Bristol Blenheim ɪᴠ/Bolingbroke ɪᴠᴛ  UK & CANADA

three-seat, twin-engined monoplane light bomber

The Blenheim was the result of a speculative private venture on the part of Bristol. Unencumbered by restrictions on the aircraft's weight, powerplants, general layout or radius of action, it produced a sleek twin-engined machine known as the Type 142. First flown at Filton on 12 April 1935, the aircraft's performance sent ripples of concern through the RAF when it was discovered that its top speed was 30 mph faster than Fighter Command's new biplane Gloster Gauntlet I. The Air Ministry ordered 150, and the first of these entered service in March 1937. By September 1939 most UK-based Blenheim squadrons had replaced their Mk ɪs with improved Mk ɪᴠs, the latter having grown out of an Air Ministry requirement for a reconnaissance type with greater crew accommodation and range. The backbone of Bomber Command at the start of hostilities, it fell to the Mk ɪᴠ to make both the first armed reconnaissance incursion over Germany and the first bombing raid. The Blenheim saw action across the globe, remaining in the frontline into 1943 in North Africa and the Far East.

SPECIFICATION:

**ACCOMMODATION:**
pilot, navigator/bomb aimer and turret gunner

**DIMENSIONS:**
LENGTH: 42 ft 7 in (12.98 m)
WINGSPAN: 56 ft 4 in (17.17 m)
HEIGHT: 9 ft 10 in (3.00 m)

**WEIGHTS:**
EMPTY: 9790 lb (4441 kg)
MAX T/O: 14,400 lb (6532 kg)

**PERFORMANCE:**
MAX SPEED: 266 mph (428 kmh)
RANGE: 1460 miles (2350 km)
POWERPLANT: two Bristol Mercury xvs
OUTPUT: 1810 hp (1350 kW)

**FIRST FLIGHT DATE:**
12 April 1935 (Blenheim I)

**ARMAMENT:**
one fixed Browning 0.303-in machine gun in port wing and one in dorsal turret; maximum bomb load of 1320-lb (600 kg) in bomb-bay

**FEATURES:**
Monoplane wing layout; rectractable landing gear; two close-cowled radial engines; fixed tailwheel; dorsal turret

# Bristol Beaufort UK & AUSTRALIA

four-seat, twin-engined monoplane torpedo/reconnaissance bomber

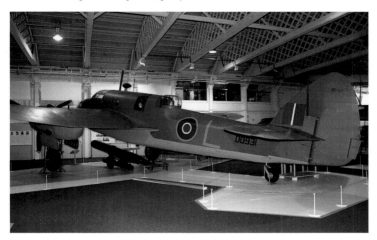

Developed from the Blenheim, the Beaufort was earmarked for use as a torpedo bomber with RAF units based in the Far East. However, following the failure of the Blackburn Botha in its intended torpedo bomber role with Coastal Command in the UK, Beauforts were issued to home-based units instead. Flown in prototype form in October 1938, the first production Beauforts entered service in December 1939. Although an excellent torpedo bomber, Beauforts were primarily used as conventional bombers. Torpedoes were used in attacks against German capital ships in 1941-42, with the mission against the *Prinz Eugen* in May 1942 being the last time the Beaufort was employed as a torpedo bomber. As Coastal Command's standard attack aircraft between 1940 and 1943, the Beaufort saw action over the North Sea, English Channel and French Atlantic coast. Overseas, units battled Axis forces from bases in the Mediterranean, India and Singapore. The Royal Australian Air Force also used locally-built Beauforts in the South-West Pacific, 700 equipping ten units from 1941 to 1946.

SPECIFICATION:

ACCOMMODATION:
pilot, navigator, wireless operator, turret gunner

DIMENSIONS:
LENGTH: 44 ft 3 in (13.49 m)
WINGSPAN: 57 ft 10 in (17.63 m)
HEIGHT: 14 ft 3 in (4.34 m)

WEIGHTS:
EMPTY: 13,100 lb (5942 kg)
MAX T/O: 21,228 lb (9629 kg)

PERFORMANCE:
MAX SPEED: 265 mph (426 kmh)
RANGE: 1600 miles (2575 km)
POWERPLANT: two Bristol Taurus VIS
OUTPUT: 2130 hp (1588 kW)

FIRST FLIGHT DATE:
15 October 1938

ARMAMENT:
one or two Browning 0.303-in machine guns in nose and one or two in dorsal turret; one 18-in torpedo or maximum bomb load of 2200-lb (998 kg) in bomb-bay

FEATURES:
Monoplane wing layout; rectractable landing gear; two close-cowled radial engines; fixed tailwheel; dorsal turret

# Bristol Beaufighter UK & AUSTRALIA

two-seat, twin-engined monoplane strike fighter

Built by Bristol using the wings, tail and rear
fuselage of the company's Beaufort torpedo
bomber, the Beaufighter proved to be one of the
best strike and nightfighters of World War 2.
Boasting a new main fuselage, Bristol Hercules
(and later Rolls-Royce Merlin) engines and a mixed
gun and cannon armament, the first Beaufighter
entered RAF service in September 1940. Soon fitted
with radar, the Mk IF (and Merlin-powered Mk IIF)
took the fight to the Luftwaffe during its nocturnal
blitz of 1940-41. Further developed into the Mk VIF
in 1942, this version of the Beaufighter had air
intercept (AI) radar fitted in a 'thimble' nose cone.
Long-range dayfighter variants also proved a staple
aircraft for Coastal Command, the Mk IC, VIC and
TF X seeing service off the coasts of Occupied
Europe from Norway to southern France,
throughout the Mediterranean and North Africa,
and against the Japanese in the Far East. A total of
5584 Beaufighters were built between 1939 and
1946, including 365 in Australia. The aircraft
remained in RAF service into the 1950s.

## SPECIFICATION:

**ACCOMMODATION:**
pilot and navigator/radar
operator/gunner

**DIMENSIONS:**
LENGTH: 41 ft 4 in (12.60 m)
WINGSPAN: 57 ft 10 in (17.63 m)
HEIGHT: 15 ft 10 in (4.83 m)

**WEIGHTS:**
EMPTY: 14 069 lb (6382 kg)
MAX T/O: 21 100 lb (9571 kg)

**PERFORMANCE:**
MAX SPEED: 323 mph (520 kmh)
RANGE: 1170 miles (1883 km)
POWERPLANT: two Bristol
Hercules XIs
OUTPUT: 3180 hp (2370 kW)

**FIRST FLIGHT DATE:**
17 July 1939

**ARMAMENT:**
four 20 mm cannon in nose, six
Browning 0.303-in machine guns
in wing and one Browning
0.303-in machine gun in dorsal
position; one 22.5/18-in torpedo
or maximum bomb/rocket load of
1000-lb (454 kg) on underwing
racks

**FEATURES:**
Monoplane wing layout; two
close-cowled radial engines;
dorsal turret; short, stub nose

# British Taylorcraft Auster I-V UK

two-seat, single-engined high-wing liaison/observation aircraft

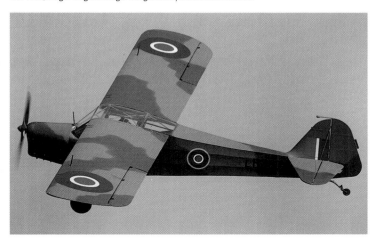

Taylorcraft was originally formed in the USA in 1936 with the express purpose of constructing light aircraft for private use. The company enjoyed so much success with its Models B, C and D that in 1938 a subsidiary firm was formed in England to build these machines under licence. Of braced, high-wing configuration and with side-by-side seating, the Taylorcraft design garnered more modest orders in the UK, however, and by September 1939 just 32 had been built. Twenty of these were impressed into RAF service upon the outbreak of war in order to assess their suitability for use in the observation and liaison roles. So successful was the aircraft that a further 100 were ordered, these being given the military designation Auster I when they entered service in August 1942. Some 1600+ Austers had been delivered by war's end, with the Mk V proving to be the most successful – 800 of this variant alone were constructed. At its peak, the Auster equipped 19 squadrons within the 2nd Tactical Air Force and the Desert Air Force.

SPECIFICATION:

ACCOMMODATION:
pilot and observer seated side-by-side

DIMENSIONS:
LENGTH: 22 ft 5 in (6.83 m)
WINGSPAN: 36 ft 0 in (10.97 m)
HEIGHT: 8 ft 0 in (2.44 m)

WEIGHTS:
EMPTY: 1100 lb (499 kg)
MAX T/O: 1850 lb (839 kg)

PERFORMANCE:
MAX SPEED: 130 mph (209 kmh)
RANGE: 250 miles (402 km)
POWERPLANT: Blackburn Cirrus Minor I (Auster I), de Havilland Gipsy Major I (Auster III) and Lycoming O-290 (Auster II, IV and V)
OUTPUT: 90 hp (67 kW) Cirrus Minor I and 130 hp (97 kW) Gipsy Major I and Lycoming O-290

FIRST FLIGHT DATE:
May 1942 (Auster I)

FEATURES:
high wing layout; side-by-side cockpit seating; fixed landing gear; extensive cockpit glazing

# Bücker BÜ 181 Bestmann/Zlin c.6/c.106

GERMANY, CZECHOSLOVAKIA & EGYPT

two-seat, single-engined monoplane primary trainer

Bücker's BÜ 181 proved to be the ideal primary trainer for the Luftwaffe, and it was produced in its thousands during the war years. Based on the company's BÜ 180, the Bestmann was the first design from Bücker to incorporate side-by-side seating. First flown in 1939, the BÜ 181 was ordered into production following flight-testing by the Luftwaffe. Once sufficient quantities of BÜ 181AS had been delivered to training units, airframes were then allocated to the communication/liaison role, whilst others became glider tugs. Aside from those aircraft built by Bücker, 708 were constructed by Fokker in the Netherlands during German occupation and 125 were produced under licence in Sweden. The Germans also opened a production line in Czechoslovakia, and aircraft continued to be built here long after VE-Day. Post-war production was also undertaken by the Heliopolis Aircraft Works in Egypt, the company building a version for the Egyptian Air Force and several Arab states. Named the Gomhouria, it remained in service into the 1980s.

SPECIFICATION:

ACCOMMODATION:
two pilots side-by-side

DIMENSIONS:
LENGTH: 25 ft 9 in (7.85 m)
WINGSPAN: 34 ft 9.25 in (10.60 m)
HEIGHT: 6 ft 8.75 in (2.05 m)

WEIGHTS:
EMPTY: 1058 lb (480 kg)
MAX T/O: 1653 lb (750 kg)

PERFORMANCE:
MAX SPEED: 134 mph (215 kmh)
RANGE: 497 miles (800 km)
POWERPLANT: Hirth HM 504
OUTPUT: 105 hp (78 kW)

FIRST FLIGHT DATE:
Early 1939

FEATURES:
Monoplane wing layout; side-by-side cockpit seating; fixed landing gear; extensive cockpit glazing; close-cowled inline engine

## CAC CA-2 **Wackett Trainer** AUSTRALIA
two-seat, single-engined monoplane primary trainer

The Wackett Trainer was the first entirely in-house design to be placed in series production by the Commonwealth Aircraft Corporation (CAC). It was also the first military aircraft of Australian design to serve with the RAAF. Named after CAC's first general manager, designer and engineer Lawrence Wackett, the CA-2 was built in response to RAAF Specification 3/38, which was issued in June 1938. The prototype, powered by a Gipsy Major engine, was successfully flown on 19 September 1939. Although the aircraft handled well, it was underpowered, and by the time a production order for 200 aircraft was placed in August 1940, the Warner Super Scarab radial engine had replaced the Gipsy Major. Although designed as an *ab initio* trainer, Wacketts served as intermediate trainers when they reached the RAAF in 1941. Flying from five locations on Australia's east coast by 1943, the Wacketts performed elementary flying training, air observer training and wireless air gunnery training. Surviving examples were sold as surplus from late 1945.

SPECIFICATION:

ACCOMMODATION:
two pilots in tandem

DIMENSIONS:
LENGTH: 26 ft 0 in (7.92 m)
WINGSPAN: 37 ft 0 in (11.28 m)
HEIGHT: 9 ft 10 in (3 m)

WEIGHTS:
EMPTY: 1910 lb (866 kg)
MAX T/O: 2590 lb (1175 kg)

PERFORMANCE:
MAX SPEED: 115 mph (185 kmh)
RANGE: 425 miles (684 km)
POWERPLANT: Warner Super Scarab 165D
OUTPUT: 175 hp (130 kW)

FIRST FLIGHT DATE:
19 September 1939

FEATURES:
Monoplane wing layout; fixed landing gear; extensive cockpit glazing; close-cowled inline engine

# CAC **Wirraway** AUSTRALIA

two-seat, single-engined monoplane trainer/dive-bomber

Essentially a licence-built North America BC-1 incorporating Australian modifications, the CAC Wirraway served not only as the RAAF's primary trainer throughout World War 2, but also as a makeshift fighter-bomber over New Guinea and Rabaul during 1942-43. The major changes carried out to the BC-1 centred around the fitment of a three-bladed propeller, the installation of machine guns in the upper engine cowling and a third weapon on a flexible mounting in the rear cockpit, and underwing stores racks for bombs. The first production Wirraway was rolled out in March 1939, and by June 1942 620 had been delivered to the RAAF. The high point of the aircraft's career came on 26 December 1942 when a Wirraway downed an A6M Zero-sen. Aside from serving with 15 squadrons in the fighter, trainer, light bomber and army co-operation roles, Wirraways also performed sterling work with Empire Air Training Scheme schools. Construction ended in mid-1946, by which time 755 had been built. The trainer remained in RAAF service until 1958.

SPECIFICATION:

**ACCOMMODATION:**
two pilots, or pilot and a rear-gunner, in tandem

**DIMENSIONS:**
LENGTH: 29 ft 6 in (8.99 m)
WINGSPAN: 43 ft 0 in (13.10 m)
HEIGHT: 12 ft 3 in (3.74 m)

**WEIGHTS:**
EMPTY: 3980 lb (1805.32kg)
MAX T/O: 6450 lb (2925.72 kg)

**PERFORMANCE:**
MAX SPEED: 205 mph (328 kmh)
RANGE: 720 miles (1152 km)
POWERPLANT: Pratt & Whitney
R-1340-47 Wasp
OUTPUT: 600 hp (447 kW)

**FIRST FLIGHT DATE:**
27 March 1939

**ARMAMENT:**
two fixed Browning 0.303-in machine guns in nose and one on a flexible mount in rear cockpit; maximum bomb load of 500-lb (227 kg) on underwing racks

**FEATURES:**
Monoplane wing layout; retractable undercarriage; extensive cockpit glazing; close-cowled inline engine

## CAC CA-12 **Boomerang** AUSTRALIA

single-seat, single-engined monoplane fighter

The only Australian-designed fighter aircraft to ever see combat, the Boomerang was built in record time in 1941-42. Realising that neither the British or American governments could spare valuable fighter aircraft to stem the Japanese tide spreading across Asia, the Australian government set about producing its own machine. The result was the Boomerang, which took to the skies for the first time just 16 weeks and three days after its design had been approved. Constructed around the largest engine then built in Australia, and incorporating as many components from the semi-indigenous Wirraway as possible, the Boomerang boasted marvellous manoeuvrability but a top speed of just 302 mph. The latter saw it relegated to the army support role when it reached the frontline in March 1943, the USAAF and RAF having since arrived in-theatre with superior fighters. A total of 250 Boomerangs were built, and the aircraft served in New Guinea, usually operating under army control. Surviving Boomerangs were retired from RAAF service soon after VJ-Day.

SPECIFICATION:

ACCOMMODATION:
pilot

DIMENSIONS:
LENGTH: 25 ft 6 in (7.77 m)
WINGSPAN: 36 ft 0 in (10.97 m)
HEIGHT: 9 ft 7 in (2.92 m)

WEIGHTS:
EMPTY: 5373 lb (2437 kg)
MAX T/O: 7699 lb (3492 kg)

PERFORMANCE:
MAX SPEED: 302 mph (486 kmh)
RANGE: 930 miles (1497 km)
POWERPLANT: Pratt & Whitney
R-1830-S3C4-G Twin Wasp
OUTPUT: 1200 hp (894 kW)

FIRST FLIGHT DATE:
28 May 1942

ARMAMENT:
two 20 mm cannon and four
Browning 0.303-in machine guns
in wings; four 20-lb (9 kg) smoke
bombs on underwing racks

FEATURES:
Monoplane wing layout;
retractable undercarriage;
extensive cockpit glazing;
close-cowled inline engine

# Cessna Model T-50 USA

five-seat, twin-engined monoplane trainer and light transport

Cessna's Model T-50 was the company's first twin-engined aircraft, being built as a five-seater for the civilian market. Within 12 months of the prototype flying, the T-50 had been chosen by the Royal Canadian Air Force as a trainer for pilots transitioning from single- to twin-engined aircraft. Some 550 Crane 1As (as they were designated) were supplied under Lend-Lease for the Commonwealth Joint Air Training Plan. The USAAC also acquired 33 T-50s for service evaluation (designated AT-8s) in 1940, after which it ordered 450.

These aircraft differed from the AT-8s in having Jacobs R-755-9 radials (245 hp) fitted in place of R-680-9s (295 hp). Designated the AT-17, the trainer was ordered in batches of 223 (AT-17A), 466 (AT-17B) and 60 (AT-17C). In 1942 the USAAF identified a role for the Cessna as a light transport, and so 1287 C-78 (later UC-78) Bobcats were bought – 2100 surplus AT-17C/Ds were also delivered in transport configuration. Finally, the US Navy procured 67 for the transportation of ferry pilots, designating these aircraft JRC-1s.

SPECIFICATION:

ACCOMMODATION:
two pilots seated side-by-side in training role, or one pilot and four passengers when in transport configuration

DIMENSIONS:
LENGTH: 32 ft 9 in (9.98 m)
WINGSPAN: 41 ft 11 in (12.78 m)
HEIGHT: 9 ft 11 in (3.02 m)

WEIGHTS:
EMPTY: 3500 lb (1588 kg)
MAX T/O: 5700 lb (2585 kg)

PERFORMANCE:
MAX SPEED: 195 mph (314 kmh)
RANGE: 750 miles (1207 km)
POWERPLANT: two Jacobs R-755-9s
OUTPUT: 490 hp (366 kW)

FIRST FLIGHT DATE:
1939 (civilian T-50)

FEATURES:
Monoplane wing layout; rectractable landing gear; two close-cowled radial engines; fixed tailwheel

# Consolidated PBY Catalina   USA

seven/nine-seat, twin-engined maritime patrol bomber, amphibian and flying boat

It is extremely unlikely that the PBY Catalina's record of being the most-built flying boat in aviation history will ever be surpassed, Consolidated constructing (or granting the licence to build in Canada and the USSR) 4000+ examples of the aircraft over a ten-year period starting in 1935. Used by virtually all the Allied nations in World War 2, the PBY flew more hours on combat patrols than any other US warplane of the period. The US Navy's VP-11F was the premier unit to receive the flying boat, taking on strength its first PBY-1 in October 1936. Such was the pace of re-equipment that by mid-1938 14 squadrons were operating PBYS, and more were scheduled to receive them. Further improvements to the engine specification resulted in new variants entering service over the next four years, Consolidated continuing to update, re-engine and improve its PBY design throughout World War 2. The final wartime variant was the PBY-6A, designated the OA-10B by the USAAF. Post-war, the Catalina remained in military service into the 1970s.

SPECIFICATION:

**ACCOMMODATION:**
pilot and co-pilot, flight engineer, radar/radio operator, navigator, nose gunner, two beam gunners

**DIMENSIONS:**
LENGTH: 63 ft 10.5 in (19.47 m)
WINGSPAN: 104 ft 0 in (31.70 m)
HEIGHT: 20 ft 2 in (6.5 m)

**WEIGHTS:**
EMPTY: 20,910 lb (9485 kg)
MAX T/O: 35,420 lb (16,066 kg)

**PERFORMANCE:**
MAX SPEED: 179 mph (288 kmh)
RANGE: 2545 miles (4096 km)
POWERPLANT: two Pratt & Whitney R-1830-92 Twin Wasps
OUTPUT: 2400 hp (1790 kW)

**FIRST FLIGHT DATE:**
21 March 1935

**ARMAMENT:**
one Browning 0.30/0.50-in machine gun in nose, each waist blister and in 'tunnel' behind hull step; maximum bomb/mine/torpedo load of 2000-lb (907 kg) on underwing racks

**FEATURES:**
High-wing monoplane layout; boat-shaped hull; two radial engines; retractable wingtip floats

# Consolidated PB2Y Coronado  USA

seven/ten-seat, four-engined long-range maritime patrol flying boat

Within months of the first PBY prototype taking to the skies, the US Navy ordered Sikorsky and Consolidated to produce prototypes of larger flying boats with better operational performance. First flown on 17 December 1937, Consolidated's aircraft was designated the XPB2Y-1 by the Navy. With almost all flying boat funding being channelled into the procurement of PBYs, Consolidated had to wait until 31 March 1939 to receive a contract for six PB2Y-2s, each of which cost as much as three PBYs. An order on 19 November 1940 established the PB2Y-3 in production, and the following month the first aircraft were issued to a frontline unit. A total of 210 PB2Y-3s were built for the Navy, with an additional ten being supplied to Britain under Lend-Lease as Coronado Is. Stripped of all military gear, these machines were used as freighters on North Atlantic routes by RAF Transport Command. Navy Coronados saw little in the way of combat in World War 2, most being converted into transports and used for evacuating wounded troops from frontline hospitals back to Hawaii or the US.

## SPECIFICATION:

**ACCOMMODATION:**
pilot and co-pilot, flight engineer, radar operator, navigator, nose, dorsal, tail and beam gunners

**DIMENSIONS:**
LENGTH: 79 ft 3 in (24.15 m)
WINGSPAN: 115 ft 0 in (35.05 m)
HEIGHT: 27 ft 6 in (8.38 m)

**WEIGHTS:**
EMPTY: 40,935 lb (18,568 kg)
MAX T/O: 68,000 lb (30,845 kg)

**PERFORMANCE:**
MAX SPEED: 213 mph (343 kmh)
RANGE: 2370 miles (3814 km)
POWERPLANT: four Pratt & Whitney R-1830-88 Twin Wasps
OUTPUT: 4800 hp (3580 kW)

**FIRST FLIGHT DATE:**
17 December 1937

**ARMAMENT:**
twin Browning 0.50-in machine guns in nose, dorsal and tail turrets and single gun in each beam position; maximum bomb/mine/torpedo load of 8000-lb (3629 kg) on underwing racks

**FEATURES:**
High-wing monoplane layout; boat-shaped hull; four radial engines; twin tail

# Consolidated B-24 Liberator USA

ten-seat, four-engined monoplane heavy bomber

Born out of an approach made by the USAAC to Consolidated for a bomber with superior performance to the B-17, the Liberator was built in near record time. The bomber was designed around the then-new long-span/low-drag Davis wing. The Army Air Corps was so impressed with the aircraft that it ordered 36 production examples before the prototype XB-24 had flown. A French purchasing mission also committed to buying 120, these aircraft later being issued to Britain following France's capitulation in 1940. Indeed, it was the British who coined the name 'Liberator'. USAAF production got into full swing with the B-24D, and it was this variant which was sent to the Middle East and Europe in 1942-43. It was superseded on all five production lines by the B-24J, which was built to the tune of 6678 airframes. The Liberator was also used by the US Navy in PB4Y form and the RAAF in the Far East. By the time production ceased on 31 May 1945, 18,475 Liberators had been built, making it the most produced American aircraft of World War 2.

SPECIFICATION:

**ACCOMMODATION:**
pilot and co-pilot, flight engineer, navigator, bombardier/nose gunner, radio operator/dorsal gunner, two waist gunners, ball turret gunner, tail gunner

**DIMENSIONS:**
LENGTH: 67 ft 2 in (20.47 m)
WINGSPAN: 110 ft 0 in (33.53 m)
HEIGHT: 18 ft 0 in (5.49 m)

**WEIGHTS:**
EMPTY: 36,500 lb (16,556 kg)
MAX T/O: 71,200 lb (32,296 kg)

**PERFORMANCE:**
MAX SPEED: 290 mph (467 kmh)
RANGE: 2100 miles (3380 km)
POWERPLANT: four Pratt & Whitney R-1830-65 Twin Wasps
OUTPUT: 4800 hp (3580 kW)

**FIRST FLIGHT DATE:**
29 December 1939

**ARMAMENT:**
four turrets with two Browning 0.50-in machine guns, and two guns in waist; maximum bomb load of 12,000-lb (5443 kg) in bomb-bay/inner wing racks

**FEATURES:**
Large-span monoplane wing; four radial engines; twin tail layout

# Consolidated PB4Y Privateer USA

eleven-seat, four-engined monoplane maritime patrol bomber

Although the US Navy had made much use of its B-24D-derived PB4Y-1 Liberators from August 1942, these aircraft had all been configured for USAAF service when originally built. It was decided in 1943 that a navalised variant would be most beneficial, and an order was placed in May for a dedicated long-range patrol bomber based on the Liberator. Three B-24DS were taken off the San Diego production line and rebuilt with lengthened fuselages, navalised interiors, greater defensive armament, modified engine cowlings and a distinctive vertical tail. The Navy ordered 739 aircraft in a single production run, 286 of which were delivered in 1944 and the remainder the following year. Few had reached the frontline by VJ-Day, although Privateer-equipped VP-24 did achieve operational status in the weeks prior to Japan's surrender. Indeed, the PB4Y went on to perform its best work in the Cold War as a radar and electronic countermeasures platform. After further service with the US Coast Guard, the final examples were retired in the early 1960s.

## SPECIFICATION:

**ACCOMMODATION:**
pilot and co-pilot, flight engineer, navigator, nose gunner, radar/radio operator, two dorsal gunners, two waist gunners, tail gunner

**DIMENSIONS:**
LENGTH: 74 ft 7 in (22.73 m)
WINGSPAN: 110 ft 0 in (33.53 m)
HEIGHT: 30 ft 1 in (9.17 m)

**WEIGHTS:**
EMPTY: 37,485 lb (17,003 kg)
MAX T/O: 65,000 lb (29,484 kg)

**PERFORMANCE:**
MAX SPEED: 237 mph (381 kmh)
RANGE: 2800 miles (4506 km)
POWERPLANT: four Pratt & Whitney R-1830-94 Twin Wasps
OUTPUT: 5400 hp (4028 kW)

**FIRST FLIGHT DATE:**
20 September 1943

**ARMAMENT:**
four turrets with two Browning 0.50-in machine guns and two guns in waist blisters; maximum bomb/depth charge/missile load of 6000-lb (2725 kg) in bomb-bay/underwing racks

**FEATURES:**
Large-span wing; four radial engines; large vertical tail

# Culver PQ-14 USA

single-seat, single-engined monoplane radio-controlled target aircraft

Culver cornered the market for unmanned aerial gunnery targets in 1940 when its Cadet light aeroplane was selected by the USAAC for conversion into a radio-controlled drone. Some 600 were built, 200 of which were issued to the Navy as training aids for anti-aircraft gunners. As the performance of manned combat aircraft increased, so the need for a more powerful gunnery target grew. To answer this demand Culver created a purpose-built machine, which entered service in 1943 as the PQ-14. Faster than its predecessor, the new design was also more manoeuvrable thanks to its larger control surfaces and retractable gear. Of the 1348 PQ-14As built, 1201 were transferred to the US Navy, where they were duly designated TD2C-1s. The final version to enter USAAF service was the heavier PQ-14B, 1112 of which were procured. A number of the latter remained in military service well into the 1950s, by which time the survivors had been redesignated Q-14A/BS. Those that were not shot down were sold into private ownership, and a number appeared on the US civil aircraft register.

SPECIFICATION:

**ACCOMMODATION:**
pilot (although usually flown unmanned)

**DIMENSIONS:**
LENGTH: 19 ft 6 in (5.94 m)
WINGSPAN: 30 ft 0 in (9.14 m)
HEIGHT: 7 ft 11 in (2.41 m)

**WEIGHTS:**
EMPTY: 1500 lb (680 kg)
MAX T/O: 1830 lb (830 kg)

**PERFORMANCE:**
MAX SPEED: 180 mph (290 kmh)
RANGE: 512 miles (824 km)
POWERPLANT: Franklin O-300-11
OUTPUT: 150 hp (112 kW)

**FIRST FLIGHT DATE:**
1942

**FEATURES:**
Monoplane wing layout; retractable undercarriage; close-cowled inline engine

# Curtiss P-40 Tomahawk USA

single-seat, single-engined monoplane fighter

Developed simply by replacing the Twin Wasp
radial engine of Curtiss's pre-war P-36 Hawk with a
supercharged Allison V-1710 inline engine, the
XP-40 prototype impressed the USAAC so much that
a contract for 524 aircraft was placed in early 1939.
This was the largest order for military aircraft
issued by the US government to a contractor since
the Great War, and the first production aircraft flew
in April 1940. A large number of P-40B/CS (no
A-models were built) had been delivered to the
USAAC by 7 December 1941. These took the fight to
the Japanese, but were soon shown to be inferior to
enemy fighters. Aside from USAAC use, the Curtiss
design also saw action with the RAF, which
christened it the Tomahawk. A total of 1180 fighters
were acquired by the British through Lend-Lease,
and these were flown by RAF, RCAF, RAAF and South
African units in North Africa and the Middle East
in 1941-42. Around 100 of these ex-British aircraft
were also issued to the American Volunteer Group
in China and Burma at around the same time.

SPECIFICATION:

**ACCOMMODATION:**
pilot

**DIMENSIONS:**
LENGTH: 31 ft 8.5 in (9.66 m)
WINGSPAN: 37 ft 3.5 in (11.37 m)
HEIGHT: 10 ft 7 in (3.22 m)

**WEIGHTS:**
EMPTY: 5812 lb (2636 kg)
MAX T/O: 8058 lb (3655 kg)

**PERFORMANCE:**
MAX SPEED: 345 mph (555 kmh)
RANGE: 1230 miles (1979 km)
POWERPLANT: Allison V-1710-33
OUTPUT: 1040 hp (775 kW)

**FIRST FLIGHT DATE:**
14 October 1938

**ARMAMENT:**
two Browning 0.50-in machine
guns in nose and two or four
Browning 0.30-in machine guns
in wings; maximum bomb load of
1600-lb (726 kg) on underwing/
fuselage racks

**FEATURES:**
Monoplane wing layout;
retractable undercarriage; close-
cowled inline engine; radiator
intake beneath propeller spinner

# Curtiss P-40 Warhawk/Kittyhawk USA

single-seat, single-engined monoplane fighter

With the further development of the Allison V-1710, Curtiss kept pace on the airframe side by producing the P-40D/E in 1941. The primary differences between these models and the earlier Tomahawk centred on a drastically revised nose shape due to the chin radiator being moved forward, which in turn allowed the propeller thrust line to be raised, the undercarriage to be shortened and fuselage top line to be lowered and recontoured. Modifications to the forward fuselage also meant that the nose guns were moved to the wings. As with the Tomahawk, the RAF was a major customer for the aircraft, which it christened the Kittyhawk. Despite suffering from poor performance at altitudes above 15,000 ft, the aircraft proved successful in the fighter-bomber role. In USAAF service, the aircraft received the appellation Warhawk, and subsequent variants were powered by Packard Merlins as well as Allison V-1710s. The last P-40 (an N-model) was built by Curtiss in December 1944, by which time 11,600+ Warhawks had been produced.

SPECIFICATION:

ACCOMMODATION:
pilot

DIMENSIONS:
LENGTH: 33 ft 4 in (10.16 m)
WINGSPAN: 37 ft 4 in (11.38 m)
HEIGHT: 12 ft 4 in (3.76 m)

WEIGHTS:
EMPTY: 6300 lb (2858 kg)
MAX T/O: 9100 lb (4128 kg)

PERFORMANCE:
MAX SPEED: 335 mph (539 kmh)
RANGE: 900 miles (1448 km)
POWERPLANT: Allison V-1710-39
OUTPUT: 1150 hp (857 kW)

FIRST FLIGHT DATE:
22 May 1941

ARMAMENT:
six Browning 0.50-in machine guns in wings; maximum bomb load of 1500-lb (681 kg) on underwing/fuselage racks

FEATURES:
Monoplane wing layout; retractable undercarriage; close-cowled inline engine; prominent radiator intake beneath propeller spinner

# Curtiss C-46 Commando  USA

54-seat, twin-engined monoplane transport

Built by Curtiss-Wright in an effort to recover
airliner sales that had been lost to monoplane
designs from Boeing, Douglas and Lockheed, the
C-46 started life as the CW-20 project in 1936. With
the prototype flying by spring 1940, its
performance figures impressed civil and military
operators alike – the USAAC placed an order for 200
in September of that year. To fulfil its military role,
the CW-20's pressurised interior was gutted and
replaced with canvas seating in an unpressurised
environment. Double cargo doors were built into
the fuselage, the floor strengthened and uprated
engines fitted. Production examples reached the
USAAF in the autumn of 1942, the type proving itself
on long-range flights transporting men and
equipment to North Africa in the wake of
Operation *Torch* landings. The C-46's 'finest hour'
came in the Far East where the India-China Wing's
aircraft formed the backbone of the 'Hump' airlift
across the Himalayas in 1943-44. Over 3000 were
built, and the aircraft continued to serve with the
USAF during the Korean and Vietnam Wars.

SPECIFICATION:

**ACCOMMODATION:**
pilot and co-pilot, navigator/radio
operator, loadmaster and up to
50 passengers

**DIMENSIONS:**
LENGTH: 76 ft 4 in (23.27 m)
WINGSPAN: 108 ft 1 in (32.94 m)
HEIGHT: 21 ft 9 in (6.63 m)

**WEIGHTS:**
EMPTY: 29,483 lb (13,373 kg)
MAX T/O: 56,000 lb (25,400 kg)

**PERFORMANCE:**
MAX SPEED: 269 mph (433 kmh)
RANGE: 1200 miles (1931 km)
POWERPLANT: two Pratt & Whitney
R-2800-51 Double Wasps
OUTPUT: 2000 hp (1491 kW)

**FIRST FLIGHT DATE:**
26 March 1940

**FEATURES:**
Monoplane wing layout;
rectractable landing gear; two
close-cowled radial engines;
retractable tailwheel; large
vertical tail surface; bulbous
fuselage

# Curtiss SB2C Helldiver USA

two-seat, single-engined monoplane dive-bomber

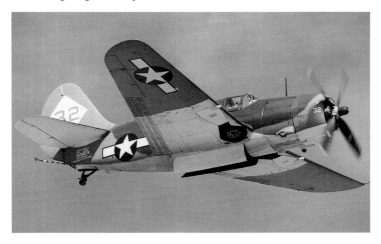

The most numerous Allied dive-bomber of World War 2, the Curtiss Helldiver endured a prolonged gestation period to mature into one of the most effective aircraft of its type. Some 7200 were built between 1942 and 1945, the aircraft making its service debut over Rabaul in November 1943 flying from the deck of USS *Bunker Hill*. At that time, the aircraft was still inferior in many respects to the Douglas SBD Dauntless, the very aircraft it was meant to replace! Despite being improved over the next two years, the Helldiver retained an unenviable reputation, with more aircraft lost in deck landing accidents than to enemy action. Indeed, its unpleasant flying characteristics near to the stall earned it the nickname 'The Beast'. Although disliked by the crews sent into combat flying it, the Helldiver was responsible for the destruction of more Japanese targets than any other dive-bomber. Post-war, a small number of aircraft saw use with the French, Italian, Greek and Portuguese navies and the Royal Thai Air Force, whilst its US Navy career lingered on until the late 1940s.

SPECIFICATION:

**ACCOMMODATION:**
pilot and gunner

**DIMENSIONS:**
LENGTH: 36 ft 8 in (11.20 m)
WINGSPAN: 49 ft 9 in (15.20 m)
HEIGHT: 16 ft 11 in (5.10 m)

**WEIGHTS:**
EMPTY: 11,000 lb (4990 kg)
MAX T/O: 16,607 lb (7550 kg)

**PERFORMANCE:**
MAX SPEED: 281 mph (452 kmh)
RANGE: 1110 miles (1786 km)
POWERPLANT: Wright R-2600-8 Cyclone
OUTPUT: 1700 hp (1267.67 kW)

**FIRST FLIGHT DATE:**
18 December 1940

**ARMAMENT:**
two 20 mm cannon or four Browning 0.50-in machine guns in wings and one flexible Browning 0.50-in machine guns in rear cockpit; maximum bomb/torpedo load of 1000-lb (454 kg) in internal bomb-bay and 1000-lb (454 kg) of bombs/rockets on underwing racks

**FEATURES:**
Monoplane wing layout; rectractable landing gear; close-cowled radial engine

147

# de Havilland Mosquito UK

two-seat, twin-engined monoplane fighter-bomber/reconnaissance aircraft

Built to replace the Blenheim, the Mosquito flew in the face of convention by utilising a wooden fuselage and wings. Initially rejected by the Air Ministry in late 1938 on the grounds of its unorthodox construction, the aircraft's wooden structure actually ensured its series production with the outbreak of war due to the fear that the supply of light alloys from abroad would be affected by the conflict. An order for 50 aircraft was received on 1 March 1940, and the prototype Mosquito took to the skies eight months later. The first Mosquito to see operational service was the photo-reconnaissance variant on 20 September 1941, whilst bomber optimised B Mk IVs began to reach the frontline two months later. While the Mosquito was being successfully blooded as a bomber, the nightfighter version was also making its mark, having been developed from the second prototype. Numerous modifications were made to the design during its production life, which eventually saw 7781 Mosquitoes built. Later versions remained in service with the RAF until 1961.

SPECIFICATION:

ACCOMMODATION:
pilot and navigator/radar operator

DIMENSIONS:
LENGTH: 40 ft 10 in (12.44 m)
WINGSPAN: 54 ft 2 in (16.51 m)
HEIGHT: 15 ft 3 in (4.65 m)

WEIGHTS:
EMPTY: 14,300 lb (6486 kg)
MAX T/O: 20,000 lb (9072 kg)

PERFORMANCE:
MAX SPEED: 370 mph (595 kmh)
RANGE: 1770 miles (2848 km) with external drop tanks
POWERPLANT: two Rolls-Royce Merlin 21s
OUTPUT: 2960 hp (2506 kW)

FIRST FLIGHT DATE:
25 November 1940

ARMAMENT:
four 20 mm cannon and four Browning 0.303-in machine guns in nose (fighter); maximum bomb load of 4000-lb (1814 kg) in internal bomb-bay and 1000-lb (454 kg) of bombs/rockets on underwing racks (bomber)

FEATURES:
Monoplane wing layout; rectractable landing gear; two close-cowled inline engines

# Dewoitine D 520 FRANCE

single-seat, single-engined monoplane fighter

Undoubtedly the best French fighter at the time of the German invasion in May 1940, the D 520 had been designed to meet an *Armée de l'Air* requirement for a monoplane fighter issued in 1936. Unfortunately for France, the first examples of the Dewoitine fighter only began to reach the frontline in December 1939. Production rates were poor, and by the eve of the *Blitzkrieg* just 36 fighters had made it into service. However, the invasion spurred a massive production programme, and by the Armistice on 30 June, 437 had been built. No further D 520s were built until June 1941, when the Vichy government ordered Dewoitine to re-open the production line. A further 478 were then built until construction ceased in mid-1943. Aside from its use by the Vichy French, the D 520 was employed as a trainer by the Luftwaffe, and others were issued to Italy, Bulgaria and Romania in the wake of the French surrender in 1940. As a fighter, the D 520 enjoyed some success, being credited with 114 German aircraft destroyed during the Battle of France.

SPECIFICATION:

ACCOMMODATION:
pilot

DIMENSIONS:
LENGTH: 28 ft 8.5 in (8.76 m)
WINGSPAN: 33 ft 5.5 in (10.20 m)
HEIGHT: 8 ft 5 in (2.56 m)

WEIGHTS:
EMPTY: 4612 lb (2092 kg)
MAX T/O: 6129 lb (2780 kg)

PERFORMANCE:
MAX SPEED: 329 mph (529 kmh)
RANGE: 777 miles (1250 km)
POWERPLANT: Hispano-Suiza 12Y-45
OUTPUT: 910 hp (678 kW)

FIRST FLIGHT DATE:
2 October 1938

ARMAMENT:
one HS 404 20 mm cannon firing through propeller hub and four MAC 34 M39 7.5 mm machine guns in wing

FEATURES:
Monoplane wing layout; rectractable landing gear; inline engine; fixed tailwheel; ventral radiator bath intake

# Douglas SBD Dauntless  USA

two-seat, single-engined monoplane dive-bomber

The SBD Dauntless was the scourge of the Japanese Imperial Fleet in the crucial years of the Pacific war. Almost single-handedly, 54 SBDs won the pivotal Battle of Midway on 4 June 1942, destroying four Japanese carriers in just 24 hours. The SBD of 1942 could trace its origins back to rival designs penned by gifted engineers John Northrop and Ed Heinemann in the mid 1930s. Northrop produced the BT-1 for the US Navy in 1938, its all-metal stressed-skin design exhibiting airframe strength that made it an ideal dive-bomber. By the time the BT-1 had evolved into the BT-2, Northrop's company had been acquired by Douglas, and the type, reworked by Heinemann, was redesignated the SBD-1. Production aircraft reached the Marine Corps in 1940, and by the spring of 1941 the definitive SBD-3 was in service. A total of 584 SBD-3s were built, and it was these machines that became the key combat aircraft in the Pacific in 1942-43. The USAAC also procured nearly 900 Dauntlesses, which it designated the A-24 – production of all variants of the SBD/A-24 totalled 5936.

## SPECIFICATION:

**ACCOMMODATION:**
pilot and gunner

**DIMENSIONS:**
LENGTH: 33 ft 0 in (10.06 m)
WINGSPAN: 41 ft 6 in (12.65 m)
HEIGHT: 12 ft 11 in (3.94 m)

**WEIGHTS:**
EMPTY: 6535 lb (2964 kg)
MAX T/O: 9519 lb (4318 kg)

**PERFORMANCE:**
MAX SPEED: 255 mph (410 kmh)
RANGE: 773 miles (1244 km)
POWERPLANT: Wright R-1820-66 Cyclone 9
OUTPUT: 1350 hp (1007 kW)

**FIRST FLIGHT DATE:**
July 1935 (XBT-1)

**ARMAMENT:**
two Browning 0.50-in machine guns in the nose and two flexible Browning 0.50-in machine guns in rear cockpit; maximum bomb load of 2250-lb (1021 kg) of bombs on underwing racks

**FEATURES:**
Monoplane wing layout; rectractable landing gear; close-cowled radial engine; aerial mast on port side forward of cockpit

# Douglas C-47 Skytrain USA

32-seat, twin-engined monoplane transport

The C-47 was the military descendant of the
Douglas Sleeper Transport. When the DC-3 entered
civilian service in 1936, the US Army Air Corps
immediately contacted Douglas and advised the
company of changes that needed to be made in
order to render the airliner suitable for military use
– these included the fitment of bigger engines, the
reinforcement of the cabin floor and the inclusion
of large cargo doors. Therefore, when the USAAC
issued contracts in 1940 for the first C-47s, Douglas
was able to get production immediately underway.
A total of 963 C-47s were built, the first aircraft
entering USAAC service in 1941. Follow-on variants
of the Skytrain included the A- and B-models,
which differed in electrical systems and
powerplant from the basic C-47. The Douglas
transport was a key factor in the success of the
Allied war effort, fulfilling the critical 'air bridge'
role with men and material to all theatres of
conflict. Some 10,926 examples were eventually
built in the USA, and a number remain in military
service across the globe today.

SPECIFICATION:

ACCOMMODATION:
pilot and co-pilot, navigator/
radio operator, loadmaster and
up to 28 passengers

DIMENSIONS:
LENGTH: 64 ft 5.50 in (19.64 m)
WINGSPAN: 95 ft 0 in (28.96 m)
HEIGHT: 16 ft 11 in (5.16 m)

WEIGHTS:
EMPTY: 16,970 lb (7700 kg)
MAX T/O: 26,000 lb (11,793 kg)

FIRST FLIGHT DATE:
17 December 1935 (Douglas
Sleeper Transport)

PERFORMANCE:
MAX SPEED: 229 mph (369 kmh)
RANGE: 2125 miles (3420 km)
POWERPLANT: two Pratt & Whitney
R-1830-93 Twin Wasps
OUTPUT: 2400 hp (1790 kW)

FEATURES:
Monoplane wing layout;
rectractable landing gear; two
close-cowled radial engines;
large vertical tail surface

# Douglas C-54 Skymaster USA

52-seat, four-engined monoplane strategic transport aircraft

Like its more famous Douglas forebear the C-47, the C-54 was a military derivative of a civilian airliner, in this case the DC-4A. Designed specifically to fulfil a specification drawn up by United Air Lines for a long-range pressurised airliner, the aircraft was ordered to the tune of 61 airframes by the US operator, followed by a further buy of 71 for the USAAC – in the event, most civilian DC-4As were requisitioned into military service. The first production C-54 made its maiden flight on 26 March 1942, and by the following October 24 were in service with Air Transport Command. The A-model was introduced in 1943, this aircraft having a cargo door, stronger floor, cargo boom hoist and larger wing tanks. The design was modified during the remaining war years to suit USAAF requirements, 1242 C-54s of varying marks being built. Included in this number were 183 for the US Navy, which operated them in the Pacific as R4DS. Post-war, the C-54/R4D enjoyed a long career with the USAF and US Navy, the final examples not being retired until the late 1960s.

SPECIFICATION:

ACCOMMODATION:
pilot and co-pilot, navigator/radio operator, loadmaster and up to 48 passengers

DIMENSIONS:
LENGTH: 93 ft 11 in (28.63 m)
WINGSPAN: 117 ft 6 in (35.81 m)
HEIGHT: 27 ft 6.25 in (8.39 m)

WEIGHTS:
EMPTY: 38,000 lb (17,237 kg)
MAX T/O: 73,000 lb (33,112 kg)

PERFORMANCE:
MAX SPEED: 274 mph (441 kmh)
RANGE: 3900 miles (6276 km)
POWERPLANT: four Pratt & Whitney R-2000-7 Twin Wasps
OUTPUT: 5400 hp (4028 kW)

FIRST FLIGHT DATE:
7 June 1938 (civilian DC-4E)

FEATURES:
Monoplane wing layout; rectractable tricycle landing gear; four close-cowled radial engines; large vertical tail surface

# Douglas A-20 Havoc  USA

three-seat, twin-engined monoplane light bomber

One of the most widely used light bombers of
World War 2, the A-20 evolved from a Douglas
design built to meet a USAAC attack specification
issued in 1938. Known as the Model 7A, the
prototype was reworked soon after its first flight in
order to make the aircraft more suitable for use in
Europe, and indeed the first order for the new
bomber came from France, not the USAAC.
Redesignated the DB-7, production of the new
bomber commenced in 1939, and 60 aircraft had
reached France prior to the *Blitzkrieg* on 10 May
1940. A handful of undelivered DB-7s were issued
to the RAF, which christened them Boston Is and
used them in the training and nightfighter roles.
The Boston became one of the mainstays of the
RAF, 1000+ being supplied through Lend-Lease.
The USAAC committed to the DB-7 (redesignated
the A-20) in May 1939, and by the time production
ended in September 1944, 7385 had been built. The
type saw combat across the globe, its ruggedness
proving particularly attractive to the Soviets, who
used 3125 A-20s.

SPECIFICATION:

**ACCOMMODATION:**
pilot and navigator/bombardier,
gunner

**DIMENSIONS:**
LENGTH: 48 ft 0 in (14.63 m)
WINGSPAN: 61 ft 4 in (18.69 m)
HEIGHT: 17 ft 7 in (5.36 m)

**WEIGHTS:**
EMPTY: 15 984 lb (7250 kg)
MAX T/O: 27 200 lb (12 338 kg)

**PERFORMANCE:**
MAX SPEED: 317 mph (510 kmh)
RANGE: 1025 miles (1650 km)
POWERPLANT: two Wright
R-2600-23 Cyclone 14 engines
(A-20G)
OUTPUT: 3200 hp (2386 kW)

**FIRST FLIGHT DATE:**
26 October 1938 (Douglas 7B)

**ARMAMENT:**
four Browning 0.30-in or 0.50-in
machine guns in nose, two
0.30-in machine guns in dorsal
and one in ventral positions;
maximum bomb load of 2000-lb
(907 kg) in bomb-bay

**FEATURES:**
Monoplane wing layout;
rectractable tricycle landing gear;
two close-cowled radial engines

# Douglas A-26 Invader USA

three-seat, twin-engined monoplane attack bomber

The A-26 Invader was designed as a natural successor to Douglas's A-20. Harnessing the power of Pratt & Whitney's new Double Wasp radial engine, prototype XP-26s were ordered by the USAAC in May 1941 in three different forms – one with a 75 mm gun, a second with a solid radar nose and armed with a quartet of 20 mm forward-firing weapons, plus four guns in an upper turret, and the third with optical sighting equipment in the nose and two defensive turrets. The latter machine was ordered first as the A-26B, and it made its combat debut on 19 November 1944. Some 1355 were built, followed by 1091 c-models (which had a transparent nose housing navigational and radar bombing equipment). The Invader enjoyed a more active post-war career with the USAF than any of its twin-engined contemporaries, 450 B-26s (the Invader was redesignated in 1948 following the retirement of the last Marauders) seeing combat in Korea, whilst the French also used them in Indo-China. Following the latter's lead, the USAF employed converted On Mark B-26Ks in Vietnam too.

SPECIFICATION:

**ACCOMMODATION:**
pilot and navigator/bombardier, gunner

**DIMENSIONS:**
LENGTH: 51 ft 3 in (15.62 m)
WINGSPAN: 70 ft 0 in (21.34 m)
HEIGHT: 18 ft 3 in (5.56 m)

**WEIGHTS:**
EMPTY: 22,850 lb (10,365 kg)
MAX T/O: 35,000 lb (15,876 kg)

**PERFORMANCE:**
MAX SPEED: 373 mph (600 kmh)
RANGE: 1400 miles (2253 km)
POWERPLANT: two Pratt & Whitney R-2800-79 Double Wasps
OUTPUT: 4000 hp (2982 kW)

**FIRST FLIGHT DATE:**
10 July 1942

**ARMAMENT:**
two Browning 0.50-in machine guns in nose and in ventral and dorsal turrets; maximum bomb load of 4000-lb (1418 kg) in bomb-bay and 2000-lb (907 kg) of bombs/rockets on underwing racks

**FEATURES:**
Monoplane wing layout; rectractable tricycle landing gear; two close-cowled radial engines; large vertical tail surface

# Fairchild C-61 Argus USA

four-seat, single-engined high-wing liaison/communications and instrument training aircraft

The Argus traced its lineage back to the Model 24C three-seater civilian tourer of 1933, Fairchild introducing the four-seat Model 24J in 1937. With the general enlarging of the US military in the late 1930s, the Model 24 was one of the numerous civilian types which found itself a role within the rapidly expanding USAAC. However, of the 163 UC-61 Forwarders (as the militarised Fairchild was designated), all bar two were passed onto the British under lend-lease. Christened Argus IS, the first examples arrived in the UK in 1941 and were issued to both the RAF and the Air Transport Auxiliary (ATA), which used them as 'aerial taxis' for its ferry pilots. A further 364 Mk IIs followed, these machines having new radios and a 24-volt electrical system – the USAAC also acquired 148 examples to this specification, which it designated UC-61AS. The final variant built was the Ranger-engined Argus III (UC-61K), of which 306 were issued to the British. Aside from USAAC and RAF/ATA use, Fairchild 24s were also supplied to the US Navy, which designated them J2KS.

SPECIFICATION:

ACCOMMODATION:
pilot and three passengers

DIMENSIONS:
LENGTH: 23 ft 9 in (7.24 m)
WINGSPAN: 36 ft 4 in (11.07 m)
HEIGHT: 7 ft 7.5 in (2.32 m)

WEIGHTS:
EMPTY: 1613 lb (732 kg)
MAX T/O: 2562 lb (1162 kg)

PERFORMANCE:
MAX SPEED: 132 mph (212 kmh)
RANGE: 640 miles (1030 km)
POWERPLANT: Warner R-500
Super Scarab or Ranger L-440-7
OUTPUT: 165 hp (123 kW) and 200
hp (149 kW) respectively

FIRST FLIGHT DATE:
1933 (civilian Model 24C)

FEATURES:
High-wing layout; fixed landing
gear; extensive cockpit glazing;
radial or inline engine

# Fairey Swordfish UK

three-seat, single-engined biplane reconnaissance/torpedo-bomber

Looking out-dated by 1939, the Fairey Swordfish somehow remained a viable weapon of war in its primary torpedo-bomber role until mid 1942. Indeed, the aircraft continued to be produced for a further two years, and was only phased out of frontline service in May 1945! The Swordfish traced its lineage back to the T.S.R.I., built by Fairey in 1933 in the hope of soliciting interest from the Air Ministry. The ploy worked, and Specification S 15/33 was issued calling for a carrier-based torpedo-spotter-reconnaissance aircraft. Following flight-testing, 86 Swordfish were ordered in 1935. The standard weapon of choice for the Swordfish was an 18-in/1610-lb torpedo.

825 Naval Air Squadron was the first unit to receive the Swordfish in July 1936, and over the next three years 12 more units re-equipped with the Fairey biplane. Aside from being the FAA's primary torpedo bomber for the first two-and-a-half years of World War 2, the Swordfish also saw combat with the RAF's Coastal Command. A total of 2391 were built over four different mark numbers.

## SPECIFICATION:

**ACCOMMODATION:**
pilot, observer, gunner in tandem

**DIMENSIONS:**
LENGTH: 35 ft 8 in (10.87 m)
WINGSPAN: 45 ft 6 in (13.87 m)
HEIGHT: 12 ft 4 in (3.76 m)

**WEIGHTS:**
EMPTY: 4700 lb (2132 kg)
MAX T/O: 7510 lb (3406 kg)

**PERFORMANCE:**
MAX SPEED: 138 mph (222 kmh)
RANGE: 1030 miles (1658 km)
POWERPLANT: Bristol Pegasus XXX
OUTPUT: 750 hp (559 kW)

**FIRST FLIGHT DATE:**
17 April 1934

**ARMAMENT:**
one fixed Browning 0.303-in machine gun in nose and one in rear cockpit on flexible mount; one 18-in/1610-lb (730 kg) torpedo or 1500-lb (680 kg) mines/bombs/rockets on underwing racks

**FEATURES:**
Biplane wing layout; fixed landing gear; close-cowled radial engine

# Fairey Albacore UK

three-seat, single-engined biplane torpedo-bomber

Conceived by Fairey as a replacement for its Swordfish, the Albacore was in fact outlasted by its legendary predecessor both in terms of its frontline service and production life. First flown on 12 December 1938, the Albacore enjoyed greater power than the Swordfish thanks to its Bristol Taurus radial engine. This allowed it to carry more weaponry and/or fuel. The first production aircraft were issued to 826 Naval Air Squadron (NAS) on 15 March 1940, and the unit gave the Albacore its combat debut on 31 May that year. The first naval action involving the Albacore took place during the Battle of Cape Matapan in March 1941, when aircraft from 826 and 820 NASs sortied from HMS *Formidable* and severely damaged the Italian battleship *Vittorio Veneto*. Subsequent operations saw units carrying out a variety of missions (attack, patrol, dive-bombing, mine-laying and target marking) in the Baltic and Mediterranean Seas and the Atlantic and Indian Oceans. Canadian Albacores participated in the D-Day operations, by which time FAA examples had been replaced by Barracudas.

SPECIFICATION:

**ACCOMMODATION:**
pilot, observer, gunner in tandem

**DIMENSIONS:**
LENGTH: 39 ft 9.5 in (12.13 m)
WINGSPAN: 50 ft 0 in (15.24 m)
HEIGHT: 15 ft 3 in (4.65 m)

**WEIGHTS:**
EMPTY: 7250 lb (3289 kg)
MAX T/O: 11,186 lb (5074 kg)

**PERFORMANCE:**
MAX SPEED: 161 mph (259 kmh)
RANGE: 930 miles (1497 km)
POWERPLANT: Bristol Taurus II
OUTPUT: 1065 hp (794 kW)

**FIRST FLIGHT DATE:**
12 December 1938

**ARMAMENT:**
one fixed Browning 0.303-in machine gun in starboard lower wing and two in rear cockpit on flexible mount; one 18-in/1610-lb (730 kg) torpedo or 2000-lb (907 kg) mines/bombs/rockets on underwing racks

**FEATURES:**
Biplane wing layout; fixed landing gear; close-cowled radial engine; enclosed cockpit

# Fairey Fulmar UK

two-seat, single-engined monoplane fighter-bomber

Developed from Fairey's P 4/34 light bomber of 1937 through the addition of folding wings, a catapult spool and an arrestor hook, the Fulmar gave the Royal Navy its first eight-gun fighter when it entered service in May 1940. Seeing action just months later when called on to protect Malta convoys from the deck of HMS *Illustrious*, the fighter provided sterling service with 11 Fleet Air Arm squadrons particularly against Italian and German opponents in the Mediterranean in 1941-42. Aside from its use in this theatre, the Fulmar also saw action off Norway and Ceylon, and completed its frontline service as a nightfighter protecting Russian convoys in 1944-45. The last Fulmar (a tropicalised Mk II) was delivered in February 1943, and by this stage of the war most Fleet Air Arm fighter units had replaced the Fairey fighter with Seafires or Corsair Is. Aside from its frontline role, the Fulmar also proved ideally suited to deck landing training, as its vice-free handling qualities and slow stalling speed made it easy for novice pilots to fly 'around the boat'.

SPECIFICATION:

**ACCOMMODATION:**
pilot and observer/gunner in tandem

**DIMENSIONS:**
LENGTH: 40 ft 3 in (12.27 m)
WINGSPAN: 46 ft 4.5 in (14.13 m)
HEIGHT: 10 ft 8 in (3.25 m)

**WEIGHTS:**
EMPTY: 6915 lb (3137 kg)
MAX T/O: 9800 lb (4445 kg)

**PERFORMANCE:**
MAX SPEED: 256 mph (412 kmh)
RANGE: 830 miles (1335 km)
POWERPLANT: Rolls-Royce Merlin VIII
OUTPUT: 1080 hp (805 kW)

**FIRST FLIGHT DATE:**
4 January 1940

**ARMAMENT:**
eight Browning 0.303-in machine guns in wings and optional single machine gun in rear cockpit; maximum bomb load of 500-lb (227 kg) on underwing racks

**FEATURES:**
Monoplane wing layout; rectractable landing gear; close-cowled inline engine; enclosed cockpit

# Fiat CR.42 ITALY

single-seat, single-engined biplane fighter

The last Fiat biplane fighter, the Falco, like the its stylish predecessor the CR.32, was obsolete before the outbreak of World War 2. Despite this, great numbers saw action during the conflict not only with the Italians, but also the Finns, Germans, Hungarians and Belgians. A development of the unsuccessful CR.41, the first CR.42 entered frontline service with the *Regia Aeronautica* in April 1939, followed by a handful of other export countries, including neutral Sweden. Built in four main variants that covered day fighter, nightfighter and close support roles, the CR.42 saw action in the Belgian, Greek, East African, Western European, Mediterranean and North African theatres. As the Fiat fighter became more and more vulnerable in its designed role, survivors were relegated to performing nocturnal patrols over northern Italy. Although production ended in early 1942, small numbers of CR.42s remained in service with the Luftwaffe as night ground attack platforms in the Balkans and northern Italy following the Italian surrender in September 1943.

SPECIFICATION:

**ACCOMMODATION:**
pilot

**DIMENSIONS:**
LENGTH: 27 ft 3 in (8.30 m)
WINGSPAN: 31 ft 10 in (9.70 m)
HEIGHT: 10 ft 10 in (3.30 m)

**WEIGHTS:**
EMPTY: 3763 lb (1707 kg)
MAX T/O: 5302 lb (2405 kg)

**PERFORMANCE:**
MAX SPEED: 266 mph (428 kmh)
RANGE: 630 miles (1014 km) with
external fuel tanks
POWERPLANT: Fiat A 74 RC38
OUTPUT: 840 hp (626 kW)

**FIRST FLIGHT DATE:**
23 May 1938

**ARMAMENT:**
two SAFAT 12.7 mm machine guns
in nose and two SAFAT 7.7 mm
machine guns in wings;
maximum bomb load of 500-lb
(227 kg) on underwing racks

**FEATURES:**
Biplane wing layout; fixed,
spatted landing gear;
close-cowled radial engine; open
cockpit; headrest behind cockpit

# Fieseler Fi 156 Storch GERMANY

three-seat, single-engined high-wing army co-operation/reconnaissance aircraft

Arguably the best army co-operation aircraft used by either side during World War 2, the Storch was the most successful product to emanate from the company founded by World War 1 ace Gerhard Fieseler. The Fi 156 boasted astounding short take-off and landing performance thanks to its unique high-lift wing devices – a fixed slot extending the span of the wing leading edge and slotted ailerons and camber-changing flaps along the length of the trailing edge. Beating off rival designs, Fieseler committed the Fi 156A-1 to production in 1937. The Storch saw action wherever the *Wehrmacht* engaged the enemy, and despite its fragile appearance, the aircraft had a frontline 'life expectancy' ten times longer than that enjoyed by a Bf 109! Indeed, it was licence-production of the latter type by Fieseler that forced the company to transfer Fi 156 construction to factories in France and Czechoslovakia in 1942. By war's end 2000+ had been built, with the C-series being the most common. Post-war, production continued in France and Czechoslovakia.

SPECIFICATION:

**ACCOMMODATION:**
one pilot and two passengers

**DIMENSIONS:**
LENGTH: 32 ft 5.75 in (9.90 m)
WINGSPAN: 46 ft 9 in (14.25 m)
HEIGHT: 10 ft 0 in (3.05 m)

**WEIGHTS:**
EMPTY: 2050 lb (930 kg)
MAX T/O: 2921 lb (1325 kg)

**PERFORMANCE:**
MAX SPEED: 109 mph (175 kmh)
RANGE: 239 miles (385 km)
POWERPLANT: Argus AS 10C-3
(Fi 156) or Salmson 9AB (MS502)
OUTPUT: 240 hp (179 kW) and
250 hp (186.4 kW) respectively

**FIRST FLIGHT DATE:**
24 May 1936

**ARMAMENT:**
one MG 17 7.9 mm machine gun
in rear cockpit on flexible mount

**FEATURES:**
high wing layout; enclosed
cockpit with extensive glazing;
fixed landing gear

# Fleet Fort CANADA

two-seat, single-engined monoplane trainer

The only aircraft designed and built by Canada during World War 2, the Fleet Fort started life as a private-venture trainer which was capable of fulfilling a variety of roles when fitted with different powerplants. As it transpired, the aircraft was only ever produced in the intermediate trainer version (the 60K). The prototype was evaluated by the RCAF in mid 1940, and following flight trials, an order for 200 was placed. Although the first production Fort was flown on 18 April 1941, the RCAF subsequently changed its mind in respect to the aircraft's ability to prepare pilots for the transition from basic to advanced types. It had found that the Fort was too easy for pilot trainees to master, thereby making it unsuitable as a transitionary step to combat aircraft. The RCAF scaled its order back to just 100 aircraft, and in 1942 it decided to convert surviving Forts into dedicated wireless trainers, installing equipment in the rear cockpit and switching the seat in this space to face aft. Most Forts were so converted, and remained in service until 1945.

SPECIFICATION:

**ACCOMMODATION:**
two pilots in tandem

**DIMENSIONS:**
LENGTH: 26 ft 10.30 in (8.18 m)
WINGSPAN: 36 ft 0 in (10.97 m)
HEIGHT: 8 ft 3 in (2.51 m)

**WEIGHTS:**
EMPTY: 2530 lb (1149 kg)
MAX T/O: 3500 lb (1589 kg)

**PERFORMANCE:**
MAX SPEED: 162 mph (260.60 kmh)
RANGE: not specified
POWERPLANT: Jacobs L-6MB
OUTPUT: 330 hp (246.18 kW)

**FIRST FLIGHT DATE:**
22 March 1940

**FEATURES:**
Monoplane wing layout; two distinctive enclosed cockpits, with the second one stepped up; fixed landing gear; close-cowled radial engine

# Focke-Wulf FW 190A/F/G GERMANY

single-seat, single-engined monoplane fighter

The FW 190 caught the RAF by surprise when it appeared over the Channel front in 1941, and it remained unmatched in aerial combat until the advent of the Spitfire Mk IX in late 1942. Powered by the compact BMW 801 radial engine, the FW 190 boasted excellent handling characteristics to match its turn of speed. The A-model FW 190s were the dedicated fighter variants, and as the design matured so more guns were fitted and more power squeezed out of the BMW engine. By the end of 1942, production of the FW 190 accounted for half of all German fighters built that year, and the fighter-bomber F/G had also been developed – F-models entered frontline service on the Eastern Front during the winter of 1942-43. All manner of ordnance from bombs to rockets could be carried by the fighter-bomber FW 190, and additional protective armour for the pilot was also added around the cockpit. Variants of the FW 190 saw action against the Allies on all fronts of the war in Europe, and the aircraft remained a deadly opponent until VE-Day.

SPECIFICATION:

**ACCOMMODATION:**
pilot

**DIMENSIONS:**
LENGTH: 29 ft 0 in (8.84 m)
WINGSPAN: 34 ft 5.50 in (10.50 m)
HEIGHT: 13 ft 0 in (3.96 m)

**WEIGHTS:**
EMPTY: 6393 lb (2900 kg)
MAX T/O: 8770 lb (3978 kg)

**PERFORMANCE:**
MAX SPEED: 382 mph (615 kmh)
RANGE: 497 miles (800 km)
POWERPLANT: BMW 801D
OUTPUT: 1700 hp (1268 kW)

**FIRST FLIGHT DATE:**
1 June 1939

**ARMAMENT:**
two MG 131 13 mm machine guns in nose, four MG 151/20 20 mm cannon in wings; one 1100 lb (500 kg) bomb under fuselage

**FEATURES:**
Monoplane wing layout; close-cowled radial engine; retractable landing gear; bulged fairings over cannon breeches forward of cockpit

# Focke-Wulf FW 190D  GERMANY

single-seat, single-engined monoplane fighter

Developed in 1942 as a replacement for the aborted
FW 190B/C high altitude fighters, the *Langnasen-
Dora* (Longnose-Dora) made use of the inverted
inline Junkers Jumo 213 engine, combined with an
MW50 water/methanol booster, to achieve an
impressive rate of climb and top speed. In total
contrast to the many models and sub-variants of
the FW 190A/F/G, only the D-9 version of the Dora
was produced in large numbers. Service entry was
achieved in August 1944, and the first fighters to
reach the *Jagdwaffe* were employed as ME 262
airfield defenders. A number of D-9s participated
in the last ditch *Bodenplatte* operation staged at
dawn on New Year's Day 1945 against numerous
Allied airfields in western Europe, and the survivors of this mission were later absorbed within the
Defence of the Reich force. In February 1945
production commenced on the D-12, which was
equipped with an uprated Jumo 213 F-1 engine, a 30
mm cannon firing through the nose and better
protective armour for the pilot, but only a handful
were built before Germany surrendered in May 1945.

SPECIFICATION:

**ACCOMMODATION:**
pilot

**DIMENSIONS:**
LENGTH: 33 ft 5.25 in (10.19 m)
WINGSPAN: 34 ft 5.5 in (10.50 m)
HEIGHT: 11 ft 0.25 in (3.36 m)

**WEIGHTS:**
EMPTY: 7964 lb (3612 kg)
MAX T/O: 10 670 lb (4840 kg)

**PERFORMANCE:**
MAX SPEED: 426 mph (685 kmh)
RANGE: 520 miles (837 km)
POWERPLANT: Junkers Jumo
213A-1
OUTPUT: 2240 hp (1670 kW)

**FIRST FLIGHT DATE:**
March 1942

**ARMAMENT:**
two MG 131 13 mm machine guns
in nose and two MG 151 20 mm
cannon in wings; one 1100 lb
(500 kg) bomb under fuselage

**FEATURES:**
Monoplane wing layout;
close-cowled inline engine;
retractable landing gear;
bulged fairings over cannon
breeches forward of cockpit;
stretched fuselage

# Grumman G-44 Widgeon USA

five-seat, twin-engined high-wing utility/ASW amphibian flying boat

The Widgeon was built as a smaller and cheaper version of the Goose amphibian for the US civil market. However, less than 40 had reached private hands when Grumman was ordered to focus production on a militarised amphibian, which the USAAC designated the OA-14 and the US Navy and Coast Guard the J4F. The latter service enjoyed its first success against the German U-boat menace in August 1942 when a J4F-1 sank U-166 off the Passes of the Mississippi. Grumman received its biggest production order (131) for the J4F-2 in early 1942, the final example of which was not delivered to the Navy until 26 February 1945. The Royal Navy also received 15 J4F-2s under Lend-Lease, these aircraft fulfilling the communications role in the West Indies. Grumman further improved the design in 1944 with the introduction of the G-44A, which boasted a deeper keel for improved hydrodynamic performance. This variant remained in production until January 1949, by which time 76 had been built – a further 41 were constructed under licence in France in 1948-49.

SPECIFICATION:

**ACCOMMODATION:**
pilot, co-pilot and three passengers

**DIMENSIONS:**
LENGTH: 31 ft 1 in (9.47 m)
WINGSPAN: 40 ft 0 in (12.19 m)
HEIGHT: 11 ft 5 in (3.48 m)

**WEIGHTS:**
EMPTY: 3189 lb (1447 kg)
MAX T/O: 4500 lb (2041 kg)

**PERFORMANCE:**
MAX SPEED: 153 mph (246 kmh)
RANGE: 920 miles (1481 km)
POWERPLANT: two Ranger L-440C-5s or Lycoming GO-480-B1DS
OUTPUT: 200 hp (149 kW) and 270 hp (201.42 kW) respectively

**FIRST FLIGHT DATE:**
28 June 1940

**ARMAMENT:**
one 325-lb (147 kg) depth charge on underwing rack

**FEATURES:**
High-wing monoplane layout; boat-shaped hull; two close-cowled engines; fixed underwing floats

# Grumman F4F Wildcat USA

single-seat, single-engined monoplane fighter

The Wildcat was the result of a study undertaken by Grumman into the feasibility of a single wing naval fighter. Designated the XF4F-2, it lost out to the rival Brewster Buffalo in a fly-off due to the latter's superior handling qualities. However, Grumman reworked the prototype into the XF4F-3 of March 1939, fitting a more powerful Twin Wasp engine with a two-stage supercharger, increasing the fighter's wing span and redesigning its tail surfaces. After flight trials, the Navy ordered 78 F4F-3s, which it christened the Wildcat. Entering service in 1940, the Wildcat proved a worthy opponent for the A6M Zero-sen during the carrier battles of 1942-43. The aircraft was also used by the Royal Navy's Fleet Air Arm in various marks from 1940 onwards. By 1943 General Motors (GM) had commenced building F4F-4s, which it redesignated FM-1s. Later that same year GM switched production to the FM-2, which utilised a turbo-charged Wright R-1820-56 Cyclone in place of the Twin Wasp. By the time production was terminated in August 1945, 4467 FM-2s had been built.

SPECIFICATION:

**ACCOMMODATION:**
pilot

**DIMENSIONS:**
LENGTH: 28 ft 9 in (8.76 m)
WINGSPAN: 38 ft 0 in (11.58 m)
HEIGHT: 11 ft 4 in (3.45 m)

**WEIGHTS:**
EMPTY: 5895 lb (2674 kg)
MAX T/O: 7952 lb (3607 kg)

**PERFORMANCE:**
MAX SPEED: 320 mph (515 kmh)
RANGE: 770 miles (1239 km)
POWERPLANT: Pratt & Whitney R-1830-76/86 Twin Wasp
OUTPUT: 1200 hp (895 kW)

**FIRST FLIGHT DATE:**
2 September 1937

**ARMAMENT:**
six Browning 0.50-in machine guns in wings; maximum bomb load of 500-lb (226 kg) on underwing racks

**FEATURES:**
Monoplane wing layout; retractable undercarriage; close-cowled radial engine; fixed tailwheel

# Grumman TBF/TBM Avenger   USA

three-seat, single-engined monoplane torpedo-bomber

Produced as a replacement for the Douglas TBD
Devastator, two prototype XTBF-1s were ordered
from Grumman in April 1940. It was distinctly
'rotund' due to its capacious internal bomb bay,
which was large enough to contain the biggest
(22-in) torpedo in the Navy arsenal. By the end of
January 1942 the first production TBF-1s were
reaching frontline units, and as its name suggested, the TBF/TBM meted out severe retribution
on the Japanese over the next three years in the
Pacific. One of the astounding features of the
Avenger story is that the aircraft changed very little
during its production life, allowing it to be built in
vast quantities over a short time scale. The Navy's
demand for the aircraft soon outstripped
Grumman's production capacity, so GM was
contracted to build the near identical TBM-1 from
September 1942 onwards. By the time production
ceased in June 1945, GM had built 7546 (of a run of
9836) TBMs. Over 1000 Avengers also saw action
with the Fleet Air Arm. Post-war, the Avenger
remained in naval service well into the 1950s.

SPECIFICATION:

**ACCOMMODATION:**
pilot, radar operator, gunner

**DIMENSIONS:**
LENGTH: 40 ft 0 in (12.19 m)
WINGSPAN: 54 ft 2 in (16.51 m)
HEIGHT: 16 ft 5 in (5.00 m)

**WEIGHTS:**
EMPTY: 10,700 lb (4853 kg)
MAX T/O: 18,250 lb (8278 kg)

**PERFORMANCE:**
MAX SPEED: 267 mph (430 kmh)
RANGE: 1130 miles (1819 km)
POWERPLANT: Wright
R-2600-20 Double Cyclone
OUTPUT: 1750 hp (1305 kW)

**FIRST FLIGHT DATE:**
1 August 1941

**ARMAMENT:**
one fixed Browning 0.30-in
machine gun in wing and single
Browning 0.30-in machine guns
in dorsal turret and ventral
position; maximum bomb/
torpedo load of 1600-lb (726 kg)
in internal bomb-bay

**FEATURES:**
Monoplane wing layout;
retractable undercarriage;
close-cowled radial engine;
gun turret

# Grumman F6F Hellcat USA

single-seat, single-engined monoplane fighter

The F6F embodied the early lessons learnt by users of the F4F Wildcat in the Pacific, as well as general pointers from the air war in Europe. Following receipt of the US Navy's order for the fighter in June 1941, Grumman modified the 'paper' aircraft by lowering the wing centre section to enable the undercarriage to be wider splayed, fitted more armour-plating around the cockpit to protect the pilot and increased the size of the fighter's ammunition magazines. Less than a year after being ordered, prototype XF6F-1 made its first flight, and it was soon realised that a more powerful engine was needed to give the fighter a combat edge – a Pratt & Whitney R-2800-10 was duly installed. The aircraft made its combat debut in August 1943, and from that point on, the question of aerial supremacy in the Pacific was never in doubt. Hellcats served aboard most US Navy carriers, being credited with the destruction of 4947 aircraft up to VJ-Day. The Fleet Air Arm was also a great believer in the Hellcat, procuring almost 1200 between 1943-45.

SPECIFICATION:

ACCOMMODATION:
pilot

DIMENSIONS:
LENGTH: 33 ft 4 in (10.16 m)
WINGSPAN: 42 ft 10 in (13.06 m)
HEIGHT: 14 ft 5 in (4.40 m)

WEIGHTS:
EMPTY: 9042 lb (4101 kg)
MAX T/O: 13 228 lb (6000 kg)

PERFORMANCE:
MAX SPEED: 376 mph (605 kmh)
RANGE: 1085 miles (1746 km)
POWERPLANT: Pratt & Whitney
R-2800-10W Double Wasp
OUTPUT: 2000 hp (1491 kW)

FIRST FLIGHT DATE:
26 June 1942

ARMAMENT:
six Browning 0.50-in machine
guns in wings; provision for six
rockets under wings or up to
2000-lb (907 kg) bombload
under centre section

FEATURES:
Monoplane wing layout;
retractable undercarriage;
close-cowled radial engine;
rectractable tailwheel

# Grumman F7F Tigercat USA

single/two-seat, twin-engined monoplane fighter

The F7F Tigercat had only just entered service by VJ-Day, despite being ordered in 1941. The fighter's long gestation period reflected the demanding US Navy specification that stipulated the aircraft must have engines that, combined, produced in excess of 4000 hp, and a weight of fire double that of the F4F. Of all-metal construction with a cantilever, shoulder-mounted wing, the Tigercat was a fast and well armed fighter of considerable dimensions – so much so that it appeared that only the proposed 45,000-ton *Midway* class 'supercarriers' would be able to operate them. Most of the 500 F7F-1s built were allocated to the Marines for use from bases in the Pacific, and just as the first units were working up for deployment Japan surrendered, leaving the Tigercat untested in World War 2. Aside from the -1, Grumman produced the -3 and F7F-3N/-4N nightfighter, equipped with a radar in a lengthened nose fairing that was operated by a second crewman. It was as a nocturnal predator that the Tigercat won its 'battle spurs' over Korea in 1951.

SPECIFICATION:

**ACCOMMODATION:**
pilot and radar operator (latter in F7F-3N/-4N only)

**DIMENSIONS:**
LENGTH: 45 ft 4.5 in (13.83 m)
WINGSPAN: 51 ft 6 in (15.70 m)
HEIGHT: 16 ft 7 in (5.05 m)

**WEIGHTS:**
EMPTY: 16,270 lb (7380 kg)
MAX T/O: 25,720 lb (11,666 kg)

**PERFORMANCE:**
MAX SPEED: 435 mph (700 kmh)
RANGE: 1200 miles (1931 km)
POWERPLANT: two Pratt & Whitney R-2800-34W Double Wasps
OUTPUT: 4200 hp (3132 kW)

**FIRST FLIGHT DATE:**
3 November 1943

**ARMAMENT:**
four Browning 0.50-in machine guns in nose and four M-2 20 mm cannon in wing roots; provision for six rockets or up to 2000-lb (907 kg) bomb load on underwing racks

**FEATURES:**
Monoplane wing layout; retractable tricycle undercarriage; two close-cowled radial engines

# Hawker Hurricane UK

single-seat, single-engined monoplane fighter

The Hurricane's arrival in the frontline in December 1937 saw the RAF make the jump from biplane to monoplane fighter, the aircraft owing much to Hawker's ultimate biplane design, the Fury. The Hurricane also benefited from Hawker's partnership with Rolls-Royce, whose Merlin I engine proved to be the ideal powerplant. Toting eight machine guns, and capable of speeds in excess of 300 mph, the Hurricane I was the world's most advanced fighter when issued to the RAF. Although eclipsed by the Spitfire come the summer of 1940, Hurricanes nevertheless outnumbered the former by three to one during the Battle of Britain, and downed more Luftwaffe aircraft than the Supermarine fighter. Even prior to its 'finest hour', Hurricanes provided the first RAF aces of the war in France during the *Blitzkrieg*. In 1941 the type was used in the Mediterranean and North Africa, before seeing action in the Far East against the Japanese. It remained in the frontline in the latter theatre until VJ-Day, despite production having ceased in September 1944.

SPECIFICATION:

ACCOMMODATION:
pilot

DIMENSIONS:
LENGTH: 31 ft 5 in (9.58 m)
WINGSPAN: 40 ft 0 in (12.19 m)
HEIGHT: 13 ft 0 in (3.96 m)

WEIGHTS:
EMPTY: 4982 lb (2260 kg)
MAX T/O: 7490 lb (3397 kg)

PERFORMANCE:
MAX SPEED: 324 mph (521 kmh)
RANGE: 600 miles (965 km)
POWERPLANT: Rolls-Royce Merlin II/III
OUTPUT: 1030 hp (768 kW)

FIRST FLIGHT DATE:
11 August 1937

ARMAMENT:
eight Browning 0.303-in machine guns in wings; maximum bomb load of 500-lb (227 kg) on underwing racks

FEATURES:
Monoplane wing layout; rectractable landing gear; close-cowled inline engine; centrally mounted cooling intake on fuselage underside

# Hawker Sea Hurricane UK

single-seat, single-engined monoplane fighter

Despite the RAF's No 46 Sqn proving that the Hurricane could take-off and land from a carrier during the ill-fated Norwegian campaign of April 1940, the first dedicated Sea Hurricanes had to wait until early 1941 to make their combat debut. The pressing need for more modern fighters for the Fleet Air Arm (FAA) resulted in a number of ex-RAF aircraft being hastily converted into Sea Hurricane IBS, the standard land-based airframe being fitted with a catapult spool and arrestor hook.

Later variants featured the engine and airframe of the Mk I combined with the Mk IIC's cannon armament, whilst the final naval Sea Hurricane (the Mk IIC) was identical to its RAF equivalent, boasting a four cannon wing and Merlin xx engine. Sea Hurricanes equipped 38 FAA units between 1941-44, and saw action over the Mediterranean and the Arctic Sea from the decks of fleet and escort carriers, as well as from land bases on Malta and along the North African coast.

SPECIFICATION:

ACCOMMODATION:
pilot

DIMENSIONS:
LENGTH: 32 ft 3 in (9.83 m)
WINGSPAN: 40 ft 0 in (12.19 m)
HEIGHT: 13 ft 3 in (4.04 m)

WEIGHTS:
EMPTY: 5800 lb (2631 kg)
MAX T/O: 7800 lb (3538 kg)

PERFORMANCE:
MAX SPEED: 322 mph (518 kmh)
RANGE: 460 miles (740 km)
POWERPLANT: Rolls-Royce Merlin xx
OUTPUT: 1460 hp (1089 kW)

FIRST FLIGHT DATE:
early 1941

ARMAMENT:
eight Browning 0.303-in machine guns in wings; maximum bomb load of 500-lb (227 kg) on underwing racks

FEATURES:
Monoplane wing layout; rectractable landing gear; close-cowled inline engine; centrally mounted cooling intake on fuselage underside, arrestor hook

# Hawker Typhoon UK

single-seat, single-engined monoplane fighter

The Typhoon was the RAF's first fighter capable of achieving speeds in excess of 400 mph in level flight. However, the aircraft was almost deemed a failure at the start of its career due to a poor rate of climb and altitude performance, unreliability of its Napier Sabre engine and suspect rear fuselage assembly. Refusing to give up on the design, Hawker and Napier spent over a year 'beefing up' the airframe and correcting engine maladies to the point where the Typhoon was found to be an excellent low altitude fighter – it defeated the Luftwaffe's FW 190 'hit and run' raiders terrorising the south coast of England in 1942-43. Its speed at low-level also made it the ideal platform for the ground attack mission, the aircraft's 20 mm cannon, rockets and bombs attacking all manner of targets across occupied western Europe. One of the key weapons in the Allied arsenal for Operation *Overlord*, the RAF could field 26 Typhoon squadrons by mid 1944. The last Typhoon was delivered to the air force in November 1945.

SPECIFICATION:

ACCOMMODATION:
pilot

DIMENSIONS:
LENGTH: 31 ft 11 in (9.73 m)
WINGSPAN: 41 ft 7 in (12.67 m)
HEIGHT: 15 ft 3.5 in (4.66 m)

WEIGHTS:
EMPTY: 9800 lb (4445 kg)
MAX T/O: 13 980 lb (6341 kg)

PERFORMANCE:
MAX SPEED: 405 mph (652 kmh)
RANGE: 980 miles (1577 km) with external tanks
POWERPLANT: Napier Sabre IIA
OUTPUT: 2180 hp (1626 kW)

FIRST FLIGHT DATE:
24 February 1940

ARMAMENT:
four 20 mm cannon in wings; maximum bomb/rocket load of 2000-lb (908 kg) on underwing racks

FEATURES:
Monoplane wing layout; retractable landing gear; close-cowled inline engine; chin-mounted air intake; cannon muzzles extending from wing leading edges

# Hawker Tempest V UK

single-seat, single-engined monoplane fighter

Based on the Typhoon, the Tempest was initially
designated the Typhoon II. The most obvious
difference between the two designs was the
adoption of a thin, elliptical, laminar flow wing for
the Tempest, which replaced the thick chord flying
surface of the earlier design. The fuel tanks
previously housed in the thick wing had to be
moved into the fuselage, resulting in the Tempest
being lengthened by two feet. A dorsal fin was also
added to the fuselage. Although several versions of
the Tempest were planned by Hawker, only the
Sabre-engined Mk v was completed in time to see
combat with the RAF. The first wing was formed in
April 1944, and by VE-Day 11 squadrons were
equipped with Tempest vs. Early aircraft suffered
from engine reliability problems caused by
overspeeding propellers, but once this was rectified,
the Tempest continued the Typhoon's tradition in
the low-level fighter-bomber role. Unlike its predecessor, the Tempest was also effective at medium to
high altitudes, and aside from downing 638 v1s, it
was credited with the destruction of 20 Me 262s.

SPECIFICATION:

ACCOMMODATION:
pilot

DIMENSIONS:
LENGTH: 33 ft 8 in (10.26 m)
WINGSPAN: 41 ft 0 in (12.50 m)
HEIGHT: 16 ft 1 in (4.90 m)

WEIGHTS:
EMPTY: 9250 lb (4196 kg)
MAX T/O: 13,640 lb (6187 kg)

PERFORMANCE:
MAX SPEED: 416 mph (669 kmh)
RANGE: 1530 miles (2462 km) with
external tanks
POWERPLANT: Napier Sabre IIA
OUTPUT: 2180 hp (1626 kW)

ARMAMENT:
four 20 mm cannon in wings;
maximum bomb/rocket load of
2000-lb (908 kg) on underwing
racks

FIRST FLIGHT DATE:
2 September 1942

FEATURES:
Monoplane wing layout;
rectractable landing gear; close-
cowled inline engine; chin-
mounted air intake; four-bladed
propeller

# Heinkel He 111 (CASA 2.111) GERMANY & SPAIN

five-seat, twin-engined monoplane medium bomber/transport

The He 111 was the staple medium bomber of the Luftwaffe's *Kampfgeschwader* throughout World War 2, 5400+ being built during its nine-year production life which spanned from 1935 to 1944. Developed from the He 70 Blitz airliner, which had entered service with Lufthansa in 1934, the He 111 retained the former's elliptical wings and tail surfaces. Whilst the transport variant was proving itself over Europe, the bomber version was also being developed by Heinkel. Squadron deliveries began in late 1936, and the following year 30 He 111B-1s saw action during the Spanish Civil War.

By the eve of World War 2, the redesigned H- and P-models had begun to enter service, the new variants having the distinctive fully glazed nose and revised ventral gondola. These versions saw action in every theatre of war in which the Luftwaffe was involved. In 1941 Spain acquired a licence to build the He 111H-16, and 236 were constructed up to 1956. Of these, 136 were fitted with Junkers Jumo 211F-2 engines (2.111A), whilst the remainder received Rolls-Royce Merlins (2.111B/D).

SPECIFICATION:

ACCOMMODATION:
pilot, navigator, bomb aimer, ventral and dorsal gunners

DIMENSIONS:
LENGTH: 53 ft 9.5 in (16.40 m)
WINGSPAN: 74 ft 1.75 in (22.60 m)
HEIGHT: 13 ft 1.25 in (4.00 m)

WEIGHTS:
EMPTY: 19,136 lb (8680 kg)
MAX T/O: 30,865 lb (14,000 kg)

PERFORMANCE:
MAX SPEED: 227 mph (365 kmh)
RANGE: 1212 miles (1950 km)
POWERPLANT: two Junkers Jumo 211F-2S
OUTPUT: 2700 hp (2014 kW)

FIRST FLIGHT DATE:
24 February 1935

ARMAMENT:
single MG 15 7.92 mm machine guns in nosecap, dorsal position and ventral gondola, two guns in waist and MG FF 20 mm cannon in ventral gondola; maximum bomb load of 4410-lb (2000 kg) in bomb-bay

FEATURES:
Monoplane wing layout; retractable undercarriage; two close-cowled radial engines; glazed nose

# Heinkel He 162 GERMANY

single-seat, single-engined jet monoplane fighter

The He 162 *Volksjäger* ('People's Fighter') was designed, built and flown in just ten weeks between October and December 1944. Of mixed construction (wooden wings, metal fuselage and metal/wood tailplane), the He 162 was powered by a BMW 003 turbojet mounted atop the fuselage. Simple to construct, the fighter was slated for production by three factories, whose combined output amounted to no fewer than 4000 He 162s a month! Faced with a shortage of pilots, the Luftwaffe was told to crew the aircraft with hastily trained members of the Hitler Youth. Ten prototypes were built prior to the definitive He 162A-1, featuring 30 mm cannon, anhedral wingtips and an increased span tailplane, going into production. Test flying revealed that the A-1 was badly afflicted by cannon vibration whenever the weapons were fired, so production was switched to the A-2, which featured 20 mm cannon. The He 162A officially entered service with I./JG 1 at Leck in January 1945, but Allied aircraft recorded few encounters with the fighter prior to VE-Day.

SPECIFICATION:

**ACCOMMODATION:**
pilot

**DIMENSIONS:**
LENGTH: 29 ft 8.5 in (9.05 m)
WINGSPAN: 23 ft 7.25 in (7.21 m)
HEIGHT: 8 ft 6 in (2.59 m)

**WEIGHTS:**
EMPTY: 4796 lb (2175 kg)
MAX T/O: 5940 lb (2694 kg)

**PERFORMANCE:**
MAX SPEED: 490 mph (788 kmh)
RANGE: 410 miles (660 km)
POWERPLANT: BMW 003E-1/2
OUTPUT: 1764 lb st (7.9 kN)

**FIRST FLIGHT DATE:**
6 December 1944

**ARMAMENT:**
two MG 151/20 20 mm cannon or two MK 108 30 mm cannon in the nose

**FEATURES:**
Monoplane wing layout; rectractable tricycle landing gear; single jet engine atop the fuselage; twin tail layout

# Ilyushin DB-3 (Il-4) USSR

four-seat, twin-engined monoplane medium bomber

The DB-3 saw combat in large numbers on the Eastern Front, flying close-support, low-level torpedo and strategic bombing missions. Originally known as the TSKB-26 by manufacturer Ilyushin when developed in 1935, the aircraft was officially designated DB-3 when it went into production in early 1937. Boasting excellent speed, bomb load, range and manoeuvrability, the DB-3 was lacking only in its defensive armament which was never increased from three manually aimed shKAS or BS machine guns.

By 1940, when the DB-3's designation changed to Il-4 (conforming to the new Soviet policy of naming aircraft after their designers), 2000+ examples had been delivered. The German invasion in June 1941 halted production of the Il-4 until new factories could be established in Siberia the following year. Aircraft emanating from the east featured the maximum amount of wood in their airframes due to a lack of steel in the USSR at the time. More than 10,000 Il-4s had been built by the time production ended in 1944.

SPECIFCATION:

**ACCOMMODATION:**
pilot, navigator, bomb aimer/nose gunner and dorsal turret gunner

**DIMENSIONS:**
LENGTH: 48 ft 6.5 in (14.80 m)
WINGSPAN: 70 ft 4.25 in (21.44 m)
HEIGHT: 13 ft 9 in (4.20 m)

**WEIGHTS:**
EMPTY: 13,230 lb (6000 kg)
MAX T/O: 22,046 lb (10,000 kg)

**PERFORMANCE:**
MAX SPEED: 255 mph (410 kmh)
RANGE: 1616 miles (2600 km)
POWERPLANT: two Tumanskii M-88BS
OUTPUT: 2200 hp (1640 kW)

**FIRST FLIGHT DATE:**
June 1935

**ARMAMENT:**
three shKAS 7.62 mm or BS 12.7 mm machine guns in nose, dorsal turret and ventral position; maximum bomb load of 2200-lb (1000 kg) in bomb-bay, or bomb load/torpedo of 3306-lb (1500 kg) on underfuselage racks

**FEATURES:**
Monoplane wing layout; retractable undercarriage; two close-cowled radial engines;

# Ilyushin Il-2 USSR

single/two-seat, single-engined monoplane close support/attack aircraft

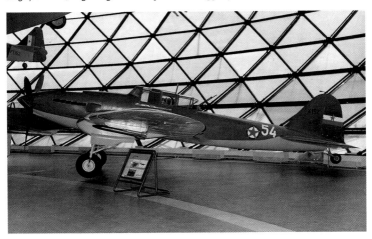

Built in greater numbers than any other combat aircraft in history, the Il-2 was one of the most important Soviet types fielded in action over the Eastern Front in World War 2. The aircraft featured a heavily armoured shell for its two-man crew which formed an integral part of the machine's structure. Although tested and initially built as a two-seater, by the time production aircraft started to reach frontline units March 1941 the Il-2 had lost the rear gunner's position. A considerable number of aircraft were serving with the various Soviet air forces by the time Germany invaded the USSR in June 1941. Armed with ground attack rockets, the aircraft proved deadly against Wehrmacht panzers as pairs of Il-2s roamed the frontline at low level. However, the *Stormoviks* (armoured attackers) were in turn vulnerable to attack from the rear by enemy fighters, so Ilyushin was ordered to revert to the two-seat layout in September 1942 with production of the Il-2M. Also produced in Il-10 form, with a more powerful engine and lighter wings, 43,100+ Il-2/10s were built between 1941 and 1955.

SPECIFICATION:

ACCOMMODATION:
pilot and rear gunner

DIMENSIONS:
LENGTH: 39 ft 4.50 in (12.00 m)
WINGSPAN: 47 ft 11 in (14.60 m)
HEIGHT: 11 ft 1.75 in (3.40 m)

WEIGHTS:
EMPTY: 7165 lb (3250 kg)
MAX T/O: 12,947 lb (5872 kg)

PERFORMANCE:
MAX SPEED: 281 mph (449 kmh)
RANGE: 373 miles (600 km)
POWERPLANT: Kontsevich AM-38F
OUTPUT: 1750 hp (1305 kW)

FIRST FLIGHT DATE:
30 December 1939

ARMAMENT:
two VYa 20/37 mm cannon in wings and one manually-aimed BS 12.7 mm machine gun in rear cockpit; maximum bomb/rocket load of 1323-lb (600 kg) on underwing racks

FEATURES:
Monoplane wing layout; retractable undercarriage; close-cowled inline engine; fixed tailwheel

# Junkers Ju 87 GERMANY

two-seat, single-engined monoplane dive-bomber

The Junkers Ju 87 Stuka (an abbreviation of *Stürzkampfflugzeug* – dive-bomber aircraft) first flew in twin-finned prototype form in late 1935, powered by a Rolls-Royce Kestrel engine. By the time it entered series production two years later, the Ju 87B had a solitary fin, a Junkers Jumo 211 engine and large-trousered landing gear. It was every inch a dive-bomber, featuring a heavy bomb crutch that swung the weapon clear of the fuselage before it was released. Capable of diving at angles of up to 80 degrees, the aircraft could deliver 1500-lb of ordnance with great accuracy. First blooded in Spain by the *Condor Legion* in 1937, the Ju 87's finest hour came during the *Blitzkrieg* campaign waged by the Wehrmacht in Poland in September 1939 and across western Europe in May-June 1940. Its vulnerability to fighter defences was exposed during the Battle of Britain, although the Stuka proved deadly against Allied troops and ships in the Mediterranean in 1941-42. In the last years of the war Ju 87 units performed close support and anti-tank missions on the Eastern Front.

SPECIFICATION:

ACCOMMODATION:
pilot and rear gunner

DIMENSIONS:
LENGTH: 37 ft 8.75 in (11.50 m)
WINGSPAN: 45 ft 3.25 in (13.80 m)
HEIGHT: 12 ft 9.25 in (3.90 m)

WEIGHTS:
EMPTY: 8600 lb (3900 kg)
MAX T/O: 14,550 lb (6600 kg)

PERFORMANCE:
MAX SPEED: 255 mph (410 kmh)
RANGE: 954 miles (1535 km)
POWERPLANT: Junkers Jumo 211J-1
OUTPUT: 1400 hp (1044 kW)

FIRST FLIGHT DATE:
Late 1935

ARMAMENT:
two fixed MG 17 7.92 mm machine guns in wings and two on flexible mounting in rear cockpit; maximum bomb load of 3968-lb (1800 kg) on centreline and various gun/bomb options up to 1102-lb (500 kg) on under wings

FEATURES:
Inverted gull monoplane wing layout; trousered fixed undercarriage; close-cowled inline engine; fixed tailwheel

# Junkers Ju 88  GERMANY

two/six-seat, twin-engined monoplane bomber and nightfighter

One of the Luftwaffe's most important, and versatile, combat aircraft types, the Ju 88 was developed as a high speed medium bomber with a dive-bombing capability. First flown in December 1936, production A-1s entered service in September 1939. Boasting a formidable bomb load and good performance, the only downside of the early Ju 88 was its poor defensive armament. Thanks to its modern design and better engines, subsequent versions of the aircraft such as the A-4, which boasted twice as many guns, still had sufficient performance available to avoid it being vulnerable to fighters. Continually upgraded, 2000 Ju 88 bombers were built each year between 1940-43. Junkers split off the Ju 188 and 388 bomber families from the parent Ju 88, allowing it to concentrate on the high-performance s-series. A variety of Ju 88 fighters were also produced, these being used as nightfighters in the defence of Germany. Fitted with radar and cannon, they proved deadly in combat until VE-Day. Close to 15,000 Ju 88s had by then been built.

## SPECIFICATION:

**ACCOMMODATION:**
pilot, navigator, bomb aimer/gunner and ventral/dorsal gunners

**DIMENSIONS:**
LENGTH: 36 ft 5 in (11.10 m)
WINGSPAN: 65 ft 10 in (20.08 m)
HEIGHT: 15 ft 11 in (4.85 m)

**WEIGHTS:**
EMPTY: 21,737 lb (9860 kg)
MAX T/O: 30,865 lb (14,000 kg)

**PERFORMANCE:**
MAX SPEED: 292 mph (470 kmh)
RANGE: 1696 miles (2730 km)
POWERPLANT: two Junkers Jumo 211FS
OUTPUT: 2680 hp (2000 kW)

**FIRST FLIGHT DATE:**
21 December 1936

**ARMAMENT:**
one MG 17 7.92 mm machine gun in cockpit, one/two on flexible mounting in nose, two in rear cockpit and one/two in ventral gondola; bomb load of 4409-lb (2000 kg) in bomb-bay, underwing racks

**FEATURES:**
Monoplane wing; two close-cowled radial engine; undernose gondola

# Kawanishi H8K JAPAN

ten-seat, four-engined monoplane maritime patrol and reconnaissance flying boat

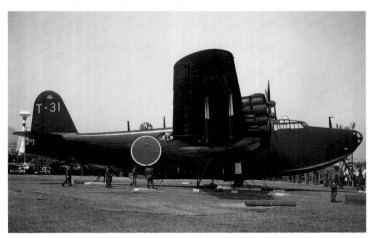

Boasting both high speed and heavy defensive armour, the H8K was arguably the best large flying boat of World War 2. Designed in 1938 by Kawanishi to replace its previous H6K design then in service with the Imperial Japanese Navy (IJN), the first of 17 H8K1 prototypes and pre-production aircraft flew on 31 December 1940. The IJN had asked for an aircraft with 30 per cent higher speed and 50 per cent greater range than the H6K, and although Kawanishi delivered on the former, it could not attain the latter. Early testing revealed that serious hull modifications were needed to eradicate chronic porpoising in the water, but once these were made the definitive H8K was the most advanced aircraft of its type. The aircraft marked its service entry with a spectacular night bombing raid on Oahu, Hawaii, on 4-5 March 1942, and by the following year the refined H8K2 variant had become the IJN's standard long-range maritime patrol flying boat. Capable of performing missions lasting up to 24 hours, the H8K was always treated with cautious respect by Allied pilots.

SPECIFICATION:

ACCOMMODATION:
pilot, co-pilot, flight engineer, radio operator, navigator, bow, dorsal, tail and beam gunners

DIMENSIONS:
LENGTH: 92 ft 4 in (28.14 m)
WINGSPAN: 124 ft 8 in (38.00 m)
HEIGHT: 30 ft 0 in (9.14 m)

WEIGHTS:
EMPTY: 40,521 lb (18,380 kg)
MAX T/O: 71,650 lb (32,500 kg)

PERFORMANCE:
MAX SPEED: 290 mph (467 kmh)
RANGE: 4460 miles (7177 km)
POWERPLANT: four Mitsubishi MK4Q Kasai 22s
OUTPUT: 7400 hp (5520 kW)

FIRST FLIGHT DATE:
31 December 1940

ARMAMENT:
single Type 99 20 mm cannon in bow, dorsal, tail turrets and beam positions, three/four Type 97 7.7 mm machine guns in cockpit, ventral and side hatches; bomb/mine load of 4408-lb (2000 kg) on underwing racks

FEATURES:
High-wing monoplane; boat-shaped hull; radial engines

# Kawanishi N1K2-J Shiden-KAI JAPAN

single-seat, single-engined monoplane fighter

Privately developed by Kawanishi from its N1K1
Kyofu floatplane fighter, the Shiden retained the
N1K1's basic airframe in combination with a
troublesome retractable undercarriage and mid-
wing layout. It was a vast improvement on the
Navy's venerable A6M and when the first Shiden
saw combat in October 1944, Allied pilots soon
learnt to respect its fighting abilities.
Acknowledging the faults of the N1K1-J before the
latter had entered production, Kawanishi
commenced work on the N1K2-J in mid-1943. To
eradicate the undercarriage problems, the wing on
the Shiden-KAI was lowered to a similar position to
that employed by the Kyofu. Other improvements
saw the engine moved forward, the fuselage
lengthened to cure a centre of gravity problem and
redesigned tail surfaces. Aircraft delivery
commenced in July 1944, and eight factories were
tooled up for mass-production of the N1K2-2, but
B-29 raids restricted output to 428 airframes. The
Shiden-KAI was the best IJN fighter of the war, and
could hold its own against any Allied foe.

SPECIFICATION:

ACCOMMODATION:
pilot

DIMENSIONS:
LENGTH: 30 ft 8 in (9.35 m)
WINGSPAN: 39 ft 4.5 in (12.00 m)
HEIGHT: 13 ft 0 in (3.96 m)

WEIGHTS:
EMPTY: 5858 lb (2657 kg)
MAX T/O: 10,714 lb (4860 kg)

PERFORMANCE:
MAX SPEED: 369 mph (594 kmh)
RANGE: 1488 miles (2395 km)
POWERPLANT: Nakajima NK9H
Homare 21
OUTPUT: 1990 hp (1484 kW)

FIRST FLIGHT DATE:
31 December 1943

ARMAMENT:
four Type 99 model 2 20 mm
cannon in wings; maximum
bomb load of 1102-lb (500 kg) on
underwing racks

FEATURES:
Monoplane layout; close-cowled
radial engine; retractable
undercarriage; four-bladed
propeller

# Kawasaki Ki-100 JAPAN

single-seat, single-engined monoplane fighter

Kawasaki's Ki-100 was born out of an urgent need for a fighter that could intercept B-29s raiding the home islands from 30,000 ft. Originally, the Ki-61-II-KAI was to fill this requirement, but problems with its inline Ha-140 resulted in 200+ engineless airframes. In November 1944 Kawasaki was ordered by the Ministry of Munitions to install a replacement powerplant, and the Mitsubishi Ha-112 radial was chosen. Engineers studied the engine mountings of an imported FW 190A to see how their German counterparts had mated a 'fat' radial to a slim fuselage. Armed with this knowledge, work proceeded on the Ki-100-I, and 271 airframes were fitted with the Ha-112 between March and June 1945. The fighter enjoyed success against B-29s, Hellcats, Mustangs and Corsairs. The Ki-100 was popular with long-suffering groundcrews too, many of whom had struggled with the Ki-61's Ha-40/-140 for two years. An all-new version of the Ki-100 entered production in May 1945, the -Ib featuring cut-down rear fuselage decking and a bubble canopy.

SPECIFICATION:

ACCOMMODATION:
pilot

DIMENSIONS:
LENGTH: 28 ft 11.25 in (8.82 m)
WINGSPAN: 39 ft 4.5 in (12.00 m)
HEIGHT: 12 ft 3.5 in (3.75 m)

WEIGHTS:
EMPTY: 5567 lb (2525 kg)
MAX T/O: 7705 lb (3495 kg)

PERFORMANCE:
MAX SPEED: 360 mph (579 kmh)
RANGE: 1367 miles (2200 km)
POWERPLANT: Mitsubishi
Ha-112-II
OUTPUT: 1500 hp (1118 kW)

FIRST FLIGHT DATE:
1 February 1945

ARMAMENT:
two HO-5 20 mm cannon in nose and two HO-103 12.7 mm machine guns in wings; maximum bomb load of 1102-lb (500 kg) on underwing racks

FEATURES:
Monoplane layout; close-cowled radial engine; retractable undercarriage; three-bladed propeller

# LaGG-3 USSR

single-seat, single-engined monoplane fighter

Built primarily of wood, the LaGG-3 can trace its origins to the I-22 fighter of 1938-39, which was subsequently designated the LaGG-1 in honour of the principal design bureau involved – Lavochkin, Gorbunov and Gudkov. Early flight trials revealed serious performance and handling deficiencies, so wing slats, new outer wing panels and aero-dynamic revisions were added. The structure of the fighter was also lightened and its armament increased. After further flight tests, the LaGG-1 went into production in late 1940, and with the fitment of the more powerful M-105PF engine, the fighter entered service as the LaGG-3 in early 1941. The aircraft proved easy to build, and by the time the last LaGG-3 left the factory in June 1942, 6527 had been built in less than two years. One of the more modern fighters in Soviet service at the time of the German invasion, the LaGG-3 earned a reputation for rugged reliability, although it was no match for Luftwaffe fighters, being underpowered and less manoeuvrable than either the Bf 109F/G or the FW 190A – both exacted a heavy toll on the LaGG-3.

SPECIFICATION:

ACCOMMODATION:
pilot

DIMENSIONS:
LENGTH: 29 ft 2.5 in (8.90 m)
WINGSPAN: 32 ft 2 in (9.80 m)
HEIGHT: 8 ft 10 in (2.69 m)

WEIGHTS:
EMPTY: 5776 lb (2620 kg)
MAX T/O: 7231 lb (3280 kg)

PERFORMANCE:
MAX SPEED: 348 mph (560 kmh)
RANGE: 497 miles (800 km)
POWERPLANT: Klimov M-105PF
OUTPUT: 1240 hp (925 kW)

FIRST FLIGHT DATE:
30 March 1940

ARMAMENT:
one ShVAK 20/23 mm cannon in propeller hub and two ShKAS 7.62 mm or Berezin UB12.7 mm machine guns in upper cowling; maximum bomb/rocket load of 440-lb (200 kg) on underwing racks

FEATURES:
Monoplane layout; close-cowled inline engine; retractable undercarriage; three-bladed propeller

# Lavochkin La-5/7 USSR

single-seat, single-engined monoplane fighter

Built as a replacement for the LaGG-3 around the Shvetsov M-82 radial in early 1942, the La-5 was not only appreciably faster than its predecessor, but also more capable at medium to high altitudes. The first examples to reach the frontline were actually re-engined LaGG-3s, and aside from the change of engine, the aircraft had two 20 mm cannon in place of the LaGG's machine guns. By late March 1943 production of the definitive La-5N had commenced, this variant featuring a fuel-injected M-82FN for better performance at altitude and cut down rear fuselage decking and a new canopy for better all round vision. The La-5FN was more than a match for the Bf 109G, and could hold its own with the FW 190. In November 1943 the further improved La-7 started flight trials, this model enjoying even greater performance thanks to the lightening of its overall structure and adoption of the metal wing spars featured in late-build La-5FNs. The La-7 entered service in the spring of 1944, and went on to become the favoured mount of most Soviet aces.

SPECIFICATION:

ACCOMMODATION:
pilot

DIMENSIONS:
LENGTH: 29 ft 2.5 in (8.90 m)
WINGSPAN: 32 ft 1.75 in (9.80 m)
HEIGHT: 8 ft 6.25 in (2.60 m)

WEIGHTS:
EMPTY: 5842 lb (2620 kg)
MAX T/O: 7496 lb (3400 kg)

PERFORMANCE:
MAX SPEED: 423 mph (680 kmh)
RANGE: 615 miles (990 km)
POWERPLANT: Shvetsov M-82FN
OUTPUT: 1850 hp (1380 kW)

FIRST FLIGHT DATE:
March 1942

ARMAMENT:
two or three ShVAK 20 mm cannon in upper cowling; maximum bomb/rocket load of 440 lb (200 kg) on underwing racks

FEATURES:
Monoplane layout; close-cowled radial engine; retractable undercarriage; three-bladed propeller

# Lisunov Li-2 USSR

27-seat, twin-engined monoplane transport

Boris Pavlovich Lisunov was the Soviet engineer assigned to supervise the licence agreement struck between the USSR and Douglas for the manufacturer of the DC-3 in the USSR. Initially bought for national carrier Aeroflot, the reverse-engineered DC-3 saw widespread use with the Soviet air forces in World War 2. Paralleling licence manufacture of the DC-3, Lisunov produced the PS-84, which embodied no fewer than 1293 engineering changes from the Douglas drawings! Redesignated the Li-2 in 1942, the aircraft had a strong external resemblance to the DC-3, but used different engines, had additional windows behind the cockpit and was fitted with a passenger door on the right side of the fuselage. Its wingspan was also reduced and the airframe locally reinforced. The first PS-84 entered service in June 1940, and in October of the following year the Lisunov production line at Chimky was evacuated to Tashkent in the face of German advances. Used by the Soviets well into the 1950s, a total of 4863 Li-2s were built between 1940-45.

SPECIFICATION:

ACCOMMODATION:
pilot and co-pilot, navigator and up to 24 passengers

DIMENSIONS:
LENGTH: 64 ft 5.50 in (19.64 m)
WINGSPAN: 94 ft 6.25 in (28.81 m)
HEIGHT: 16 ft 11 in (5.16 m)

WEIGHTS:
EMPTY: 15,653 lb (7100 kg)
MAX T/O: 24,250 lb (11,000 kg)

PERFORMANCE:
MAX SPEED: 199 mph (320 kmh)
RANGE: 1500 miles (2400 km)
POWERPLANT: two Shvetsov Ash-62IRS
OUTPUT: 2000 hp (1491 kW)

FIRST FLIGHT DATE:
Early 1940

FEATURES:
Monoplane wing layout; rectractable landing gear; two close-cowled radial engines; large vertical tail surface

# Lockheed P-38 Lightning USA

single-seat, twin-engined monoplane fighter

The P-38 Lightning was Lockheed's first venture into the world of high performance military aircraft, the company having eagerly responded to the USAAC's 1937 Request for Proposals pertaining to the acquisition of a long-range interceptor. Aside from its twin-boom and central nacelle layout, the prototype XP-38 utilised butt-joined and flush-riveted all-metal skins – a first for a US fighter. The XP-38's test programme progressed well, and aside from minor adjustments to the flying surfaces and the introduction of more powerful Allison engines, frontline P-38s differed little from the prototype throughout the aircraft's production run. The appellation 'Lightning' was coined by the RAF when the type was ordered under Lend-Lease in 1940, and duly adopted by the Americans the following year. In the event the RAF was so disappointed in the performance of the unsupercharged aircraft it received that the order was cancelled. However, definitive P-38 models fitted *with* supercharged engines proved more than a match for Axis fighters across the globe.

SPECIFICATION:

ACCOMMODATION:
pilot

DIMENSIONS:
LENGTH: 37 ft 10 in (11.53 m)
WINGSPAN: 52 ft 0 in (15.85 m)
HEIGHT: 9 ft 10 in (3.00 m)

WEIGHTS:
EMPTY: 12,780 lb (5797 kg)
MAX T/O: 21,600 lb (9798 kg)

PERFORMANCE:
MAX SPEED: 414 mph (666 kmh)
RANGE: 2260 miles (3637 km)
POWERPLANT: two Allison
V-1710-89/-91s
OUTPUT: 2850 hp (2126 kW)

FIRST FLIGHT DATE:
27 January 1939

ARMAMENT:
one AN-M2 'c' 20 mm cannon and four Browning 0.50-in machine guns in nose; maximum bomb/rocket load of 4000 lb (1814 kg) under wings

FEATURES:
Monoplane wing layout; rectractable, tricycle landing gear; twin inline engines; twin boom/tail layout; radiator housings on booms

# Lockheed Hudson USA

four/five-seat, twin-engined monoplane reconnaissance bomber

Developed from the Model 14 Super Electra airliner in response to a British Purchasing Commission order for 200 aircraft in June 1938, Lockheed's Hudson was created to perform the long-range reconnaissance mission. Lockheed had to drastically expand its Burbank, California, plant in order to manufacture these aircraft, and the first example flew on 10 December 1938. Deliveries began two months later, and by the time the final Hudson was produced in June 1943, 2000 had been received by the British. A total of 37 units were issued with Hudsons in RAF service, the bulk of these serving with Coastal Command patrolling home waters, the north and south Atlantic, the Mediterranean and the Indian Ocean. The RAAF received 247 Hudsons from January 1940, and they saw action in Malaya, the Netherlands East Indies and New Guinea. Finally, the USAAC and the US Navy bought the Hudson in modest numbers, the former purchasing 217 AT-18s for gunnery training and the latter 20 PBO-1s as an anti-submarine patrol aircraft.

SPECIFICATION:

ACCOMMODATION:
pilot and co-pilot, navigator, bomb aimer, turret gunner

DIMENSIONS:
LENGTH: 44 ft 4 in (13.51 m)
WINGSPAN: 65 ft 6 in (19.96 m)
HEIGHT: 11 ft 10.50 in (3.62 m)

WEIGHTS:
EMPTY: 12,000 lb (5443 kg)
MAX T/O: 18,500 lb (8393 kg)

PERFORMANCE:
MAX SPEED: 246 mph (394 kmh)
RANGE: 1960 miles (3150 km)
POWERPLANT: two Wright GR-1820-G102AS
OUTPUT: 2200 hp (1640 kW)

FIRST FLIGHT DATE:
10 December 1938 (Hudson I)

ARMAMENT:
two fixed Browning 0.303-in machine guns in nose, two in dorsal turret and single guns in beam windows and ventral hatch; maximum bomb/depth charge load of 750-lb (341 kg) in bomb-bay

FEATURES:
Monoplane wing layout; close-cowled twin radial engines; twin tail layout; dorsal turret

# Lockheed Model 18 Lodestar USA

17-seat, twin-engined monoplane transport aircraft

The final twin-engined commercial transporter designed by Lockheed, the Model 18 Lodestar was basically a larger version of the Model 14. Capable of accommodating up to 14 passengers in high-speed comfort in civilian guise, the Lodestar was produced in a number of versions which differed primarily in the type of engines fitted. The first military interest in the aircraft came in 1940 from the US Navy, which ordered three versions of Lodestar – the R50-4 (executive transport), R50-5 (personnel transport) and R50-6 (troop transport). The following year Lockheed built 13 Lodestars for the USAAC, these being designated C-57s. A number of civilian Lodestars were also requisitioned by the Army Air Corps after the Pearl Harbor raid, and these were given the designation C-56. The USAAF made further purchases in 1942-43, acquiring almost 350 C-60s, some of which were passed onto the RAF and Commonwealth air forces. Post-war, many surplus Lodestars reverted to their civilian role of airliner/cargo hauler, whilst a few were also converted into executive transports.

SPECIFICATION:

**ACCOMMODATION:**
pilot and co-pilot, navigator and 14 passengers

**DIMENSIONS:**
LENGTH: 49 ft 10 in (15.19 m)
WINGSPAN: 65 ft 6 in (19.96 m)
HEIGHT: 11 ft 1 in (3.38 m)

**WEIGHTS:**
EMPTY: 11,650 lb (5284 kg)
MAX T/O: 17,500 lb (7938 kg)

**PERFORMANCE:**
MAX SPEED: 253 mph (407 kmh)
RANGE: 1600 miles (2575 km)
POWERPLANT: two Wright R-1820-71S
OUTPUT: 2400 hp (1790 kW)

**FIRST FLIGHT DATE:**
21 September 1939

**FEATURES:**
Monoplane wing layout; rectractable landing gear; close-cowled twin radial engines; twin tail layout

# Lockheed B-34/PV Ventura/Harpoon  USA

four/five-seat, twin-engined bomber/reconnaissance aircraft

Spurred on by the success of the Hudson, Lockheed designed a more advanced 'bombing twin' for the RAF based on the Model 18 Lodestar. The new aircraft (designated the Ventura I by the RAF) was not only larger than its predecessor, but had more powerful engines, a ventral gun position and could carry a greater bomb load. The first examples of 675 ordered by the British made their debut with Bomber Command on 3 November 1942. Serious losses during subsequent daylight raids revealed the Ventura's vulnerability, so the survivors were passed on to Coastal Command and the balance of 350+ airframes still on order cancelled. Surplus aircraft were acquired by the USAAF, however, entering service as B-34s in the maritime patrol role. The US Navy also showed interest in the aircraft, flying no fewer than 1600 as PV-1 Venturas. The improved PV-2 Harpoon was ordered in June 1943, 500 being built from March 1944. Like the PV-1, most PV-2s saw action in the Pacific, with a number remaining in service with the Navy Reserve until the late 1940s.

SPECIFICATION:

ACCOMMODATION:
pilot, co-pilot, navigator, dorsal and ventral gunners

DIMENSIONS:
LENGTH: 51 ft 5 in (15.67 m)
WINGSPAN: 65 ft 6 in (19.96 m)
HEIGHT: 11 ft 11 in (3.63 m)

WEIGHTS:
EMPTY: 17,275 lb (7836 kg)
MAX T/O: 27,250 lb (12,360 kg)

PERFORMANCE:
MAX SPEED: 315 mph (507 kmh)
RANGE: 950 miles (1529 km)
POWERPLANT: two Pratt & Whitney R-2800-31 Double Wasps
OUTPUT: 4000 hp (2982 kW)

FIRST FLIGHT DATE:
31 July 1941

ARMAMENT:
two fixed Browning 0.50-in machine guns in nose, two in dorsal turret and two in ventral hatch; maximum bomb/depth charge load of 3000 lb (1360 kg) in bomb-bay, plus 2000-lb (907 kg) on underwing racks

FEATURES:
Monoplane wing; close-cowled twin radial engines; twin tail layout

# Macchi c.200 Saetta ITALY

single-seat, single-engined monoplane fighter

Like the majority of Italian fighters, the c.200 was a joy for its pilots to fly, possessing excellent manoeuvrability and positive handling qualities. However, like its contemporaries, the Macchi was woefully under-armed, being fitted with two 12.7 mm machine guns. The Saetta entered service with the *Regia Aeronautica* in October 1939, and by June of the following year, 156 had been delivered. The first 240 c.200s were built with enclosed canopies, although this feature was deleted when pilots complained of poor ventilation and restricted vision. Aside from this modification, the Saetta remained unchanged throughout its production career. The Saetta first saw action over Malta in 1940, and was subsequently involved in combat over the Eastern Front, North Africa, the Western Desert, Greece, Sicily and Yugoslavia. Like most surviving Italian combat aircraft, the c.200 served with both the pro-Allied Co-Belligerent Air Force and the pro-German *Aeronautica Nazionale Repubblicana* following Italy's surrender in September 1943.

SPECIFICATION:

ACCOMMODATION:
pilot

DIMENSIONS:
LENGTH: 26 ft 10.5 in (8.19 m)
WINGSPAN: 34 ft 8.5 in (10.58 m)
HEIGHT: 11 ft 6 in (3.50 m)

WEIGHTS:
EMPTY: 4451 lb (2019 kg)
MAX T/O: 5710 lb (2590 kg)

PERFORMANCE:
MAX SPEED: 312 mph (502 kmh)
RANGE: 540 miles (870 km)
POWERPLANT: Fiat A.74 RC38
OUTPUT: 870 hp (649 kW)

FIRST FLIGHT DATE:
24 December 1937

ARMAMENT:
two SAFAT 12.7 mm machine guns in nose, and later aircraft two additional Breda-SAFAT 7.7 mm machine guns in wings; maximum bomb load of 705 lb (320 kg) on underwing racks

FEATURES:
Monoplane wing layout; retractable undercarriage; close-cowled radial engine; open cockpit; headrest behind cockpit

# Macchi c.202 Folgor ITALY
single-seat, single-engined monoplane fighter

Whilst the c.200 had been a reliable fighter, it had always suffered from a lack of straightline speed. To solve this problem, Macchi chose to use Daimler-Benz's excellent DB 601A inline engine as proven in the Bf 109E. The resulting fighter was 60 mph faster than the c.200, possessed a superior rate of climb and could cruise at altitudes in excess of 37,500 ft. Designated the c.202, production aircraft reached the frontline in July 1941 fitted with imported engines, but the remaining 800+ were equipped with the licence-built Alfa Romeo version. Unfortunately for pilots, Macchi once again restricted armament to just two machine guns, although late-build examples were also fitted with underwing guns. The Folgore proved superior to both the Hurricane II and Tomahawk/ Kittyhawk during its first North African engagements, and examples saw action over the Balkans, the Western Desert, Sicily, the Eastern Front and Malta. Like the c.200, the Folgore served in modest numbers on both sides after the Italian surrender, and production of the fighter continued until 1944.

SPECIFICATION:

ACCOMMODATION:
pilot

DIMENSIONS:
LENGTH: 29 ft 0.5 in (8.85 m)
WINGSPAN: 34 ft 8.5 in (10.58 m)
HEIGHT: 9 ft 11.5 in (3.03 m)

WEIGHTS:
EMPTY: 5545 lb (2515 kg)
MAX T/O: 6766 lb (3069 kg)

PERFORMANCE:
MAX SPEED: 372 mph (598 kmh)
RANGE: 475 miles (764 km)
POWERPLANT: Alfa Romeo
RA.1000 RC41-1 Monsone
OUTPUT: 1175 hp (876 kW)

FIRST FLIGHT DATE:
10 August 1940

ARMAMENT:
two SAFAT 12.7 mm machine guns
in nose, and later aircraft two
additional 7.7 mm machine guns
in wings, and some with two MG
151 20 mm cannon under wings;
maximum bomb load of 705 lb
(320 kg) on underwing racks

FEATURES:
Monoplane wing layout; close-
cowled inline engine; headrest
behind cockpit

# Martin B-26 Marauder USA

five/seven-seat, twin-engined bomber

Martin relied on its previous experience as a successful bomber builder when it entered its Model 179 in the USAAC's 1939 Medium Bomber competition. Built around a wing optimised for high-speed cruising rather than moderate landing speeds, the new bomber won the competition and was ordered into production 'off the drawing board'. However, the manufacturers' decision to plumb for high wing loading resulted in an aircraft that initially proved too difficult for novice pilots to fly safely. The B-26 (as is was designated by the USAAC upon its entry into service in the spring of 1941) soon earned an unenviable reputation as a 'widow maker', and despite Martin improving the aircraft's handling characteristics through the fitment of increased span wings and a taller tail, the sobriquet remained with the bomber through-out its service career. It is ironic that the Marauder actually enjoyed the lowest loss rate of any USAAF bomber to see action in Europe. The Marauder also saw widespread use in the Pacific. Finally, the RAF received 522 of the 5157 Marauders that were built.

SPECIFICATION:

**ACCOMMODATION:**
pilot, co-pilot, bombardier/nose gunner, radio operator, navigator, dorsal and tail turret gunners

**DIMENSIONS:**
LENGTH: 56 ft 0 in (17 m)
WINGSPAN: 65 ft 0 in (19.80 m)
HEIGHT: 19 ft 10 in (6.04 m)

**WEIGHTS:**
EMPTY: 23 000 lb (10 433 kg)
MAX T/O: 32 000 lb (14 515 kg)

**PERFORMANCE:**
MAX SPEED: 310 mph (500 kmh)
RANGE: 1150 miles (1850 km)
POWERPLANT: two Pratt & Whitney R-2800-5 Double Wasps
OUTPUT: 3700 hp (2760.20 kW)

**FIRST FLIGHT DATE:**
25 November 1940

**ARMAMENT:**
two Browning 0.30/0.50-in machine guns in nose, two in dorsal turret, one in tail turret; maximum bomb load of 5200 lb (2539 kg) in bomb-bay

**FEATURES:**
Monoplane wing layout; close-cowled twin radial engines; dorsal and tail turrets

# Martin PBM Mariner USA

nine-seat, twin-engined maritime patrol bomber, anti-submarine flying boat/amphibian

The PBM Mariner served the US Navy well primarily in the Pacific, where it performed a variety of missions including anti-submarine warfare, maritime patrol, transport and air-sea rescue. Although 20 production aircraft were ordered by the Navy in December 1937, it was not until 1941 that the first PBM-1s finally entered service with VP-74 in 1941. Initially fitted with stabilising floats which retracted inwards into the wings, the advent of the PBM-3 the following year saw Martin revert to fixed outrigger floats, as well as the adoption of lengthened engine nacelles. The major Mariner production model was the PBM-5 of 1944, 631 of which were built. The PBM-5A amphibian was derived from this variant, featuring a retractable tricycle undercarriage. Just 36 examples were built, and these were used in the air-sea rescue role by the US Coast Guard. RAF Coastal Command received 25 PBM-3Bs in August 1943, but these were returned to the US six weeks later, while the RAAF operated 12 PBM-3Rs. A total of 1405 PBMs had been built by the time production ended in 1949.

SPECIFICATION:

**ACCOMMODATION:**
pilot, co-pilot, flight engineer, radar/radio operator, navigator, nose, dorsal and tail turret gunners, beam gunner

**DIMENSIONS:**
LENGTH: 79 ft 10 in (24.33 m)
WINGSPAN: 118 ft 0 in (35.97 m)
HEIGHT: 27 ft 6 in (8.40 m)

**WEIGHTS:**
EMPTY: 34,000 lb (15,422 kg)
MAX T/O: 60,000 lb (27,216 kg)

**PERFORMANCE:**
MAX SPEED: 205 mph (330 kmh)
RANGE: 2700 miles (4345 km)
POWERPLANT: two Pratt & Whitney R-2800-34 Double Wasps
OUTPUT: 4200 hp (3132 kW)

**FIRST FLIGHT DATE:**
18 February 1939

**ARMAMENT:**
two Browning 0.50-in machine guns in nose, dorsal and tail turrets, single gun in waist windows; maximum bomb/mine load of 4000-lb (1814 kg) in engine bays

**FEATURES:**
High-wing monoplane; boat-shaped hull; two radial engines; twin boom/tail layout

# Messerschmitt Bf 109E GERMANY

single-seat, single-engined monoplane fighter

Designed to meet a 1934 *Reichluftfahrtministerium* requirement for a single-seat monoplane fighter, the Bf 109 V1 was the winning competitor in a fly-off that involved three other designs. Production-standard Bf 109s proved their worth in the Spanish Civil War, and by the time Germany invaded Poland in September 1939, the re-engined Bf 109E was rolling off the production line in quantity, the now-familiar airframe being paired up with the Daimler-Benz DB 601 engine. This combination had been tested in June 1937, but the subsequent availability of the Bf 109E had been delayed until 1939 due to problems with the Daimler-Benz engine. Built for the fighter, reconnaissance and fighter-bomber roles, the Bf 109E proved to be the master of all of its contemporaries bar the Spitfire Mk I/II, to which it was considered an equal. Aside from fighting over Poland, the E-model saw combat throughout the *Blitzkrieg* of 1940, the Battle of Britain, in the Balkans in 1941 and in the opening phases of the North African and Soviet campaigns.

SPECIFICATION:

**ACCOMMODATION:**
pilot

**DIMENSIONS:**
LENGTH: 28 ft 0 in (8.55 m)
WINGSPAN: 32 ft 4.5 in (9.87 m)
HEIGHT: 8 ft 2 in (2.49 m)

**WEIGHTS:**
EMPTY: 4189 lb (1900 kg)
MAX T/O: 5875 lb (2665 kg)

**PERFORMANCE:**
MAX SPEED: 348 mph (560 kmh)
RANGE: 410 miles (660 km)
POWERPLANT: Daimler-Benz DB 601Aa
OUTPUT: 1175 hp (876 kW)

**FIRST FLIGHT DATE:**
June 1937 (Bf 109 V10)

**ARMAMENT:**
two MG 17 7.9 mm machine guns in upper cowling and two MG FF 20 mm cannon in wings; maximum bomb load of 551-lb (1814 kg) on under fuselage rack

**FEATURES:**
Monoplane wing layout; close-cowled inline engine; retractable landing gear; braced tailplane; fixed tailwheel

# Messerschmitt Bf 109G  GERMANY

single-seat, single-engined monoplane fighter

The Bf 109G was the most successful variant of
them all, being produced in staggering numbers
from early 1942 until war's end – 24,000+ Bf 109G/Ks
were constructed in total. Numerous modifications
to the basic G-1 were introduced either in the
factory or in the field, and these included extra
armament, additional radios, a wooden tailplane
and the installation of the boosted DB 605D engine.
In an attempt to standardise the equipment of the
frontline force, Messerschmitt produced the
Bf 109G-6 in 1942, which included many of these
previously *ad hoc* additions. Unfortunately, the
continual addition of weighty items like wing
cannon and larger engines to the slight airframe of
the Bf 109 eliminated much of the fighter's
manoeuvrability, and instead served to emphasise
the aircraft's poor low speed performance and
lateral control. The final variant to enter widespread
service was the Bf 109K-4, which incorporated all
the best parts of the late-build G-series sub-types,
including the improved vision hood, extended
tailplane and DB 605DCM engine.

SPECIFICATION:

ACCOMMODATION:
pilot

DIMENSIONS:
LENGTH: 29 ft 7.5 in (9.03 m)
WINGSPAN: 32 ft 6.5 in (9.92 m)
HEIGHT: 8 ft 2.5 in (2.50 m)

WEIGHTS:
EMPTY: 5893 lb (2673 kg)
MAX T/O: 7496 lb (3400 kg)

PERFORMANCE:
MAX SPEED: 386 mph (621 kmh)
RANGE: 620 miles (998 km)
POWERPLANT: Daimler-Benz
DB 605AM
OUTPUT: 1800 hp (1342 kW)

FIRST FLIGHT DATE:
late summer 1941

ARMAMENT:
one MG FF 20 mm cannon in
propeller hub and two under
wings, and two MG 131 13 mm
machine guns in upper cowling;
provision for various underfuselage and underwing stores

FEATURES:
Monoplane wing layout; close-
cowled inline engine; retractable
landing gear; fixed tailwheel

# Messerschmitt Bf 110 GERMANY

two/three-seat, twin-engined monoplane fighter

Designed in 1934-35 to fill the perceived need for a high-speed, long-range, heavily-armed twin-engined fighter, Messerschmitt's Bf 110 *Zerstörer* (destroyer) fulfilled all these criteria. Relying more on its firepower than manoeuvrability to survive in combat, the Bf 110 made its debut over Poland, where it dominated the skies in an environment of Luftwaffe air superiority. These successes continued in the 'Phoney War' and the early days of the *Blitzkrieg* in the west, but during the Battle of Britain, flaws in the *Zerstörer* concept were exposed. Following the loss of 200+ Bf 110s during the campaign, the day fighter role was given over to the Bf 109, and the *Zerstörer* sent to operate either on less hostile fronts like the Balkans and Mediterranean, or in the nightfighter role. The latter mission was ideally suited to a fighter like the Bf 110, and by 1943, the dedicated, radar-equipped, G-model accounted for 60 per cent of the *Nachtjagd* force. So effective was the Bf 110G in this nocturnal role that the fighter remained in production until March 1945.

SPECIFICATION:

ACCOMMODATION:
pilot, radio/radar operator and rear gunner

DIMENSIONS:
LENGTH: 39 ft 6.25 in (12.07 m)
WINGSPAN: 53 ft 3.25 in (16.25 m)
HEIGHT: 13 ft 8.50 in (4.18 m)

WEIGHTS:
EMPTY: 11,230 lb (5094 kg)
NORMAL LOADED: 21,799 lb (9888 kg)

PERFORMANCE:
MAX SPEED: 342 mph (550 kmh)
RANGE: 560 miles (900 km)
POWERPLANT: two Daimler-Benz DB 605B-1s
OUTPUT: 2950 hp (2200 kW)

FIRST FLIGHT DATE:
12 May 1936

ARMAMENT:
two MK 108 30 mm cannon and four MG 17 7.9 mm machine guns in nose and two MG 17 7.9 mm machine guns in rear cockpit; maximum bomb/rocket load of 2645-lb (1200 kg) on underwing racks

FEATURES:
Monoplane wing layout; two close-cowled inline engines; twin tail layout

# Messerschmitt Me 410 GERMANY

two-seat, twin-engined monoplane fighter-bomber

Derived from the disastrous Me 210, the Me 410 incorporated a number of significant changes to eradicate the Me 210's handling problems. The prototype Me 410 featured a lengthened and deepened rear fuselage, new outer wing panels, automatic wing slots and revised flaps and ailerons, as well as more powerful Daimler-Benz DB 603 engines. First flown in the autumn of 1942, the aircraft's development proceeded so rapidly that production aircraft reached the frontline in January 1943. The Me 410 was used for a variety of roles, including fighting-bombing, high-speed reconnaissance, heavy bomber interception and nightfighting. The aircraft made its combat debut over southern England in early 1943 in the night fighter-bomber role, and it subsequently saw action over the Eastern Front, in the Defence of the Reich and over the Mediterranean. Yet despite possessing good performance, Me 410s proved to be just as vulnerable as the Bf 110s they had replaced. Final production examples were delivered in September 1944, by which time 1160 had been built.

SPECIFICATION:

**ACCOMMODATION:**
pilot and radio/radar operator/gunner

**DIMENSIONS:**
LENGTH: 40 ft 11.50 in (12.48 m)
WINGSPAN: 53 ft 7.75 in (16.35 m)
HEIGHT: 14 ft 0.50 in (4.28 m)

**WEIGHTS:**
EMPTY: 17,598 lb (7982 kg)
NORMAL LOADED: 24,772 lb (11,236 kg)

**PERFORMANCE:**
MAX SPEED: 391 mph (629 kmh)
RANGE: 1450 miles (2333 km)
POWERPLANT: two Daimler-Benz DB 603AS
OUTPUT: 3500 hp (2610 kW)

**FIRST FLIGHT DATE:**
Autumn 1942

**ARMAMENT:**
two MG FF 20 mm cannon and two MG 17 7.9 mm machine guns in nose, two ventral 20 mm cannon and single 7.9 mm machine guns in fuselage side barbettes; maximum bomb load of 2205-lb (1000 kg) in bomb-bay

**FEATURES:**
Monoplane wing; two close-cowled inline engines; extensive cockpit glazing

# Messerschmitt Me 262 GERMANY

one/two-seat, twin-engined monoplane jet fighter

The world's first jet fighter, the Me 262 was also the most advanced aircraft of its generation to see combat. Design work commenced in 1938, and the first tailwheeled prototype, fitted with a Junkers Jumo 210 piston engine, completed its maiden flight on 4 April 1941. Unfortunately for Messerschmitt, work on the aircraft's turbojet powerplants failed to keep pace with airframe development, and it was not until 18 July 1942 that the first flight was made with the Jumo 003 turbojets.

With the engine/airframe combination sorted out, political interference from the Führer himself saw the programme side-tracked as he insisted that the aircraft be developed as a bomber. Sense prevailed in early 1944, and the first aircraft went into combat that June. Despite Germany being badly bombed during the final year of the war, 1400+ Me 262s were completed. Engine reliability and fuel shortages restricted the frontline force to 200 jets at any one time, but these accounted for 200+ Allied aircraft in day/night interceptions.

## SPECIFICATION:

**ACCOMMODATION:**
pilot, or pilot and radar operator (nightfighter)

**DIMENSIONS:**
LENGTH: 34 ft 9.5 in (10.60 m)
WINGSPAN: 41 ft 0.5 in (12.51 m)
HEIGHT: 11 ft 6.75 in (3.83 m)

**WEIGHTS:**
EMPTY: 9742 lb (4420 kg)
NORMAL LOADED: 14 101 lb (6396 kg)

**PERFORMANCE:**
MAX SPEED: 540 mph (870 kmh)
RANGE: 652 miles (1050 km)
POWERPLANT: two Junkers Jumo 004B-1/-2 or -3 turbojet engines
OUTPUT: 3960 lb st (17.8 kN)

**FIRST FLIGHT DATE:**
18 July 1942 (first all jet-powered flight)

**ARMAMENT:**
four Mk 108 30 mm cannon in nose; maximum bomb/rocket load of 1102-lb (500 kg) on underwing racks

**FEATURES:**
Swept monoplane wing layout; two jet engines in pods under wings; retractable, tricycle landing gear

# Messerschmitt ME 163 GERMANY

single-seat, single-engined monoplane rocket fighter

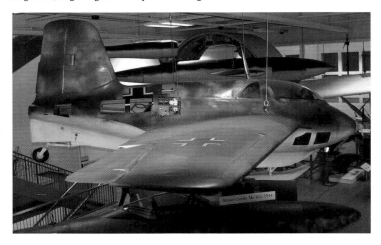

The only rocket-powered fighter of World War 2, the ME 163B was developed by Dr Alexander Lippisch from his pre-war series of tailless gliders. By 1940 Dr Lippisch and his team had come under the control of Messerschmitt, and this partnership resulted in the ME 163A, which achieved 624 mph in 1941. Messerschmitt revised the design to produce the ME 163B in 1943, and after delays waiting for a reliable Walter HWK 509 rocket motor to become available, the prototype completed its first flight on 23 June. The Walter engine was capable of outstanding performance, but ran for just eight minutes. To achieve the previously unheard of 15,950 ft per minute rate of climb, the ME 163B relied on a volatile fuel combination of T-stoff (hydrogen-peroxide and water) and C-stoff (hydrazine hydrate and methyl alcohol). In order to save weight, Messerschmitt dispensed with an undercarriage, launching the aircraft via a jettison-able trolley and relying on the pilot's skill to land using a fixed skid. Just one *gruppe* was equipped with the aircraft, making its combat debut in August 1944.

## SPECIFICATION:

**ACCOMMODATION:**
pilot

**DIMENSIONS:**
LENGTH: 19 ft 2.25 in (5.85 m)
WINGSPAN: 30 ft 7.25 in (9.33 m)
HEIGHT: 9 ft 1 in (2.77 m)

**WEIGHTS:**
EMPTY: 4206 lb (4420 kg)
NORMAL LOADED: 9502 lb (4310 kg)

**PERFORMANCE:**
MAX SPEED: 593 mph (954 kmh)
RANGE: maximum powered endurance of 8 minutes
POWERPLANT: Walter HWK 509-A2
OUTPUT: 3750 lb st (16.8 kN)

**FIRST FLIGHT DATE:**
August 1941

**ARMAMENT:**
two MK 108 30 mm cannon in wing roots

**FEATURES:**
Swept monoplane wing layout; no tailplane; landing skid; rocket engine within fuselage, exhausting through vent orifice at base of rudder

# Miles M 38 Messenger UK

four-seat, single-engined monoplane liaison/VIP communications aircraft

Designed and built at the request of senior British Army officers to fulfil the air observation post role, the Miles M 38 failed to achieve series production in substantial quantities simply because its creator, George Miles, had not obtained government authority before constructing his aircraft! The Messenger embodied all the criteria deemed desirable by operators in the frontline – an ability to carry at least two people, a radio and other military equipment, and be fitted with a modicum of armour plating. The design exhibited its ability to operate from small fields in any weather whilst being flown by pilots with limited experience and having been subjected to the minimum of servicing. The prototype had displayed all these attributes by 1943, but the only order received from the Ministry of Aircraft Production was for 21 machines to fill the VIP communications role in 1944. Amongst those deemed senior enough to receive their own personal Messengers were Field Marshal Sir Bernard Montgomery and Marshal of the RAF Lord Tedder.

SPECIFICATION:

**ACCOMMODATION:**
pilots and three passengers

**DIMENSIONS:**
LENGTH: 24 ft 0 in (7.32 m)
WINGSPAN: 36 ft 2 in (11.02 m)
HEIGHT: 9 ft 6 in (2.90 m)

**WEIGHTS:**
EMPTY: 1518 lb (689 kg)
MAX T/O: 1900 lb (862 kg)

**PERFORMANCE:**
MAX SPEED: 116 mph (187 kmh)
RANGE: 260 miles (418 km)
POWERPLANT: de Havilland Gipsy Major (Mk 1/4A) or Blackburn Cirrus Major III (Mk 2A)
OUTPUT: 140 hp (104.3 kW) and 155 hp (114.4 kW) respectively

**FIRST FLIGHT DATE:**
12 September 1942

**FEATURES:**
Monoplane wing layout; fixed landing gear; large tailplane with endplate fins and rudders and third central fin; close-cowled inline engine

# Mitsubishi A6M Zero-Sen JAPAN

single-seat, single-engined monoplane fighter

Aside from the initial surprise of the Pearl Harbor raid on 7 December 1941, perhaps the biggest shock for American forces in the Pacific was the outstanding performance of the Japan's main carrier fighter, the A6M2 Zero-Sen. It was fast, manoeuvrable, well armed and could fly an unmatched 1930 miles using a centreline drop tank. Totally dismissed by British and American intelligence in the months leading up to the attack, the Zero traced its origins back to an Imperial Navy Staff requirement issued in 1937 for an aircraft to replace the Mitsubishi A5M, then the main fleet fighter. Work progressed smoothly, with the first prototype flying on 1 April 1939 and production examples entering service the following year. Some 10,500 Zeros were built, and although outclassed by us fighters from late 1943 onwards, the Zero retained a modicum of 'combatability' due to its weight. Finally, in a last-ditch act, Zeros were converted into 'aerial bombs' and flung at the Allied invasion fleets in *kamikaze* attacks off the Philippines, Iwo Jima and Okinawa.

SPECIFICATION:

ACCOMMODATION:
pilot

DIMENSIONS:
LENGTH: 29 ft 11 in (9.12 m)
WINGSPAN: 36 ft 1 in (11.00 m)
HEIGHT: 11 ft 6 in (3.50 m)

WEIGHTS:
EMPTY: 4136 lb (1876 kg)
LOADED WEIGHT: 6025 lb (2733 kg)

PERFORMANCE:
MAX SPEED: 340 mph (548 kmh)
RANGE: 945 miles (1520 km)
POWERPLANT: Nakajima Sakae 31
OUTPUT: 1130 hp (843 kW)

FIRST FLIGHT DATE:
1 April 1939

ARMAMENT:
two Type 99 20 mm cannon and two Type 3 13 mm machine guns in wings, one Type 3 13 mm machine gun in nose; provision for one 551-lb (250 kg) bomb on underfuselage rack

FEATURES:
Monoplane layout; close-cowled radial engine; retractable undercarriage; three-bladed propeller

# Mitsubishi Ki-46 JAPAN

two-seat, monoplane strategic reconnaissance aircraft

Fast, high flying and ultra reliable, the Ki-46 was Japan's most important reconnaissance asset throughout World War 2. First flown in November 1939, initial production Ki-46-Is were powered by two Mitsubishi Ha-26-I radials which provided only modest performance. These machines were relegated to training duties as a result, frontline units being issued with the follow-on Ki-46-II instead. The latter was fitted with 1080 hp Ha-102 engines, which allowed the Ki-46 to reach speeds of up to 375 mph. The -II was the primary production variant, with 1093 being built. Frontline aircraft carried out clandestine reconnaissance flights of the Malayan Peninsula in the final months of peace, and once war had started, Ki-46s roamed across the Pacific. Some even travelled as far as northern Australia. The final variant was the Ki-46-III, which enjoyed more power from its Ha-112-II engines. The aircraft also had a redesigned forward fuselage, with a lengthened canopy. First flown in December 1942, production -IIIs (611 completed) were built alongside -IIs until VJ-Day.

## SPECIFICATION:

**ACCOMMODATION:**
pilot and observer in tandem

**DIMENSIONS:**
LENGTH: 36 ft 1 in (11.00 m)
WINGSPAN: 48 ft 2.75 in (14.70 m)
HEIGHT: 12 ft 8.75 in (3.88 m)

**WEIGHTS:**
EMPTY: 8446 lb (3831 kg)
LOADED WEIGHT: 14,330 lb (6500 kg)

**PERFORMANCE:**
MAX SPEED: 391 mph (629 kmh)
RANGE: 2485 miles (4000 km)
POWERPLANT: two Mitsubishi Ha-112-IIs
OUTPUT: 3000 hp (2236 kW)

**FIRST FLIGHT DATE:**
1 April 1939

**FEATURES:**
Monoplane layout; two close-cowled radial engines; retractable undercarriage; extensive cockpit glazing

# Morane-Saulnier MS 406 FRANCE

single-seat, single-engined monoplane fighter

The *Armée de l'Air's* staple fighter at the outbreak of World War 2, the MS 406 was outclassed by opposing German fighters in respect to its performance and armament. These deficiencies resulted in over 400 being lost during the Battle of France, with MS 406 pilots in turn claiming 175 victories. Developed from the MS 405, which had been built by Morane-Saulnier in response to a requirement issued by the *Armée de l'Air* for a modern *monoplane de chasse*, 1000 MS 406s were hastily ordered in March 1938 when the French government grew alarmed at the Nazi annexations of Czechoslovakia and Austria. Of mixed construction (steel tube framing and fabric for the fuselage, but with the rest of the structure covered in Plymax – plywood skinning bonded to metal alloy), the first production aircraft reached the frontline in late 1938. MS 406s were also sold to Finland, Turkey and Switzerland in 1939. Following the surrender of France in June 1940, surviving MS 406s were operated by both the Vichy French and the Luftwaffe.

SPECIFICATION:

ACCOMMODATION:
pilot

DIMENSIONS:
LENGTH: 26 ft 9.25 in (8.16 m)
WINGSPAN: 34 ft 9.75 in (10.61 m)
HEIGHT: 9 ft 3.75 in (2.84 m)

WEIGHTS:
EMPTY: 4189 lb (1900 kg)
MAX T/O: 6000 lb (2722 kg)

PERFORMANCE:
MAX SPEED: 302 mph (486 kmh)
RANGE: 466 miles (750 km)
POWERPLANT: Hispano-Suiza 12Y-31
OUTPUT: 860 hp (641 kW)

FIRST FLIGHT DATE:
8 August 1935 (MS 405)

ARMAMENT:
one HS 404 20 mm cannon firing through propeller hub and two MAC 1934 7.5 mm machine guns in wings

FEATURES:
Monoplane layout; close-cowled inline engine; retractable undercarriage; bulged chin housing oil cooler

# Nakajima ki-43 Hayabusa JAPAN
single-seat, single-engined monoplane fighter

The staple Japanese Army Air Force fighter of World War 2, the ki-43 was produced in greater numbers than any of its land-based contemporaries. Developed as a direct replacement for Nakajima's ki-27, the Hayabusa (Peregrine) embraced the same design philosophy in that it was built to be manoeuvrable at the expense of effective armament, protection for the pilot and structural strength. Production ki-43-is arrived in the frontline in early 1941, and the Hayabusa made its combat debut during the Japanese invasion of South-East Asia. Flying alongside the more numerous ki-27, it cleared the skies of Allied opposition. Despite these successes, pilots complained that the ki-43-i was under-powered, so Nakajima developed the re-engined ki-43-ii in 1943. Aside from the fitment of the Nakajima ha-115 radial, the new fighter had a three-bladed constant speed propeller and reduced-span 'clipped' wings. Although outclassed even after the ki-43-ii/iii had arrived in the frontline, the aircraft remained in service to war's end.

SPECIFICATION:

ACCOMMODATION:
pilot

DIMENSIONS:
LENGTH: 29 ft 3.25 in (8.92 m)
WINGSPAN: 35 ft 6.75 in (10.84 m)
HEIGHT: 10 ft 8.75 in (3.27 m)

WEIGHTS:
EMPTY: 4211 lb (1910 kg)
MAX T/O: 6450 lb (2926 kg)

PERFORMANCE:
MAX SPEED: 329 mph (529 kmh)
RANGE: 1095 miles (1762 km)
POWERPLANT: Nakajima ha-115
OUTPUT: 1150 hp (857 kW)

FIRST FLIGHT DATE:
January 1939

ARMAMENT:
two ho-103 12.7 mm machine guns in nose; maximum bomb load of 1102-lb (500 kg) on underwing racks

FEATURES:
Monoplane layout; close-cowled radial engine; retractable undercarriage; three-bladed propeller; aerial mast on right side of fuselage forward of cockpit

# Noorduyn UC-64 Norseman CANADA

eight-seat, single-engined high-wing utility transport aircraft

Based on a pre-war design from Canadian manufacturer Noorduyn, the Norseman saw widespread use with the USAAF and the RCAF during World War 2. Rugged in the extreme, the Norseman was built to withstand the rigours of a Canadian winter. Although the initial prototype and production variants came fitted with a Wright R-975-E3 radial engine of 420 hp, this was substituted by a 550 hp Pratt & Whitney Wasp. The Norseman initially enjoyed success only in the civil market, but in 1942 both the RCAF and USAAF acquired Mk VIs – 749 were built for the USAAF alone (the Americans designated their aircraft UC-64As). These machines found employment across the globe, where their sound construction, ease of maintenance and load carrying capacity made them popular with both frontline and secondary units. Perhaps the most (in)famous wartime incident involving a UC-64A was the disappearance of legendary USAAF 'Big Band' leader Major Glenn Miller in a Norseman during a flight from southern England to Paris in December 1944.

SPECIFICATION:

ACCOMMODATION:
pilots and seven passengers

DIMENSIONS:
LENGTH: 32 ft 0 in (9.75 m)
WINGSPAN: 51 ft 6 in (15.70 m)
HEIGHT: 10 ft 3 in (3.12 m)

WEIGHTS:
EMPTY: 4690 lb (2123 kg)
MAX T/O: 7400 lb (3357 kg)

PERFORMANCE:
MAX SPEED: 155 mph (249 kmh)
RANGE: 1150 miles (1851 km)
POWERPLANT: Pratt & Whitney R-1340-AN-1 Wasp
OUTPUT: 550 hp (410 kW)

FIRST FLIGHT DATE:
14 November 1935

FEATURES:
High wing layout; fixed landing gear; close-cowled radial engine

# North American AT-6 Texan/SNJ/Harvard  USA

two-seat, single-engined monoplane advanced trainer

For decades known simply as the 'pilot maker', the AT-6/SNJ/Harvard was *the* global trainer during World War 2. Derived from the NA-16, and initially designated the BC-1, the advanced trainer became the AT-6 in USAAC service. The refinement of the Texan coincided with a rapid expansion of US armed forces, and orders flowed in ranging in size from 94 basic AT-6s in 1939 to an accumulated total of 3404 AT-6DS less than five years later. In total, 17,000+ airframes were built to train USAAF and Navy pilots across the continental USA. Foreign customers also appreciated the trainer's merits, the RAF showing interest in the aircraft as early as June 1938 when the British Purchasing Commission placed an order for 200 BC-1s, dubbed 'Harvard Is'. Over the next seven years 5000+ Harvards were procured principally through Lend-Lease and issued to the RCAF and RNZAF, as well as the RAF. Although the Texan's career in the US forces ceased at the end of the 1950s, it remained the staple basic trainer for many nations across the globe well into the 1970s.

SPECIFICATION:

**ACCOMMODATION:**
two pilots in tandem

**DIMENSIONS:**
LENGTH: 29 ft 6 in (8.99 m)
WINGSPAN: 42 ft 0.25 in (12.80 m)
HEIGHT: 11 ft 9 in (3.58 m)

**WEIGHTS:**
EMPTY: 4158 lb (1886 kg)
MAX T/O: 5300 lb (2404 kg)

**PERFORMANCE:**
MAX SPEED: 205 mph (330 kmh)
RANGE: 1118 miles (1800 km)
POWERPLANT: Pratt & Whitney R-1340-AN-1 Wasp
OUTPUT: 550 hp (410 kW)

**FIRST FLIGHT DATE:**
April 1936 (NA-26)

**FEATURES:**
Monoplane wing layout; retractable undercarriage; close-cowled radial engine; fixed tailwheel

# North American B-25 Mitchell USA

four/six-seat, twin-engined bomber

Built in response to a pre-war USAAC request for a twin-engined attack bomber, the B-25 Mitchell proved to be one of the most versatile combat aircraft of World War 2. Tailored to fit USAAC Circular Proposal 38-385, the prototype completed flight trials, but North American was encouraged to improve its design by the Army, which now stated that future medium bombers would have to carry a payload of 2400 lbs – twice that originally stipulated in 38-385. Enlarged, the production airframe was designated the NA-62. Impressed with what it saw on the drawing board, the USAAC ordered 184 aircraft (designated B-25s) before metal had even been cut. Christened the Mitchell after Army bomber proponent William 'Billy' Mitchell, the bomber fought with both the USAAF in the Pacific and ETO/MTO and the US Marine Corps, British, Dutch and Australian units. By war's end the Mitchell was still in production, having outlasted rival designs to become the most prolific American medium bomber of the conflict – built to the tune of 9889 airframes.

SPECIFICATION:

ACCOMMODATION:
pilot, co-pilot, bombardier/nose gunner, navigator, dorsal and tail turret gunners

DIMENSIONS:
LENGTH: 52 ft 11 in (16.13 m)
WINGSPAN: 67 ft 7 in (20.60 m)
HEIGHT: 16 ft 4 in (4.98 m)

WEIGHTS:
EMPTY: 19,480 lb (8836 kg)
MAX T/O: 35,000 lb (15,876 kg)

PERFORMANCE:
MAX SPEED: 272 mph (438 kmh)
RANGE: 1350 miles (2173 km)
POWERPLANT: two Wright R-2600-29 Cyclones
OUTPUT: 3700 hp (2760.20 kW)

FIRST FLIGHT DATE:
January 1939

ARMAMENT:
four fixed Browning 0.50-in machine guns on fuselage sides, two on flexible mounts in nose, two in dorsal and tail turrets, two in waist; bomb load of 3000 lb (1361 kg) in bomb-bay, wing racks for rockets

FEATURES:
Monoplane wing; close-cowled twin radial engines; twin tail layout

# North American P-51A/A-36 Mustang USA

single-seat, single-engined monoplane fighter

The Mustang has its origins in a British Purchasing Commission deal struck with North American in April 1940 for an advanced fighter to supplant the Spitfire, the company having a completed prototype – tailored to the British specifications – ready for flight within 120 days of the original submission. North American had already made a start independently of the British deal, its NA-73X design incorporating lessons gleaned from aerial combat in Europe. Three days short of the required date the airframe was completed, the aircraft (christened the 'Mustang I') handling beautifully in testing thanks to its semi-laminar flow airfoil wing. However, it was soon realised that the fighter's Allison V-1710 performed poorly above 17,000 ft due to its lack of supercharging, so the Mustang Is were fitted with cameras and relegated to the low-level tactical reconnaissance and army co-operation roles. The USAAF, seeing that the Mustang I was no good as a fighter above medium altitude, ordered a small number of A-36As and P-51As for ground attack tasks instead.

## SPECIFICATION:

**ACCOMMODATION:**
pilot

**DIMENSIONS:**
LENGTH: 32 ft 3 in (9.83 m)
WINGSPAN: 37 ft 0 in (11.28 m)
HEIGHT: 12 ft 2 in (3.71 m)

**WEIGHTS:**
EMPTY: 6550 lb (2971 kg)
LOADED WEIGHT: 8800 lb (3992 kg)

**PERFORMANCE:**
MAX SPEED: 387 mph (622 kmh)
RANGE: 1250 miles (2010 km) with external tanks
POWERPLANT: Allison V-1710-81
OUTPUT: 1200 hp (1014 kW)

**FIRST FLIGHT DATE:**
26 October 1940

**ARMAMENT:**
six fixed Browning 0.50-in machine guns in wings; maximum bomb load of 2000-lb (907 kg) on underwing racks

**FEATURES:**
Monoplane wing layout; rectractable landing gear; close-cowled inline engine; ventral air intake

# North American P-51B/C/D/K Mustang USA

single-seat, single-engined monoplane fighter

Although the Mustang I's performance had let it down in the high-altitude dogfights, the airframe itself was more than sound, so the RAF searched for a replacement powerplant and came up with the Merlin 61. Once mated with this battle-proven engine, the aircraft's performance was startling. Car builder Packard licence-built the Merlin as the V-1650, and North American followed the British lead in mating surplus P-51A airframes with the 'new' powerplant. The Merlin-powered P-51B made its combat debut over Europe in December 1943, just when the USAAF's daylight bomber campaign had begun to falter due to unsustainable losses. Capable of escorting B-17s and B-24s throughout their hazardous missions, Mustangs became the dominant USAAF fighter. The RAF, too, got its hands on 1000+ Merlin-powered aircraft through Lend-Lease. In total, 14,819 P-51s were built by North American, plus a further 200 in Australia. The fighter served in a frontline capacity with the USAF into the early 1950s, and further afield in Central and South America until the 1970s.

SPECIFICATION:

ACCOMMODATION:
pilot

DIMENSIONS:
LENGTH: 32 ft 3 in (9.83 m)
WINGSPAN: 37 ft 0 in (11.28 m)
HEIGHT: 12 ft 2 in (3.71 m)

WEIGHTS:
EMPTY: 7635 lb (3463 kg)
MAX T/O: 12,100 lb (5488 kg)

PERFORMANCE:
MAX SPEED: 437 mph (703 kmh)
RANGE: 1650 miles (2655 km) with external tanks
POWERPLANT: Packard V-1650-7
OUTPUT: 1720 hp (1283 kW)

FIRST FLIGHT DATE:
13 October 1942

ARMAMENT:
six Browning 0.50-in machine guns in wings; maximum bomb/rocket load of 2000-lb (907 kg) on underwing racks

FEATURES:
Monoplane wing layout; rectractable landing gear; close-cowled inline engine; ventral air intake; four-bladed propeller

# Northrop P-61 Black Widow USA

three-seat, twin-engined monoplane fighter

The first aircraft to be designed as a radar-equipped nightfighter, Northrop's P-61 Black Widow was influenced by early RAF combat experiences with radar-equipped aircraft. Built to fulfil a 1940 USAAC requirement, the fighter was designed around the Radiation Laboratory SCR-720 radar, which was mounted in the nose. The design was accepted the following year, and Northrop immediately went to work building two XP-61 prototypes and 13 YP-61 evaluation aircraft.

The Black Widow was the largest fighter ever procured for service by the USAAF, its airframe capable of housing a dorsal barbette of four machine guns and four ventrally-mounted 20 mm cannon. After initial structural and radar problems, the aircraft was issued to frontline units in March 1944, and both ETO and Pacific squadrons went into action that spring. Some 706 Black Widows were built in three variants by Northrop, and the type saw action as a night intruder operating against ground targets as well as in its nightfighter role.

SPECIFICATION:

ACCOMMODATION:
pilot, front gunner and radio
operator/rear gunner

DIMENSIONS:
LENGTH: 49 ft 7 in (15.11 m)
WINGSPAN: 66 ft 0 in (20.11 m)
HEIGHT: 14 ft 8 in (4.47 m)

WEIGHTS:
EMPTY: 22,000 lb (9979 kg)
MAX T/O: 38,000 lb (17,237 kg)

PERFORMANCE:
MAX SPEED: 366 mph (589 kmh)
RANGE: 3000 miles (4828 km)
POWERPLANT: two Pratt & Whitney
R-2800-65 Double Wasps
OUTPUT: 4000 hp (2982 kW)

FIRST FLIGHT DATE:
26 May 1942

ARMAMENT:
four fixed ventral Browning
0.50-in machine guns and four
AN-M2 20 mm cannon in remote-
controlled dorsal turret;
bomb/rocket load of 6400-lb
(2903 kg) on underwing racks

FEATURES:
Monoplane wing layout;
close-cowled twin radial
engines; dorsal turret; twin
boom/tail layout

# Percival Proctor UK

four-seat, single-engined monoplane radio trainer and communications aircraft

Based on Percival's pre-war Vega Gull, the Proctor was tailored to an Air Ministry Specification for a communications and radio training aircraft. With the first prototype having successfully completed its service trials, production Proctor Is started reaching the RAF in mid-1940. Following the building of 247 Mk Is (all of which were configured as communications aircraft with dual flying controls), Percival commenced construction of 175 Mk IIs and 437 Mk IIIs, which were built as radio trainers. The final variant to enter RAF service was the Mk IV (258 delivered), which boasted a longer and deeper fuselage to accommodate four crew/passengers. Although built as radio trainers, some Mk IVs were later stripped of their electronic equipment and re-configured as communications hacks. After the war more than 200 Proctors were sold to civilian buyers, although some Mk IVs were retained by communications squadrons until 1955. Percival also produced 150 'civilianised' Proctors in the shape of the Mk 5, four of which were acquired by the RAF for use by air attachés.

SPECIFICATION:

**ACCOMMODATION:**
pilots and three passengers

**DIMENSIONS:**
LENGTH: 28 ft 2 in (8.59 m)
WINGSPAN: 39 ft 6 in (12.04 m)
HEIGHT: 7 ft 3 in (2.21 m)

**WEIGHTS:**
EMPTY: 2370 lb (1075 kg)
MAX T/O: 3500 lb (1588 kg)

**PERFORMANCE:**
MAX SPEED: 160 mph (257 kmh)
RANGE: 500 miles (805 km)
POWERPLANT: de Havilland Gipsy Queen II
OUTPUT: 210 hp (157 kW)

**FIRST FLIGHT DATE:**
8 October 1939

**FEATURES:**
Monoplane wing layout; fixed, spatted landing gear; close-cowled inline engine

# Petlyakov Pe-2 USSR

three/four-seat, twin-engined monoplane attack bomber

Created in 1938 as a high altitude fighter designated the vi-100, the aircraft evolved into the Pe-2 attack bomber through intensive aerodynamic refinement. Its fighter-like performance made the Pe-2 difficult to intercept, particularly in the early war years. A poor level bomber, the aircraft had dive brakes added under the wings in the early stages of its development, and the Pe-2 entered service in August 1940 as a multi-role attack and dive-bomber.

Up to 2205-lb (1000 kg) of bombs could be carried by the aircraft either on external racks or split between the bomb-bay and in the rear of the long engine nacelles. Dedicated fighter-bomber and photo-reconnaissance versions were also built. Aside from its use against Germany and its Axis allies on the Eastern Front, Soviet Pe-2s saw action against Japan in the last weeks of World War 2. A total of 11,427 Pe-2s were constructed, the final examples being built in January 1945. The aircraft also saw widespread service with Soviet Bloc countries post-war.

SPECIFICATION:

ACCOMMODATION:
pilot, rear cockpit and ventral
gunners

DIMENSIONS:
LENGTH: 41 ft 6.5 in (12.66 m)
WINGSPAN: 56 ft 3.50 in (17.16 m)
HEIGHT: 11 ft 6 in (3.50 m)

WEIGHTS:
EMPTY: 12,943 lb (5871 kg)
MAX T/O: 18,730 lb (8496 kg)

PERFORMANCE:
MAX SPEED: 336 mph (541 kmh)
RANGE: 932 miles (1500 km)
POWERPLANT: two Klimov
M-105PFS
OUTPUT: 2520 hp (1880 kW)

FIRST FLIGHT DATE:
1939

ARMAMENT:
four ShKAS 7.62 mm or
BS 12.7 mm machine guns in
nose, rear cockpit and ventral
positions; maximum bomb/
rocket load of 2200-lb (1000 kg)
in bomb-bay or on under-
fuselage racks

FEATURES:
Monoplane wing layout;
retractable undercarriage;
two close-cowled inline engines;
twin tail layout

# Piper O-59/L-4/L-18 Grasshopper USA

two-seat, single-engined high-wing liaison/observation aircraft

Piper's L-4 Grasshopper was used by the USAAC in the artillery spotting and frontline liaison roles, the aircraft being a militarised version of the Taylor Aircraft Company (later Piper) J-3 Cub of the mid-1930s. The USAAC came to realise the usefulness of the design during military manoeuvres held in August 1941, which saw 44 Cubs employed in the field. It ordered 948 O-59s (redesignated L-4s by the time they entered service), which boasted certain changes from the J-3, including a tandem cockpit arrangement. Following the attack on Pearl Harbor, hundreds of civilian Cubs were pressed into military service, and by 1943 the combined total of civil and military Cubs/Grasshoppers built was nearing 10,000. Piper also received a request by the USAAC to produce a training glider utilising the Grasshopper's airframe minus its engine and undercarriage – the Army subsequently purchased 250 examples with the designation TG-8. The L-4 remained in service post-war, with the improved L-18 variant seeing action with the USAF in the Korean War.

SPECIFICATION:

ACCOMMODATION:
pilot and passenger in tandem

DIMENSIONS:
LENGTH: 22 ft 0 in (6.71 m)
WINGSPAN: 35 ft 3 in (10.74 m)
HEIGHT: 6 ft 8 in (2.03 m)

WEIGHTS:
EMPTY: 730 lb (331 kg)
MAX T/O: 1220 lb (533 kg)

PERFORMANCE:
MAX SPEED: 85 mph (137 kmh)
RANGE: 190 miles (306 km)
POWERPLANT: Continental
O-170-3
OUTPUT: 65 hp (48 kW)

FIRST FLIGHT DATE:
1937 (Cub trainer) and 1941
(YO-59 military derivative)

FEATURES:
High-wing layout; tandem
cockpits; fixed landing gear;
extensive cockpit glazing

# Polikarpov PO-2 USSR

two-seat, single-engined biplane trainer/utility aircraft

Polikarpov's PO-2 can trace its lineage back to a Soviet air force request for a simple and reliable elementary trainer built around the M-11 radial engine. Originally designated the U-2, production aircraft were praised for their positive longitudinal stability and reluctance to spin. Aside from its instructional role, the new biplane design proved to be a veritable 'maid of all work' as it undertook agricultural flying, air ambulance tasks and civilian pilot training for Aeroflot. More than 13,500 aircraft had been built by mid-1941, and a further 6500 were completed before production ended in the USSR in 1944. That same year the aircraft was redesignated the PO-2 in honour of its designer, N N Polikarpov, who had died on 30 July 1944. Aside from its more peaceful employment, the PO-2 was also adapted for night intruder sorties over the Eastern Front – the PO-2LNB could carry 441-lb (200 kg) of ordnance. Post-war, the aircraft was returned to production in Poland in 1948. North Korean PO-2s also revived the aircraft's night intruder mission during the Korean War.

SPECIFICATION:

ACCOMMODATION:
pilot and observer/passenger in tandem

DIMENSIONS:
LENGTH: 26 ft 9.33 in (8.17 m)
WINGSPAN: 37 ft 4.75 in (11.40 m)
HEIGHT: 9 ft 1 in (2.25 m)

WEIGHTS:
EMPTY: 1631 lb (740 kg)
MAX T/O: 2756 lb (1250 kg)

PERFORMANCE:
MAX SPEED: 87 mph (140 kmh)
RANGE: 448 miles (720 km)
POWERPLANT: Shvetsov M-11/G/D/K or Okromechko-developed M-11F/FM/M/FR/FR-1/FN
OUTPUT: ranging from 100 hp (48 kW) through to 200 hp (96 kW)

FIRST FLIGHT DATE:
7 January 1928 (U-2)

ARMAMENT:
one flexibly-mounted ShKAS 7.62 mm machine gun in rear cockpit; maximum bomb load of 550-lb (250 kg) on underfuselage racks

FEATURES:
Biplane wing; tandem cockpits; fixed landing gear; N-shaped bracing struts

# Republic P-47 Thunderbolt   USA

single-seat, single-engined monoplane fighter

The original P-47 design was produced to meet a 1940 USAAC requirement for a lightweight interceptor similar in size and stature to the Spitfire and Bf 109. Powered by Allison's V-1710-39 1150 hp inline engine, the XP-47A boasted just two 0.50-in machine guns, and lacked any protective armour or self-sealing tanks. However, combat reports from Europe proved the folly of a lightweight fighter, and the USAAC modified its design requirements to include an eight-gun fitment, heavy armour plating and a self-sealing fuel system. Republic responded with an all-new design powered by the turbocharged R-2800 Double Wasp radial engine. The first P-47Bs joined the Eighth Air Force in Britain in late 1942 to perform the bomber escort role. The arrival of the definitive P-47D in late 1943 was followed by the advent of the 'bubble top' Thunderbolt, which became the favoured mount of most P-47 pilots. Some 15,677 Thunderbolts were eventually built, and a number of P-47Ns soldiered on with the Air National Guard and a handful of other air arms into the early 1950s.

SPECIFICATION:

ACCOMMODATION:
pilot

DIMENSIONS:
LENGTH: 36 ft 1 in (11.00 m)
WINGSPAN: 42 ft 7 in (12.98 m)
HEIGHT: 14 ft 8 in (4.47 m)

WEIGHTS:
EMPTY: 11,170 lb (5067 kg)
MAX T/O: 20,700 lb (9390 kg)

PERFORMANCE:
MAX SPEED: 467 mph (751 kmh)
RANGE: 2350 miles (3782 km) with
external tanks
POWERPLANT: Pratt & Whitney
R-2800-57C/-77 Double Wasp
OUTPUT: 2800 hp (2088 kW)

FIRST FLIGHT DATE:
6 May 1941 (XP-47B)

ARMAMENT:
eight Browning 0.50-in machine
guns wings in wings; maximum
bomb/rocket load of 2000-lb
(907 kg) on underwing racks

FEATURES:
Monoplane wing layout;
rectractable landing gear;
close-cowled radial engine;
four-bladed propeller

# Saab B17 SWEDEN

two-seat, single-engined monoplane light bomber/reconnaissance aircraft

The first indigenous aircraft designed and built by Saab, the B17 started life in 1937 as the L10 two-seat reconnaissance monoplane. Adhering to strict neutrality, Sweden found itself in a difficult position when it came to procuring new aircraft in the lead-up to World War 2, as traditional suppliers from Germany, the USA and Britain could not fulfil outstanding orders. Saab was therefore formed with the dual purpose of licence building foreign aircraft and working on new home-grown designs. Powered by licence-built powerplants, the B17 was a conventional aircraft capable of carrying ordnance both internally and externally.

Its rugged construction allowed it to dive-bomb too. The first version to enter service in 1941 was the B17B (powered by the Bristol Mercury XXIV), followed by the B17C (fitted with a Piaggio P XIbis RC 40) and finally the Twin Wasp-powered B17A. A total of 322 aircraft were built between 1 December 1941 and 16 September 1944, with B17s equipping six light bomber and reconnaissance wings within the Swedish Air Force.

SPECIFICATION:

ACCOMMODATION:
pilot and observer/gunner

DIMENSIONS:
LENGTH: 32 ft 2 in (9.8 m)
WINGSPAN: 45 ft 1 in (13.7 m)
HEIGHT: 13 ft 1 in (4.0 m)

WEIGHTS:
EMPTY: 5732 lb (2600 kg)
MAX T/O: 8752 lb (3970 kg)

PERFORMANCE:
MAX SPEED: 270 mph (435 kmh)
RANGE: 1120 miles (1800 km)
POWERPLANT: Pratt & Whitney R-1830 Twin Wasp
OUTPUT: 1200 hp (895 kW)

FIRST FLIGHT DATE:
18 May 1940

ARMAMENT:
two fixed 13.2 mm machine guns in wings in and one flexibly-mounted 7.9 mm machine gun in rear cockpit; maximum bomb load of 1500-lb (680 kg) in bomb-bay and on underwing racks

FEATURES:
Monoplane wing layout; rectractable landing gear; close-cowled radial engine; extensive cockpit glazing

# Savoia-Marchetti SM.79 Sparviero ITALY

four/five-seat, three-engined monoplane torpedo/reconnaissance bomber

Italy's most successful bomber, the SM.79 was also the most produced, with 1370 built between 1936 and 1944. The Sparviero (Sparrowhawk) saw combat in France, Yugoslavia, Greece, North Africa, East Africa and in the Mediterranean. Initially developed by Savoia-Marchetti as a transport, the aircraft had evolved into a dedicated medium bomber by the time the SM.79-I made its combat debut in the Spanish Civil War in 1936. The manufacturer then produced the SM.79-II torpedo-bomber, fitted with 1000 hp Piaggio or Fiat radial engines.

Entering service in 1939, the SM.79-II saw much action over the next four years, particularly in its intended torpedo bomber role against the Royal Navy in the Mediterranean. The Sparviero also performed close support, reconnaissance and transport duties. Indeed, it was in the latter role that the SM.79 enjoyed service with the post-war *Aeronautica Militare Italiana* until the 1950s. A small number of SM.79s were also sold to export customers before, during and after World War 2.

SPECIFICATION:

ACCOMMODATION:
pilot, navigator and dorsal, ventral and beam gunners

DIMENSIONS:
LENGTH: 53 ft 1.75 in (16.20 m)
WINGSPAN: 69 ft 6.75 in (21.20 m)
HEIGHT: 13 ft 5.50 in (4.10 m)

WEIGHTS:
EMPTY: 16,755 lb (7600 kg)
MAX T/O: 24,912 lb (11,300 kg)

PERFORMANCE:
MAX SPEED: 270 mph (434 kmh)
RANGE: 1180 miles (1900 km)
POWERPLANT: three Fiat A.80 RC41S
OUTPUT: 3090 hp (2304 kW)

FIRST FLIGHT DATE:
Late 1934

ARMAMENT:
one SAFAT 12.7 mm machine gun in cockpit, dorsal and ventral positions and one Breda-SAFAT 7.7 mm machine gun in beam positions; bomb load of 2755-lb (1250 kg) in bomb-bay or two 17.7-in torpedoes underwings

FEATURES:
Monoplane wing layout; retractable undercarriage; three close-cowled radial engines; ventral gondola

# Short Sunderland UK

10/13-seat, four-engined monoplane long-range maritime patrol/reconnaissance flying boat

A military development of the Imperial Airways c-Class 'Empire' flying boats of the 1930s, the Sunderland was the RAF's principal wartime maritime patrol aircraft. Flown for the first time on 16 October 1937, production examples entered frontline service in mid 1938. Established within Coastal Command ranks by World War 2, the Sunderland was soon providing convoy escort and anti-submarine cover in the Atlantic, Middle and Far East and the Mediterranean. Although seemingly vulnerable to aerial attack, the Sunderland proved difficult to shoot down thanks to its numerous machine guns – as many as 12 could be fitted in three turrets and various hatches. A total of 749 Sunderlands were built in four marks, featuring more powerful radial engines, varying degrees of protective armament, extra fuel capacity and modified hull shapes. The Mk III was the most produced, 462 examples being issued to RAF, RCAF, RNZAF and RAAF units. By war's end, 28 squadrons were flying Sunderlands, and it remained in service with Coastal Command until 1959.

## SPECIFICATION:

**ACCOMMODATION:**
pilot, co-pilot, flight engineer, radio operator, radar operator, navigator, bow, dorsal, tail/beam gunners

**DIMENSIONS:**
LENGTH: 85 ft 4 in (26.01 m)
WINGSPAN: 112 ft 9.50 in (34.38 m)
HEIGHT: 32 ft 10.50 in (10.02 m)

**WEIGHTS:**
EMPTY: 34,500 lb (15,663 kg)
MAX T/O: 58,000 lb (26,308 kg)

**PERFORMANCE:**
MAX SPEED: 210 mph (338 kmh)
RANGE: 2900 miles (4670 km)
POWERPLANT: four Bristol Pegasus XVIIIs
OUTPUT: 4260 hp (2382 kW)

**FIRST FLIGHT DATE:**
16 October 1937

**ARMAMENT:**
two Browning 0.303-in machine guns in nose/dorsal turrets, four in tail turret, two-four guns in nose/beam positions; bomb/depth charge load of 2000-lb (907 kg) on underwing racks

**FEATURES:**
High-wing monoplane; boat-shaped hull; four radial engines

# Stinson AT-19 Reliant USA

four-seat, single-engined high-wing navigation/radio trainer and communications aircraft

Derived from the successful high-wing cabin monoplane of the 1930s, the first militarised Reliants were indeed ex-civilian aircraft impressed into USAAC service at the outbreak of World War 2 – these aircraft were designated UC-81s. Two Reliants had been acquired by the US Navy in 1935, one of which was passed on to the Coast Guard. The latter was designated a RQ-1, while the Navy machine was identified as a XR3Q-1. Maintaining the nautical flavour, the largest customer for the Reliant was in fact the Royal Navy, which purchased 500 Reliant Is (the USAAF designated them AT-19s) under Lend-Lease agreements for the Fleet Air Arm.

The first examples arrived in Britain in the summer of 1943, and the aircraft subsequently served in the radio, navigational and photographic training roles, as well as performing general utility flights. A total of 12 FAA units operated Reliant Is until war's end, when around 350 were returned to the USA, reconditioned by Stinson and sold to civilian buyers.

SPECIFICATION:

ACCOMMODATION:
pilot and three passengers

DIMENSIONS:
LENGTH: 30 ft 0 in (9.14 m)
WINGSPAN: 41 ft 10.5 in (12.76 m)
HEIGHT: 8 ft 7 in (2.62 m)

WEIGHTS:
EMPTY: 2810 lb (1275 kg)
MAX T/O: 4000 lb (1814 kg)

PERFORMANCE:
MAX SPEED: 141 mph (227 kmh)
RANGE: 810 miles (1303 km)
POWERPLANT: Lycoming R-680
OUTPUT: 290 hp (216 kW)

FIRST FLIGHT DATE:
1933 (SR/SR-2 civilian variant)

FEATURES:
High-wing layout; fixed landing gear; close-cowled radial engine

# Stinson O-49/L-1 Vigilant  USA

two-seat, single-engined high-wing liaison/observation aircraft

One of three manufacturers to submit designs in response to a requirement issued by the USAAC in 1940 for a new light observation aircraft, Stinson was awarded a contract for 142 O-49s. To achieve the low-speed and high-lift performance stipulated, it fitted the leading edge of the aircraft's wing with automatically operating slats, whilst the trailing edge boasted wide-span slotted flaps and large slotted ailerons. By the time production of the Vigilant (as it was known in RAF service) had begun, Stinson had been acquired by Vultee.

A follow-on contract for 182 Vigilants saw the aircraft modified with a lengthened fuselage, resulting in a designation change to O-49A. As previously mentioned, the RAF received 100 Vigilants in 1941-42. All O-49/O-49As became L-1/L-1As in 1942, whilst aircraft modified into air ambulances (L-1B/C), glider pick-up trainers (L-1D) and floatplanes (L-1E/FS) also received designation changes. Only two batches of L-1s were acquired, as the Grasshopper family was to prove more effective in the observation role.

SPECIFICATION:

**ACCOMMODATION:**
pilot and observer/passenger in tandem

**DIMENSIONS:**
LENGTH: 34 ft 3 in (10.44 m)
WINGSPAN: 50 ft 11 in (15.52 m)
HEIGHT: 10 ft 2 in (3.10 m)

**WEIGHTS:**
EMPTY: 2670 lb (1211 kg)
MAX T/O: 3400 lb (1542 kg)

**PERFORMANCE:**
MAX SPEED: 122 mph (196 kmh)
RANGE: 280 miles (451 km)
POWERPLANT: Lycoming R-680-9
OUTPUT: 295 hp (220 kW)

**FIRST FLIGHT DATE:**
Summer 1940

**FEATURES:**
High-wing layout; fixed landing gear; close-cowled radial engine

# Stinson O-62/L-5 Sentinal  USA

two-seat, single-engined high-wing light liaison aircraft

The Stinson L-5 was derived from the successful
civilian Voyager design evaluated by the USAAC in
1941, although it was not part of the US Army trial
held that year. Six aircraft were initially acquired
(designated YO-54s), and after minor modifications
had been carried out to 'militarise' them (changing
the cabin layout from three to two seats, improving
visibility out of the cockpit and strengthening the
fuselage and undercarriage), an initial order for 275
O-62s (as they were redesignated) was placed. A
follow-on purchase of 1456 machines was received
by the manufacturer in 1942, and by the time the
first of these aircraft had reached the USAAC, all
O-62s had been redesignated L-5s. During the
type's career, modifications were carried out which
made it more suited to specific missions – an
upward-hinged door was fitted to allow the L-5B to
carry a stretcher, while a K-20 reconnaissance
camera was installed in the L-5C. The RAF also used
100 L-5s (christened Sentinals) in Burma, whilst the
Marine Corps acquired 306 as OY-1s. Post-war, the
L-5 saw further action with the USAF in Korea.

SPECIFICATION:

**ACCOMMODATION:**
pilot and observer/passenger in
tandem

**DIMENSIONS:**
LENGTH: 24 ft 1 in (7.34 m)
WINGSPAN: 34 ft 0 in (10.36 m)
HEIGHT: 7 ft 11 in (2.41 m)

**WEIGHTS:**
EMPTY: 1550 lb (703 kg)
MAX T/O: 2020 lb (916 kg)

**PERFORMANCE:**
MAX SPEED: 130 mph (209 kmh)
RANGE: 420 miles (676 km)
POWERPLANT: Lycoming O-435-1
or O-435-11 (L-5G)
OUTPUT: 185 hp (138 kW) and
190 hp (142 kW), respectively

**FIRST FLIGHT DATE:**
1940

**FEATURES:**
High-wing layout; fixed landing
gear; close-cowled engine;
extensive cockpit glazing

# Sukhoi su-2 USSR

two-seat, single-engined monoplane attack bomber

Created by Pavel Sukhoi while still a member of the Tupolev design bureau, the ANT-51 (as the su-2 was originally designated) was seen as a direct replacement for the poor Kharkov R-10 tactical attack bomber. First flown as the BB-1 in 1940, the aircraft was put into large-scale production thanks to its good armour, docile handling, adequate bomb load and reasonable performance. Initially powered by the Shvetsov M-87 radial engine, the aircraft was fitted with the more powerful M-88B in early 1941. It was at this time that a new Soviet designation system was also introduced, and the BB-1 became the su-2. Around 100 examples were in service units when the Germans invaded in June 1941, and production was dramatically increased in order to make good heavy combat losses. The evacuation of most aircraft factories in October 1941 resulted in severe disruption to su-2 production. Seen as an easy kill by Bf 109 pilots in the first year of the war, the su-2 remained in frontline service into late 1942 because there was simply nothing better to replace it.

SPECIFICATION:

ACCOMMODATION:
pilot and turret gunner

DIMENSIONS:
LENGTH: 33 ft 7.50 in (10.25 m)
WINGSPAN: 46 ft 11 in (14.30 m)
HEIGHT: 13 ft 10 in (3.94 m)

WEIGHTS:
EMPTY: 6459 lb (2930 kg)
MAX T/O: 9579 lb (4345 kg)

PERFORMANCE:
MAX SPEED: 283 mph (455 kmh)
RANGE: 528 miles (850 km)
POWERPLANT: Shvetsov M-88B
OUTPUT: 1000 hp (745 kW)

FIRST FLIGHT DATE:
August 1937 (ANT-51)

ARMAMENT:
four fixed shkas 7.62 mm
machine guns in wings and one
in dorsal turret; maximum
bomb/rocket load of 1323-lb
(600 kg) in bomb-bay and on
underwing racks

FEATURES:
Monoplane wing layout;
retractable undercarriage;
close-cowled radial engine;
dorsal turret

# Supermarine Spitfire (Merlin) UK

single-seat, single-engined monoplane fighter

The Spitfire was the only British fighter to remain in production throughout World War 2 – 22,500+ were produced in mark numbers ranging from 1 through to 24 – and its exploits are legendary. Designed by Reginald J Mitchell following his experiences with the RAF's Schneider Trophy winning Supermarine floatplanes, prototype Spitfire K5054 first took to the skies on 5 March 1936, powered by the Rolls-Royce Merlin 1 engine. However, due to production problems encountered with the fighter's revolutionary stressed-skin construction, it was to be another two-and-a-half years before the first Spitfire 1s entered service.

During its nine-year production life, the Spitfire's shape was to alter very little, but under the skin the story was very different. The power output of the Merlin was increased to allow the fighter to compete with new German types, with firstly the Mk v and then the Mk ix proving a match for the BF 109F/G and FW 190 at virtually all altitudes. The Spitfire also undertook photo-reconnaissance and fighter-bomber missions.

SPECIFICATION:

ACCOMMODATION:
pilot

DIMENSIONS:
LENGTH: 31 ft 1 in (9.47 m)
WINGSPAN: 36 ft 10 in (11.23 m)
HEIGHT: 12 ft 7.75 in (3.86 m)

WEIGHTS:
EMPTY: 6200 lb (2812 kg)
LOADED WEIGHT: 9500 lb (4309 kg)

PERFORMANCE:
MAX SPEED: 408 mph (657 kmh)
RANGE: 434 miles (698 km)
POWERPLANT: Rolls-Royce Merlin 61
OUTPUT: 1565 hp (1167 kW)

FIRST FLIGHT DATE:
5 March 1936

ARMAMENT:
two Hispano 20 mm cannon and four Browning 0.303-in machine guns in wings; maximum bomb load of 2000-lb (907 kg) on underwing racks

FEATURES:
Elliptical monoplane wing layout; rectractable landing gear; close-cowled inline engine; four-bladed propeller

# Supermarine Spitfire (Griffon) UK

single-seat, single-engined monoplane fighter

Griffon-powered Spitfires were amongst the most impressive piston-engined fighters of their time. The Spitfire Mk xɪv in particular was an awesome fighter to fly thanks to the generous levels of horsepower cranked out by its Griffon engine, which more than offset the mark's increased weight due to the strengthening of the fuselage in preparation for the fitment of the new powerplant. Only 957 production Mk xɪvs were built, with the type's finest hour coming in mid 1944 when its straight-line speed was used to counter the v1 menace during Air Defence Great Britain patrols over south-east England – the Spitfire xɪv could outpace all other frontline types. A considerable number of Griffon Spitfires were sent to units in the Far East in the final months of the war, although in the most part they arrived too late to see action. The photo-reconnaissance PR xɪx also saw service in the final weeks of the war as the first of 225 examples arrived in the frontline. Griffon Spitfires served with the RAF until the late 1950s.

SPECIFICATION:

**ACCOMMODATION:**
pilot

**DIMENSIONS:**
LENGTH: 31 ft 8 in (9.96 m)
WINGSPAN: 36 ft 10 in (11.23 m)
HEIGHT: 12 ft 8 in (3.86 m)

**WEIGHTS:**
EMPTY: 6600 lb (2994 kg)
MAX T/O: 9772 lb (4433 kg)

**PERFORMANCE:**
MAX SPEED: 448 mph (721 kmh)
RANGE: 460 miles (740 km)
POWERPLANT: Rolls-Royce Griffon 65
OUTPUT: 2050 hp (1528 kW)

**FIRST FLIGHT DATE:**
early 1943

**ARMAMENT:**
two Hispano 20 mm cannon and four Browning 0.303-in machine guns in wings; maximum bomb load of 500-lb (227 kg) on underwing racks

**FEATURES:**
Elliptical monoplane wings layout; rectractable landing gear; close-cowled inline engine; five-bladed propeller

# Taylorcraft O-57/L-2 Grasshopper USA

two-seat, single-engined high-wing light liaison aircraft

The third design in the triumvirate of civilian two-seaters trialled by the US Army in August 1941, the original Taylorcraft YO-57s were standard production Model Ds. All three aircraft were universally dubbed Grasshoppers, and similarly modified to improve crew visibility and airframe durability. An initial USAAC order for 336 O-57As was received by Taylorcraft, followed by 140 in 1942. By the time delivery of the second batch had commenced, the reclassification of aircraft of this type had taken place, resulting in all O-57/57As becoming L-2/2As. The two remaining batches of aircraft ordered comprised 490 L-2Bs optimised for field artillery spotting and 900 L-2Ms, which had cowled engines and wing spoilers. Taylorcraft was also involved in producing 253 engineless gliders based on the L-2 design. Designated ST-100s, these machines were used in the training of future frontline glider pilots. Many L-2s ended up on the US civilian register after the war, whilst other surplus Grasshoppers were supplied to air arms across the globe.

SPECIFICATION:

**ACCOMMODATION:**
pilot and observer/passenger in tandem

**DIMENSIONS:**
LENGTH: 22 ft 9 in (6.93 m)
WINGSPAN: 35 ft 5 in (10.79 m)
HEIGHT: 8 ft 0 in (2.44 m)

**WEIGHTS:**
EMPTY: 875 lb (397 kg)
MAX T/O: 1300 lb (590 kg)

**PERFORMANCE:**
MAX SPEED: 88 mph (142 kmh)
RANGE: 230 miles (370 km)
POWERPLANT: Continental O-170-3
OUTPUT: 65 hp (48 kW)

**FIRST FLIGHT DATE:**
1937

**FEATURES:**
High-wing layout; fixed landing gear; close-cowled engine; extensive cockpit glazing

# Tupolev TU-2 USSR

four-seat, twin-engined monoplane attack bomber

The TU-2 was developed by Tupolev as a successor to the PE-2. However, due to a protracted development and a slow production rate, the TU-2 never succeeded in fully replacing the Petlyakov bomber during World War 2. Designed in 1939-40 with the bureau designation ANT-58, the prototype first flew on 29 January 1941. Further pre-production development took place over the next 22 months until the first TU-2s reached the frontline in November 1942. Even then, these aircraft were far from being adequate replacements for the PE-2, and it was not until the definitive TU-2s entered service in early 1944 that the bomber made an impact on the Eastern Front. Only 1100 of the 2527 TU-2s built had been delivered by mid-1945, and the aircraft remained in service with communist air forces until 1961 – codenamed 'Bat' by NATO, it saw action in the Korean War. TU-2 sub-variants included the TU-2R reconnaissance platform, TU-10 general purpose bomber, TU-2U crew trainer, TU-1 heavy escort fighter, TU-2sh ground attack aircraft and the TU-2T torpedo-bomber.

SPECIFICATION:

ACCOMMODATION:
pilot, bomb aimer/rear cockpit gunner and dorsal and ventral gunners

DIMENSIONS:
LENGTH: 45 ft 3.5 in (13.80 m)
WINGSPAN: 61 ft 10.50 in (18.86 m)
HEIGHT: 14 ft 11 in (4.55 m)

WEIGHTS:
EMPTY: 18,200 lb (8255 kg)
MAX T/O: 28,219 lb (12,800 kg)

PERFORMANCE:
MAX SPEED: 342 mph (550 kmh)
RANGE: 1553 miles (2500 km)
POWERPLANT: two Shetsov Ash-82FNS
OUTPUT: 3700 hp (2760 kW)

FIRST FLIGHT DATE:
29 January 1941

ARMAMENT:
two fixed SHVAK 20/30 mm cannon in wing roots and single BS 12.7 mm machine guns in rear cockpit, dorsal and ventral positions; maximum bomb load of 6614-lb (3000 kg) in bomb-bay

FEATURES:
Monoplane wing layout; retractable undercarriage; two close-cowled radial engines; twin tail layout

# Vickers-Armstrongs Wellington  UK

six-seat, twin-engined monoplane bomber

Created in response to Air Ministry Specification
B 9/32, which called for an aircraft capable of
delivering a bomb load of 1000-lb and with a range
of 720 miles, the Wellington drew on Vickers'
experience with geodectic construction techniques
as used in its previous Wellesley bomber. The
prototype flew for the first time in June 1936, and
soon exceeded the specification requirements. Two
months later the Air Ministry placed an order for
180 Wellington Mk Is, and these began to reach
Bomber Command in October 1938. The aircraft
was the mainstay of the RAF's bomber efforts prior
to the arrival of the four-engined 'heavies' in 1941,
and a total of 21 British-based Bomber Command
units were equipped with Wellingtons in early 1942.
The aircraft remained in production until October
1945, by which time 11,462 had been built in 13
bomber, maritime patrol and training variants.
Having seen action across the globe against targets
on land and at sea, the Wellington saw more
peaceful service post-war in Flying Training
Command. The final examples were retired in 1953.

SPECIFICATION:

**ACCOMMODATION:**
pilot, navigator, bomb aimer,
radio operator, nose and tail
turret gunners

**DIMENSIONS:**
LENGTH: 60 ft 10 in (18.54 m)
WINGSPAN: 86 ft 2 in (26.26 m)
HEIGHT: 17 ft 5 in (5.31 m)

**WEIGHTS:**
EMPTY: 18,556 lb (8417 kg)
MAX T/O: 29,500 lb (13,381 kg)

**PERFORMANCE:**
MAX SPEED: 255 mph (410 kmh)
RANGE: 2200 miles (3540 km)
POWERPLANT: two Bristol
Hercules XIS
OUTPUT: 3000 hp (2236 kW)

**FIRST FLIGHT DATE:**
15 June 1936

**ARMAMENT:**
two Browning 0.303-in machine
guns in nose and tail turrets and
one in beam positions; maximum
bomb load of 4500-lb (2040 kg)
in bomb-bay

**FEATURES:**
Monoplane wing layout;
rectractable landing gear; two
close-cowled radial engines;
nose and tail turrets

# Vought F4U/FG-1 Corsair USA

single-seat, single-engined monoplane fighter

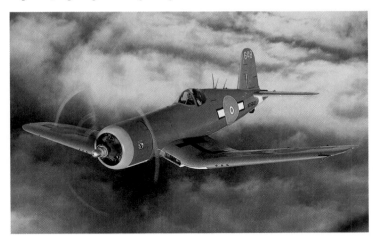

Designed as a lightweight fighter with the most powerful piston engine then available, Vought's xF4U-1 was ordered by the US Navy in June 1938. In order to harness the power of the Pratt & Whitney XR-2800 Double Wasp, one of the largest diameter propellers ever fitted to a fighter had to be used. Sufficient ground clearance for the propeller was achieved through the use of an inverted gull wing. Modifications incorporated into the design at this point following combat over Europe detrimentally affected the Corsair's handling.

No longer deemed suitable for carrier operations by the Navy, the aircraft made its combat debut with land-based Marine Corps units in 1943. The Fleet Air Arm also commenced operations with the Corsair that same year, but crucially from the decks of carriers. By mid-1944 Vought had rectified the handling problems, and the Corsair went to sea with the US Navy. It enjoyed a prosperous post-war career, with the final F4U-7 rolling off the production line in 1952. This aircraft was the 12,571st Corsair built.

SPECIFICATION:

**ACCOMMODATION:**
pilot

**DIMENSIONS:**
LENGTH: 32 ft 9.5 in (9.99 m)
WINGSPAN: 40 ft 11.75 in (12.49 m)
HEIGHT: 15 ft 0.25 in (4.58 m)

**WEIGHTS:**
EMPTY: 8873 lb (4025 kg)
MAX T/O: 13,846 lb (6280 kg)

**PERFORMANCE:**
MAX SPEED: 392 mph (631 kmh)
RANGE: 1562 miles (2514 km)
POWERPLANT: Pratt & Whitney
R-2800-8 Double Wasp
OUTPUT: 2000 hp (1491 kW)

**FIRST FLIGHT DATE:**
29 May 1940

**ARMAMENT:**
six Browning 0.50-in machine guns in wings; provision for eight rockets under wings or up to 2000-lb (907 kg) bombload under fuselage centre section

**FEATURES:**
Inverted gull-wing monoplane layout; retractable undercarriage; close-cowled radial engine; rectractable tailwheel; arrestor hook

# Vought os2u Kingfisher USA

two-seat, single-engined monoplane reconnaissance float- or landplane

Serving as the US Navy's standard scout-observation floatplane in World War 2, the Kingfisher was designed for either inshore use or for launching by catapult from capital ships. Developed in 1937, the Kingfisher embodied tried and tested techniques employed by the company in previous designs. The prototype xos2u-1 made its first flight in July 1938, and production examples reached the fleet in August 1940. The definitive Kingfisher in terms of numbers built was the os2u-3, 1006 of which were delivered up to 1942. The Naval Aircraft Factory also built 300 os2n-1 landplanes, which were used for training and coastal patrols.

Kingfishers saw action with the US Navy across the globe, being used for reconnaissance, anti-submarine patrols, air-sea rescue and artillery spotting. A small number of aircraft were also exported, with the largest customer being Britain. Exactly 100 were purchased under Lend-Lease, and the RAAF also received 18 examples. A total of 1519 Kingfishers were built.

SPECIFICATION:

ACCOMMODATION:
pilot and observer/gunner

DIMENSIONS:
LENGTH: 33 ft 10 in (10.31 m)
WINGSPAN: 35 ft 11 in (10.95 m)
HEIGHT: 15 ft 1.50 in (4.61 m)

WEIGHTS:
EMPTY: 4123 lb (1870 kg)
MAX T/O: 6000 lb (2722 kg)

PERFORMANCE:
MAX SPEED: 164 mph (264 kmh)
RANGE: 805 miles (1295 km)
POWERPLANT: Pratt & Whitney
R-985-50 Wasp Junior
OUTPUT: 450 hp (335 kW)

FIRST FLIGHT DATE:
20 July 1938

ARMAMENT:
one fixed Browning 0.30 in
machine gun in nose and one on
flexible mounting for observer;
maximum bomb load of 650-lb
(295 kg) on underwing racks

FEATURES:
monoplane wing layout; cowled
radial engine; single main float;
fixed outrigger floats

# Westland Lysander UK

two-seat, single-engined high-wing army co-operation aircraft

The first purpose-built army co-operation aircraft to enter service with the RAF, the Lysander filled a role previously performed by modified bombers. Constructed to Air Ministry Specification A 39/34, the prototype, designated P.8 by Westland, made its first flight on 15 June 1936. Within three months an order had been placed for 144 aircraft, and the first unit re-equipped with the aircraft in June 1938. By 1939 production was in full swing, the RAF receiving 66 airframes. The type first saw action in France with the British Expeditionary Force in May 1940, and the true vulnerability of the type soon came to the fore. The Lysander was quickly relegated to second-line duties, and it was whilst undertaking tasks that had never previously been thought of for the aircraft that the type came into its own. Its role with the clandestine Special Duties squadrons is the stuff of legend, the aircraft proving well suited to performing supply drops and transporting agents into and out of occupied Europe under the cover of darkness. Some 1650 Lysanders were built, including 225 in Canada.

SPECIFICATION:

**ACCOMMODATION:**
pilot and passenger/observer in tandem

**DIMENSIONS:**
LENGTH: 30 ft 6 in (9.30 m)
WINGSPAN: 50 ft 0 in (15.24 m)
HEIGHT: 14 ft 6 in (4.42 m)

**WEIGHTS:**
EMPTY: 4365 lb (1980 kg)
MAX T/O: 6318 lb (2866 kg)

**PERFORMANCE:**
MAX SPEED: 212 mph (341 kmh)
RANGE: 600 miles (966 km)
POWERPLANT: Bristol Mercury XX or XXX
OUTPUT: 870 hp (649 kW)

**FIRST FLIGHT DATE:**
15 June 1936

**ARMAMENT:**
two fixed Browning 0.30 in machine guns in upper wheel spats and one or two on flexible mounting for observer; maximum bomb load of 500-lb (227 kg) on stub wings and fuselage racks

**FEATURES:**
High-wing; tandem cockpits; spatted landing gear; v-shaped wing bracing; close-cowled radial engine

# Yakovlev Yak-3U USSR

single-seat, single-engined monoplane fighter

The second Yakovlev aircraft to be designated the Yak-3 (the first was abandoned in the autumn of 1941 due to poor engine reliability and a shortage of suitable building materials), this machine was built to fulfil a requirement for an agile fighter capable of achieving its maximum performance at low altitude. By meeting these criteria, the fighter allowed the Soviets to attain air superiority over the battlefield – something that the Luftwaffe had enjoyed for much of the war on the Eastern Front. Utilising a modified Yak-1M fitted with a smaller wing, the prototypes completed their service trials on October 1943, by which time a pre-series run of aircraft had been put into production. The Yak-3 was not officially cleared for production until June 1944, and the small number of regiments which re-equipped with the fighter soon proved its superiority in aerial combat. The Yak-3 was so dominant in combat that the Luftwaffe ordered its fighter pilots to avoid engaging the fighter below 16,000 ft. The Yak-3 remained in production until 1946, by which time 4848 had been built.

## SPECIFICATION:

**ACCOMMODATION:**
pilot

**DIMENSIONS:**
LENGTH: 27 ft 10.25 in (8.49 m)
WINGSPAN: 30 ft 2.25 in (9.20 m)
HEIGHT: 7 ft 11.25 in (2.42 m)

**WEIGHTS:**
EMPTY: 4641 lb (2105 kg)
MAX T/O: 5864 lb (2660 kg)

**PERFORMANCE:**
MAX SPEED: 407 mph (655 kmh)
RANGE: 559 miles (900 km)
POWERPLANT: Klimov M-105PF
OUTPUT: 1650 hp (1230 kW)

**FIRST FLIGHT DATE:**
late 1942

**ARMAMENT:**
one ShVAK 20 mm cannon in propeller hub and two BS 12.7 mm machine guns in upper cowling

**FEATURES:**
Monoplane layout; close-cowled inline engine; retractable undercarriage; three-bladed propeller; bubble canopy; radiator intake

# Yakovlev Yak-9U USSR

single-seat, single-engined monoplane fighter

The original Yak-9 appeared in frontline service in late 1942, the aircraft being a lightweight version of the Yak-7. By mid-1944 the Yak-9 outnumbered all other fighters on the Eastern Front, with a handful of variants fulfilling long-range interception, fighter-bomber and close-support missions. The second generation Yak-9U/P started development in late 1942, when a standard airframe had its Klimov M-105 engine replaced by the more powerful M-107 powerplant from the same manufacturer.

Aerodynamic improvements were also made to the fuselage, and plywood skinning replaced with light alloy. Designated the Yak-9U, the new fighter reached frontline units near war's end. Further development of the Yak-9 continued immediately post-war, with the cannon-armed Yak-9P being flown not only by Soviet units, but also by a number of other communist-bloc air forces, including North Korea. Production finally ceased in 1947 after 3900 Yak-9U/PS (out of an overall total of 16,769 Yak-9s built) had been delivered.

SPECIFICATION:

ACCOMMODATION:
pilot

DIMENSIONS:
LENGTH: 28 ft 0.25 in (8.55 m)
WINGSPAN: 31 ft 11.5 in (9.74 m)
HEIGHT: 9 ft 10 in (3.00 m)

WEIGHTS:
EMPTY: 5100 lb (2313 kg)
LOADED WEIGHT: 6988 lb (3170 kg)

PERFORMANCE:
MAX SPEED: 374 mph (602 kmh)
RANGE: 870 miles (1400 km)
POWERPLANT: Klimov M-105PF-3
OUTPUT: 1360 hp (1014 kW)

FIRST FLIGHT DATE:
Late December 1942

ARMAMENT:
one ShVAK 20 mm cannon in propeller hub and two BS 12.7 mm machine guns in upper cowling; maximum bomb load of 441-lb (200 kg) on underwing racks

FEATURES:
Monoplane layout; close-cowled inline engine; retractable undercarriage; three-bladed propeller; bubble canopy; radiator intake

# Yokosuka D4Y Suisei JAPAN

two-seat, single-engined monoplane reconnaissance/dive-bomber

In 1938 the Imperial Japanese Navy's Air Technical Arsenal at Yokosuka was told to design a single-engined, carrier-based bomber. An aircraft of this type was needed for the forthcoming campaign in the Pacific, and the first D4Y prototype flew in December 1941. Development problems with the aircraft's Aichi Atsuta engine (licence-built Daimler-Benz DB 601A) resulted in early D4YS being powered by the DB 600G. Testing revealed wing flutter problems with the design, which delayed production of the Suisei (Comet) dive-bomber. Indeed, the first aircraft to reach the fleet in 1942 were restricted to reconnaissance duties. Strengthened wings spars and dive brakes turned the D4Y1 into a dive-bomber, and from March 1943 it was cleared for this role. Within a year 500 had entered service, and the type's vulnerability was soon revealed. The troublesome Atsuta was replaced by the Mitsubishi Kinsei radial engine in the D4Y3, and this version was used as a Kamikaze bomber from October 1944. A vast number of the 2038 Suiseis built were lost in action.

SPECIFICATION:

ACCOMMODATION:
pilot and gunner in tandem

DIMENSIONS:
LENGTH: 33 ft 6.50 in (10.22 m)
WINGSPAN: 37 ft 8.75 in (11.50 m)
HEIGHT: 12 ft 3.25 in (3.74 m)

WEIGHTS:
EMPTY: 5379 lb (2440 kg)
LOADED WEIGHT: 9370 lb (4250 kg)

PERFORMANCE:
MAX SPEED: 343 mph (552 kmh)
RANGE: 910 miles (1465 km)
POWERPLANT: Aichi AE1A Atsuta 12
OUTPUT: 1200 hp (895 kW)

FIRST FLIGHT DATE:
December 1941

ARMAMENT:
two fixed Type 97 machine guns in nose and one Type 1 7.92 mm machine gun on flexible mount in rear cockpit; maximum bomb load of 1234-lb (560 kg) in semi-recessed bomb-bay

FEATURES:
Monoplane layout; close-cowled inline engine; retractable undercarriage; three-bladed propeller; long canopy

# Post-War Aircraft

# Aermacchi MB-326 ITALY

single/two-seat, single-engined basic/advanced trainer and ground attack aircraft

The MB-326 was the most successful creation of the Italian Aermacchi company, being built into the 1980s. The first of two prototypes flew in December 1957, the aircraft relying on the Rolls-Royce Viper turbojet for motive power. Fifteen pre-production aircraft were ordered by the *Aeronautica Militare Italiana*, and a further 85 production standard jets were procured soon after – the first of these entered service in February 1962. Suitable for all stages of military jet flying training, the MB-326 found a ready market on a global stage as air forces made the transition from World War 2 vintage piston-engined trainers to jet aircraft which boasted a performance comparable to the types then in frontline service. Aside from those aircraft supplied by Aermacchi to customers in Africa and South America, licence-built MB-326s were also produced in Australia, South Africa and Brazil. Combined production totalled 761 aircraft, with the last MB-326 being built by EMBRAER in February 1983. Single- and two-seat variants were capable of carrying weapons on six underwing hardpoints.

SPECIFICATION:

ACCOMMODATION:
two pilots in tandem, or one pilot (ground attack variant)

DIMENSIONS:
LENGTH: 34 ft 11 in (10.64 m)
WINGSPAN: 35 ft 7.25 in (10.85 m)
HEIGHT: 12 ft 2.50 in (3.72 m)

WEIGHTS:
EMPTY: 5640 lb (2558 kg)
MAX T/O: 11,500 lb (5216 kg)

PERFORMANCE:
MAX SPEED: 539 mph (867 kmh)
RANGE: 1150 miles (1850 km)
POWERPLANT: Rolls-Royce Viper 20 Mk 540
OUTPUT: 3410 lb st (15.17 kN)

FIRST FLIGHT DATE:
10 December 1957

ARMAMENT:
provision for up to 4000-lb (1815 kg) of bombs/rockets/gun pods on six underwing stores pylons

FEATURES:
Straight-wing layout; tandem cockpits; wingtip tanks; extensive cockpit glazing; tricycle landing gear; wing root engine air intakes

# Aero L-29 Delfin CZECH REPUBLIC

two-seat, single-engined basic trainer

A contemporary of the MB-326, the L-29 Delfin (Dolphin) was designed by Aero to replace piston-engined trainers then in service with the Czechoslovakian air force. Of conventional straight wing layout, the prototype XL-29 flew for the first time in April 1959, and was duly ordered into pre-production in late 1960 following the flight of a second prototype. A competition held the following year saw the L-29 chosen over the PZL Mielec TS-11 Iskra and Yakovlev Yak-30 as the standard trainer for all Warsaw Pact air forces, the aircraft's simple, robust design and docile handling characteristics being cited as significant factors in its favour. The first production L-29s entered service in 1963, and by the time Aero built its last aircraft in 1974, no fewer than 3665 had been constructed. Over 2000 of these were supplied to the former Soviet Union, whilst hundreds of others joined air forces in eastern Europe, Africa and South-east Asia. Today, a handful of countries still operate the venerable Delfin in the tuitional role.

## SPECIFICATION:

**ACCOMMODATION:**
two pilots in tandem

**DIMENSIONS:**
LENGTH: 35 ft 5.50 in (10.81 m)
WINGSPAN: 33 ft 9 in (10.29 m)
HEIGHT: 10 ft 3 in (3.13 m)

**WEIGHTS:**
EMPTY: 5027 lb (2280 kg)
MAX T/O: 7231 lb (3280 kg)

**PERFORMANCE:**
MAX SPEED: 382 mph (615 kmh)
RANGE: 397 miles (640 km)
POWERPLANT: Motorlet M 701c
OUTPUT: 1962 lb st (8.73 kN)

**FIRST FLIGHT DATE:**
5 April 1959

**ARMAMENT:**
provision for up to 440-lb (200 kg) of bombs/rockets/ gun pods on two underwing stores pylons

**FEATURES:**
Straight-wing layout; tandem cockpits; wing root engine intakes; extensive cockpit glazing; tricycle landing gear; T-tail

# Aero L-39 Albatros  CZECH REPUBLIC

two-seat, single-engined basic trainer

Aero's L-39 was built as the natural successor to the L-29, work starting on the Albatros in 1966, with representatives from the Soviet air forces (which would become the type's biggest customer) influencing the design. The key to the aircraft's superiority over the Delfin was the adoption of the AI-25 turbofan engine, which boasted virtually double the power of the L-29's Motorlet turbojet. It soon became obvious that the Albatros would enjoy a significantly improved maximum speed, a better rate of climb and the ability to carry weapons. Although the first prototype flew in November 1968, approval for production was not given until 1972, when the Soviet, Czech and East German air forces chose the L-39 to replace the L-29. Service trials were conducted the following year, and production aircraft reached the *Ceskoslovenské Letectvo* in 1974. Since then 2900+ have entered service, the training variants (C, TC and V) being joined by weapons-capable L-39s (ZA and ZO). The Albatros is still being built in modernised L-59/159 form with an uprated powerplant and Western avionics.

## SPECIFICATION:

**ACCOMMODATION:**
two pilots in tandem

**DIMENSIONS:**
LENGTH: 39 ft 9 in (12.11 m)
WINGSPAN: 29 ft 10.75 in (9.11 m)
HEIGHT: 14 ft 4.25 in (4.38 m)

**WEIGHTS:**
EMPTY: 6283 lb (2850 kg)
MAX T/O: 9480 lb (4300 kg)

**PERFORMANCE:**
MAX SPEED: 528 mph (844.80 kmh)
RANGE: 930 miles (1500 km) with full tip tanks
POWERPLANT: ZMDB Progress (Ivchenyenko) AI-25TL
OUTPUT: 3792 lb st (16.87 kN)

**FIRST FLIGHT DATE:**
4 November 1968

**ARMAMENT:**
provision for up to 2205-lb (1000 kg) of bombs/rockets/gun pods on underwing/centreline stores pylons

**FEATURES:**
Straight-wing layout; tandem cockpits; engine intakes on fuselage; extensive cockpit glazing; tricycle landing gear

# Aerospace CT-4 Airtrainer NEW ZEALAND

two-seat, single-engined basic trainer

The Airtrainer can trace its lineage to 1953 when a compact two-seat aircraft won the Light Aircraft Design Competition organised by the British Royal Aero Club. Put into production in Australia by Victa in 1960. A total of 170 Airtourers were built before Aero Engine Services Ltd (AESL) of New Zealand acquired the company in 1968. Originally constructed in wood, the aircraft was re-engineered in metal and developed into the four-seat Aircruiser, which formed the basis of the military-optimised Airtrainer. Stressed to +6/-3 G, the Airtrainer was ordered by the RAAF as the CT-4A to the tune of 37 airframes in 1972. Some 24 were purchased by the Thai Air Force (plus six more in 1992) and the RNZAF ordered 19 CT-4Bs, the latter variant boasting a higher gross weight – all were built by New Zealand Aerospace Industries, following the merger of AESL with Air Parts in 1973. Nicknamed the 'Plastic Parrot' in Australian service, the CT-4 gave sterling service in the primary training role at No 1 Flying Training School at Point Cook until retired in 1992.

SPECIFICATION:

ACCOMMODATION:
two pilots side-by-side

DIMENSIONS:
LENGTH: 23 ft 5.50 in (7.15 m)
WINGSPAN: 26 ft 0 in (7.92 m)
HEIGHT: 8 ft 6 in (2.59 m)

WEIGHTS:
EMPTY: 1460 lb (662 kg)
MAX T/O: 2400 lb (1089 kg)

PERFORMANCE:
MAX SPEED: 265 mph (426 kmh)
RANGE: 808 miles (1300 km)
POWERPLANT: Rolls-Royce
(Continental) IO-360-H
OUTPUT: 210 hp (157 kW)

FIRST FLIGHT DATE:
23 February 1972 (CT-4)

FEATURES:
Straight-wing layout; side-by-side seating; extensive cockpit glazing; fixed tricycle landing gear; two-bladed propeller

# Antonov An-2 USSR

12-seat, single-engined biplane utility aircraft

One of the last biplane designs in production, the venerable An-2 is still in widespread use with air forces worldwide. More than 18,000 'Colts' (its NATO reporting) have been built since 1947, with the bulk of these originating from the PZL Mielec factory in Poland. Indeed, the Antonov plant in Kiev built a 'mere' 5000 before production ceased in 1965. Licence production also saw 1500 completed as Harbin Y-5s in China between 1957 and the early 1970s. The aircraft's distinctively dated appearance was treated with derision in the West when the first production An-2s were reported. However, the Antonov OKB design team wanted an aircraft that created significant drag so as to allow it to boast excellent short take-off and landing characteristics. The simple construction techniques embodied in the design also meant that it was easy to maintain in the field and capable of operating from rugged terrain. Although built to fulfil a Ministry of Agriculture and Forestry requirement, the An-2 found employment in the Soviet air forces as a paratroop transport, glider tug and navigation trainer.

SPECIFICATION:

ACCOMMODATION:
two pilots and ten passengers

DIMENSIONS:
LENGTH: 42 ft 6 in (12.95 m)
WINGSPAN: 59 ft 8.50 in (18.18 m)
HEIGHT: 13 ft 9.25 in (4.20 m)

WEIGHTS:
EMPTY: 7605 lb (3450 kg)
MAX T/O: 12,125 lb (5500 kg)

PERFORMANCE:
MAX SPEED: 157 mph (253 kmh)
RANGE: 562 miles (905 km)
POWERPLANT: Shvetsov Ash-62M
or PZL Kalisz Asz-621R (Polish
licence-built Ash-62)
OUTPUT: 1000 hp (746 kW)

FIRST FLIGHT DATE:
31 August 1947

FEATURES:
Biplane wing layout; fixed
landing gear; four-bladed
propeller; close-cowled
radial engine

# Antonov An-22 Antei  USSR

35-seat, four-engined strategic freight aircraft

The largest turboprop-powered aircraft built to date, the An-22 was designed by Antonov in response to a Soviet military requirement for a strategic heavylift freighter. When it made its first flight on 27 February 1965, the An-22 was the world's largest aircraft. Powered by four Kuznetsov NK-12MA turboprop engines identical to those fitted to the Tu-95/-142 'Bear' family of bombers, the An-22 entered service with the Soviet air forces in 1971. By then pre-production aircraft had set 14 payload to height records during its proving test flights. By the time production was halted three years later, 66 An-22s had been built, of which exactly half went into service with the Soviet air forces. The remaining aircraft were supplied to Aeroflot, which used them for strategic support in Siberia. Until the introduction of the An-124 in the mid 1980s, the An-22 was the only Soviet transport capable of carrying main battle tanks and mobile missile systems. A handful of An-22s remain in service today, with most of these flown by civilian operators in the Ukraine and Russia.

SPECIFICATION:

**ACCOMMODATION:**
pilot, co-pilot, navigator, flight engineer, communications specialist and 29 passengers

**DIMENSIONS:**
LENGTH: 77 ft 3 in (25.53 m)
WINGSPAN: 95 ft 10 in (29.20 m)
HEIGHT: 27 ft 4 in (8.32 m)

**WEIGHTS:**
EMPTY: 251,325 lb (114,000 kg)
MAX T/O: 551,160 lb (250,000 kg)

**PERFORMANCE:**
MAX SPEED: 460 mph (740 kmh)
RANGE: 6804 miles (10,950 km)
POWERPLANT: four Kuznetsov (Kuibyshev) NK-12MAs
OUTPUT: 60,000 shp (44,740 kW)

**FIRST FLIGHT DATE:**
27 February 1965

**FEATURES:**
High-wing layout; four turboprop engines; twin tail layout; contra-rotating propellers; rear-loading ramp

# Armstrong Whitworth Argosy UK

91-seat, four-engined cargo aircraft

The Argosy was developed principally for airline cargo services, but enjoyed more success in a military guise for the RAF. Indeed, just 17 Argosies were sold to civilian operators in the early 1960s. Military interest in the aircraft resulted in 56 Argosy C 1s being ordered by the RAF for use with Transport Command, whose crews dubbed them 'Whistling Wheelbarrows'. The Argosy was known for being rather underpowered for many of the tasks demanded of it, and a standing joke amongst those that flew it in the RAF was that it could either carry 20,000 lbs of cargo for five miles or 5 lbs for 2000 miles! The C 1 variant entered service in March 1962, and although proving successful, the reduction in Britain's military presence overseas and budget cuts in the early 1970s saw the premature demise of the Argosy barely a decade after the type had entered service. The RAF's transport needs would be fulfilled by the Hercules instead. Most airframes were sold for scrap, although a small number saw further use with civilian operators after their demilitarisation.

SPECIFICATION:

**ACCOMMODATION:**
pilot and co-pilot and up to 89 passengers

**DIMENSIONS:**
LENGTH: 86 ft 9 in (26.44 m)
WINGSPAN: 115 ft 0 in (35.05 m)
HEIGHT: 29 ft 3 in (8.91 m)

**WEIGHTS:**
EMPTY: 50,000 lb (22,680 kg)
MAX T/O: 88,000 lb (39,915 kg)

**PERFORMANCE:**
MAX SPEED: 282 mph (455 kmh)
RANGE: 1780 miles (2865 km)
POWERPLANT: four Rolls-Royce Dart 526s
OUTPUT: 8920 shp (6654.32 kW)

**FIRST FLIGHT DATE:**
4 March 1961 (Argosy C 1)

**FEATURES:**
High-wing layout; four turboprop engines; twin boom/tail layout; rear-loading ramp

# Auster AOP 6/9/11 UK

two-seat, single-engined high-wing liaison/observation aircraft

Derived from the observation/liaison family of light aircraft built by British Taylorcraft in World War 2, the AOP 6/9/11 were improved variants of the wartime design. The AOP (Air Observation Post) Mk 6 differed from its predecessors in having a Gipsy Major engine fitted in place of the Lycoming, a larger fuel capacity and longer undercarriage legs. Its short field performance was also improved thanks to the adoption of auxiliary aerofoil flaps on the trailing edge of the wing. Production of the AOP 6 commenced in 1946, and 312 were built for the RAF – 77 dual-trainer T 7s were also delivered. The AOP 6 saw action in Korea and Malaya during the 1950s.

Twelve months after the last AOP 6 entered RAF service, Auster completed the first flight of the replacement AOP 9. This variant was the only member of the AOP family built specifically for military use, rather than having been a development of a civil design. The first AOP 9 was delivered to the RAF in 1955, and the aircraft remained in service into the late 1960s.

SPECIFICATION:

ACCOMMODATION:
pilot and observer/passenger in tandem

DIMENSIONS:
LENGTH: 23 ft 8.5 in (7.26 m)
WINGSPAN: 36 ft 5 in (11.12 m)
HEIGHT: 8 ft 5 in (2.59 m)

WEIGHTS:
EMPTY: 1461 lb (662 kg)
MAX T/O: 2130 lb (966 kg)

PERFORMANCE:
MAX SPEED: 127 mph (203 kmh)
RANGE: 246 miles (393 km)
POWERPLANT: de Havilland Gipsy Major VII (AOP 6), Blackburn Cirrus Bombardier 203 (AOP 9) and Lycoming O-360-A1D
OUTPUT: 145 hp (108.17 kW), 180 hp (134.28 kW) and 160 hp (119.36 kW) respectively

FIRST FLIGHT DATE:
1 May 1945 (AOP 6) and 19 March 1954 (AOP 9)

FEATURES:
High-wing layout; single wing bracing strut; fixed under-carriage; inline engine; extensive cockpit glazing

# Avro Lincoln UK

seven-seat, four-engined long-range bomber

Built in response to the Air Ministry's Specification B 14/43 for a long-range bomber to replace the Lancaster, the Lincoln was not as technologically advanced as Boeing's B-29 of several years earlier. However, it was an effective and cheap replacement for the Lancaster in a cash-strapped, post-war RAF. Major changes which set the Lincoln apart from the Lancaster included increased span wings of higher aspect ratio, permitting operation at greater altitudes with heavier bomb loads, high-altitude Merlin engines and four-bladed propellers. First flown on 9 June 1944, the Lincoln was rushed into production and reached the frontline in July 1945. Large orders were cancelled following VJ-Day, limiting production to 528 aircraft in Britain and 54 in Australia. A total of 20 Bomber Command units received Lincoln B I/II/IVs, and they remained in service until replaced by Boeing Washingtons in 1954. Veterans of combat against terrorists in Malaya and the Mau-Mau in Kenya, Lincolns flew with RAF Signals Command until finally retired in 1963.

## SPECIFICATION:

**ACCOMMODATION:**
pilot, flight engineer, navigator, bomb aimer/nose gunner, wireless operator, dorsal and tail turret gunners

**DIMENSIONS:**
LENGTH: 78 ft 3.50 in (23.85 m)
WINGSPAN: 120 ft 0 in (36.58 m)
HEIGHT: 17 ft 3.50 in (5.26 m)

**WEIGHTS:**
EMPTY: 44,188 lb (20,044 kg)
MAX T/O: 82,000 lb (37,194 kg)

**PERFORMANCE:**
MAX SPEED: 295 mph (475 kmh)
RANGE: 2250 miles (3620 km)
POWERPLANT: four Rolls-Royce Merlin 85s
OUTPUT: 7000 hp (5220 kW)

**FIRST FLIGHT DATE:**
9 June 1944

**ARMAMENT:**
two Browning 0.50-in machine guns in nose/tail turrets, two Hispano 20 mm cannon in dorsal turret; 14,000-lb (6350 kg) of bombs in bomb-bay

**FEATURES:**
Monoplane wing layout; four engines fitted with four-bladed propellers; twin tail layout; three gun turrets

# Avro Shackleton UK

11-seat, four-engined long-range maritime patrol/airborne early warning aircraft

The Shackleton was built as the RAF's first dedicated maritime patrol aircraft, examples entering service with Coastal Command in February 1951. The MR 1 utilised the Lincoln's mainplane and undercarriage, married to an all-new fuselage. A total of 77 MR 1s were delivered to the RAF, followed by 62 MR 2s from 1952, the latter variant boasting a longer nose and 'dustbin' radar. The final new-build version was the MR 3 of 1955, which had a tricycle undercarriage and wingtip tanks – the RAF received 34 and the South African Air Force eight. Just as the maritime patrol Shackleton was nearing the end of its career in the late 1960s, the RAF converted 12 surplus MR 2s into AEW 2 configuration through the fitment of APS-20F(I) radar into the aircraft's fuselage. Although built as a stop-gap measure, the final AEW 2 was not replaced until 1991! Converted between 1971-74, all 12 AEW 2s served exclusively with No 8 Sqn at RAF Lossiemouth, flying missions out over the North Sea, Arctic Ocean and western Atlantic that could last up to 15 hours.

SPECIFICATION:

**ACCOMMODATION:**
pilot and co-pilot, engineer and eight tactical operators/fighter controllers

**DIMENSIONS:**
LENGTH: 87 ft 4 in (26.62 m)
WINGSPAN: 120 ft 0 in (36.58 m)
HEIGHT: 16 ft 9 in (5.10 m)

**WEIGHTS:**
EMPTY: 57,000 lb (25,855 kg)
MAX T/O: 98,000 lb (44,452 kg)

**PERFORMANCE:**
MAX SPEED: 273 mph (439 kmh)
RANGE: 3050 miles (4908 km)
POWERPLANT: four Rolls-Royce Griffon 57As
OUTPUT: 9820 hp (7324 kW)

**FIRST FLIGHT DATE:**
9 March 1949 (MR 1) and 30 September 1971 (AEW 2)

**ARMAMENT:**
two 20 mm cannon in nose and dorsal turrets (MR 1/2); up to 10,000-lb (4540 kg) of bombs/depth charges/torpedoes in weapons bay (MR 1/2)

**FEATURES:**
Monoplane wing layout; four engines fitted with contra-rotating propellers; twin tail layout

# Avro York UK

29-seat, four-engined long-range transport aircraft

Designed and first flown in 1942, the Avro York did not enter large-scale service with RAF Transport Command until after World War 2. This was primarily because the British government had reached an agreement with its US counterparts that its aircraft industry would concentrate on building fighters and bombers during the war, leaving the development and construction of transports to the Americans. This meant that Avro was occupied producing Lancasters, and only a handful of Yorks made it into RAF service prior to VE-Day. Designed to Specification C 1/42, the York used the Lancaster's wing, undercarriage and engines, combined with a new fuselage that had twice the cubic capacity of the Bomber Command stalwart. The first production Yorks joined No 24 Sqn in May 1944, and by 1948 seven squadrons were flying the aircraft with Transport Command. All of these units participated in the Berlin Airlift of that same year. The 253rd, and last, York was delivered to the RAF in April 1948, the aircraft being replaced by the Hastings in the 1950s.

SPECIFICATION:

ACCOMMODATION:
pilot, co-pilot, flight engineer, navigator/wireless operator and crew chief

DIMENSIONS:
LENGTH: 78 ft 6 in (23.95 m)
WINGSPAN: 102 ft 0 in (31.10 m)
HEIGHT: 16 ft 6 in (5.05 m)

WEIGHTS:
EMPTY: 42,040 lb (19,069 kg)
MAX T/O: 68,597 lb (31,115 kg)

PERFORMANCE:
MAX SPEED: 298 mph (477 kmh)
RANGE: 2700 miles (4320 km)
POWERPLANT: four Rolls-Royce Merlin XXS
OUTPUT: 3840 hp (2863 kW)

FIRST FLIGHT DATE:
5 July 1942

FEATURES:
Monoplane, high-wing layout; four close-cowled inline engines; three-fin tail layout

# Avro Vulcan UK

five-seat, four-engined bomber

One of three jet bombers that formed the RAF's
V-Force in the early years of the Cold War, the
Vulcan was perhaps the best of the trio. Designed
as the Avro 698, the aircraft possessed fighter-like
manoeuvrability at low level despite its size. First
flown in August 1952, the Vulcan entered service in
B 1 form in February 1957. Production examples
differed from the Avro 698 in having a kinked and
cambered wing leading edge and more powerful
Olympus 101 engines. Further improvements were
introduced with the B 2, which was optimised for
high altitude performance with thinner wings of
greater span and area, as well as 17,000 lb Olympus
201 engines. Most were equipped to carry the Blue
Steel stand-off missile, but in 1966 around 50
Vulcans were redeployed in the tactical low-level
bombing role after the nuclear mission was taken
over by the Royal Navy's Polaris submarine force.
Three B 2s saw combat in May-June 1982 during
the Falklands War, and the last Vulcans in
operational service were used as aerial tankers
until retired on 1 April 1984.

SPECIFICATION:

**ACCOMMODATION:**
pilot, co-pilot, tactical navigator,
radar operator, air electronics
operator

**DIMENSIONS:**
LENGTH: 105 ft 6 in (32.15 m)
WINGSPAN: 111 ft 0 in (33.83 m)
HEIGHT: 27 ft 2 in (8.26 m)

**WEIGHTS:**
EMPTY: not disclosed
MAX T/O: approximately
250,000 lb (113,400 kg)

**PERFORMANCE:**
MAX SPEED: 640 mph (1030 kmh)
RANGE: 4600 miles (7400 km)
POWERPLANT: four Rolls-Royce
Olympus 301s
OUTPUT: 80,000 lb st (358 kN)

**FIRST FLIGHT DATE:**
30 August 1952

**ARMAMENT:**
up to 21,000-lb (9525 kg) of
bombs/missiles in internal
bomb-bay

**FEATURES:**
Monoplane, triangular wing
layout; wing root engine intakes;
no horizontal tail surfaces

# Avro Canada CF-100 UK

two-seat, twin-engined fighter

The first combat aircraft of all-Canadian design, the CF-100 was as an all-weather long-range fighter. Work commenced on the aircraft in 1946 when the RCAF realised that there was no British interceptor in the offing that fulfilled its unique demands for a jet nightfighter that could operate from Arctic airstrips. The newly formed Avro Canada design team rose to the challenge, and their Avon powered prototype flew in January 1950. By the time the CF-100 Mk 3 reached frontline units in September 1952, the aircraft had replaced its Avons with locally-built Orenda 8 engines. A total of 70 Mk 3s were built, these featuring Hughes APG-33 radar and eight Browning 0.50-cal machine guns in a ventral pack. Production was cut short to make way for the Mk 4, which featured Orenda 9s, a target interception system centred on the APG-40 radar and unguided rockets in wingtip pods and a ventral pack, the latter being interchangeable with the gun pack. The final variant produced was the Mk 5, of which 329 were produced – Belgium also bought 53 Mk 5s.

## SPECIFICATION:

**ACCOMMODATION:**
pilot and navigator

**DIMENSIONS:**
LENGTH: 54 ft 1 in (16.50 m)
WINGSPAN: 58 ft 0 in (17.7 m)
HEIGHT: 15 ft 7 in (4.72 m)

**WEIGHTS:**
EMPTY: 23,100 lb (10,478 kg)
MAX T/O: 37,000 lb (16,783 kg)

**PERFORMANCE:**
MAX SPEED: 650 mph (1046 kmh)
RANGE: 2000 miles (3200 km)
POWERPLANT: two Orenda 11s
OUTPUT: 14,550 lb st (64.5 kN)

**FIRST FLIGHT DATE:**
19 January 1950

**ARMAMENT:**
eight Browning 0.50-in machine guns or four 30 mm cannon in ventral pack, and Mighty Mouse 2.75-in rockets in wingtip pods and/or ventral pack

**FEATURES:**
Monoplane, unswept wing layout; engines either side of fuselage; tricycle undercarriage

# BAC Jet Provost UK

two-seat, single-engined basic jet trainer

Originally developed by Percival as a low cost jet-powered derivative of its piston-engined Provost, the Jet Provost wound up being a virtually new aircraft. Built as a private venture trainer at a time when the RAF used converted frontline jet types for pilot conversion, the design garnered support from the Air Force, which appreciated the Jet Provost's purpose-built, side-by-side layout. A batch of nine T 1s was purchased in 1955, and these were put to work on a new training syllabus with No 2 Flying Training School. Due to the success enjoyed with these aircraft, the RAF committed to the Jet Provost in June 1959, ordering 201 in T 3 form – these machines differed from the T 1s in having Martin-Baker ejection seats, tip tanks, updated avionics and a clear-view canopy. A follow on order for the re-engined T 4 was placed in November 1961, and 198 were built up to 1964. The final variant to enter RAF service was the T 5, which had cockpit pressurisation, a redesigned windscreen, sliding canopy and a longer nose – 110 were built from 1967.

## SPECIFCATION:

**ACCOMMODATION:**
two pilots seated side-by-side

**DIMENSIONS:**
LENGTH: 33 ft 7.5 in (10.25 m)
WINGSPAN: 35 ft 4 in (10.77 m)
HEIGHT: 10 ft 2 in (3.10 m)

**WEIGHTS:**
EMPTY: 4888 lb (2271 kg)
MAX T/O: 9200 lb (4173 kg)

**PERFORMANCE:**
MAX SPEED: 440 mph (708 kmh)
RANGE: 901 miles (1450 km)
POWERPLANT: Rolls-Royce Viper Mk 102
OUTPUT: 1750 lb st (7.80 kN)

**FIRST FLIGHT DATE:**
26 June 1954

**FEATURES:**
Straight-wing layout; side-by-side cockpit seating; extensive cockpit glazing; tricycle landing gear; wing root engine intakes

# BAC Strikemaster UK

two-seat, single-engined trainer/light strike jet aircraft

Built as a result of the export success enjoyed by
the basic Jet Provost trainer, the Strikemaster could
perform both the tuitional role and light attack
duties thanks to an uprated Viper engine, increased
stores hardpoints (eight) beneath the wings,
strengthened airframe and comprehensive
communications and navigation equipment. Based
on the pressurised T 5, and designated the BAC 167
by its manufacturer, the Strikemaster also featured
uprated Martin-Baker ejection seats, a revised fuel
layout and short landing gear designed to be more
suitable for rough field operations. Production of
the Mk 80 series Strikemaster commenced in 1968,
and over the next decade examples were sold to
Ecuador (Mk 89), Kenya (Mk 87), Kuwait (Mk 83),
New Zealand (Mk 88), Oman (Mk 82), Saudi Arabia
(Mk 80), Singapore (Mk 84) and South Yemen
(Mk 81), resulting in a total production run of 146
aircraft – final new-build Strikemasters were
constructed for Sudan (Mk 90) as late as 1984.
Examples in Oman, South Yemen and Ecuador all
saw combat during their service careers.

## SPECIFICATION:

**ACCOMMODATION:**
two pilots seated side-by-side

**DIMENSIONS:**
LENGTH: 34 ft 0 in (10.36 m)
WINGSPAN: 36 ft 10 in (11.23 m)
HEIGHT: 10 ft 2 in (3.10 m)

**WEIGHTS:**
EMPTY: 6195 lb (2810 kg)
MAX T/O: 11 500 lb (5216 kg)

**PERFORMANCE:**
MAX SPEED: 518 mph (834 kmh)
RANGE: 1382 miles (2224 km)
ferry range
POWERPLANT: Rolls-Royce
Viper 20 Mk 525
OUTPUT: 3410 lb st (15.17 kN)

**FIRST FLIGHT DATE:**
26 October 1967

**ARMAMENT:**
two FN 7.62 mm machine guns
(Mk 80); up to 3000-lb (1360 kg)
of rockets/bombs or cannon pods
on four underwing stores pylons

**FEATURES:**
Straight-wing layout; side-by-side
cockpit seating; extensive cockpit
glazing; tricycle landing gear;
wing root engine intakes;
wingtip tanks

# BAC Buccaneer UK

two-seat, twin-engined strike aircraft

Built to fulfil a 1952 Royal Navy requirement for a carrier-based attack aircraft, the Buccaneer enjoyed a long service career predominantly with the RAF. Although a big aircraft, the Buccaneer boasted modest-sized wings and tail unit thanks to the employment of boundary layer control, which restricted the amount of air flowing over the wings and tail through the use of full-span slits built into the flying surfaces. The small wing meant greater speeds at low level, and the Buccaneer remained one of the fastest combat aircraft in this environment until its retirement in 1992. The first Buccaneer s 1s entered service with the Royal Navy in July 1962, and these were followed by Spey-engined s 2s three years later. From 1969, the Navy's surviving Buccaneers were passed to the RAF in the wake of a political directive that denuded the Fleet Air Arm of conventional carriers. RAF Buccaneers saw combat in the twilight of their careers (South African Air Force Mk 50s had seen action in the 1970s and 80s) over Iraq and Kuwait in 1991 during Operation *Desert Storm*.

SPECIFICATION:

ACCOMMODATION:
pilot and navigator seated in tandem

DIMENSIONS:
LENGTH: 63 ft 5 in (19.33 m)
WINGSPAN: 44 ft 0 in (13.41 m)
HEIGHT: 16 ft 3 in (4.95 m)

WEIGHTS:
EMPTY: 29,980 lb (13,599 kg)
MAX T/O: 62,000 lb (28,123 kg)

PERFORMANCE:
MAX SPEED: 691 mph (1112 kmh)
RANGE: 600 miles (966 km) tactical range
POWERPLANT: two Rolls-Royce Spey Mk 101s
OUTPUT: 22,200 lb st (98.4 kN)

FIRST FLIGHT DATE:
30 April 1958

ARMAMENT:
4000-b (1816 kg) in bomb-bay and 12,000-lb (5444 kg) of rockets/bombs/missiles split between four underwing stores pylons

FEATURES:
Swept-wing layout; tandem cockpit seating; bulged rear fuselag; T-tail; split rear-fuselage air brake

## BAC TSR 2 UK

two-seat, twin-engined strike/reconnaissance aircraft

Designed as the replacement for the Canberra, BAC's TSR 2 was the successful tender to the Ministry of Defence's Operational Requirement 339, issued in 1956. The requirement called for an aircraft capable of high supersonic performance over long distances at low altitude, as well as short-field operating capability, inertial navigation and precision nuclear weapon delivery. British Aircraft Corporation was formed to create such a complex aircraft, the likes of which had never been built in the UK before. The combined Vickers/English Electric tender was accepted on 1 January 1959, and funding was made available for 20 development aircraft. In 1963 an order for 30 production aircraft followed at a cost of £690 million – a figure that dwarfed any previous defence programme in the UK. Problems with the Olympus engine slowed progress, and when the prototype flew on 27 September 1964, the powerplants lacked performance and flight time. Project costs proved too much for the British government to bear, and the TSR 2 was cancelled on 6 April 1965.

SPECIFICATION:

**ACCOMMODATION:**
pilot and navigator seated in tandem

**DIMENSIONS:**
LENGTH: 89 ft 0 in (27.12 m)
WINGSPAN: 37 ft 0 in (11.27 m)
HEIGHT: 24 ft 0 in (7.31 m)

**WEIGHTS:**
EMPTY: 48,900 lb (22,181 kg)
MAX T/O: 80,000 lb (36,288 kg)

**PERFORMANCE:**
MAX SPEED: 1485 mph (2376 kmh)
RANGE: 1150 miles (1840 km)
POWERPLANT: two Bristol Siddeley Olympus 320s
OUTPUT: 61,220 lb st (274 kN)

**FIRST FLIGHT DATE:**
27 September 1964

**ARMAMENT:**
6000 lb (2721 kg) in bomb-bay and 4000 lb (1814 kg) of rockets/bombs/missiles split between four underwing stores pylons

**FEATURES:**
Delta-wing layout; tandem cockpit seating; tricycle landing gear; turned down wingtips

# BAC Harrier GR 1/3 (AV-8A/C) UK

single-seat, single-engined strike aircraft

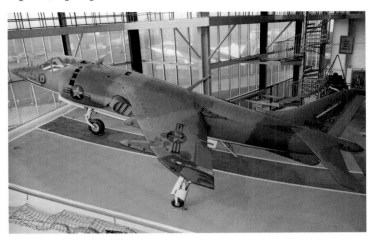

The world's first practical vertical take-off and landing fixed-wing aircraft, the Harrier was developed from the Hawker P 1127. Design of the latter started in 1957 expressly to take advantage of the Bristol BS 53 turbofan engine, which matured into the Rolls-Royce Pegasus. This powerplant was able to vector thrust from its four exhaust nozzles, which could pivot through 90° from the horizontal. Six P 1127s were built to prove the concept, followed by nine pre-production Kestrel aircraft. The Ministry of Defence then ordered six development Harriers in February 1965, the first of which flew in August 1966. The Harrier GR 1 entered frontline service as a light strike aircraft with No 1 Sqn in December 1967, and this variant was followed by the improved GR 3 in 1976 – 118 were built. The US Marine Corps had been a keen observer of the Harrier programme, and in 1969 it placed an order for 102 AV-8AS and eight two-seat TAV-8AS. RAF GR 3S saw combat in the Falklands War in 1982 and were retired in the early 1990s.

SPECIFICATION:

**ACCOMMODATION:**
pilot

**DIMENSIONS:**
LENGTH: 46 ft 10 in (14.27 m)
WINGSPAN: 37 ft 0 in (11.27 m)
HEIGHT: 22 ft 2 in (6.76 m)

**WEIGHTS:**
EMPTY: 12,300 lb (5579 kg)
MAX T/O: 25,200 lb (11,431 kg)

**PERFORMANCE:**
MAX SPEED: 730 mph (1176 kmh)
RANGE: 415 miles (667 km)
tactical range
POWERPLANT: Rolls-Royce
Pegasus Mk 103
OUTPUT: 21,500 lb st (95.64 kN)

**FIRST FLIGHT DATE:**
21 October 1960

**ARMAMENT:**
two Aden 30 mm cannon in underfuselage pods; 5000-lb (2270 kg) of rockets/bombs/missiles split between four underwing stores pylons

**FEATURES:**
Shoulder-mounted swept wing layout; centreline main undercarriage with wingtip outriggers; large air intakes either side of cockpit

# Beagle CC 1 Basset UK

six-seat, twin-engined communications aircraft

The B 206 Basset evolved from a late 1950s Bristol Aeroplane Company project for a four-seat twin-engined light aircraft. Although never built, the Bristol 220 was the basis for the prototype B 206X Basset, which made its first flight on 15 August 1961. Following flight testing, Beagle decided that the aircraft was too small, so the design grew into the B 206Y, which differed from the B 206X in having more powerful 310 hp Continental IO-470-A engines, a greater wing span, a larger cabin with seating for up to six and greater fuel capacity. These modifications now meant that the Basset met an RAF requirement for a communications aircraft capable of transporting a V-bomber support crew. Twenty were ordered for this role in preference to the de Havilland Dove, and service deliveries began in May 1965. Replacing the venerable Anson, the aircraft was designated the CC 1 by the RAF. Never a great success in the commercial marketplace, fewer than 60 B 206s were sold prior to Beagle going into liquidation in 1970. The RAF CC 1s were retired in 1975.

SPECIFICATION:

**ACCOMMODATION:**
one pilot and five passengers

**DIMENSIONS:**
LENGTH: 33 ft 8 in (10.26 m)
WINGSPAN: 45 ft 10 in (13.96 m)
HEIGHT: 11 ft 4 in (3.43 m)

**WEIGHTS:**
EMPTY: 5250 lb (2381 kg)
MAX T/O: 6310 lb (2862 kg)

**PERFORMANCE:**
MAX SPEED: 286 mph (458 kmh)
RANGE: 1995 miles (2462 km)
POWERPLANT: two Continental IO-470-AS
OUTPUT: 620 hp (460 kW)

**FIRST FLIGHT DATE:**
15 August 1961

**FEATURES:**
Straight-wing layout; side-by-side seating; extensive cockpit glazing; retractable tricycle landing gear; close-cowled engines

# Beech T-34 Mentor  USA

two-seat, single-engined primary trainer

Based on the civilian Beech Model 35 Bonanza, the Model 45 Mentor was built in 1948 in response to an expected demand by the USAF for a new primary tuitional trainer. Five years were to pass before the Beech trainer was chosen to fill the role, the USAF undertaking a fly-off that saw a wide variety of designs evaluated. As part of this process, three pre-production Mentors were acquired by the Air Force, which designated them YT-34s. Once selected, Beech supplied Training Command with 350 T-34As from its Wichita plant, deliveries commencing in 1954. That year also saw the US Navy select the Mentor as its basic trainer, 423 T-34Bs being acquired. Other foreign air arms also chose the Mentor, the Argentine firm FMA assembling 75 for its air force and Japanese manufacturer Fuji building 124 for the Air Self-Defence Force. The Mentor was replaced in USAF ranks from 1960 onwards following the adoption of an all-through jet training syllabus, whilst the Navy continued to use its T-34Bs until the late 1970s, when the T-34C Turbo Mentor entered service.

SPECIFICATION:

**ACCOMMODATION:**
two pilots in tandem

**DIMENSIONS:**
LENGTH: 25 ft 10 in (7.87 m)
WINGSPAN: 32 ft 10 in (10.01 m)
HEIGHT: 10 ft 0.25 in (3.04 m)

**WEIGHTS:**
EMPTY: 2055 lb (932 kg)
MAX T/O: 2900 lb (1315 kg)

**PERFORMANCE:**
MAX SPEED: 188 mph (302 kmh)
RANGE: 770 miles (1238 km)
POWERPLANT: Continental
O-470-13 (T-34A) or
O-470-4 (T-34B)
OUTPUT: 225 hp (168 kW)

**FIRST FLIGHT DATE:**
2 December 1948

**FEATURES:**
Straight-wing layout; tandem seating; extensive cockpit glazing; rectractable tricycle landing gear

# Beech U-8 USA

six-seat, twin-engined utility aircraft

Beech's six-seater Model 50 Twin Bonanza was the first twin-engined light aircraft to achieve quantity production in the US post-World War 2. Flown in prototype form on 15 November 1949, examples of the progressively more refined Model 50 found their way into service with several air forces in the liaison and light utility roles. The primary military operator was the US Army, which adopted the Twin Bonanza as the L-23A Seminole, 55 of which were ordered in the early 1950s. A further 40 similar L-23Bs were procured soon afterwards. In November 1956, the US Army began to receive the first of 85 L-23Ds, which were based on the civil Model E50 Twin Bonanza. This variant featured more powerful Lycoming O-480-1 engines, and the surviving 93 L-23A/Bs were also remanufactured to this standard. In 1962 all L-23Ds were redesignated U-8Ds, the U standing for Utility. The US Army used its Seminoles across the globe, the aircraft proving a favourite amongst senior officers. All U-8Ds were eventually replaced by the larger U-8F (based on the Queen Air 65) in the early 1980s.

SPECIFICATION:

**ACCOMMODATION:**
two pilots in tandem

**DIMENSIONS:**
LENGTH: 31 ft 6 in (9.61 m)
WINGSPAN: 45 ft 3 in (13.78 m)
HEIGHT: 11 ft 6 in (3.51 m)

**WEIGHTS:**
EMPTY: 5010 lb (2272 kg)
MAX T/O: 4796 lb (2175 kg)

**PERFORMANCE:**
MAX SPEED: 229 mph (366 kmh)
RANGE: 1000 miles (1600 km)
POWERPLANT: two Lycoming O-480-B1B6s
OUTPUT: 632 hp (472 kW)

**FIRST FLIGHT DATE:**
15 November 1949

**FEATURES:**
Straight-wing layout; rectractable tricycle landing gear; twin, close-cowled engines

# Beriev Be-12 Tchaika <small>USSR</small>

five-seat, twin-engined maritime patrol and ASW amphibian

Built as a replacement for the piston-engined Be-6 in the anti-submarine warfare (ASW) and maritime patrol roles, the prototype turboprop Be-12 first flew in 1960. The Beriev amphibian used the tried and tested twin tail and high cranked wing layout – the latter to give its twin Ivchenko AI-20D turboprops as much clearance from the water as possible. Selected for Soviet naval service in 1964, possibly as many as 200 Be-12s were built by Beriev, and they served with all Soviet Fleet Naval Aviation commands. Peak strength for Be-12s in the mid 1970s amounted to four aviation regiments and a number of independent squadrons. During the 1970s some of these regiments partially re-equipped with the Ilyushin Il-38 'May'. A handful of aircraft were sold to the Vietnamese People's Army Air Force and the Syrian Air Force, which used them in the search-and-rescue and maritime patrol roles. Following the break up of the USSR, a number of Be-12s were retired, although around 50 may still be in service with the Russian Northern Fleet and the Ukrainian Air Force's Black Sea Fleet.

SPECIFICATION:

ACCOMMODATION:
pilot, co-pilot, navigator, radar operator and Magnetic Anomaly Detector operator

DIMENSIONS:
LENGTH: 99 ft 0 in (30.17 m)
WINGSPAN: 97 ft 6 in (29.71 m)
HEIGHT: 23 ft 0 in (7.00 m)

WEIGHTS:
EMPTY: 47,840 lb (21,700 kg)
MAX T/O: 68,342 lb (31,000 kg)

PERFORMANCE:
MAX SPEED: 378 mph (608 kmh)
RANGE: 4660 miles (7500 km)
POWERPLANT: two Ivchenko (Progress) AI-20DS
OUTPUT: 8380 shp (6250 kW)

FIRST FLIGHT DATE:
1960

ARMAMENT:
up to 6600-lb (3000 kg) of torpedoes, depth charges and mines in internal weapons bay and on two underwing stores pylons

FEATURES:
High gull-wing layout; two turboprop engines; twin tail layout; single-step monocoque hull; fixed outrigger floats

# Blackburn Beverley UK

98-seat, four-engined transport aircraft

Designed by the General Aircraft Co in 1946 and put into production by Blackburn, the Beverley was the largest aircraft to have entered service with the RAF when production examples reached No 47 Sqn at Abingdon in March 1956. Named after the cathedral town in Yorkshire near its birthplace, the prototype GAL 60 Universal Transport completed its first flight in 1950. Following General Aircraft's merger with Blackburn, the aircraft had its quartet of Bristol Hercules radial engines replaced with more powerful Centaurus powerplants from the same manufacturer. The prototype Beverley made its first flight on 14 June 1953, and an initial contract was placed by the Ministry of Supply for 20. The first aircraft specially designed for the dropping of Army equipment through removable rear doors, it also had the ability to operate from small airfields. Aside from the transportation of vehicles, armour and artillery, the aircraft could also carry up to 70 parachute troops and casualties. Some 47 production Beverleys were built in total, and they served with Transport Command until retired in 1968.

SPECIFICATION:

ACCOMMODATION:
pilot and co-pilot, navigator, crew chief and up to 94 passengers

DIMENSIONS:
LENGTH: 99 ft 5 in (30.30 m)
WINGSPAN: 162 ft 0 in (49.38 m)
HEIGHT: 38 ft 9 in (11.81 m)

WEIGHTS:
EMPTY: 79,234 lb (35,940 kg)
MAX T/O: 143,000 lb (64,864 kg)

PERFORMANCE:
MAX SPEED: 238 mph (383 kmh)
RANGE: 3690 miles (5938 km)
POWERPLANT: four Bristol Centaurus 173s
OUTPUT: 11,400 shp (8500 kW)

FIRST FLIGHT DATE:
20 June 1950 (GAL 60)

FEATURES:
High-wing layout; four radial engines; twin tail layout; rear-loading ramp; fixed tricycle undercarriage

# Boeing C-97 Stratofreighter/Stratotanker USA

102-seat, four-engined transport/air refuelling tanker aircraft

The transport derivative of Boeing's B-29, the C-97 was appreciably bigger than the Superfortress due to the addition of a second fuselage of greater diameter on top of the existing structure. Three pre-production examples of the aircraft were designated the XC-97 by the USAAF, and although they had been ordered simultaneously with the B-29 in January 1942, the latter type took precedence in respect to its development. Boeing commenced flight trials with the XC-97s in 1944, and an order for 50 C-97As was placed. Although designed as a transporter of people and freight, it was in the role of aerial tanker for Strategic Air Command (SAC) that the C-97 achieved its greatest success. Indeed, 811 KC-97 tankers in three different variants were built. The combination of the aircraft's capacious cargo hold and Boeing's Flying Boom refuelling system allowed the Stratotanker to transfer fuel to SAC's fleet of bombers. Following their replacement by jet-powered KC-135s, KC-97s were passed onto Air National Guard units, which continued to use them into the 1970s.

SPECIFICATION:

ACCOMMODATION:
pilot and co-pilot, navigator, flight engineer, boom operator, crew chief and up to 96 passengers

DIMENSIONS:
LENGTH: 117 ft 5 in (35.8 m)
WINGSPAN: 141 ft 3 in (43.05 m)
HEIGHT: 38 ft 3 in (11.75 m)

WEIGHTS:
EMPTY: 85,000 lb (38,560 kg)
MAX T/O: 175,000 lb (78,980 kg)

PERFORMANCE:
MAX SPEED: 370 mph (595 kmh)
RANGE: 4300 miles (6920 km)
POWERPLANT: four Pratt & Whitney R-4360-59B Wasp Majors
OUTPUT: 14,000 hp (10,440 kW)

FIRST FLIGHT DATE:
15 November 1944

FEATURES:
Monoplane-wing layout; four radial engines; 'double bubble' fuselage; tricycle undercarriage; external refuelling boom (KC-97 only)

# Boeing B-47 Stratojet USA

three-seat, six-engined medium bomber

Strongly influenced by the post-war discovery of
swept wing jet aircraft in Germany, Boeing
abandoned its work on conventional straight-
winged designs and produced the Model 450. This
was ordered by the USAAF in 1945, and flight test
results proved that the jet exceeded the claims
made for it by Boeing, with drag proving to be 25
per cent lower than estimated. Although the XB-47
(USAF designation) could not fly the long missions
requested by SAC, the jet was still ordered in
quantity in 1949 – the first B-47AS reached SAC units
in late 1950. The more refined B-47B was the first
large-scale production variant, and three factories
churned these out following the escalation of
hostilities in Korea. The B-47E of 1951 featured
bigger engines, 20 mm guns in the tail turret, a
new radar bombing system, ejection seats and a
refuelling receptacle. In service with SAC
throughout the 1950s, the B-47 equipped 28 bomb
wings, each with 45 aircraft. Some 2042 Stratojets
were built, including 300+ RB-47E and ERB-47H
reconnaissance and countermeasures aircraft.

SPECIFICATION:

**ACCOMMODATION:**
pilot, co-pilot/tail gunner,
bombardier/navigator

**DIMENSIONS:**
LENGTH: 109 ft 10 in (33.50 m)
WINGSPAN: 116 ft 0 in (35.36 m)
HEIGHT: 27 ft 11 in (8.52 m)

**WEIGHTS:**
EMPTY: 78,200 lb (36,281 kg)
MAX T/O: 220,000 lb (99,790 kg)

**PERFORMANCE:**
MAX SPEED: 606 mph (980 kmh)
RANGE: 3600 miles (5794 km)
POWERPLANT: six General
Electric J47-25AS
OUTPUT: 35,820 lb st (159 kN)

**FIRST FLIGHT DATE:**
17 December 1947

**ARMAMENT:**
two M-3 20 mm cannon in
remote-controlled tail turret;
22,000-lb (9979 kg) of bombs in
bomb-bay

**FEATURES:**
Monoplane, swept-wing layout;
six turbojets in underwing pods;
'double bubble' fuselage;
fuselage-mounted undercarriage,
with wing outriggers; fighter-
style bubble cockpit

# Boeing B-50 Superfortress  USA

nine-seat, four-engined strategic bomber

SAC's standard frontline strategic bomber from the late 1940s until the early 1950s, the B-50 started life as the B-29D. Some 5152 D-models were on order when World War 2 ended, but only 50 survived cancellation to be built. Although based on the original B-29, the D-model was powered by four new and very powerful Pratt & Whitney Wasp Major engines, and also featured a lighter and stronger alloy airframe and taller tail fin. The new bomber had been redesignated the B-50 by the time the first prototype flew on 25 June 1947, and the USAF bought 80 A-models, 45 B-models, 222 D-models and 24 TB-50H dual-control trainers. A number of these were converted into WB-50s for weather reconnaissance and KB-50s for aerial refuelling following their service as bombers, and this ensured their employment with USAF and Air National Guard units until 1968. The KB-50J proved particularly successful, 112 bombers being converted into tankers through the fitment of the hose-real system or the Boeing Flying Boom – these aircraft also had two podded J47 turbojets.

SPECIFICATION:

**ACCOMMODATION:**
pilot, co-pilot, engineer, navigator, radar operator, bombardier, radio/electronic countermeasures operator, left/right side gunners, top gunner, tail gunner

**DIMENSIONS:**
LENGTH: 100 ft 0 in (30.48 m)
WINGSPAN: 141 ft 3 in (43.05 m)
HEIGHT: 34 ft 7 in (10.50 m)

**WEIGHTS:**
EMPTY: 81,000 lb (36,741 kg)
MAX T/O: 173,000 lb (78,471 kg)

**PERFORMANCE:**
MAX SPEED: 400 mph (640 kmh)
RANGE: 4900 miles (7886 km)
POWERPLANT: four Pratt & Whitney R-4360-35 Wasp Majors
OUTPUT: 14,000 hp (10,440 kW)

**FIRST FLIGHT DATE:**
25 June 1947

**ARMAMENT:**
four turrets with two/four Browning 0.50-in machine guns, tail turret with three machine guns; bomb load of 28,000-lb (12,701 kg) in bomb-bay

**FEATURES:**
Monoplane wing layout; four radial engines; very large tail

# Boeing B-52 Stratofortress USA

six-seat, eight-engined strategic bomber

Originally planned by Boeing in 1946 as a straight-wing turboprop due to the lack of available powerplants capable of propelling an inter-continental bomber, the B-52 was the direct beneficiary of Pratt & Whitney's more fuel efficient J57 turbojet. Redesigned with eight engines housed in four double pods beneath swept wings, the prototype YB-52 completed its first flight on 15 April 1952. Initially built with fighter-style tandem seating for the pilot and co-pilot, production B-52As had the revised side-by-side seating in an airliner style cockpit. Entering service in March 1955, the B-52 was produced to the tune of 744 airframes in eight sub-types. Numerically, the most important of these was the B-52D, which saw combat over Vietnam, followed by the B-52G, which had a smaller fin and remote-controlled tail guns, and the B-52H, powered by Pratt & Whitney TF33 turbofans. Today, only the H-models remain in service with the USAF, having seen combat in Iraq, Kosovo and Afghanistan. Surviving B-52s are not scheduled for retirement for at least another 20 years.

## SPECIFICATION:

**ACCOMMODATION:**
pilot, co-pilot, tail gunner, bombardier/navigator, ECM operator, radar operator

**DIMENSIONS:**
LENGTH: 157 ft 7 in (48 m)
WINGSPAN: 185 ft 0 in (56.40 m)
HEIGHT: 48 ft 3 in (14.75 m)

**WEIGHTS:**
EMPTY: 193,000 lb (87,100 kg)
MAX T/O: 450,000 lb (204,120 kg)

**PERFORMANCE:**
MAX SPEED: 630 mph (1014 kmh)
RANGE: 6200 miles (9978 km)
POWERPLANT: eight Pratt & Whitney J57-43WS
OUTPUT: 110,000 lb st (488 kN)

**FIRST FLIGHT DATE:**
15 April 1952

**ARMAMENT:**
four Browning 0.50-in machine guns (later M61A1 20 mm cannon) in remote-controlled tail turret; 70,000-lb (31,750 kg) of bombs split between bomb-bay and two underwing stores pylons

**FEATURES:**
Monoplane, shoulder-mounted swept-wing; eight turbojets in underwing pods; fuselage-mounted undercarriage

# Boeing C-135 USA

194-seat, four-engined transport/tanker/special missions/AWACS aircraft

Sired by the 367-80 civilian jet transport, the C-135 was ordered into production for the USAF following an evaluation of the prototype soon after its first flight in July 1954. Three months later Boeing received an order for 29 tanker/transport aircraft. Joining the USAF from August 1956, the jets was rarely used in the dual role, as sufficient C-135s were procured to allow KC-135 variants to operate exclusively as aerial refuellers. The system at the heart of the Stratotanker is the Boeing Flying Boom, which is flown into the receiving aircraft's refuelling receptacle by the KC-135's boom operator. The USAF bought 732 KC-135s between June 1957 and January 1965, while a further 88 were delivered as C-135 transports. More than 28 different variants of C-135 have been flown by the USAF on reconnaissance, transport and command post duties, and further examples have operated with the US Navy as E-6 Mercury submarine command aircraft. The Airborne Warning & Control System E-3 Sentry is still a crucial part of the frontline USAF force, as is the E-8 J-STARS battlefield reconnaissance platform.

## SPECIFICATION:

**ACCOMMODATION:**
pilot, co-pilot, navigator, boom operator (as tanker), and various other crew/passenger configurations depending on role

**DIMENSIONS:**
LENGTH: 136 ft 3 in (41 m)
WINGSPAN: 130 ft 10 in (39.70 m)
HEIGHT: 38 ft 4 in (11.60 m)

**WEIGHTS:**
EMPTY: 109,000 lb (49,442 kg)
MAX T/O: 297,000 lb (134,715 kg)

**PERFORMANCE:**
MAX SPEED: 600 mph (966 kmh)
RANGE: 4000 miles (6437 km)
POWERPLANT: four Pratt & Whitney J57-59WS
OUTPUT: 55,000 lb st (244 kN)

**FIRST FLIGHT DATE:**
15 July 1954

**FEATURES:**
Monoplane, swept-wing layout; four turbojets in underwing pods; tall tail fin; external refuelling boom (KC-135 only)

# Breguet Alizé  FRANCE

three-seat, single-engined ASW search and strike aircraft

The Alizé was developed from Breguet's BR 990
Vultur which had been built in 1948 following a
French Navy request for a carrier-based strike
aircraft. Powered by a turboprop engine in the nose
and a turbojet in the rear fuselage, the Vultur was
not ordered into production. Hoping for better
success with an ASW aircraft, Breguet used the
Vultur as the basis for its Alizé (tradewind),
dropping the turbojet and replacing the Rolls-
Royce Mamba turboprop with a Dart engine from
the same manufacturer. Development commenced
in 1954, and the prototype was flown on 6 October
1956. The first of 75 Alizés ordered by the French
Navy was delivered in May 1959, and the only other
customer was India, which ordered 12 – a dozen
more were bought from French stocks years later.
The French Navy operated its aircraft successfully
from the carriers *Clémenceau* and *Foch* for over 40
years. The last French Alizés were retired several
years ago, while the Indian machines spent their
final years operating from land bases until
withdrawn from service in 1992.

SPECIFICATION:

ACCOMMODATION:
pilot, radar operator, sensor
operator

DIMENSIONS:
LENGTH: 45 ft 6 in (13.86 m)
WINGSPAN: 51 ft 2 in (15.60 m)
HEIGHT: 16 ft 5 in (5.00 m)

WEIGHTS:
EMPTY: 12,565 lb (5700 kg)
MAX T/O: 18,190 lb (8250 kg)

PERFORMANCE:
MAX SPEED: 323 mph (520 kmh)
RANGE: 1553 miles (2500 km)
POWERPLANT: Rolls-Royce Dart
Rda 7 Mk 21
OUTPUT: 1975 shp (1475 kW)

FIRST FLIGHT DATE:
6 October 1956

ARMAMENT:
bomb-bay for up to 1059-lb
(480 kg) of torpedoes/depth
charges and two underwing
stores pylons for bombs/rockets
or depth charges

FEATURES:
Straight-wing layout; rectractable
tricycle landing gear; arrestor
hook; wing nacelles for gear
legs/sonobuoys

# CAC CA-25 Winjeel AUSTRALIA
two-seat, single-engined basic trainer and forward air control aircraft

Built in response to a specification issued by the RAAF in 1948 for a Tiger Moth and Wirraway replacement, the Winjeel ('young eagle') was developed as the CA-22 by the CAC. Two prototypes were delivered to the RAAF in early 1951, and after exhaustive trials, the Air Force ordered 62 production aircraft. Built between 1955 and 1958, the Winjeel that entered frontline service differed from the CA-22 primarily in its tail section, where work had been carried out to improve the trainer's spinning characteristics. Redesignated the CA-25, the Winjeel was the staple basic trainer until replaced by the Macchi in 1969 when the RAAF reverted to an all-jet syllabus. Problems with the new curriculum saw the Winjeel re-introduced as an *ab initio* trainer once again, however. It was to see a further six years of service until finally replaced for good by the CT-4 from 1975 onwards. Despite losing its training role in 1976, the Winjeel soldiered on until 1994 as a Forward Air Control platform, operating closely with the RAAF's F-111, Mirage III and F/A-18 squadrons.

SPECIFICATION:

ACCOMMODATION:
two pilots side-by-side

DIMENSIONS:
LENGTH: 28 ft 0.50 in (8.55 m)
WINGSPAN: 38 ft 7.50 in (11.77 m)
HEIGHT: 9 ft 1 in (2.77 m)

WEIGHTS:
EMPTY: 3289 lb (1492 kg)
MAX T/O: 4265 lb (1935 kg)

PERFORMANCE:
MAX SPEED: 188 mph (303 kmh)
RANGE: 550 miles (883 km)
POWERPLANT: Pratt & Whitney
R-985-AN-2 Wasp Junior
OUTPUT: 445 hp (331.97 kW)

FIRST FLIGHT DATE:
3 February 1951

FEATURES:
Straight-wing layout; side-by-side
seating; extensive cockpit glazing;
fixed landing gear

# Canadair CT-114 Tutor CANADA

two-seat, single-engined advanced jet trainer

The Tutor was originally developed in the late 1950s by Canadair independently of Canadian government interest. The prototype CL-41 flew for the first time on 13 January 1960, the aircraft differing from other jet trainers of the period in having side-by-side seating. Following an evaluation of other training aircraft as well as the CL-41, the Canadian government placed an order for 190 aircraft (designated CT-114s) in September 1961. Aircraft were delivered between December 1963 and September 1966, and they were used primarily by No 2 Flying Training School in Saskatchewan, as well as the Central Flying School and the Snowbirds aerobatic display team. Twenty CL-41Gs were also sold to the Royal Malaysian Air Force in 1967-68, and these aircraft were capable of carrying rockets and bombs attached to six wing pylons. The Malaysians retired their aircraft in the mid 1980s following fatigue and corrosion problems, while the Canadians retain a small number of CT-114s in service with the Snowbirds and the Aerospace Engineering and Test Establishment.

SPECIFICATION:

**ACCOMMODATION:**
two pilots side-by-side

**DIMENSIONS:**
LENGTH: 32 ft 0 in (9.75 m)
WINGSPAN: 36 ft 6 in (11.13 m)
HEIGHT: 9 ft 4 in (2.84 m)

**WEIGHTS:**
EMPTY: 4895 lb (2220 kg)
MAX T/O: 7788 lb (3532 kg)

**PERFORMANCE:**
MAX SPEED: 498 mph (801 kmh)
RANGE: 623 miles (1002 km)
POWERPLANT: General Electric J85-CAN-J4
OUTPUT: 2950 lb st (13.10 kN)

**FIRST FLIGHT DATE:**
10 December 1957

**ARMAMENT:**
provision for up to 4000-lb (1815 kg) of bombs/rockets/gun pods/missiles on six underwing stores pylons

**FEATURES:**
Straight-wing layout; side-by-side cockpit; extensive cockpit glazing; T-tail; tricycle landing gear; wing root engine intakes

# Cavalier F-51D Mustang Mk 2  USA

single/two-seat, single-engined monoplane fighter-bomber

The Cavalier Mustang was born out of Florida newspaper magnate David Breed Lindsay Jr's desire to convert surplus ex-military P-51s into high-performance executive transports. The first such modified aircraft were ex-RCAF P-51DS, which were rebuilt by Lindsay's company Trans Florida Aviation Inc in the late 1950s and early 1960s. Having sold the RCAF aircraft, Lindsay expanded his business and started buying up other surplus airframes and parts. In 1966 the US Department of Defense decided that the Cavalier Mustang would be ideal as a Counter Insurgency platform for 'friendly' countries in South America, and duly contracted the company to refurbish Mustangs as part of Project *Peace Condor*. These aircraft boasted Merlin 620 engines taken from ex-RCAF C-54 GM transports, a taller fin, strengthened wings for additional weapons pylons and optional tip-tanks. Customers for the aircraft were Bolivia, El Salvador, the Dominican Republic, Guatemala and Indonesia. The last of the refurbished Mustangs was retired (by the *Fuerza Aerea Dominicana*) in 1984.

SPECIFICATION:

**ACCOMMODATION:**
pilot (dual controls optional)

**DIMENSIONS:**
LENGTH: 32 ft 9.5 in (9.81 m)
WINGSPAN: 40 ft 1 in (12.10 m)
HEIGHT: 14 ft 8 in (4.51 m)

**WEIGHTS:**
EMPTY: 7635 lb (3466 kg)
MAX T/O: 10,500 lb (4762 kg)

**PERFORMANCE:**
MAX SPEED: 457 mph (731.20 kmh)
RANGE: 2000 miles (3200 km)
POWERPLANT: Packard V-1650-7 (F-51D) and Merlin 620 (Cavalier Mustang Mk 2)
OUTPUT: 1590 hp (1186.14 kW) and 1725 hp (1285.12 kW) respectively

**FIRST FLIGHT DATE:**
December 1967 (Cavalier Mustang Mk 2)

**ARMAMENT:**
six Browning 0.50-in machine guns in wings; maximum bomb/rocket load of 5000-lb (2268 kg) on underwing stores pylons pylons

**FEATURES:**
Monoplane wing; close-cowled inline engine; ventral air intake; four-bladed propeller; optional wingtip tanks; tall vertical fin

# Cessna O-1 Bird Dog USA

two-seat, single-engined high-wing liaison/Forward Air Control aircraft

Winner of a US Army competition in June 1950 for a two-seat observation and liaison aircraft, the Cessna Model 305 was based loosely on the company's highly successful Model 170 of the late 1940s. Built to replace the World War 2-vintage Grasshopper family of aircraft, the Cessna L-19 (US Army designation) was powered by a Continental O-47-11 213 hp engine, as opposed to the Continental C145-2 145 hp unit of its civil predecessor. This meant that the aircraft was better suited to military service, and particularly the Forward Air Control role that it made its own during the early years of the Vietnam War. Re-designated the O-1 in 1962, Cessna had delivered 3431 by the time production ceased that year. The bulk of these were O-1AS (L-19AS), with the later variants introducing uprated equipment and wing stores such as target marking rockets. The exploits of the O-1 over Vietnam are legendary, pilots pin-pointing enemy troop locations through communication with 'friendlies' on the ground, prior to calling in air strikes to hit targets marked with smoke rockets.

SPECIFICATION:

**ACCOMMODATION:**
pilot and observer/passenger in tandem

**DIMENSIONS:**
LENGTH: 25 ft 9 in (7.85 m)
WINGSPAN: 36 ft 0 in (10.97 m)
HEIGHT: 7 ft 3.5 in (2.22 m)

**WEIGHTS:**
EMPTY: 1614 lb (732 kg)
MAX T/O: 2400 lb (1087 kg)

**PERFORMANCE:**
MAX SPEED: 151 mph (243 kmh)
RANGE: 530 miles (853 km)
POWERPLANT: Continental O-47-11
OUTPUT: 213 hp (159 kW)

**FIRST FLIGHT DATE:**
December 1949

**ARMAMENT:**
maximum bomb/rocket load of 500-lb (226 kg) on underwing stores pylons

**FEATURES:**
High-wing layout; single wing bracing strut; fixed under-carriage; flat-six engine; extensive cockpit glazing

# Cessna O-2 Super Skymaster   USA

two-seat, twin-engined high-wing obervation/Forward Air Control aircraft

Although the war in Vietnam had provided the O-1 with its 'finest hour' in military service, it also highlighted the need for a more advanced FAC aircraft capable of greater speeds and increased weapons carriage. Once again Cessna provided the answer in the form of a 'militarised' version of the Model 337 Skymaster, known as the O-2 Super Skymaster. The unique 'push/pull' layout of the civil aircraft gave the O-2 twin-engined performance and reliability, and allowed the USAF to fit military specification radios and four weapons pylons under the wings. Further modifications for the FAC role included the addition of extra windows in the fuselage for the observer in the right-hand seat. More than 350 O-2As were delivered to the USAF following the placement of an order on 29 December 1966, and the type served as a stopgap replacement for the O-1 until the dedicated OV-10 Bronco was produced. Aside from its FAC use, the O-2 was used for psychological warfare operations. Surviving Super Skymasters were retired from USAF ANG service in the 1980s.

## SPECIFICATION:

**ACCOMMODATION:**
pilot and observer/passenger seated side-by-side

**DIMENSIONS:**
LENGTH: 29 ft 9 in (9.07 m)
WINGSPAN: 38 ft 0 in (11.58 m)
HEIGHT: 9 ft 4 in (2.84 m)

**WEIGHTS:**
EMPTY: 2848 lb (1292 kg)
MAX T/O: 5400 lb (2449 kg)

**PERFORMANCE:**
MAX SPEED: 199 mph (320 kmh)
RANGE: 1060 miles (1706 km)
POWERPLANT: two Teledyne Continental IO-360C/DS
OUTPUT: 420 hp (314 kW)

**FIRST FLIGHT DATE:**
30 March 1964 (Super Skymaster)

**ARMAMENT:**
underwing stores pylons for gun pods and rockets of undisclosed weight

**FEATURES:**
High-wing layout; single wing bracing strut; retractable, tricycle undercarriage; 'push-pull' engine layout; twin tail booms

# Cessna Model 185/U-17 Skywagon  USA

six-seat, single-engined high-wing utility/Forward Air Control aircraft

The Model 185 Skywagon was built as a multi-purpose aircraft that was both cheap to produce and operate. Both attributes made it ideally suited to the US Department of Defense's Military Assistance Program (MAP), and examples were supplied to Bolivia, Costa Rica, Laos and South Vietnam. Operators appreciated the aircraft's strengthened structure, which allowed it to be stripped out and converted into a cargo hauler that could get into and out of the most modest of landing strips – an optional glass-fibre belly Cargo-Pack could also be bolted to the Skywagon to further boost its carrying capability. The 185 was selected by the USAF for MAP in 1963, the Air Force redesignating it the U-17. Some 262 A-models were built, followed by 205 Bravos with de-rated engines. Model 185s were also procured directly from Cessna by several non-MAP countries. Aside from its use in the general utility role, the Skywagon carried on the Cessna tradition of FAC – a tasking still occasionally undertaken today by Turkish 185s. Ten other air forces also currently operate 185s/U-17s.

SPECIFICATION:

**ACCOMMODATION:**
pilot and up to five passengers

**DIMENSIONS:**
LENGTH: 25 ft 9 in (7.85 m)
WINGSPAN: 35 ft 10 in (10.92 m)
HEIGHT: 7 ft 9 in (2.36 m)

**WEIGHTS:**
EMPTY: 1585 lb (719 kg)
MAX T/O: 3350 lb (1519 kg)

**PERFORMANCE:**
MAX SPEED: 178 mph (286 kmh)
RANGE: 1035 miles (1665 km) ferry range
POWERPLANT: Teledyne Continental IO-520-D
OUTPUT: 300 hp (224 kW)

**FIRST FLIGHT DATE:**
July 1960

**FEATURES:**
High-wing layout; single wing bracing strut; fixed under-carriage; flat-six engine; extensive cockpit glazing

# Cessna T-37/A-37 Tweet/Dragonfly USA

two-seat, twin-engined advanced jet trainer/light attack aircraft

In 1952 the USAF identified a requirement for an 'all through' jet trainer that could be used to instruct pilots from basic through to wings standard. Cessna's Model 318 was duly selected, the aircraft being powered by two 920 lb st Continental J69s and featuring side-by-side seating. The prototype completed its maiden flight on 12 October 1954, and designated the T-37 in USAF service, 534 A-models were built. This variant was followed by 449 more powerful T-37Bs – all surviving A-models were upgraded to this standard. The final trainer version was the T-37C, 269 of which were constructed for export. In 1960 Cessna decided to build a combat-capable version of the Tweet, fitting 2850 lb st General Electric J85 turbojets into the aircraft. The airframe was also restressed for combat, and the first A-37As were evaluated in Vietnam in 1967. The definitive A-37B, with the bigger engines, eight underwing pylons, armoured protection and a minigun, was put into production in 1968. In all, 577 B-models were built, and these served with both the USAF and ten foreign air forces.

SPECIFICATION:

ACCOMMODATION:
two pilots side-by-side

DIMENSIONS:
LENGTH: 29 ft 4 in (8.92 m)
WINGSPAN: 35 ft 11 in (10.93 m)
HEIGHT: 8 ft 11 in (2.71 m)

WEIGHTS:
EMPTY: 6211 lb (2817 kg)
MAX T/O: 14,000 lb (6350 kg)

PERFORMANCE:
MAX SPEED: 507 mph (816 kmh)
RANGE: 1012 miles (1628 km)
POWERPLANT: two General Electric
J85-GE-17As
OUTPUT: 5700 lb st (25.40 kN)

FIRST FLIGHT DATE:
12 October 1954

ARMAMENT:
One GAU-2B/A 7.62 mm minigun
in nose; up to 5680-lb (2576 kg) of
bombs/rockets/gun pods on
eight underwing stores pylons

FEATURES:
Straight-wing layout; side-by-side
cockpit; extensive cockpit glazing;
tricycle landing gear; wing root
engine intakes; wingtip tanks
(A-37)

# Convair T-29/C-131 USA

52-seat, twin-engined trainer/transport aircraft

The T-29/C-131 trainer and transport aircraft were the military versions of Convair's 240/340/440 series of twin-engined airliners. The T-29 (based on the Convair 240) entered service with the USAF in 1949 as a navigator, bombardier and radio operator trainer. Some 48 unpressurised T-29AS were bought, followed by 105 T-29BS and 119 T-29CS. Both the B and C models featured pressurised fuselages, while the follow-on T-29D had a bombsight fitted, as well as a camera scoring capability – the first of the 93 D-models purchased flew in August 1953. The C-131 was an improved version of the T-29, 46 of which entered service with the USAF in 1950-51. Dubbed the 'Samaritan' because of its primary role of medical evacuation, the first of 26 C-131AS reached Military Air Transport Service in December 1954. Major follow-on variants included the C-131B (36 built), C-131D (ten built), VC-131D (16 built for staff/VIP transport), R4Y-1 (US Navy variant, redesignated C-131F in 1962 – 36 built) and the C-131E (SAC ECM trainer – 11 built). The last Convairs served with ANG and Navy reserve units until 1990.

## SPECIFICATION:

**ACCOMMODATION:**
pilot, co-pilot, engineer, navigator and up to 48 passengers

**DIMENSIONS:**
LENGTH: 79 ft 2 in (24.14 m)
WINGSPAN: 105 ft 4 in (32.10 m)
HEIGHT: 28 ft 2 in (8.60 m)

**WEIGHTS:**
EMPTY: 29 486 lb (13 382 kg)
MAX T/O: 52 414 lb (24 682.19 kg)

**PERFORMANCE:**
MAX SPEED: 314 mph (502 kmh)
RANGE: 2200 miles (3520 km)
POWERPLANT: two Pratt & Whitney R-2800-103WS
OUTPUT: 5000 hp (3720 kW)

**FIRST FLIGHT DATE:**
22 September 1949 (T-29A)

**FEATURES:**
Straight-wing layout; two close-cowled engines; tall fin/rudder; square fuselage windows

# Convair B-36 Peacemaker USA

15-seat, ten-engined strategic bomber

Designed to be able to operate against Nazi-held Europe from bases in North America should Britain have fallen to the Germans in World War 2, Convair's B-36 had to be able to carry a 10,000-lb bomb load to a target 5000 miles away after taking off from a 5000-ft runway. The prototype's development programme was initially slowed up by material shortages due to the demands being placed on the US aviation industry to keep pace with wartime production quotas. Indeed, it was only after VJ-Day that work gathered momentum, and when the XB-36 made its first flight on 8 August 1946, it was the world's largest aircraft. The unarmed B-36A entered service with SAC in 1947, the first production models being used as crew trainers in advance of the armed B/D-models, which started equipping bomb groups from 1948. In an effort to increase the bomber's over-target height and speed, the B-36D was fitted with two twin-jet pods. A total of 386 B-36s were built, and a significant number of them were stripped of their armament and used as reconnaissance platforms.

SPECIFICATION:

ACCOMMODATION:
pilot, co-pilot, radar/bombardier, navigator, flight engineer, two radio operators, three forward and five rear gunners

DIMENSIONS:
LENGTH: 162 ft 0 in (49.40 m)
WINGSPAN: 230 ft 0 in (70.14 m)
HEIGHT: 46 ft 9 in (14.26 m)

WEIGHTS:
EMPTY: 179,000 lb (81,200 kg)
MAX T/O: 357,500 lb (162,200 kg)

PERFORMANCE:
MAX SPEED: 439 mph (707 kmh)
RANGE: 7500 miles (12,070 km)
POWERPLANT: six Pratt & Whitney R-4360-41 Wasp Majors, four General Electric J47-GE-19s
OUTPUT: 21,000 hp (15,659 kW) and 20,800 lb st (91 kN)

FIRST FLIGHT DATE:
8 August 1946

ARMAMENT:
16 20 mm cannon in eight remotely controlled turrets; 84,000 lb (38,140 kg) bomb load in bomb-bay

FEATURES:
Monoplane, swept-wing; six radial engines in wings, four podded turbojets beneath wings

# Convair B-58 Hustler USA

three-seat, four-engined bomber

Convair's B-58 Hustler was the first aircraft of its type to reach Mach 2. To achieve this, the manufacturer included a number of structural firsts, including widespread use of stainless-steel honeycomb sandwich. It was also the first bomber to have a slim body and large payload pod (comprising ordnance and a fuel tank), the latter allowing the B-58 to become smaller once jettisoned. Numerous technical difficulties created by the state-of the-art design were rapidly overcome by Convair, and the first prototype took the skies on 11 November 1956. Production B-58AS began reaching SAC in 1959, and the 43rd and 305th Bomb Wings illustrated the Hustler's high-speed potential by setting world speed records between New York and Paris, and Tokyo and London. Despite its outstanding performance, only 116 B-58s were built as SAC had shifted its nuclear weapons focus from manned bombers to intercontinental ballistic missiles. Aside from the B-58A, Convair also built a number of TB-58 trainers. The last Hustlers were retired from the frontline in January 1970.

## SPECIFICATION:

**ACCOMMODATION:**
pilot, navigator, defence-systems operator

**DIMENSIONS:**
LENGTH: 96 ft 9 in (29.50 m)
WINGSPAN: 56 ft 10 in (17.31 m)
HEIGHT: 31 ft 5 in (9.60 m)

**WEIGHTS:**
EMPTY: 55,560 lb (25,200 kg)
MAX T/O: 163,000 lb (73,930 kg)

**PERFORMANCE:**
MAX SPEED: 1385 mph (2125 kmh)
RANGE: 5125 miles (8248 km)
POWERPLANT: four General Electric J79-GE-5BS
OUTPUT: 62,400 lb st (279 kN)

**FIRST FLIGHT DATE:**
11 November 1956

**ARMAMENT:**
one T-171 20 mm cannon in remotely controlled tail barbette; 19,450-lb (8820 kg) of bombs in bomb-bay and 7000-lb (3175 kg) on four underwing stores pylons

**FEATURES:**
Delta-wing layout; four turbojets in underwing pods; no horizontal tailplane; thin, tapered fuselage; large payload pod beneath fuselage

# Convair F-102 Delta Dagger USA

single-seat, single-engined fighter

The end result of a 1950 USAF design competition for an integral all-weather interceptor weapon system, the Convair F-102 Delta Dagger had at its heart the Hughes MX-1179 weapons system which comprised a radar, computer and Falcon missiles. Convair had experimented with delta wing designs in the late 1940s, and its prototype YF-102 completed its first flight on 24 October 1953. A further nine were built for test and evaluation purposes, and it soon became obvious that the aircraft was under-powered and incapable of level supersonic flight. Chastened by the poor performance of their design, Convair engineers applied the 'area rule' principal to the revised YF-102A, which was created in just 117 days. Cambered wings, a new canopy and a more powerful engine were also introduced, resulting in the aircraft at last meeting USAF expectations. Some 875 F-102As were built in 1955-56, and these served with 27 Air Defense Command (ADC) units well into the late 1960s. Replaced in ADC service by the F-106 in the late 1960s, Delta Daggers were then handed over to 23 Air National Guard squadrons.

SPECIFICATION:

ACCOMMODATION:
pilot

DIMENSIONS:
LENGTH: 68 ft 4.50 in (20.84 m)
WINGSPAN: 38 ft 1.50 in (11.62 m)
HEIGHT: 21 ft 2.50 in (6.46 m)

WEIGHTS:
EMPTY: 20,160 lb (9144 kg)
MAX T/O: 31,276 lb (14,187 kg)

PERFORMANCE:
MAX SPEED: 825 mph (1327 kmh)
RANGE: 1350 miles (2173 km)
POWERPLANT: Pratt & Whitney
J57-P-23
OUTPUT: 17,200 lb st (79 kN)

FIRST FLIGHT DATE:
20 December 1954
(YF-102A)

ARMAMENT:
six Hughes AIM-4 Falcon guided
missiles in weapons-bay

FEATURES:
Delta-wing layout; no horizontal
tailplane; 'area rule' fuselage;
triangular fin/tail

# Convair F-106 Delta Dart USA

single-seat, single-engined fighter

Originally designated the F-102B, the Delta Dart was the successor to the Delta Dagger. Featuring a more powerful Pratt & Whitney J75 engine and the Hughes MA-1 integrated fire-control system, the F-106 shared its delta wing with the F-102, but boasted a redesigned fuselage. The bigger engine and neater airframe gave the Delta Dart a top speed near double that of the F-102. In November 1955 the USAF ordered 17 F-102Bs, and by the time the first prototype flew on 26 December 1956, the aircraft had been redesignated the F-106. The fighter had to be able to intercept Soviet bombers in all weather up to 70,000 ft over a radius of 430 miles. Part of an integrated defence system, the F-106 was data-linked to the semi-automatic ground environment air defence network protecting North America. Early F-106s failed to meet ADC expectations and the USAF reduced its order from 1000 to 360.
Production aircraft entered service in October 1959, and 15 ADC units received F-106s. Replaced by F-15s in the late 1970s, Delta Darts soldiered on with the Air National Guard until 1988.

SPECIFICATION:

ACCOMMODATION:
pilot

DIMENSIONS:
LENGTH: 70 ft 8.50 in (21.55 m)
WINGSPAN: 38 ft 3.50 in (11.67 m)
HEIGHT: 20 ft 3.50 in (6.18 m)

WEIGHTS:
EMPTY: 23,814 lb (10,802 kg)
MAX T/O: 38,250 lb (17,350 kg)

PERFORMANCE:
MAX SPEED: 1487 mph (2393 kmh)
RANGE: 1950 miles (3138 km)
POWERPLANT: Pratt & Whitney
J75-P-17
OUTPUT: 24,500 lb st (110 kN)

FIRST FLIGHT DATE:
26 December 1956

ARMAMENT:
one M61A1 20 mm cannon in forward fuselage, four Hughes AIM-4 Falcon and two AIM-2 Genie guided missiles in weapons-bay

FEATURES:
Delta-wing layout; no horizontal tailplane; 'area rule' fuselage; squared-off fin/tail

# Dassault MD 311/312 Flamant FRANCE

12-seat, twin-engined trainer/transport/utility aircraft

One of the first post-war products of the reformed Bloch (renamed Dassault in 1945) company, the twin-engined Flamant was built to fulfil the French need for a trainer and light transport aircraft. Powered by twin Renault/SNECMA engines, the MD 311 prototype was impressive enough during flight trials to secure Dassault an initial contract for 65 aircraft in December 1947. By the time production ceased in 1952, 136 MD 311/312s had been delivered, and they would see service both in France and in its colonial territories in Africa and Asia. Used as a troop transport, freighter or air ambulance, the Flamant also saw action as a ground attack aircraft in Algeria and French Indochina. The Flamant trainer was ordered in November 1948, some 40 MD 311s (crew trainers) and 118 MD 312s (pilot trainers) being procured – the last military Flamant built (MD 312) was delivered in January 1954. Aside from Air Force aircraft, an additional 25 were built for the French Navy as MD 312Ms in 1952-53. The aircraft was finally retired in 1983.

SPECIFICATION:

ACCOMMODATION:
pilot, co-pilot and up to 10 passengers

DIMENSIONS:
LENGTH: 41 ft 11 in (12.78 m)
WINGSPAN: 66 ft 3.50 in (20.21 m)
HEIGHT: 16 ft 1 in (4.90 m)

WEIGHTS:
EMPTY: 11,245 lb (5100 kg)
MAX T/O: 14,110 lb (6400 kg)

PERFORMANCE:
MAX SPEED: 276 mph (445 kmh)
RANGE: 930 miles (1500 km)
POWERPLANT: two SNECMA 12S 02S
OUTPUT: 1060 hp (866 kW)

FIRST FLIGHT DATE:
10 February 1947

FEATURES:
Straight-wing layout; two close-cowled inline engines; twin tail layout; round fuselage windows

# Dassault MD 450 Ouragan FRANCE

single-seat, single-engined fighter

The MD 450 Ouragan (Hurricane) was the first in a long line of fighters produced by Avions Marcel Dassault. The Rolls-Royce Nene-powered Ouragan made its first flight on 28 February 1949. Three prototypes and 14 pre-production machines were subsequently used by Dassault and the French Air Force to ensure that production Ouragans enjoyed a successful introduction into frontline service in late 1951. Fifty interim standard MD 450As were built for the French Air Force, followed by 300 definitive MD 350BS powered by a lighter version of the Nene engine. Aside from the French aircraft, 71 jets were bought by the Indian Air Force in 1953-54, these MD 450BS being christened Toofanis (the Indian equivalent of Ouragan). A further 33 were procured from surplus French stocks in 1957, and they remained in frontline service until 1967. The Israelis also bought 70 surplus MD 450BS from the French in 1955-56, and they saw considerable combat over the next 15 years. The final Ouragans in military service were 18 ex-Israeli jets sold to El Salvador in 1975, which remained serviceable into the late 1980s.

SPECIFICATION:

ACCOMMODATION:
pilot

DIMENSIONS:
LENGTH: 35 ft 3 in (10.74 m)
WINGSPAN: 43 ft 2 in (13.20 m)
HEIGHT: 13 ft 7 in (4.15 m)

WEIGHTS:
EMPTY: 9150 lb (4150 kg)
MAX T/O: 14,991 lb (6800 kg)

PERFORMANCE:
MAX SPEED: 584 mph (940 kmh)
RANGE: 620 miles (1000 km)
POWERPLANT: Hispano-Suiza Nene 104B
OUTPUT: 5070 lb st (22 kN)

FIRST FLIGHT DATE:
28 February 1949

ARMAMENT:
four Hispano 404 20 mm cannon in nose; provision for up to 2200-lb (1000 kg) of bombs/rockets on four underwing stores pylons

FEATURES:
Straight-wing layout; bubble canopy; wingtip tanks; tricycle landing gear; engine air intake in nose

# Dassault Mystère IVA FRANCE

single-seat, single-engined fighter

Unlike the interim Mystère II, which was essentially a swept-wing version of the Ouragan fitted with a French-built SNECMA Atar engine and built in limited numbers, the Mystère IV was a brand new aircraft, with barely a single structural part in common between the two fighters. Its fuselage and tail were completely new, whilst the aircraft's wing was thinner, stronger and more sharply swept. The first series Mystère IVA was flown in May 1954, by which time the aircraft had been tested by the USAF prior to 225 being purchased by the US government as part of an offshore procurement contract in support of NATO nations. A further 100 jets were bought by the French government. Production aircraft began reaching frontline units in France in 1955, and the following year Mystère IVAS saw combat during the Suez Crisis. Sixty Mystère IVAS were also supplied to Israel in 1956 and 110 (67 brand new and 43 from French stocks) to India in 1957. The Israelis and Indians used their aircraft in combat as fighter-bombers into the 1970s.

SPECIFICATION:

**ACCOMMODATION:**
pilot

**DIMENSIONS:**
LENGTH: 42 ft 2 in (12.90 m)
WINGSPAN: 36 ft 5.75 in (11.10 m)
HEIGHT: 14 ft 5 in (4.40 m)

**WEIGHTS:**
EMPTY: 12,950 lb (5875 kg)
MAX T/O: 20,950 lb (9500 kg)

**PERFORMANCE:**
MAX SPEED: 696 mph (1120 kmh)
RANGE: 820 miles (1320 km)
POWERPLANT: Hispano-Suiza Verdon 350
OUTPUT: 7716 lb st (33 kN)

**FIRST FLIGHT DATE:**
28 September 1952

**ARMAMENT:**
two DEFA 551 30 mm cannon in nose; provision for up to 2000-lb (907 kg) of bombs/rockets on four underwing stores pylons

**FEATURES:**
Swept-wing layout; bubble canopy; tricycle landing gear; engine air intake in nose

# Dassault Super Mystère B2 FRANCE

single-seat, single-engined fighter

Although sharing a superficial resemblance to the Mystère II, the B2 was an all new design that featured aerodynamics copied from the F-100 Super Sabre. These combined with an Atar 101 afterburning turbojet to make the B2 the first series production Western European fighter capable of exceeding Mach 1 in level flight. Dassault produced 144 B2s for the French Air Force, the first of which was delivered in February 1957. Israel also bought 36 in 1958, and like the Ouragans and Mystère IVCS before them, the Super Mystères saw considerable combat in the Middle East over the next 15 years. Capable of carrying Sidewinder missiles, as well as bombs and rocket pods, the Super Mystère proved a capable fighter-bomber. Indeed, the Israelis rated the aircraft so highly that they re-engined their jets with Pratt & Whitney J52-P8A non-afterburning turbojets in the early 1970s in an effort to prolong their frontline life. In 1977, 18 of the re-engined machines were sold to Honduras, and these proved to be the last Super Mystères to be retired from operational service in 1989.

SPECIFICATION:

**ACCOMMODATION:**
pilot

**DIMENSIONS:**
LENGTH: 42 ft 2 in (12.90 m)
WINGSPAN: 36 ft 5.75 in (11.10 m)
HEIGHT: 14 ft 5 in (4.40 m)

**WEIGHTS:**
EMPTY: 12,950 lb (5875 kg)
MAX T/O: 20,950 lb (9500 kg)

**PERFORMANCE:**
MAX SPEED: 696 mph (1120 kmh)
RANGE: 820 miles (1320 km)
POWERPLANT: Hispano-Suiza Verdon 350
OUTPUT: 7716 lb st (33 kN)

**FIRST FLIGHT DATE:**
28 September 1952

**ARMAMENT:**
two DEFA 551 30 mm cannon in nose; provision for up to 2000-lb (907 kg) of bombs/rockets on four underwing stores pylons

**FEATURES:**
Swept-wing layout; bubble canopy; tricycle landing gear; engine air intake in nose

# Dassault Mirage III FRANCE

single-seat, single-engined fighter-bomber/reconnaissance aircraft

Conceived to meet the 1952 French Air Force light interceptor specification, the Mirage I was originally powered by two small British Viper turbojets. Dassault had little faith in the concept of low-powered lightweight fighter aircraft, however, and instead decided to develop the larger and heavier Mirage III, powered by an 8820 lb st Atar 101G. By the time the pre-production Mirage IIIA flew for the first time in May 1958, the new 13,225 lb st Atar 9 had replaced the 101G. Thanks to this powerplant, thinner wings and a revised fuselage, the Mirage IIIA-01 became the first aircraft in Western Europe to attain Mach 2 in level flight.

The production standard Mirage IIIC interceptor followed, and the first of 244 was delivered to the French Air Force in July 1961. The improved, multi-role Mirage IIIE fighter-bomber followed several years later, and this variant became the most successful, with 192 operated by the French Air Force, 98 by the RAAF (as the Mirage IIIO), 36 by the Swiss (Mirage IIIS) and over 100 exported to eight other countries.

SPECIFICATION:

**ACCOMMODATION:**
pilot

**DIMENSIONS:**
LENGTH: 49 ft 4 in (15.03 m)
WINGSPAN: 27 ft 0 in (8.22 m)
HEIGHT: 14 ft 9 in (4.50 m)

**WEIGHTS:**
EMPTY: 15,542 lb (7050 kg)
MAX T/O: 30,205 lb (13,700 kg)

**PERFORMANCE:**
MAX SPEED: 1460 mph (2350 kmh)
RANGE: 1000 miles (1610 km)
POWERPLANT: SNECMA Atar 9C-3
OUTPUT: 13,670 lb st (60.8 kN)

**FIRST FLIGHT DATE:**
17 November 1956

**ARMAMENT:**
two DEFA 552A 30 mm cannon in lower fuselage; provision for up to 8818-lb (4000 kg) of bombs/rockets/missiles on four underwing and one centreline stores pylons

**FEATURES:**
Delta-wing layout; no horizontal tail surfaces; tricycle landing gear; engine air intakes on fuselage sides aft of cockpit

# Dassault Mirage 5 FRANCE

single-seat, single-engined fighter-bomber

In 1965, the Israeli Air Force requested that Dassault build a low cost version of the Mirage III for the day fighter/ground attack mission, with the Cyrano radar and fire control avionics replaced by an extra 110 gallons of fuel and more bombs. First flown in May 1969, the Mirage 5 differed in appearance to the IIIE by having a slimmer and longer radarless nose and two extra underwing stores pylons. Israel bought the first 50 Mirage 5s built, but the imposition of an arms embargo by French President Charles de Gaulle prevented their delivery. Following the Israeli lead, a further 12 countries purchased the aircraft in varying quantities, with Dassault having built a total of 525 Mirage 5s by the time production ended in the late 1970s. Increasingly more sophisticated avionics and systems were offered as production progressed, and a number of customers bought aircraft fitted with lightweight French radar installed. The final Mirage III family variant to be built was the Mirage 50, which featured the more capable Atar engine and canards on the forward fuselage.

SPECIFICATION:

ACCOMMODATION:
pilot

DIMENSIONS:
LENGTH: 51 ft 0 in (15.55 m)
WINGSPAN: 27 ft 0 in (8.22 m)
HEIGHT: 13 ft 11.50 in (4.25 m)

WEIGHTS:
EMPTY: 14,550 lb (6600 kg)
MAX T/O: 29,760 lb (13,500 kg)

PERFORMANCE:
MAX SPEED: 1460 mph (2350 kmh)
RANGE: 1000 miles (1610 km)
POWERPLANT: SNECMA Atar 9C-3
OUTPUT: 13,670 lb st (60.8 kN)

FIRST FLIGHT DATE:
19 May 1967

ARMAMENT:
two DEFA 552A 30 mm cannon in lower fuselage; provision for up to 9260-lb (4200 kg) of bombs/rockets/missiles on six underwing and one centreline stores pylons

FEATURES:
Delta-wing layout; no horizontal tail surfaces; tricycle landing gear; engine air intakes on fuselage sides aft of cockpit

# Dassault Mirage IV FRANCE

two-seat, twin-engined strategic bomber reconnaissance aircraft

In 1954 the French government decided to create a national nuclear deterrent force, and the airborne element of this was the Mirage IV. Dassault looked at a number of designs in order to fill the Air Force requirement for a strategic bomber before settling for the Atar-powered Mirage IVA. Due to its modest size, the aircraft would have to rely on inflight refuelling to make it back to France following a strike on the USSR. Looking like a big Mirage III, the aircraft had a refuelling probe extending from the nose and surveillance and doppler radars for navigation. The Mirage IV's primary weapon was a 60 kT nuclear bomb, which was housed, semi-recessed, in an underfuselage trough. The prototype flew on 17 June 1959, and following development work with three pre-production jets, 64 Mirage IVAS were delivered between 1964 and 1968. Twelve aircraft were reconfigured as reconnaissance platforms in the 1970s, and in the late 1980s 19 jets were modified to Mirage IVP specification. Featuring new avionics and a stand-off nuclear missile capability, they are the only Mirage IVS in service today.

SPECIFICATION:

ACCOMMODATION:
pilot and navigator

DIMENSIONS:
LENGTH: 77 ft 1 in (23.50 m)
WINGSPAN: 38 ft 10.50 in (11.85 m)
HEIGHT: 17 ft 8.5 in (5.40 m)

WEIGHTS:
EMPTY: 31,967 lb (14,500 kg)
MAX T/O: 73,800 lb (33,475 kg)

PERFORMANCE:
MAX SPEED: 1454 mph (2340 kmh)
RANGE: 770 miles (1240 km)
POWERPLANT: two SNECMA
Atar 9K-50S
OUTPUT: 31,750 lb st (141.2 kN)

FIRST FLIGHT DATE:
17 June 1959

ARMAMENT:
one 60 kiloton free-fall nuclear
bomb in recessed underfuselage
trough, and up to 16,000-lb
(7257 kg) of bombs/missiles on
two underwing and one
centreline stores pylons

FEATURES:
Delta-wing layout; no horizontal
tail surfaces; tricycle landing
gear; engine air intakes on
fuselage sides aft of cockpit; twin
exhaust nozzles

# Dassault Mirage F1 FRANCE

single-seat, single-engined fighter-bomber

Dassault was awarded a development contract by the French government to develop an all weather interceptor in 1964, and the prototype F1 completed its first flight on 23 December 1966. Thanks to the F1's Atar 9K-50 engine, the aircraft was more powerful than the Mirage III, and had 43 per cent more internal fuel, which doubled the jet's combat radius. It also boasted better manoeuvrability, an improved Cyrano IV radar, slower landing approach speed and 30 per cent better short field take-off performance. The F1C was the first version to go into service, with the French Air Force receiving 100 from May 1973. Four years later production shifted to the F1C-200, which featured a fixed refuelling probe. France also took delivery of 64 reconnaissance configured F1CRs, fitted with cameras, line-scan infrared equipment and optional centreline pods. The F1 proved very popular with foreign operators, nine countries buying F1C/ES in varying quantities. The 100+ jets exported to Iraq saw considerable combat, as did South African F1AZ/CZS against Angola and Kuwaiti F1CKS in *Desert Storm*.

## SPECIFICATION:

**ACCOMMODATION:**
pilot

**DIMENSIONS:**
LENGTH: 49 ft 2.50 in (15 m)
WINGSPAN: 27 ft 6.75 in (8.40 m)
HEIGHT: 14 ft 9 in (4.50 m)

**WEIGHTS:**
EMPTY: 16,314 lb (7400 kg)
MAX T/O: 32,850 lb (14,900 kg)

**PERFORMANCE:**
MAX SPEED: 1450 mph (2335 kmh)
RANGE: 2050 miles (3300 km)
POWERPLANT: SNECMA Atar 9K-50
OUTPUT: 15,785 lb st (70.8 kN)

**FIRST FLIGHT DATE:**
23 December 1966

**ARMAMENT:**
two DEFA 553 30 mm cannon in lower fuselage; provision for up to 13,890-lb (6300 kg) of bombs/rockets/missiles on four underwing, two wingtip and one centreline stores pylons

**FEATURES:**
Shoulder-mounted wing; horizontal tail surfaces; tricycle landing gear; engine air intakes on fuselage sides aft of cockpit

# Dassault Etendard IVM/P FRANCE

single-seat, single-engined fighter-bomber

The Etendard was originally built by Dassault to
meet a NATO requirement for a light strike fighter
that had high-subsonic performance and could
operate from unpaved runways. The Fiat G 91 was
eventually chosen by NATO to fill this role, and
Dassault financed a larger machine powered by an
Atar 8 engine. The aircraft, designated the Etendard
IV, attracted the attention of the French Navy, which
was looking for a multi-role shipboard fighter. An
order was placed for a semi-navalised prototype in
December 1956, followed in May 1957 by a contract
for five pre-production aircraft. The prototype
completed its maiden flight on 21 May 1958,
followed by the first pre-production aircraft
(designated the IVM) seven months later. The
Etendard IVM featured folding wingtips, a
strengthened undercarriage and extendable nose
gear leg and an arrestor hook. A total of 69 Etendard
IVM strike and 21 IVP reconnaissance aircraft were
built for the French Navy between 1961-64, and
these served on the carriers *Foch* and *Clemenceau*
until replaced by the Super Etendard in 1991.

SPECIFICATION:

ACCOMMODATION:
pilot

DIMENSIONS:
LENGTH: 47 ft 3 in (14.40 m)
WINGSPAN: 31 ft 5.75 in (9.60 m)
HEIGHT: 14 ft 0 in (4.26 m)

WEIGHTS:
EMPTY: 12,786 lb (5800 kg)
MAX T/O: 22,486 lb (10,200 kg)

PERFORMANCE:
MAX SPEED: 683 mph (1099 kmh)
RANGE: 1056 miles (1700 km)
POWERPLANT: SNECMA Atar 8B
OUTPUT: 9700 lb st (42.4 kN)

FIRST FLIGHT DATE:
21 May 1958

ARMAMENT:
two DEFA 552 30 mm cannon in
lower fuselage; provision for up
to 3000-lb (1360 kg) of
bombs/rockets/missiles on four
underwing stores pylons

FEATURES:
Swept-wing; horizontal tail
surfaces; tricycle landing gear;
engine air intakes on fuselage
sides aft of cockpit

# Dassault/Dornier Alpha Jet FRANCE & GERMANY

two-seat, twin-engined advanced trainer and ground attack aircraft

The Alpha Jet was the end product of a combined French and German effort in the late 1960s to create a subsonic jet trainer to replace long-serving types such as the T-33 and Magister. Powered by two SNECMA Turboméca Larzac turbofans, the aircraft was named the Alpha Jet. Early in the jet's development phase the Germans changed their requirement so that the aircraft could fulfil the close support battlefield reconnaissance role as well. Development go ahead was received in February 1972, and the first prototype flew on 26 October 1973. Delivery of 175 French Alpha Jet ES commenced in 1978, while Germany's first Alpha Jet A completed its maiden flight in April 1978. Fitted with a comprehensive navigation/attack suite, the Luftwaffe received 175 Alpha Jets as G 91 replacements, although all but 35 of these (used as lead-in trainers for the Tornado) were subsequently retired in 1993. Fifty of the surplus jets were duly sold to Portugal. Nine other countries also bought a combined total of 156 A/ES, and the vast majority of these aircraft remain in service today.

## SPECIFICATION:

**ACCOMMODATION:**
two pilots in tandem

**DIMENSIONS:**
LENGTH: 43 ft 5 in (13.23 m)
WINGSPAN: 29 ft 11 in (9.11 m)
HEIGHT: 13 ft 9 in (4.19 m)

**WEIGHTS:**
EMPTY: 7750 lb (3515 kg)
MAX T/O: 17,637 lb (8000 kg)

**PERFORMANCE:**
MAX SPEED: 621 mph (1000 kmh)
RANGE: 901 miles (1450 km)
POWERPLANT: two SNECMA/
Turboméca Larzac 04-C20s
OUTPUT: 6350 lb st (28.2 kN)

**FIRST FLIGHT DATE:**
26 October 1973

**ARMAMENT:**
DEFA 30 mm or Mauser 27 mm cannon pod under fuselage; provision for up to 5510-lb (2500 kg) of bombs/rockets/missiles on four underwing stores pylons

**FEATURES:**
Shoulder-mounted swept-wing; tandem cockpits; extensive cockpit glazing; tricycle landing gear; engine air intakes on fuselage sides aft of cockpit

# de Havilland Vampire UK

single/two-seat, single-engined fighter/jet trainer

The Vampire was the second jet fighter to enter service with the RAF, being designed around de Havilland's compact Goblin turbojet engine. The thrust produced by these early powerplants was modest to say the least, so the company's design team adopted a twin-boom layout so as to keep the length of the engine's jet tailpipe – a source of much power loss – to a minimum. This worked well, for the prototype Vampire was the first Allied aircraft to exceed 500 mph. Subsequently built in numerous sub-types, the Vampire was modified to perform fighter-bomber and nightfighter (the latter boasted two seats and an Air Intercept radar in the nose) missions. Finally, a highly successful trainer variant was developed from the two-seat night-fighter, this becoming the first jet aircraft in the Air Force on which pilots could actually qualify for their 'wings' when it entered service with the RAF's Flying Training Command in 1952. Aside from the 1500+ Vampires built for the RAF, fighter and training variants were flown by the Fleet Air Arm and export models were produced in great numbers too.

SPECIFICATION:

**ACCOMMODATION:**
one pilot, or two pilots (or one navigator) seated side-by-side

**DIMENSIONS:**
LENGTH: 34 ft 6.5 in (10.51 m)
WINGSPAN: 38 ft 0 in (11.59 m)
HEIGHT: 6 ft 2 in (1.88 m)

**WEIGHTS:**
EMPTY: 7380 lb (3347 kg)
MAX T/O: 11,150 lb (5060 kg) clean

**PERFORMANCE:**
MAX SPEED: 538 mph (866 kmh)
RANGE: 853 miles (1370 km)
POWERPLANT: de Havilland Goblin 35
OUTPUT: 3500 lb st (15.57 kN)

**FIRST FLIGHT DATE:**
20 September 1943

**ARMAMENT:**
four Hispano 20 mm cannon in nose; provision for up to 2000-lb (907 kg) of bombs/rockets on two underwing stores pylons

**FEATURES:**
Straight-wing layout; twin boom/tail layout; bubble canopy; tricycle landing gear

# de Havilland Venom/Sea Venom UK

single/two-seat, single-engined fighter-bomber/nightfighter

Successor to the DH 100 Vampire, the DH 112
Venom utilised a thinner wing and more powerful
Ghost turbojet engine. De Havilland modified the
wings of the new design to boast slight quarter-
chord sweepback, plus plumbed them for the
carriage of tip tanks. The first of 375 Venom FB 1S
entered service in 1951. The FB 1 was replaced on
the production line by the FB 4, which had a larger
flat-topped fin-and-rudder design, powered
ailerons, more powerful Ghost 105 engine and
provision for underwing drop tanks. Some 150
were delivered to the RAF from May 1954 onwards.
Export orders for both versions were also secured,
with the Swiss EFW consortium building 100 FB 1S
and 150 FB 4S for its air force. A two-seat
nightfighter variant was also developed as the
NF 2/3, which replaced the Vampire NF 10 in service
from 1953 (90 NF 2S and 129 NF 3S were built).
Finally, the Fleet Air Arm bought the Sea Venom
all-weather fighter, which featured a tailhook,
strengthened undercarriage and folding wings –
217 were built (FAW 20S and 21S).

SPECIFICATION:

ACCOMMODATION:
one pilot, or a pilot and navigator
seated side-by-side

DIMENSIONS:
LENGTH: 36 ft 8 in (11.21 m)
WINGSPAN: 41 ft 9 in (12.80 m)
HEIGHT: 8 ft 6 in (2.59 m)

WEIGHTS:
EMPTY: 8800 lb (4000 kg)
MAX T/O: 15,800 lb (7167 kg) clean

PERFORMANCE:
MAX SPEED: 590 mph (950 kmh)
RANGE: 1000 miles (1610 km)
POWERPLANT: de Havilland
Ghost 104
OUTPUT: 4950 lb st (21.9 kN)

FIRST FLIGHT DATE:
22 August 1950

ARMAMENT:
four Hispano Mk 5 20 mm
cannon in nose; provision for up
to 2000-lb (907kg) of
bombs/rockets/missiles on two
underwing stores pylons

FEATURES:
Straight-wing layout; twin
boom/tail layout; bubble canopy;
tricycle landing gear; tip tanks

# de Havilland Sea Vixen UK

two-seat, twin-engined fighter-bomber

Built in response to joint 1946 Air Ministry and Admiralty requirements for a nightfighter, the first of two DH 110 prototypes was flown on 26 September 1951. Although the aircraft adhered to the company's tried and tested twin boom layout, the jet had a highly swept wing, all-metal structure, powered controls and a horizontal tail atop sharply raked fins. Initial flight trials proved the worthiness of the design, but a crash at the 1952 Farnborough airshow slowed progress to such a degree that six years would pass before production standard Sea Vixen FAW 1s entered service with the Royal Navy in November 1958.

Although no longer the world-beater that it may once have been, the aircraft nevertheless gave the Fleet Air Arm a formidable all-weather interception capability when paired with the new air-to-air missiles that were entering service at this time. Also capable of carrying 1000-lb of bombs or rockets, the Sea Vixen FAW 1 was replaced by the FAW 2 in October 1962. A total of 146 Sea Vixens were built, and these remained in fleet service until 1971.

SPECIFICATION:

**ACCOMMODATION:**
pilot and navigator

**DIMENSIONS:**
LENGTH: 55 ft 7 in (17 m)
WINGSPAN: 50 ft 0 in (15.24 m)
HEIGHT: 10 ft 9 in (3.30 m)

**WEIGHTS:**
EMPTY: 22,000 lb (9979 kg)
MAX T/O: 36,000 lb (16,329 kg) clean

**PERFORMANCE:**
MAX SPEED: 650 mph (1050 kmh)
RANGE: 800 miles (1280 km)
POWERPLANT: two Rolls-Royce Avon 208s
OUTPUT: 22,500 lb st (104 kN)

**FIRST FLIGHT DATE:**
26 September 1951

**ARMAMENT:**
four Red Top or Firestreak missiles on four inboard underwing pylons; provision for up to 1000-lb (454 kg) of bombs/missiles on two outboard underwing stores pylons

**FEATURES:**
Swept-wing layout; twin boom/tail layout; bubble canopy; tricycle landing gear; high horizontal tail

# de Havilland Devon/Sea Devon   UK

13-seat, twin-engined executive transport aircraft

The first post-war design to be produced in quantity by de Havilland, and built as a replacement for the company's pre-war Dragon Rapide, the Dove made little sales impact until bought in quantity by the RAF in 1948 for use as a general communications aircraft. Based on the Dove 4, and christened the Devon C 1, the first military examples were issued to No 31 Sqn at Hendon. With a production life lasting from 1945 to 1968, 544 Doves were built to eight separate series specifications – varying levels of horsepower from the aircraft's Gipsy Queen engines provided the major difference between variants. Aside from use by the RAF in Devon C 1 (Gipsy Queen 71s) and C 2 (Gipsy Queen 175s) configuration, the Royal Navy also operated a small number of Sea Devon C 20s as 'admirals' barges' well into the 1970s. Overseas, modest numbers of Doves found military application with the air forces of Ethiopia, India, Ireland, Jordan, the Lebanon, Malaysia, Paraguay and Sri Lanka, whilst RAF-specification Devons were used by India and New Zealand.

## SPECIFICATION:

**ACCOMMODATION:**
pilot and co-pilot and up to 11 passengers

**DIMENSIONS:**
LENGTH: 39 ft 4 in (11.99 m)
WINGSPAN: 57 ft 0 in (17.37 m)
HEIGHT: 13 ft 4 in (4.06 m)

**WEIGHTS:**
EMPTY: 6580 lb (2985 kg)
MAX T/O: 8950 lb (4060 kg)

**PERFORMANCE:**
MAX SPEED: 210 mph (338 kmh)
RANGE: 880 miles (1415 km) with maximum fuel
POWERPLANT: two de Havilland Gipsy Queen 70-3 engines
OUTPUT: 800 hp (596 kW)

**FIRST FLIGHT DATE:**
25 September 1945

**FEATURES:**
Unswept wing layout; two close-cowled inline engines; retractable tricycle landing gear

# de Havilland Canada DHC-1 Chipmunk CANADA/UK

two-seat, single-engined basic training aircraft

The first aircraft designed by de Havilland Canada (DHC), the Chipmunk was developed to replace the Tiger Moth in the primary training role. The aircraft was ordered into series production as the T 1 for the RCAF, DHC building 218 Chipmunks to this standard, including military examples for Egypt, Chile and Thailand. With the introduction of the Gipsy Major 10, the aircraft's RCAF designation changed to T 2. Following flight trials in the UK, Specification 8/48 was issued by the Air Ministry to cover the purchase 735 Chipmunk T 10s, which were issued to most primary flying training units in the RAF. The British Chipmunk differed from its Canadian forbear in being fully aerobatic and having a multi-panelled sliding canopy rather than a single-piece sliding unit – the Gipsy Major 8 engine was also used. Aside from those supplied to the RAF (and Army Air Corps and Fleet Air Arm), de Havilland UK also produced 217 for export, whilst a further 60 were built under-licence by OGMA in Portugal. The RAF and Army Air Corps retired its last Chipmunks in 1996.

SPECIFICATION:

**ACCOMMODATION:**
two pilots in tandem

**DIMENSIONS:**
LENGTH: 25 ft 5 in (7.75 m)
WINGSPAN: 34 ft 4 in (10.45 m)
HEIGHT: 7 ft 0 in (2.13 m)

**WEIGHTS:**
EMPTY: 1425 lb (646 kg)
MAX T/O: 2014 lb (914 kg)

**PERFORMANCE:**
MAX SPEED: 138 mph (222 kmh)
RANGE: 280 miles (451 km)
POWERPLANT: de Havilland Gipsy Major 8 or 10
OUTPUT: both 145 hp (108 kW)

**FIRST FLIGHT DATE:**
22 May 1946

**FEATURES:**
Unswept wing layout; close-cowled inline engine; fixed undercarriage

# de Havilland Canada DHC-2 Beaver   CANADA

eight-seat, single-engined high-wing utility light transport

The first of DHC's 'bush' aircraft, the Beaver was a rugged, reliable, 'go anywhere' machine, boasting incredible Short Take-Off and Landing (STOL) characteristics and the ability to carry a useful payload. The Beaver's big break came in 1951 when it was selected to fulfil a joint US Army/Air Force requirement for a liaison aircraft. By the time the order had been completed in 1960, 968 L-20A Beavers had been delivered, the bulk of these (three-quarters) going to the Army. The Beaver proved popular in frontline service, and saw action in the Korean and Vietnam Wars.

Redesignated the U-6A in 1962, the Beaver remained in the employ of the Army and Air Force into the 1970s. Today only the US Navy uses the type, operating three examples with its Test Pilot's School. Other nations to buy the Beaver in quantity included Britain, which purchased 46 AL 1s for the Army Air Corps, Chile with 15 and Colombia 18, although few of these remain in service– a handful are reportedly still flying in Colombia. Total Beaver production reached 1691 aircraft.

SPECIFICATION:

**ACCOMMODATION:**
pilot and up to seven passengers

**DIMENSIONS:**
LENGTH: 30 ft 4 in (9.24 m)
WINGSPAN: 48 ft 0 in (14.64 m)
HEIGHT: 9 ft 0 in (2.75 m)

**WEIGHTS:**
EMPTY: 2850 lb (1293 kg)
MAX T/O: 5100 lb (2313 kg)

**PERFORMANCE:**
MAX SPEED: 140 mph (225 kmh)
RANGE: 778 miles (1252 km) with maximum fuel
POWERPLANT: Pratt & Whitney R-985-AN Wasp Junior
OUTPUT: 450 hp (336 kW)

**FIRST FLIGHT DATE:**
August 1947

**FEATURES:**
High-wing layout; close-cowled radial engine; fixed undercarriage

# de Havilland Canada DHC-4 Caribou   CANADA

34-seat, twin-engined tactical transport aircraft

Built in an effort to combine the load carrying
capacity of the C-47 with the STOL performance of
the Beaver, the DHC-4 Caribou relied on a high-
aspect-ratio cranked wing fitted with full-span
double-slotted flaps to perform the latter portion of
its mission. The Caribou was both robust and agile,
its STOL performance being unmatched. Even
before the prototype aircraft had flown, the US
Army had committed to five aircraft and, following
trials, ordered 159 – total Caribou production
numbered 304. As the largest fixed-wing type flown
by the Army, the first aircraft entered service in
1961. Capable of carrying 32 troops, 26 paratroops,
22 stretchers, two fully-loaded Jeeps or three tons
of cargo, the Caribou operated into forward
landing strips. Such missions were undertaken in
Vietnam, where US Army aircraft flew alongside
RAAF Caribou. In 1967 the responsibility for all
fixed-wing transports was transferred to the USAF,
and surviving Caribou were redesignated C-7AS.
Retired from USAF service in the late 1970s, a
handful of Caribou remain in use with the RAAF.

SPECIFICATION:

**ACCOMMODATION:**
pilot, co-pilot, loadmaster and up
to 32 passengers

**DIMENSIONS:**
LENGTH: 72 ft 7 in (22.13 m)
WINGSPAN: 95 ft 7.5 in (29.15 m)
HEIGHT: 31 ft 9 in (9.70 m)

**WEIGHTS:**
EMPTY: 18,260 lb (8283 kg)
MAX T/O: 31,300 lb (14,197 kg)

**PERFORMANCE:**
MAX SPEED: 216 mph (347 kmh)
RANGE: 1307 miles (2103 km)
POWERPLANT: two Pratt & Whitney
R-2000-7M2 Twin Wasps
OUTPUT: 2900 hp (2162 kW)

**FIRST FLIGHT DATE:**
30 July 1958

**FEATURES:**
High-wing layout; high beaver
tail; two close-cowled radial
engines; retractable tricycle
undercarriage

# Douglas A-1 Skyraider  USA

single/three-seat, single-engined attack/AEW aircraft

Initially dubbed the 'Dauntless II', the A-1 had the reputation of the Douglas dive-bomber to live up to. That the aircraft broke all records for frontline longevity for a piston-engined attack type, and served with distinction in Korea and Vietnam, proves that the Skyraider's reputation as a tough workhorse was equal to its initial Dauntless sobriquet. The success of the Skyraider was due as much to its engine – the Wright R-3350 – as to its airframe. That same engine delayed the aircraft's entry into service long enough for it to miss World War 2. Indeed, it seemed that the aircraft would remain unproven in action with the US Navy. However, the Skyraider refused to become obsolete, and fought in the Korean War. With the advent of jet types like the Skyhawk, the life of the A-1 seemed limited by the late 1950s. However, the Vietnam War gave the it a new lease of life – so much so that both the USAF and South Vietnamese Air Force used ex-Navy A-1s in action from 1964. The Navy retired its last Skyraiders in April 1968.

SPECIFICATION:

ACCOMMODATION:
pilot, or pilot and three radar operators seated side-by-side

DIMENSIONS:
LENGTH: 40 ft 1 in (12.19 m)
WINGSPAN: 50 ft 9 in (15.47 m)
HEIGHT: 15 ft 10 in (4.83 m)

WEIGHTS:
EMPTY: 12,313 lb (5585 kg)
MAX T/O: 25,000 lb (11,340 kg)

PERFORMANCE:
MAX SPEED: 311 mph (501 kmh)
RANGE: 3000 miles (4828 km)
POWERPLANT: Wright R-3350-26W or R-3350-26WB
OUTPUT: 3020 hp (2252 kW) and 3050 hp (2271 kW)

FIRST FLIGHT DATE:
18 March 1945

ARMAMENT:
four 20 mm cannon in outer wings; provision for up to 8000-lb (3630 kg) of bombs/ torpedoes/rockets on 14 underwing and one centre fuselage stores pylons

FEATURES:
Straight-wing layout; close-cowled radial engine; retractable undercarriage; bubble canopy; arrestor hook

# Douglas A-3 Skywarrior  USA

seven-seat, twin-engined bomber/electronic warfare aircraft

The Skywarrior was the world's first carrier-based strategic bomber. Designed around both the predicted size of future thermonuclear bombs and the strength and length of the *Forrestal* class 'supercarriers', the jet boasted a large bomb-bay, blind bombing radar and an Aero-21B remote tail turret. Douglas was contracted to build 280 Skywarriors, and the last of these being completed in January 1961. Performing the heavy bomber mission for a decade, the Skywarrior was replaced in its intended role by the more agile, and more survivable, A-6 Intruder in the mid-1960s, although the A-3's fleet service continued for another 25 years. Thanks to its size, the Skywarrior was suited to performing other tasks such as aerial refuelling (KA-3B), reconnaissance (RA-3B), radar/navigation training (TA-3B) and electronic countermeasures (EA-3B). Seeing action throughout the Vietnam War, the Skywarrior disappeared from carrier decks in the late 1980s, although a handful of EA-3BS survived long enough to see action in *Desert Storm* in 1991, flying from shore bases.

## SPECIFICATION:

**ACCOMMODATION:**
pilot, co-pilot, bombardier and four systems operators

**DIMENSIONS:**
LENGTH: 76 ft 6 in (23.35 m)
WINGSPAN: 72 ft 5 in (22.10 m)
HEIGHT: 23 ft 4 in (7.13 m)

**WEIGHTS:**
EMPTY: 41,193 lb (18,685 kg)
MAX T/O: 78,000 lb (35,380 kg)

**PERFORMANCE:**
MAX SPEED: 557 mph (1032 kmh)
RANGE: 1110 miles (2057 km)
POWERPLANT: two Pratt & Whitney J57-10S
OUTPUT: 20,400 lb st (95 kN)

**FIRST FLIGHT DATE:**
28 June 1954

**ARMAMENT:**
remotely controlled 20 mm cannon in tail turret; provision for up to 15,000-lb (6804 kg) of bombs in bomb-bay

**FEATURES:**
Swept shoulder-mounted wing; retractable tricycle undercarriage; two podded engines below wings

# Douglas B-66 Destroyer   USA

seven-seat, twin-engined bomber/electronic warfare aircraft

Built by Douglas's Long Beach, California, plant, the B-66 started life as a slightly modified Skywarrior that was tailored to meet a USAF requirement for a tactical attack bomber. Yet, despite looking outwardly similar, the Destroyer had hardly a single airframe part or system common with the A-3! This in turn meant that the B-66 was expensive both to construct and maintain. Built as reconnaissance tactical/nuclear bombers, 145 RB-66BS were produced for the USAF's Tactical Air Command, followed by 72 B-66BS. Although the reconnaissance bomber variant saw only brief service, the electronic intelligence-optimised RB-66C proved far more successful, the B-66's bomb-bay having been replaced by a pressurised compartment for electronic warfare (EW) systems. Some 36 RB-66CS were built, and an identical number of WB-66D weather reconnaissance jets were also delivered to the USAF. The Destroyer saw considerable combat over Vietnam, with the EW-configured EB-66C/ES (rebuilt B/RB-66S) providing electronic countermeasures.

## SPECIFICATION:

**ACCOMMODATION:**
pilot, co-pilot, bombardier and four systems operators

**DIMENSIONS:**
LENGTH: 75 ft 2 in (22.90 m)
WINGSPAN: 72 ft 5 in (22.10 m)
HEIGHT: 23 ft 7 in (7.19 m)

**WEIGHTS:**
EMPTY: 44,771 lb (20,308 kg)
MAX T/O: 76,967 lb (34,912 kg)

**PERFORMANCE:**
MAX SPEED: 700 mph (1127 kmh)
RANGE: 2035 miles (3275 km)
POWERPLANT: two Allison J71-13S
OUTPUT: 24,800 lb st (111.17 kN)

**FIRST FLIGHT DATE:**
28 October 1952

**ARMAMENT:**
remotely controlled 20 mm cannon in tail turret; provision for up to 12,000-lb (5443 kg) of bombs in bomb-bay

**FEATURES:**
Swept shoulder-mounted wing; retractable tricycle undercarriage; arrestor hook; two podded engines below wings

# Douglas A-4 Skyhawk USA

single/two-seat, single-engined attack/advanced training aircraft

Bucking the trend for ever-larger combat aircraft when built in the early 1950s, the Douglas A-4 weighed less than half the specified weight (of 30,000 lbs) stipulated by the US Navy for its new jet attack bomber, yet was still capable of undertaking all the missions required of it. The first A-4As (then designated A4D-1s) entered service in October 1956, and by the time of the Vietnam War all carrier air wings included at least two squadrons of Skyhawks.

The B-, C- and E-models had all seen the capabilities (and weight) of the A-4 increase since the first examples were built, and the aircraft was in the vanguard of Navy and Marine Corps light attack strikes on Vietnam. Export success was also enjoyed by the Skyhawk, with substantial numbers being sold to Indonesia, Australia, Malaysia, Singapore, New Zealand, Kuwait, Israel and Argentina. In 1965 Douglas produced the two-seat TA-4, and 555 were subsequently built for the US Navy, Marine Corps and export customers. Of the 2405 attack models produced between 1954 and 1979, a handful are still in frontline service today.

SPECIFICATION:

ACCOMMODATION:
pilot, or two pilots in tandem

DIMENSIONS:
LENGTH: 39 ft 6 in (12.04 m)
WINGSPAN: 27 ft 6 in (8.38 m)
HEIGHT: 15 ft 0 in (4.57 m)

WEIGHTS:
EMPTY: 9284 lb (4211 kg)
MAX T/O: 22,000 lb (9979 kg)

PERFORMANCE:
MAX SPEED: 676 mph (1088 kmh)
RANGE: 920 miles (1480 km)
POWERPLANT: Wright J65-16A
(A-4B/C) or Pratt & Whitney
J52-P-8A (TA-4J)
OUTPUT: 7700 lb st (33.8 kN) and
9300 lb st (41.4 kN) respectively

FIRST FLIGHT DATE:
22 June 1954

ARMAMENT:
two Mk 12 20 mm cannon in
wing roots; 9155-lb (4153 kg) of
bombs/rockets/missiles on four
underwing/one centre fuselage
stores pylons

FEATURES:
Delta-wing; delta tailplane;
bubble canopy; arrestor
hook; engine air intakes on
fuselage sides

# Douglas R4D-8/C-117 USA

41-seat, twin-engined transport aircraft

Dubbed the Super DC-3 by manufacturer Douglas, the R4D-8 was the military version of the reworked transport classic that had so revolutionised both civil and military air transport. Rather than produce an all-new design, Douglas was convinced that all the market wanted was another variant of the Dakota. Accordingly, the aircraft was revised through the fitment of a squared off tail section and a more aerodynamic wing (slightly swept and squared off). Further streamlining was achieved by fully enclosing the main gear legs, whilst the aircraft's performance was improved through the replacement of its Twin Wasp engines with more powerful Wright Cyclones. Despite an exhaustive American sales tour, the Super DC-3 evoked little interest – indeed, if it had not been for the US Navy ordering 100 as the R4D-8 (only 17 were built, with the remainder being converted from standard R4DS), it is unlikely that the Super DC-3 would have entered series production. In military service, the R4D-8 (redesignated the C-117D in 1962) was employed in cargo hauling and VIP tasks.

SPECIFICATION:

**ACCOMMODATION:**
pilot, co-pilot, navigator and 38 passengers

**DIMENSIONS:**
LENGTH: 71 ft 1 in (21.67 m)
WINGSPAN: 93 ft 0 in (28.34 m)
HEIGHT: 18 ft 11 in (5.51 m)

**WEIGHTS:**
EMPTY: 21,470 lb (9738 kg)
MAX T/O: 30,500 lb (13,834 kg)

**PERFORMANCE:**
MAX SPEED: 270 mph (432 kmh)
RANGE: 2125 miles (3420 km)
POWERPLANT: two Wright R-1820-80 Cyclones
OUTPUT: 3070 hp (2290.22 kW)

**FIRST FLIGHT DATE:**
June 1949

**FEATURES:**
Straight-wing layout, but with swept leading edge; two close-cowled radial engines; tall tailfin; low-set tailplane, fully retractable undercarriage

# Douglas R6D/C-118 Liftmaster USA

78-seat, four-engined transport aircraft

The C-118 was the end result of a USAAF requirement for a C-54 Skymaster successor which provided the advantages of a greater payload, higher performance and, most importantly, full pressurisation so that the aircraft could attain higher altitudes, and thus be flown over adverse weather. Initially designated the XC-112A, the transport completed its first flight in February 1946. However, with World War 2 now over, the USAAF had lost interest in the new aircraft, and the transport duly became the civil DC-6 airliner instead. Essentially an enlarged version of the DC-4/C-54, the DC-6 initially shared its wing and fuselage structure, although later A/B models were twelve feet longer. The first DC-6 to enter military service was the 26th production example built, which the USAAF bought in 1947 for use as a presidential transport for President Harry S Truman. Designated a C-118, this aircraft paved the way for future orders from both the Air Force and the Navy, the former buying 101 C-118As and the latter 65 R6D-1s (which were redesignated C-118Bs in 1962) for personnel and logistic transportation.

SPECIFICATION:

ACCOMMODATION:
pilot, co-pilot, navigator, engineer and 74 passengers

DIMENSIONS:
LENGTH: 105 ft 7 in (32.21 m)
WINGSPAN: 117 ft 6 in (35.81 m)
HEIGHT: 28 ft 8 in (8.77 m)

WEIGHTS:
EMPTY: 49,767 lb (22,574 kg)
MAX T/O: 107,000 lb (48,535 kg)

PERFORMANCE:
MAX SPEED: 315 mph (504 kmh)
RANGE: 4720 miles (7552 km)
POWERPLANT: four Pratt & Whitney R-2800-52WS
OUTPUT: 10,000 hp (7457 kW)

FIRST FLIGHT DATE:
15 February 1946

FEATURES:
Straight-wing layout; tricycle landing gear; four close-cowled radial engines; tall tailfin; low-set tailplane

# Douglas C-124 Globemaster USA

205-seat, four-engined strategic transport aircraft

Using the DC-4 as a base, Douglas commenced work on a giant military transport in 1942 after securing an order for a prototype from the USAAF. Designated the XC-74, the prototype flew on 3 September 1945. With the war now all but over, the emphasis for the aircraft shifted to civil transoceanic employment. Pan American ordered 26, but then pulled out of the project, while a large-scale USAAF buy was reduced to 14 aircraft. These were delivered in 1946-47, and had almost circular-section fuselages due to the fact that the civilian C-74 was to have been pressurised. This proved impractical on the military variant due to its freight doors, so the pressurisation was deleted and the C-74 redesigned with a fuselage that offered twice the internal volume. The nose was fitted with clamshell doors for loading vehicles and heavy freight. Designated the YC-124 Globemaster, the first prototype flew on 27 November 1949, and production examples reached the USAF in May 1950. A total of 204 C-124As and 243 C-124Cs were built, and they saw service into the 1970s.

SPECIFICATION:

ACCOMMODATION:
pilot, co-pilot, navigator, engineer, loadmaster and 200 passengers

DIMENSIONS:
LENGTH: 130 ft 5 in (39.75 m)
WINGSPAN: 174 ft 1.50 in (53.08 m)
HEIGHT: 48 ft 3.50 in (14.70 m)

WEIGHTS:
EMPTY: 101,165 lb (45,887 kg)
MAX T/O: 194,500 lb (88,223 kg)

PERFORMANCE:
MAX SPEED: 304 mph (489 kmh)
RANGE: 6820 miles (10,975 km)
POWERPLANT: four Pratt & Whitney R-4360-20WAS
OUTPUT: 14,000 hp (10,440 kW)

FIRST FLIGHT DATE:
17 November 1949 (YC-124)

FEATURES:
Straight-wing layout; tricycle landing gear; four close-cowled radial engines; tall tailfin; large, double-deck fuselage; clamshell doors in nose

# Douglas C-133 Cargomaster USA

five/six-seat, four-engined heavy logistic freighter

Developed by Douglas to fulfil a USAF requirement for a logistic transporter capable of lifting strategic cargo that could not be easily 'broken down' for carriage in the C-124 or C-130, the C-133 went straight into production from the drawing board. The first C-133A doubled as the prototype, the aircraft's pressurised fuselage of circular section being able to accept the new Atlas and Titan ICBMS through full width rear cargo doors. The first of 35 A-models was delivered to the USAF in August 1957, and these were followed by 15 C-133BS from 1959, the latter variant boasting a more powerful version of the T34 engine and a revised rear fuselage combining clamshell doors. It was estimated at the time that roughly 96 per cent of all US military equipment could be carried by the Cargomaster. This was put to the test during the American build up in South Vietnam in the mid-1960s. The advent of the C-5 Galaxy in 1969 eased the overworked C-133's burden, the Lockheed transporter replacing the Cargomaster. The last C-133s were retired in 1979.

SPECIFICATION:

**ACCOMMODATION:**
pilot, co-pilot, navigator, two flight engineers, loadmaster

**DIMENSIONS:**
LENGTH: 157 ft 6.5 in (48.02 m)
WINGSPAN: 179 ft 8 in (54.75 m)
HEIGHT: 48 ft 3 in (14.7 m)

**WEIGHTS:**
EMPTY: 120,263 lb (54,550 kg)
MAX T/O: 286,000 lb (129,727 kg)

**PERFORMANCE:**
MAX SPEED: 359 mph (578 kmh)
RANGE: 4300 miles (6920 km)
POWERPLANT: four Pratt & Whitney T34-7S (C-133A) or T34-9WS (C-133B)
OUTPUT: 28,000 shp (20,879 kW) and 30,000 shp (22,368 kW) respectively

**FIRST FLIGHT DATE:**
23 April 1956

**FEATURES:**
Shoulder-mounted straight-wing; tricycle landing gear; four close-cowled turboprop engines; tall tailfin; rear cargo doors

# Douglas F3D Skynight USA

two-seat, twin-engined fighter

On 3 April 1946 Douglas received a contract from the US Navy to produce an all-weather jet fighter for use from its new large aircraft carriers. Designated the XF3D-1, the prototype made its first flight on 23 March 1948, after which work commenced on 28 F3D-1 Skynights. Production aircraft reached VC-3 in 1951, by which time testing of the F3D-2 had begun. This version became the definitive variant, with 237 built. Deemed unsuitable for carrier operations, most F3D-2s were passed on to the US Marine Corps, which sent Skynights into action in Korea. Thanks to its radar equipment and all-weather interception capabilities, the jet proved successful in the nightfighter role, downing MiG-15s and a PO-2 in 1952-53. A number of F3D-2s were modified for different roles in the 1950s, 35 receiving electronic reconnaissance and countermeasures equipment as F3D-2Qs and 55 being converted into F3D-2T radar controller trainers. Surviving jets became F/TF/EF-10Bs in September 1962, and the latter variant was the first tactical EW jet aircraft to see service in Vietnam.

SPECIFICATION:

ACCOMMODATION:
pilot and radar operator

DIMENSIONS:
LENGTH: 45 ft 5 in (13.84 m)
WINGSPAN: 50 ft 9 in (15.24 m)
HEIGHT: 16 ft 1 in (4.90 m)

WEIGHTS:
EMPTY: 14,989 lb (6799 kg)
MAX T/O: 26,731 lb (12,125 kg)

PERFORMANCE:
MAX SPEED: 490 mph (788 kmh)
RANGE: 1146 miles (1844 km)
POWERPLANT: two Westinghouse J34-WE-36s
OUTPUT: 6800 lb st (15.4 kN)

FIRST FLIGHT DATE:
23 March 1948

ARMAMENT:
four 20 mm cannon under nose and four Sparrow missiles on four underwing stores pylons

FEATURES:
Straight-wing; tricycle landing gear; engines located under wing centre section

# Douglas F4D Skyray USA

single-seat, single-engined fighter

Influenced by wartime work carried out by German scientists on delta-winged aircraft, the US Navy issued a proposal for a short-range interceptor with a similar layout. Two XF4D-1 prototypes were ordered in December 1948, although development was delayed by problems with the aircraft's ill-fated Westinghouse J40 turbojet. Using an Allison J35 instead, the prototype flew for the first time on 23 January 1951. By the time production aircraft began to be assembled at Douglas in late 1954 the Skyray featured a Pratt & Whitney J57-P-2. Further flight test problems delayed delivery of jets to the Navy until April 1956, after which large numbers were handed over in a short space of time. All 420 aircraft on order had been built by December 1958, and all to F4D-1 standard. Flown by eleven Navy and six Marine Corps fighter squadrons, as well as three reserve units and several specialised squadrons, the Skyray enjoyed only a brief career due to its modest armament and engine performance. Redesignated the F-6A in September 1962, final examples were retired 18 months later.

SPECIFICATION:

ACCOMMODATION:
pilot

DIMENSIONS:
LENGTH: 45 ft 8 in (13.90 m)
WINGSPAN: 33 ft 6 in (10.20 m)
HEIGHT: 13 ft 0 in (3.96 m)

WEIGHTS:
EMPTY: 16,030 lb (7250 kg)
MAX T/O: 27,000 lb (12,250 kg)

PERFORMANCE:
MAX SPEED: 725 mph (1167 kmh)
RANGE: 950 miles (1530 km)
POWERPLANT: Pratt & Whitney
J57-P-8
OUTPUT: 16,000 lb st (74.5 kN)

FIRST FLIGHT DATE:
23 January 1951

ARMAMENT:
four 20 mm cannon in outer
wings; provision for up to
4000-lb (1814 kg) of bombs/
rockets on six underwing/
fuselage stores pylons

FEATURES:
Delta-wing; no horizontal
tailplane; tricycle landing gear;
engine; arrestor hook; engine air
intakes on fuselage sides aft
of cockpit

# English Electric Canberra UK

two-seat, twin-engined bomber/reconnaissance aircraft

Aside from being the RAF's first jet bomber, the Canberra has also proved to be Britain's most durable frontline type, with a handful of reconnaissance PR 9s still soldiering on 55 years after the prototype's first flight. Built to Air Ministry Specification B 3/45, the Canberra was also built for speed, and aside from its bombload, carried no other weapons. Although ordered as a 'light bomber', many B 2s went into service as Avro Lincoln replacements. Indeed, the RAF was so pleased with the aircraft that 546 were constructed, and 30+ RAF units equipped with the type. The key to the Canberra's success was its low-aspect wing, which gave outstanding fuel economy at a maximum cruising altitude that far exceeded the ceiling of contemporary NATO fighters of the period. This essentially meant that for a number of years prior to the advent of the air-to-air missile, the Canberra was immune to manned inter-ception. The aircraft also enjoyed great export success, with 49 B 20s being assembled in Australia and UK-built jets being sold to nine other countries.

## SPECIFICATION:

**ACCOMMODATION:**
pilot and navigator

**DIMENSIONS:**
LENGTH: 65 ft 6 in (19.96 m)
WINGSPAN: 63 ft 11.5 in (19.50 m)
HEIGHT: 15 ft 8 in (4.77 m)

**WEIGHTS:**
EMPTY: 27,950 lb (12,678 kg)
MAX T/O: 56,250 lb (25,514 kg)

**PERFORMANCE:**
MAX SPEED: 518 mph (834 kmh)
RANGE: 3630 miles (5842 km)
ferry range
POWERPLANT: two Rolls-Royce
Avon 109s
OUTPUT: 7400 lb st (32.92 kN)

**FIRST FLIGHT DATE:**
13 May 1949

**ARMAMENT:**
provision for up to 3000-lb
(1362 kg) of bombs/flares in
bomb-bay and up to 2000-lb
(908 kg) of bombs/rockets on two
underwing stores pylons

**FEATURES:**
Straight-wing; tricycle landing
gear; two mid-wing mounted
engines

# English Electric Lightning UK

single-seat, twin-engined fighter

Tracing its lineage back to the P 1 supersonic research aircraft of 1954, which was itself built to satisfy a 1947 contract for a supersonic jet, the Lightning was the most revered British jet fighter of the modern age. The RAF had issued Specification F 23/49 in 1949, calling for the production of a supersonic fighter. With the P 1 well placed to answer this requirement, English Electric set about reworking the aircraft into the production-capable P 1B. First flown in April 1957, the prototype achieved Mach 2 in November 1958. Such a performance saw the RAF commit to 20 pre-production aircraft, followed by 47 Lightning F 1/1AS in 1959-60. Development of the F 2 was funded in 1961, the aircraft featuring variable afterburner and all-weather radar – 42 were built, and most served with the RAF in Germany. The interim F 3 featured bigger engines, while the definitive F 6 of 1965 made the jet a truly effective interceptor. Some 338 were built, with export examples sold to Kuwait and Saudi Arabia. The last RAF Lightnings were retired in 1988.

SPECIFICATION:

ACCOMMODATION:
pilot

DIMENSIONS:
LENGTH: 53 ft 3 in (16.25 m)
WINGSPAN: 34 ft 10 in (10.60 m)
HEIGHT: 19 ft 7 in (5.95 m)

WEIGHTS:
EMPTY: 28,000 lb (12,700 kg)
MAX T/O: 50,000 lb (22,680 kg)

PERFORMANCE:
MAX SPEED: 1500 mph (2415 kmh)
RANGE: 800 miles (1290 km)
POWERPLANT: two Rolls-Royce Avon 302S
OUTPUT: 31,360 lb st (139.4 kN)

FIRST FLIGHT DATE:
4 April 1957 (P 1B)

ARMAMENT:
two air-to-air missiles on fuselage stores pylons; optional Aden 30 mm cannon in forward part of belly tank; provision for up to 6000-lb (2722 kg) of bombs/rockets four over/underwing stores pylons

FEATURES:
Mid-mounted swept-wing; tricycle landing gear; engines in fuselage, one atop the other; bulged ventral fuel tank

# Fairchild A-10 Thunderbolt II  USA

single-seat, twin-engined close air support attack aircraft

Conceived during the Vietnam War, the A-10 was designed to operate in low intensity conflicts as a close support aircraft for troops. The Fairchild jet was the winner of the USAF's AX competition, which called for a jet with good endurance, a potent weapons suite and exceptional survivability. Constructed with the latter aspect in mind, the Thunderbolt II had a low-set straight wing which not only made it highly manoeuvrable, but also shielded the aircraft's podded General Electric TF34 turbofan engines from ground fire – the engines were also widely spaced, so that damage to one would not knock out the other. Finally, the pilot was sat in a titanium armour 'bathtub'. Able to carry up to 16,000-lb of ordnance, the A-10 also boasts the General Electric GAU-8 seven-barrel 30 mm cannon buried in its forward fuselage. A total of 707 A-10s were built for the USAF in the late 1970s, and these saw action in both Gulf Wars. A number of aircraft were also redesignated as OA-10s in the late 1980s to perform the forward air controlling mission.

SPECIFICATION:

**ACCOMMODATION:**
pilot

**DIMENSIONS:**
LENGTH: 53 ft 4 in (16.26 m)
WINGSPAN: 57 ft 6 in (17.53 m)
HEIGHT: 14 ft 8 in (4.47 m)

**WEIGHTS:**
EMPTY: 21,540 lb (9770 kg)
MAX T/O: 50,000 lb (22,680 kg)

**PERFORMANCE:**
MAX SPEED: 518 mph (835 kmh)
RANGE: 620 miles (1000 km)
POWERPLANT: two General Electric TF34-GE-100S
OUTPUT: 18,130 lb st (80.6 kN)

**FIRST FLIGHT DATE:**
5 April 1972

**ARMAMENT:**
one General Electric GAU-8 Avenger 30 mm cannon in nose; provision for up to 16,000-lb (7257 kg) of bombs/rockets/missiles on 11 underwing and underfuselage stores pylons

**FEATURES:**
Low 'plank' unswept wing; tricycle landing gear; podded turbofan engines; bubble canopy; twin tail fins

# Fairchild C-119 Flying Boxcar USA

66-seat, twin-engined tactical transport aircraft

Developed from Fairchild's C-82 Packet, the C-119 maintained its predecessor's highly valued near-ground level loading/unloading attributes, but had its flightdeck moved ahead of the cargo hold rather than sat on top of it. The Flying Boxcar also had a wider fuselage, strengthened wings and more powerful R-3350 engines. The first C-119Bs entered service with the USAF in December 1949, and by the time production ceased in 1955, 946 had been accepted into the USAF. A further 141 were sold overseas through various assistance programmes. The aircraft saw action in the Korean and Vietnam Wars, with heavily-armed nocturnal interdiction variants fitted with Gatling guns and night sensor giving the Flying Boxcar an offensive role in the latter conflict – 26 AC-119G and a similar number of jet-assisted AC-119K were converted from standard C-119s in 1966-67. Relegated to the Air National Guard by the early 1970s, many early C-119s had been upgraded to J-model specification (featuring a 'beaver-tail' rear door) by this stage. The aircraft was retired in September 1975.

SPECIFICATION:

ACCOMMODATION:
pilot, co-pilot, flight engineer, loadmaster

DIMENSIONS:
LENGTH: 86 ft 6 in (26.36 m)
WINGSPAN: 109 ft 3 in (33.30 m)
HEIGHT: 26 ft 4 in (8.03 m)

WEIGHTS:
EMPTY: 39,982 lb (18,136 kg)
MAX T/O: 74,400 lb (33,748 kg)

PERFORMANCE:
MAX SPEED: 296 mph (476 kmh)
RANGE: 2280 miles (3669 km)
POWERPLANT: two Wright R-3350-89W Cyclones
OUTPUT: 6800 hp (5070 kW)

FIRST FLIGHT DATE:
November 1947

ARMAMENT:
two 20 mm cannon and four 7.62 mm machine guns on flexible mounts in fuselage

FEATURES:
Shoulder-mounted straight-wing; tricycle landing gear; two close-cowled radial engines; twin boom/tail layout; rear-loading ramp

# Fairchild C-123 Provider USA

65-seat, twin-engined transport aircraft

The Provider was developed from the Chase Aircraft XG-20 all-metal troop/cargo glider of 1949. The USAF expressed interest in a powered version of the design, so the company fitted two Double Wasp engines to the second prototype glider and redesignated it the XC-123 Avitruc. In 1953 a contract for 300 C-123BS was awarded to Kaiser-Frazer, although the latter company soon ran into production difficulties and Fairchild stepped in to fulfil the order. Production aircraft reached the USAF in 1954, and the aircraft's rugged build and excellent handling characteristics made it popular with aircrew. The Provider became the first USAF transport committed to the Vietnam War, and aside from hauling troops and cargo, UC-123B variants were also used to spray pesticides. The C-123's performance was greatly improved with the fitment of two podded J85 turbojets during the reworking of B-models into K-specification aircraft in the early 1960s, whilst the specialist H/J version received a similar boost in power, but with Fairchild J44 turbojets fitted in wingtip pods.

SPECIFICATION:

ACCOMMODATION:
pilot and co-pilot, flight engineer, loadmaster

DIMENSIONS:
LENGTH: 75 ft 3 in (23.25 m)
WINGSPAN: 110 ft 0 in (33.35 m)
HEIGHT: 34 ft 1 in (10.38 m)

WEIGHTS:
EMPTY: 35,336 lb (16,042 kg)
MAX T/O: 60,000 lb (27,240 kg)

PERFORMANCE:
MAX SPEED: 245 mph (392 kmh)
RANGE: 1470 miles (2365 km)
POWERPLANT: two Pratt & Whitney R-2800-99w Cyclones and two General Electric J85-GE-17S
OUTPUT: 5000 hp (3730 kW) and 5700 lb st (25.35 kN) respectively

FIRST FLIGHT DATE:
1 September 1954

FEATURES:
Shoulder-mounted straight-wing; tricycle landing gear; two close-cowled radial engines; tall tail; rear-loading ramp

# Fairey Firefly AS 5/6 UK
two-seat, single-engined fighter-bomber and ASW aircraft

Enjoying one of the longest production runs of any piston-engined naval fighter, the Firefly evolved from the Fulmar fleet fighter of 1940. Soon after the first production examples of the latter type had entered fleet service, Fairey commenced work on a revised design powered by a Griffon engine, which was subsequently christened the Firefly. Reaching Royal Navy carriers in the summer of 1943, the Firefly I equipped eight squadrons by war's end. Despite the more powerful Griffon engine, the Fairey fighter could still not better 290 mph, so the design was revised once again and the clipped wing, Griffon 74-powered Mk 5 was created.

Realising that the aircraft's day as a pure fighter had passed, the Navy re-rolled the 'new' Firefly 5 as a fighter-bomber, purchasing 352. Seeing combat in Korea, the Firefly was also bought by the Dutch, Canadian and Australian navies. The final two variants – the AS 6/7 – were dedicated ASW aircraft, and 284 were produced by Fairey. More than 400 Fireflies were rebuilt in the 1950s as training aircraft and target drones.

SPECIFICATION:

**ACCOMMODATION:**
pilot and observer in tandem

**DIMENSIONS:**
LENGTH: 38 ft 0 in (11.58 m)
WINGSPAN: 41 ft 0 in (12.49 m)
HEIGHT: 13 ft 11 in (4.24 m)

**WEIGHTS:**
EMPTY: 9859 lb (4472 kg)
MAX T/O: 15,600 lb (7076 kg)

**PERFORMANCE:**
MAX SPEED: 316 mph (509 kmh)
RANGE: 1070 miles (1722 km)
POWERPLANT: Rolls-Royce Griffon 74
OUTPUT: 2245 hp (1674 kW)

**FIRST FLIGHT DATE:**
22 December 1941 (Firefly I) and 12 December 1947 (first production Firefly 5)

**ARMAMENT:**
four Hispano 20 mm cannon in wings; 2000-lb (907 kg) of bombs/rockets on two under-wing and one underfuselage stores pylons

**FEATURES:**
Straight wing; wing leading edge oil and coolant radiator; radiator intake at wing root; close-cowled inline engines; arrestor hook

# Fairey Gannet UK

three-seat, single-engined ASW, AEW and utility aircraft

Designed to fulfil naval Specification GR 17/45, issued in October 1945, the Gannet combined the strike and ASW roles in an aircraft built to operate from carrier decks. Its unique engine was the key to the aircraft's service success, as it boasted two independent power sections driving separate propellers combined in a co-axial arrangement. This meant that after both sections had been used during take-off, one could be shut down to improve fuel consumption and extend range/patrol time. Some 256 AS 1/4s were built, with the first examples reaching the fleet in January 1955. T 2/T 5 dual control trainers (46 in total) then followed, and both variants were sold to the Australian, West German and Indonesian navies. In a major revision of roles, 44 new-build AEW 3 aircraft were completed for the Royal Navy between 1958-61, these aircraft being fitted with a dome beneath the fuselage to house the radome for the APS-20 surveillance radar. These airborne early warning aircraft were the last Gannets retired from service upon the decommissioning of HMS *Ark Royal* in 1978.

## SPECIFICATION:

**ACCOMMODATION:**
pilot and two radar plotters

**DIMENSIONS:**
LENGTH: 43 ft 0 in (13.10 m)
WINGSPAN: 54 ft 4 in (16.50 m)
HEIGHT: 13 ft 8 in (4.16 m)

**WEIGHTS:**
EMPTY: 14,069 lb (6382 kg)
MAX T/O: 22,506 lb (10,208 kg)

**PERFORMANCE:**
MAX SPEED: 311 mph (500 kmh)
RANGE: 662 miles (1066 km)
POWERPLANT: Armstrong Siddeley Double Mamba 100
OUTPUT: 2950 shp (2199 kW)

**FIRST FLIGHT DATE:**
17 September 1949

**ARMAMENT:**
provision for up to 2000-lb (907 kg) of bombs/depth charges/mines in bomb-bay and/or rockets on two underwing stores pylons

**FEATURES:**
Gull-wing; contra-rotating propellers; close-cowled turboprop engine; arrestor hook; rectractable tricycle undercarriage

# Fiat G 46 ITALY

two-seat, single-engined trainer

The G 46 was built as an intermediate trainer for the post-war *Aeronautica Militare Italiano* (AMI). The first batch of Series 1 aircraft reached AMI flying schools in 1949, where they proved to be the ideal 'stepping stone' for pilots recently graduated from the Stinson L-5 Sentinel (then the AMI's basic trainer) and heading for the T-6 Texan or Fiat G 55. After almost a decade in this role, the G 46 was rendered redundant after the AMI embraced the jet age and duly restructured its syllabus. More than 150 Fiat trainers were built, and some of these remained in AMI service with obscure units like the officer currency training flight and numerous communications squadrons. However, the bulk of the aircraft were supplied to aero clubs across Italy following their 'demilitarisation'. Aside from AMI examples, the Syrian Air Force ordered 11 G 46s (powered by de Havilland Gipsy Queen 30 engines), Argentina received 70 (again Gipsy Queen-powered) and the Austrian Air Force five, bringing total G 46 construction to 223 airframes.

## SPECIFICATION:

**ACCOMMODATION:**
two pilot in tandem

**DIMENSIONS:**
LENGTH: 27 ft 10 in (8.47 m)
WINGSPAN: 34 ft 1 in (10.30 m)
HEIGHT: 7 ft 10 in (2.37m)

**WEIGHTS:**
EMPTY: 2442 lb (1107 kg)
MAX T/O: 3102 lb (1407 kg)

**PERFORMANCE:**
MAX SPEED: 196 mph (315 kmh)
RANGE: 570 miles (917 km)
POWERPLANT: Alfa 115ter
OUTPUT: 225 hp (167 kW)

**FIRST FLIGHT DATE:**
25 February 1948

**FEATURES:**
Straight-wing; close-cowled inline engine; rectractable undercarriage; fixed tailwheel

# Fiat G 59 ITALY

single/two-seat, single-engined fighter

The G 59 was created due to a shortage of war-surplus Daimler-Benz DB 603A engines for the company's remaining G 55A airframes. The aircraft was duly modified to accept a Rolls-Royce Merlin T 24-2 inline engine, the first converted G 55B (two-seater trainer variant) flying in 1948 with the designation G 59BM. Egypt initially showed interest in purchasing 20 G 55AM/BMs, but following the cessation of hostilities with Israel decided not to proceed with the purchase. However, 12 G 55AS were rebuilt as AMS for the AMI, which redesignated them G 59-1AS and used them as fighter-trainers.

A further 15 G 59-1AS and two-seat -1BS were also built for AMI service in 1950, followed by 40 armed G 59-2s. Twenty-six examples of the latter variant were delivered to the Syrian Air Force. The final version built was the G 59-4A/B trainer, again for the AMI, which purchased twenty single- and ten two-seaters. These aircraft differed from previous models by having cut-down rear fuselage decking and bubble canopies. The G 59s were retired in the mid 1950s.

SPECIFICATION:

**ACCOMMODATION:**
pilot/two pilots in tandem

**DIMENSIONS:**
LENGTH: 31 ft 0.75 in (9.47 m)
WINGSPAN: 38 ft 10.5 in (11.85 m)
HEIGHT: 12 ft 4 in (3.76 m)

**WEIGHTS:**
EMPTY: 6041 lb (2740 kg)
MAX T/O: 7496 lb (3400 kg)

**PERFORMANCE:**
MAX SPEED: 368 mph (593 kmh)
RANGE: 882 miles (1420 km)
POWERPLANT: Rolls-Royce Merlin T.24-2 and Merlin 500 (G.59-4A/4B)
OUTPUT: 1610 hp (1200 kW) and 1490 hp (1111 kW) respectively

**FIRST FLIGHT DATE:**
early 1948

**ARMAMENT:**
four Hispano 20 mm cannon in wings; up to 705-lb (320 kg) of bombs on two underwing stores pylons

**FEATURES:**
Straight-wing; close-cowled inline engine; rectractable undercarriage; fixed tailwheel; ventral radiator intake

# Fiat G 91R/T ITALY
single/two-seat, single-engined advanced trainer and ground attack aircraft

Robust, simple to maintain and capable of operating from rough airstrips, the Fiat G 91 was the design chosen to answer the 1953 NATO specification for a light tactical strike aircraft. Based on the F-86, the Fiat saw off three French contenders to secure production status. Although ordered by the Italians and Germans, remaining NATO nations chose not to buy the G 91 even though the aircraft was supposedly a key part of the organisation's Mutual Weapons Programme! Italy bought 98 G 91RS, which were also reconnaissance capable, and 76 G 91T two-seat advanced trainers.

Germany acquired no fewer than 395 G 91RS, 295 of which were built under licence by Messerschmitt, Heinkel and Dornier in 1961-66. Greece and Turkey were originally to receive 100 of the German machines, but these were retained for Luftwaffe use. Some 44 G 91T trainers were also procured by the Germans. Forty G 91RS were sold to Portugal in 1965, followed by 14 in 1976 and 20 in 1981. The Portuguese saw combat with their aircraft in Angola in the 1970s.

SPECIFICATION:

**ACCOMMODATION:**
one pilot, or two pilots in tandem (trainer variant)

**DIMENSIONS:**
LENGTH: 33 ft 9.25 in (10.31 m)
WINGSPAN: 28 ft 1 in (8.57 m)
HEIGHT: 13 ft 1.50 in (4 m)

**WEIGHTS:**
EMPTY: 7275 lb (3300 kg)
MAX T/O: 12,500 lb (5695 kg)

**PERFORMANCE:**
MAX SPEED: 675 mph (1086 kmh)
RANGE: 1150 miles (1850 km)
POWERPLANT: Rolls-Royce Orpheus 80302
OUTPUT: 5000 lb st (23 kN)

**FIRST FLIGHT DATE:**
9 August 1956

**ARMAMENT:**
four Colt-Browning 0.5-in machine guns or two DEFA 552 30 mm cannon in nose; provision for up to 1000-lb (454 kg) of bombs/rockets on four underwing stores pylons

**FEATURES:**
Swept-wing layout; bubble canopy; tricycle landing gear; chin engine air intake; nose-mounted camera

311

# Fiat G 91Y   ITALY

single-seat, twin-engined ground fighter-bomber

Although an evolution of the G 91R based on the airframe of the G 91T, the twin-engined G 91Y shared only a superficial resemblance with its predecessor as the finished aircraft was a total redesign. Built exclusively for the AMI, the first of two prototype G 91Ys completed its maiden flight on 27 December 1966. At the heart of the new aircraft were two afterburning General Electric J85-GE-13A turbojets, which gave the jet almost double the thrust of the G 91R/T. This allowed the jet to carry up to 4000-lb of ordnance, as well as the internally mounted Aden 30 mm cannon. Like the G 91R, the G 91Y also had a nose-mounted Vinten camera fitted as standard.

Twenty pre-series aircraft were delivered to the AMI by Aeritalia (formed in 1969 through the merger of Fiat and Finmeccanica-IRI) from 1968, and they entered service in May 1970. A further 45 production standard G 91Ys were delivered during 1971-76. The G 91Y equipped just two AMI *gruppi*, and these were eventually replaced in the late 1980s by the AMX.

SPECIFICATION:

ACCOMMODATION:
pilot

DIMENSIONS:
LENGTH: 38 ft 3.50 in (11.67 m)
WINGSPAN: 29 ft 6.50 in (9.01 m)
HEIGHT: 14 ft 6 in (4.43 m)

WEIGHTS:
EMPTY: 8598 lb (3900 kg)
MAX T/O: 19,180 lb (8700 kg)

PERFORMANCE:
MAX SPEED: 690 mph (1110 kmh)
RANGE: 2175 miles (3500 km)
POWERPLANT: two General Electric J85-GE-13AS
OUTPUT: 8160 lb st (35.8 kN)

FIRST FLIGHT DATE:
27 December 1966

ARMAMENT:
two Aden 30 mm cannon in nose; provision for up to 4000-lb (1814 kg) of bombs/rockets on four underwing stores pylons

FEATURES:
Swept-wing layout; bubble canopy; tricycle landing gear; chin engine air intake; nose-mounted camera

# FMA IA-58 Pucará UK

two-seat, twin-engined light ground attack aircraft

The Pucará was developed to meet an Argentinian Air Force requirement for a counter insurgency/ light attack aircraft. Having struggled to fight guerrillas in northern Argentina in the early 1960s, the Air Force realised that it needed an aircraft tailored to its requirements. The job was given to Argentina's state-run Fabrica Militar de Aviones, and a prototype was flown on 20 August 1969. The IA-58 was built to be manoeuvrable, survivable and rough field capable, and be able to carry bombs and rockets. Production Pucarás entered service in 1976, and the aircraft soon saw action against rebels in north-west Argentina. Further combat followed in May-June 1982 when Argentinian forces, including 24 Pucarás, occupied the Falkland Islands. These aircraft faired poorly in the war, with all two-dozen aircraft either being destroyed by ground fire or sabotaged by the SAS. In the wake of the conflict the Argentinian Air Force lost faith in the IA-58, and 40 were withdrawn from service in 1986. A handful of Pucará also serve with the air forces of Colombia, Sri Lanka and Uruguay.

SPECIFICATION:

ACCOMMODATION:
pilot and observer in tandem

DIMENSIONS:
LENGTH: 46 ft 9 in (14.25 m)
WINGSPAN: 47 ft 7 in (14.50 m)
HEIGHT: 17 ft 7 in (5.36 m)

WEIGHTS:
EMPTY: 8862 lb (4020 kg)
MAX T/O: 14,990 lb (6800 kg)

PERFORMANCE:
MAX SPEED: 466 mph (750 kmh)
RANGE: 2305 miles (3710 km)
POWERPLANT: two Turboméca Astazou XVIGS
OUTPUT: 1956 hp (1458 kW)

FIRST FLIGHT DATE:
20 August 1969

ARMAMENT:
two Hispano HS-284 20 mm cannon and four Browning 7.62 mm machine guns in nose; provision for up to 3307-lb (1500 kg) of bombs/rocket pods on two underwing and one underfuselage stores pylons

FEATURES:
Low, straight 'plank' wing; T-tail; wing-mounted, close-cowled turboprop engines; stalky tricycle undercarriage

# Fokker S-11 Instructor THE NETHERLANDS

two-seat, single-engined basic trainer

One of the first post-war products of the now-defunct Dutch aircraft manufacturer Fokker, the modest s-11 was designed as a primary trainer for either military or civilian use. It was to enjoy some success in the former role, with 40 Instructors being purchased by the Royal Netherlands Air Force (deliveries began in 1949) and 41 by the Israeli Defence Force. Licence-production of the aircraft was also undertaken in Italy for the AMI by Macchi (150 built as M 416s) and in Brazil by the specially-created Fokker Industria Aeronautica SA (100 delivered). The Brazilian company also developed the s-12 variant of the Instructor, which utilised a tricycle undercarriage – 50 were built for the Brazilian Air Force. In Dutch service, the s-11s also performed the primary training role for the naval component until finally retired, along with the surviving Air Force examples, in late 1973. A significant number of ex-military s-11s subsequently made their way onto the European civil register during the 1970s, the aircraft proving particularly popular with flying clubs.

SPECIFICATION:

**ACCOMMODATION:**
two pilots seated side-by-side

**DIMENSIONS:**
LENGTH: 26 ft 8 in (8.18 m)
WINGSPAN: 36 ft 1 in (11.00 m)
HEIGHT: 7 ft 10.5 in (2.70 m)

**WEIGHTS:**
EMPTY: 1785 lb (810 kg)
MAX T/O: 2425 lb (1100 kg)

**PERFORMANCE:**
MAX SPEED: 130 mph (209 kmh)
RANGE: 430 miles (695 km)
POWERPLANT: Lycoming O-435A
OUTPUT: 190 hp (141 kW)

**FIRST FLIGHT DATE:**
18 December 1947

**FEATURES:**
Low, straight wing; close-cowled engine; fixed undercarriage; extensive cockpit glazing

# Folland Gnat F 1  UK

single-seat, single-engined fighter-bomber

The private venture Folland Gnat F 1 was created in an effort to reverse the trend of ever larger, and more complex, combat aircraft. Design work commenced on the FO 139 Midge – as it was dubbed by Folland – in 1951, with a one-off prototype flying for the first time on 11 August 1954. The company finally convinced the British Ministry of Supply (MOS) to fund the building of six aircraft for evaluation by the RAF, and the first of these flew on 18 July 1955. Although failing to impress the RAF, the jet proved attractive to export customers, with Yugoslavia buying two and Finland twelve (plus an ex-MOS aircraft). A further two MOS machines were supplied to India, which also received 23 UK-built Gnat F 1s and 20 sets of components for assembly by Hindustan Aircraft (later Aeronautics) Ltd. Licence production was subsequently undertaken by HAL, which built 195 Gnat F 1s between November 1959 and January 1974. These aircraft saw considerable action as fighter-bombers with the Indian Air Force during the 1965 and 1971 wars with Pakistan.

SPECIFICATION:

**ACCOMMODATION:**
pilot

**DIMENSIONS:**
LENGTH: 29 ft 9 in (9.06 m)
WINGSPAN: 22 ft 2 in (6.75 m)
HEIGHT: 8 ft 10 in (2.69 m)

**WEIGHTS:**
EMPTY: 4850 lb (2200 kg)
MAX T/O: 8885 lb (4030 kg)

**PERFORMANCE:**
MAX SPEED: 714 mph (1150 kmh)
RANGE: 1180 miles (1900 km)
POWERPLANT: Rolls-Royce Orpheus 701
OUTPUT: 4520 lb st (19 kN)

**FIRST FLIGHT DATE:**
11 August 1954 (Midge)

**ARMAMENT:**
two Aden 30 mm cannon in fuselage; provision for up to 1000-lb (454 kg) of bombs/rockets on four underwing stores pylons

**FEATURES:**
Shoulder-mounted swept-wing layout; bubble canopy; tricycle landing gear; engine air intakes on fuselage sides aft of cockpit; small vertical tail

# Folland Gnat T 1 UK

two-seat, single-engined advanced trainer

Derived from the FO 139 Midge, the Gnat T 1 proved to be a success with the RAF where its single-seat predecessor had not. Despite the Air Force showing little interest in the 'cheap' fighter, all was not lost for Folland as the RAF had been attracted to the two-seat advanced trainer variant because of its ability to achieve near-supersonic speeds. The Air Force committed to the Gnat T 1 by placing an order for 14 pre-production machines in January 1958, which was followed by a contract for 91 aircraft. Once in service, the Gnat was found to be over-complex, resulting in engineering headaches for maintainers – particularly in respect to its longitudinal control runs and supporting systems. The small rear cockpit provided the instructor with virtually no forward visibility, and its use as a platform for weapons instruction was spoiled by pitch control difficulties that were never solved. Indeed, the Gnat's greatest contribution to the RAF during its two decades of service was as a recruiting tool with the Red Arrows. The T 1 was retired in 1979.

SPECIFICATION:

**ACCOMMODATION:**
two pilots in tandem

**DIMENSIONS:**
LENGTH: 31 ft 9 in (9.65 m)
WINGSPAN: 24 ft 0 in (7.32 m)
HEIGHT: 10 ft 6 in (3.20 m)

**WEIGHTS:**
EMPTY: 5613 lb (2546 kg)
MAX T/O: 9350 lb (4240 kg)

**PERFORMANCE:**
MAX SPEED: 636 mph (1026 kmh)
RANGE: 1180 miles (1900 km)
POWERPLANT: Bristol Siddeley Orpheus 101
OUTPUT: 4230 lb st (18.84 kN)

**FIRST FLIGHT DATE:**
31 August 1959 (T 1)

**ARMAMENT:**
provision for up to 1000-lb (454 kg) of bombs/rockets on four underwing stores pylons

**FEATURES:**
Shoulder-mounted swept-wing layout; bubble canopy; tricycle landing gear; engine air intakes on fuselage sides aft of cockpit; larger vertical tail than fitted to F 1

# Fouga CM 170 Magister FRANCE

two-seat, twin-engined basic trainer

As the world's first jet trainer to enter production, the Magister was built to a French Air Force specification. The prototype CM 170 relied on two Turboméca Marboré IIA turbojet engines to provide motive power, and the Air Force was so impressed that ten pre-production jets were followed by large orders. Some 400 Magisters were delivered to the Air Force, with a further 32 'navalised' (boasting an arrestor hook) CM 175 Zéphyrs bought by the French Navy. Production continued through to 1970, the aircraft enjoying remarkable export success. Aside from those CM 170s built in France for foreign customers (190 aircraft), Flugzeug Union Sud completed 188 in Germany, Valmet of Finland 62 and Israeli Aircraft Industries 36. The Magister remained little changed throughout its production life, with the later CM 170-2 featuring uprated Marboré VICS engines and the CM 170-3 increased fuel capacity and Martin-Baker ejection seats. Although all French aircraft have now been retired, others remain in active service across the globe.

SPECIFICATION:

ACCOMMODATION:
two pilots in tandem

DIMENSIONS:
LENGTH: 33 ft 0 in (10.06 m)
WINGSPAN: 37 ft 5 in (11.40 m)
HEIGHT: 9 ft 2 in (2.80 m)

WEIGHTS:
EMPTY: 4740 lb (2150 kg)
MAX T/O: 7055 lb (3200 kg)

PERFORMANCE:
MAX SPEED: 444 mph (715 kmh)
RANGE: 746 miles (1200 km)
POWERPLANT: two Turboméca
Marboré IIAS
OUTPUT: 1764 lb st (7.84 kN)

FIRST FLIGHT DATE:
23 July 1952

ARMAMENT:
two 7.62 mm machines guns in
nose; provision for up to 220-lb
(100 kg) of bombs/rockets on two
underwing stores pylons

FEATURES:
Mid-mounted straight-wing
layout; tandem, bubble canopy;
tricycle landing gear; engine air
intakes on fuselage sides;
butterfly tail; wingtip tanks

# General Dynamics F-16A/B Fighting Falcon USA

single-seat, single-engined multi-role fighter

Although still very much a frontline fighter with
numerous air forces across the globe, a number of
older General Dynamics-built F-16A/B Fighting
Falcons have now been retired to museum
collections in Europe and North America, hence the
type's inclusion in this volume. Built in the early
1970s for inclusion in the USAF's Lightweight Fighter
Program, the F-16 beat the rival Northrop YF-17
(forerunner to the F/A-18) in a fly-off that lasted
almost a year. Eight development jets were then
built, with the first production F-16A reaching the
USAF in August 1978. By then the aircraft had also
been selected by four NATO countries as a replacement for the ageing F-104 Starfighter. Production
lines were set up in the USA, the Netherlands and
Belgium (and latterly in Turkey for the F-16C), and
more than 1800 F-16A/BS had been churned out by
the time production switched to the more capable,
and heavier, F-16C in the early 1990s. Early-model
Fighting Falcons have seen combat in the Middle
East, Afghanistan and the Balkans, and over 1000
examples remain in frontline service today.

SPECIFICATION:

ACCOMMODATION:
pilot

DIMENSIONS:
LENGTH: 49 ft 4 in (15.03 m)
WINGSPAN: 32 ft 10 in (10 m)
HEIGHT: 16 ft 5 in (5.01 m)

WEIGHTS:
EMPTY: 14,567 lb (6607 kg)
MAX T/O: 33,000 lb (14,968 kg)

PERFORMANCE:
MAX SPEED: 1333 mph (2145 kmh)
RANGE: 2418 miles (3869 km)
POWERPLANT: Pratt & Whitney
F100-PW-100
OUTPUT: 23,830 lb st (106 kN)

ARMAMENT:
one M61A1 Vulcan 30 mm cannon
in fuselage; provision for up to
12,000-lb (5435 kg) of
bombs/rockets/missile on six
underwing, one underfuselage
and two wingtip stores pylons

FIRST FLIGHT DATE:
20 January 1974

FEATURES:
Mid-mounted swept-wings;
bubble canopy; tricycle
landing gear; chin air intake;
ventral strakes

# General Dynamics F-111  USA
two-seat, twin-engined strategic/tactical strike aircraft

The F-111 was originally developed to meet a
Department of Defense edict that the USAF's
requirement for a new fighter-bomber and the US
Navy's need for a new fleet air defence fighter
should be met by a single aircraft – the TFX.
Designated the F-111 by General Dynamics, the
prototype flew for the first time on 21 December
1964. Although the overweight F-111B naval fighter
was cancelled in 1968, the USAF's F-111A showed
greater promise. Despite development problems,
General Dynamics persisted with the design and
eventually handed over the first of 141 A-models in
1967. The F-111 duly evolved into the most capable
medium range strike bomber of its generation. The
A-model was followed into service by 94 F-111ES,
with revised inlets and better engines, 96 F-111DS,
with improved avionics, and finally 106 F-111FS,
which boasted new engines and still better avionics.
SAC also received 76 FB-111S, which replaced the
B-58. Finally, the Australians bought 24 F-111CS. With
the retirement of all USAF F-111s in 1998, only the
Australian jets remain in service today.

SPECIFICATION:

**ACCOMMODATION:**
pilot and weapons systems
officer/navigator sat side-by-side

**DIMENSIONS:**
LENGTH: 73 ft 6 in (22.40 m)
WINGSPAN: 63 ft 0 in (19.20 m)
HEIGHT: 17 ft 1 in (5.22 m)

**WEIGHTS:**
EMPTY: 47,480 lb (21,537 kg)
MAX T/O: 100,000 lb (45,360 kg)

**PERFORMANCE:**
MAX SPEED: 1450 mph (2335 kmh)
RANGE: 3165 miles (5093 km)
POWERPLANT: two Pratt & Whitney
TF30-P-100S
OUTPUT: 50,200 lb st (223.4 kN)

**FIRST FLIGHT DATE:**
21 December 1964

**ARMAMENT:**
1500-lb (682 kg) of bombs in
bomb-bay and 31,500-lb (14,290
kg) of bombs/rockets/missile on
eight underwing stores pylons

**FEATURES:**
Mid-mounted variable geometry
wings; bubble canopy; tricycle
landing gear; wing root engine
intakes; wide, sleek nose

# Gloster Javelin UK

two-seat, twin-engined fighter

Built in response to RAF Specification F 4/48, the Javelin was the first aircraft of its type designed in Britain specifically to perform night and all-weather fighter interception missions. Enduring a lengthy gestation period which saw three prototypes written off in accidents, the Javelin FAW 1 finally entered production in July 1954, although examples did not reach the frontline (with No 46 Sqn) until February 1956. A total of 381 aircraft were delivered to the RAF in no fewer than nine different variants. This often meant that just as one mark had become established in Fighter Command it would be superseded by the next version of Javelin newly rolled out from the Gloster factory. Better radar, improved flight controls, increased fuel tankage, bigger engines and compatibility with air-to-air missiles were examples of the changes introduced to the Javelin during its seven-year production run. The final variant was the FAW 9, which embodied all of these improvements, plus numerous others. Entering service in 1961, it was the last Javelin variant retired seven years later.

SPECIFICATION:

ACCOMMODATION:
pilot and navigator

DIMENSIONS:
LENGTH: 56 ft 3.25 in (17.15 m)
WINGSPAN: 52 ft 0 in (15.85 m)
HEIGHT: 16 ft 3 in (4.98 m)

WEIGHTS:
EMPTY: 27,800 lb (12,610 kg)
MAX T/O: 38,400 lb (17,418 kg)

PERFORMANCE:
MAX SPEED: 680 mph (1014 kmh)
RANGE: 950 miles (1530 km)
POWERPLANT: two Bristol Siddeley Sapphire 203s
OUTPUT: 26,780 lb st (121.8 kN)

FIRST FLIGHT DATE:
26 November 1951

ARMAMENT:
two Aden 30 mm cannon in outer wings and four Firestreak air-to-air missiles on four underwing stores pylons

FEATURES:
Thick delta wing; swept-wing; delta tailplane atop large swept vertical tail; round-lipped engine air intakes either side of cockpit; bulbous ventral fuel tank

# Gloster Meteor UK

single/two-seat, twin-engined fighter/advanced trainer

The only Allied jet combat design to see action in World War 2, the Meteor was initially handicapped because its large size and generous wing area had a detrimental affect on the modest power output of its Welland engines. However, these features came into their own following development work undertaken by Rolls-Royce which resulted in the Meteor being fitted with Derwent turbojets from the F 3 onwards. The standard day fighter of Fighter Command into the early 1950s, the Meteor's ability to perform other roles saw the development of the T 7 advanced trainer and the radar-equipped Armstrong Whitworth two-seat nightfighters, the first of which (NF 11) made its service debut in 1951. The ultimate dayfighter variant was the F 8, which dominated Fighter Command ranks between 1950 and 1955. The final versions to enter RAF service were the FR 9 tactical fighter-reconnaissance and PR 10 high-altitude strategic reconnaissance aircraft. More than a dozen export countries received Meteors of varying marks, and with the completion of the final T 7 in 1954, production had totalled 3947.

SPECIFICATION:

**ACCOMMODATION:**
pilot (dayfighter), pilot/navigator (nightfighter) and two pilots seated in tandem (trainer)

**DIMENSIONS:**
LENGTH: 44 ft 7 in (13.59 m)
WINGSPAN: 37 ft 2 in (11.30 m)
HEIGHT: 13 ft 10 in (4.22 m)

**WEIGHTS:**
EMPTY: 10,626 lb (4820 kg)
MAX T/O: 19,100 lb (8664 kg)

**PERFORMANCE:**
MAX SPEED: 595 mph (958 kmh)
RANGE: 1000 miles (1610 km)
POWERPLANT: two Rolls-Royce Derwent 8s
OUTPUT: 7200 lb st (32 kN)

**FIRST FLIGHT DATE:**
5 March 1943

**ARMAMENT:**
four Hispano 20 mm cannon in nose; provision for up to 2000-lb (907 kg) of bombs/rockets on two underwing stores pylons

**FEATURES:**
Thick straight wing; engines mounted within wing structure; high-mounted horizontal tailplane; bubble canopy

# Grumman F8F Bearcat  USA

single-seat, single-engined fighter-bomber

The last piston-engined Grumman fighter, the Bearcat bucked the unwritten law of the day which stated that a new fighter had to be larger in order to be better than its predecessor. The Bearcat was shorter and lighter than the F6F Hellcat it replaced, and although both types were powered by the R-2800 Double Wasp engine, the Bearcat could easily out-perform the F6F thanks to its compact design. The Navy was so pleased with the F8F that it ordered 2023, with delivery commencing in January 1945. VF-19 was the first unit to receive Bearcats, and it was just completing work-ups when the A-bomb raids brought the war to a dramatic end.

Post-war, the contract was slashed by 1258 aircraft, and production ceased in May 1949 following the delivery of 1266 F8Fs. Some 24 active and reserve units flew Bearcats with the US Navy, the last F8Fs being retired in late 1952. A number of surplus aircraft were sold to the French and Thai air forces, and whilst serving with these countries, the Bearcat saw action in South-East Asia.

SPECIFICATION:

**ACCOMMODATION:**
pilot

**DIMENSIONS:**
LENGTH: 28 ft 3 in (8.61 m)
WINGSPAN: 35 ft 10 in (7.87 m)
HEIGHT: 13 ft 10 in (4.2 m)

**WEIGHTS:**
EMPTY: 7070 lb (3206 kg)
MAX T/O: 12 947 lb (5873 kg)

**PERFORMANCE:**
MAX SPEED: 421 mph (680 kmh)
RANGE: 1105 miles (1775 km)
POWERPLANT: Pratt & Whitney R-2800-34W Double Wasp
OUTPUT: 2800 hp (2087 kW)

**FIRST FLIGHT DATE:**
21 August 1944

**ARMAMENT:**
four Colt-Browning 0.50-in machine guns in wings; up to 2000-lb (907 kg) of bombs/ rockets on six underwing and one underfuselage stores pylons

**FEATURES:**
Straight-wing; close-cowled radial engine; rectractable undercarriage; arrestor hook; bubble canopy

# Grumman AF-2 Guardian USA

two/four-seat, single-engined ASW/strike aircraft

Built to counter the Soviet submarine threat, the AF-2 entered production in two separate variants which combined to perform the ASW mission. The AF-2W (153 built) was the 'hunter' element of the team, its four-man crew searching for submarines with the aircraft's belly-mounted APS-20 radar and other dedicated sensors, calling in the two-man AF-2S 'killer' when a contact was encountered. The latter aircraft would then 'locally acquire' the target using APS-31 radar, an AVQ-2 searchlight and sonobuoys, before despatching the submarine with bombs/ torpedo/depth charges – all of which could be carried in the aircraft's weapon bay (which contained the APS-20 radar equipment on the -2W). An initial run of 193 AF-2Ss was undertaken by Grumman, with the first examples reaching the fleet in October 1950. A follow-on batch of 40 MAD-equipped S-models completed the production run in 1953. Replaced in the fleet by a single ASW platform in the form of the S-2 Tracker, the Guardian had been consigned to the Navy Reserve by 1955.

SPECIFICATION:

ACCOMMODATION:
pilot and navigator (AF-2S), pilot, navigator and two radar operators (AF-2W)

DIMENSIONS:
LENGTH: 43 ft 4 in (13.2 m)
WINGSPAN: 60 ft 8 in (18.49 m)
HEIGHT: 16 ft 2 in (4.93 m)

WEIGHTS:
EMPTY: 14,580 lb (6613 kg)
MAX T/O: 25,500 lb (11,567 kg)

PERFORMANCE:
MAX SPEED: 317 mph (510 kmh)
RANGE: 1500 miles (2415 km)
POWERPLANT: Pratt & Whitney R-2800-48W Double Wasp
OUTPUT: 2400 hp (1789 kW)

FIRST FLIGHT DATE:
19 December 1946

ARMAMENT:
(AF-2S only) up to 4000-lb (1814 kg) of bombs/torpedo/ depth charges in bomb-bay

FEATURES:
Straight-wing; close-cowled radial engine; rectractable undercarriage; arrestor hook

# Grumman UF-1/U-16 Albatross USA

four/six-seat, twin-engined rescue, utility and ASW amphibian

Having gained a wealth of experience building amphibians thanks to the huge number of JRF Goose aircraft supplied to the Allies in World War 2, Grumman decided to embark on a study to replace its earlier aircraft with an all-new type which was three times the size of is predecessors. The result was the G-64 Albatross, which retained a link with previous Grumman amphibians through the employment of a trademark cantilever high wing and main gear retraction into the fuselage sides. Both the US Navy and the USAF were so impressed by the Albatross prototype that they each ordered their own variants into series production. Whilst the Air Force adopted the designation SA-16A, which later changed to HU-16, the Navy opted initially for JR2F-1 and then UF-1 (also later redesignated to U-16). The first of 418 production aircraft entered service in July 1949, and the improved SA-16B/UF-2 followed in 1955. USAF, US Navy and US Coast Guard aircraft saw combat in Korea and Vietnam, and surviving HU-16s remained in the US inventory well into the 1970s.

SPECIFICATION:

**ACCOMMODATION:**
pilot, co-pilot, navigator, crew chief, radar operator

**DIMENSIONS:**
LENGTH: 62 ft 10 in (19.18 m)
WINGSPAN: 96 ft 8 in (29.46 m)
HEIGHT: 25 ft 10 in (7.87 m)

**WEIGHTS:**
EMPTY: 22,883 lb (10,380 kg)
MAX T/O: 37,500 lb (17,010 kg)

**PERFORMANCE:**
MAX SPEED: 236 mph (379 kmh)
RANGE: 2850 miles (4587 km)
POWERPLANT: two Wright R-1820-82S
OUTPUT: 3050 hp (2274 kW)

**FIRST FLIGHT DATE:**
24 October 1947

**ARMAMENT:**
four Mk 43 torpedoes or two depth charges

**FEATURES:**
High-mounted straight-wing; two close-cowled radial engines; rectractable undercarriage; boat-shaped hull; fixed outriggers

# Grumman F9F Panther USA

single-seat, single-engined fighter-bomber

As Grumman's first jet fighter, the F9F was originally designed to be powered by four Westinghouse 19XB (J30) engines. However, the US Navy had been monitoring the performance of the Rolls-Royce Nene and had two shipped to the Naval Air Center in Philadelphia for bench testing. The engine's performance was so revelatory that it was placed into production by Pratt & Whitney as the J42. The prototype XF9F-1 Panther used a Nene to complete its flight trials in 1947-48. A conventional design with excellent low speed handling for carrier operations, the first of 567 F9F-2s reached the fleet in May 1949. The Panther was the first carrier-based jet to see action over Korea, the aircraft performing almost half the attack mission flown by Navy/Marine Corps units. The later -5 introduced the more powerful J48 turbojet, and this went some way to improving the Panther's poor top speed, although this problem was not solved until the advent of the swept-wing Cougar. The Panther was also a popular photo-reconnaissance platform, with 100 of the 761 F9F-5s built converted into -5Ps.

SPECIFICATION:

**ACCOMMODATION:**
pilot

**DIMENSIONS:**
LENGTH: 37 ft 3 in (11.4 m)
WINGSPAN: 38 ft 0 in (11.58 m)
HEIGHT: 11 ft 4 in (3.47 m)

**WEIGHTS:**
EMPTY: 11,000 lb (4990 kg)
MAX T/O: 19,494 lb (8840 kg)

**PERFORMANCE:**
MAX SPEED: 526 mph (849 kmh)
RANGE: 1353 miles (2164 km)
POWERPLANT: Pratt & Whitney J42-P-2
OUTPUT: 5000 lb st (22.26 kN)

**FIRST FLIGHT DATE:**
24 November 1947

**ARMAMENT:**
four M-2 20 mm cannon in nose; provision for up to 2000-lb (907 kg) of bombs/rockets on six underwing stores pylons

**FEATURES:**
Straight wing; engine air intakes on fuselage sides below cockpit; high-mounted horizontal tailplane; bubble canopy; arrestor hook; wingtip tanks

# Grumman F9F/F-9 Cougar  USA

single/two-seat, single-engined fighter-bomber/advanced trainer

Proving the soundness of Grumman's original jet fighter design, the F9F Panther was developed into the swept-wing F9F-8 Cougar and remained in production for a further seven years. Grumman had first proposed making a swept-wing Panther in 1950, and in March of the following year the US Navy contracted for three prototypes to be built. The 'new' aircraft, designated the XF9F-6, comprised a Panther fuselage and tail unit, an uprated J48-P-8 engine and a new wing with 35 degrees sweepback. The prototype made its maiden flight in September 1951, and 646 F9F-6s, 168 near-identical F9F-7s and 60 F9F-6P photo-reconnaissance aircraft were built. The F9F-8 introduced a lengthened fuselage, modified canopy and larger wings. Of the 711 built, 110 were configured as F9F-8P photo-reconnaissance jets. The final variant was the stretched two-seat F9F-8T advanced trainer, 399 of which were delivered in 1956-59. Redesignated F/RF/TF-9s in 1962, Cougars served with numerous frontline, training and reserve units until 1974.

SPECIFICATION:

ACCOMMODATION:
pilot, or two pilots in tandem
(F9F-8T/TF-9)

DIMENSIONS:
LENGTH: 42 ft 7 in (13 m)
WINGSPAN: 36 ft 4 in (11.10 m)
HEIGHT: 15 ft 0 in (4.45 m)

WEIGHTS:
EMPTY: 13,000 lb (5897 kg)
MAX T/O: 20,000 lb (9072 kg)

PERFORMANCE:
MAX SPEED: 690 mph (1110 kmh)
RANGE: 1000 miles (1610 km)
POWERPLANT: Pratt & Whitney
J48-P-8
OUTPUT: 7200 lb st (32 kN)

FIRST FLIGHT DATE:
20 September 1951

ARMAMENT:
four M-2 20 mm cannon in nose;
provision for up to 4000-lb
(1814 kg) of bombs/rockets/
missiles on six underwing
stores pylons

FEATURES:
Swept wing; engine air intakes in
wing root; high-mounted
horizontal tailplane; bubble
canopy; arrestor hook

# Grumman s-2 Tracker/c-1 Trader USA

four/eleven-seat, twin-engined ASW/AEW/utility aircraft

Built as a replacement for the 'hunter/killer' Guardian, the Tracker was developed over an incredibly short time span. Despite being of modest dimensions, the s-2's airframe nevertheless proved more than capable of housing all the ASW radar, sensor equipment and weaponry deemed necessary to locate and destroy submarines. A combination of fuel-efficient Wright Cyclone radials and long span wings gave the aircraft a superb loitering ability and good handling characteristics 'around the boat'. With space at a premium aboard ship, all the s-2's mission equipment was installed in such a way so as to allow its retraction back into the fuselage when not in use – the APS-38 was housed in a ventral 'bin', the MAD boom retracted into the tail and eight sonobuoys were stored in the rear engine nacelles. The first s2F-1 (redesignated s-2A in 1962) entered service in February 1954, and when production ceased in 1968, Grumman had built 1181 Trackers/Traders. The Tracker also formed the basis for the specialist E-1B Tracer AEW aircraft and the C-1A Trader Carrier On-board Delivery transport.

SPECIFICATION:

ACCOMMODATION:
pilot, co-pilot/tactical operator and two radar operators (s-2/E-1), or pilot, co-pilot and nine passengers (c-1)

DIMENSIONS:
LENGTH: 42 ft 3 in (12.88 m)
WINGSPAN: 69 ft 8 in (21.23 m)
HEIGHT: 16 ft 3.5 in (4.96 m)

WEIGHTS:
EMPTY: 17,357 lb (7873 kg)
MAX T/O: 26,300 lb (11,929 kg)

PERFORMANCE:
MAX SPEED: 287 mph (462 kmh)
RANGE: 900 miles (1448 km)
POWERPLANT: two Wright R-1820-82WA Cyclones
OUTPUT: 3050 hp (2274 kW)

FIRST FLIGHT DATE:
4 December 1952

ARMAMENT:
provision for up to 4810-lb (2181 kg) of torpedoes/depth charges/rockets in weapons bay and on six underwing stores pylons

FEATURES:
Shoulder-mounted straight-wing; two close-cowled radial engines; rectractable undercarriage; arrestor hook

# Grumman F11F/F-11 Tiger USA

single-seat, single-engined fighter

Intended to be a development of the Panther/ Cougar family, the Tiger eventually became an all new fighter. Taking shape with incredible speed, Grumman's G-98 (as it was designated in-house) prototype completed its first flight on 30 July 1954. Christened the Tiger, the fighter featured a waisted body to allow for the volume of the wing as per NACA's area rule for minimum transonic and supersonic drag. Powered by a Wright J65 turbojet with afterburner, the F11F-1 (as it was designated by the Navy in April 1955) entered production in 1956. Delayed by engine performance and reliability issues, 42 short-nose F11F-1s were built, and the first of these entered fleet service with VA-156 (a day fighter unit despite its attack designation) in March 1957. The radar-capable (never fitted) long-nose F11F-1 variant soon followed, and 157 had been delivered to the Navy by the time production ended in December 1958. Although only five fighter units made brief use of the Tiger in fleet service, the Navy's *Blue Angels* formation display team was equipped with the redesignated F-11A until 1968.

SPECIFICATION:

ACCOMMODATION:
pilot

DIMENSIONS:
LENGTH: 44 ft 11 in (13.7 m)
WINGSPAN: 31 ft 7.50 in (9.63 m)
HEIGHT: 13 ft 3 in (4.05 m)

WEIGHTS:
EMPTY: 13,428 lb (6092 kg)
MAX T/O: 22,160 lb (10,052 kg)

PERFORMANCE:
MAX SPEED: 890 mph (1432 kmh)
RANGE: 700 miles (1130 km)
POWERPLANT: Wright J65-W-18
OUTPUT: 11,000 lb st (49.2 kN)

FIRST FLIGHT DATE:
30 July 1954

ARMAMENT:
four M-2 20 mm cannon in fuselage and up to four AIM-9 Sidewinder missiles on four underwing stores pylons

FEATURES:
Mid-mounted swept wing; engine air intakes on fuselage sides either side of cockpit; low-mounted horizontal tailplane; bubble canopy; arrestor hook

# Grumman A-6 Intruder USA

two-seat, twin-engined bomber

Built to meet a US Navy requirement for a carrier-based long-range, low-level attack aircraft, the Intruder was chosen over nine other designs from seven rival manufacturers. The first of six A2F-1 development aircraft flew on 19 April 1960, and by the time the first of 482 production aircraft was delivered in 1963, the jet's designation had changed to A-6A. Making its combat debut over Vietnam in 1965, the Intruder saw much action in the conflict with both the Navy and Marine Corps. Capable of carrying up to 18,000-lb of bombs and missiles, the aircraft's usefulness was enhanced by its all-weather attack navigation equipment. The improved A-6E was delivered in 1970, this aircraft featuring more powerful engines and upgraded avionics. Of the 445 acquired, 240 were new build jets and 205 A-6A conversions. A further 78 A-models were reconfigured as KA-6D tankers. Periodically upgraded in the 1980s and early 1990s, A-6s saw further action over Libya, Lebanon, the Persian Gulf and in *Desert Storm*, before retiring in 1997.

SPECIFICATION:

**ACCOMMODATION:**
pilot and bombardier-navigator

**DIMENSIONS:**
LENGTH: 54 ft 9 in (16.69 m)
WINGSPAN: 53 ft 0 in (16.15 m)
HEIGHT: 16 ft 2 in (4.93 m)

**WEIGHTS:**
EMPTY: 27,613 lb (12,525 kg)
MAX T/O: 58,600 lb (26,580 kg)

**PERFORMANCE:**
MAX SPEED: 685 mph (1037 kmh)
RANGE: 1077 miles (1733 km)
POWERPLANT: two Pratt & Whitney
J52-P-8Bs
OUTPUT: 18,600 lb st (82.8 kN)

**FIRST FLIGHT DATE:**
19 April 1960

**ARMAMENT:**
up to 18,000-lb (8165 kg) of
bombs/missiles four underwing/
one centreline stores pylons

**FEATURES:**
Mid-mounted swept wing;
engine air intakes on fuselage
sides either side of cockpit; low-mounted horizontal tailplane;
bubble canopy; arrestor hook;
refuelling probe immediately in
front of cockpit

# Grumman EA-6B Prowler USA

four-seat, twin-engined electronic warfare aircraft

The US Navy and Marine Corps' standard tactical electronic warfare (EW) aircraft, the EA-6B traces its lineage back to the EF-10 Skynight of the early 1960s. The latter type was initially replaced in Marine Corps service by the EA-6A Intruder, 27 of which were built for service in Vietnam. This interim EW aircraft sired the purpose-built Prowler in the late 1960s, which the Navy used to replace its EKA-3B Skywarriors on carrier decks. Based on the A-6, the EA-6B had a stretched forward fuselage for a four-man crew consisting of a pilot and three electronic warfare officers. EW antenna were fitted into a bulbous fin tip fairing, while radar jamming equipment was carried in underwing pods. This EW mission equipment combined to form the Tactical Jamming System.

First flown on 25 May 1968, production Prowlers began reaching the fleet in 1971. Some 170 aircraft were built in a production run that lasted until 1991. One of the most highly valued assets in the US armed forces, the surviving 100 Prowlers remain in the forefront of current combat operations.

SPECIFICATION:

**ACCOMMODATION:**
pilot and three electronic warfare officers

**DIMENSIONS:**
LENGTH: 59 ft 10 in (18.24 m)
WINGSPAN: 53 ft 0 in (16.15 m)
HEIGHT: 16 ft 3 in (4.95 m)

**WEIGHTS:**
EMPTY: 31,572 lb (14,320 kg)
MAX T/O: 65,000 lb (29,895 kg)

**PERFORMANCE:**
MAX SPEED: 599 mph (958 kmh)
RANGE: 1106 miles (1770 km)
POWERPLANT: two Pratt & Whitney J52-P-408s
OUTPUT: 22,400 lb st (99.6 kN)

**FIRST FLIGHT DATE:**
25 May 1968

**ARMAMENT:**
up to four AGM-88 HARM anti-radar missiles on four underwing stores pylons

**FEATURES:**
Mid-mounted swept wing; engine air intakes on fuselage sides either side of cockpit; low-mounted horizontal tailplane; bubble canopy; arrestor hook; refuelling probe immediately in front of cockpit; bulbous fin tip fairing

# Grumman F-14 Tomcat  USA

two-seat, twin-engined fighter-bomber

Emerging from the failed F-111 fleet fighter programme, the F-14 Tomcat was for many years the world's best long-range defence fighter. Grumman, as lead contractor for the US Navy's version of the F-111, had independently begun work on the G-303 air defence fighter long before the cancellation of the General Dynamics project, and this was duly selected in January 1969. Built to replace the F-4, the aircraft featured key systems from the F-111B, including the AWG-9 radar, AIM-54 Phoenix missile, TF30 engines and swing wings. Designated the F-14 by the Navy, the prototype undertook its maiden flight on 12 December 1970, and the first of 556 production aircraft reached the fleet in 1972. A further 79 F-14As were sold to pre-revolutionary Iran in the mid 1970s.

Fifty A-models were re-engined and redesignated as F-14B/DS in the late 1980s and 76 new build jets delivered. With its principle fighter mission disappearing with the ending of the Cold War, the Tomcat has seen much combat of late as a precision bomber. All Navy F-14s will be retired by 2006.

SPECIFICATION:

ACCOMMODATION:
pilot and radar intercept officer in tandem

DIMENSIONS:
LENGTH: 62 ft 8 in (19.10 m)
WINGSPAN: 64 ft 2 in (19.54 m)
HEIGHT: 16 ft 0 in (4.88 m)

WEIGHTS:
EMPTY: 40,105 lb (18,190 kg)
MAX T/O: 74,349 lb (33,724 kg)

PERFORMANCE:
MAX SPEED: 1553 mph (2485 kmh)
RANGE: 2012 miles (3220 km)
POWERPLANT: two Pratt & Whitney TF30-P-412S
OUTPUT: 41,800 lb st (186 kN)

FIRST FLIGHT DATE:
12 December 1970

ARMAMENT:
one M61A1 Vulcan 20 mm cannon in forward fuselage; up to six air-to-air missiles on four underwing/fuselage stores pylons, or 14,500-lb (6577 kg) of bombs

FEATURES:
Variable-sweep wings; low-mounted horizontal tailplane; bubble canopy; arrestor hook; twin fins, underfuselage strakes

# Grumman OV-1 Mohawk USA

two-seat, twin-engined battlefield surveillance aircraft

The OV-1 Mohawk was built to fulfil the US Army's need for a dedicated battlefield observation platform. Boasting STOL capability, crew armour and systems redundancy in order to allow it to remain operational after having been hit by small-arms fire, the Mohawk proved itself to be the ideal aircraft for the task. Its twin turboprop engines combined with the aircraft's short high-lift wings to make the OV-1 an agile battlefield interdictor, whilst its long-stroke undercarriage allowed for rough-field operations. The first OV-1AS entered Army service in February 1961, and by the time of the Vietnam War, more than 150 had been delivered. The final OV-1s were delivered in 1970, bringing production to a close after the 375th airframe had been completed. The Mohawk's passive electronic intelligence role saw the D-model become an important weapon in the 'Cold War' arsenal, aircraft being converted to carry infrared linescan and side-looking radar. The surviving OV-1D/RV-1S were retired from US Army service in 1996 when fatigue lives were reached.

SPECIFICATION:

**ACCOMMODATION:**
pilot and observer, seated
side-by-side

**DIMENSIONS:**
LENGTH: 41 ft 0 in (12.50 m)
WINGSPAN: 42 ft 0 in (12.80 m)
HEIGHT: 12 ft 8 in (3.86 m)

**WEIGHTS:**
EMPTY: 9937 lb (4507 kg)
MAX T/O: 15,031 lb (6818 kg)

**PERFORMANCE:**
MAX SPEED: 310 mph (500 kmh)
RANGE: 1410 miles (2270 km)
POWERPLANT: two Lycoming
T53-701S
OUTPUT: 2800 shp (2087.96 kW)

**FIRST FLIGHT DATE:**
14 April 1959

**ARMAMENT:**
Gun/rocket pods and grenade
launchers occasionally fitted on
two underwing stores pylons

**FEATURES:**
Straight, mid-mounted wings;
two turboprop engines mounted
atop wings; bulged, side-by-side
canopy; triple tail fin

# Grumman E-2 Hawkeye USA

five-seat, twin-engined airborne early warning aircraft

The E-2 Hawkeye was developed to replace Grumman's E-1 Tracer, which was an AEW derivative of the S-2. The US Navy announced in March 1957 that it had chosen the Grumman design, combined with the digital processors and the General Electric APS-96 surveillance radar. The resulting W2F-1 (redesignated the E-2 in 1962) featured the radar housed in a rotodome above the fuselage. Tailored to fit within a carrier hangar deck, the aircraft had high-mounted, folding wings and a four-finned tailplane with significant dihedral. The first of 59 E-2As was delivered to the Navy in 1961, and the aircraft saw much service during the Vietnam War. E-2As were upgraded to E-2B standard from 1969, while the definitive E-2C made its fleet debut in 1971. The latter variant was initially fitted with APS-125 radar and improved signal processing equipment, and over the years the aircraft has been upgraded with better radar. Still in production for the US Navy today, more than 170 E-2Cs have been built to date. Export versions of the aircraft have also been sold to seven countries.

SPECIFICATION:

**ACCOMMODATION:**
pilot, co-pilot, combat information centre officer, air control operator, radar operator

**DIMENSIONS:**
LENGTH: 57 ft 7 in (17.54 m)
WINGSPAN: 80 ft 7 in (24.56 m)
HEIGHT: 18 ft 4 in (5.58 m)

**WEIGHTS:**
EMPTY: 39,373 lb (17,860 kg)
MAX T/O: 53,267 lb (24,160 kg)

**PERFORMANCE:**
MAX SPEED: 390 mph (625 kmh)
RANGE: 1784 miles (2855 km)
POWERPLANT: two Allison T56-A-425s
OUTPUT: 10,200 shp (7610 kW)

**FIRST FLIGHT DATE:**
21 October 1960

**FEATURES:**
Straight, high-mounted wings; two turboprop engines mounted beneath wings; four tail fins; radome atop fuselage; arrestor hook

# Grumman C-2 Greyhound USA

42-seat, twin-engined carrier onboard delivery aircraft

Grumman's tradition of building Carrier Onboard Delivery (COD) aircraft for the US Navy stretched back to its cargo-carrying Avenger of World War 2 and similarly configured C-1 Trader version of the S-2 Tracker of the 1950s. The final example of Grumman's COD 'craft' came in the form of the C-2 Greyhound, which was derived from the E-2. Whereas the Avenger and the C-1 had simply been passenger/cargo-configured versions of frontline types, the Greyhound was significantly different from its donor airframe. Although retaining the E-2's powerplants and wings, its fuselage was much broader, and featured a rear-loading cargo ramp and upturned tail. The first of two YC-2A prototypes made its first flight on 18 November 1964, after which a follow-on batch of 17 C-2As was built. Entering fleet service in 1966, the Greyhound has been a constant feature on US Navy carrier decks across the globe ever since. An additional 39 C-2s were built in 1985-89 as replacements for the recently retired C-1 Traders. The humble Greyhound is set to remain in Navy service for the foreseeable future.

## SPECIFICATION:

**ACCOMMODATION:**
pilot, co-pilot, crew chief and 39 passengers

**DIMENSIONS:**
LENGTH: 56 ft 10 in (17.32 m)
WINGSPAN: 80 ft 7 in (24.56 m)
HEIGHT: 15 ft 11 in (4.84 m)

**WEIGHTS:**
EMPTY: 36,345 lb (16,485 kg)
MAX T/O: 57,500 lb (26,080 kg)

**PERFORMANCE:**
MAX SPEED: 359 mph (575 kmh)
RANGE: 1806 miles (2890 km)
POWERPLANT: two Allison T56-A-425S
OUTPUT: 9824 shp (7330 kW)

**FIRST FLIGHT DATE:**
18 November 1964

**FEATURES:**
Straight, high-mounted wings; two turboprop engines mounted beneath wings; four tail fins; rear-loading cargo ramp; arrestor hook

# HAL HF-24 Marut INDIA

single-seat, twin-engined fighter-bomber

The first indigenous fighter to emerge from India, the stylish HF-24 Marut (Wind Spirit) was designed by a team lead by Dr Kurt Tank of Focke-Wulf fame. Work on the aircraft had commenced in 1956, with Tank's brief being to produce a Mach 2-capable multi-role fighter. The first of two prototypes was flown on 17 June 1961, and the first of 18 pre-production Marut Mk 1s began flight testing in April 1963. Powered by two HAL-built Bristol Orpheus 703 turbojets, a total of 112 production aircraft were delivered to the Indian Air Force from November 1967 onward – a dozen two-seat Marut Mk 1T trainers were also built. The installation of Orpheus 703s was originally intended to be only a temporary measure following the cancellation of the more powerful Orpheus BOr 12, but the former remained in place throughout the Marut's service life, restricting its top speed to just Mach 1.02. Three squadrons received Maruts, and they saw action as fighter-bombers in the 1971 Indo-Pakistan War. All surviving HF-24s had been replaced by licence-built MiG-23BNs by 1985.

## SPECIFICATION:

**ACCOMMODATION:**
pilot

**DIMENSIONS:**
LENGTH: 52 ft 0.75 in (15.87 m)
WINGSPAN: 29 ft 6.33 in (9.00 m)
HEIGHT: 11 ft 9.75 in (3.60 m)

**WEIGHTS:**
EMPTY: 13,658 lb (6195 kg)
MAX T/O: 24,048 lb (10,908 kg)

**PERFORMANCE:**
MAX SPEED: 705 mph (1134 kmh)
RANGE: 480 miles (772 km)
POWERPLANT: two Bristol Orpheus 703s
OUTPUT: 9700 lb st (41 kN)

**FIRST FLIGHT DATE:**
17 June 1961

**ARMAMENT:**
four Aden 20 mm cannon in forward fuselage; up to 4000-lb (1814 kg) of bombs/rocket pods on four underwing stores pylons

**FEATURES:**
Low-mounted swept wings; low-mounted horizontal tailplane; bubble canopy; engine air intakes on fuselage sides just aft of cockpit

# HAL Ajeet INDIA

single-seat, single-engined fighter-bomber

Although a derivative of the licence-built Gnat, the Ajeet (Sanskrit for Invincible) lightweight fighter-bomber featured less than 60 per cent commonality with its Folland predecessor. Unlike the British aircraft, the HAL-designed Ajeet had integral wing tanks, new avionics, more sophisticated control systems (those in the Gnat were chronically unreliable) and a new Martin-Baker ejection seat. The final two production Gnats served as the Ajeet prototypes, with the first of these taking to the sky on 5 March 1975. The first production Ajeet was flown on 30 September 1976. Although featuring many new systems, and expanded capabilities, the Ajeet was powered by the same Orpheus 701 turbojet as had featured in the Gnat. The Indian aircraft also boasted identical twin 30 mm Aden cannon. A total of 79 Ajeets were built for the Indian Air Force, with the last example being delivered in February 1982. Ten HAL-built Gnats were also converted into Ajeets. The final Ajeets in frontline service were retired by No 2 on 25 March 1991.

SPECIFICATION:

**ACCOMMODATION:**
pilot

**DIMENSIONS:**
LENGTH: 29 ft 8 in (9.04 m)
WINGSPAN: 22 ft 1 in (6.73 m)
HEIGHT: 8 ft 1 in (2.46 m)

**WEIGHTS:**
EMPTY: 5086 lb (2307 kg)
MAX T/O: 9195 lb (4171 kg)

**PERFORMANCE:**
MAX SPEED: 685 mph (1102 kmh)
RANGE: 1300 miles (2080 km)
POWERPLANT: Rolls-Royce Orpheus 701-01
OUTPUT: 4520 lb st (19 kN)

**FIRST FLIGHT DATE:**
5 March 1975

**ARMAMENT:**
two Aden 30 mm cannon in fuselage; provision for up to 1000-lb (454 kg) of bombs/rockets on four underwing stores pylons

**FEATURES:**
Shoulder-mounted swept-wing layout; bubble canopy; tricycle landing gear; engine air intakes on fuselage sides aft of cockpit; small vertical tail

# Handley Page Hastings UK

55-seat, four-engined long-range transport

Built to replace the Avro York in the long-range transport role within the RAF, the prototype Hastings made its maiden flight on 7 May 1946. Transport Command's No 47 Sqn became the first unit to receive Hasting C 1s in October 1948, and it was joined by aircraft of No 297 Sqn the following year when the RAF helped keep Berlin supplied during Operation *Plainfare*, better known as the Berlin Airlift. Indeed, it was a Hastings that made the last sortie of the lift on 6 October 1949.

The C 2 variant was introduced into RAF service in late 1950, this version differing from the Mk 1 in having a wider-span tailplane mounted lower on the rear fuselage (standard on all remaining variants) and additional fuel capacity. A total of 147 Hastings aircraft was built for the RAF (100 C 1s, 43 C 2s and four C 4s), as well as four Hastings C 3s for the RNZAF. The Hastings was retired from RAF service in early 1968, being replaced by the Lockheed Hercules.

SPECIFICATION:

**ACCOMMODATION:**
pilot, co-pilot, navigator, engineer, crew chief and 50 troops

**DIMENSIONS:**
LENGTH: 82 ft 8 in (25.23 m)
WINGSPAN: 113 ft 0 in (34.44 m)
HEIGHT: 22 ft 6 in (6.88 m)

**WEIGHTS:**
EMPTY: 48,427 lb (21,966 kg)
MAX T/O: 80,000 lb (36,288 kg)

**PERFORMANCE:**
MAX SPEED: 348 mph (557 kmh)
RANGE: 4250 miles (6800 km)
POWERPLANT: four Bristol Hercules 106s
OUTPUT: 6700 hp (4996 kW)

**FIRST FLIGHT DATE:**
7 May 1946

**FEATURES:**
Low-mounted straight-wing; large tail; four wing-mounted radial engines; circular fuselage; 'taildragger' undercarriage configuration

# Handley Page Victor  UK

five-seat, four-engined bomber/tanker/strategic reconnaissance aircraft

Designed to meet the same specification (B 35/46) as the Vulcan, the Victor was built for high altitude flight at high speeds. It did this thanks to its 'crescent' shape wing, which was sharply swept but with a thicker inner section which housed the aircraft's four Rolls-Royce Sapphire engines. The last of the RAF's V-bombers to enter service with Bomber Command in 1955-58, the 50 B 1s were progressively upgraded to B 1A standard with better electronic countermeasures equipment. The survivors were converted into dedicated K 1A tankers in 1965-67 after the nuclear deterrent mission was passed on to the Royal Navy's Polaris missile submarine force. The more powerful B 2, fitted with Rolls-Royce Conways, entered service in the early 1960s, 34 aircraft being built. These were used in the low-level strike/reconnaissance role, carrying the British-built Blue Steel missile. Twenty aircraft became K 2 tankers once the bomber role was taken away from the Victor in the 1970s, and the last jets were retired in October 1993 following service in the first Gulf War.

SPECIFICATION:

ACCOMMODATION:
pilot, co-pilot, tactical navigator, radar operator, air electronics operator

DIMENSIONS:
LENGTH: 114 ft 11 in (35.05 m)
WINGSPAN: 120 ft 0 in (36.58 m)
HEIGHT: 30 ft 1.50 in (9.20 m)

WEIGHTS:
EMPTY: 91,000 lb (41,277 kg)
MAX T/O: 233,000 lb (101,150 kg)

PERFORMANCE:
MAX SPEED: 640 mph (1030 kmh)
RANGE: 4600 miles (7400 km)
POWERPLANT: four Rolls-Royce Conway 201s
OUTPUT: 82,400 lb st (366 kN)

FIRST FLIGHT DATE:
24 December 1952

ARMAMENT:
up to 35,000-lb (15,890 kg) of bombs/missiles in internal bomb-bay

FEATURES:
Swept wing of variable thickness; engines housed within wing roots; upswept T-tail; tadpole-shaped fuselage

# Hawker Tempest II UK

single-seat, single-engined fighter-bomber

The RAF's last single-seat, single-piston-engined fighter to enter production, the Tempest II can trace its origins to the capture of an airworthy Focke-Wulf FW 190 in June 1942. Prior to the arrival of this aircraft, British designers had considered air-cooled radial engines inferior to liquid-cooled inline powerplants. However, the performance derived from the FW 190's compact BMW 801D dispelled previous beliefs, and resulted in the RAF requesting that a radial engine be developed for fitment to Hawker's Tempest fighter then under development as Specification F 10/41, powered by the troublesome Napier Sabre inline engine. Intended primarily for service with the RAF's Tiger Force in operations against the Japanese, the first of two Tempest II prototypes flew on 28 June 1943. However, technical delays with the potentially awesome Bristol Centaurus 5/6 radial engine meant that the Napier-powered Tempest V entered service in April 1944 – a full six months before the Tempest II. Failing to see action in World War 2, the bulk of the 452 Tempest IIs built survived in RAF service until 1953.

SPECIFICATION:

ACCOMMODATION:
pilot

DIMENSIONS:
LENGTH: 34 ft 5 in (10.50 m)
WINGSPAN: 41 ft 0 in (12.50 m)
HEIGHT: 15 ft 10 in (4.81 m)

WEIGHTS:
EMPTY: 8900 lb (4037 kg)
MAX T/O: 13,250 lb (6010 kg)

PERFORMANCE:
MAX SPEED: 440 mph (708 kmh)
RANGE: 820 miles (1319 km)
POWERPLANT: Bristol Centaurus 5/6
OUTPUT: 2526 hp (1883 kW)

FIRST FLIGHT DATE:
28 June 1943

ARMAMENT:
Four wing-mounted Hispano Mk v 20 mm cannon; up to 2000-lb (907 kg) of bombs/rockets on four underwing stores pylons

FEATURES:
Straight wing; close-cowled radial engine; bubble canopy; propeller spinner

# Hawker Fury/Sea Fury UK

single-seat, single-engined fighter-bomber

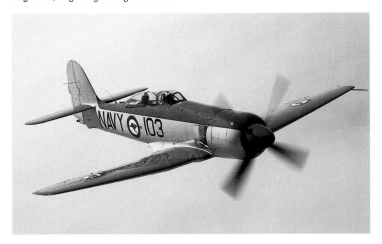

Using the wings of the Tempest II without the
centre section, which were joined under an all-new
monocoque fuselage, the Sir Sydney Camm-
designed Fury was the second Hawker aircraft to
make use of the powerful, but complex, Centaurus
radial engine. The Fleet Air Arm (FAA) showed great
interest in the new Hawker fighter, and Boulton
Paul duly developed a navalised version for carrier
deployment. Hefty orders for the RAF were
summarily cancelled in the wake of VE-Day, and
only 65 Furies were completed for Iraq, Egypt and
Pakistan. Fortunately, the FAA remained committed
to the Sea Fury variant, and purchased 50 F 10s and
615 FB 11s. Export sales of the Sea Fury were also
achieved in Australia, Canada, the Netherlands,
West Germany, Burma and Cuba. The FB 11 saw
much action in Korea with the British, Australian
and Canadian fleets, and although most Sea Furies
had been phased out of frontline service by the late
1950s, Pakistani Furies remained active in the
various wars with India until 1973.

SPECIFICATION:

**ACCOMMODATION:**
pilot (two pilots in tandem in
TT 20 trainer variant)

**DIMENSIONS:**
LENGTH: 34 ft 8 in (10.56 m)
WINGSPAN: 38 ft 4.75 in (11.69 m)
HEIGHT: 15 ft 10 in (4.81 m)

**WEIGHTS:**
EMPTY: 8977 lb (4090 kg)
MAX T/O: 12,500 lb (5669 kg)

**PERFORMANCE:**
MAX SPEED: 460 mph (740 kmh)
RANGE: 760 miles (1223 km)
POWERPLANT: Bristol
Centaurus 18
OUTPUT: 2550 hp (1901 kW)

**FIRST FLIGHT DATE:**
1 September 1944

**ARMAMENT:**
four wing-mounted Hispano
Mk v 20 mm cannon; up to
2000-lb (907 kg) of bombs/
rockets on four underwing
stores pylons

**FEATURES:**
Straight, folding wing; close-
cowled radial engine; arrestor
hook (Sea Fury only); bubble
canopy

# Hawker Sea Hawk  UK

single-seat, single-engined fighter-bomber

Hawker's first jet fighter, the Sea Hawk, was of
conventional appearance but internally unique in
having a jet pipe that split to serve two propelling
nozzles – one on each side of the wing trailing
edge. Although initially designed for the RAF as the
P.1040, the Sea Hawk was developed for the FAA
following the Air Force's decision to wait for the
Hunter. The first of 161 production F 1s was issued
to the fleet in March 1953. After the delivery of the
95th F 1, production switched first to the F 2 (40)
and then the bomb rack-equipped FB 3 (116).
Further new-builds were to follow, with 90 FGA 4s
and 86 FGA 6s also being delivered. Part of the FAA
for over a decade, British Sea Hawks saw action
during the Suez Crisis of 1956 and with the Indian
Navy (which had 74 examples) in the wars against
Pakistan in 1965 and 1971. The Royal Netherlands
Navy (22) and the West German Marineflieger (68)
also flew the Sea Hawk.

SPECIFICATION:

ACCOMMODATION:
pilot

DIMENSIONS:
LENGTH: 39 ft 8 in (12.08 m)
WINGSPAN: 39 ft 11 in (11.89 m)
HEIGHT: 8 ft 8 in (2.79 m)

WEIGHTS:
EMPTY: 9720 lb (4410 kg)
MAX T/O: 16,200 lb (7355 kg)

PERFORMANCE:
MAX SPEED: 599 mph (958 kmh)
RANGE: 1400 miles (2253 km)
POWERPLANT: Rolls-Royce
Nene 103
OUTPUT: 5400 lb st (24.05 kN)

FIRST FLIGHT DATE:
2 September 1947

ARMAMENT:
four fuselage-mounted Hispano
Mk v 20 mm cannon; up to
2000-lb (907 kg) of
bombs/rockets on four
underwing stores pylons

FEATURES:
Straight, folding wing; tricyle
undercarriage; arrestor hook;
bubble canopy; wing root engine
air intakes

# Hawker Hunter UK

single/two-seat, single-engined fighter-bomber/advanced trainer

The most successful post-war British fighter, the Hunter was built to Specification F 4/48. Capable of attaining supersonic speeds in a shallow dive, and as manoeuvrable as any other jet fighter of the period, the first of 139 production F 1s was issued to Fighter Command in mid-1953, followed by 45 improved F 2s later that year. Early Hunters suffered engine reliability problems, particularly when the Aden guns were fired, but gas ingestion difficulties were overcome with the definitive F 4 (365 built), F 5 (105) and F 6 (383). The power of the jet's Avon (and Sapphire in the F 5) engine steadily increased with every new variant, and by the time the ground-attack optimised FGA 9 appeared, the Avon 207 powerplant was good for 10,150 lb st. Using the F 4 as a basis, Hawker also built the T 7 advanced trainer variant in 1957. The last Hunter was completed in 1966, which brought total production to 1985. Aside from its use by the RAF, the Hunter was also flown by 17 foreign air forces.

SPECIFICATION:

**ACCOMMODATION:**
pilot, or two pilots seated side-by-side (T 7 trainer)

**DIMENSIONS:**
LENGTH: 45 ft 10.5 in (13.98 m)
WINGSPAN: 33 ft 8 in (10.26 m)
HEIGHT: 13 ft 2 in (4.01 m)

**WEIGHTS:**
EMPTY: 14,400 lb (6532 kg)
MAX T/O: 24,600 lb (11,158 kg)

**PERFORMANCE:**
MAX SPEED: 620 mph (978 kmh)
RANGE: 1840 miles (2961 km)
POWERPLANT: Rolls-Royce Avon RA.28 Mk 207
OUTPUT: 10,150 lb st (45.15 kN)

**FIRST FLIGHT DATE:**
20 June 1951

**ARMAMENT:**
four fuselage-mounted Aden 30 mm cannon; up to 2000-lb (907 kg) of bombs/rockets on four underwing stores pylons

**FEATURES:**
Mid-mounted swept wing; swept fin; tricyle undercarriage; bubble canopy; wing root engine air intakes

# Helio AU-24 Stallion USA

six-seat, single-engined, high-winged light utility aircraft

A military derivative of Helio's STOL family of civil utility aircraft, the Kaman-developed Stallion was built specifically for the counter-insurgency role in South-east Asia. To achieve its incredible short-field performance, the aircraft was equipped with full-span automatic leading-edge slats, an augmented lateral control system and slotted flaps. Unlike Helio's H-250 and H-295 Courier (the U-10 Super Courier version of which was used extensively by the USAF and allied air forces in Vietnam), the Stallion relied on a turboprop engine to offset its increased all up weight. Much of the latter took the form of six underwing hardpoints and 1900 lbs of assorted weaponry (rockets, bombs, flares and other 'goodies'), plus a cabin-mounted machine-gun or M197 20 mm cannon. Designated the H-550A by Helio, 15 were ordered as the AU-24A by the USAF with 1972 funds, these aircraft being sent to South Vietnam and evaluated during Project Credible Chase. Fourteen unarmed Stallions were subsequently handed over to the Khmer (Cambodian) Air Force in 1973.

SPECIFCATION:

**ACCOMMODATION:**
pilot and five passengers

**DIMENSIONS:**
LENGTH: 39 ft 7 in (12.07 m)
WINGSPAN: 41 ft 0 in (12.50 m)
HEIGHT: 9 ft 3 in (2.81 m)

**WEIGHTS:**
EMPTY: 2860 lb (1297 kg)
MAX T/O: 6300 lb (2857 kg)

**PERFORMANCE:**
MAX SPEED: 216 mph (348 kmh)
RANGE: 1090 miles (1755 km)
POWERPLANT: Pratt & Whitney
(UACL) PT6A-27
OUTPUT: 680 shp (507 kW)

**FIRST FLIGHT DATE:**
5 June 1964

**ARMAMENT:**
cabin-mounted M197 20 mm
cannon or machine gun; up to
1900-lb (862 kg) of bombs/
rockets/flares on six underwing
stores pylons

**FEATURES:**
High-mounted, unbraced
straight wing; fixed taildragger
undercarriage; three-bladed
propeller; close-cowled
turboprop engine

# Hispano HA-1112 Buchón SPAIN

single-seat, single-engined fighter-bomber

Although the Spanish government had agreed a licence-production deal with Messerschmitt for the Bf 109G-2 in 1942, finished aircraft only started trickling out of the Hispano Aviación plant in 1945, delayed by a lack of complete technical drawings and appropriate jigs. Easily the most important 'piece' missing from the Gustav 'puzzle' was the Daimler-Benz DB 605 engine, which had been withheld in Germany because of a shortage of powerplants. The Spanish were forced to use the less powerful, French-built, Hispano Suiza HS 12Z 17 instead, and 69 HA-1112-K1Ls were built. Production of airframes outstripped engine availability, and with the thawing of relations between Spain and the West from 1952, more powerful Rolls-Royce Merlin 500/45 engines were sourced from Britain to create the Buchón (Pigeon). Despite the advent of jet fighters rendering the HA-1112-M1L obsolete before it had reached service, the Spanish saw the aircraft as a valuable fighter-bomber and 171 were completed between 1955-58. The Buchón remained in service until 1965.

## SPECIFICATION:

**ACCOMMODATION:**
pilot

**DIMENSIONS:**
LENGTH: 29 ft 10 in (9.10 m)
WINGSPAN: 32 ft 6.5 in (9.92 m)
HEIGHT: 8 ft 6.5 in (2.60 m)

**WEIGHTS:**
EMPTY: 5855 lb (2656 kg)
MAX T/O: 7011 lb (3180 kg)

**PERFORMANCE:**
MAX SPEED: 419 mph (674 kmh)
RANGE: 476 miles (766 km)
POWERPLANT: Rolls-Royce Merlin 500-45
OUTPUT: 1632 hp (1217 kW)

**FIRST FLIGHT DATE:**
30 December 1954

**ARMAMENT:**
two 20 mm cannon in wings; provision for various underfuselage and underwing stores (bombs/rockets)

**FEATURES:**
Monoplane wing layout; close-cowled inline engine; retractable landing gear; fixed tailwheel; heavily framed canopy

# Hispano HA-200/-220 Saetta/Super Saetta SPAIN

single/two-seat, twin-engined trainer/light attack aircraft

Built under the guidance of Willy Messerschmitt as a basic jet trainer by Hispano for the Spanish Air Force, the Saetta (Arrow) relied on the same Marboré turbojet engines as used by Fouga's Magister. Production was relatively slow, with just ten HA-200s being delivered to 1960, when work commenced on the improved A-model. The latter variant enjoyed greater success with the Air Force, 30 being built as T-6G Texan replacements in the 1960s. The heavily-armed HA-200D was placed in production in 1965, 55 being completed. The Saetta's ground attack capabilities were increased during 1965 when Hispano fitted the HA-200DS with uprated Marboré VI engines and doubled the number of underwing hardpoints. The success of the Saetta in this role prompted the manufacture of the dedicated HA-220 Super Saetta single-seat ground attack variant. Boasting better armour protection, machine guns and six hardpoints, 25 Super Saettas were built for the Spanish, and these saw action over the Sahara in 1974-75. The last HA-220s were retired in December 1981.

SPECIFICATION:

ACCOMMODATION:
two pilots in tandem (HA-200), or pilot only (HA-220)

DIMENSIONS:
LENGTH: 29 ft 5 in (8.97 m)
WINGSPAN: 34 ft 2 in (10.42 m)
HEIGHT: 9 ft 4 in (2.85 m)

WEIGHTS:
EMPTY: 4035 lb (1830 kg)
MAX T/O: 7385 lb (3350 kg)

PERFORMANCE:
MAX SPEED: 404 mph (650 kmh)
RANGE: 930 miles (1500 km)
POWERPLANT: two Turboméca Marboré IIS
OUTPUT: 1760 lb st (15.50 kN)

FIRST FLIGHT DATE:
12 August 1955

ARMAMENT:
two Browning M3 0.50-in machine guns or 20 mm cannon in upper nose; provision for up to 2954-lb (1340 kg) of bombs/rockets on four underwing and two underfuselage pylons

FEATURES:
Straight-wing layout; bubble canopy; wingtip tanks; tricycle landing gear; engine air intake in nose

# Hunting Percival Provost UK

two-seat, single-engined basic trainer

As the wholesale re-equipment of the RAF's frontline force with jets got into its stride in the late 1940s, the Air Staff soon realised that the Prentice/Harvard sequence in its training programme was not providing fast jet pilots with sufficient experience for frontline flying. In order to solve this problem the Air Ministry issued Operational Requirement OR 257, which detailed the need for a new piston-engined trainer with greater performance. Percival's response was the Provost. The competition for the Prentice replacement was fierce, with 15 companies submitting proposals. However, Percival was the only one who could guarantee delivery of a prototype within the time specified, and it received an order for 200 machines in May 1951. Production-standard Provosts made their service debut with the Central Flying School's Basic Training Squadron two years later. More than 330 Provosts were eventually delivered over a three-year period, and these remained in service until progressively replaced by Hunting's follow-on Jet Provost trainer in the late 1950s.

SPECIFICATION:

ACCOMMODATION:
two pilots seated side-by-side

DIMENSIONS:
LENGTH: 28 ft 8 in (8.74 m)
WINGSPAN: 35 ft 2 in (10.72 m)
HEIGHT: 12 ft 2.5 in (3.73 m)

WEIGHTS:
EMPTY: 3350 lb (1519 kg)
MAX T/O: 4400 lb (1996 kg)

PERFORMANCE:
MAX SPEED: 201 mph (322 kmh)
RANGE: 648 miles (1036 km)
POWERPLANT: Alvis Leonides 126
OUTPUT: 550 hp (410 kW)

FIRST FLIGHT DATE:
23 February 1950

FEATURES:
Straight-wing layout; side-by-side seating; extensive cockpit glazing; fixed landing gear

# IAI **Nesher** ISRAEL

single-seat, single-engined fighter-bomber

The Nesher (Eagle) was hastily built as a result of the French government's refusal to deliver the Mirage 5Js that Israel had ordered and paid for following its involvement in the Six Day War of June 1967. An unlicensed Israeli Aircraft Industries (IAI) copy of the Mirage 5 (which had been developed by Dassault specially for Israel), the Nesher was powered by an IAI Bedek Aviation Division-built SNECMA Atar 9C engine. Unlike the Mirage 5, the Nesher was fitted with locally-developed avionics and a Martin-Baker JM 6 zero-zero ejection seat, and it could also carry AIM-9 Sidewinder or Rafael Shafrir (Dragonfly) air-to-air missiles. The prototype Nesher (a modified Mirage IIICJ) flew in September 1969, and the first of 51 single-seat and ten two-seat aircraft reached the Israeli Air Force in 1971. Seeing combat in the 1973 Yom Kippur War, surviving Neshers (35 single-seaters and four two-seaters) were refurbished and sold as Daggers to the Argentine Air Force in 1978-79 and 1981-82. These saw further combat during the Falklands War of 1982.

SPECIFICATION:

ACCOMMODATION:
pilot

DIMENSIONS:
LENGTH: 51 ft 0 in (15.55 m)
WINGSPAN: 27 ft 0 in (8.22 m)
HEIGHT: 13 ft 11.50 in (4.25 m)

WEIGHTS:
EMPTY: 14,550 lb (6600 kg)
MAX T/O: 29,760 lb (13,500 kg)

PERFORMANCE:
MAX SPEED: 1460 mph (2350 kmh)
RANGE: 1000 miles (1610 km)
POWERPLANT: SNECMA Atar 9C-3
OUTPUT: 13,670 lb st (60.8 kN)

FIRST FLIGHT DATE:
September 1969

ARMAMENT:
two DEFA 552A 30 mm cannon in lower fuselage; provision for up to 9260-lb (4200 kg) of bombs/rockets/missiles on six underwing and one centreline stores pylons

FEATURES:
Delta-wing layout; no horizontal tail surfaces; tricycle landing gear; engine air intakes on fuselage sides aft of cockpit

# IAI **Kfir** ISRAEL

single-seat, single-engined fighter-bomber

Using the same basic airframe as the Nesher, the
Kfir (Lion Cub) had a shorter and wider-diameter
rear fuselage which allowed an IAI Bedek Division-
built J79-IAI-J1E engine to be fitted in place of the
SNECMA 9C. Based on the General Electric turbojet
engine fitted into the F-4 Phantom II, the new
engine produced an extra 5100 lb st thrust in
afterburner. Following an exhaustive test flight
programme in the early 1970s, the first of 27
production Kfir-C1s was delivered in April 1975. The
definitive C2 soon replaced the C1 in production,
the former featuring canard surfaces, nose strakes
and 'dog tooth' outer wing extensions in an effort
to improve the fighter's manoeuvrability in low
speed dogfights and reduce the jet's take-off run.
Some 185 C2s were built, and most of the C1s
upgraded to this specification. From 1983, all
surviving C2s were upgraded to C7 specification,
featuring two extra wing pylons and improved
avionics. The Kfir saw combat over Lebanon in
1182, after which refurbished jets were sold to
Ecuador, Colombia and Sri Lanka.

SPECIFICATION:

ACCOMMODATION:
pilot

DIMENSIONS:
LENGTH: 51 ft 4 in (15.65 m)
WINGSPAN: 27 ft 0 in (8.22 m)
HEIGHT: 14 ft 11 in (4.55 m)

WEIGHTS:
EMPTY: 16,060 lb (7285 kg)
MAX T/O: 36,375 lb (16,500 kg)

PERFORMANCE:
MAX SPEED: 1464 mph (2440 kmh)
RANGE: 711 miles (1185 km)
POWERPLANT: IAI Bedek Division
J79-IAI-J1E
OUTPUT: 17,860 lb st (79.4 kN)

FIRST FLIGHT DATE:
September 1969

ARMAMENT:
two DEFA 552A 30 mm cannon in
lower fuselage; provision for up
to 13,415-lb (6085 kg) of bombs/
rockets/missiles on four
underwing and four
underfuselage stores pylons

FEATURES:
Delta-wing layout; no horizontal
tail surfaces; intake-mounted
canards (C2/C7); tricycle landing
gear; engine air intakes on
fuselage sides aft of cockpit; fin
root intake

# Ilyushin Il-14 USSR

30-seat, twin-engined transport

The Il-12 was developed as a replacement for the war-weary Li-2, which was the workhorse of the Soviet Union's immediate post-war airline system. Development started as early as 1943, although production Il-12s did not enter service until 1946. The Il-14 was essentially an improved development of this design, featuring a new wing of more efficient aerofoil section, as well as more powerful Shvetsov engines and a cleaner airframe. The prototype Il-14 was first flown on 15 July 1950, and production commenced in June 1953. Initial service models were designated Il-14P, and they were configured to seat 18. Two years after entry into service, most Il-14Ps were configured to seat 24 passengers in a higher density configuration. By 1956 a stretched development – the Il-14M – had appeared. Few modifications were made during its production run of 3500 examples. While most Il-14s were constructed in the USSR, aircraft were also built under licence by VEB Flugzeugwerke (80) in East Germany and by Avia in Czechoslovakia (203).

SPECIFICATION:

**ACCOMMODATION:**
pilot, co-pilot, navigator, engineer and 26 passengers

**DIMENSIONS:**
LENGTH: 73 ft 2.25 in (22.31 m)
WINGSPAN: 104 ft 0 in (31.70 m)
HEIGHT: 25 ft 11 in (7.90 m)

**WEIGHTS:**
EMPTY: 27,998 lb (12,700 kg)
MAX T/O: 40,785 lb (18,500 kg)

**PERFORMANCE:**
MAX SPEED: 267 mph (430 kmh)
RANGE: 932 miles (1500 km)
POWERPLANT: two Shvetsov Ash-82TS
OUTPUT: 3750 hp (2794 kW)

**FIRST FLIGHT DATE:**
15 July 1950

**FEATURES:**
Straight-wing layout; tricycle landing gear; close-cowled, engine-mounted radial engines; six/seven passenger windows in fuselage

# Ilyushin Il-28 USSR

three-seat, twin-engined bomber

Effectively a Soviet Canberra bomber, the Il-28 was built to replace the USSR's vast fleet of World War 2 vintage piston-engined TU-2 medium bombers. The programme to produce the aircraft was launched in December 1947, and the prototype was powered by two RD-10 turbojets (reverse-engineered Junkers Jumo 004 turbojets). Flown for the first time on 8 August 1948, the aircraft was initially underpowered, but this problem was rectified with the installation of copied British Nene engines (known as the Klimov VK-1 in the USSR). Known to NATO as 'Beagle', over 2000 Il-28s were subsequently built, and aside from being used as tactical bombers, the aircraft proved suited to torpedo bombing, electronic warfare/reconnaissance, target towing and crew training. Ilyushin ceased production of the aircraft in 1955, although Chinese manufacturer Harbin licence-built 500+ Il-28s (as H-5s) into the 1960s. Although retired from the frontline Soviet Air Force in 1970, the survivors of the 1000 exported Il-28/H-5s remained in service across the globe with 21 air arms into the late 1990s.

SPECIFICATION:

**ACCOMMODATION:**
pilot, navigator, tail gunner

**DIMENSIONS:**
LENGTH: 57 ft 10.75 in (17.65 m)
WINGSPAN: 70 ft 4.75 in (21.45 m)
HEIGHT: 22 ft 0 in (6.70 m)

**WEIGHTS:**
EMPTY: 28,417 lb (12,890 kg)
MAX T/O: 46,297 lb (21,000 kg)

**PERFORMANCE:**
MAX SPEED: 559 mph (900 kmh)
RANGE: 684 miles (1100 km)
POWERPLANT: two Klimov VK-1S
OUTPUT: 11,904 lb st (52.5 kN)

**FIRST FLIGHT DATE:**
8 August 1948

**ARMAMENT:**
two NR-23 23 mm fixed cannon in nose and in tail turret; provision for up to 4410-lb (2000 kg) of bombs/rockets/torpedoes split between bomb-bay and two underwing stores pylons

**FEATURES:**
High-mounted straight-wing layout; tricycle landing gear; engines-mounted beneath wings; manned tail turret; glazed nose; swept-back horizontal tailplane

# Lavochkin La-9 USSR

single-seat, single-engined fighter

Developed from the wartime La-5/7, the La-9 was Lavochkin's penultimate piston-engined fighter. Starting with a standard La-7 in mid-1944, the design reworked the fuselage both in terms of its appearance and construction. Changes included a wider canopy with a frameless hood, deeper rear fuselage, larger vertical and horizontal tail surfaces, and revised wingtips. The prototype La-9 completed its maiden flight on 16 June 1946 and series production commenced five months later, although the numbers built were drastically scaled back following the advent of the first generation of Soviet jet fighters. Some 1630 La-9s were built before it was replaced on the production line by the near-identical La-11. Aside from its use with the Soviet Air Force, surplus La-9s were supplied to Eastern Bloc countries including Bulgaria and Romania. In early 1952 nearly 100 La-9s were sent to China, where they were thrown into action against United Nations forces during the Korean War. Surviving Chinese examples remained in service with training units into the early 1960s.

SPECIFICATION:

ACCOMMODATION:
pilot

DIMENSIONS:
LENGTH: 29 ft 6.50 in (9 m)
WINGSPAN: 34 ft 9.50 in (10.62 m)
HEIGHT: 9 ft 8 in (2.95 m)

WEIGHTS:
EMPTY: 5816 lb (2638 kg)
MAX T/O: 8104 lb (3676 kg)

PERFORMANCE:
MAX SPEED: 429 mph (690 kmh)
RANGE: 1078 miles (1735 km)
POWERPLANT: Shvetsov ASh-82FN
OUTPUT: 1870 hp (1394 kW)

FIRST FLIGHT DATE:
16 June 1946

ARMAMENT:
four ShVAK 20 mm cannon on top decking of nose

FEATURES:
Straight-wing layout; retractable landing gear; close-cowled radial engine; engine oil cooler inlet below centre fuselage

# Lockheed c-69/c-121 USA

93-seat, four-engined transport and airborne early warning aircraft

Developed for Howard Hughes' TWA, the majestic Constellation donned drab olive rather than red and white airliner trim as the first production aircraft were requisitioned as strategic transports for the USAAF, designated c-69s. Just 22 were taken on charge, but these aircraft made a big impression, and a number of longer-range c-121s were bought post-war. With the development of the stretched Super Constellation in 1950, the full military potential of the aircraft was realised, as specialist AEW (dubbed Warning Stars) and Elint variants were procured by the USAF and the US Navy – 20 distinct sub-types would eventually see operational service. The aircraft's 'finest hour' came during the Vietnam War, when seven variants of c-121 were used for radar/electronic surveillance, airborne early warning and fighter control, airborne radio relay, weather reconnaissance and troop transportation (with the Military Air Transport Service). The US Navy was the final military operator of the aircraft in American service, the last of its 142 Warning Star surveillance aircraft finally being retired in 1982.

SPECIFICATION:

ACCOMMODATION:
four/five-man crew and 64 (c-69) or 88 passengers (c-121), or 22-26 systems operators (EC-121)

DIMENSIONS:
LENGTH: 116 ft 2 in (35.41 m)
WINGSPAN: 123 ft 0 in (37.49 m)
HEIGHT: 27 ft 0 in (8.1 m)

WEIGHTS:
EMPTY: 80,611 lb (36,275 kg)
MAX T/O: 143,600 lb (64,620 kg)

PERFORMANCE:
MAX SPEED: 321 mph (517 kmh)
RANGE: 4600 miles (7405 km)
POWERPLANT: four Wright R-3350-34S
OUTPUT: 8800 hp (6562 kW)

FIRST FLIGHT DATE:
9 January 1943 (c-69), 1953 (RC-121)

FEATURES:
Straight-wing layout; retractable landing gear; four close-cowled radial engines; wingtip tanks; three-finned tail; large radomes above and below fuselage (AEW variants only)

# Lockheed P-2 Neptune USA

seven-seat, twin-engined maritime patrol and anti-submarine warfare aircraft

Designed with extreme range and endurance in mind, the P-2 was the end result of development work carried out by Lockheed subsidiary Vega into an aircraft combining a high aspect ratio wing with two then new R-3350 radial engines. With Lockheed focusing its efforts on other high-priority designs like the P-38 and Ventura, it was not until the last months of the war that the prototype XP2V-1 Neptune finally flew. Aside from the previously mentioned features, the aircraft also had large Fowler flaps for good short-field performance, a capacious weapons bay and two defensive turrets. The first of 838 Neptunes was delivered to the US Navy in March 1947, and the aircraft went on to become the staple ASW platform for many Western countries into the 1960s. Built in seven sub-types, the Neptune evolved into a superb maritime patrol aircraft, which was also produced by Kawasaki in Japan. Aside from its maritime use, modified OP-2E Elint and AP-2H 'gunship' versions were also employed to great effect by the USAF and Army in Vietnam.

SPECIFICATION:

ACCOMMODATION:
pilot, co-pilot, navigator, engineer, three sensor operators

DIMENSIONS:
LENGTH: 91 ft 8 in (27.94 m)
WINGSPAN: 103 ft 10 in (31.65 m)
HEIGHT: 29 ft 4 in (8.94 m)

WEIGHTS:
EMPTY: 49,935 lb (22,650 kg)
MAX T/O: 79,895 lb (36,240 kg)

PERFORMANCE:
MAX SPEED: 356 mph (573 kmh)
RANGE: 2500 miles (4000 km)
POWERPLANT: two Wright R-3350-30W Turbo-Compounds and two Westinghouse J34-36s
OUTPUT: 6500 hp (4847 kW) and 6800 lb st (30.24 kN)

FIRST FLIGHT DATE:
17 May 1945

ARMAMENT:
six fixed and two turret-mounted 20 mm cannon and two 0.5-in machine guns; up to 8000-lb (3629 kg) of bombs/rockets/depth charges in bomb-bay and on underwing pylons

FEATURES:
Straight-wing layout; retractable landing gear; two close-cowled radial engines; wingtip tanks

# Lockheed F-80 Shooting Star USA

single-seat, single-engined fighter-bomber

Lockheed's first jet fighter was designed by chief engineer Clarence L 'Kelly' Johnson and built within a 180-day time limit in 1943. Lacking a suitable American engine, the prototype XP-80 was powered by a de Havilland Goblin engine supplied by the British. The aircraft completed its first flight on 8 January 1944, and by January of the following year two YP-80As had been sent to Italy to operate in combat conditions. Although production aircraft failed to see action in World War 2, the F-80 (as the type was designated post-war) bore the brunt of the early fighting with USAF units in Korea in 1950-51, flying 15,000 sorties in the first four months of the war. A Shooting Star also shot down the first MiG-15 to fall to the USAF on 8 November 1950 in the world's first jet-versus-jet combat. A total of 1718 Shooting Stars were built, and a number were converted into RF-80 photo-reconnaissance platforms. Having served with 13 fighter groups in the frontline, surviving F-80s were relegated to the Air National Guard post-Korea.

SPECIFICATION:

**ACCOMMODATION:**
pilot

**DIMENSIONS:**
LENGTH: 34 ft 5 in (10.49 m)
WINGSPAN: 38 ft 9 in (11.81 m)
HEIGHT: 11 ft 3 in (3.43 m)

**WEIGHTS:**
EMPTY: 8420 lb (3819 kg)
MAX T/O: 16,856 lb (7646 kg)

**PERFORMANCE:**
MAX SPEED: 606 mph (975 kmh)
RANGE: 825 miles (1328 km)
POWERPLANT: Allison J33-A-35
OUTPUT: 5400 lb st (24 kN)

**FIRST FLIGHT DATE:**
8 January 1944

**ARMAMENT:**
six fixed Browning 0.5-in machine guns; up to 2000-lb (908 kg) of bombs/rockets on four underwing pylons

**FEATURES:**
Straight-wing layout; retractable landing gear; wingtip tanks; low lateral engine intakes; bubble canopy

# Lockheed T-33 and Canadair CL-30 USA & CANADA

two-seat, single-engined trainer

Boasting the title of the world's most populous jet trainer, the T-33 (of which the CL-30 is a Canadian derivative) was built to the tune of 6750 airframes during the 1950s. Sired by the F-80, the prototype T-33 was a stretched F-80C fitted with a second seat and a long canopy. First examples were designated TF-80Cs, and these entered service with the USAF in the late 1940s as replacements for the veteran T-6 Texan. Dubbed the 'T-Bird' following the type's redesignation as the T-33, the trainer proved to be so successful that production of the two-seater soon outstripped that of the F-80. Canada secured a licence (as did Kawasaki in Japan) to build its own variant, replacing the aircraft's Allison J33-A-35 turbojet powerplant with a Rolls-Royce Nene 10. Total CL-30 production ran to 656 aircraft between 1952-59, and although the last T-33s were retired from the USAF's Training Command in 1974, the CT-133 (as Canadian survivors were redesignated) soldiered on as electronic warfare, target tug and general utility aircraft into the late 1990s.

SPECIFICATION:

**ACCOMMODATION:**
two pilots in tandem

**DIMENSIONS:**
LENGTH: 37 ft 9 in (11.48 m)
WINGSPAN: 38 ft 10.5 in (11.85 m)
HEIGHT: 11 ft 8 in (3.55 m)

**WEIGHTS:**
EMPTY: 8084 lb (3667 kg)
MAX T/O: 14,442 lb (6551 kg)

**PERFORMANCE:**
MAX SPEED: 600 mph (960 kmh)
RANGE: 1345 miles (2165 km)
POWERPLANT: Allison J33-A-35 or Rolls-Royce Nene 10
OUTPUT: 5200 lb st (23.16 kN) and 5100 lb st (22.71 kN) respectively

**FIRST FLIGHT DATE:**
22 March 1948 (TF-80C)

**FEATURES:**
Straight-wing layout; retractable landing gear; wingtip tanks; low lateral engine intakes; long bubble canopy

# Lockheed TV-1/2 Seastar   USA

two-seat, single-engined trainer

The US Navy procured 53 single-seat F-80CS from
the USAF in 1948, which it designated TO/TV-1S.
These were used as advanced jet trainers until the
advent of the dedicated two-seat TF-80C in 1949,
which the Navy bought as the TO/TV-2. The early
aircraft were identical to the USAF's T-33, and they
proved unsuitable for carrier operations due to a
lack of forward visibility for the instructor in the
rear cockpit – the Navy/Marine Corps procured 699
examples nevertheless! Lockheed modified a TV-2
in late 1953 with a humped cockpit to give the rear
seat occupant a better view. The lower landing and
take-off speeds necessary for carrier operation
were achieved through the fitment of leading- and
trailing-edge flaps and a blown-flaps system of
boundary layer control. The reworked TV-2 also
featured a more powerful J33-A-24 engine. First
flown on 16 December 1953, the T2V-1 Seastar was
ordered into production and the first of 150
delivered in 1956. The aircraft was redesignated
the T-1A in 1962, and retired from service in the
early 1970s.

SPECIFICATION:

ACCOMMODATION:
two pilots in tandem

DIMENSIONS:
LENGTH: 38 ft 6.50 in (11.70 m)
WINGSPAN: 42 ft 10 in (12.83 m)
HEIGHT: 13 ft 4 in (4.08 m)

WEIGHTS:
EMPTY: 11,965 lb (5427 kg)
MAX T/O: 15,800 lb (7167 kg)

PERFORMANCE:
MAX SPEED: 580 mph (928 kmh)
RANGE: 970 miles (1552 km)
POWERPLANT: Allison J33-A-24
OUTPUT: 6100 lb st (27.18 kN)

FIRST FLIGHT DATE:
16 December 1953 (T2V-1)

FEATURES:
Straight-wing layout; retractable
landing gear; wingtip tanks; low
lateral engine intakes; long,
humped bubble canopy
(T2V-1 only)

# Lockheed F-94 Starfire USA

two-seat, single-engined fighter

The ultimate development of the long-lived F-80/T-33 series, the F-94 Starfire was the best known all-weather interceptor of the 1950s. Equipped with APG-33 radar in the nose, and a Sperry Zero-reader flight director, the prototype YF-94 (a modified TF-80C) made its first flight on 16 April 1949. Driven by the threat of Soviet long-range bombers attacking North America under the cover of the darkness, Lockheed completed the maiden flight of the first production F-94A just five months later. Equipping Air Defense Command units from December 1949, 110 F-94As and 357 F-94Bs served with over 24 frontline squadrons in the USA and Alaska. Despite fears of a radar-equipped jet coming down over enemy territory, the jet made its combat debut over Korea in late 1952. The revised F-94C was effectively an all-new aircraft, featuring a bigger engine, thinner wing, redesigned fuselage with a longer rear section, stepped cockpits and a swept tailplane. Some 387 C-models were built, and they ended their days with the Air National Guard in the late 1950s.

SPECIFICATION:

ACCOMMODATION:
pilot and radar observer in tandem

DIMENSIONS:
LENGTH: 44 ft 6 in (13.56 m)
WINGSPAN: 42 ft 5 in (12.93 m)
HEIGHT: 14 ft 11 in (4.55 m)

WEIGHTS:
EMPTY: 12,700 lb (5760 kg)
MAX T/O: 24,200 lb (10,977 kg)

PERFORMANCE:
MAX SPEED: 585 mph (941 kmh)
RANGE: 1200 miles (1931 km)
POWERPLANT: Pratt & Whitney
J48-P-5
OUTPUT: 8750 lb st (38 kN)

FIRST FLIGHT DATE:
16 April 1949

ARMAMENT:
four fixed Browning 0.5-in machine guns in nose (F-94A/B), or 24/48 2.75-in Mighty Mouse air-to-air rocket projectiles in nose and in wing pods (F-94C)

FEATURES:
Straight-wing layout; retractable landing gear; wingtip tanks; low lateral engine intakes; bubble canopy; swept tailplane (F-94C)

# Lockheed C-130 Hercules  USA

97-seat, four-engined tactical transport aircraft

A radical and bold design when built in the early 1950s, Lockheed's long-lived C-130 Hercules was in fact a clever synthesis of known techniques that had been featured in isolation in previous transport types. For example, the aircraft featured full size, rear-loading cargo doors, rough field landing gear, a pressurised fuselage and four turboprop engines. The prototype YC-130 flew for the first time on 23 August 1954, and A-models entered service with the USAF from December 1956. The Hercules made its combat debut in Vietnam in the early 1960s, and has remained at the heart of America's tactical transport force ever since. Over 2200 C-130s have been built to date in various guises, with the most popular variant being the C-130H, introduced in 1965. Aside from its use as a transport, the aircraft has also been modified to perform missions such as command and control, search and rescue, signal intelligence, aerial tanking and as an armed gunship. In service with over 60 countries worldwide, the Hercules remains in production today in its comprehensively updated C-130J form.

SPECIFICATION:

ACCOMMODATION:
pilot, co-pilot, navigator, flight engineer, loadmaster, 92 passengers

DIMENSIONS:
LENGTH: 97 ft 9 in (29.79 m)
WINGSPAN: 132 ft 7 in (40.41 m)
HEIGHT: 38 ft 3 in (11.66 m)

WEIGHTS:
EMPTY: 76,470 lb (34,685 kg)
MAX T/O: 175,000 lb (79,380 kg)

PERFORMANCE:
MAX SPEED: 376 mph (602 kmh)
RANGE: 4918 miles (7870 km)
POWERPLANT: four Allison T56-A-15s
OUTPUT: 18,032 shp (13,448 kW)

FIRST FLIGHT DATE:
23 August 1954

ARMAMENT:
Two M61 Vulcan 20 mm cannon, two 7.62 mm miniguns, two 40 mm Bofors cannon and a 105 mm howitzer, all mounted on left side of fuselage (AC-130 variant)

FEATURES:
Shoulder-mounted straight wing layout; retractable landing gear in fairings; four close-cowled turboprop engines

# Lockheed F-104 Starfighter USA

single-seat, single-engined fighter

Designed by Clarence L 'Kelly' Johnson, the xF-104 Starfighter compromised everything (manoeuvrability, weapons carriage and endurance) in search of superior flight performance. To achieve Mach 2.2 and an impressive initial rate of climb, the Starfighter combined the power of the J79 with a wing of minuscule span and razor-thin chord. With such features, the Starfighter was on the limits of available technology, which caused delays in the development of production aircraft. When the F-104A reached the USAF's Air Defense Command in 1958, just 153 were purchased. Later, the tactically-optimised c-model was also procured (77 aircraft), and this variant saw combat over Vietnam. The aircraft would have been deemed a commercial failure had it not been for Lockheed securing sales to NATO countries in 1959 for the strengthened and totally re-equipped F-104G. European air forces and Canada procured 1466 aircraft, and others were sold to Japan, Pakistan, Jordan and Taiwan. The last frontline F-104s were retired by Italy in 2004.

SPECIFICATION:

**ACCOMMODATION:**
pilot

**DIMENSIONS:**
LENGTH: 54 ft 9 in (16.69 m)
WINGSPAN: 21 ft 11 in (6.68 m)
HEIGHT: 13 ft 6 in (4.11 m)

**WEIGHTS:**
EMPTY: 14,082 lb (6387 kg)
MAX T/O: 28,779 lb (13,054 kg)

**PERFORMANCE:**
MAX SPEED: 1450 mph (2330 kmh)
RANGE: 1380 miles (2220 km) with drop tanks
POWERPLANT: General Electric J79-GE-11A
OUTPUT: 15,800 lb st (70.28 kN)

**FIRST FLIGHT DATE:**
7 February 1954

**ARMAMENT:**
one fixed T171E2 Vulcan cannon in fuselage; up to 7495-lb (3400 kg) of bombs/rockets/missiles on six underwing/wingtip and three underfuselage pylons

**FEATURES:**
Small, unswept wings with anhedral; retractable landing gear; wingtip tanks; lateral engine intakes; bubble canopy; T-tail

# Lockheed U-2 USA

single-seat, single-engined reconnaissance aircraft

The U-2 was designed by Lockheed's secretive 'Skunk Works' department in response to a request by the US government for a purpose-built reconnaissance aircraft that would hopefully be immune from interception by communist fighters. It would achieve its immunity by flying at extremely high altitudes (90,000 ft). The 'black' nature of the programme resulted in the aircraft's U-2 designation (U for utility, rather than R for reconnaissance). Resembling a powered glider, the first prototype completed its maiden flight in extreme secrecy on 1 August 1955, and production U-2AS were delivered to remote Watertown Strip, in Nevada, where Central Intelligence Agency (CIA) pilots converged onto them and prepared to fly missions over communist countries. Others were issued to the USAF, Lockheed building a total of 48 U-2A/B/CS and five two-seat DS. Flown extensively throughout the 1950s and 60s, additional, larger, U-2RS (12 built from 1967) were followed by 37 TR-1s in 1979. These were redesignated U-2RS in the 1980s, and the survivors remain in service with the USAF and NASA today.

SPECIFCATION:

ACCOMMODATION:
pilot

DIMENSIONS:
LENGTH: 62 ft 9 in (19.13 m)
WINGSPAN: 103 ft 0 in (31.39 m)
HEIGHT: 16 ft 0 in (4.88 m)

WEIGHTS:
EMPTY: 10,000 lb (4355 kg)
MAX T/O: 41,300 lb (18,735 kg)

PERFORMANCE:
MAX SPEED: 431 mph (690 kmh)
RANGE: 3019 miles (4830 km)
POWERPLANT: Pratt & Whitney J75-P-13B
OUTPUT: 17,000 lb st (75.6 kN)

FIRST FLIGHT DATE:
1 August 1955

FEATURES:
Shoulder-tapered, unswept, long-span wings; retractable landing gear on fuselage centreline; wing pods on some aircraft; engine air intakes on fuselage sides aft of cockpit; long nose

# Lockheed C-140 JetStar USA

12-seat, four-engined VIP transport aircraft

The Lockheed Model 1329 light jet transport was built to participate in a competition being staged by the USAF to find a general Utility Transport Category aeroplane. The twin-engined JetStar flew in prototype form for the first time on 4 September 1957, only 241 days after design completion. The aircraft was beaten in the competition by the rival North American Saberliner, but all was not lost for Lockheed as the Kennedy White House chose the re-engined JetStar (fitted with four JT12A-6s) as a Presidential/VIP transport to augment the first Boeing VC-135s then being used as Air Force One aircraft. Designated C-140A/BS, the USAF bought 16 JetStars, the first of which was delivered in late 1961. Five C-140AS were assigned to Air Force Communications Command for use in evaluating military navigation aids and operations, and the remaining eleven C-140BS were issued to Miltary Airlift Command for operational support airlift. Six of the latter jets were flown as VC-140BS on special government and White House airlift missions. All were retired by the early 1990s.

## SPECIFICATION:

**ACCOMMODATION:**
pilot, co-pilot, ten passengers

**DIMENSIONS:**
LENGTH: 60 ft 5 in (18.42 m)
WINGSPAN: 53 ft 8 in (16.37 m)
HEIGHT: 20 ft 5 in (6.23 m)

**WEIGHTS:**
EMPTY: 18,450 lb (8376 kg)
MAX T/O: 38,940 lb (17,678 kg)

**PERFORMANCE:**
MAX SPEED: 575 mph (920 kmh)
RANGE: 2865 miles (4585 km)
POWERPLANT: four Pratt & Whitney JT12-A-6s
OUTPUT: 13,200 lb st (58.80 kN)

**FIRST FLIGHT DATE:**
4 September 1957

**FEATURES:**
Low-mounted swept wings; mid-wing external fuel tanks; four podded engines attached to rear fuselage

# Lockheed P-3 Orion  USA

ten-seat, four-engined maritime patrol and anti-submarine warfare aircraft

Derived from Lockheed's less than successful L-188 Electra passenger airliner as an 'off-the-shelf' replacement for the P-2 Neptune, the P-3 Orion has proven to be so successful that well over 500 have been built in a handful of different variants. The first of 157 P-3As entered US Navy service in August 1962, this variant duly being followed by the improved B-model (124) in 1965, which boasted uprated engines and the provision to carry the Bullpup missile. The final ASW version built was the P-3C, which made its frontline debut in 1969. Progressively upgraded over the intervening three decades, the P-3C Upgrade III is still the most effective maritime patrol and ASW platform in today's US Navy, with in excess of 12 frontline and reserve units equipped with the aircraft.

Specialist Elint and Sigint versions have also been acquired by the Navy, whilst 21 foreign air arms have also bought either new or second-hand P-3A/B/CS. More than 700 Orions have been built to date, including 100 under licence by Kawasaki in Japan.

SPECIFICATION:

ACCOMMODATION:
pilot, co-pilot, navigator, flight engineer, tactical coordinator, three sensor operators, two observers/sonobuoy loaders

DIMENSIONS:
LENGTH: 116 ft 10 in (35.61 m)
WINGSPAN: 99 ft 8 in (30.37 m)
HEIGHT: 33 ft 8.5 in (10.27 m)

WEIGHTS:
EMPTY: 61,491 lb (27,890 kg)
MAX T/O: 142,000 lb (64,410 kg)

PERFORMANCE:
MAX SPEED: 473 mph (761 kmh)
RANGE: 2383 miles (3853 km)
POWERPLANT: four Allison T56-A-14S
OUTPUT: 18,040 shp (13,452 kW)

FIRST FLIGHT DATE:
19 August 1958

ARMAMENT:
internal bomb-bay can carry eight torpedoes or eight depth charges and ten underwing pylons can carry up to eight Harpoon missiles or ten torpedoes or ten mines

FEATURES:
Low tapered wing; four wing-mounted turboprop engines, tail MAD boom

# Lockheed SR-71 USA

two-seat, twin-engined reconnaissance aircraft

The ultimate high speed manned reconnaissance aircraft, the SR-71 was unique in being able to cruise at a sustained Mach 3. The aircraft evolved from the CIA-sponsored A-12 programme, which was created in secrecy by Lockheed's 'Skunk Works' under the direction of Clarence L 'Kelly' Johnson. Eighteen A-12s were built in the early 1960s, and following flight testing, the USAF committed to the creation of the larger SR-71. The first of 31 A-models (including three SR-71B trainers) flew on 22 December 1964, and these served exclusively with the 9th Strategic Reconnaissance Wing at Beale AFB, California – detachments were also maintained at Mildenhall, in Suffolk, and Kadena, on Okinawa. Involved in numerous Cold War missions across the USSR and Eastern Europe, China, North Africa and the Middle East, the SR-71 was eventually retired in 1990 due to budgetary constraints. NASA continued to operate several jets for research purposes, and in 1995 two jets were briefly brought back into USAF service to plug the gap in US reconnaissance capabilities. They were permanently retired in 1996.

SPECIFCATION:

**ACCOMMODATION:**
pilot and reconnaissance systems operator

**DIMENSIONS:**
LENGTH: 107 ft 5 in (37.74 m)
WINGSPAN: 55 ft 7 in (16.95 m)
HEIGHT: 18 ft 6 in (5.64 m)

**WEIGHTS:**
EMPTY: 60,000 lb (27,215 kg)
MAX T/O: 170,000 lb (77,110 kg)

**PERFORMANCE:**
MAX SPEED: 2012 mph (3220 kmh)
RANGE: 3018 miles (4830 km)
POWERPLANT: two Pratt & Whitney J58-1s
OUTPUT: 65,000 lb st (291.2 kN)

**FIRST FLIGHT DATE:**
22 December 1964

**FEATURES:**
Low-mounted delta-shaped wings; engines built into wings; angular fuselage; inward-canted twin fins

# Lockheed s-3 Viking  USA

four-seat, twin-engined maritime patrol, anti-submarine warfare and aerial tanking aircraft

In 1967 the us Navy issued a requirement for a replacement for the s-2 Tracker. Five us manufacturers submitted designs, and in 1969 the ys-3A Viking from the Lockheed/Ling Temco Vought team was selected as the winner. The first of eight service evaluation aircraft made its maiden flight on 21 January 1972. Powered by two turbofan engines mounted to a high wing, the Viking featured a large internal weapons bay, seating for four crewmen and extensive asw equipment crammed into its portly fuselage. The s-3A entered fleet service in July 1974, and 187 examples were built. The upgraded s-3B variant was created in the early 1980s, the aircraft featuring improved avionics and an expanded weapons suite, including air-to-surface missiles. All surviving s-3As were upgraded to this specification. Aside from four us-3A Carrier Onboard Delivery aircraft used into the early 1990s, the only other Viking variant was the short-lived es-3A electronic warfare aircraft, 16 of which were converted from s-3As in the 1990s. Today used primarily as an aerial tanker, all s-3s will be retired by 2008.

SPECIFICATION:

ACCOMMODATION:
pilot, co-pilot, tactical coordinator and sensor operator

DIMENSIONS:
LENGTH: 53 ft 4 in (16.26 m)
WINGSPAN: 68 ft 8 in (20.93 m)
HEIGHT: 22 ft 9 in (6.93 m)

WEIGHTS:
EMPTY: 26,650 lb (12,088 kg)
MAX T/O: 52,540 lb (23,832 kg)

PERFORMANCE:
MAX SPEED: 679 mph (815 kmh)
RANGE: 3803 miles (6085 km)
POWERPLANT: two General Electric
TF34-GE-2S
OUTPUT: 18,550 lb st (82.6 kN)

FIRST FLIGHT DATE:
21 January 1972

ARMAMENT:
internal bomb-bay can carry four torpedoes or four depth charges, bombs or mines, and two underwing pylons can carry two Harpoon/Maverick missiles or two torpedoes/mines/bombs/rocket pods

FEATURES:
Shoulder-mounted swept wings; two podded turbofan engines under wings; arrestor hook; tall folding tail

# Martin JRM Mars USA

186-seat, four-engined long-range maritime transport flying boat

The original Mars was ordered on 23 August 1938 by the US Navy as a flying boat patrol bomber. However, progress was slowed by war priorities, and the first XPB2M-1 did not fly until July 1942. By that time the aircraft's long-range patrol mission was being performed by navalised Liberators (PB4YS) and the PBY Catalina, forcing Martin to convert the huge flying boat into a troop transport. Redesignated the JRM-1, 20 Mars were ordered by the US Navy in January 1945, but only five were built before VJ-Day, followed by a sixth JRM-2 powered by uprated R4360 Wasp Major engines. The earlier aircraft were also subsequently re-engined, and all six machines given the designation JRM-3. Production JRMs differed from the XPB2M by having a longer nose and a single tailfin in place of the traditional Martin endplate-type fins and rudders. The aircraft were issued to Navy Air Transport Service unit VR-2, and the four survivors (one was lost in an accident in 1945 and another in a fire in 1950) were declared obsolete in 1956.

SPECIFICATION:

ACCOMMODATION:
pilot, co-pilot, flight engineer, radio operator, navigator, crew chief and 180 passengers

DIMENSIONS:
LENGTH: 120 ft 3 in (36.66 m)
WINGSPAN: 200 ft 0 in (60.96 m)
HEIGHT: 47 ft 11 in (14.35 m)

WEIGHTS:
EMPTY: 77,920 lb (35,344 kg)
MAX T/O: 165,000 lb (74,844 kg)

PERFORMANCE:
MAX SPEED: 220 mph (352 kmh)
RANGE: 3315 miles (5304 km)
POWERPLANT: four Pratt & Whitney R4360 Wasp Majors
OUTPUT: 14,000 hp (10,439 kW)

FIRST FLIGHT DATE:
21 July 1945 (JRM-1)

FEATURES:
High-wing monoplane; boat-shaped hull; four radial engines; large single tail fin/rudder; fixed outrigger floats

# Martin P5M Marlin USA

11-seat, twin-engined maritime patrol flying boat

A post-war evolution of Martin's PBM Mariner, the Marlin proved to be the US Navy's last operational flying boat. Indeed, Martin made use of the Mariner's distinctive gull wing and upper fuselage, combined with a new lower hull, when it built the prototype XP5M-1. The latter flew on 30 May 1948, and featured Wright R-3350 engines with twice the horsepower of the Mariner's R-2600s. The Marlin also had radar-operated nose/tail turrets, as well as a power-operated dorsal turret. By the time production commenced in 1951, the Marlin had had its nose turret replaced by an APS-80 search radar, the dorsal turret had been removed and the flight deck raised for better visibility. The first of 114 P5M-1s reached the frontline on 23 April 1952. The following year Martin redesigned the Marlin in P5M-2 form, the aircraft featuring a T-tail, lower bow chine and more powerful engines. By the time production of the aircraft ended in 19650, 145 had been built. Redesignated the P-5B in 1962, the Marlin remained in the frontline until 1966.

## SPECIFICATION:

**ACCOMMODATION:**
pilot, co-pilot, flight engineer, radio operator, navigator, crew chief, three sensor operators, two observers/sonobuoy loaders

**DIMENSIONS:**
LENGTH: 100 ft 7 in (30.66 m)
WINGSPAN: 118 ft 2 in (36.02 m)
HEIGHT: 32 ft 8.50 in (9.97 m)

**WEIGHTS:**
EMPTY: 50,485 lb (22,900 kg)
MAX T/O: 85,000 lb (38,555 kg)

**PERFORMANCE:**
MAX SPEED: 251 mph (404 kmh)
RANGE: 2050 miles (3300 km)
POWERPLANT: two Wright R-3350-32WAS
OUTPUT: 6900 hp (5146 kW)

**FIRST FLIGHT DATE:**
30 May 1948

**ARMAMENT:**
internal bomb-bay and two underwing stores pylons capable of carrying up to 8000-lb (3629 kg) of bombs/torpedoes/depth charges/mines/rockets

**FEATURES:**
High-wing monoplane; boat-shaped hull; two radial engines; large single tail fin (P5M-1), or T-tail (P5M-2)

# Martin B-57 Canberra  USA

two-seat, twin-engined bomber

When the USAF chose the English Electric Canberra to serve as a tactical attack bomber in the late 1940s, it was the first time a foreign combat aircraft had been chosen for frontline service with the US military in large numbers since 1918. Martin was chosen to manufacture the British jet under licence. The moderately Americanised B-57A entered service in late July 1953, with the bulk of the 75 built being re-rolled as RB-57 photo-reconnaissance platforms as soon as they entered service. Martin heavily modified the follow-on B-57B in order to make it a more adaptable attack aircraft, particularly at low level. Featuring a fighter-style canopy and no nose glazing, the aircraft had additional underwing pylons, a rotary bomb-bay door and improved avionics. A total of 202 B-57Bs were built, followed by 38 B-57C trainers, 20 RB-57D high altitude reconnaissance platforms and 68 B-57E target tugs. Seeing extensive combat in Vietnam, the final modified B-57G precision bombers were retired in 1974, but specialist electronic warfare and reconnaissance variants served into the early 1980s.

SPECIFICATION:

**ACCOMMODATION:**
pilot and navigator

**DIMENSIONS:**
LENGTH: 65 ft 6 in (19.96 m)
WINGSPAN: 64 ft 0 in (19.50 m)
HEIGHT: 15 ft 7 in (4.75 m)

**WEIGHTS:**
EMPTY: 26,800 lb (12,200 kg)
MAX T/O: 55,000 lb (24,950 kg)

**PERFORMANCE:**
MAX SPEED: 582 mph (937 kmh)
RANGE: 2100 miles (3380 km)
POWERPLANT: two Wright J65-5s
OUTPUT: 14,440 lb st (33 kN)

**FIRST FLIGHT DATE:**
20 July 1953

**ARMAMENT:**
provision for four 20 mm cannon or eight 0.50-in machine guns in outer wings; bomb-bay load of 5000-lb (2268 kg), plus rockets/bombs on eight underwing and two wingtip stores pylons

**FEATURES:**
Straight-wing; tricycle landing gear; two mid-wing mounted engines; fighter type bubble canopy

# Max Holste M.H.1521M Broussard FRANCE

six-seat, single-engined high wing light utility transport and AOP aircraft

Developed from the smaller and less powerful M.H.152 Air Observation Post (AOP) prototypes of the late 1940s, the M.H.1521 was built as a private-venture by small French manufacturer Max Holste. Dubbed the Broussard (Bushman), the aircraft was a rugged machine that combined the reliability of the Wasp radial engine with a sturdy airframe of useful size. Of the initial batch of 24 built by the manufacturer, 18 were sold to the French Army, where they received the designation M.H.1521M. Further orders from both the Army and Air Force kept Max Holste busy for five years between 1954-59, as 363 Broussards were completed. Following its military use as a utility 'hack' and occasional artillery spotter in France, surplus Broussards were supplied to many former colonies in Africa for use by their embryonic air arms – the air forces of Cameroon, Ivory Coast, Mauritania, Niger, Senegal, Togo and Upper Volta were amongst those that received examples. The final French M.H.1521MS were retired from military service in the very early 1980s.

SPECIFICATION:

ACCOMMODATION:
pilot and five passengers

DIMENSIONS:
LENGTH: 28 ft 2.5 in (8.60 m)
WINGSPAN: 45 ft 1 in (13.75 m)
HEIGHT: 9 ft 2 in (2.79 m)

WEIGHTS:
EMPTY: 3373 lb (1530 kg)
MAX T/O: 5953 lb (2700 kg)

PERFORMANCE:
MAX SPEED: 168 mph (270 kmh)
RANGE: 745 miles (1200 km)
POWERPLANT: Pratt & Whitney
R-985-AN-1 Wasp
OUTPUT: 450 hp (335 kW)

FIRST FLIGHT DATE:
17 November 1952

FEATURES:
High-mounted, braced straight wing; fixed taildragger undercarriage; two-bladed propeller; close-cowled radial engine; twin fins

# McDonnell F2H Banshee USA

single-seat, twin-engined fighter

Derived from the McDonnell's pioneering US Navy FD-1 Phantom jet fighter, the Banshee retained the former's unswept wing and two Westinghouse axial engines housed within fattened wing roots. The Phantom had been the world's first operational naval jet fighter to operate from an aircraft carrier, although its service life had been restricted by a limited production run of just 60 jets due to the modest power produced by its J30 engines. The J34 cured these problems, and the Navy ordered 56 F2H-1s following the successful testing of the prototype XF2D-1 in 1947. The first examples reached the fleet in March 1949, by which time McDonnell had commenced development of the improved F2H-2, with its longer fuselage for extra fuel and 200 US gal wingtip tanks. Some 188 were built, followed by 146 -2N/2P nightfighters and photo-reconnaissance aircraft. Seeing action in the Korean War with both the Navy and Marine Corps, the Banshee remained in naval service into the late 1950s. The final frontline variants were the radar-equipped F2H-3 (250 built) and re-engined F2H-4 (150 built).

SPECIFICATION:

ACCOMMODATION:
pilot

DIMENSIONS:
LENGTH: 47 ft 6 in (14.48 m)
WINGSPAN: 44 ft 10 in (13.67 m)
HEIGHT: 14 ft 6 in (4.40 m)

WEIGHTS:
EMPTY: 12,790 lb (5800 kg)
MAX T/O: 22,312 lb (10,270 kg)

PERFORMANCE:
MAX SPEED: 610 mph (982 kmh)
RANGE: 2000 miles (3220 km)
POWERPLANT: two Westinghouse
J34-WE-34S
OUTPUT: 7200 lb st (16.5 kN)

FIRST FLIGHT DATE:
11 January 1947

ARMAMENT:
four M-2 20 mm cannon in nose;
up to 4000-lb (1814 kg) of
bombs/rockets/missiles on eight
underwing pylons

FEATURES:
Straight, folding wing; tricycle
landing gear; engines housed
within wing roots; fighter type
bubble canopy; arrestor hook;
wingtip tanks

# McDonnell F3H Demon   USA

single-seat, single-engined fighter

Designed as the first naval jet aircraft to be equal in performance to the fastest land-based fighters, the Demon promised to be the most advanced machine of its generation. However, in reality, the aircraft was badly let down by its original engine, the unreliable Westinghouse J40. The F3H had been designed around the J40, and the prototype XF3H-1 flew with the XJ40-WE-6 engine in place on 7 August 1951. By the time production aircraft were being built, the fighter's weight had increased to the point where the more powerful J40-WE-24 was needed, but this proved unreliable, and the underpowered J40-WE-22 was used instead. The Navy responded by cutting its order from 529 F3H-1s to 56, and these were issued to training units only. McDonnell reworked the jet to allow the Allison J71 to be fitted, and the first of 459 F3H-2s entered fleet service in 1956. This variant could carry both the AIM-7C and AIM-9C missiles, and featured an APG-51 radar. Redesignated the F-3B in 1962, the Demon remained in frontline service until 1965.

SPECIFICATION:

ACCOMMODATION:
pilot

DIMENSIONS:
LENGTH: 58 ft 11 in (17.95 m)
WINGSPAN: 35 ft 4 in (10.76 m)
HEIGHT: 14 ft 7 in (4.45 m)

WEIGHTS:
EMPTY: 22,300 lb (10,115 kg)
MAX T/O: 33,900 lb (15,376 kg)

PERFORMANCE:
MAX SPEED: 647 mph (1040 kmh)
RANGE: 1370 miles (2200 km)
POWERPLANT: Allison J71-A-2E
OUTPUT: 14,250 lb st (32.5 kN)

FIRST FLIGHT DATE:
7 August 1951

ARMAMENT:
four M-2 20 mm cannon in nose;
up to 6600-lb (2994 kg) of
bombs/rockets/missiles on four
underwing pylons

FEATURES:
Mid-mounted, swept wing;
tricycle landing gear; engines
housed within wing roots; fighter
type bubble canopy; arrestor
hook; swept tail

# McDonnell F-101 Voodoo USA

single/two-seat, twin-engined fighter-bomber/reconnaissance aircraft

Easily the biggest and most powerful fighter of its days, the F-101 was developed from the XF-88 Voodoo prototype first flown on 20 October 1948. Initially built to serve as a long-range escort for Strategic Air Command's nuclear bombers, the F-101A evolved into an attack aircraft for Tactical Air Command (TAC). The first A-model flew on 29 September 1954, and when SAC dropped its requirement for the F-101A, all 77 Voodoos were issued to TAC from May 1957 onwards. The follow-on C-model (47 built) was capable of carrying a tactical nuclear weapon. Photo-reconnaissance variants of the single-seat jet (RF-101A/C) saw combat with the USAF over Cuba and Vietnam, no fewer than 32 of the 201 delivered being lost in action. The F-101B two-seat Voodoo was built specially for Air Defense Command (ADC), the aircraft featuring a second cockpit for the operator of the MG-13 fire-control radar. Some 478 were built, and these equipped 16 ADC squadrons – 66 were also supplied to the Canadians. The last Voodoos were retired from Canadian service in the early 1990s.

SPECIFICATION:

ACCOMMODATION:
pilot, and pilot and radar operator (F-101B/F)

DIMENSIONS:
LENGTH: 67 ft 4.75 in (20.55 m)
WINGSPAN: 39 ft 8 in (12.09 m)
HEIGHT: 18 ft 0 in (5.49 m)

WEIGHTS:
EMPTY: 28,000 lb (12,700 kg)
MAX T/O: 51,000 lb (23,133 kg)

PERFORMANCE:
MAX SPEED: 1220 mph (1963 kmh)
RANGE: 1550 miles (2500 km)
POWERPLANT: two Pratt & Whitney J57-PW-53s
OUTPUT: 29,980 lb st (129.5 kN)

FIRST FLIGHT DATE:
29 September 1954 (F-101A)

ARMAMENT:
three M-39 20 mm cannon in fuselage; up to 2000-lb (907 kg) of bombs/rockets/missiles on four underwing/underfuselage pylons, or in semi-recessed underfuselage troughs

FEATURES:
Low-mounted, swept wing; tricycle landing gear; air intakes at wing roots; fighter type bubble canopy; swept tail, with high-mounted tailplane

# McDonnell Douglas F-4 Phantom II   USA

two-seat, twin-engined fighter-bomber/reconnaissance aircraft

The most famous post-World War 2 fighter, the F-4 Phantom II is still a part of today's military scene. However, this number is shrinking by the year, with most of the 5195 built during a 19-year production run having now been retired. Initially developed as a company private venture by McDonnell, the Phantom II was an advanced, gunless, all-weather interceptor boasting state-of-the-art radar and advanced missiles. Ordered by the US Navy for deployment aboard its carriers, the first production F-4Bs were delivered in December 1960. The following year the USAF ordered the aircraft in slightly modified form as the F-4C, and the jet went on to equip 16 of its 23 TAC fighter wings. The advent of the Vietnam War saw the Phantom II thrust into action, and the design's multi-role capability saw it deliver tons of bombs in large-scale attack formations. Improved versions of the Phantom II (F-4E and F-4J) also made their debut in combat in the late 1960s, whilst foreign customers like Britain, Israel, Germany and Japan purchased the F-4 in large numbers.

SPECIFICATION:

ACCOMMODATION:
pilot and navigator in tandem

DIMENSIONS:
LENGTH: 58 ft 3 in (17.76 m)
WINGSPAN: 38 ft 5 in (11.7 m)
HEIGHT: 16 ft 3 in (4.96 m)

WEIGHTS:
EMPTY: 28,000 lb (12,700 kg)
MAX T/O: 58,000 lb (26,308 kg)

PERFORMANCE:
MAX SPEED: 1500 mph (2414 kmh)
RANGE: 2300 miles (3700 km)
POWERPLANT: two General Electric
J79-GE-15S
OUTPUT: 34,000 lb st (151 kN)

FIRST FLIGHT DATE:
27 May 1958

ARMAMENT:
one M-61 20 mm cannon in nose
(F-4E only); up to 16,000-lb
(7257 kg) of bombs/rockets/
missiles on four underwing
pylons, or in semi-recessed
underfuselage troughs
(missiles only)

FEATURES:
Low-mounted, swept wing with
dihedral outer panels; fuselage
air intakes below cockpit; fighter
type bubble canopy; swept tail,
with anhedral tailplane

# McDonnell Douglas F-15A Eagle USA

single/two-seat, twin-engined fighter-bomber

The world's pre-eminent air superiority fighter since its introduction into service, the F-15 was the end result of the USAF's F-X requirement launched in the mid-1960s. Embodying lessons learned from air combat in Vietnam, the winning design had to have a thrust to weight ratio in excess of unity, and be able to out-turn any opponent in order to bring its missiles to bear first. McDonnell Douglas' F-15 beat off rivals from Fairchild-Republic and North American Rockwell, and the prototype was first flown on 27 July 1972. Powered by purpose-built Pratt & Whitney F100 turbofans, and featuring the Hughes APG-63 radar, the Eagle was a compelling package. The first production A-models entered service in January 1976, and a total of 355 single-seat and 57 two-seat F-15Bs were built prior to production switching to the improved F-15C/D in 1979. Also purchased by Israel, the A-models were upgraded under the Multi Stage Improvement Program in the 1980s. Today, only a small number of F-15A/BS remain in service with the Air National Guard, although Israel still flies 35+.

SPECIFICATION:

**ACCOMMODATION:**
pilot, or two pilots in tandem (F-15B)

**DIMENSIONS:**
LENGTH: 63 ft 9.75 in (19.45 m)
WINGSPAN: 42 ft 9.75 in (13.05 m)
HEIGHT: 18 ft 7.50 in (5.68 m)

**WEIGHTS:**
EMPTY: 28,600 lb (12,793 kg)
MAX T/O: 68,000 lb (30,845 kg)

**PERFORMANCE:**
MAX SPEED: 1659 mph (2655 kmh)
RANGE: 1228 miles (1965 km)
POWERPLANT: two Pratt & Whitney F100-PW-100S
OUTPUT: 47,620 lb st (211.8 kN)

**FIRST FLIGHT DATE:**
27 July 1972

**ARMAMENT:**
one M-61 20 mm cannon in right wing root; up to 16,000-lb (7257 kg) of missiles in four semi-recessed underfuselage troughs and on two wing stores pylons

**FEATURES:**
Shoulder-mounted, swept wing; fuselage air intakes below cockpit; fighter type bubble canopy; twin fins; prominent nose radome

# McDonnell Douglas F/A-18A/B Hornet USA

single/two-seat, twin-engined fighter-bomber

Following the cancellation of the US Navy's VFAX lightweight multi-role fighter programme by US Congress in 1974, the latter recommended that the service should focus on a navalised General Dynamics YF-16 or Northrop YF-17 which had been built for the USAF. The latter design was chosen on 2 May 1975, and Northrop paired up with naval manufacturer McDonnell Douglas to produce fleet capable aircraft. Initially, separate F-18 fighter and A-18 attack jets were to be built, but these were combined as a cost-cutting measure to create the F/A-18A Hornet. The first of 11 development jets flew on 18 November 1978. Powered by two General Electric F404 turbofans, and featuring APG-65 radar, production aircraft reached the US Navy in May 1980. The Marine Corps received Hornets two years later. Some 371 A-models and 40 F/A-18BS were delivered to the Navy up to 1986, when production switched to the F/A-18C/D. Seeing combat over Libya in 1986 and Iraq in 1991, most Navy/Marine F/A-18A/BS have now been retired, although Spain, Canada and Australia continue to fly them.

SPECIFICATION:

ACCOMMODATION:
pilot, or two pilots in tandem
(F/A-18B)

DIMENSIONS:
LENGTH: 56 ft 0 in (17.07 m)
WINGSPAN: 37 ft 6 in (11.43 m)
HEIGHT: 15 ft 3.50 in (4.66 m)

WEIGHTS:
EMPTY: 28,000 lb (12,700 kg)
MAX T/O: 48,253 lb (21,888 kg)

PERFORMANCE:
MAX SPEED: 1185 mph (1900 kmh)
RANGE: 636 miles (1018 km)
POWERPLANT: two general Electric
F404-GE-400S
OUTPUT: 32,000 lb st (142.4 kN)

FIRST FLIGHT DATE:
9 June 1974 (YF-17)

ARMAMENT:
one M-61 20 mm cannon in nose;
17,000-lb (7711 kg) of bombs/
rockets/missiles missiles on four
underwing, two wingtip (missiles)
and one underfuselage stores
pylons; two missiles in two semi-
recessed underfuselage troughs

FEATURES:
Shoulder-mounted, swept wing;
fighter type bubble canopy; twin
fins; long leading edge root
extensions

# Mikoyan MiG-15 USSR & POLAND

single/two-seat, single-engined fighter/trainer

As the first truly successful Soviet jet fighter, the MiG-15 arrived virtually unannounced in the skies over war-torn Korea in 1950 and provided UN pilots with a rather unpleasant shock. With its all-swept wing and aerodynamic design, the MiG could easily out-climb, out-dive, out-manoeuvre and out-pace all of its US and British opponents bar the F-86 Sabre. At the 'heart' of the nimble fighter was the Klimov RD-45F engine, which was a direct descendent of the Rolls-Royce Nene. Examples of the latter had been sent to the USSR by the British government in 1947, and these solved the powerplant problems that had afflicted early Soviet jet fighter development. Mikoyan's designers were also influenced by German data captured during the final days of World War 2. Following flight-testing in early 1948, the MiG-15 was placed into series production, and within five years 8000 had been built in the USSR. Further improved variants (including the two-seat UTI trainer) were ushered into service in the 1950s, with licence production continuing in Poland into the early 1960s.

SPECIFICATION:

**ACCOMMODATION:**
pilot, and two pilots in tandem (MiG-15UTI)

**DIMENSIONS:**
LENGTH: 35 ft 7.50 in (10.86 m)
WINGSPAN: 33 ft 1 in (10.08 m)
HEIGHT: 12 ft 1.7 in (3.70 m)

**WEIGHTS:**
EMPTY: 8115 lb (3681 kg)
MAX T/O: 11,861 lb (5380 kg)

**PERFORMANCE:**
MAX SPEED: 667 mph (1076 kmh)
RANGE: 826 miles (1330 km)
POWERPLANT: Klimov VK-1
OUTPUT: 5952 lb st (26.4 kN)

**FIRST FLIGHT DATE:**
20 December 1947

**ARMAMENT:**
one N-37 37 mm cannon and two NS-23 23 mm cannon in nose

**FEATURES:**
Mid-mounted swept-wing layout; tricycle landing gear; engine air intake in nose; fighter type bubble canopy; swept tail; high-mounted tailplane

# Mikoyan MiG-17 USSR, POLAND & CHINA

single-seat, single-engined fighter-bomber

Built in order to overcome the MiG-15's snaking and pitching at high speed, which rendered the fighter near-useless as a gun platform, the MiG-17 was an all-new design, despite Western reports at the time that the fighter was little more than an enlarged version of the earlier aircraft. Although physically resembling the MiG-15, the MiG-17 had a reduced-thickness wing which vastly improved the jet's high-speed handling. Other external changes saw the angle of sweep of the vertical tail surface increased and the fuselage lengthened by three feet. MiG-17s began replacing MiG-15s in Soviet service in October 1952, and definitive F-models (introducing the afterburning VK-1F) made their frontline debut in February 1953. Numerous versions of the MiG-17 were to follow, some fitted with radar for use with early air-to-air missiles. Production in the USSR totalled 8000+, and as with the MiG-15, licence-built examples were churned out in Poland (1000) as Lim-5/6s and, on this occasion, in China as J-5/F-5s (767). The aircraft was used to great effect by the North Vietnamese in the Vietnam War.

SPECIFCATION:

**ACCOMMODATION:**
pilot

**DIMENSIONS:**
LENGTH: 38 ft 0 in (11.59 m)
WINGSPAN: 31 ft 7 in (9.62 m)
HEIGHT: 11 ft 0 in (3.35 m)

**WEIGHTS:**
EMPTY: 8373 lb (3798 kg)
MAX T/O: 13,078 lb (5932 kg)

**PERFORMANCE:**
MAX SPEED: 671 mph (1080 kmh)
RANGE: 1230 miles (1880 km)
POWERPLANT: Klimov VK-1F
OUTPUT: 7451 lb st (33.14 kN)

**FIRST FLIGHT DATE:**
29 September 1951

**ARMAMENT:**
three NS-23 23 mm cannon in nose; provision for up to 2200-lb (1000 kg) of bombs/rockets on four underwing stores pylons

**FEATURES:**
Mid-mounted swept-wing layout; tricycle landing gear; engine air intake in nose; fighter type bubble canopy; swept tail; high-mounted tailplane; wing fences

# Mikoyan MiG-19 USSR, CZECHOSLOVAKIA & CHINA

single-seat, single-engined fighter-bomber

The first Soviet fighter to be able to achieve supersonic speeds in level flight, the MiG-19 started life as Mikoyan's I-350 in 1950. Five prototypes were ordered in July of the following year, and the first of these flew on 5 January 1954. Powered by two afterburning Mikulin AM-5 engines, production standard MiG-19s entered frontline service in 1955. Steadily improved over the following three years through the introduction of new engines and better armament (including missiles guided by radar fitted into the aircraft's upper inlet lip), the MiG-19 remained in production until 1958, by which time 2000+ had been built. Production was also undertaken in Czechoslovakia (103 S-105s built) until 1963, and in China. Built in the latter country by Shenyang as the J/F-6, it is estimated that more than 4000 had been delivered in several variants by the time production ended in the mid-1980s. Supplied to both the Chinese People's Republic Air Force and Navy, a vast number of J/F-6s are still in service today. More than 16 countries also operated Soviet- or Chinese-built aircraft.

SPECIFICATION:

**ACCOMMODATION:**
pilot

**DIMENSIONS:**
LENGTH: 42 ft 11.25 in (13.08 m)
WINGSPAN: 29 ft 6.5 in (9 m)
HEIGHT: 13 ft 2.25 in (4.02 m)

**WEIGHTS:**
EMPTY: 12,698 lb (5760 kg)
MAX T/O: 20,944 lb (9500 kg)

**PERFORMANCE:**
MAX SPEED: 920 mph (1480 kmh)
RANGE: 1367 miles (2200 km)
POWERPLANT: two Klimov RD-9BS
OUTPUT: 14,330 lb st (63.8 kN)

**FIRST FLIGHT DATE:**
5 January 1954

**ARMAMENT:**
one NR-30 30 mm cannon in nose and two in wing roots; provision for up to 1100-lb (500 kg) of bombs/rockets/ missiles on four underwing stores pylons

**FEATURES:**
Mid-mounted swept-wing layout; tricycle landing gear; engine air intake in nose; fighter type bubble canopy; swept tail; fuselage-mounted tailplane; wing fences

# Mikoyan MiG-21 USSR, CZECHOSLOVAKIA & CHINA

single-seat, single-engined fighter-bomber

The MiG-21 is still very much a frontline fighter type in service on a wide scale across the globe. Indeed, with well over 10,000 examples built in multifarious variants in the former Soviet Union alone (not to mention the improved Chinese F-7 version which is still in production), the legendary delta-winged design will feature in military circles well into the next century. Designed in the immediate aftermath of the Korean War as a small day interceptor with the best possible performance, the MiG-21 was developed over a series of prototypes and no less than 40 pre-production aircraft during the mid-1950s. The end result was the definitive MiG-21F-13, which began to enter Soviet service in 1958. This variant was also built under licence in both Czechoslovakia and China. Later models saw the lightweight fighter interceptor develop into a multi-role combat aircraft, boasting more internal fuel, heavier armament and vastly superior avionics. Although now a rarity in Russia, versions of the MiG-21 remain very much frontline equipment in more than 40 countries.

SPECIFICATION:

ACCOMMODATION:
pilot

DIMENSIONS:
LENGTH: 51 ft 8.5 in (15.76 m)
WINGSPAN: 23 ft 5.7 in (7.15 m)
HEIGHT: 13 ft 6.2 in (4.12 m)

WEIGHTS:
EMPTY: 11,795 lb (5350 kg)
MAX T/O: 20,018 lb (9080 kg)

PERFORMANCE:
MAX SPEED: 1320 mph (2125 kmh)
RANGE: 808 miles (1300 km)
POWERPLANT: MNPK 'Soyuz'
(Tumanskii) R-11F2S-300
OUTPUT: 13,613 lb st (60.5 kN)

FIRST FLIGHT DATE:
16 June 1955

ARMAMENT:
one GSH-23 23 mm cannon in centre fuselage; provision for up to 3307-lb (1500 kg) of bombs/rockets/missiles on four underwing stores pylons

FEATURES:
Mid-mounted delta wing layout; tricycle landing gear; engine air intake in nose; swept tail; fuselage-mounted tailplane

# Mikoyan MiG-23 USSR & INDIA

single-seat, single-engined fighter-bomber

The USSR's most capable tactical fighter during the height of the Cold War, the MiG-23 was developed by Mikoyan to replace the MiG-21. Both swept-wing and swing-wing prototypes were built by Mikoyan in the early stages of the MiG-23's development, and the variable sweep 23-11 aircraft was chosen thanks to its better short-field performance. The prototype flew for the first time on 10 April 1967, and 50 production MiG-23Ss (fitted with the MiG-21S's RP-22 radar) were built for further evaluation. The MiG-23M was the first production version built with the dedicated Sapfir-23 pulse Doppler radar in an enlarged radome, this aircraft also having a more powerful engine and R-23 air-to-air missile capability. A further three interceptor variants were produced into the 1980s. Ground attack versions of the MiG-23 were also built in great number, the radarless MiG-23B being the first of these. The most effective models were the MiG-23BK and BM, which featured navigation-attack systems taken from the ground attack-dedicated MiG-27. MiG-23s were also exported to 20 nations in the 1970s and 80s.

SPECIFICATION:

ACCOMMODATION:
pilot

DIMENSIONS:
LENGTH: 52 ft 1 in (15.88 m)
WINGSPAN: 45 ft 10 in (13.97 m)
HEIGHT: 15 ft 10 in (4.82 m)

WEIGHTS:
EMPTY: 22,485 lb (10,200 kg)
MAX T/O: 39,250 lb (17,800 kg)

PERFORMANCE:
MAX SPEED: 1562 mph (2500 kmh)
RANGE: 719 miles (1150 km)
POWERPLANT: 'Soyuz' (Tumanskii) R-35-300
OUTPUT: 28,660 lb st (127.5 kN)

FIRST FLIGHT DATE:
10 April 1967

ARMAMENT:
two GSh-23 23 mm cannon in ventral gun pack; provision for up to 4410-lb (2000 kg) of bombs/rockets/missiles on two underwing, one centreline and two underfuselage stores pylons

FEATURES:
Shoulder-mounted, variable-geometry wing layout; tricycle landing gear; fuselage air intakes behind cockpit; swept tail; fuselage-mounted tailplane; ventral fin

# Mikoyan MiG-25 USSR

single-seat, twin-engined fighter-bomber/reconnaissance aircraft

Created to counter the still-born XB-70 Valkyrie bomber under development in the US in the early 1960s, the MiG-25 was built with high speed and high altitude performance firmly in mind. Having to withstand the high temperatures associated with high-speed flight, the airframe was built mainly of nickel steel, with titanium used in the leading edges of the wings and twin fins. The first prototype MiG-25 flew on 6 March 1964. Numerous climb to height and speed records were set by development aircraft in the 1960s, and many of these remain unbeaten. Production MiG-25P interceptors entered service in 1973, and by the time the last fighter variant was delivered nine years later, 900 had been built. The initial MiG-25R reconnaissance variant was soon replaced by the MiG-25RB, which also had a ground attack capability. Finally, dedicated defence suppression MiG-25BMs were also produced in small numbers. The final production total numbered 1200+ aircraft. MiG-25P/RBs were also supplied to Algeria, India, Iraq, Libya and Syria.

SPECIFICATION:

ACCOMMODATION:
pilot

DIMENSIONS:
LENGTH: 78 ft 2 in (23.82 m)
WINGSPAN: 46 ft 0 in (14.02 m)
HEIGHT: 20 ft 0 in (6.10 m)

WEIGHTS:
EMPTY: 44,136 lb (20,020 kg)
MAX T/O: 80,952 lb (36,720 kg)

PERFORMANCE:
MAX SPEED: 1875 mph (3000 kmh)
RANGE: 1081 miles (1730 km)
POWERPLANT: two 'Soyuz'
(Tumanskii) R-15BD-300
OUTPUT: 49,380 lb st (219.6 kN)

FIRST FLIGHT DATE:
6 March 1964

ARMAMENT:
provision for up to 9635-lb
(4000 kg) of bombs/missiles on
four underwing stores pylons

FEATURES:
Shoulder-mounted swept wing
layout; tricycle landing gear;
fuselage air intakes below
cockpit; twin tail fins, twin ventral
fins; low-mounted tailplane

# Mikoyan MiG-27 USSR & INDIA

single-seat, single-engined ground attack aircraft

Based on the swing-wing MiG-23, the MiG-27 was a dedicated strike and ground attack aircraft. The aircraft replaced interim ground attack optimised MiG-23s in the frontline from the mid-1970s. Unlike the latter type, the MiG-27 featured simplified air intakes and more basic two-stage afterburner nozzles. An additional underfuselage stores pylon and strengthened main undercarriage boosted the aircraft's weapons carrying ability also. The MiG-27's most recognisable feature was its flat 'duckbill' nose (also fitted to the MiG-23 ground attack variants), which housed a laser rangefinder and other bombing sensors. Advanced navigation attack systems and an ability to carry tactical reconnaissance pods made the MiG-27 one of the most effective weapons in the Soviet inventory. First flown in prototype form in 1973, five differing variants entered service from 1975 onwards with Soviet units based in Warsaw Pact countries. India built 165 MiG-27Ms under licence, while small numbers were also inherited by Kazakhstan and Ukraine following the break up of the USSR.

SPECIFICATION:

ACCOMMODATION:
pilot

DIMENSIONS:
LENGTH: 56 ft 0 in (17.08 m)
WINGSPAN: 45 ft 10 in (13.97 m)
HEIGHT: 16 ft 5 in (5 m)

WEIGHTS:
EMPTY: 26,252 lb (11,910 kg)
MAX T/O: 44,753 lb (20,300 kg)

PERFORMANCE:
MAX SPEED: 1178 mph (1885 kmh)
RANGE: 337 miles (540 km)
POWERPLANT: 'Soyuz' (Tumanskii)
R-29B-300
OUTPUT: 25,353 lb st (112.8 kN)

FIRST FLIGHT DATE:
1973

ARMAMENT:
one GSh-6-30 30 mm cannon in fuselage; provision for up to 8820-lb (4000 kg) of bombs/ rockets/missiles on two underwing, one centreline and five underfuselage stores pylons

FEATURES:
Shoulder-mounted, variable-geometry wing layout; tricycle landing gear; fuselage air intakes behind cockpit; swept tail; fuselage-mounted tailplane; ventral fin; flat 'duckbill' nose

# Mikoyan MiG-29 USSR

single-seat, twin-engined fighter

Russia's principal tactical fighter, more than 600 MiG-29s remain in service today in the former USSR. An additional 500+ are also in use with at least 15 export customers in Europe, Africa, Asia, the Middle East and South America. Development began on the MiG-29 in 1974 in response to a Soviet Air Force requirement for a highly manoeuvrable lightweight fighter capable of beating modern Western types such as the F-15 and F-16. Chosen to replace the MiG-21, MiG-23 and Su-15 in Frontal Aviation service, the first of 14 prototypes flew on 6 October 1977. Service entry commenced in 1984, production aircraft boasting an excellent high-angle-of-attack and low speed performance, plus an impressive thrust to weight ratio. The fighter's RP-29 radar was also an improvement on previous Soviet systems. The original MiG-29 was joined by the 'Fulcrum-c' and MiG-29s in the early 1990s, this variant having increased fuel and improved avionics. Although a number of early MiG-29s have been retired both in Russia and in former eastern bloc countries such as Romania, Mikoyan continues low-rate production.

SPECIFICATION:

**ACCOMMODATION:**
pilot

**DIMENSIONS:**
LENGTH: 56 ft 10 in (17.32 m)
WINGSPAN: 37 ft 3 in (11.36 m)
HEIGHT: 15 ft 6 in (4.73 m)

**WEIGHTS:**
EMPTY: 24,030 lb (10,900 kg)
MAX T/O: 40,785 lb (18,500 kg)

**PERFORMANCE:**
MAX SPEED: 1528 mph (2445 kmh)
RANGE: 937 miles (1500 km)
POWERPLANT: two Klimov/
Sariskov RD-33s
OUTPUT: 36,600 lb st (162.8 kN)

**FIRST FLIGHT DATE:**
6 October 1977

**ARMAMENT:**
one GSH-6-30 30 mm cannon in leading edge root extension; provision for up to 6615-lb (3000 kg) of bombs/rockets/ missiles on six underwing stores pylons

**FEATURES:**
Mid-mounted wing layout; tricycle landing gear; fuselage air intakes below leading edge root extensions; swept twin fins; fighter style bubble canopy

# Mikoyan MiG-31 USSR

two-seat, twin-engined fighter

The MiG-31 was developed to specifically counter cruise missiles and low-flying strike aircraft. Construction commenced in the early 1970s, and the first example flew on 16 September 1975. Production MiG-31s entered service in 1979, Mikoyan building a total of 280 aircraft to replace su-15s and MiG-23s. Although bearing a superficial resemblance to the MiG-25, the MiG-31 was a totally new machine, featuring afterburning turbofan engines and greater use of light alloy and titanium in its construction. The aircraft was also the world's first frontline fighter type to feature electronically scanned phased array radar. The latter is employed by a dedicated weapon system operator, and can track up to ten targets and engage four simultaneously. The MiG-31 also featured an inflight refuelling probe, tandem main undercarriage and an internal 23 mm cannon. Serving both in eastern and western Russia, the MiG-31 has performed the ultra-long-range interception mission for over 20 years, filling the gaps in Russia's ground-based radar chain.

SPECIFICATION:

**ACCOMMODATION:**
pilot and weapon system operator in tandem

**DIMENSIONS:**
LENGTH: 74 ft 5 in (22.69 m)
WINGSPAN: 44 ft 2 in (13.46 m)
HEIGHT: 20 ft 2 in (6.15 m)

**WEIGHTS:**
EMPTY: 48,115 lb (21,825 kg)
MAX T/O: 101,850 lb (46,200 kg)

**PERFORMANCE:**
MAX SPEED: 1875 mph (3000 kmh)
RANGE: 2062 miles (3300 km)
POWERPLANT: two Aviadvigital (Soloviev) D-30F6s
OUTPUT: 68,340 lb st (303.8 kN)

**FIRST FLIGHT DATE:**
16 September 1975

**ARMAMENT:**
one GSh-6-23 23 mm cannon in rear fuselage; provision for four air-to-air missiles in four underfuselage troughs and four missiles on four underwing stores pylons

**FEATURES:**
Shoulder-mounted swept wing layout; tricycle landing gear; fuselage air intakes below cockpit; twin tail fins, twin ventral fins; low-mounted tailplane

383

# Morane-Saulnier MS.760 Paris FRANCE

four-seat, twin-engined basic trainer, light strike and liaison aircraft

The MS.760 was a direct descendent of MS.755 Flueret, which had been of the first light aircraft to embrace jet power. Relying on the small Turboméca Marboré IICs working in tandem, the Paris was bought by the French Air Force for use in the communications role. The first aircraft entered service in 1958, being designated the MS.760A Paris I. A small number of aircraft were also supplied to the French Navy to perform a similar role, whilst the Paris I and uprated II also enjoyed export successes in Argentina and Brazil. Argentinean manufacturer FAMA assembled 48 Paris Is for use as both trainers and ground attack platforms, as well as liaison duties. Neighbour Brazil acquired an identical number of more powerful Paris IIs, which were also used for similar roles. Argentine aircraft were later re-engined with Marboré VIs to upgrade them to Paris II specification. Paris production numbered 150 MS.760AS and 63 MS.760BS, and they were retired from French service in 1997. Roughly 20 can still be found performing multifarious tasks for the Argentine Air Force .

SPECIFICATION:

**ACCOMMODATION:**
pilot and three passengers seated side-by-side in two rows

**DIMENSIONS:**
LENGTH: 33 ft 7.10 in (10.24 m)
WINGSPAN: 33 ft 3.6 in (10.15 m)
HEIGHT: 8 ft 6.4 in (2.60 m)

**WEIGHTS:**
EMPTY: 4557 lb (2067 kg)
MAX T/O: 8642 lb (3920 kg)

**PERFORMANCE:**
MAX SPEED: 432 mph (695 kmh)
RANGE: 1081 miles (1740 km)
POWERPLANT: two Turboméca Marboré VIs
OUTPUT: 2116 lb st (9.42 kN)

**FIRST FLIGHT DATE:**
29 July 1954

**ARMAMENT:**
provision for two underwing 7.62 mm gun pods or up to 896-lb (400 kg) of bombs/rockets on four underwing/wingtip stores pylons

**FEATURES:**
Mid-mounted straight-wing layout; bubble canopy with side-by-side seating; tricycle landing gear; wing root engine air intakes; T-tail tail; wingtip tanks

# Myasishchev M-4/3M USSR

seven-seat, four-engined bomber/tanker/reconnaissance aircraft

In the late 1940s Myasishchev was tasked with producing a bomber capable of attacking targets in North America. However, this proved to be an impossible task using the Soviet technology at the time, so the company chose to build the M-4 medium-range bomber instead. The end product was as good an aircraft as any in its class when flown in prototype on 20 January 1953. Indeed, it was a better medium bomber than its TU-16 rival. However, the political leadership were unhappy at its perceived limited range, and only 200 were ever built. The basic M-4 was the strategic bomber version, which made its debut at the 1954 May Day flypast. This was soon superseded by the re-engined 3M, which was in turn replaced by the still more powerful 3MD. The last aircraft were delivered in the early 1960s, by which time all surviving M-4/3Ms had been converted into tankers (with a hose-drogue unit in the bomb-bay) or maritime reconnaissance platforms. Most examples were retired in the late 1980s.

## SPECIFICATION:

**ACCOMMODATION:**
pilot, co-pilot, communications operator, navigator, defensive systems operator, flight engineer, tail gunner

**DIMENSIONS:**
LENGTH: 169 ft 7.5 in (51.70 m)
WINGSPAN: 174 ft 4 in (32.14 m)
HEIGHT: 46 ft 3 in (14.10 m)

**WEIGHTS:**
EMPTY: 166,975 lb (75,740 kg)
MAX T/O: 423,280 lb (192,000 kg)

**PERFORMANCE:**
MAX SPEED: 620 mph (998 kmh)
RANGE: 7705 miles (12,400 km)
POWERPLANT: four MNPK 'Soyuz' (Mikulin) RM-3M-500AS
OUTPUT: 83,776 lb st (372.8 kN)

**FIRST FLIGHT DATE:**
20 January 1953

**ARMAMENT:**
four remote-controlled (dorsal/ventral) and one manned (tail) turrets with twin NR-23 23 mm cannon; 22,050 lb (10000 kg) of bombs in bomb-bay

**FEATURES:**
Shoulder-mounted swept wing; engines-mounted in wing roots; manned tail turret; swept-back horizontal tailplane

# North American AJ Savage  USA

three-seat, three-engined bomber/aerial tanker

On 13 August 1945, just a week after the first atomic
bomb was dropped on Hiroshima, the US Navy
initiated a design competition for a carrier-based
attack aircraft that could deliver a 10,000-lb
payload – the weight of the plutonium-based 'Fat
Man' Nagasaki bomb. North American's NA-146
design was selected as the winner of the
competition, and the Navy ordered it into
production in June 1946. Equipped with two
2400 hp Pratt & Whitney R-2800 engines as well as
a 4600-lb thrust Allison J33 auxiliary jet in the tail,
the first AJ Savages were delivered three years later.
With the completion of carrier suitability tests in
1950, the AJ-1 was introduced into operational
service with the fleet as the largest (at the time)
nuclear strike aircraft ever to fly from an aircraft
carrier. In addition to the nuclear strike role, the
Savage was also modified for use as a carrier-based
flight-refuelling tanker. Some 55 AJ-1s, 55 AJ-2s and
30 AJ-2Ps were built, and they were replaced by
A3D Skywarriors in the late 1950s.

SPECIFCATION:

ACCOMMODATION:
pilot, co-pilot, navigator/engineer

DIMENSIONS:
LENGTH: 63 ft 1 in (19.23 m)
WINGSPAN: 71 ft 4.5 in (21.77 m)
HEIGHT: 21 ft 5 in (6.55 m)

WEIGHTS:
EMPTY: 30,800 lb (13,970 kg)
MAX T/O: 54,000 lb (24,494 kg)

PERFORMANCE:
MAX SPEED: 449 mph (718 kmh)
RANGE: 2475 miles (3960 km)
POWERPLANT: two Pratt & Whitney
R-2800-44W radials and one
Allison J33-A-10 turbojet
OUTPUT: 4600 hp (3430 kW) and
4600 lb st (20.47 kN)

FIRST FLIGHT DATE:
3 July 1948

ARMAMENT:
up to 12,000-lb (5443 kg) of
bombs in bomb-bay and on
underwing stores pylons

FEATURES:
Straight, shoulder-mounted wing
layout; retractable landing gear;
two close-cowled radial engines
under wings, with turbojet in rear
fuselage; wingtip tanks; arrestor
hook; heavily glazed canopy

# North American B-45 Tornado USA

four-seat, four-engined bomber/reconnaissance aircraft

At the end of 1944, the US Army issued a design competition for a jet-powered bomber, and the end result was the B-45 Tornado – the world's first effective jet bomber. Although in effect little more than a conventional medium bomber of the time fitted with jet rather than piston engines, the Tornado proved to be a tough and reliable workhorse for the USAF. The first of 96 B-45AS entered service between February 1948 and June 1949, and these were followed by ten B-45CS and 33 RB-45CS. The B-45 served well as a reconnaissance aircraft during the Korean War, while several units also served with the USAF in Europe well into the 1950s. Although the bomber version of the Tornado never saw combat, the photo-reconnaissance variant – assigned to Strategic Air Command – performed classified, deep penetration photographic intelligence missions over many Cold War communist countries from bases in Europe, Asia and North America. Indeed, the RB-45 was the forerunner of the U-2 and SR-71 surveillance aircraft. Surviving Tornados were retired in the late 1950s.

SPECIFICATION:

**ACCOMMODATION:**
pilot, co-pilot, bombardier/navigator, tail gunner (B-45 only)

**DIMENSIONS:**
LENGTH: 75 ft 4 in (22.98 m)
WINGSPAN: 89 ft 0 in (27.12 m)
HEIGHT: 25 ft 2 in (7.68 m)

**WEIGHTS:**
EMPTY: 47,775 lb (21,671 kg)
MAX T/O: 92,745 lb (42,069 kg)

**PERFORMANCE:**
MAX SPEED: 570 mph (917 kmh)
RANGE: 1910 miles (3056 km)
POWERPLANT: four General Electric J47-GE-9AS
OUTPUT: 20,800 lb st (93.25 kN)

**FIRST FLIGHT DATE:**
17 March 1947

**ARMAMENT:**
two Browning M-3 machine guns in tail turret; maximum bomb load of 22,000-lb (9979 kg) in bomb-bay

**FEATURES:**
Shoulder-mounted straight-wing; tricycle landing gear; engines-mounted beneath wings; manned tail turret; glazed nose; tailplane with dihedral

# North American F-82 Twin Mustang USA

two-seat, twin-engined monoplane fighter

Although often referred to simply as two P-51s joined by a single wing, the F-82 was a wholly new design which used the twin boom configuration to achieve long range and good endurance. Created in 1943 as an escort fighter for long range bombing missions in the Pacific War, the two-man P-82 (as then designated) would have a navigator who could also help fly the aircraft for brief periods in order to allow the pilot to rest during the course of eight-hour missions. When built, the XP-82 featured new fuselages (booms) which differed significantly from the P-51 that they were based on. The prototype first flew on 15 April 1945, and only 20 P-52Bs had been built by war's end. North American reconfigured the aircraft as a nightfighter, equipped with a search radar in a central pod. This proved highly successful, with 100 F-82E day escort fighters and 100 F-82F and 50 F-82G nightfighters being built. The F-82 saw brief action in the early weeks of the Korean War, prior to being retired by the mid-1950s.

SPECIFICATION:

ACCOMMODATION:
pilot and navigator

DIMENSIONS:
LENGTH: 42 ft 5 in (12.93 m)
WINGSPAN: 51 ft 3 in (11.28 m)
HEIGHT: 13 ft 10 in (4.22 m)

WEIGHTS:
EMPTY: 15,997 lb (7256 kg)
MAX T/O: 25,591 lb (11,608 kg)

PERFORMANCE:
MAX SPEED: 461 mph (742 kmh)
RANGE: 2240 miles (3605 km)
POWERPLANT: two Allison
V-1710-143
OUTPUT: 3200 hp (2386 kW)

ARMAMENT:
six Browning 0.50-in machine
guns in wings; maximum
bomb/rocket load of 4000-lb
(1816 kg) on underwing stores
pylons

FIRST FLIGHT DATE:
15 April 1945

FEATURES:
Monoplane wing layout;
rectractable landing gear; two
close-cowled inline engines;
twin fuselages ('booms'); central
radar pod

# North American F-86 Sabre  USA & CANADA

single-seat, single-engined fighter-bomber

Aside from the Bell UH-1 Huey, no other post-war Western combat aircraft has been built in as great a numbers as the F-86. Total production amounted to 9502 airframes covering no less than 13 separate land- and sea-based variants. The first contracts for the fighter were placed jointly by the USAAF and US Navy in 1944, although the initial design featured unswept wings and a fuselage of greater diameter to allow it to house the Allison J35-2 engine. Following examination of captured German jet aircraft and related documentation, North American radically altered the design's shape to produce the XP-86 a vastly superior machine. F-86A Sabres were thrust into battle over Korea in December 1950, where the aircraft soon achieved the status of 'ace maker' in battles against the MiG-15. Combat ushered in further improvements to the aircraft, whilst the radar-equipped F-86D also enjoyed widespread use with Air Defense Command as its first all-weather interceptor. Examples of the F-86 remained in the active inventory of a number of air forces into the early 1990s.

SPECIFICATION:

**ACCOMMODATION:**
pilot

**DIMENSIONS:**
LENGTH: 37 ft 6 in (11.43 m)
WINGSPAN: 39 ft 1 in (11.90 m)
HEIGHT: 14 ft 8.75 in (4.47 m)

**WEIGHTS:**
EMPTY: 11,125 lb (5045 kg)
MAX T/O: 20,611 lb (9350 kg)

**PERFORMANCE:**
MAX SPEED: 678 mph (1091 kmh)
RANGE: 850 miles (1368 km)
POWERPLANT: General Electric J47-GE-27
OUTPUT: 5970 lb st (26.56 kN)

**FIRST FLIGHT DATE:**
27 November 1946

**ARMAMENT:**
six Browning M-2 0.50-in machine guns in nose; maximum bomb/rocket load of 2000-lb (908 kg) on two underwing stores pylons

**FEATURES:**
Low-mounted swept-wing layout; tricycle landing gear; engine air intake in nose; fighter type bubble canopy; swept tail; low-mounted tailplane

# North American FJ Fury USA

single-seat, single-engined fighter-bomber

An aircraft that was significantly revised during its long career with the US Navy, the first jet to carry the appellation Fury was a straight wing subsonic fighter. Designed by North American in response to a joint Navy and Army Air Force request for a jet-powered fighter, the NA-134 (redesignated the FJ-1 Fury in Navy service) featured unswept wings and a fuselage of large diameter. Following examination of captured German jet aircraft post-war, North American radically altered the NA-134's shape, although the Navy still received 30 FJ-1 Furys, which featured the original wing, fuselage and powerplant. Fleet deliveries began in March 1948. The Navy chose to order a navalised F-86 as the FJ-2 in 1951, and 200 were built for Marine Corps use only. The completely revised FJ-3 followed in 1954, this aircraft being better suited for carrier operations than the FJ-2. A total of 538 were built, and these equipped 17 Navy and four Marine units. The final Fury variants built were the FJ-4 and FJ-4B, 372 of which were delivered between 1955-58.

SPECIFICATION:

ACCOMMODATION:
pilot

DIMENSIONS:
LENGTH: 37 ft 7 in (11.45 m)
WINGSPAN: 37 ft 1.50 in (11.31 m)
HEIGHT: 13 ft 8 in (4.16 m)

WEIGHTS:
EMPTY: 12,205 lb (5536 kg)
MAX T/O: 17,189 lb (7797 kg)

PERFORMANCE:
MAX SPEED: 681 mph (1096 kmh)
RANGE: 990 miles (1593 km)
POWERPLANT: Wright J65-W-2
OUTPUT: 7200 lb st (31.3 kN)

FIRST FLIGHT DATE:
27 November 1946

ARMAMENT:
six Browning M-2 0.50-in machine guns (FJ-1) or four M-24 20 mm cannon (FJ-2/3/4) in nose; maximum bomb/rocket/missile load of 3000-lb (1362 kg) on six underwing stores pylons

FEATURES:
Low-mounted straight (FJ-1) or swept-wing layout (FJ-2/3/4); tricycle landing gear; engine air intake in nose; fighter type bubble canopy; low-mounted tailplane

# North American F-100 Super Sabre USA

single/two-seat, single-engined fighter-bomber

The natural successor to the F-86, the F-100 Super Sabre was both larger and more powerful than its famous forebear – and capable of breaking the sound barrier in level flight, which was a first for any combat aircraft. Development on the F-100 had commenced as early as February 1949, and the overall size and shape of the fighter was barely influenced by air combat over Korea. The Super Sabre made rapid progress through flight-testing to the point where it was declared frontline capable in early 1954. However, a series of flight control-related crashes saw the F-100A grounded in November of that same year, North American rectifying these problems by lengthening both the wings and the vertical fin. A total of 2294 F-100s were built in five different variants, the USAF's C/D-models and two-seat F-100F 'Wild Weasel I' seeing considerable service as fighter-bombers and anti-SAM missile platforms in the Vietnam War. Super Sabres also served with the French, Turkish, Danish and Taiwanese air forces, with the last examples being retired in the late 1980s.

SPECIFICATION:

**ACCOMMODATION:**
pilot, or two pilots in tandem
(F-100F)

**DIMENSIONS:**
LENGTH: 52 ft 6 in (16 m)
WINGSPAN: 38 ft 9.5 in (11.81 m)
HEIGHT: 16 ft 2.75 in (4.96 m)

**WEIGHTS:**
EMPTY: 22,300 lb (10,115 kg)
MAX T/O: 30,700 lb (13,925 kg)

**PERFORMANCE:**
MAX SPEED: 864 mph (1390 kmh)
RANGE: 1500 miles (2415 km)
POWERPLANT: Pratt & Whitney
J57-PW-21A
OUTPUT: 16,950 lb st (75.18 kN)

**FIRST FLIGHT DATE:**
25 May 1953

**ARMAMENT:**
four M-39E 20 mm cannon in nose; maximum bomb/rocket/ missile load of 7500-lb (3402 kg) on six underwing stores pylons

**FEATURES:**
Low-mounted swept-wing layout; tricycle landing gear; engine air intake in nose; swept tail; fighter type bubble canopy; low-mounted tailplane

# North American Sabreliner USA

ten-seat, twin-engined crew trainer/VIP transport

The T-39 was developed by North American as a
private venture to meet a USAF requirement
announced in 1956 for an off-the-shelf twin utility
jet transport and trainer. Although eight companies
submitted proposals, the NA246 Sabreliner was the
only one to actually be flown in prototype form
(from 16 September 1958 onwards), and the USAF
informed North American that it had won the
competition. The first of several production orders
was duly placed, and a total of 143 T-39AS, six T-39BS
and three T-39FS were built for the USAF. These
were used as radar trainers for pilots destined to fly
the F-105D, with the F-models specialist F-105F
'Wild Weasel' trainers, as well as staff transports.
The US Navy ordered 42 navalised T-39DS in 1961,
these being used to train pilots and radar intercept
officers destined to fly fighters. A further 17 were
bought in the late 1960s for fleet support missions,
being designated CT-39E/GS. Although the USAF
have retired its Sabreliners, around 30 are still
used by the Navy/Marines for crew training and
utility work.

SPECIFCATION:

**ACCOMMODATION:**
pilot, co-pilot and eight
passengers

**DIMENSIONS:**
LENGTH: 43 ft 9 in (13.33 m)
WINGSPAN: 44 ft 5 in (13.53 m)
HEIGHT: 16 ft 0 in (4.88 m)

**WEIGHTS:**
EMPTY: 9257 lb (4200 kg)
MAX T/O: 17,760 lb (8055 kg)

**PERFORMANCE:**
MAX SPEED: 540 mph (869 kmh)
RANGE: 1950 miles (3130 km)
POWERPLANT: two Pratt & Whitney
J60-P-3S
OUTPUT: 6000 lb st (29 kN)

**FIRST FLIGHT DATE:**
16 September 1958

**FEATURES:**
Low-mounted swept-wing;
tricycle landing gear; twin
podded engines attached to rear
fuselage; triangular windows
in fuselage

# North American T-28 Trojan USA

two-seat, single-engined trainer/light attack aircraft

The T-28 was designed to answer a USAAF request for an aircraft to replace North American's legendary T-6 Texan. The resulting aircraft featured a tricycle undercarriage, frameless canopy and a Wright R-1300 radial engine, which gave the Trojan (as it was named) a top speed of 280+ mph. Some 1194 T-28As were procured from 1950, and the type was also bought by the US Navy. It re-engined its Trojans with 1425 hp R-1820-86 Cyclones, which drove a three-bladed propeller as opposed the T-28A's 'two-blader'. Designated the T-28B, 489 were acquired, followed by 299 carrier-capable C-models. Foreign sales were also secured, with the French alone purchasing in excess of 250 aircraft. In 1960 the USAF acquired an armed variant for use in the close-support role, and several hundred surplus T-28As were modified by North American and Fairchild into AT-28D Nomads. These aircraft featured the R-1820 engine and six underwing hardpoints, and were used extensively in South-East Asia. The French carried out similar modifications to their T-28s, which saw action in North Africa.

SPECIFICATION:

ACCOMMODATION:
two pilots in tandem

DIMENSIONS:
LENGTH: 32 ft 10 in (10 m)
WINGSPAN: 40 ft 0 in (12.19 m)
HEIGHT: 12 ft 8 in (8.36 m)

WEIGHTS:
EMPTY: 7750 lb (3515 kg)
MAX T/O: 15,600 lb (7075 kg)

PERFORMANCE:
MAX SPEED: 346 mph (554 kmh)
RANGE: 1060 miles (1696 km)
POWERPLANT: Wright R-1820-86 Cyclone
OUTPUT: 1425 hp (1062 kW)

FIRST FLIGHT DATE:
26 September 1949

ARMAMENT:
up to 4000-lb (1814 kg) of bombs/rockets/gun pods on six underwing stores pylons

FEATURES:
Low-mounted straight-wing; large canopy; tricycle landing gear; close-cowled radial engine

# North American L-17 Navion  USA

four-seat, single-engined liaison and light utility aircraft

With previously massive contracts for military aircraft like the P-51 and B-25 cancelled soon after VJ-Day, North American was forced to broaden it manufacturing base by breaking into the civilian market. Its first attempt was the NA-145 Navion four-seater, which enjoyed great success in 1946-47 – 1100+ plus were built almost exclusively for the domestic market. The USAAF also showed an interest in the Navion, and a prototype was flown in April 1946. Later that year the first of 83 L-17As (as the type was designated in USAAF service) was delivered, the aircraft being employed as liaison 'hacks' personnel/cargo carriers and trainers within the USAF University Reserve Officers' Training Corps programme. In 1947 Ryan Aeronautical Company acquired the design and manufacturing rights for the Navion, selling a further 158 improved L-17Bs to the newly created USAF. The first of these was delivered in November 1948, and a further order for five was placed in 1949. Surviving L-17s became U-18s following the 1962 overhaul of all US military aircraft designations.

SPECIFICATION:

**ACCOMMODATION:**
pilot and three passengers seated side-by-side in two rows

**DIMENSIONS:**
LENGTH: 27 ft 6 in (8.38 m)
WINGSPAN: 33 ft 5 in (10.19 m)
HEIGHT: 8 ft 7 in (2.65 m)

**WEIGHTS:**
EMPTY: 1945 lb (882 kg)
MAX T/O: 2950 lb (1338 kg)

**PERFORMANCE:**
MAX SPEED: 163 mph (260 kmh)
RANGE: 700 miles (1120 km)
POWERPLANT: Continental O-470-7
OUTPUT: 185 hp (140 kW)

**FIRST FLIGHT DATE:**
April 1946

**FEATURES:**
Low-mounted straight-wing; large canopy; rectractable tricycle undercarriage; close-cowled engine; wingtip tanks

# North American A-5/RA-5 Vigilante USA

two-seat, twin-engined bomber/reconnaissance aircraft

One of the most advanced aircraft of its time, the Vigilante introduced a wealth of new technologies when it entered service in 1961. Designed as a carrier-based attack jet, the A-5 featured automatically scheduled engine inlets and nozzles, a single surface vertical tail, differential slab tailplanes, a comprehensive radar-inertial navigation system and a linear bomb-bay between the engines. Flap and leading edge blowing was also introduced to make the weighty aircraft carrier deck-capable. Just 59 A-5A/B bombers had been built when Navy carriers gave up the strategic nuclear role, leaving the Vigilantes to be re-rolled as photographic intelligence gathering platforms. Aside from those bombers modified through the fitment of cameras and electronic surveillance equipment, a further 63 RA-5Cs were built in 1962-66, followed by 46 Phase II jets in 1969-71. The first frontline RA-5C unit carried out its maiden cruise in 1964. The Navy's premier reconnaissance asset during the Vietnam War, the Vigilante remained in fleet service until finally retired in 1979.

SPECIFICATION:

ACCOMMODATION:
pilot and observer/radar operator

DIMENSIONS:
LENGTH: 75 ft 10 in (23.11 m)
WINGSPAN: 53 ft 0 in (16.15 m)
HEIGHT: 19 ft 5 in (5.92 m)

WEIGHTS:
EMPTY: 38,000 lb (17,240 kg)
MAX T/O: 80,000 lb (36,285 kg)

PERFORMANCE:
MAX SPEED: 1385 mph (2230 kmh)
RANGE: 3200 miles (5150 km)
POWERPLANT: two General Electric
J79-GE-10S
OUTPUT: 35,720 lb st (159 kN)

FIRST FLIGHT DATE:
31 August 1958

ARMAMENT:
one nuclear weapon in linear
bomb-bay and 6000-lb (2722 kg)
on four underwing stores pylons
(A-5A/B only)

FEATURES:
Shoulder-mounted swept-wing;
tricycle landing gear; engine air
intakes behind cockpit; swept
tail; low-mounted tailplane;
arrestor hook

# North American (Rockwell) T-2 Buckeye   USA

two-seat, single/twin-engined trainer

Built as a result of a US Navy study into pilot
training, which identified the need for an aircraft
capable of taking a student that had graduated
from the *ab initio* phase through to the point of
initial carrier qualification, the T-2A Buckeye
incorporated many features seen on previous
North American designs – the T-28C's flight control
system and the wing of the FJ-1 Fury. The Buckeye
featured robust landing gear, powered flight
controls, large trailing edge flaps and airbrakes on
either side of the rear fuselage. The single-engined
T-2A entered service in July 1959, and some 201
were eventually delivered. The original Buckeye
was underpowered, so North American
commenced work on a twin-engined version soon
after the first A-models had been delivered. The
T-2B was powered by two J60-P-6s, and 97 were
built. Another engine change saw J85-GE-4s fitted
in pairs into the T-2C, of which 231 were procured
by the Navy in 1969-75. The C-model is the only
variant still in service today, and is now on the
verge of retirement.

SPECIFICATION:

**ACCOMMODATION:**
two pilots in tandem

**DIMENSIONS:**
LENGTH: 38 ft 3.5 in (11.67 m)
WINGSPAN: 38 ft 1.5 in (11.62 m)
HEIGHT: 14 ft 9.5 in (4.51 m)

**WEIGHTS:**
EMPTY: 8115 lb (3680 kg)
MAX T/O: 13,179 lb (5977 kg)

**PERFORMANCE:**
MAX SPEED: 540 mph (840 kmh)
RANGE: 1047 miles (1685 km)
POWERPLANT: one Westinghouse
J34-WE-36/-48 (T-2A) or two Pratt
& Whitney J60-P-6 (T-2B) or
General Electric J85-GE-4 (T-2C)
turbojets
OUTPUT: 3400 lb st (15.4 kN),
6000 lb st (26.68 kN) and
5900 lb st (26.2 kN) respectively

**FIRST FLIGHT DATE:**
31 January 1958

**FEATURES:**
Mid-mounted tapered wings;
bubble canopy; tricycle landing
gear; fuselage chin engine air
intakes; wingtip tanks; arrestor
hook

# North American (Rockwell) OV-10 Bronco  USA

two-seat, twin-engined forward air control/close-air support aircraft

The OV-10 Bronco was a purpose-built close-air support aircraft derived from Department of Defense studies carried out between 1959-65. North American's NA-300 had been one of several aircraft put forward by US manufacturers to meet the Marine Corps' LARA (Light Armed Recon Aircraft) specification, the Bronco being chosen the winner in August 1965. An initial batch of 271 OV-10AS was delivered in 1967-68, of which 157 were supplied to the USAF for use in the forward air control (FAC) role in place of O-1/2s. Surviving OV-10CS soldiered on with both the USAF and Marine Corps into the early 1990s, with the latter service developing a specialised night FAC variant that drew on experience gained by the USAF in Vietnam. Designated the OV-10D, and featuring a modified nose housing sensor equipment, a 20 mm cannon turret and uprated engines, 17 OV-10AS were converted in 1979-80. These aircraft subsequently saw action in the 1991 Gulf War. Although all American Broncos were retired in 1994, a small number remain in frontline service with a handful of air forces.

SPECIFICATION:

ACCOMMODATION:
pilot and observer

DIMENSIONS:
LENGTH: 41 ft 7 in (12.67 m)
WINGSPAN: 40 ft 0 in (12.19 m)
HEIGHT: 15 ft 2 in (4.62 m)

WEIGHTS:
EMPTY: 6893 lb (3127 kg)
MAX T/O: 14,444 lb (6552 kg)

PERFORMANCE:
MAX SPEED: 281 mph (452 kmh)
RANGE: 1428 miles (2298 km)
POWERPLANT: two Garrett
T76-G-416/417S
OUTPUT: 1430 shp (1066 kW)

FIRST FLIGHT DATE:
16 July 1965

ARMAMENT:
four M60C 7.62 mm machine
guns in sponsons, and one
20 mm cannon in ventral turret
(OV-10D only); up to 3600-lb
(1632 kg) of bombs/rockets/
flares/missiles on four under-
sponson, two underwing and one
underfuselage stores pylons

FEATURES:
high-mounted straight wing;
twin boom tail, containing
turboprop engines; podded
fuselage; large blown canopy

# Northrop F-89 Scorpion  USA

two-seat, twin-engined fighter

The USAF's first two-seat all-weather interceptor, the F-89 Scorpion was designed specifically for the newly formed Air Defense Command (ADC). Two prototypes were ordered in December 1946, and the first of these made its maiden flight on 16 August 1948. The delivery of 18 production standard F-89AS began in June 1950, although, a further year would pass before ADC got its hands on the Scorpion. Once in service, these aircraft were charged with the responsibility of protecting North America from attack by Soviet bombers. A further 30 improved F-89BS followed, before production of 164 F-89CS. The most produced variant was the F-89D, which featured wingtip-mounted rockets – 682 were built. This version was used to equip the vast majority of ADC squadrons from 1954. The final new-build Scorpion variant was the F-89H, which featured wingtip-mounted Hughes Falcon missiles. A number of D-models were rebuilt as F-89JS, fitted with Genie and Falcon missiles. Relegated to Air National Guard duty by the F-102 in the late 1950s, the last F-89s were retired in the mid-1960s.

SPECIFICATION:

ACCOMMODATION:
pilot and radar observer in tandem

DIMENSIONS:
LENGTH: 53 ft 10 in (16.41 m)
WINGSPAN: 59 ft 8 in (18.19 m)
HEIGHT: 17 ft 7 in (5.36 m)

WEIGHTS:
EMPTY: 25,194 lb (11,428 kg)
MAX T/O: 42,241 lb (19,160 kg)

PERFORMANCE:
MAX SPEED: 636 mph (1023 kmh)
RANGE: 2600 miles (4184 km)
POWERPLANT: two Allison J35-A-47S
OUTPUT: 14,400 lb st (62.5 kN)

FIRST FLIGHT DATE:
16 August 1948

ARMAMENT:
104 2.75-in Mighty Mouse air-to-air rocket projectiles in wingtip pods and four air-to-air missiles on four underwing stores pylons

FEATURES:
Mid-mounted straight wing; retractable landing gear; wingtip rocket pods/fuel tanks; low lateral engine intakes; bubble canopy; high-mounted tailplane

# Northrop T-38 Talon/F-5A Freedom Fighter  USA

single/two-seat, twin-engined fighter-bomber/advanced trainer

As the first supersonic aircraft designed from scratch as a trainer, the T-38 has enjoyed a long and successful career primarily with the USAF. Developed by Northrop as the N-156T, the Talon was a spin-off product from the company's lightweight fighter programme (N-156C), which eventually saw the F-5 Freedom Fighter produced in large numbers for export. As with its forebear, work on the N-156T proceeded for two years as a private venture before the USAF finally announced a requirement for just such a supersonic advanced trainer. The first contract issued in May 1956 was for six YT-38 pre-production aircraft, whilst the premier production example completed its first flight in May 1960. By the time the final Talon had been delivered in January 1972, 1187 had been constructed. The F-5A/B fighter-bomber was the result of a 1954 US government initiative to produce a simple lightweight fighter that could be exported through the Military Assistance Program. The N-156C was officially chosen in 1962, and 1000+ were produced and supplied to more than a dozen air forces worldwide.

SPECIFICATION:

ACCOMMODATION:
two pilots in tandem (T-38/F-5B) and one pilot (F-5A)

DIMENSIONS:
LENGTH: 46 ft 4.5 in (14.14 m)
WINGSPAN: 25 ft 3 in (7.70 m)
HEIGHT: 12 ft 10.5 in (3.92 m)

WEIGHTS:
EMPTY: 7174 lb (3254 kg)
MAX T/O: 12,050 lb (5465 kg)

PERFORMANCE:
MAX SPEED: 858 mph (1381 kmh)
RANGE: 1094 miles (1761 km)
POWERPLANT: two General Electric J85-GE-5s
OUTPUT: 7700 lb st (34.2 kN)

FIRST FLIGHT DATE:
10 April 1959

ARMAMENT:
two M39A2 20 mm cannon in nose; up to 4400-lb (1994 kg) of bombs/rockets/missiles on four underwing, one underfuselage and two wingtip (missiles only) stores pylons

FEATURES:
Low-mounted swept wing; retractable landing gear; wingtip tanks; fuselage air intakes below cockpit; bubble canopy; low-mounted tailplane

# Northrop F-5E Tiger II   USA

single/two-seat, twin-engined fighter-bomber/reconnaissance aircraft

Developed by Northrop as an improved version of its highly successful F-5A Freedom Fighter, the F-5E Tiger II featured more powerful engines, enlarged wing leading edge extensions, permanent wingtip missile rails and better avionics. A dedicated photo-reconnaissance variant, designated the RF-5E Tigereye, was also built, featuring a four-camera photo nose. The first Tiger II took the form of a converted F-5A prototype, which made its maiden flight in March 1969, soon after which it was submitted for the US Government's International Fighter Competition (IFC), managed by the USAF. Beating off the F-8, F-104 and F-4, the F-5E was officially selected in November 1970. The first production single-seat Tiger II took to the skies on 11 August 1972, followed by the F-5F two-seater two years later. Like the F-5A, the F-5E/F proved popular, with Northrop building 1300 between 1972 and 1986. 20 foreign air forces received Tiger IIs, while the USAF and US Navy acquired over 100 for use as aggressor/adversary trainers. Indeed, the USAF was the first operator to receive jets in early 1973.

SPECIFCATION:

**ACCOMMODATION:**
pilot (F/RF-5E), or two pilots in tandem (F-5F)

**DIMENSIONS:**
LENGTH: 47 ft 5 in (14.45 m)
WINGSPAN: 28 ft 0 in (8.53 m)
HEIGHT: 13 ft 5 in (4.08 m)

**WEIGHTS:**
EMPTY: 9558 lb (4350 kg)
MAX T/O: 24,664 lb (11,187 kg)

**PERFORMANCE:**
MAX SPEED: 1081 mph (1730 kmh)
RANGE: 2325 miles (3720 km)
POWERPLANT: two General Electric J85-GE-21BS
OUTPUT: 10,000 lb st (44.8 kN)

**FIRST FLIGHT DATE:**
March 1969

**ARMAMENT:**
two M39A2 20 mm cannon in nose; up to 7000-lb (3195 kg) of bombs/rockets/missiles on four underwing, one underfuselage and two wingtip (missiles only) stores pylons

**FEATURES:**
Low-mounted swept wing; retractable landing gear; wingtip missile rails; fuselage air intakes below cockpit; bubble canopy; low-mounted tailplane

# Panavia Tornado GR 1 UK, GERMANY & ITALY

two-seat, twin-engined fighter-bomber/reconnaissance aircraft

The Tornado was the end product of a late 1960s feasibility study carried out by Belgium, Canada, Germany, Italy, the Netherlands and the UK for a multi-role combat aircraft (MRCA). Germany, Italy and the UK duly formed Panavia in March 1969, and development of the MRCA commenced in 1970. The first of nine prototypes flew on 14 August 1974 and production aircraft were delivered from July 1980. The aircraft featured variable geometry wings, two specially developed Turbo-Union RB199 engines, terrain-following radar and a digital inertial navigation system. The most advanced tactical interdictor/strike (IDS) aircraft built in Europe, the Tornado IDS can carry almost every air-launched weapon in the NATO arsenal. Aircraft reached the Trinational Tornado Training Establishment in the UK in July 1980, and the first RAF unit was established two years later. A total of 828 IDS aircraft were built, and RAF and Italian aircraft saw combat in the 1991 Gulf War. A number of older GR 1s have now been retired by the RAF, although more than 120 GR 4s remain in frontline service.

SPECIFICATION:

ACCOMMODATION:
pilot and navigator in tandem

DIMENSIONS:
LENGTH: 54 ft 10 in (16.72 m)
WINGSPAN: 45 ft 8 in (13.91 m)
HEIGHT: 19 ft 6 in (5.95 m)

WEIGHTS:
EMPTY: 30,620 lb (13,890 kg)
MAX T/O: 61,620 lb (27,950 kg)

PERFORMANCE:
MAX SPEED: 921 mph (1482 kmh)
RANGE: 2431 miles (3890 km)
POWERPLANT: two Turbo-Union
RB199-34R Mk 103s
OUTPUT: 32,150 lb st (143 kN)

FIRST FLIGHT DATE:
14 August 1974

ARMAMENT:
two IWKA-Mauser 27 mm cannon in nose; up to 19,840-lb (9000 kg) of bombs/rockets/missiles on four underwing and eight underfuselage stores pylons

FEATURES:
Shoulder-mounted variable-sweep wing; fuselage air intakes below cockpit; bubble canopy; low-mounted tailplane; large fin

# Percival Prentice UK

three-seat, single-engined monoplane basic trainer

Built in the immediate post-war years as a modern replacement in the basic flying training role for the venerable Tiger Moth, the Prentice was designed to meet Air Ministry Specification T 23/43, issued in late 1943. It incorporated many features deemed necessary following several years of wartime pilot training, including a variable-pitch propeller, radios, flaps and a more powerful engine than that fitted to either the Tiger Moth or Magister. With pilot and instructor seated side-by-side, the Prentice was also the first of its type to feature such an arrangement in RAF service. Air Force trials were conducted with 30 aircraft at the Central Flying School (CFS) in November 1947, and following several modifications to the design in order to improve its general handling qualities, the first of 370 production T 1s was delivered in 1948. Well liked by both students and instructors, the Prentice was used by the Basic Training Squadron of the CFS and numerous flying training schools. The aircraft was replaced by the Percival Provost from 1953 onwards.

SPECIFICATION:

**ACCOMMODATION:**
two pilots seated side-by-side and one passenger

**DIMENSIONS:**
LENGTH: 31 ft 6.5 in (9.60 m)
WINGSPAN: 46 ft 0 in (14.02 m)
HEIGHT: 12 ft 10 in (3.68 m)

**WEIGHTS:**
EMPTY: 3140 lb (1424 kg)
MAX T/O: 4100 lb (1859 kg)

**PERFORMANCE:**
MAX SPEED: 143 mph (230 kmh)
RANGE: 466 miles (745 km)
POWERPLANT: de Havilland Gipsy Queen 32
OUTPUT: 251 hp (187 kW)

**FIRST FLIGHT DATE:**
31 March 1946

**FEATURES:**
Monoplane wing layout; fixed, spatted landing gear; close-cowled inline engine

# Percival Pembroke/Sea Prince UK

ten-seat, twin-engined light utility/transport aircraft

Derived from the civilian Percival Prince of the late
1940s, the Pembroke entered service with the RAF
as an Anson replacement in 1953. Slightly larger,
boasting an increased wing span and with the
interior passenger seating facing aft in line with
standard RAF practice, 45 Pembroke C 1s were
acquired, and they were used in a variety of roles
ranging from air freight through to photo-
reconnaissance and aerial survey taskings until
1988. Preceding the RAF's use of the Pembroke by
three years, the Royal Navy's Fleet Air Arm (FAA)
acquired three Sea Prince C 1s in late 1950. Unlike
the Pembroke, these aircraft were near-identical to
the civilian Prince Series II, and were used for
communications duties, including serving as an
'Admiral's Barge'. The follow-on Sea Prince T 1
resembled the Pembroke C 1, and was used as a
'flying classroom' to teach navigation techniques
and ASW warfare to would-be FAA aircrew. Some 41
T 1s were delivered from 1953 onwards, and the last
examples were replaced by Jetstream T 2s in 1979.

SPECIFCATION:

**ACCOMMODATION:**
pilot, co-pilot and up to eight
passengers

**DIMENSIONS:**
LENGTH: 46 ft 0 in (14.02 m)
WINGSPAN: 64 ft 6 in (19.66 m)
HEIGHT: 16 ft 0 in (4.87 m)

**WEIGHTS:**
EMPTY: 9589 lb (4349 kg)
MAX T/O: 13,500 lb (6125 kg)

**PERFORMANCE:**
MAX SPEED: 224 mph (360 kmh)
RANGE: 1150 miles (1850 km)
POWERPLANT: two Alvis Leonides
127s
OUTPUT: 1120 hp (835 kW)

**FIRST FLIGHT DATE:**
13 May 1948 (civilian Prince)

**FEATURES:**
Shoulder-mounted straight-wing
layout; two close-cowled radial
engines hung beneath wings;
rectractable tricycle
undercarriage; tall tail fin

# Piaggio P.149D   ITALY

four/five-seat, single-engined basic trainer and light communications aircraft

Piaggio initially developed this aircraft as a civilian four-seater, using many structural components from its 'tail-dragging' P.148 in service with the Italian Air Force. Small numbers were initially built in the mid-1950s, although production only increased to profitable levels following an order for 72 from the Luftwaffe in 1956. A licence deal was then struck between Piaggio and Focke-Wulf which saw 190 aircraft constructed by the famous German manufacturer. Designated the P.149D in Luftwaffe service, the aircraft was used for both training and liaison tasks, and was eventually used by three schools teaching future piston-engined pilots – the aircraft supplanted the T-6 Texan in this role. Surplus P.149Ds were subsequently transferred to the air forces of Nigeria, Tanzania and Uganda as part of the German military assistance programmes of the late 1960s and early 1970s. The last German examples were retired in the early 1980s, while those in Africa had been declared unserviceable some years earlier.

SPECIFICATION:

ACCOMMODATION:
two pilots seated side-by-side and two/three passengers

DIMENSIONS:
LENGTH: 28 ft 9.5 in (8.80 m)
WINGSPAN: 36 ft 6 in (11.12 m)
HEIGHT: 9 ft 6 in (2.90 m)

WEIGHTS:
EMPTY: 2557 lb (1160 kg)
MAX T/O: 3704 lb (1680 kg)

PERFORMANCE:
MAX SPEED: 192 mph (304 kmh)
RANGE: 680 miles (1090 km)
POWERPLANT: Lycoming GO-480-B1A6
OUTPUT: 270 hp (201 kW)

FIRST FLIGHT DATE:
19 June 1953

FEATURES:
Low-mounted straight-wing; large canopy; rectractable tricycle undercarriage; close-cowled engine

# Pilatus P-2 SWITZERLAND

two-seat, single-engined basic trainer

Designed specifically to operate from the high altitude airfields found in Switzerland, the P-2 relied heavily on German engineering technology brought into the country with the securing of a licence to build Bf 109ES in the late 1930s. Serving exclusively with the Swiss Air Force as a basic trainer, the P-2 initially prepared pilots for eventual postings to Bf 109E and Morane-Saulnier MS.406 units, but this changed to Vampire and Venom units in the late 1950s. The first 27 aircraft delivered to the Swiss from 1946 were dedicated pilot trainers, boasting full night flying equipment, a high-altitude oxygen system and comprehensive radios, whilst the second batch of 26 were completed as weapons and observer trainers. To this end, the latter P-2s were fitted with a single 7.92 mm machine-gun and underwing racks for practice bombs and unguided rockets. Despite the advent of the more advanced Pilatus P-3 in Swiss Air Force service from the late 1950s onwards, P-2s were retained as aerobatics trainers (a role in which they excelled) until 1981.

SPECIFICATION:

**ACCOMMODATION:**
two pilots in tandem

**DIMENSIONS:**
LENGTH: 29 ft 9 in (9.07 m)
WINGSPAN: 36 ft 1 in (11 m)
HEIGHT: 13 ft 4 in (4.08 m)

**WEIGHTS:**
EMPTY: 3040 lb (1378 kg)
MAX T/O: 4335 lb (1966 kg)

**PERFORMANCE:**
MAX SPEED: 211 mph (340 kmh)
RANGE: 535 miles (860 km)
POWERPLANT: Argus AS 410
OUTPUT: 465 hp (346 kW)

**FIRST FLIGHT DATE:**
1945

**ARMAMENT:**
one 7.92 mm machine gun in wing; practice bombs/rockets on two underwing stores pylons

**FEATURES:**
Low-mounted straight-wing; large canopy; rectractable taildragger undercarriage; close-cowled inline engine

# PZL PZL-104 **Wilga** POLAND

four-seat, single-engined, high-winged light utility aircraft

A purpose-built utility aircraft designed by PZL, the Wilga boasts an impressive STOL performance. First flown on 24 October 1962, the aircraft has proven to be very popular with flying clubs across the former Eastern Bloc, particularly as a glider tug thanks to its short take-off roll and the excellent 'pulling power' of its radial or inline engine. It has also been used for parachuting and air ambulance duties. The advent of the Wilga 3 in 1967 saw PZL redesign the fuselage to improve the cabin accommodation for up to three passengers, plus modify the undercarriage. The PZL-104 has enjoyed limited success in military ranks, with a version known as the Lipnur Gelatik (Rice Bird) 32 being built under-licence in Indonesia in the early 1970s – 56 were constructed and 24 supplied to the Indonesian Army. A further 15 are also operated by the Polish Air Force, and others have seen military service in Mongolia and Egypt. Continually updated and re-engined during its 40+ years in production, over 900 Wilgas have been built by PZL.

SPECIFCATION:

**ACCOMMODATION:**
pilot and up to three passengers

**DIMENSIONS:**
LENGTH: 26 ft 6.75 in (8.10 m)
WINGSPAN: 36 ft 5.75 in (11.12 m)
HEIGHT: 9 ft 8.5 in (2.75 m)

**WEIGHTS:**
EMPTY: 1918 lb (870 kg)
MAX T/O: 2866 lb (1300 kg)

**PERFORMANCE:**
MAX SPEED: 173 mph (279 kmh)
RANGE: 317 miles (510 km)
POWERPLANT: PZL (Ivchyenko)
AI-14RA or M-14P
OUTPUT: 260 hp (194 kW) and 360 hp (261 kW) respectively

**FIRST FLIGHT DATE:**
24 April 1962

**FEATURES:**
High-mounted, unbraced straight wing; fixed taildragger undercarriage; two-bladed propeller; close-cowled engine

# PZL TS-11 Iskra POLAND

two-seat, single-engined trainer

Placing second in the early 1960s competition to provide the Warsaw Pact air forces with a jet basic trainer, the Iskra (Spark) was nevertheless chosen ahead of the winning L-29 by the Polish Air Force in an effort to keep the country's aircraft industry in business. The type entered service in 1964, where its viceless design and rugged construction soon made it very popular with students and instructors alike. Indeed, the aircraft was used from its service introduction to provide an all through jet training syllabus. The TS-11 was built in a number of sub-variants, with the primary differences centring around the number of hardpoints available for weapons or the fitment of photo-reconnaissance training equipment. TS-11 production ended in 1978 following the delivery of 500 aircraft (including 50 Iskra-Bis DS to India), although a small number of Iskra-Bis DF photo-reconnaissance trainers were subsequently built post-1982. Polish aircraft were retired in the late 1990s by PZL Iryda and Orlik trainers, although the Indian aircraft still remain in daily use.

SPECIFICATION:

ACCOMMODATION:
two pilots in tandem

DIMENSIONS:
LENGTH: 36 ft 7.75 in (11.17 m)
WINGSPAN: 33 ft 0 in (10.06 m)
HEIGHT: 11 ft 5.5 in (3.50 m)

WEIGHTS:
EMPTY: 5644 lb (2560 kg)
MAX T/O: 8465 lb (3840 kg)

PERFORMANCE:
MAX SPEED: 466 mph (750 kmh)
RANGE: 776 miles (1250 km)
POWERPLANT: IL SO-3
OUTPUT: 2205 lb st (9.81 kN)

FIRST FLIGHT DATE:
5 February 1960

ARMAMENT:
one NS-23 23 mm cannon in forward fuselage; up to 440-lb (200 kg) of bombs/rockets on four underwing stores pylons

FEATURES:
Mid-mounted straight-wing layout; tricycle landing gear; engine air intakes in wing roots; fighter type bubble canopy

# Republic F-84 Thunderjet USA

single-seat, single-engined fighter-bomber

Initially planned as nothing more than a jet-powered Thunderbolt, Republic's XP-84 Thunderjet ended up being a wholly new design powered by the then unfashionable Allison TG-180 (J35) axial flow jet engine. The aircraft's contemporaries all used centrifugal-flow turbine turbojets. Rolled out in February 1945, the prototype XP-84 flew for the first time on 28 February 1946. Following the construction of 16 YP-84AS, the first of 226 P-84BS entered frontline service in November 1947. Redesignated the F-84 in June 1948, the Thunderjet was not easy to fly, but nevertheless proved popular with USAF pilots. A further 191 F-84CS were built in 1948-49, followed by 154 F-84DS. This variant became the first to deploy overseas, when the 27th Fighter Escort Group moved to Korea in 1950. The stretched F-84E proved to be the definitive Thunderjet model in USAF service, 743 being built – the E-model was also the Air Force's principal fighter-bomber in the Korean War. The final straight wing F-84 was the G-model, of which no fewer than 3025 were constructed, and 1900 supplied to NATO nations.

SPECIFICATION:

ACCOMMODATION:
pilot

DIMENSIONS:
LENGTH: 38 ft 1 in (11.60 m)
WINGSPAN: 36 ft 5 in (11.09 m)
HEIGHT: 12 ft 7 in (3.83 m)

WEIGHTS:
EMPTY: 11,095 lb (5033 kg)
MAX T/O: 23,525 lb (10,670 kg)

PERFORMANCE:
MAX SPEED: 622 mph (1001 kmh)
RANGE: 1330 miles (2140 km)
POWERPLANT: Allison J35-A-29
OUTPUT: 5600 lb st (25.8 kN)

FIRST FLIGHT DATE:
28 February 1946

ARMAMENT:
four Browning M-3 0.50-in machine guns in nose and two in wing roots; maximum bomb/rocket load of 4000-lb (1814 kg) on four underwing stores pylons

FEATURES:
Centrally-mounted straight wings; tricycle landing gear; engine air intake in nose; fighter type bubble canopy; wingtip tanks

# Republic F-84F Thunderstreak USA

single-seat, single-engined fighter-bomber

Essentially a brand new aircraft, the Thunderstreak shared its F-84 designation with its Thunderjet predecessor. Originally designated the YF-96A, the prototype flew for the first time on 3 June 1950. Featuring swept back wing and tail surfaces and a Wright J65 turbojet engine, the Thunderstreak bore little resemblance to the Thunderjet. The first service test YF-84F flew on 14 February 1951, and problems with high-g stall pitch-up soon occurred. The fitment of a powered 'slab' surface horizontal tailplane partially solved the problem, but the F-84F was hampered by manoeuvrability restrictions throughout its service career. With no other fighter type available, the Thunderstreak entered service with Strategic Air Command as a bomber escort in January 1954. A total of 2348 F-84Fs were built, with the type being supplied in great numbers to NATO countries. A dedicated photo-reconnaissance variant was also built as the RF-84F, the jet boasting six cameras as well as four machine guns. Of the 715 built, 386 were exported to NATO operators. Both versions were retired in the 1970s.

## SPECIFICATION:

**ACCOMMODATION:**
pilot

**DIMENSIONS:**
LENGTH: 43 ft 4.75 in (13.23 m)
WINGSPAN: 33 ft 7.25 in (10.24 m)
HEIGHT: 14 ft 4.75 in (4.39 m)

**WEIGHTS:**
EMPTY: 13,830 lb (6273 kg)
MAX T/O: 28,000 lb (12,700 kg)

**PERFORMANCE:**
MAX SPEED: 695 mph (1118 kmh)
RANGE: 810 miles (1304 km)
POWERPLANT: Wright J65-W-3
OUTPUT: 5600 lb st (25.8 kN)

**FIRST FLIGHT DATE:**
3 June 1950

**ARMAMENT:**
four Browning M-3 0.50-in machine guns in nose and two in wing roots; maximum bomb/rocket load of 6000-lb (2721 kg) on four underwing stores pylons

**FEATURES:**
Centrally-mounted swept wings and tailplane; tricycle landing gear; engine air intake in nose; fighter type bubble canopy; swept tail

# Republic F-105 Thunderchief USA

single/two-seat, single-engined fighter-bomber

Conceived by Republic in 1951 as the model AP-63 nuclear strike fighter-bomber with an internal bomb-bay, the F-105 Thunderchief which actually entered service seven years later was to win fame as a conventional tactical bomber hauling ordnance hung beneath its wings. Flight-testing began with two YF-105AS in October 1955, and following technical delays, the first of 75 B-models entered service in May 1958. It took two years to work up with the new aircraft due to further production problems, and it was not until the F-105D made its debut in 1960 that the aircraft's fortunes began to improve. Flown by USAF units both at home and in Europe and Japan, a total of 610 D-models were built up to 1965. These aircraft would bear the brunt of the USAF bombing campaign in Vietnam from 1965, and 397 would be lost in combat. Joining the D-models in South-east Asia were two-seat F-105FS, 143 of which were built – 61 of these were later modified as electronic warfare F-105G 'Wild Weasels'. Surviving Thunderchiefs were retired in the early 1980s.

SPECIFICATION:

**ACCOMMODATION:**
pilot, and pilot and weapon systems officer in tandem (F-105F/G)

**DIMENSIONS:**
LENGTH: 64 ft 4 in (19.61 m)
WINGSPAN: 34 ft 9 in (10.59 m)
HEIGHT: 19 ft 7 in (5.97 m)

**WEIGHTS:**
EMPTY: 27,500 lb (12,474 kg)
MAX T/O: 52,838 lb (23,967 kg)

**PERFORMANCE:**
MAX SPEED: 1390 mph (2237 kmh)
RANGE: 2390 miles (3846 km)
POWERPLANT: Pratt & Whitney J75-P-19W
OUTPUT: 24,500 lb st (99.25 kN)

**FIRST FLIGHT DATE:**
22 October 1955

**ARMAMENT:**
one M61A1 20 mm cannon; maximum bomb/rocket/missile load of 20,000-lb (9072 kg) on four underwing and two underfuselage stores pylons

**FEATURES:**
Mid-mounted swept wings; low-mounted swept tailplane; wing root engine air intakes; fighter type bubble canopy; swept tail; ventral fin

# Saab J 29 SWEDEN

single-seat, single-engined fighter-bomber

Western Europe's first swept-wing fighter to reach series production, the portly J 29 'Tunnan' (barrel) was designed as a replacement for the Saab 21A/R and the P-51 Mustang. Combining a solid swept wing with the power of the licence-built de Havilland Ghost (produced as the Svenska Flygmotor RM2), the J 29A entered frontline service in May 1951. A total of 224 A-models were produced before production switched to the improved J 29B, which could carry external stores and drop tanks – 360 were duly delivered. Further improvements saw the aircraft fitted with a 'dog tooth' wing and an afterburning version of the RM2. The combination of the two resulted in production of the definitive J 29F, the 308 aircraft so designated being reworked J 29B/ES. The last new aircraft was delivered by Saab in March 1956. The 'Tunnan' saw action during UN peace-keeping operations in the Congo in 1961-63, whilst the only export customer was Austria, which acquired 30 surplus Swedish J 29FS in 1961. The 'Tunnan' remained in Swedish service until August 1976.

SPECIFICATION:

**ACCOMMODATION:**
pilot

**DIMENSIONS:**
LENGTH: 33 ft 2.5 in (10.12 m)
WINGSPAN: 36 ft 1 in (11 m)
HEIGHT: 12 ft 3.5 in (3.75 m)

**WEIGHTS:**
EMPTY: 10,141 lb (4600 kg)
MAX T/O: 17,637 lb (8000 kg)

**PERFORMANCE:**
MAX SPEED: 659 mph (1060 kmh)
RANGE: 1678 miles (2700 km)
POWERPLANT: Svenska Flygmotor RM2B
OUTPUT: 6170 lb st (27.4 kN)

**FIRST FLIGHT DATE:**
1 September 1948

**ARMAMENT:**
four Hispano Mk V 20 mm cannon in nose; maximum bomb/rocket/missile load of 1100-lb (500 kg) on four underwing stores pylons

**FEATURES:**
High-mounted swept wings; swept tailplane; tricycle landing gear; engine air intake in nose; fighter type bubble canopy

# Saab A/J 32 Lansen  SWEDEN

two-seat, single-engined fighter-bomber

The Type 32 Lansen (Lance) was a swept wing design produced well in advance of other similar aircraft in Western Europe. Work on the aircraft commenced in 1946, with permission to begin construction following two years later. Seating two crewman in tandem, the Lansen was a deceptively large aircraft, and Saab utilised every inch of its airframe size to produce three variants capable of performing vastly different roles. The dedicated A 32A bomber was the first to enter squadron service in 1956, 287 A-models being built between December 1955 and June 1957. These were followed by 44 S 32C reconnaissance aircraft, fitted with a battery of different cameras and radar equipment in place of the integral cannon. Finally, 120 J 32B night and all-weather fighters were constructed between July 1958 and May 1960, these aircraft being shared between three fighter wings. In the early 1970s 24 surplus Lansens were modified into target tugs (redesignated J 32DS) and ECCM trainers (J 32E), and these aircraft were only retired from Air Force service in October 1997.

SPECIFICATION:

**ACCOMMODATION:**
pilot and navigator in tandem

**DIMENSIONS:**
LENGTH: 49 ft 0.75 in (14.94 m)
WINGSPAN: 42 ft 7.75 in (13 m)
HEIGHT: 15 ft 3 in (4.65 m)

**WEIGHTS:**
EMPTY: 16,398 lb (7438 kg)
MAX T/O: 28,660 lb (13,600 kg)

**PERFORMANCE:**
MAX SPEED: 692 mph (1114 kmh)
RANGE: 2000 miles (3220 km)
POWERPLANT: Svenska Flygmotor RM5A2
OUTPUT: 10,362 lb st (42.1 kN)

**FIRST FLIGHT DATE:**
3 November 1952

**ARMAMENT:**
four Hispano Mk V 20 mm cannon in nose; maximum bomb/rocket/missile load of 3000-lb (1361 kg) on four underwing stores pylons

**FEATURES:**
Low-mounted swept wings; swept tailplane; tricycle landing gear; fuselage air intakes below cockpit; fighter type bubble canopy

# Saab J/F 35 Draken SWEDEN

single-seat, single-engined fighter-bomber

Developed in response to a challenging 1949 Swedish Air Force requirement for an advanced interceptor to replace the J 29, Saab's J 35 Draken (Dragon) was once again an innovative design. The Air Force wanted an aircraft with 50 per cent better performance than any other fighter then entering service. It also had to be all-weather and short-field capable. The resulting J 35 featured a unique double delta wing which gave the fighter Mach 2 performance, and it possessed a shorter take-off run than the Mirage III or F-104. The first of three Draken prototypes flew on 25 October 1955, and production J 35As entered service in 1960. New build and converted J 35Bs followed, this version featuring a lengthened rear fuselage. The J 35D was powered by an improved version of the RM6C engine, and the final new build variant was the J 35F, which boasted improved avionics. A total of 606 Drakens were built, with 40 being supplied to Denmark, 12 to Finland and 24 to Austria. Only the latter remain in service.

SPECIFICATION:

**ACCOMMODATION:**
pilot, or two pilots in tandem (sk 35)

**DIMENSIONS:**
LENGTH: 50 ft 4 in (15.35 m)
WINGSPAN: 30 ft 10 in (9.40 m)
HEIGHT: 12 ft 9 in (3.89 m)

**WEIGHTS:**
EMPTY: 18,188 lb (8250 kg)
MAX T/O: 35,275 lb (16,000 kg)

**PERFORMANCE:**
MAX SPEED: 1328 mph (2125 kmh)
RANGE: 2031 miles (3250 km)
POWERPLANT: Volvo Flygmotor RM6C
OUTPUT: 17,650 lb st (78.5 kN)

**FIRST FLIGHT DATE:**
25 October 1955

**ARMAMENT:**
two Aden 30 mm cannon in wings; maximum bomb/rocket/ missile load of 9000-lb (4086 kg) on nine underwing stores pylons

**FEATURES:**
Mid-mounted cranked double delta wings; swept tailplane; tricycle landing gear; fuselage air intakes below cockpit; fighter type bubble canopy; no tailplane

# Saab 91 Safir  SWEDEN

four-seat, single-engined basic trainer and communications aircraft

Built as a basic trainer/tourer for both civil and
military use, the Safir was developed in 1944-45.
Quantity production of the Saab 91 commenced in
the spring of 1946 but sales were slow, and only 46
de Havilland Gipsy Major x A-models were built.
Most were sold to the Ethiopian Air Force as part of
a package of Swedish military equipment bought
by the African country in 1947. Two years later the
more powerful 91B was put into production, its flat
six Lycoming O-435A significantly improving the
Safir's performance. In 1951 the Swedish Air Force
ordered the aircraft for use as its new basic trainer,
Saab building 74. Most of these were constructed
under-licence by De Schelde in The Netherlands
because of capacity problems at Saab's Linköping
plant. Total Dutch production numbered 120 Safirs
between 1951-55, after which all remaining Safirs
were built in Sweden. Saab had constructed 323
Safirs in all variants by the time the last aircraft was
delivered to Ethiopia in 1966. Other military users
were Finland, Tunisia and Austria.

SPECIFICATION:

**ACCOMMODATION:**
two pilots seated in tandem with
two passengers

**DIMENSIONS:**
LENGTH: 26 ft 4 in (8.03 m)
WINGSPAN: 34 ft 9 in (10.60 m)
HEIGHT: 7 ft 2.66 in (2.20 m)

**WEIGHTS:**
EMPTY: 1570 lb (710 kg)
MAX T/O: 2660 lb (1205 kg)

**PERFORMANCE:**
MAX SPEED: 165 mph (265 kmh)
RANGE: 660 miles (1062 km)
POWERPLANT: Lycoming
O-360-A1A
OUTPUT: 180 hp (134 kW)

**FIRST FLIGHT DATE:**
20 November 1945

**FEATURES:**
Low-mounted straight-wing;
large canopy; rectractable tricycle
undercarriage; close-cowled flat
four engine

# Scottish Aviation Pioneer CC 1 UK

five-seat, single-engined, high-winged light utility aircraft

The first aircraft built by Scottish Aviation Ltd, the appropriately named Pioneer was designed in response to Air Ministry Specification A 4/45 for a light communication aircraft capable of operating from confined spaces. Although the original three-seat, de Havilland Gipsy Queen-powered Pioneer I failed to receive a production contract, it sired the bigger, Alvis Leonides-powered Pioneer II, which made its first flight in June 1950. This aircraft boasted remarkable short field performance thanks to its wing, which was fitted with full-span controlled leading-edge slates and large-area Fowler-type trailing edge flaps. With a take-off run of 225 ft and a landing run of just 198 ft, the Pioneer II had a stalling speed of 36 mph! The RAF was clearly impressed, and 40 Pioneer CC 1s were purchased. Entering service in August 1953, these aircraft proved invaluable for casualty evacuation work in the Malayan jungles with No 267 Sqn. Five other squadrons received Pioneer CC 1s in Aden, Singapore and the UK. Suffering a high attrition rate in service, the survivors had been retired by 1970.

SPECIFICATION:

ACCOMMODATION:
pilot and four passengers

DIMENSIONS:
LENGTH: 34 ft 4 in (10.48 m)
WINGSPAN: 49 ft 9 in (15.20 m)
HEIGHT: 10 ft 3 in (3.13 m)

WEIGHTS:
EMPTY: 3835 lb (1739 kg)
MAX T/O: 5800 lb (2631 kg)

PERFORMANCE:
MAX SPEED: 162 mph (259 kmh)
RANGE: 420 miles (672 km)
POWERPLANT: Alvis Leonides 502/4
OUTPUT: 520 hp (387 kW)

FIRST FLIGHT DATE:
June 1950

FEATURES:
high-mounted, braced straight wing; fixed taildragger undercarriage; three-bladed propeller; close-cowled radial engine; large fin

# Scottish Aviation Twin Pioneer cc 1/2 UK

18-seat, twin-engined, high-winged utility transport aircraft

Designed by specialist STOL manufacturer Scottish Aviation in the early 1950s as a natural successor to its single-engined high-wing Pioneer CC 1, the larger 'Twin Pin' looked assured of a healthy production run when first unveiled in 1955. However, just 87 examples were eventually built between 1956-64, the bulk of these being supplied as CC 1/2s to the RAF. The Air Force's initial order was for 20 aircraft, which were supplied to No 78 Sqn in Aden in 1958. A further 19 were subsequently acquired, and these saw extensive use primarily with the overseas Commands in Bahrain, Singapore, Borneo and, of course, Aden. Like the Pioneer CC 1, the aircraft was used for a variety of general utility roles including para-trooping (11 fully equipped paratroops could be carried) and medical evacuation (six stretchers and five sitting casualties/medical attendants). Budget cuts saw the shrinking of the overseas force, and the 'Twin Pin' was withdrawn from service in late 1968. A handful of aircraft were also sold to the Malaysian Air Force.

SPECIFICATION:

**ACCOMMODATION:**
two pilots and sixteen passengers

**DIMENSIONS:**
LENGTH: 45 ft 3 in (13.80 m)
WINGSPAN: 76 ft 6 in (23.33 m)
HEIGHT: 12 ft 3 in (3.74 m)

**WEIGHTS:**
EMPTY: 10,200 lb (4630 kg)
MAX T/O: 14,600 lb (6628 kg)

**PERFORMANCE:**
MAX SPEED: 165 mph (266 kmh)
RANGE: 791 miles (1287 km)
POWERPLANT: two Alvis Leonides 531s
OUTPUT: 1280 hp (950 kW)

**FIRST FLIGHT DATE:**
25 June 1955

**FEATURES:**
High-mounted, braced straight wing; fixed taildragger undercarriage; close-cowled radial engines; three-finned tail

# Scottish Aviation Bulldog UK

two-seat, single-engined basic trainer

The Bullog was a militarised version of Beagle's civil B 121 Pup, which flew for the first time in April 1967. Although popular with private pilots, sales of the Pup failed to save Beagle, which went into liquidation in January 1970 after building 152 aircraft. Seven months earlier, on 19 May 1969, the company had flown a military trainer variant of the Pup, which it called the Bulldog. Differing little from the civil aircraft, the Bulldog featured a rearward sliding canopy, a Lycoming IO-360 engine and a fixed undercarriage. Following the collapse of Beagle, Scottish Aviation purchased the design rights to the Bulldog and built 98 Series 100 aircraft for export to Kenya, Malaysia and Sweden. The Series 120 aircraft which followed was fully aerobatic up to a higher weight, and the RAF purchased 130. Designated Bulldog T 1s, these aircraft were issued to University Air Squadrons to train sponsored undergraduates – a task they performed until retired in 2001. Series 120 aircraft were also sold to seven export customers, with overall Beagle production numbering 328.

SPECIFICATION:

**ACCOMMODATION:**
two pilots seated side-by-side

**DIMENSIONS:**
LENGTH: 23 ft 3 in (7.09 m)
WINGSPAN: 33 ft 0 in (10.60 m)
HEIGHT: 7 ft 6 in (2.28 m)

**WEIGHTS:**
EMPTY: 1430 lb (650 kg)
MAX T/O: 2350 lb (1065 kg)

**PERFORMANCE:**
MAX SPEED: 150 mph (240 kmh)
RANGE: 625 miles (1000 km)
POWERPLANT: Lycoming
IO-360-A1B6
OUTPUT: 200 hp (150 kW)

**FIRST FLIGHT DATE:**
19 May 1969

**ARMAMENT:**
maximum bomb/rocket/gun pod/missile load of 640-lb (290 kg) on four underwing stores pylons

**FEATURES:**
Low-mounted straight-wing with slight dihedral; side-by-side cockpit with large canopy; fixed tricycle undercarriage; close-cowled flat four engine

# SEPECAT Jaguar FRANCE & UK

single/two-seat, twin-engined ground attack aircraft

The Jaguar was the end result of the world's first bi-national military aircraft programme. The British and French air forces had originally issued a requirement for an advanced supersonic jet trainer, and the SEPECAT (*Société Européené de Production de l'Avion de Ecole de Combat et Appui Tactique*) teaming of Breguet and the British Aircraft Corporation was duly formed in 1966 to meet this requirement. The first of eight prototypes flew on 8 September 1968, and by the time service deliveries began in 1973 (to the French), the Jaguar had exclusively become a ground attack aircraft. A total of 200 Jaguars (165 GR 1s and 35 two-seat T 2s) were delivered to the RAF, and 160 Jaguar As and 40 two-seat Jaguar ES to the French Air Force. British-built export examples were also sold to India, Ecuador, Nigeria and Oman. British and French Jaguars saw combat in the first Gulf War, and RAF aircraft were also involved in combat in the Balkans. All British and French Jaguars are due for retirement in 2005.

SPECIFICATION:

**ACCOMMODATION:**
pilot, or two pilots in tandem (T 2 and Jaguar E)

**DIMENSIONS:**
LENGTH: 55 ft 3 in (16.83 m)
WINGSPAN: 28 ft 6 in (8.69 m)
HEIGHT: 16 ft 1 in (4.89 m)

**WEIGHTS:**
EMPTY: 16,975 lb (7700 kg)
MAX T/O: 34,612 lb (15,700 kg)

**PERFORMANCE:**
MAX SPEED: 1062 mph (1700 kmh)
RANGE: 2203 miles (3525 km)
POWERPLANT: two Rolls-Royce/ Turboméca Adour Mk 104s
OUTPUT: 16,080 lb st (71.6 kN)

**FIRST FLIGHT DATE:**
8 September 1968

**ARMAMENT:**
two Aden 30 mm cannon in lower fuselage; maximum bomb/ rocket/missile load of 10,000-lb (4540 kg) on four underwing, two overwing (missiles) and one underfuselage stores pylons

**FEATURES:**
Shoulder-mounted swept wings; swept tailplane; square lateral fuselage air intakes below cockpit

# Shorts Belfast C 1 UK

four-seat, four-engined strategic freight aircraft

Weighing in at over 100 tonnes at maximum take-off weight, the Belfast was one of the largest turboprop-powered aircraft ever built. It was developed in response to an RAF requirement for a heavylift freighter large enough to transport all manner of military hardware, including tanks and artillery pieces, 200+ troops, ground-to-air guided missile batteries and helicopters over long distances. After studying numerous freighter designs, Shorts settled on the SC 5/10 in February 1959. The first of only ten Belfasts to be built took to the skies on 5 January 1964, the aircraft being powered by four Rolls-Royce Tyne turboprops. The Belfast had an 18-wheel undercarriage, as well as a beaver tail rear entry door. When the first Belfast C 1 joined No 53 Sqn at Fairford in January 1966 it became the largest aircraft to be operated by the RAF. The Belfast proved expensive to maintain in service, and with the Air Force's overseas commitments rapidly shrinking, all ten aircraft were prematurely retired in September 1976. Two remain in civil use today.

SPECIFCATION:

ACCOMMODATION:
pilot, co-pilot, navigator, flight engineer, loadmaster

DIMENSIONS:
LENGTH: 136 ft 5 in (41.58 m)
WINGSPAN: 158 ft 10 in (48.41 m)
HEIGHT: 47 ft 0 in (14.33 m)

WEIGHTS:
EMPTY: 130,000 lb (34,685 kg)
MAX T/O: 230,000 lb (104,325 kg)

PERFORMANCE:
MAX SPEED: 354 mph (566 kmh)
RANGE: 3875 miles (6200 km)
POWERPLANT: four Rolls-Royce Tyne RTYS
OUTPUT: 22,920 shp (17,100 kW)

FIRST FLIGHT DATE:
5 January 1964

FEATURES:
Shoulder-mounted straight wing layout; retractable landing gear in fairings; four close-cowled turboprop engines; large tail; rear-loading ramp

# Shorts Skyvan  UK

24-seat, twin-engined utility transport aircraft

Shorts' Skyvan was the end product of a decision made in 1959 to make a small utility transport with a square-sided fuselage in order to accommodate oversized loads. The first Series 1 Skyvans entered production powered by Continental GTSIO-520 piston engines, but these were swiftly replaced in Series 2 aircraft by Astazou XII turboprops. Finally, Shorts settled on the Garrett TWP331-2-201AS in the mid-1960s, the re-engined aircraft being designated the Skyvan 3M. Military sales were achieved at an early stage in the aircraft's production life, with Oman being one of the first customers with an order for 16 3MS. A further 11 countries acquired Skyvans in smaller quantities. Most military aircraft have been used as utility transports, although the six acquired by Singapore had a radar fitted in a thimble nose blister for SAR/coastal patrol duties. Skyvan production ended in 1987, by which time Shorts had built 150 examples, of which around 60 were supplied to military customers. The aircraft is still in limited use today with both military and civilian operators.

## SPECIFICATION:

**ACCOMMODATION:**
pilot, co-pilot and 22 passengers

**DIMENSIONS:**
LENGTH: 40 ft 1 in (12.21 m)
WINGSPAN: 64 ft 11 in (19.79 m)
HEIGHT: 15 ft 1 in (4.60 m)

**WEIGHTS:**
EMPTY: 7400 lb (3355 kg)
MAX T/O: 14,500 lb (6577 kg)

**PERFORMANCE:**
MAX SPEED: 203 mph (327 kmh)
RANGE: 694 miles (1115 km)
POWERPLANT: two Garrett
TPE 331-2-201AS
OUTPUT: 1430 shp (1070 kW)

**FIRST FLIGHT DATE:**
17 January 1963

**FEATURES:**
Braced high straight wing; fixed tricycle landing gear; slab-sided fuselage, with upswept rear loading ramp; twin wing-mounted close-cowled turboprop engines; large tail; twin square-sided tail units

# SIAI Marchetti S.211 ITALY

two-seat, single-engined trainer

Built as a private venture in Italy to fulfil basic/intermediate, weapons training and light ground attack tasks, models of the S.211 were first displayed at the Paris Airshow in 1977. However, a further four years were to pass before the prototype conducted its first flight on 10 April 1981. Only three customers committed to the design, with the Philippines buying 24 and Singapore 30. A further four S.211s were also bought by Haiti, but these were soon sold on to private buyers in the USA. Both Singapore and the Philippines assembled the bulk of their aircraft locally. Singapore has based the bulk of its jets at RAAF Pearce, in Western Australia, since 1993, where they conduct training for the Air Force in less congested skies. The Philippines uses its aircraft for both training and ground attack, with aircraft seeing combat against communist rebels throughout the country. The S.211 can carry up to 1455-lb of ordnance (bombs, rockets and machine pods) on four underwing pylons.

SPECIFICATION:

ACCOMMODATION:
two pilots in tandem

DIMENSIONS:
LENGTH: 31 ft 2 in (9.50 m)
WINGSPAN: 27 ft 8 in (8.43 m)
HEIGHT: 13 ft 0 in (3.96 m)

WEIGHTS:
EMPTY: 4078 lb (1850 kg)
MAX T/O: 6955 lb (3150 kg)

PERFORMANCE:
MAX SPEED: 416 mph (667 kmh)
RANGE: 1040 miles (1665 km)
POWERPLANT: Pratt & Whitney JT15D-4C
OUTPUT: 3190 lb st (14.2 kN)

FIRST FLIGHT DATE:
10 April 1981

ARMAMENT:
up to 1455-lb (660 kg) of bombs/rockets/gun pods on four underwing stores pylons

FEATURES:
shoulder-mounted swept wing; engine air intakes on fuselage below cockpit wing roots; fighter type bubble canopy; swept fin

# Soko G-2A/J-1 Galeb YUGOSLAVIA

single/two-seat, single-engined trainer/light attack aircraft

The Galeb (Seagull) was the first indigenous Yugoslav jet design to enter series production, initially being built as a two-seat trainer but later being developed into a single-seat light strike aircraft. Similar in both powerplant and configuration to the MB-326 Macchi, the Galeb entered service with the Yugoslav Air Force in 1965, which procured 120+ for use by the Air Academy and fighter and ground-attack schools. Export orders were also received from Zambia (six G-2s and 20 single-seat J-1s), and Libya, the latter nation buying 120 G-2As in two batches. Production ended in 1985. With the break up of the Yugoslavia into numerous independent states during the bloody civil war of the early 1990s, surviving G-2As were impressed into offensive action with the newly-created Serbian Air Force, equipping the 105th Fighter-Bomber Regiment. These aircraft saw action between 1991-95, attacking Muslim forces in Bosnia-Herzegovina. Other Galebs remain in service in their designed role with the 'new' Yugoslavian Air Force and its Croatian counterpart.

SPECIFICATION:

ACCOMMODATION:
pilot (J-1) or two pilots in tandem (G-2A)

DIMENSIONS:
LENGTH: 33 ft 11 in (10.34 m)
WINGSPAN: 34 ft 4.5 in (10.47 m)
HEIGHT: 10 ft 9 in (3.28 m)

WEIGHTS:
EMPTY: 5775 lb (2620 kg)
MAX T/O: 7690 lb (3488 kg)

PERFORMANCE:
MAX SPEED: 470 mph (756 kmh)
RANGE: 770 miles (1240 km)
POWERPLANT: Rolls-Royce Viper II Mk 22-6
OUTPUT: 2500 lb st (11.12 kN)

FIRST FLIGHT DATE:
May 1961

ARMAMENT:
two 12.7 mm machine guns in nose; up to 440-lb (200 kg) of bombs/rockets on eight underwing stores pylons

FEATURES:
Low-mounted straight-wing layout; tricycle landing gear; lateral engine air intakes below cockpit; fighter type bubble canopy; wingtip tanks

# Soko J-20 Kraguj YUGOSLAVIA

single-seat, single-engined counter-insurgency/weapons training aircraft

Created specifically for the counter-insurgency mission, the J-20 Kraguj (Sparrowhawk) was designed for the Yugoslavian Air Force by the Aeronautical Research Establishment at Beograd in the mid-1960s. Built by the government-owned Soko factory at Mostar, the prototype aircraft flew for the first time in 1966. Of simple all-metal construction, with a fixed undercarriage and Lycoming GSO-480 flat six piston engine, the Kraguj could take off and land on grass fields or unprepared airstrips of less than 395 ft in length. The Kraguj had a fixed armament of two wing-mounted Colt-Browning 7.7 mm machine-guns and six underwing attachment points for weapon pylons. The Kraguj entered production in 1968, and was flown by several weapons training squadrons within the Yugoslav Air Force. Surviving examples were retired in 1990, with a number of J-20s being passed on to the Slovenian national guard. However, these were repossessed by the Yugoslav Air Force in June 1991 and used by Bosnian Serb militia forces against Muslim and Croat forces.

SPECIFICATION:

**ACCOMMODATION:**
pilot

**DIMENSIONS:**
LENGTH: 26 ft 0.25 in (7.93 m)
WINGSPAN: 34 ft 11 in (10.64 m)
HEIGHT: 9 ft 10 in (3 m)

**WEIGHTS:**
EMPTY: 2491 lb (1130 kg)
MAX T/O: 3580 lb (1624 kg)

**PERFORMANCE:**
MAX SPEED: 183 mph (295 kmh)
RANGE: 497 miles (800 km)
POWERPLANT: Lycoming GSO-480-B1A6
OUTPUT: 340 hp (253.3 kW)

**FIRST FLIGHT DATE:**
1966

**ARMAMENT:**
two Colt-Browning 7.7 mm machine guns in wings; maximum bomb/rocket load of 660-lb (300 kg) on six underwing stores pylons

**FEATURES:**
Low-mounted straight-wing; large canopy; fixed taildragger undercarriage; close-cowled flat six engine; three-bladed propeller

# Sud-Ouest so.4050 Vautour II FRANCE

single/two-seat, twin-engined fighter-bomber

One of the most successful of the early post-war crop of aircraft designed by the re-born French aviation industry, the so.4050 was the creation of the SNCASO (south-west) nationalised group in 1951. Built to meet a requirement issued by the French Air Force for an all-weather day/night fighter, close support aircraft and bomber, the first of nine Vautour (Vulture) prototypes was flown on 16 October 1952. Following three years of testing, production aircraft were delivered to the French Air Force in early 1956. The Vautour proved to be a versatile design capable of carrying a handy warload over significant distances. Thirty IIA single-seat attack bombers were built, 25 of which were supplied to Israel. These saw much action over the next 15 years, being supplanted by a number of ex-French IIB (two-seat) bombers in 1960 – 40 IIBs had been acquired by the French for its Strategic Air Command. A further 70 II.1N nightfighters were also bought, and these remained in frontline service with the French Air Force until replaced by Mirage F1CS in 1973-76.

SPECIFICATION:

**ACCOMMODATION:**
pilot (IIA), and pilot navigator (IIB/II.1N)

**DIMENSIONS:**
LENGTH: 51 ft 11.75 in (15.84 m)
WINGSPAN: 49 ft 6.50 in (15.10 m)
HEIGHT: 16 ft 2.50 in (4.95 m)

**WEIGHTS:**
EMPTY: 24,250 lb (11,000 kg)
MAX T/O: 45,635 lb (20,700 kg)

**PERFORMANCE:**
MAX SPEED: 684 mph (1100 kmh)
RANGE: 1990 miles (3200 km)
POWERPLANT: two SNECMA Atar 101E-3s
OUTPUT: 15,432 lb st (68.1 kN)

**FIRST FLIGHT DATE:**
16 October 1952

**ARMAMENT:**
four DEFA 553 30 mm cannon in nose; up to 8500-lb (3854 kg) of bombs/rockets/missiles split between bomb-bay and two underwing stores pylons (missiles only)

**FEATURES:**
Mid-mounted swept-wing layout; bicycle landing gear with outriggers; engines-mounted beneath wings; swept-back horizontal tailplane; ventral fin

# Sukhoi su-7 USSR

single-seat, single-engined fighter-bomber

The su-7 was designed by the Sukhoi bureau
during its time assigned to Tupolev after it had
been closed down by Stalin in December 1949
following the failure of a jet fighter prototype. The
aircraft progressed to s-1 prototype form following
Sukhoi's reopening in the wake of Stalin's death,
and on 8 September 1955 it flew for the first time.
Initially designed as a fighter, just 100 su-7s were
built to serve in this role in 1958-59 following the
Soviet Air Force's decision to choose the faster
mig-21 as its frontline interceptor. The Sukhoi
design was duly developed into the su-7b
(b standing for Bombardirovschkik, or fighter-
bomber), the aircraft needing only minor changes
to perform this mission. It proved extremely
popular with its pilots, the Sukhoi's speed, strength
and manoeuvrability all being greatly appreciated.
The more powerful su-7bm was introduced in 1961,
and this provided the basis for the export-standard
su-7bmk – at least 11 countries were supplied with
this variant. The Soviet Air Force retired its last
su-7bms from frontline service in 1986.

SPECIFICATION:

ACCOMMODATION:
pilot

DIMENSIONS:
LENGTH: 57 ft 0 in (17.37 m)
WINGSPAN: 29 ft 3.5 in (8.93 m)
HEIGHT: 15 ft 5 in (4.70 m)

WEIGHTS:
EMPTY: 19,000 lb (8620 kg)
MAX T/O: 29,750 lb (13,500 kg)

PERFORMANCE:
MAX SPEED: 1055 mph (1700 kmh)
RANGE: 900 miles (1450 km)
POWERPLANT: Lyulka AL-7F
OUTPUT: 22,046 lb st (97.9 kN)

FIRST FLIGHT DATE:
8 September 1955

ARMAMENT:
two NR-30 30 mm cannon in
wing roots; provision for up to
5510-lb (2499 kg) of bombs/
rockets/missiles on four
underwing and one
underfuselage stores pylons

FEATURES:
Mid-mounted swept wing;
tricycle landing gear; engine air
intake in nose; swept tail; mid-
mounted tailplane; fighter style
bubble canopy

# Sukhoi su-15 USSR

single-seat, twin-engined fighter

Based on the su-11, which was itself a delta winged fighter interceptor version of the su-7, the su-15 boasted genuine Mach 2 performance. Bigger than either the su-7 or -11, and using lateral engine intakes, the prototype su-15 (designated the т-58 by Sukhoi) flew for the first time on 30 May 1962. Development of production-standard aircraft was a drawn out affair, with su-15s finally reaching frontline units in 1969. Further development saw the introduction of the 'second generation' su-15M in the early 1970s, this aircraft featuring an improved wing and tailplane. The Soviet Air Force employed the su-15 as its standard interceptor across the length and breadth of the USSR during the height of the Cold War. Indeed, an su-15 was responsible for shooting down the Korean Airlines Boeing 747 that strayed into Soviet airspace in September 1983. Further improvements to the aircraft saw bigger engines fitted, extra wing pylons added and fuel capacity increased. The su-15TM was the final version to enter frontline ranks from 1974, and all had been retired by the mid-1990s.

SPECIFICATION:

ACCOMMODATION:
pilot

DIMENSIONS:
LENGTH: 67 ft 3 in (20.50 m)
WINGSPAN: 34 ft 6.6 in (10.53 m)
HEIGHT: 16 ft 5 in (5 m)

WEIGHTS:
EMPTY: 27,006 lb (12,250 kg)
MAX T/O: 44,092 lb (20,000 kg)

PERFORMANCE:
MAX SPEED: 1650 mph (2655 kmh)
RANGE: 1398 miles (2250 km)
POWERPLANT: two MNPK 'Soyuz'
(Tumanskii) R-13F2-300s
OUTPUT: 31,306 lb st (139.26 kN)

FIRST FLIGHT DATE:
30 May 1962

ARMAMENT:
up to four air-to-air missiles on
four underwing stores pylons

FEATURES:
Low-mounted delta wing; tricycle
landing gear; lateral engine air
intakes below cockpit; swept tail;
low-mounted tailplane; fighter
style bubble canopy; large
radome

# Sukhoi su-17/20/22  USSR

single-seat, single-engined fighter-bomber

The end result of Sukhoi's refinement of the venerable su-7, the su-17 was the staple ground-attack aircraft for the Warsaw Pact air forces for over 20 years. Although the su-7 had been a robust, rugged aircraft, it had poor short take-off/landing performance and limited range. Sukhoi saw the introduction of variable sweep outer wings as the answer to these problems, and the resulting su-17 prototype made its maiden flight on 2 August 1966. Production aircraft reached frontline Soviet units in eastern Europe in the early 1970s, and export examples (designated su-20) were supplied to a dozen air forces. The improved, and shortened, su-17m-2/2d was introduced by Sukhoi from 1974, followed by the su-17m-3 and finally the su-17m-4 from 1980. Export versions were designated the su-22m-3/4, and again they were supplied to air forces in eastern Europe, Africa, the Middle East and Asia. The later m-3/4 variants of the su-17/22 boasted better avionics and improved low-level performance. All Russian su-17s have now been retired, and only a small number remain in service in other countries.

SPECIFICATION:

ACCOMMODATION:
pilot

DIMENSIONS:
LENGTH: 52 ft 1 in (15.87 m)
WINGSPAN: 44 ft 11 in (13.68 m)
HEIGHT: 16 ft 10 in (5.13 m)

WEIGHTS:
EMPTY: 23,737 lb (10,767 kg)
MAX T/O: 42,770 lb (19,400 kg)

PERFORMANCE:
MAX SPEED: 1156 mph (1850 kmh)
RANGE: 1594 miles (2550 km)
POWERPLANT: Lyulka AL-21F-3
OUTPUT: 24,800 lb st (110.3 kN)

FIRST FLIGHT DATE:
2 August 1966

ARMAMENT:
two NR-30 30 mm cannon in wing roots; provision for up to 8820-lb (4000 kg) of bombs/rockets/missiles on four underwing and five underfuselage stores pylons

FEATURES:
Mid-mounted variable-sweep wing; tricycle landing gear; engine air intake in nose; swept tail; mid-mounted tailplane; fighter style bubble canopy; wing fences

# Sukhoi su-24 USSR

two-seat, twin-engined strike/reconnaissance fighter

Still very much a part of today's Russian Air Force, and in service with the air forces of Algeria, Iran, Libya, Syria and Ukraine, the formidable su-24 is one of the world's most capable long-range strike fighters. Developed to replace the il-28 and yak-28, the su-24 was equipped with a swing wing by Sukhoi so as to allow the aircraft to meet the strict take-off requirements set down by the Soviet Air Force in the late 1960s. The prototype su-24 flew for the first time on 17 January 1970, and production aircraft began to enter service with Soviet units in the USSR in 1974. It remained strictly within Soviet territory until 1979, when a regiment deployed to then East Germany. In 1984 the aircraft made its combat debut over Afghanistan, by which time Soviet su-24s had also been moved to bases in Hungary and Poland. The improved su-24M entered service in 1986, this aircraft having terrain following radar, an inflight refuelling probe, and improved avionics. Still in production today, 950+ su-24s have been built to date.

SPECIFICATION:

ACCOMMODATION:
pilot and weapons systems operator sat side-by-side

DIMENSIONS:
LENGTH: 80 ft 8 in (24.60 m)
WINGSPAN: 57 ft 11 in (17.64 m)
HEIGHT: 20 ft 4 in (6.19 m)

WEIGHTS:
EMPTY: 49,163 lb (22,300 kg)
MAX T/O: 87,235 lb (39,570 kg)

PERFORMANCE:
MAX SPEED: 1441 mph (2320 kmh)
RANGE: 1562 miles (2500 km)
POWERPLANT: two Saturn/Lyulka AL-21F-3AS
OUTPUT: 49,380 lb st (219.60 kN)

FIRST FLIGHT DATE:
17 January 1970

ARMAMENT:
one GSh-6 23 mm cannon in fuselage; provision for up to 17,635-lb (8000 kg) of bombs/rockets/missiles on three underfuselage and four underwing stores pylons

FEATURES:
Shoulder-mounted variable-sweep wing; lateral engine air intake behind cockpit; swept tail; mid-mounted all-moveable tailplane; side-by-side cockpit

# Sukhoi su-25 USSR

single-seat, twin-engined ground attack aircraft

The Russian equivalent of the A-10 Thunderbolt II, the su-25 was designed specifically for the close air support of troops on the ground. Sukhoi started development of the aircraft in 1968, the design team being heavily influenced by the experiences of the USAF in Vietnam. Seen as a modern successor to the legendary Il-2 Stormovik, the prototype su-25 flew for the first time on 22 February 1975. Pre-production aircraft saw combat in Afghanistan in the early 1980s, and the end result of this was the fitment of better chaff/flare protection, engine exhaust infrared suppressors and titanium engine shielding to production aircraft. The latter reached Soviet units in 1984, and the jet was subsequently built in single- and two-seat variants. Ten countries have bought su-25s to date, with a number of surplus aircraft from former eastern bloc air forces being refurbished and sold in Africa. A total of 330 su-25s were built up to 1989, and the aircraft remains in frontline service in Russia today. Sukhoi continues to build modernised su-25TS on a low-rate production line.

SPECIFICATION:

ACCOMMODATION:
pilot

DIMENSIONS:
LENGTH: 50 ft 11.5 in (15.53 m)
WINGSPAN: 47 ft 1.4 in (14.36 m)
HEIGHT: 15 ft 9 in (4.80 m)

WEIGHTS:
EMPTY: 21,605 lb (9800 kg)
MAX T/O: 41,005 lb (18,600 kg)

PERFORMANCE:
MAX SPEED: 590 mph (950 kmh)
RANGE: 308 miles (495 km)
POWERPLANT: two MNPK 'Soyuz'
Tumanskii R-195S
OUTPUT: 19,842 lb st (88.26 kN)

FIRST FLIGHT DATE:
22 February 1975

ARMAMENT:
one AO-17A 30 mm cannon in fuselage; provision for up to 9700-lb (4400 kg) of bombs/rockets/missiles on ten underwing stores pylons

FEATURES:
Shoulder-mounted swept wing; lateral engine air intakes behind cockpit; tailplane with dihedral; ECM pods on wingtips

# Supermarine Spitfire Mk XVIII/XIX UK

single-seat, single-engined monoplane fighter/photo reconnaissance aircraft

The final Griffon-engined development of the Spitfire, the Mk XVIII and photo-reconnaissance PR XIX looked remarkably similar to the interim Mk XIV, which had been rushed into service with the RAF in early 1944 whilst design work continued on the definitive Griffon Spitfires. The resulting delay in service entry of these marks meant that only the PR XIX saw action during World War 2. Unlike the 'temporary' Mk XIV, the Mk XVIII/XIX had specially strengthened wings in place of the universal flying surfaces used by the earlier variant, a more robust undercarriage and a rear-view 'bubble' hood. Produced as either a standard fighter (F XVIII – 100 built) or fighter-reconnaissance (FR XVIII – 200 built) platform, the aircraft reached the frontline in mid-1945 and was issued primarily to units in the Far East. The last RAF Spitfire variant to fire its guns in anger, the FR XVIII was retired in 1952. The unarmed PR XIX remained in service for a few more years as the PR 19, 225 having been built.

SPECIFICATION:

ACCOMMODATION:
pilot

DIMENSIONS:
LENGTH: 32 ft 8 in (9.99 m)
WINGSPAN: 36 ft 10 in (11 m)
HEIGHT: 12 ft 8 in (3.9 m)

WEIGHTS:
EMPTY: 6550 lb (3016 kg)
MAX T/O: 10,450 lb (4740 kg)

PERFORMANCE:
MAX SPEED: 460 mph (736 kmh)
RANGE: 1550 miles (800 km)
POWERPLANT: Rolls-Royce
Griffon 65/66
OUTPUT: 2050 hp (1528 kW)

FIRST FLIGHT DATE:
Spring 1945

ARMAMENT:
(Mk XVIII only) two Hispano
20 mm cannon and two
Browning 0.50-in machine guns
in wings; maximum bomb
load of 1000-lb (454 kg) on two
underwing racks

FEATURES:
Elliptical monoplane wings;
rectractable landing gear; close-
cowled inline engine; five-bladed
propeller; bubble canopy
(Mk XVIII only)

# Supermarine Attacker UK

single-seat, single-engined fighter-bomber

The Attacker was the Fleet Air Arm's first jet fighter to reach frontline service, the aircraft originally being conceived in response to Air Ministry Specification E 10/44 for an RAF day fighter. Incorporating the laminar flow, unswept wing fitted to the Supermarine Spiteful piston-engined fighter, the prototype made its first flight on 27 July 1946. The first British aircraft to be powered by the Rolls-Royce Nene turbojet, the Attacker failed to elicit any orders from the RAF. However, the Royal Navy showed great interest, and Supermarine modified the second and third prototypes to feature long-stroke undercarriages, deck arrestor hooks and wing lift spoilers in order to meet naval requirements for carrier operations. The first of 61 Attacker F 1/FB 1s was issued to 800 Naval Air Squadron in August 1951, thus ushering in the jet age to the Fleet Air Arm. By 1953, three frontline units had received Attackers, with the last of 84 FB 2s being delivered that year. Passed on to naval reserve units in 1954, all Attackers had been retired by 1957.

SPECIFICATION:

ACCOMMODATION:
pilot

DIMENSIONS:
LENGTH: 37 ft 6 in (11.43 m)
WINGSPAN: 36 ft 11 in (11.25 m)
HEIGHT: 9 ft 11 in (3.02 m)

WEIGHTS:
EMPTY: 8434 lb (3825 kg)
MAX T/O: 11,500 lb (5216 kg)

PERFORMANCE:
MAX SPEED: 590 mph (950 kmh)
RANGE: 1190 miles (1915 km)
POWERPLANT: Rolls-Royce Nene 3
OUTPUT: 5100 lb st (24.15 kN)

FIRST FLIGHT DATE:
27 July 1946

ARMAMENT:
four Hispano Mk 5 20 mm cannon in wings; maximum bomb/rocket load of 2000-lb (907 kg) on four underwing stores pylons

FEATURES:
Low-mounted straight laminar flow wing; retractable taildragger undercarriage; lateral engine air intakes below cockpit; fighter type bubble canopy; tailplane with dihedral; arrestor hook

# Supermarine Swift  UK

single-seat, single-engined fighter-bomber/reconnaissance aircraft

The first British swept-wing jet fighter to enter
frontline service, the Swift was developed over
many years from the Attacker. Although inferior in
many ways to contemporary designs both in
Europe and the US, the Swift was ordered into
production in 1950 as a safeguard against the
possible failure of the Hawker Hunter. The
prototype made its first flight on 5 August 1951, and
production aircraft reached the RAF in late 1952.
Control restrictions prevented the Swift F 1 from
making supersonic dives, and this was corrected
with the hastily reworked F 2, which also featured
additional guns and a cranked wing leading edge.
No 56 Sqn became the only fighter unit to receive
Swifts in February 1954, although it flew the aircraft
for little more than a year. The afterburning
equipped F 3 and variable tailplane F 4 were never
released for frontline use, despite huge numbers
being in production. The most successful variant
was the camera-equipped FR 5 (62 built), which flew
with Nos 2 and 79 Sqns in Germany until 1960.

SPECIFICATION:

ACCOMMODATION:
pilot

DIMENSIONS:
LENGTH: 42 ft 3 in (12.88 m)
WINGSPAN: 32 ft 4 in (9.85 m)
HEIGHT: 12 ft 6 in (3.8 m)

WEIGHTS:
EMPTY: 12,800 lb (5800 kg)
MAX T/O: 21,400 lb (9706 kg)

PERFORMANCE:
MAX SPEED: 685 mph (1100 kmh)
RANGE: 480 miles (772 km)
POWERPLANT: Rolls-Royce
Avon 114
OUTPUT: 9450 lb st (41.4 kN)

FIRST FLIGHT DATE:
5 August 1951

ARMAMENT:
two Aden 30 mm cannon in
fuselage; maximum bomb/rocket
load of 2000-lb (907 kg) on four
underwing stores pylons

FEATURES:
Low-mounted swept wing; lateral
engine air intakes below cockpit;
fighter type bubble canopy;
tailplane with dihedral; swept tail

# Supermarine Scimitar UK

single-seat, twin-engined fighter-bomber

The Scimitar was the first swept-wing single-seat fighter delivered to the Fleet Air Arm, and it was also the first British naval jet capable of supersonic flight, albeit in a shallow dive. Designed to meet naval specification N 113D, the Scimitar evolved from the Supermarine Types 508, with thin straight wings and a butterfly tail, through the 525, with swept wings and a conventional tail, to the near definitive Type 544. The latter, flown for the first time on 20 January 1956, had blown flaps, a slab tail, an area-ruled fuselage and dog-tooth swept wings. All these innovations made the fighter more suited to carrier operations. The Royal Navy ordered 100+ Scimitar F 1s, and the first production aircraft reached the fleet in August 1957. Only 76 were eventually delivered, however, and these were used primarily as reconnaissance fighters, with an interchangeable camera nose, and aerial tankers, fitted with an inflight refuelling 'buddy store'. Lacking radar, the Scimitar F 1 proved to be of limited value as a fighter interceptor and was retired in 1969.

SPECIFICATION:

ACCOMMODATION:
pilot

DIMENSIONS:
LENGTH: 55 ft 4 in (16.87 m)
WINGSPAN: 37 ft 2 in (11.33 m)
HEIGHT: 15 ft 3 in (4.65 m)

WEIGHTS:
EMPTY: 21,000 lb (9525 kg)
MAX T/O: 40,000 lb (18,144 kg)

PERFORMANCE:
MAX SPEED: 710 mph (1143 kmh)
RANGE: 600 miles (966 km)
POWERPLANT: two Rolls-Royce
Avon 202s
OUTPUT: 22,500 lb st (100 kN)

FIRST FLIGHT DATE:
27 April 1954

ARMAMENT:
four Aden 30 mm cannon under
nose; maximum bomb/rockets/
missiles load of 4000-lb (1814 kg)
on four underwing stores pylons

FEATURES:
Mid-mounted swept wing; lateral
engine air intakes below cockpit;
fighter type bubble canopy;
swept tail; long dorsal spine;
arrestor hook

# Tupolev тu-4 USA

eleven-seat, four-engined monoplane heavy bomber

Based on the в-29, the тu-4 was developed after the
ussr acquired three intact Superfortresses that were
'lost' during raids on Manchuria in 1944. Far in
advance of anything then in service with the Soviet
Air Force, the в-29s proved hugely influential in
allowing the ussr to develop a strategic bombing
capability. The reversed engineered тu-4 made its
public debut on 3 August 1947 at the Aviation Day
parade over Moscow's Tushino Airport. Powered by
Shvetsov versions of the Wright Duplex Cyclone
(known as the ash-73тk), these aircraft had been
constructed in two purpose-built factories in the
Urals. Despite numerous teething problems with
both the тu-4 and the ash-73тk engines, aircraft
begin to enter service with the Soviet strategic
bombing arm in 1948. By the end of 1949 300 тu-4s
had entered service, and approximately 1200 were
eventually built in the Soviet Union, with some of
these being passed on to China. The тu-4 was
retired from frontline use in the ussr in the early
1960s, although Chinese aircraft remained in
service into the 1970s.

## SPECIFICATION:

**ACCOMMODATION:**
pilot, co-pilot, flight engineer,
navigator, bombardier/nose
gunner, radar operator, radio
operator, central fire controller/
top gunner, right and left
gunners, tail gunner

**DIMENSIONS:**
LENGTH: 99 ft 0 in (30.18 m)
WINGSPAN: 141 ft 3 in (43.05 m)
HEIGHT: 29 ft 7 in (9.02 m)

**WEIGHTS:**
EMPTY: 77,756 lb (35,270 kg)
MAX T/O: 145,500 lb (65,999 kg)

**PERFORMANCE:**
MAX SPEED: 347 mph (558 kmh)
RANGE: 3170 miles (5100 km)
POWERPLANT: four Shvetsov
ash-73тks
OUTPUT: 9600 hp (7159 kW)

**FIRST FLIGHT DATE:**
19 May 1947

**ARMAMENT:**
four remote-controlled and two
manned (ball/tail) turrets with
twin в-20e 0.50-in machine guns
on top/bottom of fuselage;
17,636 lb (8000 kg) bombs in
bomb-bay

**FEATURES:**
Monoplane wing; radial engines

# Tupolev Tu-16 USSR

four-seat, twin-engined bomber/tanker/reconnaissance aircraft

One of Russia's most effective, and enduring, jet bombers, the TU-16 was developed as a twin-engined medium bomber to complement the strategic Myasischev M-4 and Tupolev TU-95. The creation of the bomber was made possible by the advent of the Mikulin AM-3 turbojet, and the prototype made its maiden flight on 27 April 1952. The aircraft's bomb-bay was sized to accommodate the Soviet Union's largest bomb (20,000-lb FAB-9000), with the layout of the rest of the fuselage being strongly influenced by Tupolev's experience with the TU-4. Early production TU-16A nuclear bombers entered service in 1954, and they were followed by a multitude of types which served with the Soviet Air Force for much of the Cold War. The TU-16T torpedo bomber soon followed, as did the TU-16N tanker. The aircraft was modified to carry air-to-surface missiles in the late 1950s, and electronic intelligence gathering and maritime reconnaissance versions were also soon in production. Built under licence in China as the Xian H-6, over 2000 TU-16/H-6s were produced.

SPECIFICATION:

**ACCOMMODATION:**
pilot, co-pilot, navigator/bombardier, tail gunner

**DIMENSIONS:**
LENGTH: 114 ft 2 in (34.80 m)
WINGSPAN: 108 ft 3 in (32.99 m)
HEIGHT: 34 ft 0 in (10.36 m)

**WEIGHTS:**
EMPTY: 82,012 lb (37,200 kg)
MAX T/O: 167,110 lb (75,800 kg)

**PERFORMANCE:**
MAX SPEED: 652 mph (1050 kmh)
RANGE: 4474 miles (7200 km)
POWERPLANT: two MNPK 'Soyuz' (Mikulin) AM-3M-500s
OUTPUT: 41,890 lb st (186.4 kN)

**FIRST FLIGHT DATE:**
27 April 1952

**ARMAMENT:**
two remote-controlled (dorsal/ventral) and one manned (tail) turrets with twin NR-23 23 mm cannon; 19,800 lb (9000 kg) of bombs/missiles in bomb-bay or on two underwing stores pylons

**FEATURES:**
Mid-mounted swept wing with trailing edge fairings; engines-mounted in wing roots

# Tupolev Tu-95/142 USSR

seven-seat, four-engined bomber/maritime patrol aircraft

Developed in the early 1950s to take advantage of new turboprop engines then becoming available, the Tu-95 was powered by four KKBM NK-12MVS driving eight-bladed counter-rotating propellers. Thanks to these, and the aircraft's unique swept wing layout, the aircraft boasted a decent top speed and substantial range. Like the Tu-16, the Tu-95 featured a fuselage cross-section identical to the Tu-4. The prototype flew for the first time on 12 November 1952, and Tu-95M nuclear bombers reached the Soviet Air Force four years later. As with the Tu-16, these aircraft were converted to carry Kh-series cruise missiles, while others became maritime reconnaissance Tu-95MR/RTS. The final bomber variant built was the Tu-95MS, which entered service in 1983. The Tu-142 was a dedicated ASW platform developed from the Tu-95 in the late 1960s, the aircraft featuring a stretched fuselage, search radar, fin tip MAD boom and sonobuoys/mines/torpedoes. This version was also sold to India. Tu-95s and Tu-142s remain in service today in Russia, Ukraine and India.

SPECIFICATION:

ACCOMMODATION:
pilot, co-pilot, communications operator, navigator, defensive systems operator, flight engineer, tail gunner

DIMENSIONS:
LENGTH: 161 ft 2 in (49.13 m)
WINGSPAN: 164 ft 2 in (50.04 m)
HEIGHT: 43 ft 8 in (13.30 m)

WEIGHTS:
EMPTY: 264,550 lb (120,000 kg)
MAX T/O: 412,258 lb (187,000 kg)

PERFORMANCE:
MAX SPEED: 575 mph (925 kmh)
RANGE: 9197 miles (14,800 km)
POWERPLANT: four KKBM (Kuznetsov) NK-12MVS
OUTPUT: 59,180 shp (44,140 kW)

FIRST FLIGHT DATE:
12 November 1952

ARMAMENT:
one manned 23 mm cannon in tail turret; 24,244 lb (11,000 kg) of bombs/missiles in bomb-bay or on two underwing stores pylons

FEATURES:
Shoulder-mounted swept wings; wing-mounted turboprop engines with counter-rotating propellers on wings; manned tail turret; swept-back tailplane

# Tupolev **TU-22**  USSR

three-seat, twin-engined bomber/reconnaissance/electronic warfare aircraft

The original TU-22 (as opposed to the current TU-22M) was the first supersonic Soviet bomber, the aircraft stemming from a 1955 study undertaken by Tupolev to produce an aircraft capable of penetrating modern defences at high speed with a payload similar to the subsonic TU-16. Flown in prototype form in September 1959, the TU-22 remained unknown in the west until the Tushino Aviation Day flypast of 1961. The TU-22 boasted an efficient wing derived from Sukhoi's TU-28P all-weather fighter, and two Dobrynin RD-7M-2 engines mounted at the base of the fin. The positioning of the latter left the fuselage free for fuel and gave both engines undisturbed airflow. Only 250 TU-22s were built, the initial production variant being a conventional/nuclear bomber. The bulk of the aircraft built were KH-22 cruise missile-capable, and 17 examples of this version were supplied to Libya and nine to Iraq. Some 60 TU-22R reconnaissance aircraft were also built, and most surviving examples were converted into electronic warfare platforms in the 1980s. All have now been retired.

## SPECIFICATION:

**ACCOMMODATION:**
pilot, co-pilot, navigator/systems operator

**DIMENSIONS:**
LENGTH: 139 ft 9 in (42.60 m)
WINGSPAN: 77 ft 0 in (23.50 m)
HEIGHT: 35 ft 0 in (10.67 m)

**WEIGHTS:**
EMPTY: 83,995 lb (38,100 kg)
MAX T/O: 207,230 lb (94,000 kg)

**PERFORMANCE:**
MAX SPEED: 920 mph (1480 kmh)
RANGE: 1926 miles (3100 km)
POWERPLANT: two Dobrynin RD-7M-2S
OUTPUT: 72,750 lb st (326 kN)

**FIRST FLIGHT DATE:**
September 1959

**ARMAMENT:**
one remote-controlled NR-23 23 mm cannon in tail; 17,600 lb (7983 kg) of bombs/missiles in bomb-bay

**FEATURES:**
Low-mounted swept wing with trailing edge fairings; engines-mounted at base of fine; unmanned tail barbette; low-mounted swept-back horizontal tailplane, nose-mounted refuelling probe

# Vickers Valetta UK

38-seat, twin-engined transport aircraft

Derived from the Vickers Viking civil airliner (four of which had been supplied to the RAF for use by the King's Flight in 1947), the Valetta prototype flew for the first time on 30 June 1947. In order to render the civilian design suitable for military use, Vickers fitted a strengthened fuselage floor, large loading doors on the port side, longer stroke landing gear oleos and a modified fuel system. The aircraft also had more powerful Bristol Hercules 230s fitted in place of the Viking's 634s. Valetta C 1s entered service in 1948, the aircraft being equipped for troop-carrying, glider-towing, supply dropping, air ambulance duties and general freighting. The follow-on C 2 was configured for VIP transportation duties, while the T 3 was fitted out as a 'flying classroom' for the training of navigators. The latter version was the last of 250+ Valettas built for the RAF, with the final example being delivered in September 1952. Supplanting Dakotas and Hastings within Transport Command, Valettas served across the globe until retired in 1966-67.

SPECIFICATION:

ACCOMMODATION:
pilot, co-pilot, navigator, crew chief and up to 34 passengers

DIMENSIONS:
LENGTH: 62 ft 11 in (18.93 m)
WINGSPAN: 89 ft 3 in (27.21 m)
HEIGHT: 19 ft 6 in (5.97 m)

WEIGHTS:
EMPTY: 24,854 lb (11,274 kg)
MAX T/O: 36,500 lb (16,556 kg)

PERFORMANCE:
MAX SPEED: 294 mph (470 kmh)
RANGE: 1410 miles (2256 km)
POWERPLANT: two Bristol Hercules 230s
OUTPUT: 3950 hp (2945 kW)

FIRST FLIGHT DATE:
30 June 1947

FEATURES:
Mid-mounted straight-wing layout; two close-cowled radial engines; oval-sectioned fuselage; rectractable taildragger undercarriage; tall tail fin

# Vickers Varsity UK

nine-seat, twin-engined training aircraft

Built as a post-war replacement for the Wellington T 10 crew trainer within the RAF, the Varsity was designed to meet Air Ministry Specification T 13/48. The Varsity had a tricycle undercarriage, giving it landing characteristics more akin to the modern bomber and transport types it was charged with representing within Flying Training Command. In order to accommodate the new undercarriage, the aircraft's nose was lengthened – the wingspan was also increased by six feet. A pannier was added beneath the fuselage to provide facilities for bomb-aiming practice, the forward section housing the bomb-aiming position and the rear section stowage for 24 25-lb practice bombs. Full radar and radio equipment, including H2S and Rebecca, was also carried. The prototype Varsity made its first flight on 17 July 1949, and production orders for 162 T 1s then followed. Pilots, navigators and bomb-aimers destined for multi-engined types all received advanced instruction on the Varsity from 1951 onwards with Flying Training Command. Surviving examples were retired in the early 1970s.

SPECIFICATION:

**ACCOMMODATION:**
pilot, co-pilot, student signaller, instructor signaller, student bomb-aimer, instructor bomb-aimer, two student navigators and one instructor navigator

**DIMENSIONS:**
LENGTH: 67 ft 6 in (20.60 m)
WINGSPAN: 95 ft 7 in (29.16 m)
HEIGHT: 19 ft 6 in (7.04 m)

**WEIGHTS:**
EMPTY: 27,040 lb (12,265 kg)
MAX T/O: 37,500 lb (17,010 kg)

**PERFORMANCE:**
MAX SPEED: 288 mph (461 kmh)
RANGE: 2648 miles (4237 km)
POWERPLANT: two Bristol Hercules 264s
OUTPUT: 3900 hp (2908 kW)

**FIRST FLIGHT DATE:**
17 July 1949

**ARMAMENT:**
maximum bomb load of 600-lb (272 kg) in underfuselage pannier

**FEATURES:**
Mid-mounted straight-wing layout; two close-cowled radial engines; oval-sectioned fuselage; rectractable tricycle under-carriage; tall tail fin; pannier under fuselage

# Vickers Valiant UK

five-seat, four-engined bomber/tanker/strategic reconnaissance aircraft

The first of three v-bombers to enter frontline service with the RAF, the Valiant was designed to meet Air Ministry Specification B 9/48. Despite it being less capable than either the Vulcan or Victor which followed, the more conventional Valiant was nevertheless ordered into production because it would be ready sooner. The prototype made its first flight on 18 May 1951, and production Valiant B 1s were delivered to Bomber Command in early 1955. The following year Valiants dropped bombs on Egyptian Air Force airfields during the opening phase of the Suez campaign. Befitting its v-bomber role, B 1s conducted all live trials for the British air-dropped nuclear weapons programme. Interspersed within the B 1 production line at Weybridge were 11 B(PR) 1 photo-reconnaissance Valiants and 14 B(PR)K tankers. The final 48 Valiants (which brought total production to 107 aircraft) were delivered as B(K) bomber-tankers. Switched to the low-level interdictor mission in 1963, the Valiant fleet experienced chronic fatigue problems the following year and were hastily scrapped.

SPECIFICATION:

ACCOMMODATION:
pilot, co-pilot, tactical navigator, radar operator, air electronics operator

DIMENSIONS:
LENGTH: 108 ft 3 in (33 m)
WINGSPAN: 114 ft 4 in (34.85 m)
HEIGHT: 32 ft 2 in (9.80 m)

WEIGHTS:
EMPTY: 75,881 lb (34,419 kg)
MAX T/O: 175,000 lb (79,378 kg)

PERFORMANCE:
MAX SPEED: 567 mph (912 kmh)
RANGE: 4500 miles (7242 km)
POWERPLANT: four Rolls-Royce Avon 204s
OUTPUT: 40,200 lb st (180.5 kN)

FIRST FLIGHT DATE:
18 May 1951

ARMAMENT:
up to 21,000-lb (9525 kg) of bombs in internal bomb-bay

FEATURES:
Shoulder-mounted swept wing; engines housed within wing roots; swept tail; wing-mounted drop tanks

# Vought F7U Cutlass  USA

single-seat, single-engined fighter-bomber

Its layout strongly influenced by experimental tailless designs built by Arado in World War 2, the Cutlass appeared to offer the US Navy an ideal solution to its unique requirements for carrier-based fighters. Theoretically boasting a high rate of climb and high top speed, all in a comparatively small package, three XF7U-1 prototypes were ordered in June 1946. These were to be powered by two Westinghouse J34 engines. The first example flew on 29 September 1948, and it was followed by 14 F7U-1s in 1950-51. Severe problems with the J34 resulted in the engine's cancellation, and an overall redesign of the Cutlass in light of poor handling characteristics saw the F7U-3 produced from late 1951. This aircraft featured a new nose shape and redesigned fins and, eventually, Westinghouse J46 engines. Some 180 were built, and these equipped four fleet squadrons. The final production variant was the missile-armed F7U-3M, 98 of which were constructed up to December 1955. Difficult to fly, and a maintenance nightmare, surviving Cutlasses were replaced by the Crusader in the late 1950s.

SPECIFICATION:

ACCOMMODATION:
pilot

DIMENSIONS:
LENGTH: 44 ft 3 in (13.48 m)
WINGSPAN: 38 ft 8 in (11.78 m)
HEIGHT: 14 ft 7 in (4.48 m)

WEIGHTS:
EMPTY: 15,900 lb (7212 kg)
MAX T/O: 31,642 lb (14,353 kg)

PERFORMANCE:
MAX SPEED: 695 mph (1120 kmh)
RANGE: 1400 miles (2250 km)
POWERPLANT: two Westinghouse J46-W-8Bs
OUTPUT: 12,000 lb st (54 kN)

FIRST FLIGHT DATE:
29 September 1948

ARMAMENT:
four M-24 20 mm cannon in fuselage; maximum bomb/rocket/missile load of 5500-lb (2495 kg) on four underwing stores pylons

FEATURES:
Mid-mounted swept-wing; tricycle landing gear, with extended nose gear leg; lateral engine air intakes behind cockpit; tailless fuselage (no horizontal tailplanes)

# Vought F-8 Crusader USA

single-seat, single-engined fighter-bomber/reconnaissance aircraft

The US Navy's first supersonic day interceptor and its last single-engined, single-seat fighter, the Crusader was built in response to a 1952 naval requirement for an aircraft with high-speed performance, but a 115-mph landing speed. The Crusader achieved the desired recovery speed through the employment of a unique high-mounted variable incidence wing which angled up to increase drag – it was also employed during take-off, as it greatly increased lift. The prototype flew for the first time on 25 March 1955, and service deliveries commenced in March 1957. Arguably the world's best fighter at the time, no fewer than 1259 Crusaders were built. This number included unarmed photo-reconnaissance RF-8s, which were used into the 1980s. A veteran of combat in Vietnam, where it was flown by both the Navy and Marines, the Crusader proved so popular that 446 airframes were refurbished to allow them to serve until the mid-1970s. Second-hand jets were also supplied to the Philippines, and France acquired 42 F-8(FN)s, which it flew from its carriers until 2000.

SPECIFICATION:

ACCOMMODATION:
pilot

DIMENSIONS:
LENGTH: 54 ft 3 in (16.54 m)
WINGSPAN: 35 ft 8 in (10.87 m)
HEIGHT: 15 ft 9 in (4.80 m)

WEIGHTS:
EMPTY: 19,700 lb (8935 kg)
MAX T/O: 34,000 lb (14,420 kg)

PERFORMANCE:
MAX SPEED: 1105 mph (1780 kmh)
RANGE: 1400 miles (2250 km)
POWERPLANT: Pratt & Whitney
J57-PW-20A
OUTPUT: 18,000 lb st (80.1 kN)

FIRST FLIGHT DATE:
25 March 1955

ARMAMENT:
four Colt Mk 12 20 mm cannon in
fuselage; maximum bomb/
rocket/missile load of 5000-lb
(2268 kg) on two underwing and
four fuselage side stores pylons

FEATURES:
High-mounted swept-wing, with
variable incidence; engine air
intake below nose; fighter style
canopy; ventral fins; all-moving
tailplanes

# Vought A-7 Corsair II USA

single-seat, single-engined attack aircraft

The A-7 Corsair II was the winner of the US Navy's 1963 light attack aircraft competition, which sought to find a replacement for the A-4 Skyhawk. By restricting its performance to high subsonic speed, the A-7 was ideally suited to the role of carrier-based 'bomb truck', as it could carry nearly twice as much ordnance as the A-4 over vast distances. The prototype Corsair II completed its first flight on 27 September 1965, and two years later the A-7A made its combat debut over Vietnam. By then, in a rare example of cross-service unity, the USAF had also selected the Corsair II to fill a requirement for a tactical attack aircraft. Some 380 A-7DS were bought, and these served into the late 1980s. This variant introduced the definitive Allison TF41 (licence-built Rolls-Royce Spey) turbofan in place of the Pratt & Whitney TF30, and the Navy purchased 535 similarly powered A-7ES up to 1983. Retired from fleet service in 1991, a handful of Corsair IIS still serve with the Greek Air Force and Thai Navy.

SPECIFICATION:

**ACCOMMODATION:**
pilot

**DIMENSIONS:**
LENGTH: 46 ft 1.5 in (14.06 m)
WINGSPAN: 38 ft 9 in (11.80 m)
HEIGHT: 16 ft 0.75 in (4.90 m)

**WEIGHTS:**
EMPTY: 19,781 lb (8972 kg)
MAX T/O: 42,000 lb (19,050 kg)

**PERFORMANCE:**
MAX SPEED: 698 mph (1123 kmh)
RANGE: 2878 miles (4605 km)
POWERPLANT: Allison TF41-A-1
OUTPUT: 15,000 lb st (66.7 kN)

**FIRST FLIGHT DATE:**
27 September 1965

**ARMAMENT:**
one M61 Vulcan 20 mm cannon in fuselage; maximum bomb/rocket/missile load of 20,000-lb (9072 kg) on six underwing and two fuselage side stores pylons

**FEATURES:**
High-mounted wing; engine air intake below nose; fighter style canopy; all-moving tailplanes

# Westland Wyvern UK

single-seat, single-engined attack aircraft

One of the heaviest and most complex single-engined combat aircraft to enter frontline service, the Wyvern was designed to meet challenging 1944 Royal Navy Specification N 11/44 covering the production of a day fighter which could carry a torpedo. Following years of agonising work at Westland with the temperamental Rolls-Royce Eagle sleeve valve engine, and its eventual abandonment in favour of the newly developed Armstrong Siddeley Python turboprop, the first Wyvern s 4 production aircraft finally reached the fleet in mid-1953! By then the fighter requirement had long since been fulfilled by jet-powered aircraft, so the brutish Wyvern was used exclusively in the ground-attack role. Boasting contra-rotating propellers, a total of just 107 production aircraft were built, and these were flown by four frontline units from 1953 until replaced by Sea Hawks in 1958. The high point of the aircraft's brief frontline career came in November 1956 when 830 and 831 Naval Air Squadrons were involved in the Suez campaign, flying from the deck of HMS *Eagle*.

SPECIFICATION:

**ACCOMMODATION:**
pilot

**DIMENSIONS:**
LENGTH: 42 ft 3 in (12.88 m)
WINGSPAN: 44 ft 0 in (13.41 m)
HEIGHT: 15 ft 9 in (4.80 m)

**WEIGHTS:**
EMPTY: 15,608 lb (7080 kg)
MAX T/O: 24,500 lb (11,115 kg)

**PERFORMANCE:**
MAX SPEED: 440 mph (704 kmh)
RANGE: 900 miles (1450 km)
POWERPLANT: Armstrong Siddeley Python 101
OUTPUT: 4110 shp (3065 kW)

**FIRST FLIGHT DATE:**
12 December 1946

**ARMAMENT:**
Four wing-mounted Hispano Mk v 20 mm cannon; up to 3000-lb (1361 kg) of bombs/rockets/torpedoes on one underfuselage and two underwing stores pylons

**FEATURES:**
Straight, folding wing; close-cowled turboprop engine; arrestor hook; bubble canopy; tall tail fin; tailplane with dihedral and auxiliary fins

# Yakovlev Yak-11 USSR & CZECHOSLOVAKIA

two-seat, single-engined intermediate trainer

Designed as an advanced fighter/trainer variant of the Yak-3 for use with the Soviet Air Force, the concept of the Yak-11 was first discussed officially in mid-1944. Given a low production priority, a converted Yak-3 prototype (designated Yak-3UTI) finally flew in 1945. A definitive Yak-11 made its first flight 12 months later, the aircraft utilising many slightly modified Yak-3 parts. Powered by a Shvetsov ASh-21 radial engine, the aircraft was put into series production in early 1947, with the first completed aircraft being delivered by the middle of that year. Yakovlev produced 3859 basic Yak-11s before progressing to the U-model, which featured a nosewheel for the training of jet fighter pilots. This variant replaced many standard Yak-11s during 1958. With production of the latter aircraft having ceased in the USSR in 1954, LET of Czechoslovakia commenced building the aircraft under licence with the designation C.11 that same year. Some 707 were constructed, and aside from its use by Warsaw Pact nations, the aircraft was also exported to numerous communist countries.

SPECIFCATION:

ACCOMMODATION:
two pilots seated in tandem

DIMENSIONS:
LENGTH: 27 ft 10.7 in (8.50 m)
WINGSPAN: 30 ft 10 in (9.40 m)
HEIGHT: 10 ft 9 in (3.28 m)

WEIGHTS:
EMPTY: 4189 lb (1900 kg)
MAX T/O: 5379 lb (2440 kg)

PERFORMANCE:
MAX SPEED: 295 mph (475 kmh)
RANGE: 800 miles (1290 km)
POWERPLANT: Shvetsov ASl-21
OUTPUT: 730 hp (425 kW)

FIRST FLIGHT DATE:
1946

ARMAMENT:
one UBS 12.7 mm machine gun on top decking of nose; up to 360-lb (200 kg) of bombs/rockets on two underwing racks

FEATURES:
Straight-wing layout; retractable taildragger landing gear; close-cowled radial engine; long canopy

# Yakovlev Yak-18/Nanchang CJ-5/6    USSR & CHINA

two-seat, single-engined basic trainer

Derived from the pre-war Yak UT-2, the Yak-18 was built from the outset as a dedicated basic trainer for the Soviet Air Force. The first production aircraft entered service in the USSR in 1947. In 1955 the Yak-18U was introduced, the new aircraft featuring a lengthened fuselage and semi-retractable tricycle undercarriage. Wing dihedral was also increased, but despite a considerable increase in all up weight, the aircraft still relied on the venerable Shvetsov M-11FR radial. This engine was replaced with the advent of the Yak-18A in 1957, the new aircraft boasting a 260 hp Ivchyenko AI-14R radial in a revised cowling. By this time licence-production had begun in China on the CJ-5, followed by the improved CJ-6/6A (total production of the later aircraft came to 1800+). The final Yakovlev-built variant to enter production was the four-seat Yak-18T tourer, which first appeared in 1967 with side-by-side seating for both the pilot(s) and passengers. Production of the Yak-18 trainer stopped in late 1967 after the delivery of 6760 aircraft, many of which had been exported.

SPECIFICATION:

ACCOMMODATION:
two pilots seated in tandem, one pilot (Yak-18PM) or two pilots seated side-by-side and two passengers (Yak-18T)

DIMENSIONS:
LENGTH: 28 ft 0 in (8.53 m)
WINGSPAN: 34 ft 9.25 in (10.60 m)
HEIGHT: 11 ft 0 in (3.35 m)

WEIGHTS:
EMPTY: 2259 lb (1025 kg)
MAX T/O: 2900 lb (1316 kg)

PERFORMANCE:
MAX SPEED: 163 mph (263 kmh)
RANGE: 630 miles (1015 km)
POWERPLANT: Shvetsov M-11FR (Yak-18/18U) or Ivchyenko AI-14R (Yak-18A/P)
OUTPUT: 160 hp (119 kW) and 260 hp (193 kW) respectively

FIRST FLIGHT DATE:
1946

FEATURES:
Straight-wing; retractable landing gear (variants with taildragger and tricycle undercarriage); close-cowled radial engine; long canopy

# Yakovlev Yak-17 USSR

single/two-seat, single-engined fighter/trainer

A more refined version of the pioneering Yak-15 fighter, which was in itself little more than a Yak-3 that had hastily had its piston engine replaced with a Soviet copy (RD-10) of the German Jumo 004 turbojet engine, the Yak-17 was flown in prototype form in early 1947. This aircraft featured a tricycle undercarriage (the Yak-15 was a taildragger), wingtip tanks, a redesigned tail fin and an improved RD-10A engine. The Yak-17 replaced the Yak-15 on the production line in late 1947, and 430 were built in the space of a year. At least 150 of these were two-seat Yak-17UTI trainers, 20 of which were exported to Poland. The Polish government actually committed to licence production of the single-seat Yak-17 and its RD-10A engine, but the programme was abandoned in early 1951 before any aircraft had actually been built due to the availability of the far superior MiG-15. The Yak-17 was phased out of Soviet service in 1951, followed by the UTI variant two years later. Polish Yak-17UTIs lingered on until 1955.

SPECIFICATION:

ACCOMMODATION:
pilot, and two pilots in tandem
(Yak-17UTI)

DIMENSIONS:
LENGTH: 28 ft 9.66 in (8.78 m)
WINGSPAN: 30 ft 2.25 in (9.20 m)
HEIGHT: 6 ft 10 in (2.10 m)

WEIGHTS:
EMPTY: 5357 lb (2430 kg)
MAX T/O: 7326 lb (3323 kg)

PERFORMANCE:
MAX SPEED: 466 mph (750 kmh)
RANGE: 446 miles (717 km)
POWERPLANT: RD-10A
OUTPUT: 2205 lb st (9.7 kN)

FIRST FLIGHT DATE:
Early 1947

ARMAMENT:
two NS-23 23mm cannon in nose

FEATURES:
Mid-mounted straight wing
layout; tricycle landing gear;
engine air intake in nose;
fighter type bubble canopy;
wingtip tanks

# Yakovlev yak-23 USSR

single-seat, single-engined fighter

Although looking outwardly similar to the YAK-15/17 due to its adoption of the so-called redan (stepped) configuration that saw the engine mounted ahead of the cockpit, the YAK-23 was in fact a new design that owed nothing to the piston-engined heritage of the first Yakovlev jet fighters. Of all-metal stressed-skin construction, and powered by a vastly superior Rolls-Royce Derwent engine, the first prototype was flown on 17 June 1947. Seen as a back-up for the much more advanced Nene-engined MIG-15 and YAK-30 swept-wing designs then under development, the YAK-23 made it into limited production thanks to its outstanding agility. Aircraft started to reach the frontline in early 1949, and a total of 310 YAK-23s had been built by the time production was terminated in favour of the MIG-15 in 1950. YAK-23s replaced YAK-17s within the Soviet Air Force, while Czechoslovakia, Romania and Bulgaria each received 12 jets, and Poland 95. All surviving YAK-23s had been replaced in Soviet and Warsaw Pact service by MIG-15s come the mid-1950s.

SPECIFICATION:

ACCOMMODATION:
pilot

DIMENSIONS:
LENGTH: 26 ft 9.25 in (8.16 m)
WINGSPAN: 28 ft 6 in (8.69 m)
HEIGHT: 9 ft 10 in (3 m)

WEIGHTS:
EMPTY: 6395 lb (2900 kg)
MAX T/O: 10,990 lb (4985 kg)

PERFORMANCE:
MAX SPEED: 550 mph (885 kmh)
RANGE: 870 miles (1400 km)
POWERPLANT: Klimov RD-500
OUTPUT: 3527 lb st (15.6 kN)

FIRST FLIGHT DATE:
17 June 1947

ARMAMENT:
two NS-23 23mm cannon in nose

FEATURES:
Mid-mounted straight wing layout; tricycle landing gear; engine air intake in nose; fighter type bubble canopy

# Yakovlev Yak-28 USSR

two-seat, twin-engined fighter/attack/reconnaissance/EW aircraft

The final evolution of Yakovlev's long-lived family of twin-engined combat aircraft, the supersonic-capable YAK-28 multi-role aircraft was flown in tactical attack bomber form on 5 March 1958. The first version to enter frontline service was the YAK-28B, fitted with an RBR-3 radar bombing system in the nose. This was followed by the YAK-28I/L tactical attack aircraft and, in 1961, the YAK-28P all-weather interceptor. Intended for low and medium altitude operation, the latter featured Orel-D radar in an ogival, solid radome. The fighter variant was improved during its production life, and by the time the last examples reached the frontline in 1967, its radome had been drastically lengthened and overall performance significantly improved. A dedicated photo-reconnaissance variant was also produced in 1963, the YAK-28R spawning the late-build YAK-28PP electronic warfare platform. Created in order to provide ECM jamming for bombers and strike aircraft, these aircraft were finally replaced by dedicated SU-24 EW variants in 1989.

SPECIFICATION:

ACCOMMODATION:
pilot, navigator/bomb aimer/
radar-sensor operator

DIMENSIONS:
LENGTH: 71 ft 0.5 in (17.65 m)
WINGSPAN: 42 ft 6 in (12.95 m)
HEIGHT: 12 ft 11.5 in (3.95 m)

WEIGHTS:
EMPTY: 24,250 lb (11,000 kg)
MAX T/O: 41,000 lb (18,600 kg)

PERFORMANCE:
MAX SPEED: 1174 mph (1890 kmh)
RANGE: 1634 miles (2630 km)
POWERPLANT: two Tumanskii
R-11AF-2-300S
OUTPUT: 26,984 lb st (119.75 kN)

FIRST FLIGHT DATE:
5 March 1958

ARMAMENT:
two NR-30 30 mm cannon in
fuselage; provision for up to
4400-lb (2000 kg) of bombs/
rockets/missiles split between
bomb-bay and two underwing
stores pylons

FEATURES:
Shoulder-mounted swept-wing
layout; bicycle landing gear with
wingtip outriggers; engines-
mounted beneath wings; swept
tail fin

# Yakovlev Yak-38 USSR

single-seat, three-engined fighter

Russia's first, and only, operational v/STOL aircraft, the Yak-38 enjoyed only modest success during its 20-year frontline career. Developed from the Yak-36 research platform, which undertook its first flight in 1966, the Yak-38 featured two vertically-mounted lift jets behind the cockpit entirely separate to the main Tumanskii turbojet in the centre fuselage. The prototype Yak-38 (designated Yak-36M at the time) flew for the first time on 28 May 1970, and sea trials took place aboard the STOL carrier *Moskva* in 1972, followed by more deck time on *Kiev* two years later. By 1976 a test squadron of Yak-36Ms were being regularly flown at sea, and aircraft (redesignated Yak-38) entered frontline Soviet Navy service in 1978. The improved Yak-38M was introduced following evaluation of the original Yak-38 in operational conditions in Afghanistan in 1980. This variant had more power, more fuel and increased armament. A total of 100 Yak-38s had been built by the time production ended in 1987, with 20 of these being two-seat Yak-38U trainers. All had been withdrawn by the late 1990s.

SPECIFICATION:

ACCOMMODATION:
pilot

DIMENSIONS:
LENGTH: 50 ft 10 in (15.50 m)
WINGSPAN: 24 ft 0 in (7.32 m)
HEIGHT: 14 ft 4 in (4.37 m)

WEIGHTS:
EMPTY: 16,500 lb (7485 kg)
MAX T/O: 28,660 lb (13,000 kg)

PERFORMANCE:
MAX SPEED: 628 mph (1010 kmh)
RANGE: 231 miles (370 km)
POWERPLANT: one Tumanskii
R-27V-300 and two RKBM
RD-36-35FVRS
OUTPUT: 14,990 lb st (66.7 kN) and
14,350 lb st (63.8 kN) respectively

FIRST FLIGHT DATE:
28 May 1970

ARMAMENT:
provision for up to 4400-lb
(2000 kg) of bombs/rockets/
missiles/gun pods on four
underwing stores pylons

FEATURES:
Shoulder-mounted swept-wing
layout; two lift engines behind
cockpit and one centrally-
mounted engine; swept tail fin;
lateral engine air intakes behind
cockpit

# Yakovlev Yak-50   USSR

single-seat, single-engined aerobatic aircraft

Derived from the Yak-18 family of basic training aircraft, the single-seat Yak-50 was built specially for the Soviet aerobatic team to use in competition in the 1976 aerobatic championship, held in Kiev. The aircraft was based on the taildragger, aft cockpit Yak-18PS, but with a new stress-skinned airframe and wings inspired by the Yak-20 of 1950. Boasting a tear-drop canopy and Yak-18T M-14P engine, the prototype flew in mid-1975. Cleared to unrestricted +9/-6 g manoeuvres, six production Yak-50s swept the board in the Kiev championship the following year – a Yak-50 also won the 1982 championship as well. In the wake of its success, substantial numbers of Yak-50s were subsequently built. Although it was never directly introduced into Soviet military service, military pilots who were trained in state-sponsored aeroclubs flew the Yak-50 prior to entering the Air Force. It was also used as a primary aerobatic trainer by air forces throughout the Warsaw Pact.

SPECIFICATION:

ACCOMMODATION:
pilot

DIMENSIONS:
LENGTH: 25 ft 7 in (7.80 m)
WINGSPAN: 31 ft 2 in (9.50 m)
HEIGHT: 10 ft 6 in (3.20 m)

WEIGHTS:
EMPTY: 1683 lb (765 kg)
MAX T/O: 1980 lb (900 kg)

PERFORMANCE:
MAX SPEED: 200 mph (320 kmh)
RANGE: 630 miles (1015 km)
POWERPLANT: VMKB (Vedenyev)
M-14P
OUTPUT: 360 hp (268 kW)

FIRST FLIGHT DATE:
Summer 1975

FEATURES:
Straight-wing; retractable taildragger landing gear; close-cowled radial engine; bubble canopy

# Yakovlev YAK-52 USSR & ROMANIA

two-seat, single-engined basic trainer

Built as the successor to the YAK-18 family by
Yakovlev in the mid-1970s, the YAK-52 bore a strong
family resemblance to its predecessor despite
having been totally redesigned by the
manufacturer. Its stressed-skin airframe derived
from the YAK-50 and production YAK-52s were built
by the IAV factory at Bacau, in Romania. Work
commenced on the first aircraft in 1979, and
deliveries to the USSR began the following year. By
mid-1992 1600+ had been constructed primarily for
use in the former Soviet Union. Like the YAK-50, the
aircraft is fully aerobatic, and one of its unique
features centres on its tricycle undercarriage,
whose tyres remain exposed when the gear is
retracted so as to give the fuselage some protection
in the event of a wheels-up landing. IAV became
Aerostar following the removal of the communist
regime in Romania, and the type remains in
production today. Aside from its employment with
the Russian and Romanian air forces, a dozen
YAK-52s were also been supplied to the Hungarian
Air Force in 1994.

SPECIFICATION:

**ACCOMMODATION:**
two pilots in tandem

**DIMENSIONS:**
LENGTH: 25 ft 5 in (7.75 m)
WINGSPAN: 30 ft 6.25 in (9.30 m)
HEIGHT: 8 ft 10.25 in (2.70 m)

**WEIGHTS:**
EMPTY: 2238 lb (1015 kg)
MAX T/O: 2877 lb (1305 kg)

**PERFORMANCE:**
MAX SPEED: 223 mph (360 kmh)
RANGE: 310 miles (500 km)
POWERPLANT: VMKB (Vedenyev)
M-14P
OUTPUT: 360 hp (268 kW)

**FIRST FLIGHT DATE:**
1976

**FEATURES:**
Straight-wing; retractable tricycle
landing gear; close-cowled radial
engine; bubble canopy

# Helicopters

# Aérospatiale Alouette II FRANCE & INDIA

five-seat, single-engined light utility helicopter

Developed from Sud-Est's three-seater SE 3120 of 1952, the Alouette II was totally redesigned to incorporate the more powerful Artouste I turboshaft in place of the former's Salmson 9NH radial piston engine. Flown for the first time in March 1955, the helicopter was put into production the following year. The type's designation changed to SE 313B following SNCASE's merger with Sud Aviation, which was in turn absorbed by Aérospatiale in 1970. Re-engining in 1961 saw the introduction of the SA 318C with its Astazou IIA powerplant, and production of this version boosted total numbers to 1303. The final variant was the 'hot and high' optimised SA 315B Lama built for the Indian Army, which combined the Alouette II airframe with the larger powerplant and dynamic components of the Alouette III. Aérospatiale built 407 up to 1989, whilst Indian manufacturer HAL continues low-rate licence production. Over 50 countries have used the Alouette II in military service, with the German Army being the biggest employer with 226 SA 315BS and 54 SA 318CS.

SPECIFICATION:

ACCOMMODATION:
pilot and four passengers

DIMENSIONS:
LENGTH: 31 ft 11.75 in (9.75 m)
ROTOR DIAMETER: 33 ft 5 in (10.20 m)
HEIGHT: 9 ft 0 in (2.75 m)

WEIGHTS:
EMPTY: 1961 lb (890 kg)
MAX T/O: 3630 lb (1650 kg)

PERFORMANCE:
MAX SPEED: 127 mph (205 kmh)
RANGE: 447 miles (720 km)
POWERPLANT: Turboméca Artouste IIC6
OUTPUT: 360 shp (270 kW)

FIRST FLIGHT DATE:
12 March 1955

FEATURES:
Bubble canopy; open rear fuselage; skid undercarriage; exposed engine

# Aérospatiale Alouette III  FRANCE, INDIA & ROMANIA

seven-seat, single-engined light utility helicopter

Effectively an enlarged version of the Alouette II, the Alouette III also traces its history back to the efforts of the Sud-Est company – and its SE 3101 prototypes – of the early 1950s. As the largest member of the Alouette family of helicopters, the SE 316 flew in prototype form for the first time on 28 February 1959. Although larger and capable of seating seven, the Alouette III in SA 316A form shared the same Turboméca Artouste turboshaft engine as the lighter Alouette II. This variant remained in production until 1969, when it was replaced by the SA 316B, which featured a greater maximum take-off weight and strengthened transmission. That same year the SA 319 Alouette III Astazou was also introduced, this helicopter featuring the more powerful Turboméca Astazou XIV turboshaft in place of the Artouste. Both the SA 319 and SA 316B remained in production in France into the 1980s, while 230 were constructed under licence in Romania up to 1989. HAL of India continues to build the SA 319 in low rate production.

SPECIFICATION:

ACCOMMODATION:
pilot and six passengers

DIMENSIONS:
LENGTH: 32 ft 11 in (10.03 m)
ROTOR DIAMETER: 36 ft 2 in (11.02 m)
HEIGHT: 9 ft 10 in (3 m)

WEIGHTS:
EMPTY: 2513 lb (1140 kg)
MAX T/O: 4960 lb (2250 kg)

PERFORMANCE:
MAX SPEED: 131 mph (210 kmh)
RANGE: 300 miles (480 km)
POWERPLANT: Turboméca Astazou XIV
OUTPUT: 600 shp (450 kW)

FIRST FLIGHT DATE:
28 February 1959

ARMAMENT:
one tripod-mounted 7.62 mm machine gun in right doorway and 20 mm cannon fixed to left side of fuselage; provision for up to four AS.11 anti-tank missiles or two Mk 44 torpedoes on external stores pylons

FEATURES:
Rounded glazed nose; enclosed rear fuselage; wheeled undercarriage; exposed engine

# Aérospatiale SA 321 Super Frelon FRANCE & CHINA

32-seat, three-engined multi-role utility helicopter

The largest helicopter ever built in western Europe, the Super Frelon was developed from the mid-sized SA 3200 Frelon (Hornet), which first flew on 19 June 1959. Built in response to a French military requirement for a transport helicopter, the SA 3200 was not ordered into production. However, all was not lost, as the helicopter formed the basis of the appreciably larger Super Frelon, which Sud Aviation created with the help of American manufacturer Sikorsky. The latter was responsible for developing the main and tail rotor systems, Italian company Fiat assisted with the production of the gearbox and main transmission. The prototype SA 3210-01 flew for the first time on 7 December 1962, and 99 production aircraft were built by Aérospatiale up to 1983. A total of 26 SA 321Gs were acquired by the French Navy from 1963 for use as ASW helicopters, while Iraq, Libya, Israel and South Africa also bought small numbers of Super Frelons. China entered into SA 321Ja series production when it commenced construction of the Changhe Z-8 in 1989.

SPECIFICATION:

**ACCOMMODATION:**
pilot, co-pilot and three tactical/sonar operators in ASW fit, or flightcrew of two and 30 passengers in utility configuration

**DIMENSIONS:**
LENGTH: 75 ft 7 in (23.03 m)
ROTOR DIAMETER: 62 ft 0 in (18.90 m)
HEIGHT: 21 ft 10 in (6.66 m)

**WEIGHTS:**
EMPTY: 14,775 lb (6700 kg)
MAX T/O: 28,660 lb (13,000 kg)

**PERFORMANCE:**
MAX SPEED: 155 mph (248 kmh)
RANGE: 637 miles (1020 km)
POWERPLANT: three Turboméca Turmo IIICS
OUTPUT: 4890 shp (3645 kW)

**FIRST FLIGHT DATE:**
10 June 1959

**ARMAMENT:**
provision for up to four torpedoes or two AM39 Exocet anti-ship missiles on external stores pylons

**FEATURES:**
Boat hull bottom to fuselage; wheeled undercarriage; enclosed engines

# Bell Model 47/H-13 Sioux USA, BRITAIN, JAPAN & ITALY

three-seat, single-engined light utility helicopter

The world's first truly successful helicopter, the diminutive Bell Model 47 was built to the tune of 5000+ airframes between the late 1940s and the early 1970s, with production lines being set up by Augusta in Italy, Westland in the UK and Kawasaki in Japan. The helicopter can trace its lineage back to the Model 30 of 1943, which the US Army ordered for evaluation. Following service recommendations for general improvements, Bell created the Model 47 in 1945, and this became the first helicopter certificated by the American Civil Aeronautics Administration. Military orders followed in 1947, with both the USAAF and the US Navy acquiring examples as the YR-13 and HTL-1 respectively. The US Army followed suit the following year by purchasing 65 H-13BS. Bell continued to improve the helicopter, and by 1953 it had focused production on the Model 47G. The military H-13 saw widespread use in the medevac role in Korea, and numerous other air arms also experienced the versatility of the helicopter for the first time with the Bell 47.

SPECIFICATION:

ACCOMMODATION:
pilot and two passengers

DIMENSIONS:
LENGTH: 32 ft 7 in (11.31 m)
ROTOR DIAMETER: 37 ft 1.5 in (11.31 m)
HEIGHT: 9 ft 3.75 in (2.82 m)

WEIGHTS:
EMPTY: 1936 lb (877 kg)
MAX T/O: 2850 lb (1293 kg)

PERFORMANCE:
MAX SPEED: 105 mph (169 kmh)
RANGE: 324 miles (521 km)
POWERPLANT: Lycoming TVO-435-FIA
OUTPUT: 280 shp (210 kW)

FIRST FLIGHT DATE:
8 December 1945

FEATURES:
Blown bubble canopy; lattice frame tail boom; skid undercarriage; exposed engine

# Bell UH-1 Iroquois USA, JAPAN, TAIWAN, ITALY & GERMANY

15-seat, single/twin-engined utility and battlefield helicopter

Built in greater numbers than any other military aircraft since World War 2, the UH-1 family of helicopters has also seen service with more air forces than any other type. Developed from the XH-40 prototype, which had been built by Bell in response to a US Army requirement for a general utility and medevac helicopter, the first production HU-1A (Model 204) entered service in the late 1950s. In 1961 Bell modified the design into the Model 205 through the adoption of a longer fuselage and more powerful engine, and the resulting UH-1D/H went on to become the most popular variant in military service. The mainstay of the air mobile units in Vietnam, the Iroquois was also armed with gun packs, rocket pods and hand-held machine-guns and used in the helicopter gunship role. Further modifications have seen the helicopter fitted with twin engines for naval use, ASW radar for sea search duties, and drastically enlarged so as to be able to carry up to 17 troops. The UH-1 is still in widespread military service today.

SPECIFICATION:

ACCOMMODATION:
pilot and up to 14 passengers
(UH-1H)

DIMENSIONS: (FOR UH-1H)
LENGTH: 41 ft 10 in (12.77 m)
ROTOR DIAMETER: 48 ft 0 in
(14.63 m)
HEIGHT: 14 ft 5.5 in (4.41 m)

WEIGHTS:
EMPTY: 5210 lb (2363 kg)
MAX T/O: 9500 lb (4309 kg)

PERFORMANCE:
MAX SPEED: 127 mph (204 kmh)
RANGE: 318 miles (511 km)
POWERPLANT: Textron Lycoming
T53-L-13
OUTPUT: 1400 shp (1044 kW),

FIRST FLIGHT DATE:
22 October 1956 (XH-40)

ARMAMENT:
pintle-mounted Browning
0.50-in machine gun in doorway,
7.62 mm miniguns/grenade
launchers/rockets on fuselage-
mounted stub wings

FEATURES:
Squat fuselage; skid
undercarriage; enclosed engine

# Bell 206 JetRanger USA

five-seat, single-engined utility/training helicopter

Despite being a losing contender in the US Army's 1960 four-seat light observation helicopter competition, the OH-4 nevertheless matured into the world's most successful light turbine helicopter. Unperturbed by the Army's selection of the Hughes UH-6 Cayuse, Bell developed its submission into the civilian 206 five-seater. The OH-4 had flown in prototype form in December 1962, and it took three years for the 206 to reach a similar stage, making its maiden flight on 10 January 1966. Christened the JetRanger, the helicopter has been in production ever since. In 1967 the US Army reopened the Light Observation Helicopter competition because of rising costs and late delivery of the OH-6, and this time Bell received orders for the 206A in OH-58A Kiowa form. No fewer than 2200 were delivered to the Army from May 1968. That same year, the US Navy ordered 200+ TH-57 SeaRangers to fulfil its requirement for a light turbine primary training helicopter. Still flown in large numbers by the US Army/Navy, the utility/trainer Kiowa remains in military service with 29 countries worldwide.

SPECIFICATION:

**ACCOMMODATION:**
pilot and up to four passengers

**DIMENSIONS:**
LENGTH: 32 ft 4 in (9.84 m)
ROTOR DIAMETER: 35 ft 4 in (10.77 m)
HEIGHT: 9 ft 7 in (2.91 m)

**WEIGHTS:**
EMPTY: 1582 lb (718 kg)
MAX T/O: 3000 lb (1360 kg)

**PERFORMANCE:**
MAX SPEED: 122 mph (196 kmh)
RANGE: 300 miles (480 km)
POWERPLANT: Allison T63-A-700
OUTPUT: 317 shp (237 kW),

**FIRST FLIGHT DATE:**
10 January 1966

**FEATURES:**
Tadpole fuselage; skid undercarriage; enclosed engine; large glazed cockpit area

# Bell AH-1 HueyCobra USA & JAPAN

two-seat, single/twin-engined attack helicopter

The world's first dedicated attack helicopter to achieve operational status, the HueyCobra was chosen as a stopgap until the Lockheed AH-56 Cheyenne became available. However, the rugged simplicity of the AH-1, and the escalating conflict in Vietnam, saw the long-delayed Cheyenne cancelled in favour of the Bell product. The AH-1 had started life as the private venture 209, created in 1965 when Bell mated the powerplant, transmission and rotor system of the UH-1B/C with a new fuselage featuring tandem seating, a nose-mounted turret and stub wings. The prototype was flown on 7 September 1965, and the US Army ordered the helicopter into production as the AH-1G for employment in Vietnam as an escort for troop-carrying UH-1s. The Army received 1078 G-models, and improved variants featured in its arsenal in large numbers well into the 1990s. Although now retired from Army service, the AH-1W SuperCobra is still very much a part of the US Marine Corps' frontline force. AH-1F/SS also remain in service with seven foreign air arms.

SPECIFICATION:

**ACCOMMODATION:**
pilot and gunner in tandem

**DIMENSIONS:**
LENGTH: 53 ft 1 in (16.18 m)
ROTOR DIAMETER: 44 ft 0 in (13.41 m)
HEIGHT: 13 ft 5 in (4.09 m)

**WEIGHTS:**
EMPTY: 6698 lb (2993 kg)
MAX T/O: 10,000 lb (4535 kg)

**PERFORMANCE:**
MAX SPEED: 142 mph (227 kmh)
RANGE: 317 miles (507 km)
POWERPLANT: Textron Lycoming T53-L-703
OUTPUT: 1800 shp (1340 kW),

**FIRST FLIGHT DATE:**
7 September 1965 (XH-40)

**ARMAMENT:**
M197 20 mm cannon in nose turret; grenade launchers/ rockets/anti-armour missiles on fuselage-mounted stub wings

**FEATURES:**
Lateral engine intakes behind tandem cockpit; slim fuselage; skid undercarriage; enclosed engine/s; gun turret beneath nose

# Boeing (Vertol) H-46 Sea Knight  USA & JAPAN

28-seat, twin-engined multi-role utility helicopter

Tried and tested in combat, the H-46 has been the US Marine Corps' primary assault troop transport since 1964. Developed as a private venture by Vertol (later acquired by Boeing), the H-46 evolved from the Model 107, which flew in prototype form on 22 April 1958. Vertol adopted the tandem main rotor layout so as to avoid the need for an anti-torque tail rotor, thus creating a helicopter with an unobstructed main cabin and rear loading freight ramp. The US Army initially looked into buying the 107, but chose the larger CH-47 Chinook instead. However, the US Marines selected the CH-46 as a replacement for its US-34s, and the first of 160 A-models entered service in June 1964. A further 266 CH-46DS and 174 CH-46FS were also bought, and the survivors were all upgraded to CH-46E standard from 1977 onwards. The US Navy acquired 24 Sea Knights too, and these were finally retired in 2004. The helicopter was also exported as the KV-107 to Canada, Sweden, Saudi Arabia and Japan.

SPECIFICATION:

ACCOMMODATION:
pilot, co-pilot, crew chief and up
to 25 passengers

DIMENSIONS:
LENGTH: 83 ft 4 in (25.40 m)
ROTOR DIAMETER: 50 ft 0 in
(15.24 m)
HEIGHT: 16 ft 9 in (5.09 m)

WEIGHTS:
EMPTY: 11,585 lb (5255 kg)
MAX T/O: 24,300 lb (11,022 kg)

PERFORMANCE:
MAX SPEED: 166 mph (267 kmh)
RANGE: 694 miles (1110 km)
POWERPLANT: two General Electric
T58-GE-16s
OUTPUT: 3740 shp (2790 kW),

FIRST FLIGHT DATE:
22 April 1958

FEATURES:
Twin rotor configuration; fixed
tricycle undercarriage; enclosed
engines; rear fuselage sponsons

# Bristol Sycamore UK

five-seat, single-engined light utility helicopter

Designed to Air Ministry Specification E 20/45, the Bristol Sycamore was the first British helicopter to go into service with the RAF. The prototype Type 171 Mk 1, from which the Sycamore was derived, made its first flight on 24 July 1947. The civilian-optimised Sycamore Mk III went into production in 1949, and the RAF's HC 10 ambulance and HR 12 search and rescue variants, as well as the British Army's HC 11 communications helicopter were all based on this version. The Army received its first Sycamores in September 1951, followed by HR 12s for RAF Coastal Command in February 1952. Following trials with the latter type, improved HR 13/14s were acquired in quantity. This allowed Fighter Command's No 275 Sqn to become the RAF's first dedicated search and rescue unit. Of the 178 Sycamores built, a significant number were sold to the Belgian and German air forces, as well as the Royal Australian Navy and Air Force. The RAF retired its last Sycamores (from Support Command) in the early 1970s.

SPECIFICATION:

ACCOMMODATION:
pilot, aircrewman and three passengers

DIMENSIONS:
LENGTH: 46 ft 2 in (14.08 m)
ROTOR DIAMETER: 48 ft 7 in (14.84 m)
HEIGHT: 12 ft 2 in (3.71 m)

WEIGHTS:
EMPTY: 3810 lb (1728 kg)
MAX T/O: 5400 lb (2449 kg)

PERFORMANCE:
MAX SPEED: 127 mph (203 kmh)
RANGE: 312 miles (500 km)
POWERPLANT: Alvis Leonides 73
OUTPUT: 550 shp (410 kW)

FIRST FLIGHT DATE:
24 July 1947

FEATURES:
Tadpole-like fuselage; wheeled undercarriage; enclosed engine; bulged windows in fuselage sides

# Bristol Belvedere UK

21-seat, twin-engined tactical transport helicopter

The Belvedere was the RAF's first twin-engined and twin-rotor helicopter, being derived from Bristol's experimental Type 173, which made its maiden flight on 3 January 1952. With the helicopter maturing into a viable combat type by the early 1950s, the RAF announced a requirement for an all-purpose transport that could carry 18 troops or 6000-lb of internal freight or a 5250-lb underslung load. The 173 seemed broadly suited to the task, and the company refined the helicopter into the Type 192, which went on to form the basis of the Belvedere HC 1 in RAF service. Freight and passengers were loaded through a large cargo door in the starboard side of the helicopter. Although the Belvedere's twin-unit landing gear appeared to be almost comically flimsy, it proved to be more than up to the task once the helicopter entered service in 1958. Just 24 HC 1s were acquired, the last of which was delivered in June 1962. Three units flew the Belvedere in the UK, Aden and Singapore, and all had been retired by 1969.

SPECIFICATION:

ACCOMMODATION:
pilot, co-pilot, crew chief and up to 18 passengers

DIMENSIONS:
LENGTH: 54 ft 4 in (16.56 m)
ROTOR DIAMETER: 48 ft 11 in (14.91 m)
HEIGHT: 17 ft 0 in (5.18 m)

WEIGHTS:
EMPTY: 11,085 lb (5028 kg)
MAX T/O: 20,000 lb (9072 kg)

PERFORMANCE:
MAX SPEED: 138 mph (221 kmh)
RANGE: 445 miles (712 km)
POWERPLANT: two Napier Gazelle NGa 2 Mk 101s
OUTPUT: 3300 shp (2460 kW),

FIRST FLIGHT DATE:
3 January 1952

FEATURES:
Twin rotor configuration; fixed undercarriage; enclosed engines; large tailplane

# Hiller UH-12 Raven   USA

three-seat, single-engined light utility helicopter

Adopted as the standard US Army observation helicopter in 1950, the UH-12 was the end product of pioneering helicopter development carried out by Stanley Hiller Jr in 1944. Designated the H-23 by the Army, 100 were initially acquired with optional dual controls and associated equipment for carrying two stretcher casualties in external panniers. The US Navy also opted for 16 HTE-1s as helicopter trainers, followed by a larger purchase of the quad landing gear or skid-equipped HTE-2. The Army re-ordered again with the advent of the H-23B, buying 273 fitted with skids rather than the A-model's tricycle gear. The three-seater, one-piece canopy H-23C followed (145 built), again for the Army, but by far the largest order received by Hiller for the Raven was that placed for the D-model, which had an uprated engine. Some 483 were acquired, and these served on into the 1970s. The helicopter was also used by a number of foreign countries. Over 2600 have been built, and the type remains in production in UH-12E form with Hiller Aircraft Corporation of California.

SPECIFICATION:

ACCOMMODATION:
pilot and two passengers

DIMENSIONS:
LENGTH: 27 ft 9.5 in (8.45 m)
ROTOR DIAMETER: 35 ft 0 in
(10.67 m)
HEIGHT: 9 ft 9.5 in (2.98 m)

WEIGHTS:
EMPTY: 1816 lb (824 kg)
MAX T/O: 2700 lb (1225 kg)

PERFORMANCE:
MAX SPEED: 95 mph (153 kmh)
RANGE: 205 miles (330 km)
POWERPLANT: Lycoming
O-540-23B
OUTPUT: 250 shp (186 kW)

FIRST FLIGHT DATE:
January 1948

FEATURES:
Bubble canopy; thin, sloped tail boom; skid undercarriage; exposed engine

# Hughes OH-6 Cayuse USA & JAPAN

six-seat, single-engined light utility helicopter

In 1960 the US Army drew up a specification calling for the production of a four-seat light observation helicopter to replace its ageing Bell and Hiller types. The new aircraft had to have high performance, turboshaft power, easy maintenance and a low purchase cost. All the major manufacturers submitted proposals, and the Hughes OH-6A (based on the Model 369 and flown for the first time on 27 February 1963) was declared the winner in May 1965. Entering Army service four months later, 1415 would be acquired, and of this number 658 were lost in combat in Vietnam and a further 297 written off in accidents. The survivors were handed over the Reserve and National Guard following the selection of the OH-58 to replace the OH-6 from 1967. A number of Cayuse were modified into MH/AH-6s for use with Special Forces, and these were amongst the last to be retired from Army ranks in 1997 following the delivery of new-build T-tailed MD500s. Bahrain, Brazil, Colombia, Dominican Republic, Honduras, Nicaragua and Taiwan also received OH-6s.

SPECIFICATION:

**ACCOMMODATION:**
pilot and four passengers

**DIMENSIONS:**
LENGTH: 30 ft 3.75 in (9.24 m)
ROTOR DIAMETER: 26 ft 4 in (8.03 m)
HEIGHT: 8 ft 1.4 in (2.48 m)

**WEIGHTS:**
EMPTY: 1229 lb (557 kg)
MAX T/O: 2700 lb (1225 kg)

**PERFORMANCE:**
MAX SPEED: 150 mph (241 kmh)
RANGE: 1560 miles (2510 km)
POWERPLANT: Allison T63-A-5A
OUTPUT: 317 shp (236 kW)

**FIRST FLIGHT DATE:**
27 February 1963

**ARMAMENT:**
XM27E1 7.62 mm machine gun or XM75 40 mm grenade launcher on port stub wing, with flexibly-mounted gun in starboard cabin door

**FEATURES:**
Egg-shaped cabin; thin tail boom; skid undercarriage; enclosed engine

# Kaman H-43 Huskie USA

four/eight-seat, single-engined light utility/search and rescue helicopter

The H-43 Huskie gained famed for its combat search and rescue missions during the Vietnam War. Although best known for its service with the USAF, the first Huskies were actually acquired by the US Navy for shipboard use. Featuring Kaman's distinctive contra-rotating and intermeshing twin-rotor system, 29 three-seat HTKs were bought for training purposes in the early 1950s. The Navy followed this up with an order for 29 larger HUK-1s and 81 HOK-1s for the Marines – these were delivered between 1956-58. It was at this stage that the USAF took an interest in the helicopter, buying 175 turbine-engined HH-43Bs (the naval version was piston-engined). By using this more compact type of powerplant, and mounting it above the cabin, rather than in it, Air Force Huskies were more roomy, and they also boasted clam-shell rear doors. This made the HH-43B (and the improved F-model which followed) ideal for local crash rescue work, and examples could be found at USAF bases worldwide. All USAF/Navy Huskies had been retired by the mid-1970s.

SPECIFICATION:

ACCOMMODATION:
pilot, aircrewman and two/four passengers

DIMENSIONS:
LENGTH: 25 ft 2 in (7.68 m)
ROTOR DIAMETER: 47 ft 0 in (14.32 m)
HEIGHT: 15 ft 6.5 in (4.73 m)

WEIGHTS:
EMPTY: 4469 lb (2027 kg)
MAX T/O: 5969 lb (2707 kg)

PERFORMANCE:
MAX SPEED: 120 mph (192 kmh)
RANGE: 277 miles (445 km)
POWERPLANT: Lycoming T53-L-1B
OUTPUT: 1825 shp (1361 kW)

FIRST FLIGHT DATE:
27 September 1956 (HH-43)

FEATURES:
Rounded glazed nose; twin contra-rotating intermeshing rotor blades; twin tail booms; wheeled undercarriage; engine partially exposed to rear of cabin

# Kaman H-2 Seasprite USA

three-seat, twin-engined utility/ASW helicopter

The Seasprite was built by Kaman to fulfil a 1956 US Navy requirement for a long range, all weather multi-role utility helicopter. The company's K-20 design was chosen for development, and the prototype completed its maiden flight on 2 July 1959. A total of 190 UH-2A/BS were built in the early 1960s, with helicopters reaching the fleet in December 1962. Capable of carrying up to 11 passengers, these machines were used as fleet utility transports, performing the search-and-rescue and vertical replenishment missions. In October 1970 the UH-2 was chosen as the basis for the ASW Light Airborne Multi-Purpose System (LAMPS) helicopter, and 20 Seasprites were converted into SH-2DS through the fitment of search radar and dedicated ASW equipment. In May 1973 Kaman converted 88 UH-2/SH-2DS into LAMPS 2 SH-2FS, with bigger engines and improved ASW avionics. A further 52 new build helicopters were delivered from 1981, followed by six re-engined SH-2GS and 18 converted SH-2FS in 1991. The US Navy retired its Seasprites in 2001, but four foreign navies continue to use them.

## SPECIFICATION:

**ACCOMMODATION:**
pilot, co-pilot and sensor operator (SH-2D/F/G), or pilot and 11 passengers (UH-2A/B)

**DIMENSIONS:**
LENGTH: 40 ft 6 in (12.34 m)
ROTOR DIAMETER: 44 ft 0 in (13.41 m)
HEIGHT: 15 ft 2 in (4.62 m)

**WEIGHTS:**
EMPTY: 9200 lb (4173 kg)
MAX T/O: 13,500 lb (6125 kg)

**PERFORMANCE:**
MAX SPEED: 160 mph (256 kmh)
RANGE: 553 miles (885 km)
POWERPLANT: two General Electric T700-GE-401S
OUTPUT: 3446 shp (2570 kW),

**FIRST FLIGHT DATE:**
2 July 1959

**ARMAMENT:**
7.62 mm machine gun on pintle mounting in each cabin doorway; two Mk 46/50 torpedoes on external stores pylons

**FEATURES:**
Rectractable wheeled under-carriage; podded engines; four-bladed main rotor; radome under nose

# Kamov Ka-25 USSR

14-seat, twin-engined utility/ASW helicopter

A faithful servant to the Soviet Navy for over 30 years, the Ka-25 was the end result of a 1957 requirement for a shipborne ASW/utility helicopter. Kamov's Ka-20 was chosen to fill this role soon after its first flight in 1960, and over the next six years of development testing the helicopter evolved into the definitive Ka-25. The most distinguishing feature of this helicopter and, indeed, all Kamov products, was its counter-rotating coaxial main rotors, which meant that the Ka-25 dispensed with the need for a tail rotor. The helicopter's tail could be kept shorter as a result, which made it ideal for shipboard operations. Some 460 Ka-25s were built for the Soviet Navy between 1966-75, and these replaced the Mil Mi-4 as the service's primary shipborne helicopter. Around 25 different versions of the Ka-25 were built, with the most common being the ASW optimised Ka-25BSh and the utility Ka-25PS. The helicopter has now been replaced in Russian service by the Ka-27, although a handful remain in use in Syria, India and Vietnam.

**ACCOMMODATION:**
pilot, co-pilot and up to 12 passengers

**DIMENSIONS:**
LENGTH: 32 ft 0 in (9.75 m)
ROTOR DIAMETER: 51 ft 8 in (15.74 m)
HEIGHT: 17 ft 8 in (5.37 m)

**WEIGHTS:**
EMPTY: 10,505 lb (4765 kg)
MAX T/O: 16,535 lb (7500 kg)

**PERFORMANCE:**
MAX SPEED: 130 mph (209 kmh)
RANGE: 406 miles (650 km)
POWERPLANT: two Glushenkov (OMKB Mars) GTD-3FS
OUTPUT: 1800 shp (1340 kW),

**FIRST FLIGHT DATE:**
1960 (Ka-20)

**ARMAMENT:**
weapons bay capable of carrying two torpedoes or conventional/nuclear-tipped depth charges

**FEATURES:**
Fixed wheeled undercarriage; podded engines above cabin; counter-rotating coaxial rotor blades; radome under nose; triple tail fins

# Kellett YG-1B Autogiro USA

two-seat, single-engined artillery-spotting helicopter

Forerunner to the helicopter, the Kellett family of Autogiros could trace its lineage back to the late 1920s when brothers Rod and Wallace Kellett commenced experimentation with the K-1X. By the mid-1930s the company had made such advances with the Autogiro that 20 K-2/-3s had been sold to both civil and military buyers. The advent of the all-new KD-1 in the mid-1930s attracted much interest across the USA, with the USAAC deciding that it should evaluate the Autogiro for possible military applications. A single KD-1 was obtained in 1936 and redesignated the YG-1. The following year seven YG-1BS were also purchased, these having additional radio equipment and reduced fuel capacity. Five of the seven YG-1BS were placed in a standard training programme for pilot-artillery spotters and liaison duties, whilst the remaining two were bailed back to Kellett for further development work. After comprehensive tests, USAAC pilots reported that the YG-1B offered no great advantage over fixed-wing aircraft at the time, and the Autogiros were duly passed on to the US Border Patrol in Texas.

SPECIFICATION:

ACCOMMODATION:
pilot and passenger in tandem

DIMENSIONS:
LENGTH: 21 ft 0 in (6.40 m)
ROTOR DIAMETER: 40 ft 0 in (12.19 m)
HEIGHT: 10 ft 3 in (3.13 m)

WEIGHTS:
EMPTY: 1315 lb (596 kg)
MAX T/O: 2250 lb (1020 kg)

PERFORMANCE:
MAX SPEED: 120 mph (192 kmh)
RANGE: 200 miles (320)
POWERPLANT: Jacobs L-4MA
OUTPUT: 225 hp (167 kW)

FIRST FLIGHT DATE:
mid-1930s

FEATURES:
Aircraft-style fuselage; fixed taildragger undercarriage; fully exposed radial engine; open cockpits

# Mil Mi-1 USSR & POLAND

four-seat, single-engined light utility helicopter

Mil has been Russia's pre-eminent builder of helicopters for over half a century, and the company's first type to reach series production was the modest Mi-1. Design work on the helicopter, which was originally designated the GM-1, began in September 1947, and exactly 12 months later the first prototype completed its maiden flight. Although the first two GM-1s were lost in crashes, Mil persevered, and by 1951 the definitive Mi-1 was in full-scale production. Both civil and military variants were built side-by-side in the USSR up to 1954, when Mil transferred production to the WSK factory in Poland. From then on all helicopters were designated SM-1s to denote their place of manufacture. Several thousand Mi-1/SM-1s had been built by the time production ended in 1965, and many were exported to countries across the globe. Most had been withdrawn by 1983, although a handful served on into the 1990s in the USSR, China and Cuba. WSK developed the Mi-1 inspired SM-2, which was the same in layout but with a lengthened, five-seat forward fuselage.

SPECIFICATION:

**ACCOMMODATION:**
pilot and three passengers

**DIMENSIONS:**
LENGTH: 39 ft 9 in (12.11 m)
ROTOR DIAMETER: 47 ft 1 in (14.35 m)
HEIGHT: 10 ft 10 in (3.30 m)

**WEIGHTS:**
EMPTY: 4035 lb (1831 kg)
MAX T/O: 5325 lb (2416 kg)

**PERFORMANCE:**
MAX SPEED: 111 mph (180 kmh)
RANGE: 340 miles (550 km)
POWERPLANT: Ivchenko AI-26V
OUTPUT: 575 shp (429 kW),

**FIRST FLIGHT DATE:**
September 1948

**FEATURES:**
Fixed wheeled undercarriage, with single nosewheel; thin tail boom; enclosed engine

# Mil (PZL) Mi-2  USSR & POLAND

eight-seat, twin-engined light utility helicopter

Mil began work on a replacement for its Mi-1 in the late 1950s, and the culmination of the company's efforts was the Mi-2, which flew for the first time in September 1961. In January 1964 Mil reached an agreement with the Polish government that saw full responsibility for the development, manufacture and marketing of the Mi-2 passed on to PZL. The Swidnik-based company had by then built 1700 Mi-1s, and it test flew its first production Mi-2 in November 1965. Aside from building the basic Mi-2T military transport and Mi-2RM naval variant, PZL also developed a number of armed derivatives based on these machines. The Mi-2US gunship was fitted with a 23 mm cannon beneath the fuselage and had door-mounted machine guns, while the Mi-2URN combat support/reconnaissance variant retained the cannon and added 57 mm Mars 2 rocket pods on stub pylons. Finally, the Mi-2URP anti-tank helicopter could employ 9M14M Malyutka missiles. By the time production ended in 1991, PZL had manufactured 5250+ Mi-2s, and at least 16 countries received examples in varying quantities.

SPECIFICATION:

**ACCOMMODATION:**
pilot and seven passengers

**DIMENSIONS:**
LENGTH: 37 ft 4.75 in (11.40 m)
ROTOR DIAMETER: 47 ft 6.75 in (14.50 m)
HEIGHT: 12 ft 3.50 in (3.75 m)

**WEIGHTS:**
EMPTY: 5180 lb (2350 kg)
MAX T/O: 8157 lb (3700 kg)

**PERFORMANCE:**
MAX SPEED: 130 mph (210 kmh)
RANGE: 360 miles (580 km)
POWERPLANT: two Izotov GTD-350S
OUTPUT: 800 shp (600 kW),

**FIRST FLIGHT DATE:**
September 1961

**ARMAMENT:**
fixed NS-23 23 mm cannon on port fuselage and pintle-mounted 7.62 mm machine guns in cabin doors; four 9M14M Malyutka anti-tank missiles or two 57 mm rocket pods mounted on lower fuselage

**FEATURES:**
Fixed wheeled undercarriage, with single gear/dual tyre nosewheel; pod and boom configuration

# Mil Mi-4 USSR & CHINA

14-seat, single-engined utility helicopter

Development of the Mi-4 followed a direct request by Premier Josef Stalin in September 1951 for a helicopter capable of carrying a significant number of troops quickly across a battlefield. Mil was given a year to build such a machine, and the prototype made its first flight in May 1952. Looking a lot like a Sikorsky S-55, but closer in size to a S-58, the Mi-4 was powered by a single radial piston engine mounted in the nose, which drove the four-bladed main rotor (initially made out of wood) via a shaft passing between the raised cockpit and the main cabin. The latter could accommodate 12 troops, who entered the cabin via rear clamshell doors. Some 3500 Mi-4s had been built in the USSR (and widely exported) by the time production ended in 1969, the basic troop-carrying variant serving as the basis for a dedicated search-radar equipped ASW helicopter, a battlefield ECM platform and a cannon-armed assault gunship. China also built the Mi-4 under licence as the Harbin Z-5 between 1965-79, delivering 545.

## SPECIFICATION:

**ACCOMMODATION:**
pilot, co-pilot and 12 passengers

**DIMENSIONS:**
LENGTH: 82 ft 1 in (25.02 m)
ROTOR DIAMETER: 68 ft 11 in (21 m)
HEIGHT: 14 ft 5 in (4.40 m)

**WEIGHTS:**
EMPTY: 10,802 lb (4900 kg)
MAX T/O: 16,645 lb (7550 kg)

**PERFORMANCE:**
MAX SPEED: 130 mph (210 kmh)
RANGE: 250 miles (400 km)
POWERPLANT: Shvetsov Ash-82v
OUTPUT: 1700 shp (1270 kW),

**FIRST FLIGHT DATE:**
May 1952

**ARMAMENT:**
fixed NS-23 23 mm cannon and pintle-mounted 7.62 mm machine guns in cabin; gun/rocket pods mounted on lower fuselage

**FEATURES:**
Fixed wheeled undercarriage; pod and boom configuration; enclosed engine in nose; raised cockpit

# Mil Mi-6 USSR

95-seat, twin-engined heavylift transport helicopter

The Mi-6 was developed in response to a joint request put forward by the Soviet Air Force and state airline Aeroflot in June 1954. The prototype made its first flight in September 1957, at which point it became the world's largest and fastest helicopter. It was also the first Soviet rotary-winged designed to boast turboshaft powerplants. The standard Mi-6T entered military service in the late 1950s, this variant being cleared to carry up to 90 troops at speeds in excess of 180 mph. Aside from the basic troop transport Mi-6, several Mi-6VKP and Mi-22 command support aircraft were also produced. These were capable of acting as portable command posts, being fitted with various communications systems. One of the Mi-6's unique features was its fuselage-mounted wings, which provided 20 per cent of the helicopter's total lift when in cruising flight. Mil had produced 800 Mi-6s by the time production ended in 1981 in favour of the even larger Mi-26. Thirteen countries were supplied with Mi-6s, and examples remain in frontline service across the globe.

SPECIFICATION:

**ACCOMMODATION:**
pilot, co-pilot, flight engineer, radio operator, navigator/gunner and 90 passengers

**DIMENSIONS:**
LENGTH: 137 ft 0 in (41.74 m)
ROTOR DIAMETER: 114 ft 0 in (35 m)
HEIGHT: 32 ft 4 in (9.86 m)

**WEIGHTS:**
EMPTY: 60,055 lb (27,240 kg)
MAX T/O: 93,700 lb (42,500 kg)

**PERFORMANCE:**
MAX SPEED: 186 mph (300 kmh)
RANGE: 620 miles (1000 km)
POWERPLANT: two Soloviev D-25VS
OUTPUT: 10,850 shp (8090 kW),

**FIRST FLIGHT DATE:**
September 1957

**ARMAMENT:**
12.7 mm machine gun in nose

**FEATURES:**
Long fuselage and tail boom; fixed wheeled undercarriage, with single gear/dual tyre nosewheel; enclosed engines, with intakes above cockpit; shoulder-mounted wings

# Mil mi-8 USSR

31-seat, twin-engined multi-role transport helicopter

The mi-8/17 family of utility helicopters have become the most-produced rotary-winged aircraft in Russian history, with more than 10,000 built to date. Work on the mi-8 began in 1960, as Mil sought to develop a replacement for its mi-4. The resulting machine retained the latter's dynamic systems, but housed in an all-new fuselage and powered by a single turboshaft engine. The prototype mi-8 completed its first flight in June 1961, and it was soon realised that the helicopter was underpowered. Its Solviev turboshaft engine was duly replaced by two Isotov tv2s, and its four-bladed main rotor swapped for a five-bladed hub. The revised mi-8 flew again in August 1962, and the helicopter's configuration has essentially remained unchanged ever since. Built in myriad variants, the primary types to enter military service were the mi-8t troop transport, mi-8tb assault helicopter and numerous radio relay/command and ecm jamming platforms. In 1976 the tv3-powered mi-17 was introduced, and this remains in low rate production today. mi-8/17s are currently flown by at least 50 countries worldwide.

SPECIFICATION:

ACCOMMODATION:
pilot, co-pilot, loadmaster and 28 passengers

DIMENSIONS:
LENGTH: 82 ft 10 in (25.24 m)
ROTOR DIAMETER: 69 ft 11 in (21.29 m)
HEIGHT: 18 ft 7 in (5.65 m)

WEIGHTS:
EMPTY: 16,007 lb (7600 kg)
MAX T/O: 26,455 lb (12,000 kg)

PERFORMANCE:
MAX SPEED: 155 mph (250 kmh)
RANGE: 290 miles (465 km)
POWERPLANT: two Isotov TV2-117AS
OUTPUT: 2962 shp (2208 kW),

FIRST FLIGHT DATE:
June 1961

ARMAMENT:
Afanasayev 12.7 mm machine gun on flexible mounting in nose; six uv-32-57 rocket pods or four 9m17 Falanga anti-tank missiles on braced outriggers

FEATURES:
Pod and boom configuration; fixed wheeled undercarriage, with single gear/dual tyre nosewheel; clamshell rear entry doors; enclosed engines

# Mil Mi-14 USSR

four-seat, twin-engined ASW and search-and-rescue helicopter

A navalised variant of the Mi-8, the Mi-14 was developed by Mil to replace the Mi-4 in service with the Soviet Navy. Development work started in 1968, and the prototype M-14, featuring TV2 turboshafts, flew for the first time in 1973. However, by the time the Mi-14 reached the fleet in 1976, the helicopter had been fitted with TV3s, as per the Mi-17. The Mi-14's most notable features were its boat-like hull, flotation equipment and retractable undercarriage. Three versions were built by Mil, with the Mi-14PL being the dedicated ASW platform equipped with MAD, dipping sonar, sonobuoys and search radar. This was followed in 1983 by the Mi-14BT mine countermeasures helicopter, equipped to tow a mine-clearing sled. Only 25 were built, six going to the East German Navy. Finally, the Mi-14PS was the dedicated search-and-rescue variant, capable of carrying ten survivors. The helicopter had an enlarged sliding door, a rescue hoist and extra searchlights. Bulgaria, Cuba, Libya and Syria all received Mi-14PLs, while Poland bought this variant and the Mi-14PS.

## SPECIFICATION:

**ACCOMMODATION:**
pilot, co-pilot and two sensor operators (Mi-14PL/BT), or pilot, co-pilot, aircrewman and 10 passengers (Mi-14PS)

**DIMENSIONS:**
LENGTH: 83 ft 1 in (25.32 m)
ROTOR DIAMETER: 69 ft 11 in (21.29 m)
HEIGHT: 22 ft 9 in (6.93 m)

**WEIGHTS:**
EMPTY: 19,625 lb (8900 kg)
MAX T/O: 30,865 lb (14,000 kg)

**PERFORMANCE:**
MAX SPEED: 143 mph (230 kmh)
RANGE: 578 miles (925 km)
POWERPLANT: two Isotov TV3-117AS
OUTPUT: 3400 shp (2536 kW),

**FIRST FLIGHT DATE:**
1973

**ARMAMENT:**
weapons bay capable of carrying two torpedoes, bombs or depth charges

**FEATURES:**
Pod and boom configuration; retractable undercarriage; boat-like hull; enclosed engines, with intakes above cockpit; podded flotation gear

# Mil мi-24 USSR

ten-seat, twin-engined armed assault/attack helicopter

The мi-24 was originally developed by Mil as a
flying armoured personnel carrier for a squad of
soldiers. Capable of defending itself, and providing
suppressive fire for the troops it was inserting, its
role was to support an armoured push by
mechanised forces on the ground or participate in
independent airborne assaults. Based on the мi-8,
the prototype v-24 first flew in early 1970, and
production мi-24as entered service in 1973.
Operational experience soon showed that this
concept of a combined assault/attack helicopter
was flawed, and troop transportation was left to
less agile types like the мi-8. The мi-24 was
redesigned with a twin bubble nose replacing the
greenhouse canopy of the мi-24a, and its offensive
armament was greatly increased through the
fitment of a jakв 12.7 mm Gatling gun in a nose
turret. Additional 23/30 mm cannon was also made
available, and rocket pods and anti-tank missiles
carried on underwing hardpoints. Blooded in
combat in Afghanistan, the 'Devil's Chariot' has
been widely exported. Over 1000 remain in service.

SPECIFICATION:

ACCOMMODATION:
pilot, weapon operator and eight
passengers

DIMENSIONS:
LENGTH: 70 ft 1 in (21.35 m)
ROTOR DIAMETER: 56 ft 9 in
(17.30 m)
HEIGHT: 13 ft 1 in (3.97 m)

WEIGHTS:
EMPTY: 18,078 lb (8200 kg)
MAX T/O: 27,557 lb (12,500 kg)

PERFORMANCE:
MAX SPEED: 192 mph (310 kmh)
RANGE: 466 miles (750 km)
POWERPLANT: two Klimov TV3-117s
OUTPUT: 4380 shp (3270 kW),

FIRST FLIGHT DATE:
Early 1970

ARMAMENT:
jakв 12.7 mm machine gun or
23/30 mm cannon in undernose
turret, or cannon rigidly
mounted; four rocket/gun pods
on four underwing stores pylons,
and two anti-tank missiles on
stub wing endplates

FEATURES:
Tandem cockpit with bubble
canopies; retractable
undercarriage; undernose turret;
intakes above cockpit; stub wings

# Piasecki HUP/H-25 Retriever USA

seven-seat, single-engined utility/rescue helicopter

Piasecki's response to a 1945 US Navy requirement issued in 1945 for a helicopter designed for seaborne operations, the HUP was both compact enough to fit aboard a variety of ships, yet capable of performing vertical replenishment, casevac, rescue and plane-guard duties. Known for its work with tandem rotor designs, Piasecki duly adopted just such a layout for the HUP, which was placed into series production in 1948 following receipt of an order for 32 HUP-1 Retrievers. With space for five passengers or three stretchers, the HUP-1s made their fleet debut in early 1949. Continued development work by Piasecki resulted in the Sperry autopilot-equipped HUP-2, of which 165 were delivered (some of which were fitted with ASW equipment). US Army interest in the helicopter saw the company produce the H-25A, which had boosted flight controls and a strong cargo floor – 70 were constructed alongside the final Navy order for 50 HUP-3s. Surviving HUP-2/3s remained in service long enough to be redesignated UH-25B/CS in 1962, although they were retired soon after.

SPECIFICATION:

ACCOMMODATION:
pilot, co-pilot and five passengers

DIMENSIONS:
LENGTH: 31 ft 10 in (9.7 m)
ROTOR DIAMETER: 35 ft 0 in (10.67 m)
HEIGHT: 13 ft 2 in (4.01 m)

WEIGHTS:
EMPTY: 3938 lb (1782 kg)
MAX T/O: 6100 lb (2767 kg)

PERFORMANCE:
MAX SPEED: 108 mph (174 kmh)
RANGE: 340 miles (547 km)
POWERPLANT: Continental R-975-34
OUTPUT: 525 shp (391 kW)

FIRST FLIGHT DATE:
March 1948

FEATURES:
Twin rotor configuration; fixed undercarriage, with single wheel at rear; enclosed engine in tail

# Piasecki (Vertol) H-21 Shawnee  USA

22-seat, single-engined transport/assault/rescue helicopter

The HRP-2 was the end result of a 1948 US Navy order for a replacement for Piasecki's pioneering HRP-1 'Flying Banana' of the late 1940s. The new helicopter featured an all-metal fuselage of greater diameter and length, its smooth exterior finish greatly improving the helicopter's flight performance in comparison with the fabric-covered HRP-1. Despite these modifications, the Navy ordered only a handful of HRP-2s, and it was left to the USAF, which acquired 18 YH-21S, 38 H-21A Work Horses and 163 H-21BS (with more powerful engines), and the US Army, with a large purchase of 334 H-21C Shawnees, to make the most of the Piasecki design. The Air Force used a number of its H-21S in the utility role in Alaska supporting various bases and radar sites being built in the area, whilst the Army sent 33 H-21Cs to South Vietnam as early as December 1961, making the Shawnee one of the first US military aircraft to arrive in-theatre. More than 90 would see action over Vietnam up to their final retirement in 1969.

SPECIFICATION:

**ACCOMMODATION:**
pilot, co-pilot and 20 passengers

**DIMENSIONS:**
LENGTH: 52 ft 4 in (15.98 m)
ROTOR DIAMETER: both 44 ft 6 in (13.56 m)
HEIGHT: 15 ft 1 in (4.6 m)

**WEIGHTS:**
EMPTY: 8700 lb (3946 kg)
MAX T/O: 13,500 lb (6124 kg)

**PERFORMANCE:**
MAX SPEED: 130 mph (209 kmh)
RANGE: 300 miles (482 km)
POWERPLANT: Wright Cyclone R-1820-103
OUTPUT: 1425 shp (1062 kW)

**FIRST FLIGHT DATE:**
11 April 1952

**FEATURES:**
Banana-shaped fuselage; twin rotor configuration; fixed undercarriage, with single wheel at front; enclosed engine in tail; prominent tailfins

# Saro Skeeter UK

two-seat, single-engined light utility helicopter

Originally designed by Autogiro specialists Cierva, the W 14 Skeeter 1 completed its initial flight trials powered by a Jameson FF-1 engine. This rather limited horsepower engine was soon replaced by the Gipsy Major 10, with the resulting powerplant/airframe combination being designated the Skeeter 2. Cierva was acquired by Saunders-Roe in 1951, and development continued on the Skeeter through Mks 3 to 6, all with more powerful engines. Further refinement produced the Mk 6, and four of these were delivered to the British Army for service evaluation – three Skeeter AOP 10s and one dual-control T 11 trainer. The Army duly purchased 64 AOP 12s, of which a handful were supplied to the RAF for training purposes. Entering service with the Army Air Corps in 1957, the Skeeter flew as a utility type until given the task of immediate battlefield support in place of the Auster AOP 9 in 1961. However, performance deficiencies with the Skeeter meant that the AOP 9 remained in service until 1966. All Skeeters were replaced by Westland Sioux in 1968.

SPECIFICATION:

ACCOMMODATION:
pilot and passenger

DIMENSIONS:
LENGTH: 26 ft 6 in (8.08 m)
ROTOR DIAMETER: 32 ft 0 in (9.75 m)
HEIGHT: 7 ft 6 in (2.31 m)

WEIGHTS:
EMPTY: 3938 lb (1782 kg)
MAX T/O: 2200 lb (998 kg)

PERFORMANCE:
MAX SPEED: 101 mph (161 kmh)
RANGE: 215 miles (344 km)
POWERPLANT: de Havilland Gipsy Major 200 Mk 30
OUTPUT: 200 shp (149 kW)

FIRST FLIGHT DATE:
October 1948

FEATURES:
Tadpole-like fuselage; wheeled undercarriage, with single wheel at front; enclosed engine; heavily glazed cockpit

# Sikorsky R-4 Hoverfly USA

two-seat, single-engined light utility helicopter

The world's first operational helicopter, the R-4 was a production development of Sikorsky's VS-300, which made its first tethered flight on 14 September 1939. By the spring of 1941 the VS-300 was achieving free flight at forward speeds up to 70 mph, thus proving the soundness of Igor Sikorsky's brilliant anti-torque tail rotor system. Vought-Sikorsky duly received a contract from the US government to build a development of the VS-300, which was designated the XR-4. This helicopter boasted a two-seat, enclosed cockpit, and was powered by a Warner R-500 engine driving both the main and tail rotors through gearboxes and driveshafts. First flown on 14 January 1942, the prototype ushered in the age of the helicopter. Thirty production R-4s were ordered by the USAAF, and these soon proved the versatility of the helicopter by carrying out shipboard landings and aircrew rescues. The US Navy also ordered 25 R-4s in 1942-44, these being designated HNS-1s in frontline service. Finally, the RAF and Fleet Air Arm also received 45 R-4s in 1945-46, which were christened Hoverfly Is.

## SPECIFICATION:

**ACCOMMODATION:**
pilot and passenger

**DIMENSIONS:**
LENGTH: 48 ft 2 in (14.68 m)
ROTOR DIAMETER: 38 ft 0 in (11.58 m)
HEIGHT: 12 ft 5 in (3.78 m)

**WEIGHTS:**
EMPTY: 2020 lb (916 kg)
MAX T/O: 2535 lb (1150 kg)

**PERFORMANCE:**
MAX SPEED: 75 mph (121 kmh)
RANGE: 130 miles (209 km)
POWERPLANT: Warner R-550-1
OUTPUT: 180 shp (134 kW)

**FIRST FLIGHT DATE:**
14 January 1942

**FEATURES:**
Fabric-covered, lattice frame fuselage; fixed undercarriage, with single wheel at rear; heavily glazed cockpit

# Sikorsky s-51/Westland Dragonfly USA & UK

four-seat, single-engined light utility helicopter

Having proved the viability of the helicopter with the R-4, Sikorsky set about developing a machine better suited to the operational requirements of the USAAF and US Navy. The company came up with the VS-337, which was designated the R-5 by the USAAF. The prototype made its first flight on 18 August 1943, and the USAAF acquired 65 for evaluation and service use. Unlike the R-4, the R-5 had an all-metal fuselage, and also reaped the benefits of a more powerful engine. A number of R-5s were fitted with litter carriers and issued to the USAAF's Air Rescue Service. In 1946 Sikorsky test flew a four-seat version of the R-5 for the civil market, designated the s-51. This proved more popular with the military than the R-5, and of the 379 built, 66 went to the USAAF as H-5s. A further 88 were procured by the US Navy as HO3s in 1947-48, and 165 were built under licence by Westland as the Dragonfly for both the RAF and Fleet Air Arm.

SPECIFICATION:

ACCOMMODATION:
pilot and three passengers

DIMENSIONS:
LENGTH: 40 ft 10 in (12.45 m)
ROTOR DIAMETER: 49 ft 0 in (14.94 m)
HEIGHT: 12 ft 11 in (3.69 m)

WEIGHTS:
EMPTY: 4397 lb (1993 kg)
MAX T/O: 5500 lb (2495 kg)

PERFORMANCE:
MAX SPEED: 103 mph (165 kmh)
RANGE: 300 miles (480 km)
POWERPLANT: Pratt & Whitney R-985-AN-5
OUTPUT: 450 shp (336 kW)

FIRST FLIGHT DATE:
18 August 1943

FEATURES:
All-metal fuselage; fixed undercarriage, with single wheel at front; heavily glazed cockpit

# Sikorsky HO5S USA

four-seat, single-engined light utility helicopter

Derived from the Sikorsky's s-52, which was the first US helicopter to feature metal rotor blades, the HO5S was procured by the US Navy in order to replace the HO3S in service with the Marine Corps. The s-52 had been built as a two-seater, powered by a 178 shp Franklin engine, and following Navy interest in the helicopter, Sikorsky doubled its seating capacity and fitted a 245 shp Franklin o-245-1 engine instead. The s-52 prototype had initially flown in February 1947, and the four-seat variant was produced several years later. The first HO5Ss reached the Marine Corps in March 1952, and the helicopter saw extensive combat in the Korean War in the scout and observation roles. Like the HO3S, the HO5S proved invaluable in the day/night evacuation of wounded personnel from the frontline. Eight of the 79 HO5S-1s supplied to the Navy saw service with the US Coast Guard as HO5S-1GS from September 1952. Finally, the USAF and US Army evaluated the s-52 under the designation YH-18. The Marine Corps retired its surviving HO5Ss in 1958.

SPECIFICATION:

**ACCOMMODATION:**
pilot and three passengers

**DIMENSIONS:**
LENGTH: 27 ft 5 in (8.38 m)
ROTOR DIAMETER: 33 ft 0 in (10.05 m)
HEIGHT: 10 ft 4 in (3.16 m)

**WEIGHTS:**
EMPTY: 2000 lb (907 kg)
MAX T/O: 2770 lb (1256 kg)

**PERFORMANCE:**
MAX SPEED: 105 mph (168 kmh)
RANGE: 190 miles (304 km)
POWERPLANT: Franklin O-245-1
OUTPUT: 245 shp (182 kW)

**FIRST FLIGHT DATE:**
12 February 1947 (S-52)

**FEATURES:**
All-metal, pod and boom fuselage; fixed undercarriage; heavily glazed cockpit

# Sikorsky CH-37 Mojave   USA

22-seat, twin-engined transport helicopter

The first in a series of large Sikorsky transport helicopters built for the Marine Corps, the CH-37 was created following the issuing of a requirement for just such a machine in 1950. For more than a decade after its first flight, on 18 December 1953, the Mojave was the world's largest non-Soviet helicopter. Both the US Army and Marines wanted a rotary-winged aircraft that could carry around 26 troops or soft-skinned vehicles and other military equipment. Although featuring standard Sikorsky single rotor layout, a helicopter of this size needed two engines. In order to keep the fuselage clear for cargo, the engines were located in nacelles on stub wings, into which the main legs of the landing gear retracted. Clamshell doors in the nose aided the straight-in loading of freight. Initially designated the HR2S-1 by the Marine Corps, the first of 55 production aircraft was delivered in July 1956. The US Army also received a small number of Mojaves, which saw combat in Vietnam alongside their Marine counterparts. All had been redesignated CH-37s in 1962.

SPECIFICATION:

**ACCOMMODATION:**
pilot, co-pilot and 20 passengers

**DIMENSIONS:**
LENGTH: 64 ft 3 in (19.50 m)
ROTOR DIAMETER: 72 ft 0 in (21.95 m)
HEIGHT: 22 ft 0 in (6.07 m)

**WEIGHTS:**
EMPTY: 21,502 lb (9753 kg)
MAX T/O: 31,000 lb (14,061 kg)

**PERFORMANCE:**
MAX SPEED: 121 mph (195 kmh)
RANGE: 335 miles (540 km)
POWERPLANT: two Pratt & Whitney R2800-PW-54S
OUTPUT: 4200 shp (3132 kW),

**FIRST FLIGHT DATE:**
18 December 1953

**FEATURES:**
Twin engines, mounted in nacelles on stub wings; retractable undercarriage; clamshell doors in nose; fixed tailwheel

# Sikorsky s-55/Westland Whirlwind USA, UK & JAPAN

12-seat, single-engined utility helicopter

Few designs advanced the cause of rotary-winged flight as much as the Sikorsky s-55, which was built in previously unheard of numbers for a helicopter – 1700+ in the USA, UK and Japan. Used by all three services and the Coast Guard in the USA, the first production examples (HO4S-1s) reached the US Navy in December 1950. The USAF's H-19B introduced detail changes to the tail boom and stabilisers, and utilised the more powerful Wright Cyclone in place of the HO4S-1's Wasp engine. Built as the H-19D Chickasaw for the Army and the HO4S-3/HRS-3 for the Marines, this version of the helicopter accounted for the bulk of the s-55's huge production run. UK-based Westland Helicopters produced its first licence-built Whirlwind in 1952, and over the next ten years 400 more were delivered to the RAF and Fleet Air Arm in a handful of versions. Easily the best of these was the turboshaft-powered HAR 9/10, which remained in service into the late 1970s. Both the s-55 and Whirlwind enjoyed considerable export success.

SPECIFICATION:

**ACCOMMODATION:**
pilot, co-pilot and ten passengers

**DIMENSIONS:**
LENGTH: 42 ft 3 in (12.88 m)
ROTOR DIAMETER: 53 ft 0 in (16.16 m)
HEIGHT: 13 ft 4 in (4.07 m)

**WEIGHTS:**
EMPTY: 5250 lb (2381 kg)
MAX T/O: 7900 lb (3583 kg)

**PERFORMANCE:**
MAX SPEED: 112 mph (180 kmh)
RANGE: 360 miles (578 km)
POWERPLANT: Wright R-1300-3 Cyclone
OUTPUT: 800 hp (596 kW)

**FIRST FLIGHT DATE:**
10 November 1949

**FEATURES:**
Pod and boom fuselage, with ventral fairing joining pod with boom; fixed undercarriage; engine in nose; raised cockpit above cabin

# Sikorsky s-58/Westland Wessex USA, UK & FRANCE

18-seat, single-engined utility helicopter

The s-58 was created by Sikorsky following the us Navy's tabling of a requirement for an ASW helicopter in 1951 to replace the HO4S-1. Flown in prototype form on 8 March 1954, the s-58 had already been ordered into production 'off the drawing board' by the Navy, which was feeling the pressure being exerted by an ever growing Soviet submarine force. The first of 350 HSS-1 Seabats reached fleet units in August 1955, by which time the Marine Corps had also chosen the s-58 in HUS-1 form as its new troop transport helicopter. Christened the Choctaw, some 603 examples were built for the Corps, and these entered service from February 1957. Seabats began to be replaced by the HSS-2 Sea King in 1961, and the surplus machines (redesignated UH-34s in 1962) were stripped of their ASW gear and turned into utility helicopters. In the UK, Westland commenced license production of the s-58 in 1957, building 350+ ASW and utility Wessex helicopters for the RAF, Royal Navy and export customers over the next ten years.

## SPECIFICATION:

**ACCOMMODATION:**
pilot, co-pilot and 16 passengers

**DIMENSIONS:**
LENGTH: 65 ft 9 in (20.04 m)
ROTOR DIAMETER: 56 ft 0 in (17.07 m)
HEIGHT: 14 ft 5 in (4.39 m)

**WEIGHTS:**
EMPTY: 8304 lb (3767 kg)
MAX T/O: 13,500 lb (6123 kg)

**PERFORMANCE:**
MAX SPEED: 123 mph (197 kmh)
RANGE: 185 miles (300 km)
POWERPLANT: Wright R-1820-84
OUTPUT: 1525 shp (1137 kW)

**FIRST FLIGHT DATE:**
8 March 1954

**ARMAMENT:**
Two homing torpedoes, bombs or depth charges on fuselage pylons

**FEATURES:**
Engine in nose; raised cockpit above cabin; four-bladed rotor; fixed undercarriage, with single wheel at rear; engine mounted in nose

# Sikorsky s-62 Seaguard  USA

14-seat, single-engined search-and-rescue helicopter

In 1962, the US Coast Guard selected a version of the commercial Sikorsky s-62 to replace its small fleet of HH-34 search-and-rescue helicopters. The prototype s-62 had first flown on 24 May 1958, and it had the distinction of being the first amphibious helicopter produced by Sikorsky. Utilising the standard single turbine-powered engine and rotor design synonymous with previous Sikorsky types, the s-62's unique features were its watertight fuselage and two outrigger floats which housed retractable landing gear. On 9 January 1963 the Coast Guard received the first of 99 s-62s, which were given the designation HH-52A and christened Seaguards. Thanks to its ability to land on water, along with its unique folding rescue platform and overhead winch, the HH-52A has the honour of having rescued more people at sea than any other helicopter in the world. Aside from being based at locations along the vast US seaboard, a number of HH-52AS also flew from Coast Guard cutters and ice breakers. Seaguards were replaced by HH-65A Dolphins in the 1980s.

## SPECIFICATION:

**ACCOMMODATION:**
pilot, co-pilot and 12 passengers

**DIMENSIONS:**
LENGTH: 44 ft 7 in (13.62 m)
ROTOR DIAMETER: 53 ft 0 in (18.44 m)
HEIGHT: 16 ft 0 in (4.88 m)

**WEIGHTS:**
EMPTY: 5083 lb (2305 kg)
MAX T/O: 8100 lb (3674 kg)

**PERFORMANCE:**
MAX SPEED: 109 mph (174 kmh)
RANGE: 474 miles (758 km)
POWERPLANT: General Electric T58-GE-8B
OUTPUT: 1250 shp (932 kW)

**FIRST FLIGHT DATE:**
24 May 1958 (s-62)

**FEATURES:**
Single engine above cockpit; fixed undercarriage, with single wheel at rear; boat-like hull, flotation gear in undercarriage sponsons

# Sikorsky s-61/Westland Sea King  USA, UK, JAPAN & ITALY

19-seat, twin-engined ASW/utility/search-and-rescue helicopter

The Sea King was the end result of a US Navy requirement for a single helicopter that could both hunt and kill enemy submarines. Sikorsky received a contract to develop the aircraft in 1957, and the HSS-2 prototype made its first flight on 11 March 1959. Based on the civil s-62, and powered by two turboshaft engines above the cabin, leaving the latter free for ASW gear, dunking sonar and radar, the helicopter featured a boat hull for amphibious operations. Fleet deliveries began in September 1961, and 245 SH-3AS were built. A further 73 re-engined SH-3DS were acquired from 1966, and in 1970 105 airframes were upgraded to SH-3G standard. The final Navy variant was the SH-3H, 145 being created through upgrades. A handful of these remain in service as UH-3s today. The USAF bought a number of stretched HH-3s with a rear-loading ramp for search-and-rescue duties, while Westland built its own Sea Kings (over 150) for the Royal Navy and RAF. Westland, Sikorsky and Augusta-built examples were exported to 22 countries.

SPECIFICATION:

ACCOMMODATION:
pilot, co-pilot, two sensor operators and 15 passengers

DIMENSIONS:
LENGTH: 72 ft 8 in (22.15 m)
ROTOR DIAMETER: 62 ft 0 in (18.90 m)
HEIGHT: 16 ft 10 in (5.13 m)

WEIGHTS:
EMPTY: 12,530 lb (5600 kg)
MAX T/O: 21,000 lb (9525 kg)

PERFORMANCE:
MAX SPEED: 166 mph (266 kmh)
RANGE: 628 miles (1005 km)
POWERPLANT: two General Electric T58-GE-10S
OUTPUT: 2800 shp (2090 kW)

FIRST FLIGHT DATE:
11 March 1959 (s-62)

ARMAMENT:
two homing torpedoes or depth charges on fuselage pylons up to weight of 840-lb (380 kg)

FEATURES:
Twin engines above cockpit; retractable main undercarriage, with single wheel at rear; boat-like hull, flotation gear in undercarriage sponsons

# Sikorsky CH-54 Tarhe USA

five-seat, twin-engined heavy crane helicopter

Built specifically as a crane helicopter, the CH-54 Tarhe had its fuselage replaced by a slim beam, which was left as unobstructed as possible so as to allow bulky loads to be slung centrally from it. The helicopter was operated by a three-man crew, one of whom faced aft at all times watching the load and manipulating the hooks and winches. Sikorsky built six YCH-54A pre-production helicopters in 1962-63, five of which were issued to the US Army for evaluation. An order for 54 A-models was soon received, and the first of these entered service in 1964. A further 37 CH-54BS were subsequently delivered, these featuring uprated engines and twin-wheel landing gear. A series of purpose-built Universal Military Pods were also acquired, these being configured either for the carriage of 46 troops or 24 stretchers. Others were kitted out as mobile command posts or surgical hospitals. The Tarhe saw considerable use in Vietnam, lifting M114 howitzers, armoured vehicles, bulldozers, troops and 380 damaged aircraft. The helicopter retired from Army National Guard service in the 1990s.

SPECIFICATION:

ACCOMMODATION:
pilot, co-pilot, loadmaster and jump seats for two loader/technicians

DIMENSIONS:
LENGTH: 70 ft 3 in (21.41 m)
ROTOR DIAMETER: 72 ft 0 in (21.95 m)
HEIGHT: 25 ft 5 in (7.75 m)

WEIGHTS:
EMPTY: 19,234 lb (8724 kg)
MAX T/O: 42,000 lb (19,050 kg)

PERFORMANCE:
MAX SPEED: 126 mph (203 kmh)
RANGE: 230 miles (370 km)
POWERPLANT: two Pratt & Whitney T73-1S
OUTPUT: 9000 shp (6711 kW)

FIRST FLIGHT DATE:
9 May 1962

FEATURES:
Cockpit pod and beam-type fuselage; twin (exposed) engines above cockpit; fixed under-carriage, with single wheel at front; starboard stabiliser on top of tail unit

# Sikorsky S-65　USA & GERMANY

58-seat, twin-engined medium/heavy lift helicopter

The s-65 was developed by Sikorsky in response to a 1960 requirement issued by the Marine Corps for a replacement for its CH-37 Mojave. Using the CH-54 as a basis, the company combined the Tarhe's proven dynamic systems with an all-new watertight fuselage that featured a rear-loading freight ramp. Capable of carrying (underslung) a 1-1/2 ton truck and trailer, 105 mm howitzer, Hawk missile system or 55 troops, the first of two prototypes flew on 14 October 1964, and production deliveries commenced in 1966. Within 12 months the CH-53A Sea Stallion, as the helicopter was called in Marine service, was proving its worth in Vietnam. A total of 139 CH-53As had been built by the time production switched to the improved CH-53D, 174 of which were built up to 1972. The USAF ordered 52 S-65s as the HH-53B/C in 1966 for combat rescue, and Germany built 112 CH-53GS under licence. Finally, Israel also acquired 45 CH-53s. A number of early-build CH-53s have now been retired both by the Marines and the Israelis.

SPECIFICATION:

ACCOMMODATION:
pilot, co-pilot, aircrewman and 55 passengers

DIMENSIONS:
LENGTH: 88 ft 3 in (26.90 m)
ROTOR DIAMETER: 72 ft 3 in (22.02 m)
HEIGHT: 17 ft 2 in (5.22 m)

WEIGHTS:
EMPTY: 23,485 lb (10,653 kg)
MAX T/O: 42,000 lb (19,050 kg)

PERFORMANCE:
MAX SPEED: 196 mph (315 kmh)
RANGE: 259 miles (415 km)
POWERPLANT: two General Electric T64-GE-413S
OUTPUT: 7850 shp (5860 kW)

FIRST FLIGHT DATE:
14 October 1964

ARMAMENT:
single 12.7 mm machine gun and 7.62 minigun on pintle mounts in fuselage ramp/doorways

FEATURES:
Long cabin with tail ramp; twin podded engines on upper fuselage sides; retractable undercarriage; starboard stabiliser on top of tail unit; centre fuselage sponsons

# Westland AH 1 Scout/Wasp  UK

five-seat, single-engined ASW/utility helicopter

The AH 1 Scout started life in 1956 as Saunders-Roe light helicopter proposal P 531, with work commencing on the first two prototypes two years later. Following the company's acquisition by Westland, development of the helicopter progressed to the point where the British Army Air Corps ordered a batch of pre-production aircraft. The first of these was delivered in August 1960, followed a month later by several production orders. Christened the Scout AH 1, the helicopter commenced Army service in 1963 – 150 were eventually delivered, these machines being used for all manner of roles ranging from forward utility taskings to the anti-tank mission. Scouts saw action in the Falklands War in liaison and medevac roles. The last Scouts were retired in 1994. A naval version of the AH 1, known as the Wasp, was also built in significant numbers (133), and served with distinction aboard numerous Royal Navy vessels for over 25 years. Fitted with four castoring wheels in place of the fixed skids, the Wasp also saw action in the Falklands War.

## SPECIFICATION:

**ACCOMMODATION:**
pilot and four passengers

**DIMENSIONS:**
LENGTH: 30 ft 4 in (9.24 m)
ROTOR DIAMETER: 32 ft 3 in (9.83 m)
HEIGHT: 11 ft 8 in (3.56 m)

**WEIGHTS:**
EMPTY: 3232 lb (1465 kg)
MAX T/O: 5300 lb (2404 kg)

**PERFORMANCE:**
MAX SPEED: 131 mph (211 kmh)
RANGE: 314 miles (505 km)
POWERPLANT: Rolls-Royce Nimbus Mk 101
OUTPUT: 1050 shp (783 kW)

**ARMAMENT:**
two Mk 44 torpedoes (Wasp) or two AS 12 anti-tank/ship missiles on fuselage pylons

**FIRST FLIGHT DATE:**
20 July 1958

**FEATURES:**
Pod and boom fuselage; single exposed engine behind cockpit; fixed wheeled undercarriage (Wasp) or skids (Scout); heavily glazed cockpit

# Photo
# Credits

# Photo Credits

| | |
|---|---|
| **Shlomo Aloni** | 279, 458, 459, 489 |
| **Daniel Brackx** | 26 |
| **Rob Fox** | 135, 136, 137, 153, 186, 263, 268, 269, 285, 310, 321, 446 |
| **Cory Graff** | 22 |
| **Tony Holmes** | 15, 57, 61, 74, 108, 140, 148, 155, 163, 178, 192, 205, 207, 208, 222, 223, 227, 234, 236, 254, 257, 259, 260, 264, 277, 286, 290, 293, 300, 305, 313, 329, 330, 331, 333, 334, 354, 361, 364, 366, 367, 368, 371, 372, 374, 377, 390, 392, 395, 397, 410, 420, 438, 442, 443, 460, 461, 466, 467, 484, 487 |
| **Mike Hooks** | 59, 132, 162, 172, 177, 196, 201, 242, 256, 417, 424, 432, 486 |
| **Phil Jarrett** | 18, 19, 21, 32, 34, 35, 38, 40, 50, 51, 92, 109, 121 |
| **Otger van der Kooij** | 276, 311, 312, 315, 345, 349, 425, 427 |
| **Cliff Knox** | 36, 39, 43, 43, 46, 47, 54, 55, 71, 82, 90, 91, 96, 110, 130, 133, 156, 160, 164, 170, 194, 199, 212, 213, 229, 235, 241, 245, 247, 266, 275, 288, 302, 314, 316, 338, 341, 351, 403, 404, 412, 414, 423, 430, 439, 451, 455, 457, 471, 479, 490 |
| **Phil Makanna** | 89 |
| **Peter March** | 20, 23, 24, 25, 27, 31, 33, 41, 42, 44, 49, 52, 58, 60, 63, 64, 65, 70, 72, 76, 79, 86, 87, 88, 93, 94, 95, 97, 100, 102, 103, 104, 105, 111, 112, 113, 114, 118, 119, 122, 126, 128, 129, 131, 134, 143, 147, 149, 157, 158, 159, 171, 173, 175, 180, 189, 190, 195, 197, 203, 204, 209, 210, 211, 215, 220, 224, 225, 228, 230, 237, 238, 239, 244, 246, 248, 249, 251, 255, 258, 261, 265, 272, 282, 287, 291, 294, 296, 299, 301, 303, 309, 320, 322, 323, 326, 328, 336, 337, 339, 346, 352, 360, 369, 370, 373, 376, 386, 388, 394, 401, 405, 406, 408, 411, 426, 431, 434, 440, 441, 444, 447, 452, 463, 464, 465, 470, 477, 478, 480, 481, 482, 483, 488 |